This book is dedicated to

my longtime wonderful friend

Irene A. Fogarty

who shared the faith,

the dream and the sweat.

In memoriam
May 9, 1937 - December 30, 1995

The wonderful thing about books is that they allow us to enter imaginatively into someone else's life. And when we do that, we learn to sympathize with other people. But the real surprise is that we also learn truths about ourselves, about our own lives, that somehow we hadn't been able to see before.

—Katherine Womeldorf Paterson (1923–)
U.S. children's writer in *The Horn Book* (1991)

Detecting Women 2

ISBN: 0-9644593-1-0

Printed on recycled paper and bound in the USA by Bookcrafters of Chelsea, Michigan.
♻

Cover design by Jacqué Consulting, Inc. of Dearborn, Michigan.
Electronic prepress and text design by Publitech of Ann Arbor, Michigan.

Cataloging-in-Publication Data

Heising, Willetta L., 1947-

       Detecting women 2: a reader's guide and checklist for mystery series
       written by women / Willetta L. Heising
       384 p. 28 cm.
       Includes index and bibliographic references.
       ISBN 0-9644593-0-2 (alk. paper)
       1. Detective and mystery stories, American—Women authors—Bibliography.
  2. Detective and mystery stories, English—Women authors—Bibliography.
  I. Title.   1996   016.8

The paper used in this publication meets the minimum requirements of American National Standard for Information Sciences—Permanence of Paper for Printed Library Materials. ANSI Z39.48-1984

First printing February 1996

Detecting Women 2

A Reader's Guide and Checklist
for Mystery Series Written by Women

WILLETTA L. HEISING

1996–97 edition

Purple Moon Press

Colophon

The database used to compile the Master List for the original **Detecting Women** was constructed in 1994 using an Excel spreadsheet (hard to believe). But we worked a lot smarter in 1995 (thanks to a push from Bill Albert) and converted the database to Claris FileMaker Pro—Windows version for the author and Mac version for our design consultant.

Text for the Master List and other chapters was composed by the author using Microsoft Word for Windows (version 6.0) operating on her 486-33i PC. These files were later transferred on disk to Publitech where they were consolidated, sorted, edited and massaged using the Macintosh applications for FileMaker and Word. The use of compatible software allowed us to move files back and forth, editing and revising relentlessly, but never re-entering data or text.

Text was later imported into PageMaker (version 5.0) on a PowerMac 6112CD for page composition. PostScript files were delivered on a 100MB Iomega Zip disk to BookCrafters for final output to film by a Linotronic 530.

The cover was designed by Jacqué Consulting, Inc. in Illustrator (version 5.5) on a Macintosh Quadra 840AV and delivered to BookCrafters on a 44MB SyQuest cartridge. Color separations were completed by BookCrafters before final output. Fonts used on the cover are Pepita, Futura, Matrix Tall, Myriad and Mistral.

The fonts used inside the book are Bookman (body text), Helvetica (page headers and tables), Mistral (numbers), Pepita (accent text) and Gill Sans Ultra (accent text). The pen nib is a Zapf Dingbat.

The paper is 60-pound Glatfelter Offset. The cover is 10-point C1S with GBC Lay Flat gloss film lamination.

Printing and binding was done by BookCrafters of Chelsea, Michigan, using a state-of-the-art Otabind™ lay-flat binding.

Contents

A letter to mystery lovers 9

Acknowledgments 12

How to use this book 15

Lists, lists and more lists

1   Master list 19

2   Mystery types 203

3   Series characters 223

4   Settings 243

5   Mystery chronology 261

6   Alphabetical list of titles 295

7   Pseudonyms 327

Where to look for more

8   Short stories 331

9   Awards and organizations 341

10   Other resources 345

Extras

11   Glossary 355

12   Bibliography 361

13   Index 363

14   About the author 375

Appendices

A   Preview of future editions 377

B   Pocket guide changes 381

A Letter to Mystery Lovers

I love mysteries. You love mysteries. We all love mysteries. And some of us are downright fanatical about reading our favorite mystery series in the proper order. But determining the correct order can sometimes be difficult. Just tracking down all the titles can be tricky. So what's a body to do? You could start keeping track for yourself—which is exactly what I did in 1992 when I resumed serious mystery reading after a long lapse.

I was thrilled to discover that while I wasn't looking, Nancy Drew grew up, hung out a shingle and got her own gun. Sharon McCone, Kinsey Millhone and V. I. Warshawski inspired me during my first summer of self-employment after 20 years of corporate soldiering. I was thankful that my work was a lot easier than theirs. And one thing I didn't have to worry about was getting beat up or shot at—not literally anyway. By comparison, my clients were pretty mild-mannered.

Initially, one of the things I did worry about was running out of detective stories. Little did I know my standard fare of four and five books each week was barely keeping pace with the release of new series titles by women mystery writers. In both 1993 and 1994, well over 200 new titles were released by women authors with series detective characters. How was I going to find time for all the new books, plus the great ones I'd missed in past years? And what about the wonderful series written by men and non-series mysteries and other fiction written by women and men? The phrase "So many books, so little time" took on a whole new meaning for me.

List-making seemed like a good way to get organized. But the real bonus came from sharing the lists with friends. From a practical point of view, sharing increased our chances of finding new and not-to-be-missed series. We had more readers on the job. And they started sharing with their friends and before long, people I'd never met were calling to ask when I was going to put these lists between two covers.

So, here it is—THE list of mystery series written by women. A great place to start your mystery reading if you're new at the game. A great way to get organized if you're a serious reader. Toss a copy of *Detecting Women* in your briefcase, your purse or the back seat of your car. And the next time you visit your favorite bookstore or library, you'll be more than just prepared, you'll be well-armed.

To those who ask (and I know you will), "Where are the men?" I say, "Just about everywhere you look." Dozens of fascinating male detectives have been created by women mystery writers. Some of them are legends of crime fiction. Certainly

Hercule Poirot and Lord Peter Wimsey come immediately to mind. Also Reginald Wexford, Roderick Alleyn, Luis Mendoza and more recently, Milt Kovak, J. P. Beaumont and many others.

Curiously, or maybe not so curiously, very few men writing mysteries have chosen a woman detective as their protagonist. In fact, there's a chapter already in progress for the next edition of *Detecting Women* titled "Men Who Write Women Series Characters." Starting with Warren Adler's homicide detective, Fiona Fitzgerald, through R. D. Zimmerman's blind paraplegic psychologist and stock-trading genius, Dr. Madeline Phillips, we pose the question, "If the author's identity were unknown, could you spot a woman protagonist written by a man?" My reading experience tells me sometimes yes, sometimes no.

But this is a book about detecting women. The women who write crime fiction of all types. Police procedurals, private eye novels and traditional or cozy mysteries—with protagonists from all walks of life in every period in history, with settings around the world. Their detectives are men and women, old and young, gay, straight, black, white, married, single, widowed, divorced. With and without families, children, parents, siblings and companion animals. In short, they're all of us—the women who write and read mysteries. And we want to know who they are, where they come from, what issues concern them, how they got to where they are now and what has affected their lives.

I am no apologist for gender-specific interests. We read what we like. What interests us. What stretches our minds and captures our imagination. And yes, that often includes fiction and nonfiction written by men. But with all the wonderful stuff written by the women of this world, I intend to do my part to promote their work. To make sure that every woman who doesn't already know what great stories are out there for the reading, might renew her interest in reading after paging through this book. Reading is fundamental for all of us—not just the kids. So dust off your library card and don't wait until your next vacation to bring home a sackful of books. Ready, set, read!

—*Willetta L. Heising*
November 1994

Postscript

January 1996

It's hard to believe only 14 months have passed since I wrote my first Letter to Mystery Lovers, reprinted here as part of the story behind **Detecting Women**. This book has literally changed my life. Since 1994 I've found a new career—it's starting to look like my life's work, actually—new friends, new knowledge and skills (acquired from the seat-of-the-pants school of learn-from-an-expert and then-do-it-yourself) and more fun than I've had in 20 years.

Part of the surprise was how quickly things changed. Within weeks of the release of **Detecting Women** on January 25, 1995, the mail started (fax, phone, e-mail and the old fashioned kind). These wonderful notes of thanks and praise were my biggest surprise and greatest encouragement. Never having received printed ovations (at least not in this quantity), I saved each one and started a collection that I kept in a box labelled FAN MAIL. Whenever things weren't going well and I was sure I'd lost my mind to even think I could pull this off, I would retreat to a comfortable chair and sit with the box on my lap, reading letters until my energy picked up and I could get happily back to work. I still keep the box handy.

But these letters weren't just hurrahs. It seems mystery lovers (particularly the women) are some pretty opinionated folks. From the beginning, the mail was full of suggestions, directions and specific orders to "Do this" and "Do that." The suggestion to do a pocket guide came early and often, until I had no choice but to start the search for a manufacturer. What a surprise to find the company that prints the boring pocket calendar used by the bank where I previously worked was capable of a lot more flash and dazzle.

Only slightly less vocal than the pocket guide proponents were the Detecting Men enthusiasts. To the first 100 suggestions of "Do Detecting Men" my retort was "Not my job. Not my book. Not my problem." Until a clever friend pointed out that I owned the franchise. "Just think," she said, "you'll end up a series mystery writer after all—series reference."

Detecting Men will be a tougher job simply because I am woefully under-read in this department. And to keep this book a manageable size, we are limiting it to series authors currently writing. Perhaps in the future we can produce **Detecting Classics** with all the mystery writers who are no longer with us (men and women together), but for the present, we'll concentrate on the living. Our current schedule calls for release of **Detecting Men** by year-end 1996. All contributions will be gleefully accepted and acknowledged. Stay tuned.

One of my favorite queries—the Scarlett letter—came in early May from an 11-year-old girl in Clarksville, Indiana, whose mother had bought a copy of **Detecting Women**. What Scarlett Harrod (I predict her name will be on a book cover someday) wanted to know was when were we going to produce a Young Adult edition? I was relieved she liked our working title—**Detecting Kids**—and am delighted she and her friends have already sent several lists of their YA favorites. My niece Kelly Barlow's 6th grade class in Charlottesville, Virginia, has also expressed interest, as have school teachers and library professionals in several states. As soon as **Detecting Men** is underway we will commence formal planning for the 1997 production of **Detecting Kids**.

And last but not least among the projects spawned by **Detecting Women** is our forthcoming newsletter—**Detecting News**. A quarterly print piece for starters, the first issue should be out before mid-year. Once we made the decision to alternate titles between Detecting Men and Women (it's impossible to do more than one big book and one pocket guide a year and keep the creative control we want), a newsletter seemed the best way to fill the gaps in the two-year stretch between Detecting Women 2 and 3, and Detecting Men 1 and 2. If you'd like to receive a complimentary copy of the first newsletter, just let us know.

We hope you'll keep sending comments, suggestions, and yes, even orders to "Do this" and "Do that." I can hardly wait to see where you're taking us next!

— Willetta L. Heising
Dearborn, Michigan

Acknowledgments

∾ First and foremost, to the mystery booksellers who were enthusistic and supportive in the early days when no one knew who we were. Thank you.

∾ To those who sent comments, suggestions, corrections and ideas (see *Other Contributors* on page 14). Thank you.

∾ To Miskit Airth and Betsy Caprio for wit, wisdom and special assistance. Thank you.

∾ To Kate and Doug Bandos for skill and daring. Thank you.

∾ To Nevada Barr for unsolicited advice that saved me from myself. Thank you.

∾ To Alice Ann Carpenter and John Leininger, expert booksellers, fact-finders and friends extraordinaire. Thank you.

∾ To Dennis Drabelle for making possible our first big break in print. Thank you.

∾ To Wendy Everett who is still performing heroic feats with deadlines and not complaining (at least not to me). Thank you.

∾ To Geraldine Galentree of the Dallas Mystery Bookstore whose enthusiasm for mystery books is as big as Texas. Thank you.

∾ To Claudia Gordon and Joan Hollingsworth for unwavering moral support. Thank you.

❧ To Liz Hennessey and everyone at Borders for treating us as if we were big-time. Thank you.

❧ To Sue Henry for insisting that I drop everything and head for Nottingham and Chester. Thank you.

❧ To Allen J. Hubin who is surely the most generous bibliographer ever. For 25 pages of notes early on and for everything since. Thank you.

❧ To Anne Hughes, Tom Dorow and everyone at BookCrafters. Thank you.

❧ To Don Onesi of Forbes for being the pocket guide champion. Thank you.

❧ To everyone at Powell's Books in Portland, Oregon, for their enthusiasm and support. Thank you.

❧ To Jane Troxell of Lammas Women's Books & More for intervening when we needed help. Thank you.

❧ To Ann Williams who generously reviewed the pocket guide manuscript at the eleventh hour. Any errors are entirely ours and no fault of hers. Thank you.

❧ To Margaret Southworth who is still pushing, prodding, affirming and magnifying my efforts. You're the best.

❧ And to my senior partners who make it all possible. My love and everlasting thanks.

Other Contributors

Airth, Miskit
Barlow, Ellen
Bayne, Josephine
Black, Lyndee J.
Brady, Joy
Brinkman-Viall, Amy
Brown, Jeanette
Bryan, Peggy
Bryant, Libby
Bursaw, Jenny
Caprio, Betsy
Carpenter, Mary Jane
Chadwick, Carol S.
Corrigan, Maureen
Creagan, Jennifer
Cromwell, Joyce
DeLucia, Carmella
Diaz, Victoria
Drescher, Margaret
Drew, Nancy
Durack, Eve
Easter, George
Eggers, Susan
Faucett, Barbara
Ford, Evelyn
Fox, Jane
Frank, Norma J.
Freedman, Barbara
Funk, Vicky
Galentree, Geraldine
Gardner, Barry
Gauntt, Barbara
Glasby, Jan
Glass, Mary Kay
Gnau, Tara
Goldman, Richard
Gordon, Claudia B.
Greenup, Nadine
Hardy, Margaret
Harig, Kathy
Harrod, Scarlett
Hart, Maryelizabeth
Hausauer, Barbara Lee

Heising, Willetta B., Rev.
Henderson, Marilyn
Hill, Christine Nyback
Hollingsworth, Joan
Hutchins, Janice L.
Kelly, Vicki M.
Korosa, Sue
Koupal, Marla
Lampe, Betsy
McClain, Michele
McDaniel, Pat
Napier, Cap'n Bob
Nissenbaum, Robert
Panszczyk, Linda
Potts, Rinehart S.
Power, Margo
Randig, Linda
Rose, Paige
Rose, Susan
Sandstrom, Don
Sapp, Molly
Sharrow, Marilyn J.
Shellhorn, Charles
Shutts, Diane
Siciliano, Kathy
Simpson, Helen
Stay, Harriett & Larry
Thompson, Janis A.
Tocalis, Tom
Troxell, Jane
Tuggle, Mary Brandreth
Van Hyning, Gretchen
Villines, Sharon
Warner, Phyllis K.
Wasserman, Jan
Watson, Carol
Weber, Deborah
Weston, Molly
Wood, Kathleen
Wright, Anne & Gordon
Wright, Betty
Wunsch, Joan
Zappen, R. G.

How to use this book

No matter what your preference for hunting mysteries—by author, character, type, background, setting, title, or date—*Detecting Women 2* has a list for you. The Master List, presented in *Chapter 1*, contains all the information which is later re-presented in different formats in other lists. The Master List—complete with boxes to check for every series title—is designed to keep track of books you've read, books you own, books you intend to buy, books you especially like, or anything about mystery series written by women that you'd like to keep track of.

Master List–Chapter 1

In the Master List, authors appear in alphabetical order by last name, according to the name under which their series mysteries are published. For example, you will find Marion Chesney listed as M. C. Beaton, the pseudonym under which her Hamish MacBeth and Agatha Raisin series are published. An author profile with information about her life and work is followed by her series character(s) and book titles in order of appearance. The date that follows the title is intended to be the earliest date of publication.

For books first published in Britain, Canada or Australia, you should expect that the U. S. edition may not appear until a year or more later. In fact, the U. S. title might differ from the British, Canadian or Australian title, or the book may not even be published in the United States. There may also be differences between hardcover and paperback editions. But whenever more than one title is known, both titles will be listed, with a notation indicating whether the second title is U. S., British or another alternate title. APA is used to indicate "also published as."

When an author has more than one series detective, the characters are listed in alphabetical order by first name. An abbreviated character description, including the primary

series setting, follows the character's name. This may not be the setting for every book in the series, but it is typically the home base of the protagonist.

Whenever a book has been nominated or awarded recognition for a major prize or award in the mystery field, the book title appears in demi-bold type followed by the specific nomination or award and a star. If you're interested in reading award-winning authors, just scan the pages of *Chapter 1* looking for starred demi-bold titles. Solid stars indicate award winners and open stars indicate nominations. Because these awards are a fairly recent phenomenon, you should not overlook titles which predate awards. A description of the various mystery awards can be found in both the *Glossary* and *Chapter 9, Awards and Organizations.*

Mystery Types–Chapter 2

Simply for the purpose of organization, the 681 mystery series presented in *Detecting Women 2* have been slotted into three groups, based on the standard definitions for police procedurals, P. I. novels and traditional mysteries with amateur detectives. Those group totals are shown below:

Police	154	(23%)
P. I.s	115	(17%)
Amateurs	412	(60%)
Total Series	**681**	**(100%)**

Traditional mystery series are further classified using 47 categories of backgrounds, listed on the following page. These categories have also been applied to private eye and police series whenever such a background is important to the series. For example, historical private eye series appear in the P. I. section and again in the appropriate historical section. Thus, you will find Lynda Robinson's Lord Meren series grouped with other private eyes and listed again in the section for "Historical, Ancient."

Mystery Backgrounds

Academic
Animals, cats
_____, dogs
_____, horses
_____, other
Art & Antiques
Authors & Writers
Bed & Breakfast
Black
Books & Libraries
Botanical
Business & Finance
Computers & Technology
Criminal
Cross Genre
Domestic
Ecclesiastical & Religious
Environment & Wilderness
Ethnic & Native American
Gay & Lesbian
Gourmet & Food
Government
Historical, ancient
_____, medieval
_____, renaissance
_____, 18th century
_____, 19th century
_____, 1920s
_____, other
Journalism, magazine
_____, newspaper
_____, photography
_____, radio & television
Legal, attorney
_____, judge
Medical
Military
Miscellaneous
Occult
Romantic
Secret Agents
Senior Sleuths
Small Town
Sports
Suburban
Theatre & Performing Arts
Travelers

You will notice we have included a category for black, gay & lesbian and senior sleuths.

However inappropriate it may seem at first, it was decided to include these categories as long as they were not the only category in which a particular character appears. Hence, black cops and black P. I.s are listed first as cops and P. I.s and secondly as black detectives. If it's important that you know the protagonist's age, sexual orientation or skin color, this information is included. If you think it unimportant, please ignore it.

If you count the number of entries in the "Amateurs" category, you'll find more than the 412 series identified earlier. This is because many series have more than one "background." For example, Lilian Jackson Braun's "Cat Who" series is listed under "Animals" and again under "Journalism" which is Qwill's line of work. Judith Van Gieson's Neil Hamel series is listed under "Attorney" and also under "Environment & Wilderness." After finding a series that interests you, don't forget to return to the Master List for more information about the author and series character.

We have included a "Cross Genre" category for the first time, in order to highlight a few series which are not typical mysteries but which might pique your interest. The Cross Genre group includes science fiction police series, vampire P. I.s, practicing witch investigators, and a western private eye series.

Another new feature of the Mystery Types chapter is the designation for date-of-the-first-book-in-the-series and number-of-books-in-the-series. When you see '29-66, for example, you will know the series begins in 1929 and runs for 66 books, as does Gladys Mitchell's series featuring Beatrice Lestrange Bradley. This two-part column, included in all table-format lists (types, series characters, settings, chronology and alphabetical listing), makes it easy to spot the long-running series.

Please note that whenever a collection of short stories featuring a series character appears in the series list, it will be listed in the order in which it was published, but will be unnumbered so as not to confuse the number of book-length series installments. For example, *The McCone Files* (1995)—15 short stories featuring Sharon McCone—was published in between books #15 and #16 and is listed with

Marcia Muller's Sharon McCone title list as a numberless entry.

Series Characters–Chapter 3

This list was first requested by someone who wanted to know—just for fun, she said—if there was a detective who shared her name. She was certain there wasn't. Saying she was pleased to find one is an understatement. She was so excited by the news that we showed the list to others, wondering if we'd get a similar reaction. We're now convinced that finding a same-name heroine is a secret desire for many. So for those who always wished that Nancy Drew had been "your-name" Drew, here's your chance to find her.

This list will also prove useful for anyone who remembers a character's first name but hasn't a clue about the author. Whenever the series character is actually a pair, each of the partners is listed separately. For example, both Leslie Wetzon and Xenia Smith from Annette Meyers' Wall Street series appear in the character listing. The partner's name is always attached so you know the character is part of a series pair.

Settings–Chapter 4

As mentioned earlier, the settings identified in the Master List and in Chapter 4 are not necessarily the setting for each book in the series, but typically the home base of the series character(s). Often the setting will change from book to book. When world travel is part of the story line, we classify the series as such. And whenever a sufficient number of books exists so that a primary location can be determined, we choose the most frequent setting. When there are only two books in the series, each with a different location, we try to specify the current location.

States of the U. S. are listed in alphabetical order. Within each state, cities and towns appear in alphabetical order, with fictional towns included as if they were real. Unspecified locations are grouped together at the beginning of each section. Locations outside the United States are presented alphabetically by country and further by city, province or region alphabetically.

Mystery Chronology–Chapter 5

The Mystery Chronology is another list that resulted from the enthusiastic response of one reader, later seconded by others, who ordered us to "keep that one; I need that list." Some fascinating patterns emerge from arranging titles by decade and charting their numbers. See Chapter 5 for the charts, graphs and every-title list of the more than 3,500 series mysteries written by women since 1878.

Within the chronological list, series titles are grouped by year within each decade—presented in alphabetical order according to the author's last name. For example, in 1928 Agatha Christie's *The Mystery of the Blue Train* is listed ahead of Patricia Wentworth's *Grey Mask*. Whenever a title is the first book in a new series, it is designated with a ◼ which appears in front of the title.

Black header bars separate the decades. Each header includes the name of the decade (1920s for example) along with the number of new titles published that decade and the number of new series introduced. Returning to the 1920s as our example, the 1920s header bar shows 46 titles and 10 new series. The number of new series is represented by the same icon used to denote first-in-a-series.

Titles nominated or awarded prizes are marked with open and solid stars, but since these prizes are a fairly recent phenomenon, stars do not start to appear until the 1960s. Whenever a book is reissued with a different title at a later date, alternate titles are listed in the appropriate year with a cross-reference to the corresponding title.

Alphabetical Title List–Chapter 6

Chapter 6 is the alphabetical list of almost 3,600 series mystery titles written by women, presented by decade through the 1980s and by year starting in 1990. Within the time period (decade or year), titles are listed alphabetically by the author's last name, so that titles from a single author in a given year will be listed together. Whenever a title is the first book in a new series, it is designated with a ◼. And whenever a book is reissued with a different title, you will find both titles listed alphabetically, with a cross-reference to the corresponding title. Titles are also starred to indicate award winners and nominations.

Pseudonyms–Chapter 7

Pseudonyms used by the women who write mystery series are presented in *Chapter 7* in a simple table format showing the author's true identity and the corresponding pseudonym for each series and nonseries mysteries, historical novels or romantic suspense. Please note that the author entry in the Master List is based on the name under which a mystery series is published.

Short Stories–Chapter 8

If you are looking for short stories by your favorite author or curious about the style of an author you are not familiar with, the 25 anthologies presented in *Chapter 8* are a great place to start. A summary of award-winning stories from these anthologies is provided at the end of the chapter, along with the short story bibliography. Award winners and nominees are also easy to identify within the table formats by the solid and open stars used throughout the book.

Awards & Organizations–Chapter 9

More information about awards and organizations can be found in *Chapter 9* as well as the *Glossary*.

Other Resources–Chapter 10

Other Resources focuses on mystery periodicals and reference books which can add to your enjoyment of mystery reading. Because of their frequent and timely publication, mystery magazines and newsletters are the best source for up-to-date information on conferences and conventions, book reviews, and announcements of forthcoming books of interest. Information about the fast-growing and rapidly-changing world of cyber resources [have you lurked on DorothyL or visited *Murderous Intent's* homepage on the World Wide Web?] can also be found in mystery periodicals.

Glossary—Chapter 11

The glossary provides definitions for more than 100 terms you are likely to come across in your mystery reading, including a list of police officer ranks in both U. S. and British police departments (especially useful for the hierarchically-challenged).

Index–Chapter 13

The index includes authors (last name first), series characters (first name first), awards, organizations and periodicals. Index entries for authors included in the Master List are marked with little pen nibs for easy identification. The first index entry for each of these authors typically identifies her location in the Master List. Multiple mentions of an author on a single page are not separately identified.

Preview of Future Editions–Appendix A

A preview of future editions is provided to encourage feedback and participation from anyone who has information to share about authors, series characters, organizations, publications or other matters of interest to mystery readers. A fax-back or mail-back form is included. We look forward to hearing from you.

Pocket Guide Changes–Appendix B

Appendix B is a list of 116 series titles added after publication of the Pocket Guide edition of *Detecting Women 2*. It also includes several titles found to be nonseries titles. Please use this list to make corrections to your Pocket Guide. Whenever there is a discrepancy between the Pocket Guide and the full-size edition, use the full-size edition as your guide. Because the big book went to press three months after the Pocket Guide, it includes corrections that became available later.

 Master List

■ **Deborah ADAMS** is a seventh-generation Tennessean and creator of the Jesus Creek series featuring a small town with a large cast of colorful characters who take turns narrating these rollicking whodunits. Adams credits a late-night misread highway sign with her inspiration for Jesus Creek. At the age of 14, she was the youngest charter member of the Carroll County Historical Society, but more recently her extracurricular interests have turned to endurance riding. In 1995 she and her horse Sundance completed a novice's 25-mile trail ride, where despite a raging thunderstorm, they proudly finished the race and were not last. Adams' short story "Cast Your Fate to the Wind" in *Malice Domestic 3* won the 1995 Macavity Award for best short story which she shared with Jan Burke.

> **Jesus Creek, Tennessee** . . . eccentric small town
> ❑ ❑ 1 - **All the Great Pretenders** (1992) *Agatha nominee* ☆
> ❑ ❑ 2 - All the Crazy Winters (1992)
> ❑ ❑ 3 - All the Dark Disguises (1993)
> ❑ ❑ 4 - All the Hungry Mothers (1993)
> ❑ ❑ 5 - All the Deadly Beloved (1995)

■ **M. J. ADAMSON** is Mary Jo Adamson, author of a police series set in Puerto Rico featuring NYPD homicide detective Balthazar Marten and Puerto Rican cop Sixto Cardenas. The Spanish-speaking Marten is sent to Puerto Rico on an exchange program while recovering from the bombing which killed his young wife. Under the shared pseudonym of Yvonne Adamson, she writes historical romance (*Bridey's Mountain*) with fellow Denver novelist Yvonne Montgomery. Adamson, who holds a PhD from the University of Denver, grew up in Illinois and later lived in London, Los Angeles, northern California, southeast Missouri and central Wyoming. These days she prefers spending her winters in Puerto Rico and summers in Colorado.

> **Balthazar Marten & Sixto Cardenas** . . . NYPD homicide detective & Puerto Rican cop
> ❑ ❑ 1 - Not Till a Hot January (1987)
> ❑ ❑ 2 - A February Face (1987)
> ❑ ❑ 3 - Remember March (1988)
> ❑ ❑ 4 - April When They Woo (1988)
> ❑ ❑ 5 - May's Newfangled Mirth (1989)

■ **Catherine AIRD** is the pseudonym of Kinn Hamilton McIntosh, creator of Inspector C. D. Sloan, aptly nicknamed "Seedy" by his friends. Launched in 1966 with *The Religious Body*, this series is set in the fictitious county of Calleshire. Included in that first book is a map depicting all the geographical features and fictional landmarks of Calleshire—towns, farms, factories, schools, and, of course, Berebury police headquarters. Each detective's character is fully described in book #1 and even after 30 years of police work, they've changed not one bit. Aird is also the author of *A Most Contagious Game* (1967) involving a secret room, a murdered wife and a 200-year-old skeleton. She lives in Kent, England and is vice-chairman of the British Crime Writers Association.

    Christopher Dennis "Seedy" Sloan . . . Berebury CID department head in West Calleshire, England

        ❑ ❑ 1 - The Religious Body (1966)
        ❑ ❑ 2 - Henrietta Who? (1968)
        ❑ ❑ 3 - The Complete Steel (1969) [U.S.–The Stately Home Murder]
        ❑ ❑ 4 - A Late Phoenix (1970)
        ❑ ❑ 5 - His Burial Too (1973)
        ❑ ❑ 6 - Slight Mourning (1975)
        ❑ ❑ 7 - Parting Breath (1977)
        ❑ ❑ 8 - Some Die Eloquent (1979)
        ❑ ❑ 9 - Passing Strange (1980)
        ❑ ❑ 10 - Last Respects (1982)
        ❑ ❑ 11 - A Dead Liberty (1987)
        ❑ ❑ 12 - A Going Concern (1993)
        ❑ ❑ 13 - After Effects (1996)

■ **Susan Wittig ALBERT** is a former Texas university professor and administrator whose China Bayles mystery series is a corporate leave-taking story not unlike her own. A former fast-track attorney, China ditches the rat race for an herb shop in the Hill Country of west Texas, specifically the fictional town of Pecan Springs. Once a fast tracker herself, Albert now writes full time and produces *China's Garden*, an herb and literary newsletter which is a delightful blend of her many interests. She holds a PhD from Berkeley and is the author of numerous books and articles about literature and writing, over 60 novels for young readers and *Work of Her Own, A Woman's Guide to Success off the Career Track*. Albert and her husband Bill recently launched a Victorian mystery series under the pseudonym Robin Paige.

    China Bayles . . . herb shop owner & former attorney in Pecan Springs, Texas

        ❑ ❑ 1 - **Thyme of Death** (1992) *Agatha & Anthony nominee* ☆ ☆
        ❑ ❑ 2 - Witches' Bane (1993)
        ❑ ❑ 3 - Hangman's Root (1994)
        ❑ ❑ 4 - Rosemary Remembered (1995)

■ **Irene ALLEN** is the pseudonym of Elsa Kirsten Peters, a Harvard- and Princeton-educated geologist and creator of a new mystery series featuring Elizabeth Elliot, widowed Pennsylvania Quaker meeting clerk. Elliot's first appearance *Quaker Silence* (1992) is followed by *Quaker Witness* (1993). The author lives in Washington State.

    Elizabeth Elliot . . . widowed Pennsylvania Quaker meeting clerk

        ❑ ❑ 1 - Quaker Silence (1992)
        ❑ ❑ 2 - Quaker Witness (1993)

■ **Kate ALLEN** is the pseudonym of a Denver author and creator of a police series featuring lesbian cop Alison Kaine, whose first appearance is *Tell Me What You Like* (1993).

Alison Kaine . . . lesbian "leather" cop in Denver, Colorado
    ❑ ❑ 1 - Tell Me What You Like (1993)
    ❑ ❑ 2 - Give My Secrets Back (1995)

■ **Margery ALLINGHAM** (1904-1966) published her first novel at the age of 19 and four years later married the artist and magazine editor who had designed its cover, Philip Youngman Carter (1904-1970). She was best known for her series detective Albert Campion who first appeared in 1929 and was thought by some to be an over-the-top caricature of Lord Peter Wimsey. Campion claimed family connections to the royal throne, yet his house-man was an ex-burglar. He later married a titled aviation engineer (Lady Amanda Fitton) and their son Rupert eventually enrolled in Harvard. After Allingham's death, her husband completed the title she had last worked on (*Cargo of Eagles*) and added two of his own creation before his death. In 1988 British television created a Campion series which was shown in the U.S. on the PBS *Mystery!* series. As a result of revived American interest, many of these titles have been reprinted in paperback and are widely available.

Albert Campion . . . suave sleuth with noble blood in London
    ❑ ❑ 1 - The Crime at Black Dudley (1929)
                  [U.S.–The Black Dudley Murder]
    ❑ ❑ 2 - Mystery Mile (1930)
    ❑ ❑ 3 - Look to the Lady (1931) [U.S.–The Gryth Chalice Mystery]
    ❑ ❑ 4 - Police at the Funeral (1931)
    ❑ ❑ 5 - Sweet Danger (1933) [U.S.–Kingdom of Death] [APA–The Fear Sign]
    ❑ ❑ 6 - Death of a Ghost (1934)
    ❑ ❑ 7 - Flowers for the Judge (1936) [APA–Legacy in Blood]
    ❑ ❑ 8 - Dancers in Mourning (1937) [APA–Who Killed Chloe?]
    ❑ ❑ 9 - The Case of the Late Pig (1937)
    ❑ ❑ 10 - The Fashion in Shrouds (1938)
    ❑ ❑ 11 - Traitor's Purse (1941) [APA–The Sabotage Murder Mystery]
    ❑ ❑ 12 - Coroner's Pidgin (1945) [U.S.–Pearls Before Swine]
    ❑ ❑ 13 - More Work for the Undertaker (1949)
    ❑ ❑ 14 - The Tiger in the Smoke (1952)
    ❑ ❑ 15 - No Love Lost (1954)
    ❑ ❑ 16 - The Beckoning Lady (1955) [U.S.–The Estate of the Beckoning Lady]
    ❑ ❑ 17 - **Hide My Eyes** (1958) [U.S.–**Tether's End**] [APA–**Ten Were Missing**]
                  Silver Dagger ★
    ❑ ❑ 18 - The China Governess (1962)
    ❑ ❑ 19 - The Mind Readers (1965)
    ❑ ❑ 20 - Cargo of Eagles (1968) [with Philip Youngman Carter]
    ❑ ❑ 21 - Mr. Campion's Farthing (1969) [Philip Youngman Carter]
    ❑ ❑ 22 - Mr. Campion's Falcon (1970) [U.S.–Mr. Campion's Quarry] [Philip Youngman Carter]

■ **Linda AMEY** of Austin, Texas is a mortician and funeral home director as well as the author of a new series featuring Austin funeral director Blair Emerson. The series debuts with *Bury Her Sweetly* (1992) and later moves to Live Oak, Texas with *Dead of Night* (1995). Amey, who operates the family business with her husband, is also the author of four mystery suspense novels published by a Christian press.

Blair Emerson . . . funeral director in Austin, Texas
    ❑ ❑ 1 - Bury Her Sweetly (1992)
    ❑ ❑ 2 - At Dead of Night (1995)

■ **Christine ANDREAE**, of Bentonville, Virginia, is a freelance writer and adjunct professor of English as well as the creator of a series featuring English professor and poet Lee Squires. To escape the summer heat of Washington DC, Squires signs on as the substitute cook for a Montana trail ride in the first installment which was nominated for an Edgar for best first novel.

> **Lee Squires** . . . English professor & poet
> ❑ ❑ 1 - **Trail of Murder** (1992) *Edgar nominee* ☆
> ❑ ❑ 2 - Grizzly, A Murder (1994)

■ **Sarah ANDREWS** of Sebastopol, California, is a working geologist with a series detective who also works in the oil business. In her first appearance, Em Hansen is working on a Wyoming drilling rig, looking for oil in Tensleep sandstone—a 400-million-year-old formation rich in petroleum. Book #2 takes her to the Denver headquarters of Blackfeet Oil Company. The author has traveled to remote parts of the U.S. as well as South America and Australia for a variety of assignments with the federal government, oil producers and environmental services. She holds both a bachelor's and master's degree in geology and is a veteran of the U.S. Geological Survey, Amoco and ANGUS Petroleum.

> **Em Hansen** . . . oil worker in Wyoming
> ❑ ❑ 1 - Tensleep (1994)
> ❑ ❑ 2 - A Fall in Denver (1995)

■ **Charlotte ARMSTRONG** (1905-1969) was born in an iron-mining town in Michigan's Upper Peninsula and later attended the University of Wisconsin and Barnard College. She published poetry in the *New Yorker* and wrote two plays produced on Broadway before trying her hand at mystery writing in a short series featuring college professor MacDougal Duff. She later turned to psychological suspense with titles such as *A Dram of Poison* which earned her the Edgar award for best novel in 1956. From the late 1940s until her death she produced 20 nonseries novels, several collections of short stories, a pair of novelettes and several scripts for *Alfred Hitchcock Presents*.

> **MacDougal Duff** . . . retired history professor in New York city
> ❑ ❑ 1 - Lay on, Mac Duff! (1942)
> ❑ ❑ 2 - The Case of the Weird Sisters (1943)
> ❑ ❑ 3 - The Innocent Flower (1945)

■ **Margot ARNOLD** is the pseudonym of Petronelle Cook for her series featuring the 60-something academic crime-solving twosome of American anthropologist Penelope Spring and British archaeologist Tobias Glendower. Arnold brings her lifelong interest in archaeology, anthropology and travel to the globe-trotting adventures of Penny and Sir Toby. In addition to this series Arnold has written several novels of romantic suspense. A longtime resident of Cape Cod, she was educated at Oxford and has lived and traveled extensively abroad. She currently resides in Pennsylvania.

> **Penny Spring & Sir Toby Glendower** . . . American anthropologist & British
> archeologist
> ❑ ❑ 1 - Exit Actors, Dying (1979)
> ❑ ❑ 2 - Zadock's Treasure (1979)
> ❑ ❑ 3 - The Cape Cod Caper (1980)
> ❑ ❑ 4 - Death of a Voodoo Doll (1982)
> ❑ ❑ 5 - Lament for a Lady Laird (1982)
> ❑ ❑ 6 - Death on a Dragon's Tongue (1982)
> ❑ ❑ 7 - The Menehune Murders (1989)

❏ ❏   8 - Toby's Folly (1990)
❏ ❏   9 - The Catacomb Conspiracy (1991)
❏ ❏ 10 - Cape Cod Conundrum (1992)
❏ ❏ 11 - Dirge for a Dorset Druid (1994)
❏ ❏ 12 - The Midas Murders (1995)

■ **Nancy ATHERTON**, born and raised in the Chicago area, now lives and writes in the corner of a cornfield in central Illinois. After working at a dude ranch, a ski lodge, and a day care center, Atherton was a freelance proofreader and a rare book bibliographer. Clearly in love with England, she says she's traveled from Land's End to John o' Groats by rail, car, thumb and foot. Her Aunt Dimity creations—both the ghost and the cottage—were greeted with rave reviews when the series debuted in 1992. It seems almost incongruous that her creator is a serious fan of science fiction who's lived in Brooklyn, Boston, Washington DC and south Florida, but never in an enchanted cottage.

Aunt Dimity . . . romantic English ghost
❏ ❏   1 - Aunt Dimity's Death (1992)
❏ ❏   2 - Aunt Dimity and the Duke (1994)
❏ ❏   3 - Aunt Dimity's Good Deed (1996)

■ **Noreen AYRES**, of Mission Viejo, California, is the creator of the Smokey Brandon series featuring a forensic expert and civilian employee of the Orange County sheriff's department. The series was recently optioned for film and television. Ayres is a former technical writer and editor of aircraft maintenance manuals and computer reference guides. She has a master's degree in English and has won awards for her short fiction and poetry. Among her previous jobs she lists fish cleaner, bookbinder, door-to-door photography salesperson, theatre cashier, sign painter, insurance rater, convalescent home bookkeeper, trademark docket clerk, church secretary, proofreader, personnel clerk, brokerage receptionist and science teacher.

Samantha "Smokey" Brandon . . . Orange County, California sheriff's forensic expert
❏ ❏   1 - A World the Color of Salt (1992)
❏ ❏   2 - Carcass Trade (1994)
❏ ❏   3 - The Long Slow Whistle of the Moon (1996)

■ **Jacqueline BABBIN**, long-time producer of the daytime drama *All My Children* on ABC-TV, is the creator of a mystery series featuring Clovis Kelly, ex-homicide detective turned television crime consultant in New York City. Kelly lands a role in the series when he visits the set and a crime is committed. Babbin, who worked on the original Broadway production of *Streetcar Named Desire*, spent 14 years with David Susskind, first as story editor and later as producer. She produced and won an Emmy for the NBC-drama *Sybil*, starring Joanne Woodward and Sally Field. She currently resides in Connecticut.

Clovis Kelly . . . ex-NYPD homicide detective & TV crime consultant in New York city
❏ ❏   1 - Prime Time Corpse (1972) [APA–Bloody Special ('89)]
❏ ❏   2 - Bloody Soaps (1989)

■ **Marian BABSON** is an American-born author who has lived in London for more than 30 years and writes mysteries in the English style. In addition to more than 20 nonseries novels she is the creator of two mystery series. The first features Doug Perkins, co-owner of a London public relations firm. The second more humorous cast of characters is headed by a pair of aging Hollywood movie queens—Eve Sinclair and Trixie Dolan—who are looking to jump-start their careers on the London stage. In 1985 Babson received a special award for ten years of magnificent secretaryship to the British Crime Writers Association, a post she continues to hold. She is currently working on a new series to be called Babson's Cats, although she says it is unlikely there will be a single continuing cat character.

Douglas Perkins . . . London-based travel agent
- ❑ ❑ 1 - Cover-up Story (1971)
- ❑ ❑ 2 - Murder on Show (1972) [U.S.–Murder at the Cat Show]
- ❑ ❑ 3 - Tourists are for Trapping (1989)
- ❑ ❑ 4 - In the Teeth of Adversity (1990)

Eve Sinclair & Trixie Dolan . . . aging British ex-movie queens in London
- ❑ ❑ 1 - Reel Murder (1986)
- ❑ ❑ 2 - Encore Murder (1989)
- ❑ ❑ 3 - Shadows in Their Blood (1993)
- ❑ ❑ 4 - Even Yuppies Die (1993)
- ❑ ❑ 5 - Break a Leg Darlings (1995)

■ **Nikki BAKER** is the pseudonymous author of a new mystery series featuring lesbian stockbroker Virginia Kelly. The first appearance of this black, gay woman broker from Chicago is titled *In the Game* (1991).

Virginia Kelly . . . black lesbian stockbroker in Chicago, Illinois
- ❑ ❑ 1 - In the Game (1991)
- ❑ ❑ 2 - The Lavender House Murder (1992)
- ❑ ❑ 3 - Long Goodbyes (1993)

■ **Mignon F. BALLARD**, a native of Calhoun, Georgia, is the author of several romantic suspense novels reminiscent of the Southern gothic style. She is also the creator of a new mystery series featuring former Georgia Peace Corps volunteer Eliza Figg. Ballard says it is little wonder she is fascinated with ghost stories and mysteries—growing up across the street from a funeral home with a birthday just two days before Halloween. Currently a resident of Fort Mill, South Carolina, Ballard has served as chairman of the Fort Mill Community Playhouse and member of the South Carolina Arts Commission's Artists-in-Education Program.

Eliza Figg . . . former Peace Corps volunteer in Georgia
- ❑ ❑ 1 - Minerva Cries Murder (1993)

■ **Carolyn BANKS** is the creator of a new mystery series set in the Texas horse world of equestrienne sleuth Robin Vaughn. *Death by Dressage* (1993) is followed by *Groomed for Death* (1994) and *Murder Well-Bred* (1995).

Robin Vaughn . . . Texas equestrienne sleuth
- ❑ ❑ 1 - Death by Dressage (1993)
- ❑ ❑ 2 - Groomed for Death (1994)
- ❑ ❑ 3 - Murder Well-Bred (1995)

■ **Jo BANNISTER** is a writer and newspaper editor in Northern Ireland where she won the United Kingdom's Royal Society of Arts bronze medal for excellence in journalism. She has written three mystery series, including her earliest featuring Dr. Clio Rees who leaves her medical practice to write mysteries, and the local chief inspector, Harry Marsh, who later becomes Clio's husband. They make their first appearance in *Striving with Gods* (1984). Bannister's most recent series involves several Castlemere cops, including Frank Shapiro,

Cal Donovan and Liz Graham, who debut in *A Bleeding of Innocents* (1993). Bannister also wrote a pair of high-action novels starring American photojournalist Mickey Flynn, who photographs a Middle Eastern terrorist training camp in *Shards* (1990) and deals with arson at his London home in *Death and Other Lovers* (1991). Bannister's nonseries novels include *Mosaic* (1986) and *The Mason Codex* (1988).

Dr. Clio Rees & Harry Marsh . . . physician/mystery writer & chief inspector in England
- ❏ ❏ 1 - Striving with Gods (1984)
- ❏ ❏ 2 - Gilgamesh (1989)
- ❏ ❏ 3 - The Going Down of the Sun (1990)

Frank Shapiro, Cal Donovan & Liz Graham . . . cops in Castlemere, England
- ❏ ❏ 1 - A Bleeding of Innocents (1993)
- ❏ ❏ 2 - Charisma (1994) [Britain–Sins of the Heart]
- ❏ ❏ 3 - A Taste for Burning (1995) [Britain–Burning Desires]
- ❏ ❏ 4 - No Birds Sing (1996)

■ **Willetta Ann BARBER**, along with her husband Rudolph F. Schabelitz (1884-1959), is the creator of Christopher "Kit" Storm, a New York City police (and later FBI) artist whose sketches provide important clues. Each of the seven books in this series, narrated by Kit's secretary (and later wife) Sherry Locke, is illustrated with Kit's drawings of the murder scene, suspects and other evidence. The back cover of the dust jacket for book #5, *The Noose is Drawn* (1945), shows a profile sketch of Willetta Ann drawn by her husband, who was the illustrator for their seven mystery collaborations.

Christopher "Kit" Storm . . . police illustrator for the NYPD
- ❏ ❏ 1 - Murder Draws a Line (1940)
- ❏ ❏ 2 - Pencil Points to Murder (1941)
- ❏ ❏ 3 - Drawn Conclusion (1942)
- ❏ ❏ 4 - Murder Enters the Picture (1942)
- ❏ ❏ 5 - The Noose Is Drawn (1945)
- ❏ ❏ 6 - Drawback to Murder (1947)
- ❏ ❏ 7 - The Deed Is Drawn (1949)

■ **Linda BARNES** is best known for Carlotta Carlyle, the red-headed cab-driving private eye first seen in the Edgar-award winning short story, "Lucky Penny" (1985). Her novel debut, *A Trouble of Fools* (1987), was Edgar- and Shamus-nominated and won the American Mystery Award. According to her creator, Carlotta is not casually named. She's capable, caring and competent. At 6' 1", she's a natural at volleyball, her sport of choice. She and her 5' 10" creator share a passion for blues guitar and a tendency toward righteous indignation. Barnes' earlier series character, Michael Spraggue, is passionate about the theatre world, not unlike his creator who once taught high school drama and worked briefly as a playwright. Spraggue's delightful Aunt Mary is the bonus in this series, introduced in 1982 and recently reissued in paperback. Unfortunately Barnes won't be writing any more Spraggue books because she says he was getting too depressed. As an amateur sleuth, many of the bodies he encountered were friends and associates. To keep Michael supplied with "cases," everybody around him was dying. Born and raised in Detroit, Barnes earned her BA in fine arts from Boston University. She lives outside Boston.

Carlotta Carlyle . . . 6' 1" cab-driving ex-cop P. I. in Boston
- ❏ ❏ 1 - **A Trouble of Fools** (1987) *American Mystery Award winner* ★
      Edgar & Shamus nominee ☆ ☆
- ❏ ❏ 2 - The Snake Tattoo (1989)

    ❑ ❑ 3 - Coyote (1990)
    ❑ ❑ 4 - Steel Guitar (1991)
    ❑ ❑ 5 - Snapshot (1993)
    ❑ ❑ 6 - Hardware (1995)

Michael Spraggue III . . . Boston, Massachusetts wealthy actor & ex-P. I.
    ❑ ❑ 1 - Blood Will Have Blood (1982)
    ❑ ❑ 2 - Bitter Finish (1983)
    ❑ ❑ 3 - Dead Heat (1984)
    ❑ ❑ 4 - Cities of the Dead (1986)

■ **Nevada BARR** is a U. S. park ranger whose *Track of the Cat* (set in Guadalupe Mountains National Park in Texas) was awarded both the Agatha and Anthony for best first novel in 1993. Her second outing, in northern Michigan's Isle Royale National Park, is a stunning tribute to the natural beauty of the Great Lakes. Although she worked boat patrol in the park, the author never dove in the icy waters of Lake Superior. She relied instead on the expertise of another park service officer who is named in the book's credits. Book #3 moves to the arid Anasazi ruins of Colorado's Mesa Verde National Park and then on to Lassen Volcanic National Park in northern California for book #4. Although she grew up near Lassen, Barr has not been assigned there, but used her fire-fighting experience from Idaho's Horse-fly Fire Camp. In addition to a master's degree in acting and 18 years of commercial theatre experience, Barr brings a certain genetic strength to her novel writing. She describes her grandmother, the globe-trotting missionary, as a fighting Quaker Democrat. Her mother, a licensed airplane pilot and mechanic, is also a carpenter who still ranches on the eastern edge of the Sierras. And like Anna Pigeon, the author has a sister named Molly, but Barr's sister is not a Manhattan psychologist—she is a commercial pilot for USAir.

    Anna Pigeon . . . U.S. park ranger
    ❑ ❑ 1 - **Track of the Cat** (1993) *Agatha & Anthony winner* ★ ★
    ❑ ❑ 2 - A Superior Death (1994)
    ❑ ❑ 3 - Ill Wind (1995)
    ❑ ❑ 4 - Firestorm (1996)

■ **M. C. BEATON** is the pseudonym of Scotland native Marion Chesney for her Hamish Macbeth series featuring a village constable in the highlands of Scotland. She says the idea for the first Hamish (pronounced HAY-mish) story—now a BBC television series—came to her while learning to fly cast for salmon at a fishing school in northern Scotland. Her newer mystery series stars Agatha Raisin, who like the author, lives in a charming cottage in the English Cotswolds. Chesney is best known as the author of over 100 novels of historical romance written under her own name and the various pseudonyms of Helen Crampton, Ann Fairfax, Jennie Tremaine and Charlotte Ward. Of her most recent Regency series—*The Banishment, Being the First Volume of the Daughters of Mannerling* (1995)—one reviewer declared that nobody writes Jane Austen like Marion Chesney. Her Regency novels are noted for their historical accuracy and a fondness for such period details as clothing, decor, cuisine and manners. No small surprise that Chesney was once the women's fashion editor of *Scottish Field* magazine. She also worked as a theatre critic and crime reporter on the *Scottish Daily Express* in Glasgow and later chief reporter for the *Daily Express* in London.

    Agatha Raisin . . . London advertising retiree in the Cotswolds
    ❑ ❑ 1 - Agatha Raisin and the Quiche of Death (1992)
    ❑ ❑ 2 - Agatha Raisin and the Vicious Vet (1993)
    ❑ ❑ 3 - Agatha Raisin and the Potted Gardener (1994)
    ❑ ❑ 4 - Agatha Raisin and the Walkers of Dembley (1995)

Hamish Macbeth . . . Scottish police constable
- ❑ ❑ 1 - Death of a Gossip (1985)
- ❑ ❑ 2 - Death of a Cad (1987)
- ❑ ❑ 3 - Death of an Outsider (1988)
- ❑ ❑ 4 - Death of a Perfect Wife (1989)
- ❑ ❑ 5 - Death of a Hussy (1990)
- ❑ ❑ 6 - Death of a Snob (1991)
- ❑ ❑ 7 - Death of a Prankster (1992)
- ❑ ❑ 8 - Death of a Glutton (1993)
- ❑ ❑ 9 - Death of a Travelling Man (1993)
- ❑ ❑ 10 - Death of a Charming Man (1994)
- ❑ ❑ 11 - Death of a Nag (1995)

■ **K. K. BECK** is the pseudonym of Seattle native Katherine Marris who has a background in advertising and previously edited a trade magazine. Beck's Iris Cooper series set in the 1920s, features a Stanford University coed. Her Jane da Silva series features a former lounge singer in present-day Seattle who collects money from her uncle's estate as payment for solving crimes on behalf of those who can't afford a private investigator. In addition to her two series mysteries, Beck has written several nonseries mysteries and survived an appearance on the TV game show *Jeopardy*.

Iris Cooper . . . Roaring 20s co-ed at Stanford University in Palo Alto, California
- ❑ ❑ 1 - Death in a Deck Chair (1984)
- ❑ ❑ 2 - Murder in a Mummy Case (1985)
- ❑ ❑ 3 - Peril Under the Palms (1989)

Jane da Silva . . . former lounge singer in Seattle, Washington
- ❑ ❑ 1 - A Hopeless Case (1992)
- ❑ ❑ 2 - Amateur Night (1993)
- ❑ ❑ 3 - Electric City (1994)
- ❑ ❑ 4 - Cold Smoked (1995)

■ **Jean BEDFORD** was born in England and moved to Australia the following year. She grew up in Victoria, graduated in Arts from Monash University, and later worked as a journalist, publisher's editor, and teacher of creative writing and English as a second language. Her mystery series features Sydney private eye Anna Southwood introduced in *To Make a Killing* (1990). Author of a number of short stories, Bedford currently divides her time between Sydney and the Illwarra Coast.

Anna Southwood . . . P. I. in Sydney Australia
- ❑ ❑ 1 - To Make a Killing (1990)
- ❑ ❑ 2 - Worse Than Death (1992)
- ❑ ❑ 3 - Signs of Murder (1993)

■ **Rose BEECHAM** is the creator of Amanda Valentine, ex-New York City cop turned Detective Inspector in New Zealand. *Introducing Amanda Valentine* (1992) and *Second Guess* (1994) are followed by *Fair Play* (1995).

Amanda Valentine . . . ex-NYPD cop now a detective inspector in New Zealand
- ❑ ❑ 1 - Introducing Amanda Valentine (1992)
- ❑ ❑ 2 - Second Guess (1994)
- ❑ ❑ 3 - Fair Play (1995)

■ **Sophie BELFORT** is the pseudonym of Massachusetts historian Kate Auspitz, who is the creator of a Boston mystery series featuring Molly Rafferty, professor of Renaissance and Reformation history, and Catholic cop Nick Hannibal. Introduced in *Lace Curtain Murders*, Molly makes her third appearance is *Eyewitness to Murder* (1992) which takes her to the Soviet Union.

    Molly Rafferty . . . Boston, Massachusetts college history professor
      ❏ ❏ 1 - The Lace Curtain Murders (1986)
      ❏ ❏ 2 - The Marvell College Murders (1991)
      ❏ ❏ 3 - Eyewitness to Murder (1992)

■ **Josephine BELL** is the pseudonym of Doris Bell Collier Ball (1897-1987), English physician and author of historical, true crime and mystery novels who attended Newnham College, Cambridge and then University College Hospital in London. She married Dr. Norman Dyer Ball in 1923 and they practiced medicine together until his death in 1936. After closing her solo medical practice at the age of 57, she continued writing until she was 85, producing more than 40 crime novels. One of the founders of the British Crime Writers Association, she chaired the organization in 1959. Many of her books feature medical mysteries and physician sleuths, like her series detectives, Drs. Wintringham and Frost. Her favorite police inspector, Steven Mitchell, appears in eight Wintringham books, three Warrington-Reeve titles and one of his own.

    Amy Tupper . . . amateur sleuth in London
      ❏ ❏ 1 - Wolf! Wolf! (1979)
      ❏ ❏ 2 - A Question of Inheritance (1980)

    Claude Warrington-Reeve . . . London barrister
      ❏ ❏ 1 - Easy Prey (1959)
      ❏ ❏ 2 - A Well-Known Face (1960)
      ❏ ❏ 3 - A Flat Tire in Fulham (1963) [U.S.–Fiasco in Fulham]
                   [APA–Room for a Body]

    David Wintringham, Dr. . . . British physician
      ❏ ❏ 1 - Murder in Hospital (1937)
      ❏ ❏ 2 - Death on the Borough Council (1937)
      ❏ ❏ 3 - Fall Over Cliff (1938)
      ❏ ❏ 4 - Death at Half-Term (1939) [APA–Curtain Call for a Corpse]
      ❏ ❏ 5 - From Natural Causes (1939)
      ❏ ❏ 6 - All Is Vanity (1940)
      ❏ ❏ 7 - Death at the Medical Board (1944)
      ❏ ❏ 8 - Death in Clairvoyance (1949)
      ❏ ❏ 9 - The Summer School Mystery (1950)
      ❏ ❏ 10 - Bones in the Barrow (1953)
      ❏ ❏ 11 - Fires at Fairlawn (1954)
      ❏ ❏ 12 - Death in Retirement (1956)
      ❏ ❏ 13 - The China Roundabout (1956)
                   [U.S.–Murder on the Merry-Go-Round]
      ❏ ❏ 14 - The Seeing Eye (1958)

    Henry Frost, Dr. . . . British physician
      ❏ ❏ 1 - The Upfold Witch (1964)
      ❏ ❏ 2 - Death on the Reserve (1966)

    Steven Mitchell . . . Scotland Yard Inspector
      ❏ ❏ 1 - The Port of London (1938)

■ **Liza BENNETT** is the author of two mysteries featuring Peg Goodenough, creative director at a New York advertising agency. Peg's first case is *Madison Avenue Murder* (1989) followed by *Seventh Avenue Murder* (1990).

> **Peg Goodenough** . . . New York City ad agency creative director
> ❑ ❑ 1 - Madison Avenue Murder (1989)
> ❑ ❑ 2 - Seventh Avenue Murder (1990)

■ **Laurien BERENSON**, of New Canaan, Connecticut, is the creator of a new dog series featuring Melanie Travis, divorced special education teacher posing as a poodle breeder. Melanie and her Aunt Peg, introduced in *A Pedigree to Die For* (1995) also appear in *Underdog* (1996) and *Dog Eat Dog* (1996). Berenson, the author of 15 novels, including romance, young adult and mystery, has 20 years' experience as a dog breeder and exhibitor. Her mother bred and showed dogs and her grandmother was a dog show judge. Berenson currently owns four miniature poodles, who are three generations of the same family. Her nonfiction has appeared in a variety of magazines and *The New York Times*.

> **Gwen Harding** . . . New York city journalist turned suburban wife & mother in upstate New York
> ❑ ❑ 1 - Deep Cover (1994)
>
> **Melanie Travis** . . . special ed teacher posing as poodle breeder in Connecticut
> ❑ ❑ 1 - A Pedigree to Die For (1995)
> ❑ ❑ 2 - Underdog (1996)
> ❑ ❑ 3 - Dog Eat Dog (1996)

■ **Carole BERRY** is the creator of a series featuring Bonnie Indermill, a Manhattan office temp with a love for tap dancing. Each one of Bonnie's work assignments provides a new setting and different cast of characters for murder and mayhem. Bonnie's sixth adventure, *The Death of a Dancing Fool* (1996), finds her sorting out the filing for old friend "Fast Eddie" Fong at the behest of NYPD's Captain Lee. Like her fictional sleuth, Berry has had a number of jobs—waitress, teacher, publisher's assistant, office manager, sales clerk and temporary typist. But unlike her heroine, she has been employed for a number of years by the same New York City law firm where she works as a legal secretary.

> **Bonnie Indermill** . . . tap-dancing Manhattan office temp
> ❑ ❑ 1 - The Letter of the Law (1987)
> ❑ ❑ 2 - The Year of the Monkey (1988)
> ❑ ❑ 3 - Good Night, Sweet Prince (1990)
> ❑ ❑ 4 - Island Girl (1991)
> ❑ ❑ 5 - The Death of a Difficult Woman (1994)
> ❑ ❑ 6 - The Death of a Dancing Fool (1996)

■ **Claudia BISHOP** is the pseudonym of Mary Stanton, creator of a new bed and breakfast series featuring sisters Sarah and Meg Quilliam. Sarah runs the Hemlock Falls Inn in a picturesque little town in upstate New York where sister Meg toils as the inn's chef. After growing up in Hawaii and Japan, Stanton started her writing career contributing nonfiction articles to national magazines. In 1993 she switched to fiction-writing full time after the sale of her process assessment business to a large corporation. She currently lives in upstate New York where she has also written young adult fiction and a novel of hardboiled suspense under the name Anne Craig.

Sarah & Meg Quilliam . . . Hemlock Falls, New York inn owner & chef (sisters)
- ❏ ❏ 1 - A Taste for Murder (1994)
- ❏ ❏ 2 - A Dash of Death (1995)
- ❏ ❏ 3 - A Pinch of Poison (1995)
- ❏ ❏ 4 - Murder Well-Done (1996)

■ **Veronica BLACK** is the pseudonym of English romance writer Maureen Peters for her mystery series featuring British investigative nun, Sister Joan first appears in *Vow of Silence* (1990). One of the founding members of the Romantic Novelists Association (1970), she is a prolific writer with more than 60 titles under a variety of pseudonyms—Catherine Darby, Judith Rothman, Sharon Whitby and Veronica Black. She has been a teacher of English to retarded children and includes among her interests the Tudor period, hagiography and theatre. She says she writes everything in longhand, often working eight to ten hours a day.

Sister Joan . . . British investigative nun in Cornwall England
- ❏ ❏ 1 - A Vow of Silence (1990)
- ❏ ❏ 2 - A Vow of Chastity (1992)
- ❏ ❏ 3 - A Vow of Sanctity (1993)
- ❏ ❏ 4 - A Vow of Obedience (1993)
- ❏ ❏ 5 - A Vow of Penance (1994)
- ❏ ❏ 6 - A Vow of Devotion (1994)
- ❏ ❏ 7 - A Vow of Poverty (1995)
- ❏ ❏ 8 - A Vow of Felicity (1996)

■ **L. L. BLACKMUR** is the pseudonym of Lydia Long, creator of New England writer Galen Shaw and financier Julian Baugh, introduced in *Love Lies Slain* (1989), later reappearing in *Love Lies Bleeding* (1989)

Galen Shaw & Julian Baugh . . . New England writer & financier
- ❏ ❏ 1 - Love Lies Slain (1989)
- ❏ ❏ 2 - Love Lies Bleeding (1989)

■ **Eleanor Taylor BLAND**, of Waukegan, Illinois, is the creator of Marti MacAlister, mystery fiction's first black woman homicide detective. MacAlister is a former Chicago cop and widowed mother of two who moves 60 miles out of the city to join the suburban Lincoln Prairie police force and start over after her husband is killed. Bland has managed to produce a book each year since the series was introduced in 1992, despite still working nine-to-five as an auditor. She says it works because Marti is always several chapters ahead of her.

Marti MacAlister . . . black police detective in Lincoln Prairie, Illinois
- ❏ ❏ 1 - Dead Time (1992)
- ❏ ❏ 2 - Slow Burn (1993)
- ❏ ❏ 3 - Gone Quiet (1994)
- ❏ ❏ 4 - Done Wrong (1995)

■ **Barbara BLOCK**, of Syracuse, New York, is the creator of a new mystery series featuring Robin Light, the recently widowed owner of Noah's Ark, a Syracuse pet shop. Robin's first appearance, *Chutes and Adders* (1994) is followed by *Twister* (1994). Block is an ex-Manhattanite whose past pets have included various reptiles and other exotic wildlife.

Robin Light . . . Syracuse, New York pet store owner
- ❏ ❏ 1 - Chutes and Adders (1994)
- ❏ ❏ 2 - Twister (1994)

■ **J. S. BORTHWICK** is the pseudonym of Joan Scott Creighton from Thomaston, Maine, creator of series pair Sarah Deane and Alex McKenzie—Boston graduate student in English literature and bird-watching Boston physician. Their adventures begin in Texas with the death of Sarah's boyfriend, but they return to home ground after successfully solving their first case. Later in the series, Sarah becomes a professor. The author describes herself as the "old lady of Medium Egg Cozies—yolk runny, white firm."

Sarah Deane & Dr. Alex McKenzie . . . English professor & internist in Boston, Massachusetts

- ❏ ❏ 1 - The Case of the Hook-Billed Kites (1982)
- ❏ ❏ 2 - The Down East Murders (1985)
- ❏ ❏ 3 - The Student Body (1986)
- ❏ ❏ 4 - Bodies of Water (1990)
- ❏ ❏ 5 - Dude on Arrival (1992)
- ❏ ❏ 6 - The Bridled Groom (1994)
- ❏ ❏ 7 - Dolly Is Dead (1995)

■ **D. B. BORTON** is the pseudonym of Ohio Wesleyan English professor Dr. Lynette Carpenter, creator of Cincinnati P. I.-in-training Cat Caliban, introduced in *One for the Money* (1993). After 38 years of marriage, Cat buys an apartment building and starts work on her P. I. license. Along the way she manages to demolish all the stereotypes about mothers and women of a certain age in a series of adventures which now numbers five. In her academic guise, the author teaches American literature, film, composition and women's studies and has written film and literary criticism for academic journals. She is editor with Wendy K. Kolmar of *Haunting the House of Fiction: Feminist Perspectives on Ghost Stories by American Women* (1991). A native of Houston, she earned a BA at the University of Texas and an MA and PhD at Indiana University.

Cat Caliban . . . 60-something P. I.-in-training in Cincinnati, Ohio

- ❏ ❏ 1 - One for the Money (1993)
- ❏ ❏ 2 - Two Points for Murder (1993)
- ❏ ❏ 3 - Three Is a Crowd (1994)
- ❏ ❏ 4 - Four Elements of Murder (1995)
- ❏ ❏ 5 - Five Alarm Fire (1996)

■ **Gail BOWEN** of Regina, Saskatchewan, is the creator of Canadian political science professor Joanne Kilbourn, introduced in 1990 with *Deadly Appearances*. Book #4, *A Colder Kind of Death* (1994) won the Ellis Awards for best novel, awarded by the Crime Writers of Canada.

Joanne Kilbourn . . . political science professor in Regina, Saskatchewan

- ❏ ❏ 1 - Deadly Appearances (1990)
- ❏ ❏ 2 - Love and Murder (1991) [APA–Murder at the Mendel]
- ❏ ❏ 3 - The Wandering Soul Murders (1993)
- ❏ ❏ 4 - **A Colder Kind of Death** (1994) *Ellis winner* ★

■ **Elisabeth BOWERS** is the creator of a mystery series set in Vancouver, British Columbia, featuring private investigator Meg Lacey, mother of a college-age son. The series opener, *Ladies' Night* (1988), is followed by *No Forwarding Address* (1991).

Meg Lacey . . . Vancouver, British Columbia P. I.

- ❏ ❏ 1 - Ladies' Night (1988)
- ❏ ❏ 2 - No Forwarding Address (1991)

■ **Eleanor BOYLAN** is the creator of the Agatha-nominated Clara Gamadge series featuring a character who first appeared as the wife of Henry Gamadge, the New York bibliophile created by Boylan's aunt, Elizabeth Daly, said to be the favorite American writer of Agatha Christie. By 1989 when Boylan's series begins, Clara has become Henry's widow. The family adventures continue, but this time around, Clara's the one doing the detecting. Boylan is a New York native who lives on Anna Maria Island in Florida where she also writes short stories for mystery magazines.

    Clara Gamadge . . . New York City widow of Henry, the forgery expert
      ❑ ❑ 1 - **Working Murder** (1989) *Agatha nominee* ☆
      ❑ ❑ 2 - Murder Observed (1990)
      ❑ ❑ 3 - Murder Machree (1992)
      ❑ ❑ 4 - Pushing Murder (1993)

■ **Lynn BRADLEY**, of Sugar Land, Texas, is the creator of a new Houston P. I. series featuring Cole January, a specialist in insurance investigations, introduced in the 1994 title *Stand-in for Murder*.

    Cole January . . . Houston, Texas insurance investigator
      ❑ ❑ 1 - Stand-in for Murder (1994)

■ **Christianna BRAND** is the pseudonym of Mary Christianna Lewis (1907-1985) who was born in Malaya and educated in India before being sent to a Franciscan convent in England. Family financial problems forced her to leave school in her late teens after which she worked in a variety of unfulfilling jobs. While employed as a salesgirl she developed a strong dislike for one of her coworkers and wrote her first novel (*Death in High Heels*, 1941) to murder the woman on paper. The book was not finished until after her marriage to surgeon Ronald S. Lewis, whose father was said to be her inspiration for Inspector Cockrill, Kent County constable. In addition to the six-book Cockrill series, Brand wrote romantic suspense, historical thrillers and near-fantasy.

    Inspector Cockrill . . . Kent County, England constable
      ❑ ❑ 1 - Heads You Lose (1941)
      ❑ ❑ 2 - Green for Danger (1944)
      ❑ ❑ 3 - Suddenly at His Residence (1946) [U.S.–The Crooked Wreath]
      ❑ ❑ 4 - Death of a Jezebel (1948)
      ❑ ❑ 5 - London Particular (1953) [U.S.–Fog of Doubt]
      ❑ ❑ 6 - Tour de Force (1955)

■ **Lilian Jackson BRAUN**, a Michigan native and former writer for the *Detroit Free Press*, is widely acknowledged as the originator of the cat craze in contemporary mysteries with her Cat Who series featuring newspaper columnist Jim Qwilleran and his Siamese cats Koko and Yum Yum. The first three installments appeared in the late 1960s, but almost 20 years passed before she revived the series in 1986 with the title that won an Edgar nomination. The following year, book #5 was nominated for an Anthony. Braun, her husband Earl and their two Siamese cats Koko III and Pitti Sing divide their time between Michigan and North Carolina.

    Jim Qwilleran, Koko & Yum Yum . . . Midwestern ex-police reporter & cats
      ❑ ❑ 1 - The Cat Who Could Read Backwards (1966)
      ❑ ❑ 2 - The Cat Who Ate Danish Modern (1967)
      ❑ ❑ 3 - The Cat Who Turned On and Off (1968)
      ❑ ❑ 4 - **The Cat Who Saw Red** (1986) *Edgar nominee* ☆
      ❑ ❑ 5 - **The Cat Who Played Brahms** (1987) *Anthony nominee* ☆

❑	❑	6	-	The Cat Who Played Post Office (1987)
❑	❑	7	-	The Cat Who Knew Shakespeare (1988)
❑	❑	8	-	The Cat Who Sniffed Glue (1988)
❑	❑	9	-	The Cat Who Went Underground (1989)
❑	❑	10	-	The Cat Who Talked to Ghosts (1990)
❑	❑	11	-	The Cat Who Lived High (1990)
❑	❑	12	-	The Cat Who Knew a Cardinal (1991)
❑	❑	13	-	The Cat Who Moved a Mountain (1992)
❑	❑	14	-	The Cat Who Wasn't There (1993)
❑	❑	15	-	The Cat Who Came to Breakfast (1994)
❑	❑	16	-	The Cat Who Went into the Closet (1994)
❑	❑	17	-	The Cat Who Blew the Whistle (1995)
❑	❑	18	-	The Cat Who Said Cheese (1996)

■ **Carol BRENNAN**, who lives in Dutchess County, New York, is a public relations consultant who took a two-year break to sell luxury Manhattan real estate before writing the second installment in her series featuring Liz Wareham, Manhattan PR consultant. Brennan, whose newer series features New York actress Emily Silver, has herself worked as an actress, a spokesperson and a speech therapist.

Emily Silver . . . New York actress

❑	❑	1	-	In the Dark (1994)
❑	❑	2	-	Chill of Summer (1995)

Liz Wareham . . . Manhattan public relations consultant

❑	❑	1	-	Headhunt (1991)
❑	❑	2	-	Full Commission (1992)

■ **Ann BRIDGE** is the pseudonym of Lady Mary Dolling Saunders O'Malley (1889-1974), wife of a British diplomat and creator of Julia Probyn Jamieson, freelance journalist and part-time British Intelligence agent. Jamieson appeared in seven novels from 1956 to 1969 beginning with *The Lighthearted Quest*, set in North Africa. Julia's later adventures included trips to Portugal (books #2 and #7), Switzerland (#3), the Hebrides (#4), France (#5) and Spain (#6). As Ann Bridge, the author also wrote two nonseries novels set in Hungary— *A Place to Stand* (1953) and *The Tightening String* (1962).

Julia Probyn Jamieson . . . freelance journalist & part-time British Intelligence agent

❑	❑	1	-	The Lighthearted Quest (1956)
❑	❑	2	-	The Portuguese Escape (1958)
❑	❑	3	-	The Numbered Account (1960)
❑	❑	4	-	The Dangerous Islands (1963)
❑	❑	5	-	Emergency in the Pyrenees (1965)
❑	❑	6	-	The Episode at Toledo (1966)
❑	❑	7	-	The Malady in Madeira (1969)

■ **Emily BRIGHTWELL** is the pseudonym of Cheryl Arguiles for the historical mystery series she writes for Berkley. These Victorian mysteries, featuring police Inspector Witherspoon and his sleuthing housekeeper Mrs. Jeffries, were originated by Berkley, who owns the copyrights. Arguiles has thus far written all the Inspector Witherspoon installments and expects to continue producing them at the rate of at least two titles a year.

Inspector Witherspoon & Mrs. Jeffries . . . Victorian inspector & housekeeper

❏	❏	1	-	The Inspector and Mrs. Jeffries (1993)
❏	❏	2	-	Mrs. Jeffries Dusts for Clues (1993)
❏	❏	3	-	The Ghost and Mrs. Jeffries (1993)
❏	❏	4	-	Mrs. Jeffries Takes Stock (1994)
❏	❏	5	-	Mrs. Jeffries on the Ball (1994)
❏	❏	6	-	Mrs. Jeffries on the Trail (1995)
❏	❏	7	-	Mrs. Jeffries Plays the Cook (1995)

■ **Toni BRILL** is the pseudonym used by a husband and wife writing team for their mystery series featuring Midge Cohen, New York city children's author fluent in Russian, who first appears in *Date with a Dead Doctor* (1991), followed by *Date with a Plummeting Publisher* (1993).

Midge Cohen . . . New York City children's author fluent in Russian

❏	❏	1	-	Date with a Dead Doctor (1991)
❏	❏	2	-	Date with a Plummeting Publisher (1993)

■ **D. C. BROD** is Deborah Cobban Brod, creator of the Quint McCauley series set in the western suburbs of Chicago. Described as a medium-boiled P. I., the ex-big city cop starts the series as a department store security chief and turns to private investigation in book #2, Error in Judgment (1990). Brod is currently at work on a novel of suspense set in the British Isles.

Quint McCauley . . . ex-cop turned P. I. in suburban Chicago

❏	❏	1	-	Murder in Store (1989)
❏	❏	2	-	Error In Judgment (1990)
❏	❏	3	-	Masquerade in Blue (1991) [APA–Framed in Blue]
❏	❏	4	-	Brothers in Blood (1993)

■ **Lizbie BROWN** is the pseudonym of Mary Marriott, creator of a quilting mystery series featuring Elizabeth Blair, American widow from Turkey Creek, Virginia, transplanted to Bath, England. The series opener, *Broken Star* (1992) is followed by *Turkey Tracks* (1994).

Elizabeth Blair . . . American widow from Turkey Creek, Virginia selling quilts in Bath, England

❏	❏	1	-	Broken Star (1992)
❏	❏	2	-	Turkey Tracks (1994)

■ **Rita Mae BROWN**, of Charlottesville, Virginia, is a best-selling author, Emmy-nominated screenwriter, poet and adopted mother of Sneaky Pie Brown, her tiger cat collaborator. Brown and Sneaky Pie are the creators of a mystery series featuring postmistress Mary Minor Haristeen (Harry to her friends) of Crozet, Virginia, and her tiger cat Mrs. Murphy, along with their friends Tee Tucker (a Welsh corgi), Simon the possum and Harry's ex-husband, the local veterinarian. Brown was an established novelist with more than six other titles to her credit before launching this series which the *New York Times Review of Books* called "charming...with wise, disarming wit."

Mary Minor Haristeen . . . small-town postmistress & cat in Crozet, Virginia

❏	❏	1	-	Wish You Were Here (1990)
❏	❏	2	-	Rest in Pieces (1992)
❏	❏	3	-	Murder at Monticello (1994)
❏	❏	4	-	Pay Dirt (1995)

■ **Edna BUCHANAN** won a Pulitzer Prize for her police-beat reporting for *The Miami Herald* and is the creator of the Edgar-nominated series featuring Miami crime reporter Britt Montero. Buchanan is also the author of true crime and autobiographical work including *Never Let Them See You Cry*, *The Corpse Had a Familiar Face* and *Nobody Lives Forever*.

    Britt Montero . . . Miami, Florida newspaper crime reporter
- ❏ ❏ 1 - Contents Under Pressure (1992)
- ❏ ❏ 2 - **Miami, It's Murder** (1994) *Edgar nominee* ☆
- ❏ ❏ 3 - Suitable for Framing (1995)
- ❏ ❏ 4 - Act of Betrayal (1996)

■ **Kathryn BUCKSTAFF** is the creator of a new series featuring Florida-based travel writer Morgana Dalton, who heads for Branson, Missouri, in the series opener, to report on the country music awards.

    Morgana Dalton . . . Florida-based travel writer
- ❏ ❏ 1 - No One Dies in Branson (1994)

■ **Pat BURDEN** is the creator of a cozy English mystery series featuring retired constable Henry Bassett who is perfectly content in his Herefordshire cottage, tending his pigs, chickens and garden. The tale of a bizarre crime (*Screaming Bones*) which upsets his domesticity earned Burden an Agatha nomination for best first traditional mystery in 1990.

    Henry Bassett . . . retired cop in Herefordshire, England
- ❏ ❏ 1 - **Screaming Bones** (1990) *Agatha nominee* ☆
- ❏ ❏ 2 - Wreath of Honesty (1990)
- ❏ ❏ 3 - Bury Him Kindly (1992)
- ❏ ❏ 4 - Father, Forgive Me (1993)

■ **Jan BURKE** and her newspaper reporter character, Irene Kelly, both live and work on the southern California coast. Burke's first manuscript was bought unagented and unsolicited by Simon & Schuster and went on to earn Agatha and Anthony nominations for best first mystery novel and accolades from President Bill Clinton, who mentioned in a television interview that it was on his reading list. In addition to her journalist-sleuth series, Burke writes a book column for the *Long Beach Press-Telegram* and chairs several promotional programs for Sisters in Crime. Her 1994 short story "Unharmed" was a winner of both the Ellery Queen Mystery Magazine Readers Award and the Macavity award which she shared with Deborah Adams.

    Irene Kelly . . . southern California newspaper reporter
- ❏ ❏ 1 - **Goodnight, Irene** (1993) *Agatha & Anthony nominee* ☆ ☆
- ❏ ❏ 2 - Sweet Dreams, Irene (1994)
- ❏ ❏ 3 - Dear Irene, (1995)
- ❏ ❏ 4 - Remember Me, Irene (1996)

■ **Anne BURTON** is one of the pseudonyms of Sara Hutton Bowen-Judd (1922-1985) who also wrote as Sara Woods, Mary Challis and Margaret Leek. As Anne Burton she wrote a three-part series featuring British banker Richard Trenton who was introduced in the 1980 title *The Dear Departed*. Although educated in Yorkshire, she did not begin writing until she moved to Nova Scotia. And despite the fact that all her novels are set in England, she is often considered Canada's most successful writer of detective fiction.

Richard Trenton . . . banker in England
- ❏ ❏ 1 - The Dear Departed (1980)
- ❏ ❏ 2 - Where There's a Will (1980)
- ❏ ❏ 3 - Worse Than a Crime (1981)

■ **Agnes BUSHELL** is the creator of a pair of private eye novels starring Wilson and Wilder, two Maine investigators whose first appearance, *Shadowdance* (1989) is followed by *Death by Chrystal* (1993).

Wilson & Wilder . . . private investigators in Maine
- ❏ ❏ 1 - Shadowdance (1989)
- ❏ ❏ 2 - Death by Chrystal (1993)

■ **Gwendoline BUTLER** has published almost 60 novels since 1956 and is the author of a long-running series featuring London Inspector John Coffin, who is more enthusiastically received in the author's native England than in the U.S. Coffin's actress wife, Stella Pinero, is both likable and theatrical according to *Publisher's Weekly* and can be counted on to bring some light to these often dark tales. Butler has also written seven nonseries novels, including the historical mystery that won a Silver Dagger in 1973 (*A Coffin for Pandora*)—not part of the Inspector Coffin series despite the title. Under the pseudonym Jennie Melville she writes another police series and numerous titles of romantic suspense and historical fiction.

Inspector John Coffin . . . London police inspector
- ❏ ❏ 1 - Dead in a Row (1957)
- ❏ ❏ 2 - The Dull Dead (1958)
- ❏ ❏ 3 - The Murdering Kind (1958)
- ❏ ❏ 4 - Death Lives Next Door (1960)
- ❏ ❏ 5 - Make Me a Murderer (1961)
- ❏ ❏ 6 - Coffin in Oxford (1962)
- ❏ ❏ 7 - A Coffin for Baby (1963)
- ❏ ❏ 8 - Coffin Waiting (1964)
- ❏ ❏ 9 - A Nameless Coffin (1966)
- ❏ ❏ 10 - Coffin Following (1968)
- ❏ ❏ 11 - Coffin's Dark Number (1969)
- ❏ ❏ 12 - A Coffin from the Past (1970)
- ❏ ❏ 13 - A Coffin for the Canary (1974) [U.S.–Sarsen Place]
- ❏ ❏ 14 - Coffin on the Water (1986)
- ❏ ❏ 15 - Coffin in Fashion (1987)
- ❏ ❏ 16 - Coffin Underground (1988)
- ❏ ❏ 17 - Coffin in the Black Museum (1989)
- ❏ ❏ 18 - Coffin in the Museum of Crime (1989)
- ❏ ❏ 19 - Coffin and the Paper Man (1991)
- ❏ ❏ 20 - Coffin on Murder Street (1992)
- ❏ ❏ 21 - Cracking Open a Coffin (1993)
- ❏ ❏ 22 - A Coffin for Charley (1994)
- ❏ ❏ 23 - The Coffin Tree (1994)
- ❏ ❏ 24 - A Dark Coffin (1995)

■ **Carol CAIL** is the creator of a new Colorado mystery series featuring investigative reporter Maxey Burnell who first appears in *Private Lies* (1993).

Maxey Burnell . . . investigative reporter in Colorado
- ❏ ❏ 1 - Private Lies (1993)
- ❏ ❏ 2 - Unsafe Keeping (1995)

■ **Dorothy CANNELL** (rhymes with channel), born in Nottingham, England, came to the U.S. in 1963 and currently lives in Peoria, Illinois, where she writes a series she calls deliciously malicious, set almost entirely in England. This Agatha- and Anthony-nominated series features Ellie and Ben Haskell and the dotty Tramwell sisters who pop in and out after their introduction in the second installment. Ellie is an unmarried overweight interior decorator in the first outing where she hires an escort to hunt treasure and ends up marrying him and inheriting the castle. He's an aspiring chef who writes trashy novels to support his later works of literature. Cannell has written a number of short stories including the Agatha award-winning "The Family Jewels" (*Malice Domestic 3*).

    Ellie & Ben Haskell & the Tramwells . . . interior decorator & writer/chef with a pair of sister sleuths in Chitterton Falls, England

      ❑ ❑ 1 - The Thin Woman (1984)
      ❑ ❑ 2 - Down the Garden Path: A Pastoral Mystery (1985)
      ❑ ❑ 3 - **The Widow's Club** (1988) *Agatha & Anthony nominee* ☆ ☆
      ❑ ❑ 4 - Mum's the Word (1990)
      ❑ ❑ 5 - Femmes Fatal (1992)
      ❑ ❑ 6 - How to Murder Your Mother-in-law (1994)
      ❑ ❑ 7 - How to Murder the Man of Your Dreams (1995)

■ **Taffy CANNON** is the author name used by Eileen E. Cannon for her mystery series featuring Los Angeleno, Nan Robinson, attorney-investigator for the California State Bar. Before launching the series, Cannon wrote *Convictions: A Novel of the Sixties* and an Academy-Award nominated short film titled *Doubletalk*. Like many writers, Cannon has worked a variety of jobs but is pleased that her epitaph can read "She Never Waitressed." She did, however, correctly wager everything on a *Jeopardy* Daily Double when she identified Shirley Jackson in the category Women Writers. Cannon lives in Carlsbad, California.

    Nan Robinson . . . Los Angeles investigator for the California State Bar

      ❑ ❑ 1 - A Pocketful of Karma (1993)
      ❑ ❑ 2 - Tangled Roots (1995)
      ❑ ❑ 3 - Class Reunions are Murder (1996)

■ **P. M. CARLSON** is Patricia M. Carlson, who taught psychology and statistics at Cornell University before introducing her statistician sleuth, Maggie Ryan, in 1985. Nominated for Anthony, Edgar and Macavity awards, the series opens with Maggie as a college student and follows her through marriage and motherhood. In 1992, Carlson launched the Marty Hopkins series featuring a young woman sheriff in southern Indiana. A past president of Sisters in Crime, Carlson lives in Brooklyn where she also writes short stories featuring Bridget Mooney, 19th century guttersnipe and would-be actress.

    Maggie Ryan . . . college student turned statistician & mother in New York City

      ❑ ❑ 1 - Audition for Murder (1985)
      ❑ ❑ 2 - **Murder Is Academic** (1985) *Anthony nominee* ☆
      ❑ ❑ 3 - Murder is Pathological (1986)
      ❑ ❑ 4 - **Murder Unrenovated** (1987) *Anthony & Macavity nominee* ☆ ☆
      ❑ ❑ 5 - Rehearsal for Murder (1988)
      ❑ ❑ 6 - **Murder in the Dog Days** (1990) *Edgar nominee* ☆
      ❑ ❑ 7 - Murder Misread (1990)
      ❑ ❑ 8 - Bad Blood (1991)

    Martine LaForte Hopkins . . . southern Indiana deputy sheriff

      ❑ ❑ 1 - Gravestone (1992)
      ❑ ❑ 2 - Bloodstream (1995)

■ **Sarah CAUDWELL** is the pseudonym of English barrister Sarah Cockburn for her mystery series featuring Oxford professor Hilary Tamar, an expert in medieval law frequently called upon to assist five young barristers who practice together in a London firm. Many of Caudwell's fans continue to puzzle over the question—Is the wise professor a woman or a man? Thus far, the author has declined to settle the debate. Caudwell is the daughter of writer Claud Cockburn and actress and journalist Jean Ross who is generally regarded as the original Sally Bowles in Christopher Isherwood's *Goodbye to Berlin*. Caudwell graduated in Classics from Aberdeen University before studying law at St. Ann's College, Oxford.

  Hilary Tamar . . . Oxford professor of medieval law
  ❑ ❑ 1 - Thus Was Adonis Murdered (1981)
  ❑ ❑ 2 - The Shortest Way to Hades (1985)
  ❑ ❑ 3 - **The Sirens Sang of Murder** (1989) *Anthony winner* ★
         Agatha nominee ☆

■ **Mary CHALLIS** is one of the pseudonyms of Sara Hutton Bowen-Judd (1922-1985) who also wrote as Sara Woods and Margaret Leek. As Mary Challis she wrote a four-book series featuring barrister Jeremy Locke who first appeared in *Burden of Proof* (1980). Far better known is her 48-book series featuring Antony Maitland, often called the British Perry Mason.

  Jeremy Locke . . . attorney in England
  ❑ ❑ 1 - Burden of Proof (1980)
  ❑ ❑ 2 - Crimes Past (1980)
  ❑ ❑ 3 - The Ghost of an Idea (1981)
  ❑ ❑ 4 - A Very Good Hater (1981)

■ **Sally CHAPMAN** spent nine years with IBM and was well acquainted with life in the Silicon Valley before launching her mystery series featuring computer investigator Juliet Blake, introduced in *Raw Data* (1991).

  Juliet Blake . . . Silicon Valley fraud investigator in California
  ❑ ❑ 1 - Raw Data (1991)
  ❑ ❑ 2 - Love Bytes (1994)
  ❑ ❑ 3 - Cyber Kiss (1996)

■ **Kate CHARLES** is a pseudonym of Carol Chase, an American living in England who brings personal experience as a church administrator to her ecclesiastical mystery series featuring solicitor David Middleton-Brown and artist Lucy Kingsley. David and Lucy meet in the first installment when David is hired by a priest who is being blackmailed. Anglican politics and church art and architecture play dominant roles in this series. Charles was born in Cincinnati and holds a BA from Illinois State University and an MA from Indiana University. Having worked as a librarian and in public relations for public radio, she currently writes full time from her home outside London.

  Lucy Kingsley & David Middleton-Brown . . . London artist & solicitor
  ❑ ❑ 1 - A Drink of Deadly Wine (1991)
  ❑ ❑ 2 - The Snares of Death (1993)
  ❑ ❑ 3 - Appointed to Die (1994)
  ❑ ❑ 4 - A Dead Man Out of Mind (1995)
  ❑ ❑ 5 - Evil Angels Among Them (1995)

■ **Elaine Raco CHASE** is a best-selling romance writer turned mystery writer and 1995-96 president of Sisters in Crime International. Her twelve romance novels, with over three million copies in print, were published in 24 countries in 14 languages. She is the author of two essays in *The Fine Art of Murder* (1993) and editor of the short story anthology *Partners in Crime* (1994). She is also the creator of Florida reporter Nikki Holden and private eye Roman Cantrell who first appeared in *Dangerous Places* (1987) and later in *Dark Corners* (1988). Their adventures will continue.

> **Nikki Holden & Roman Cantrell** . . . reporter & P. I. in Florida
>
> ❑ ❑ 1 - Dangerous Places (1987)
> ❑ ❑ 2 - Dark Corners (1988)

■ **P. F. CHISHOLM** is the pseudonym of English historical writer Pauline Finney, creator of a new mystery series featuring Sir Robert Carey, Elizabethan nobleman, who first appears in 1592 as told in *A Famine of Horses* (1995). Finney was only 17 when she completed her first novel, *A Shadow of Gulls* (1977), published two years later after winning the prestigious David Higham Award. Set in second century Ireland, the book is based on the Ulster cycle of Celtic Hero Tales featuring Lugh the Harper as the hero. The saga continues with *The Crow Goddess* (1978). Her recent historical fiction includes *Firedrake's Eye* set amidst Tudor politics of 1583 London and a plot to kill Queen Elizabeth I. Finney says she plans to write screenplays, science fiction, children's books and history. She also intends to learn several languages, including Hungarian, so she can translate the novels of her Hungarian grand-mother, Dr. Lilla Veszy-Wagner. Born in London, where she now lives, Finney earned a BA (with honors) at Wadham College, Oxford.

> **Sir Robert Carey** . . . Elizabethan nobleman (1592) in England
>
> ❑ ❑ 1 - A Famine of Horses (1995)
> ❑ ❑ 2 - A Season of Knives (1996)
> ❑ ❑ 3 - A Surfeit of Guns (1997)

■ **Agatha CHRISTIE** (1890-1976) is undoubtedly the world's best-known woman mystery writer, with two of the all-time best-loved series characters ever created, Hercule Poirot and Miss Jane Marple. In addition to being the undisputed master of the cozy mystery, she is one of the best-selling authors in the history of the world. Twenty years after her death, her books continue to sell millions of copies and her life's work has inspired more than 20 critical and biographical works. It is reported that this shy, quiet woman wrote many of her novels in the bathtub and learned much about drugs and poisons while working as a hos-pital volunteer during the First World War. She later became a top mystery playwright and is credited with writing the longest running play in London history (*The Mousetrap*, 1954). Six titles of romantic suspense written under the name Mary Westmacott were later reprinted under her own name. And in 1945 she published *Come Tell Me How You Live*, a humorous nonfiction account of her archaeological adventures with her second husband, Sir Max Mallowan. She served as president of the Detection Club in 1954 and that same year was the first to be named Grand Master by the Mystery Writers of America. In 1971 she was made a Dame Commander of the Order of the British Empire. Her full name was Dame Agatha Mary Clarissa Miller Christie Mallowan.

> **Hercule Poirot** . . . former Belgian cop turned London-based private detective
>
> ❑ ❑ 1 - The Mysterious Affair at Styles (1920)
> ❑ ❑ 2 - Murder on the Links (1923)
> ❑ ❑ 3 - Poirot Investigates (1924)
> ❑ ❑ 4 - The Murder of Roger Ackroyd (1926)
> ❑ ❑ 5 - The Big Four (1927)

❑ ❑ 6 - The Mystery of the Blue Train (1928)
❑ ❑ 7 - Peril at End House (1932)
❑ ❑ 8 - Lord Edgeware Dies (1933) [U.S.–Thirteen at Dinner]
❑ ❑ 9 - Three-Act Tragedy (1934) [U.S.–Murder in Three Acts]
❑ ❑ 10 - Murder on the Orient Express (1934)
       [U.S.–Murder in the Calais Coach]
❑ ❑ 11 - Death in the Clouds (1935) [U.S.–Death in the Air]
❑ ❑ 12 - The ABC Murders (1935) [APA–The Alphabet Murders]
❑ ❑ 13 - Murder in Mesopotamia (1936)
❑ ❑ 14 - Cards on the Table (1936)
❑ ❑ 15 - Dumb Witness (1937) [U.S.–Poirot Loses a Client]
❑ ❑ 16 - Death on the Nile (1937)
❑ ❑   - Murder in the Mews [3 stories] (1937) [U.S.–Dead Man's Mirror]
❑ ❑ 17 - A Holiday for Murder (1938)
❑ ❑ 18 - Appointment with Death (1938)
❑ ❑ 19 - Hercule Poirot's Christmas (1938) [U.S.–Murder for Christmas]
❑ ❑ 20 - Sad Cypress (1939)
❑ ❑ 21 - One, Two, Buckle My Shoe (1940) [U.S.–The Patriotic Murders]
❑ ❑ 22 - Evil Under the Sun (1941)
❑ ❑ 23 - Five Little Pigs (1941) [U.S.–Murder in Retrospect]
❑ ❑ 24 - The Hollow (1946) [U.S.–Murder After Hours]
❑ ❑ 25 - Taken at the Flood (1948) [U.S.–There is a Tide]
❑ ❑ 26 - Mrs. McGinty's Dead (1952) [U.S.–Blood Will Tell]
❑ ❑ 27 - After the Funeral (1953) [U.S.–Funerals are Fatal]
❑ ❑ 28 - Hickory, Dickory, Dock (1955) [U.S.–Hickory, Dickory, Death]
❑ ❑ 29 - Dead Man's Folly (1956)
❑ ❑ 30 - Cat Among the Pigeons (1959)
❑ ❑ 31 - The Clocks (1963)
❑ ❑ 32 - Third Girl (1966)
❑ ❑ 33 - Hallowe'en Party (1969)
❑ ❑ 34 - Elephants Can Remember (1972)
❑ ❑ 35 - Curtain (1975)

Miss Jane Marple . . . elderly spinster living in St. Mary's Mead, England
❑ ❑ 1 - The Murder at the Vicarage (1930)
❑ ❑ 2 - The Body in the Library (1942)
❑ ❑ 3 - The Moving Finger (1942)
❑ ❑ 4 - A Murder is Announced (1950)
❑ ❑ 5 - They Do It with Mirrors (1952) [U.S.–Murder with Mirrors]
❑ ❑ 6 - A Pocket Full of Rye (1953)
❑ ❑ 7 - 4:50 from Paddington (1957) [U.S.–What Mrs. McGillicuddy Saw!]
❑ ❑ 8 - The Mirror Crack'd from Side to Side (1962)
       [U.S.–The Mirror Crack'd]
❑ ❑ 9 - A Caribbean Mystery (1964)
❑ ❑ 10 - At Bertram's Hotel (1965)
❑ ❑ 11 - Nemesis (1971)
❑ ❑ 12 - Sleeping Murder (1976)

Tuppence & Tommy Beresford . . . English adventurers for hire; intelligence agents
❑ ❑ 1 - The Secret Adversary (1922)
❑ ❑   - Partners in Crime [short stories] (1929)
❑ ❑ 2 - N or M? (1941)
❑ ❑ 3 - By the Pricking of My Thumbs (1968)
❑ ❑ 4 - Postern of Fate (1973)

■ **Joyce CHRISTMAS** is the author of two mystery series featuring women of accomplishment who find themselves in sleuthing roles—New York socialite Lady Margaret Priam and retired Connecticut office manager Betty Trenka. Lady Margaret, who will make her eighth appearance in 1996, is an English noblewoman living in New York City. Her friends are socialites and royalty but she pursues a romantic relationship with a police detective. Christmas is currently an executive with a hotel consulting firm where she edits a monthly newsletter. A former book and magazine editor, she is also the author of three other novels (*Blood Child*, *Dark Tide* and *Hidden Assets*) and several children's plays.

Betty Trenka . . . retired Connecticut office manager
❏ ❏ 1 - This Business Is Murder (1993)
❏ ❏ 2 - Death at Face Value (1995)

Lady Margaret Priam . . . English noblewoman in New York City
❏ ❏ 1 - Suddenly in Her Sorbet (1988)
❏ ❏ 2 - Simply to Die For (1989)
❏ ❏ 3 - A Fete Worse than Death (1990)
❏ ❏ 4 - A Stunning Way to Die (1991)
❏ ❏ 5 - Friend or Faux (1991)
❏ ❏ 6 - It's Her Funeral (1992)
❏ ❏ 7 - A Perfect Day for Dying (1994)

■ **Jill CHURCHILL** is the pseudonym of Janice Young Brooks, author of more than a dozen historical novels, one gothic and numerous nonfiction books and articles. She chose her pseudonym with the expectation that her books would be shelved alongside Agatha Christie's, so it's no surprise that her charming mysteries feature Jane Jeffry, a young, suburban Miss Jane Marple with kids, a dog and the busy schedule of a single mother. Jane's first adventure *Grime & Punishment* (1989) was awarded an Agatha for best first traditional mystery. Each of this series' titles is a humorous play on the words of a favorite classic such as #6, *From Here to Paternity*, which includes a wonderful genealogy sub-plot. If you share Brooks' love for ancestor hunting, you'll want to check out her list of surnames at the front of the book. You just might detect a relative.

Jane Jeffry . . . Chicago, Illinois suburban single mother
❏ ❏ 1 - **Grime & Punishment** (1989) *Agatha & Macavity winner* ★ ★
     Anthony nominee ☆
❏ ❏ 2 - A Farewell to Yarns (1991)
❏ ❏ 3 - A Quiche Before Dying (1993)
❏ ❏ 4 - The Class Menagerie (1993)
❏ ❏ 5 - A Knife to Remember (1994)
❏ ❏ 6 - From Here to Paternity (1995)
❏ ❏ 7 - Silence of the Hams (1996)

■ **Carol Higgins CLARK**, daughter of famed suspense writer Mary Higgins Clark, is a graduate of Mount Holyoke College. Before launching her Regan Reilly series—nominated for an Agatha as best first novel—the younger Clark worked as her mother's research assistant. She has acted professionally on stage, film and television. Fictional private eye Regan Reilly, daughter of famous mystery novelist Nora Regan Reilly, wraps up her third case (*Iced*) in the glamorous winter setting of Aspen, Colorado.

Regan Reilly . . . Los Angeles P. I.
❏ ❏ 1 - **Decked** (1992) *Agatha nominee* ☆
❏ ❏ 2 - Snagged (1993)
❏ ❏ 3 - Iced (1995)

■ **Carolyn Chambers CLARK**, of St. Petersburg, Florida, is the creator of two new series with women protagonists—St. Petersburg RN Megan Baldwin and Florida P. I. Theresa Franco.

    Megan Baldwin . . . St. Petersburg, Florida registered nurse
       ❑ ❑ 1 - Deadlier Than Death (1993)

    Theresa Franco . . . P. I. in Florida
       ❑ ❑ 1 - Dangerous Alibis (1994)

■ **Anna CLARKE** has written numerous nonseries mysteries set in the literary world, so it is no surprise that her series detective is an English professor at the University of London. Writer and professor Paula Glenning's first appearance is *Last Judgment* (1985) and her seventh and most recent is *The Case of the Ludicrous Letters* (1994).

    Paula Glenning . . . British professor & writer in London
       ❑ ❑ 1 - Last Judgment (1985)
       ❑ ❑ 2 - Cabin 3033 (1986)
       ❑ ❑ 3 - The Mystery Lady (1986)
       ❑ ❑ 4 - Last Seen in London (1987)
       ❑ ❑ 5 - Murder in Writing (1988)
       ❑ ❑ 6 - The Whitelands Affair (1989)
       ❑ ❑ 7 - The Case of the Paranoid Patient (1991)
       ❑ ❑ 8 - The Case of the Ludicrous Letters (1994)

■ **Melissa CLEARY** is the author of a new mystery series for dog lovers, featuring college film instructor Jackie Walsh, her ten-year-old son Peter and their Alsatian shepherd Jake—a retired police dog who is rescued by Jackie and Peter in the first installment entitled *A Tail of Two Murders* (1992).

    Jackie Walsh & Jake . . . college film instructor with her ex-police dog in the bustling small town of Palmer, Massachusetts
       ❑ ❑ 1 - A Tail of Two Murders (1992)
       ❑ ❑ 2 - Dog Collar Crime (1993)
       ❑ ❑ 3 - Hounded to Death (1993)
       ❑ ❑ 4 - Skull and Dog Bones (1994)
       ❑ ❑ 5 - First Pedigree Murder (1994)
       ❑ ❑ 6 - Dead and Buried (1994)
       ❑ ❑ 7 - The Maltese Puppy (1995)
       ❑ ❑ 8 - Murder Most Beastly (1996)

■ **Ann CLEEVES** is perhaps best known for her bird-watching series featuring George Palmer-Jones, an official of the Home Office, and his wife Molly whose first appearance is *A Bird in the Hand* (1986). Cleeves' second series featuring Inspector Stephen Ramsey is a traditional British police mystery which debuts with *A Lesson in Dying* (1990). Ramsay's fourth appearance in *Killjoy* (1994).

    George & Molly Palmer-Jones . . . ex-Home Office official/bird-watcher & wife in Surrey England
       ❑ ❑ 1 - A Bird in the Hand (1986)
       ❑ ❑ 2 - Come Death and High Water (1987)
       ❑ ❑ 3 - Murder in Paradise (1989)
       ❑ ❑ 4 - A Prey to Murder (1989)
       ❑ ❑ 5 - Sea Fever (1991)
       ❑ ❑ 6 - Another Man's Poison (1993)

❑ ❑ 7 - The Mill on the Shore (1994)
❑ ❑ 8 - High Island Blues (1996)

Stephen Ramsey . . . British Inspector
   ❑ ❑ 1 - A Lesson in Dying (1990)
   ❑ ❑ 2 - Murder in My Backyard (1991)
   ❑ ❑ 3 - A Day in the Death of Dorothea Cassidy (1992)
   ❑ ❑ 4 - Killjoy (1995)

■ **Liza CODY** is the pseudonym of Liza Nassim, probably the only mystery writer who has studied painting at the Royal Academy School of Art and worked at Madame Tussaud's Wax Museum. Cody's hard-boiled detective Anna Lee is an operative with a London security firm, while her newer detective is a female wrestler, junkyard security guard and small-time criminal. Both series have won awards including a Silver Dagger for *Bucket Nut*.

Anna Lee . . . P. I. for small London firm
   ❑ ❑ 1 - **Dupe** (1980) *Creasey winner* ★ *Edgar nominee* ☆
   ❑ ❑ 2 - Bad Company (1982)
   ❑ ❑ 3 - Stalker (1984)
   ❑ ❑ 4 - Head Case (1985)
   ❑ ❑ 5 - Under Contract (1986)
   ❑ ❑ 6 - **Backhand** (1991) *Edgar nominee* ☆

Eva Wylie . . . London wrestler & security guard
   ❑ ❑ 1 - **Bucket Nut** (1993) *Silver Dagger* ★
   ❑ ❑ 2 - Monkey Wrench (1994)

■ **Margaret COEL** is the creator of a new Wyoming series featuring Jesuit missionary John Aloysius O'Malley and Vicky Holden, Arapaho attorney on the Wind River Reservation. Their first appearance in this critically-acclaimed Native American series is *The Eagle Catcher* (1995) followed by *The Ghost Walker* (1996). Coel is the author of five nonfiction books on the American West, including *Chief Lefthand*, *Southern Arapaho*, and *Goin' Railroading*. Her articles on the West have appeared in numerous publications, including *The New York Times* and *American Heritage*.

John Aloysius O'Malley & Vicky Holden . . . Jesuit missionary & Arapaho attorney in Wind River Reservation, Wyoming
   ❑ ❑ 1 - The Eagle Catcher (1995)
   ❑ ❑ 2 - The Ghost Walker (1996)

■ **Anthea COHEN** is the pseudonym of nurse and medical writer Doris Simpson, creator of a medical mystery series featuring Agnes Carmichael, British hospital staff nurse. Nurse Carmichael is introduced in *Angel Without Mercy* as an awkward, slightly pathetic women who one day decides she will no longer be bullied. In *Angel of Vengeance* she is assigned to a case of suspected child abuse and clashes violently with the parents involved.

Agnes Carmichael . . . hospital staff nurse in England
   ❑ ❑ 1 - Angel Without Mercy (1982)
   ❑ ❑ 2 - Angel of Vengeance (1982)
   ❑ ❑ 3 - Angel of Death (1983)
   ❑ ❑ 4 - Fallen Angel (1984)
   ❑ ❑ 5 - Guardian Angel (1985)
   ❑ ❑ 6 - Hell's Angel (1986)
   ❑ ❑ 7 - Ministering Angel (1986)

❑ ❑ 8 - Destroying Angel (1988)
❑ ❑ 9 - Angel Dust (1989)
❑ ❑ 10 - Recording Angel (1991)
❑ ❑ 11 - Angel in Action (1992)
❑ ❑ 12 - Angel in Love (1993)
❑ ❑ 13 - Angel in Autumn (1995)

■ **Carolyn COKER** is the creator of a mystery series set in the art world with Andrea Perkins, restorer of paintings for a Boston Museum, whose first appearance is *The Other David* (1984). Coker has extensive television experience both on camera and off as an administrator.

Andrea Perkins . . . museum art historian & restorer of paintings at a Boston museum
❑ ❑ 1 - The Other David (1984)
❑ ❑ 2 - The Hand of the Lion (1987)
❑ ❑ 3 - The Balmoral Nude (1990)
❑ ❑ 4 - Appearance of Evil (1993)

■ **Anna Ashwood COLLINS**, of Jekyll Island, Georgia, is the creator of amateur sleuth and efficiency expert, Abby Doyle, who specializes in crime solving for the affluent. Collins is a past executive director of the International Association of Crime Writers and a former field agent for the U.S. Department of Labor. She currently works as a columnist (*Crime by Collins*) and freelance interviewer for various publications. The second installment in her series—*Red Roses for a Dead Trucker*—is likely to appear first in Japan, perhaps in 1996.

Abigail Doyle . . . New York City efficiency expert
❑ ❑ 1 - Deadly Resolutions (1994)
❑ ❑ 2 - Red Roses for a Dead Trucker (1996)

■ **Barbara COMFORT** is the creator of a Vermont series featuring 70-something artist and painter Tish McWhinney. A portrait and landscape painter who has exhibited in galleries from Boston to Honolulu, Comfort studied painting at New York's National Academy, Massachusetts' Cape School of Art and the Ecole des Beaux Arts in France. During the Second World War, while operating her own welding company, she bought five acres of land in Vermont for $100. On this site overlooking the Bromley and Tabor Mountains, she later built the house which became her summer studio where she continues to paint. In the winter she writes from her apartment in a historic house in Greenwich Village. Comfort is also the author of *Vermont Village Murder* (1982) and *Green Mountain Murder* (1984).

Tish McWhinney . . . 70-something Vermont artist & painter
❑ ❑ 1 - Phoebe's Knee (1986)
❑ ❑ 2 - Grave Consequences (1989)
❑ ❑ 3 - The Cashmere Kid (1993)
❑ ❑ 4 - Elusive Quarry (1995)

■ **Susan CONANT** is the creator of a popular mystery series featuring Holly Winter, magazine columnist for *Dog's Life* and owner of the lovable malamute Rowdy. Set in Cambridge, Massachusetts, this series involves varied aspects of the dog world. Conant and her husband, along with their two cats and two Alaskan malamutes, live in Massachusetts where she serves as state coordinator of the Alaskan Malamute Protection League.

Holly Winter . . . 30-something dog trainer & magazine columnist in Cambridge, Massachusetts
- ❏ ❏ 1 - A New Leash on Death (1989)
- ❏ ❏ 2 - Dead and Doggone (1990)
- ❏ ❏ 3 - A Bite of Death (1991)
- ❏ ❏ 4 - Paws Before Dying (1992)
- ❏ ❏ 5 - Gone to the Dogs (1992)
- ❏ ❏ 6 - Bloodlines (1992)
- ❏ ❏ 7 - Ruffly Speaking (1993)
- ❏ ❏ 8 - Black Ribbon (1995)

■ **Natasha COOPER** is the pseudonym of Daphne Wright, successful romance novelist and creator of an amateur sleuth who leads a double life. As Willow King, British civil service administrator, she works Tuesday through Thursday for the Department of Old Age Pensions (DOAP) and her wardrobe and flat are as drab as her job. After leaving the office on Thursday evening, a manicure, make-up and new hair transform her into Cressida Woodruffe, writer of romance novels with a glamorous apartment and housekeeper cook.

Willow King & Cressida Woodruffe . . . British civil servant & romance novelist
- ❏ ❏ 1 - Festering Lilies (1990) [U.S.–A Common Death]
- ❏ ❏ 2 - Poison Flowers (1991)
- ❏ ❏ 3 - Bloody Roses (1992)
- ❏ ❏ 4 - Bitter Herbs (1993)
- ❏ ❏ 5 - Rotten Apples (1995)

■ **Susan Rogers COOPER** is the creator of Milt Kovak, Oklahoma sheriff's deputy, who unexpectedly meets the woman who'll change his life in *Chasing Away the Devil* (1991). You'll want to read this delightful series just for the titles, especially *Man in the Green Chevy* (1988) and *Houston in the Rear View Mirror* (1990). Cooper later introduced E. J. (Eloise Janine) Pugh, Texas housewife, mother and romance novelist in *One Two, What Did Daddy Do?* (1992). Although Cooper never intended E. J. to be a series character, this Texas mom makes her second appearance in *Hickory, Dickory Stock* (1996). Cooper's most recent series features Kimmey Kruse, a young stand-up comic introduced in *Funny as a Dead Comic* (1993) followed by *Funny as a Dead Relative* (1994).

E. J. Pugh . . . Texas housewife & mother & romance writer
- ❏ ❏ 1 - One, Two, What Did Daddy Do? (1992)
- ❏ ❏ 2 - Hickory, Dickory, Stock (1996)

Kimmey Kruse . . . stand-up comic in Austin, Texas
- ❏ ❏ 1 - Funny as a Dead Comic (1993)
- ❏ ❏ 2 - Funny as a Dead Relative (1994)

Milton Kovak . . . Prophesy County, Oklahoma chief deputy
- ❏ ❏ 1 - The Man in the Green Chevy (1988)
- ❏ ❏ 2 - Houston in the Rear View Mirror (1990)
- ❏ ❏ 3 - Other People's Houses (1990)
- ❏ ❏ 4 - Chasing Away the Devil (1991)
- ❏ ❏ 5 - Dead Moon on the Rise (1994)
- ❏ ❏ 6 - Doctors and Lawyers and Such (1995)

■ **Patricia Daniels CORNWELL** is a former crime reporter for the *Charlotte Observer* who, after six years in the Virginia Medical Examiner's Office, launched her best-selling series starring Dr. Kay Scarpetta, Medical Examiner. Scarpetta works closely with the Richmond police department and the Behavioral Sciences Division of the FBI. Her first case swept the mystery awards for 1990 and book #4, *Cruel and Unusual* (1993), won a Gold Dagger. Before creating her forensic series, Cornwell wrote the 1983 biography of Ruth Graham, wife of evangelist Billy Graham.

> **Dr. Kay Scarpetta** . . . Richmond, Virginia chief medical examiner
> ❑ ❑ 1 - **Postmortem** (1990) *Edgar, Creasey, Anthony & Macavity winner* ★ ★ ★
> ❑ ❑ 2 - Body of Evidence (1991)
> ❑ ❑ 3 - All That Remains (1992)
> ❑ ❑ 4 - **Cruel and Unusual** (1993) *Gold Dagger* ★
> ❑ ❑ 5 - The Body Farm (1994)
> ❑ ❑ 6 - From Potter's Field (1995)

■ **Alisa CRAIG** is the pseudonym of Charlotte MacLeod for her two Canadian mystery series. The more traditional series features Royal Canadian Mounted Police (RCMP) officer Madoc Rhys and his wife Janet. The Grub-and-Stakers series, set in Lobelia Falls, Ontario, features without a doubt the zaniest character names in mystery fiction. This series tells the adventures of Dittany Henbit Monk and her husband Osbert, a writer of westerns, along with his aunt Arethusa, writer of romance novels.

> **Dittany Henbit Monk & Osbert Monk** . . . garden club member & western author husband in Lobelia Falls, Ontario Canada
> ❑ ❑ 1 - The Grub-and-Stakers Move a Mountain (1981)
> ❑ ❑ 2 - The Grub-and-Stakers Quilt a Bee (1985)
> ❑ ❑ 3 - The Grub-and-Stakers Pinch a Poke (1988)
> ❑ ❑ 4 - The Grub-and-Stakers Spin a Yarn (1990)
> ❑ ❑ 5 - The Grub-and-Stakers House a Haunt (1993)

> **Madoc & Janet Rhys** . . . RCMP Inspector & wife
> ❑ ❑ 1 - A Pint of Murder (1980)
> ❑ ❑ 2 - Murder Goes Mumming (1981)
> ❑ ❑ 3 - A Dismal Thing To Do (1986)
> ❑ ❑ 4 - Trouble in the Brasses (1989)
> ❑ ❑ 5 - The Wrong Rite (1992)

■ **Frances CRANE** was born in Lawrenceville, Illinois, but lived in Europe for many years where she wrote articles and short stories for American publications. After her return to Lawrenceville in her early 40s, she started the long-running series featuring globe-trotting husband and wife detectives Pat and Jean Abbot. The two meet over murder on their first vacation and for 24 years and 26 books they look everywhere for a vacation without homicide.

> **Pat & Jean Abbot** . . . husband & wife traveling detection team from San Francisco
> ❑ ❑ 1 - The Turquoise Shop (1941)
> ❑ ❑ 2 - The Golden Box (1942)
> ❑ ❑ 3 - The Yellow Violet (1943)
> ❑ ❑ 4 - The Pink Umbrella (1943)
> ❑ ❑ 5 - The Applegreen Cat (1943)
> ❑ ❑ 6 - The Amethyst Spectacles (1944)
> ❑ ❑ 7 - The Indigo Necklace (1945)
> ❑ ❑ 8 - The Cinnamon Murder (1946)
> ❑ ❑ 9 - The Shocking Pink Hat (1946)

❏ ❏ 10 - Murder on the Purple Water (1947)
❏ ❏ 11 - Black Cypress (1948)
❏ ❏ 12 - The Flying Red Horse (1949)
❏ ❏ 13 - The Daffodil Blonde (1950)
❏ ❏ 14 - Murder in Blue Street (1951) [Britain–Murder in Blue Hour]
❏ ❏ 15 - The Polkadot Murder (1951)
❏ ❏ 16 - Thirteen White Tulips (1953)
❏ ❏ 17 - Murder in Bright Red (1953)
❏ ❏ 18 - The Coral Princess Murders (1954)
❏ ❏ 19 - Death in Lilac Time (1955)
❏ ❏ 20 - Horror on the Ruby X (1956)
❏ ❏ 21 - The Ultraviolet Widow (1956)
❏ ❏ 22 - The Man in Gray (1958) [Britain–The Gray Stranger]
❏ ❏ 23 - The Buttercup Case (1958)
❏ ❏ 24 - Death Wish Green (1960)
❏ ❏ 25 - The Amber Eyes (1962)
❏ ❏ 26 - The Body Beneath a Mandarin Tree (1965)

■ **Hamilton CRANE** is the pseudonym of Sarah J. Mason for her work continuing the Miss Seeton series featuring English spinster and retired art teacher Emily Dorothea Seeton. The series was originated by Heron Carvic, who wrote the first five novels before his death in 1980. Hampton Charles wrote another three titles in this series before Mason took over and quickened the pace with her first Miss Seeton title in 1991. Mason has another series under her own name featuring Detective Superintendent Trewley and Sergeant Stone of the Allingham police department.

Miss Emily D. Seeton . . . retired British art teacher in Kent, England
❏ ❏ 1 - **Picture Miss Seeton (1968)** *Edgar nominee* ☆ [Heron Carvic]
❏ ❏ 2 - Miss Seeton Draws the Line (1969) [Heron Carvic]
❏ ❏ 3 - Witch Miss Seeton (1971) [Brit–Miss Seeton, Bewitched] [H. Carvic]
❏ ❏ 4 - Miss Seeton Sings (1973) [Heron Carvic]
❏ ❏ 5 - Odds on Miss Seeton (1975) [Heron Carvic]
❏ ❏ 6 - Advantage Miss Seeton (1990) [Hampton Charles]
❏ ❏ 7 - Miss Seeton at the Helm (1990) [Hampton Charles]
❏ ❏ 8 - Miss Seeton, by Appointment (1990) [Hampton Charles]
❏ ❏ 9 - Miss Seeton Cracks the Case (1991)
❏ ❏ 10 - Miss Seeton Paints the Town (1991)
❏ ❏ 11 - Miss Seeton Rocks the Cradle (1992)
❏ ❏ 12 - Hands up, Miss Seeton (1992)
❏ ❏ 13 - Miss Seeton by Moonlight (1992)
❏ ❏ 14 - Miss Seeton Plants Suspicion (1993)
❏ ❏ 15 - Miss Seeton Goes to Bat (1993)
❏ ❏ 16 - Starring Miss Seeton (1994)
❏ ❏ 17 - Miss Seeton Undercover (1994)
❏ ❏ 18 - Miss Seeton Rules (1994)
❏ ❏ 19 - Sold to Miss Seeton (1995)

■ **Camilla T. CRESPI** was born in Prague to an American mother and Italian father who served in the diplomatic corps. She came to the U.S. as a teenager and later earned degrees from Barnard College and Columbia University, before returning to Italy. While in Rome she dubbed films for Fellini, Germi, Visconti, Wertmuller and other directors. Not unlike the author, Crespi's series detective Simono Griffo is a food-loving Italian who works as an art buyer for a New York advertising agency. Crespi is a past president of the New York chapter of Mystery Writers of America and lives in New York City.

Simona Griffo . . . New York City advertising executive & gourmet cook
- ❑ ❑ 1 - The Trouble with a Small Raise (1991)
- ❑ ❑ 2 - The Trouble with Moonlighting (1991)
- ❑ ❑ 3 - The Trouble with Too Much Sun (1992)
- ❑ ❑ 4 - The Trouble with Thin Ice (1993)
- ❑ ❑ 5 - The Trouble with Going Home (1995)
- ❑ ❑ 6 - The Trouble with a Bad Fit (1996)

■ **Deborah CROMBIE** writes a British police series featuring Superintendent Duncan Kincaid and Sergeant Gemma James introduced in the Agatha-nominated *A Share in Death* (1993). Crombie worked in advertising and publishing before moving to Edinburgh after marrying a Scot. She later lived in Chester, England, before returning to Texas. Her first Kincaid and James title was also nominated for a Macavity for best first novel. She lives in Trophy Club, Texas.

Duncan Kincaid & Gemma James . . . Scotland Yard superintendent & sergeant
- ❑ ❑ 1 - **A Share in Death** (1993) *Agatha & Macavity nominee* ☆ ☆
- ❑ ❑ 2 - All Shall Be Well (1994)
- ❑ ❑ 3 - Leave the Grave Green (1995)

■ **Amanda CROSS** is the pseudonym of Carolyn G. Heilbrun, Phi Beta Kappa from Wellesley College with MA and PhD degrees in English from Columbia University. She has taught at Brooklyn College and Columbia, served as president of the Modern Language Association, been awarded five honorary doctorates and published numerous scholarly works in addition to her Edgar-nominated mystery series featuring English professor Kate Fansler introduced in *In the Last Analysis* (1964).

Kate Fansler . . . New York City university English professor
- ❑ ❑ 1 - **In the Last Analysis** (1964) *Edgar nominee* ☆
- ❑ ❑ 2 - The James Joyce Murder (1967)
- ❑ ❑ 3 - Poetic Justice (1970)
- ❑ ❑ 4 - The Theban Mysteries (1972)
- ❑ ❑ 5 - The Question of Max (1976)
- ❑ ❑ 6 - Death in a Tenured Position (1981) [Britain–A Death in the Faculty]
- ❑ ❑ 7 - Sweet Death, Kind Death (1984)
- ❑ ❑ 8 - No Word from Winifred (1986)
- ❑ ❑ 9 - A Trap for Fools (1989)
- ❑ ❑ 10 - The Players Come Again (1990)
- ❑ ❑ 11 - An Imperfect Spy (1995)

■ **Ann CROWLEIGH** is the joint pseudonym of Barbara Cummings and Jo-Ann Power for their new historical mystery series set in Victorian London. Featuring twin sisters Miranda and Claire Clively, the series opens with *Dead as Dead Can Be* (1993).

Mirinda & Clare Clively . . . Victorian London twin sisters
- ❑ ❑ 1 - Dead as Dead Can Be (1993)
- ❑ ❑ 2 - Wait for the Dark (1993)

■ **Laura CRUM** grew up in horse country—Santa Cruz, California—where she is a regular competitor on the cutting and team-roping circuit. Owner of three quarter horses and a pair of Queensland heelers, Crum is the creator of a new mystery series featuring 30-something northern California horse veterinarian Gail McCarthy. The horse vet's first adventure, set in the cutthroat world of cowhorse competition, is followed by *Hoofprints* (1996).

Gail McCarthy . . . Santa Cruz, California horse veterinarian
- ❏ ❏ 1 - Cutter (1994)
- ❏ ❏ 2 - Hoofprints (1996)

■ **Clare CURZON** began writing imaginative stories at the age of five, but didn't see publication of her first novel until 36 years later. The book was *Death in Deakins Wood* (1963), the first of her police procedurals featuring Inspector Marcus MacLurg, written as Rhona Petrie. During the 1970s she wrote a number of dark suspense novels as Marie Buchanan, the most successful of which was *Anima* (1972). But this author is better known in the U.S. as Clare Curzon, creator of the Thames Valley mystery series featuring Detective Superintendent Mike Yeadings. As director of the Serious Crimes Squad, Yeadings makes his tenth appearance in *Nice People* (1995). Born in Sussex, with a BA (honors) from the University of London, this author has worked throughout Europe as an interpreter, translator, probation officer and social secretary. She is Eileen-Marie Duell Buchanan.

Mike Yeadings . . . Thames Valley, England detective superintendent of Serious Crimes Squad
- ❏ ❏ 1 - I Give You Five Days (1983)
- ❏ ❏ 2 - Masks and Faces (1984)
- ❏ ❏ 3 - The Trojan Hearse (1985)
- ❏ ❏ 4 - The Quest for K (1986)
- ❏ ❏ 5 - Three-Core Lead (1988)
- ❏ ❏ 6 - The Blue-Eyed Boy (1990)
- ❏ ❏ 7 - Cat's Cradle (1992)
- ❏ ❏ 8 - First Wife, Twice Removed (1993)
- ❏ ❏ 9 - Death Prone (1994)
- ❏ ❏ 10 - Nice People (1995)

■ **Barbara D'AMATO** won both the Anthony and Agatha for her true crime title *The Doctor, The Murder, The Mystery* featured on *Unsolved Mysteries*. She has written musical comedies, suspense and crime fiction, including two early titles starring forensic pathologist Dr. Gerritt DeGraaf. Her Cat Marsala series features a Chicago freelance magazine writer who investigates big stories like gambling, prostitution and most recently, Christmas tree farming. A past president of Sisters in Crime, D'Amato is also the author of Anthony-nominated *On My Honor* written under the pseudonym Malacai Black. Her newest series features a pair of Chicago cops who've been featured in several of her short stories. Suze Figueroa and Norm Bennis make their first book-length appearance in the technothriller *KILLER.app* (1996).

Cat Marsala . . . Chicago, Illinois freelance investigative journalist
- ❏ ❏ 1 - Hardball (1990)
- ❏ ❏ 2 - Hard Tack (1991)
- ❏ ❏ 3 - Hard Luck (1992)
- ❏ ❏ 4 - Hard Women (1993)
- ❏ ❏ 5 - Hard Case (1994)
- ❏ ❏ 6 - Hard Christmas (1995)

Dr. Gerritt DeGraaf . . . forensic pathologist in Chicago, Illinois
- ❏ ❏ 1 - The Hands of Healing Murder (1980)
- ❏ ❏ 2 - The Eyes on Utopia Murders (1981)

Suze Figueroa & Norm Bennis . . . pair of Chicago cops
- ❏ ❏ 1 - KILLER.app (1996)

■ **Mary DAHEIM** (pronounced DAY-hime) is a Seattle native and former journalist who writes two Agatha-nominated mystery series. Her lighter series features Judith McMonigle, owner and operator of a Seattle bed & breakfast, while the Alpine series features Emma Lord, small-town newspaper editor and publisher. Since 1991 Daheim has produced a combined 16 titles in the two series. Although the town of Alpine no longer exists, it was a thriving mill center in western Washington until the late 1920s. The mill's owner, Carl Clemans, was a cousin of Mark Twain's despite the spelling discrepancy between the two branches of the Clemens family. When the logging operation shut down, Alpine was intentionally burned to the ground to prevent transients from starting forest fires. In the intervening 60-some years, a second stand of timber has completely obliterated the original town. Daheim's mother grew up in Alpine and because local lore played such a large part in her life, she felt the town deserved to live again. A graduate of the University of Washington, Daheim is the author of several historical romances, including *Love's Pirate*, *Destiny's Pawn* and *Sound of Surrender*.

Emma Lord . . . small-town newspaper owner & editor in Alpine, Washington
- ❑ ❑ 1 - **The Alpine Advocate** (1992) *Agatha nominee* ☆
- ❑ ❑ 2 - The Alpine Betrayal (1993)
- ❑ ❑ 3 - The Alpine Christmas (1993)
- ❑ ❑ 4 - The Alpine Decoy (1994)
- ❑ ❑ 5 - The Alpine Escape (1995)
- ❑ ❑ 6 - The Alpine Fury (1995)
- ❑ ❑ 7 - The Alpine Gamble (1996)

Judith McMonigle . . . Seattle, Washington bed & breakfast owner
- ❑ ❑ 1 - **Just Desserts** (1991) *Agatha nominee* ☆
- ❑ ❑ 2 - Fowl Prey (1991)
- ❑ ❑ 3 - Holy Terrors (1992)
- ❑ ❑ 4 - Dune to Death (1993)
- ❑ ❑ 5 - Bantam of the Opera (1993)
- ❑ ❑ 6 - Fit of Tempera (1994)
- ❑ ❑ 7 - Major Vices (1995)
- ❑ ❑ 8 - Murder My Suite (1995)
- ❑ ❑ 9 - Auntie Mayhem (1996)

■ **Catherine DAIN** is the pseudonym of Judith Garwood, creator of the Freddie O'Neal series featuring a hard-boiled Reno private eye with a love for flying, a weakness for Keno and a gun in her cowboy boot. Twice nominated for a Shamus award, Freddie's adventures have been optioned for television. With a theatre arts degree from UCLA and a graduate degree from the University of Southern California, Dain worked as a TV newscaster before turning to mystery writing. She was managing editor of USC's *New Management* magazine and edited two books on leadership and a book on global business for the USC International Business Education and Research Center. Like Freddie O'Neal, the author was raised in Reno and lives with two cats.

Freddie O'Neal . . . Reno, Nevada plane-flying P. I.
- ❑ ❑ 1 - **Lay It on the Line** (1992) *Shamus nominee* ☆
- ❑ ❑ 2 - Sing a Song of Death (1993)
- ❑ ❑ 3 - Walk a Crooked Mile (1994)
- ❑ ❑ 4 - **Lament for a Dead Cowboy** (1994) *Shamus nominee* ☆
- ❑ ❑ 5 - Bet Against the House (1995)

■ **Elizabeth DALY** (1878-1967), reported to be Agatha Christie's favorite American mystery writer, earned a BA from Bryn Mawr in 1901 and an MA from Columbia the following year. She was a tutor in English and French and for many years a producer and director of amateur theatre. She was also the creator of 16 novels featuring New York bibliophile and forgery expert Henry Gamadge—a series she started at the age of 61. Twenty-one years later, she was awarded a special Edgar by the Mystery Writers of America in recognition of her entire body of work. The Gamadge stories continue with Henry's widow Clara, in a series written by Daly's niece, Eleanor Boylan.

Henry Gamadge . . . New York City author & bibliophile
- ❑ ❑ 1 - Unexpected Night (1940)
- ❑ ❑ 2 - Deadly Nightshade (1940)
- ❑ ❑ 3 - Murder in Volume 2 (1941)
- ❑ ❑ 4 - The House Without the Door (1942)
- ❑ ❑ 5 - Nothing Can Rescue Me (1943)
- ❑ ❑ 6 - Evidence of Things Seen (1943)
- ❑ ❑ 7 - Arrow Pointing Nowhere (1944) [APA–Murder Listens In ('49)]
- ❑ ❑ 8 - The Book of the Dead (1944)
- ❑ ❑ 9 - Any Shape or Form (1945)
- ❑ ❑ 10 - Somewhere in the House (1946)
- ❑ ❑ 11 - The Wrong Way Down (1946) [APA–Shroud for a Lady ('56)]
- ❑ ❑ 12 - Night Walk (1947)
- ❑ ❑ 13 - The Book of the Lion (1948)
- ❑ ❑ 14 - And Dangerous to Know (1949)
- ❑ ❑ 15 - Death and Letters (1950)
- ❑ ❑ 16 - The Book of the Crime (1951)

■ **Gloria DANK** is the creator a Connecticut mystery series featuring Bernard Woodrull and Arthur "Snooky" Randolph, a writer of children's books and his visiting brother-in-law, introduced in *Friends Till the End* (1989). With her physicist father Milton Dank, she is the author of several mysteries, including *The Computer Caper* (1983), *A UFO Has Landed* (1983), *The 3-D Traitor* (1984), *The Treasure Code* (1985) and *The Computer Game Murder* (1985). Her fantasy novels for young adults include *The Forest of App* (1983) and *The Changeling*. Phi Beta Kappa at Princeton, Dank studied at Cambridge University as a George C. Marshall scholar in England. After graduate school she worked briefly as a computer programmer and research analyst.

Bernard Woodrull & Arthur "Snooky" Randolph . . . writer of children's books & visiting brother-in-law in Connecticut
- ❑ ❑ 1 - Friends Till the End (1989)
- ❑ ❑ 2 - Going Out in Style (1990)
- ❑ ❑ 3 - As the Sparks Fly Upward (1992)
- ❑ ❑ 4 - The Misfortune of Others (1993)

■ **Denise DANKS** is the creator of a mystery series featuring London computer journalist Georgina Powers introduced in *User Deadly* (1989). Like her heroine, Danks has worked as a journalist specializing in information technology and spent much of 1994 traveling and researching in the U.S., after being awarded the Raymond Chandler Fulbright Award. She lives in London.

Georgina Powers . . . British computer journalist in London
- ❑ ❑ 1 - User Deadly (1989) [Britain–The Pizza House Crash]
- ❑ ❑ 2 - Frame Grabber (1992)
- ❑ ❑ 3 - Wink a Hopeful Eye (1994)

■ **Diane Mott DAVIDSON** is the creator of Colorado's culinary sleuth Goldy Bear, owner of Goldilocks' Catering, "Where everything is just right." Goldy's debut, *Catering to Nobody*, was nominated for Agatha, Anthony and Macavity awards as best first mystery novel of 1990. In addition to her catering adventures, the books contain original recipes created especially for this series. The supporting cast includes police detective Tom Schulz, Goldy's son Arch, one ex-husband and Goldy's dessert-loving best friend Marla, who happens to be another ex-wife of the same ex-husband. Before writing full time, Davidson was a prep school teacher, volunteer counselor, tutor and licensed lay preacher in the Episcopal church. She also worked as a caterer and completed what she describes as "the police academy without pushups." Born in Honolulu and raised in Maryland and Virginia, Davidson has a BA from Stanford and an MFA from Johns Hopkins. She currently lives in Evergreen, Colorado, her inspiration for Aspen Meadow.

Goldy Bear . . . Aspen Meadow, Colorado caterer & single mother
- ❑ ❑ 1 - **Catering to Nobody** (1990)
    - ***Agatha, Anthony & Macavity nominee*** ☆ ☆ ☆
- ❑ ❑ 2 - Dying for Chocolate (1992)
- ❑ ❑ 3 - Cereal Murders (1993)
- ❑ ❑ 4 - The Last Suppers (1994)
- ❑ ❑ 5 - Killer Pancake (1995)
- ❑ ❑ 6 - The Main Course (1996)

■ **Dorothy Salisbury DAVIS**, author of more than 20 mystery novels, is a seven-time Edgar nominee, past president of the Mystery Writers of America and one of the founding directors of Sisters in Crime. She was named Grand Master in 1984 and later received a lifetime achievement Anthony Award in 1989. Her first crime novel, *The Judas Cat*, was published in 1949, but the majority of her work is nonseries except for three books featuring DA's investigator Jasper Tully and his Scottish housekeeper Mrs. Norris and four with Julie Hayes, former New York City actress and columnist who tells fortunes in Times Square. Her seven Edgar nominations include four for novels and three for short stories. She cites as her best work *A Gentle Murderer* (1951), *The Pale Betrayer* (1965) and *God Speed the Night* (1958). A native of Chicago and graduate of Barat College in Lake Forest, Illinois, Davis currently lives in Palisades, New York.

Jasper Tully & Mrs. Norris . . . DA's investigator & his Scottish housekeeper in New York City
- ❑ ❑ 1 - Death of an Old Sinner (1957)
- ❑ ❑ 2 - A Gentleman Called (1958)
- ❑ ❑ 3 - Old Sinners Never Die (1959)

Julie Hayes . . . former actress & columnist in New York City
- ❑ ❑ 1 - A Death in the Life (1976)
- ❑ ❑ 2 - Scarlet Night (1980)
- ❑ ❑ 3 - Lullaby of Murder (1984)
- ❑ ❑ 4 - The Habit of Fear (1987)

■ **Lindsey DAVIS**, born and raised in Birmingham, England, joined the civil service after reading English at Oxford. She currently lives in London where she writes a brilliant historical series featuring Marcus Didius Falco and the world of first century Rome. Falco is a plebeian P. I. and staunch republican who much to his own discomfort finds himself in the employ of the emperor Vespasian. Falco's love interest is the patrician Helena Justina.

Marcus Didius Falco . . . P. I. in ancient Rome
- ❑ ❑ 1 - Silver Pigs (1989)
- ❑ ❑ 2 - Shadows in Bronze (1990)

		3	-	Venus in Copper (1991)
❏	❏	4	-	Iron Hand of Mars (1992)
❏	❏	5	-	Poseidon's Gold (1993)
❏	❏	6	-	Last Act in Palmyra (1994)
❏	❏	7	-	Time to Depart (1995)
❏	❏	8	-	A Dying Light in Corduba (1996)

■ **Janet DAWSON** is the creator of Oakland P. I. Jeri Howard, whose first case, *Kindred Crimes* (1990), won the St. Martin's Press/Private Eye Writer's Association contest for best first P. I. novel. It was also nominated for the Anthony, Shamus and Macavity awards. Dawson lives in Alameda, California where she has been a newspaper reporter, an enlisted journalist and an officer in the U.S. Navy.

Jeri Howard . . . Oakland, California P. I.

		1	-	**Kindred Crimes** (1990) *SMP/PWA winner* ★
				Anthony, Macavity & Shamus nominee ☆ ☆ ☆
❏	❏	2	-	Till the Old Men Die (1993)
❏	❏	3	-	Take a Number (1993)
❏	❏	4	-	Don't Turn Your Back on the Ocean (1994)
❏	❏	5	-	Nobody's Child (1995)

■ **Dianne DAY** is the creator of a new mystery series featuring Caroline Fremont Jones, 20-something owner of a San Francisco typewriting service at the turn-of-the-century. Armed with her typewriting machine and a degree from Wellesley, she leaves Boston for Bagdad by the Bay and business success at ten cents a page. Among the clients in her first adventure, *The Strange Files of Fremont Jones* (1995), are a handsome young attorney who encourages her to rethink her vow of celibacy, an older Chinese gentleman whose will needs typing, and the mysterious manuscript owner, Edgar Allen Partridge. Day is the author of seven novels of romantic suspense written under the now-retired pseudonyms of Madelyn Sanders and Diana Bane. She has worked as a psychologist, psychotherapist and health services administrator in northern California and the eastern and southeastern U.S. In 1993 she returned to California where she combines her writing with work at a Monterey historical museum.

Fremont Jones . . . owner of a typewriting service at the turn of the century in San Francisco, California

		1	-	The Strange Files of Fremont Jones (1995)
❏	❏	2	-	Fire and Fog (1996)
❏	❏	3	-	The Bohemian Murders (1997)

■ **Marele DAY** is the creator of Australia's first woman private eye, Claudia Valentine, introduced in *The Life and Crimes of Harry Lavender* (1988). Claudia's third appearance, *The Last Tango of Delores Delgado* (1992), was the Shamus winner for best paperback original that year. An honors graduate of the University of Sydney, Day grew up in Sydney but has traveled extensively and lived in Italy, France and Ireland. She once took a voyage by yacht from Cairns to Singapore which resulted in a near shipwreck in the Java Sea. Her work experience ranges from fruit picking to academic teaching and she is currently a freelance editor. She is the author of *Successful Promotion by Writers* in "The Art of Self Promotion" series.

Claudia Valentine . . . Australian P. I.

		1	-	The Life and Crimes of Harry Lavender (1988)
❏	❏	2	-	The Case of the Chinese Boxes (1990)
❏	❏	3	-	**The Last Tango of Delores Delgado** (1992) *Shamus winner* ★
❏	❏	4	-	The Disappearance of Madalena Grimaldi (1994)

■ **Lillian DE LA TORRE** is the pseudonym of Lillian de la Torre Bueno McCue (1902-1993), creator of 29 stories of histo-detection featuring the real-life 18th century lexicographer and sage, Dr. Samuel Johnson, narrated by his biographer, that fascinating rake James Boswell. The mysteries, characters and settings are all real but the solutions are only rarely something other than fiction. She called herself a histo-detector, engaged in the craft of solving mysteries of the long-ago. Born in New York City, she earned a BA from College of New Rochelle (1921) and master's degrees from Columbia (1927) and Harvard (1933). She also attended the University of Munich and the University of Colorado where she later worked as an instructor. She once taught high school in New York City and in 1945 served as a technical advisor to Twentieth Century Fox.

Samuel Johnson, Dr. & James Boswell . . . 18th century English lexicographer & his biographer in London
- ❑ ❑ 1 - Dr. Sam: Johnson, Detector (1946)
- ❑ ❑ 2 - The Detections of Dr. Sam: Johnson (1960)
- ❑ ❑ 3 - The Return of Dr. Sam: Johnson, Detector (1984)
- ❑ ❑ 4 - The Exploits of Dr. Sam: Johnson (1987)

■ **Sandy DENGLER** is the creator of two mystery series featuring law enforcement officers. Jack Prester is a U.S. park ranger whose four adventures are set in Death Valley (1993), Acadia National Park in Maine (1993), Mt. Ranier National Park in Washington state (1994) and Great Smoky Mountain National Park in Tennessee (1995). Dengler's Arizona police series features Sgt. Joe Rodriguez of the Phoenix police deparment, introduced in *Cat Killer* (1993). Armed with a master's degree in desert ecology, she has milked scorpions, plucked chickens and wrangled cows. The author of more than 40 nonmysteries, Dengler lives in Ashford, Washington, where her park ranger husband is based at Mt. Ranier National Park.

Jack Prester . . . U. S. park ranger
- ❑ ❑ 1 - Death Valley (1993)
- ❑ ❑ 2 - A Model Murder (1993)
- ❑ ❑ 3 - Murder on the Mount (1994)
- ❑ ❑ 4 - The Quick and the Dead (1995)

Sergeant Joe Rodriguez . . . police officer in Phoenix, Arizona
- ❑ ❑ 1 - Cat Killer (1993)
- ❑ ❑ 2 - Mouse Trapped (1993)
- ❑ ❑ 3 - The Last Dinosaur (1994)
- ❑ ❑ 4 - Gila Monster (1994)

■ **Jane DENTINGER** has a BFA in acting and directing from Ithaca College and has worked professionally in regional theatre, Off Broadway and Joe Papp's Shakespeare in the Park. While writing the Jocelyn O'Roarke series featuring a working actor and director, Dentinger herself has continued to work as a director and acting coach. Getting to know theatrical statesman Frederick Revere, lover of Shakespeare and limericks, is the unexpected bonus of this wonderful series and worth twice the price of every installment, even in hard cover.

Jocelyn O'Roarke . . . Broadway actress & director in New York City
- ❑ ❑ 1 - Murder on Cue (1983)
- ❑ ❑ 2 - First Hit of the Season (1984)
- ❑ ❑ 3 - Death Mask (1988)
- ❑ ❑ 4 - Dead Pan (1992)
- ❑ ❑ 5 - The Queen Is Dead (1994)
- ❑ ❑ 6 - Who Dropped Peter Pan? (1995)

■ **Jo DERESKE** is the creator of a new library series featuring the always correct and always correcting Helma Zukas, librarian extraordinare, making her fourth appearance in *Miss Zukas and the Raven's Dance* (1996). In the series opener Helma is joined by her friend since tenth grade, six-foot, free-spirited Ruth, an artist. There is also just a hint of potential romance between Helma and Police Chief Wayne Gallant. A native of western Michigan who has lived in Washington for 20 years, Dereske worked in both university and corporate libraries before turning to writing full time. She is the author of three fantasy novels for young adults and in 1996 will introduce a new series with forgery expert Ruby Crane. From her home base in rural western Michigan, Ruby will be involved in cases requiring her expertise as a questioned-documents specialist. Dereske lives in Bellingham, Washington, also the home of mystery writers Linda Mariz and Audrey Peterson.

Helma Zukas . . . Washington State librarian
- ❏ ❏ 1 - Miss Zukas and the Library Murders (1994)
- ❏ ❏ 2 - Miss Zukas and the Island Murders (1995)
- ❏ ❏ 3 - Miss Zukas and the Stroke of Death (1996)
- ❏ ❏ 4 - Miss Zukas and the Raven's Dance (1996)

■ **Denise DIETZ** is the creator of diet group leader and dessert-maven sleuth Ellie Bernstein introduced in *Throw Darts at a Cheesecake* (1993). Dietz says her writing is inspired by her experience as a waitress, Weight Watchers lecturer, professional singer, newspaper reporter and film extra at Paramount. In addition to her food mysteries, she is the author of a 1995 mystery-romance titled *Johnny Angel*. A graduate of the University of Wisconsin, Dietz currently lives in Denver where she still can't get enough of the Broncos.

Ellie Bernstein . . . diet group leader
- ❏ ❏ 1 - Throw Darts at a Cheesecake (1993)
- ❏ ❏ 2 - Beat Up a Cookie (1994)

■ **Doris Miles DISNEY** (1907-1976) was born in rural Connecticut and worked in the insurance business in Hartford before starting her writing career with an early series featuring small-town cop Jim O'Neill. Her best known series detective is Boston-based insurance investigator Jefferson Di Marco who falls in love with a murderer in the opening title, *Dark Road* (1946). She also wrote a 1950s trilogy with postal inspector David Madden and 30 other nonseries mysteries.

Jeff Di Marco . . . Boston, Massachusetts insurance investigator
- ❏ ❏ 1 - Dark Road (1946)
- ❏ ❏ 2 - Family Skeleton (1949)
- ❏ ❏ 3 - Straw Man (1951) [Britain–The Case of the Straw Man]
- ❏ ❏ 4 - Trick or Treat (1955) [Britain–The Halloween Murder]
- ❏ ❏ 5 - Method in Madness (1957) [Britain–Quiet Violence]
- ❏ ❏ 6 - Did She Fall or Was She Pushed? (1959)
- ❏ ❏ 7 - Find the Woman (1962)
- ❏ ❏ 8 - The Chandler Policy (1971)

Jim O'Neill . . . small town policeman in Connecticut
- ❏ ❏ 1 - Compound for Death (1943)
- ❏ ❏ 2 - Murder on a Tangent (1945)
- ❏ ❏ 3 - Appointment at Nine (1947)
- ❏ ❏ 4 - Fire at Will (1950)
- ❏ ❏ 5 - The Last Straw (1954) [Britain–Driven to Kill]

■ **Hildegarde DOLSON** (1908-1981) was a New York advertising copywriter before her 1965 marriage to widower Richard Lockridge, who along with his first wife Frances created the immensely popular Mr. and Mrs. North mystery series. Dolson launched her own mystery series in 1971 with feisty Connecticut illustrator Lucy Ramsdale and her tenant, homicide inspector James McDougal. McDougal arrives in Wingate after resigning his post as head of the Connecticut State Police homicide division but gets pressed into service by local authorities. Lucy's witty repartee, especially in the first two installments, is well worth the trouble to locate these little gems. Dolson also wrote six nonmystery novels, several young adult novels, her autobiography, *We Shook the Family Tree* (1946), and with Elizabeth Stevenson Ives, *My Brother Adlai* (1956).

    Lucy Ramsdale & James McDougal . . . Wingate, Connecticut illustrator & homicide inspector

        ❑ ❑ 1 - **To Spite Her Face** (1971) *Edgar nominee* ☆
        ❑ ❑ 2 - A Dying Fall (1973)
        ❑ ❑ 3 - Please Omit Funeral (1975)
        ❑ ❑ 4 - Beauty Sleep (1977)

■ **R. B. DOMINIC** is the pseudonym used by Mary Latsis and Martha Henissart to create the Ben Safford series featuring a Democratic congressman from Ohio. Although they jealously guard their personal privacy, Latsis and Henissart are known to be an economist and attorney, respectively, living in Massachusetts. They also write the John Putnam Thatcher series under another pseudonym, Emma Lathen. Ben Safford, like John Putnam Thatcher, is ably assisted in his detecting by clever colleagues.

    Ben Safford . . . Ohio Democratic congressman

        ❑ ❑ 1 - Murder Sunny Side Up (1968)
        ❑ ❑ 2 - Murder in High Place (1970)
        ❑ ❑ 3 - There is No Justice (1971)
        ❑ ❑ 4 - Epitaph for a Lobbyist (1974)
        ❑ ❑ 5 - Murder Out of Commission (1976)
        ❑ ❑ 6 - The Attending Physician (1980)
        ❑ ❑ 7 - Unexpected Developments (1984)

■ **Anabel DONALD** is the creator of London television researcher and part-time private eye Alex Tanner introduced in *Smile, Honey* (1991). Alex later appears in *An Uncommon Murder* (1993), *In at the Deep End* (1994) and *The Glass Ceiling* (1995) where she finds herself with a brilliant 17-year-old orphan assistant who doesn't speak and an anonymous client who sends money and threats by messenger.

    Alex Tanner . . . part-time P. I. & TV researcher in London

        ❑ ❑ 1 - Smile, Honey (1991)
        ❑ ❑ 2 - An Uncommon Murder (1993)
        ❑ ❑ 3 - In at the Deep End (1994)
        ❑ ❑ 4 - The Glass Ceiling (1995)

■ **Carole Nelson DOUGLAS** is the author of more than 30 novels of mystery, fantasy, science fiction and romance, as well as historical and mainstream. A former journalist, Douglas is the creator of diva-detective Irene (pronounced Eye-REE-nee) Adler, the only woman to outwit Sherlock Holmes, first appearing in *Good Night, Mr. Holmes*, winner of the 1991 American Mystery Award. Among cat lovers, this author is best known for her series featuring Las Vegas publicist Temple Barr and Midnight Louie, the big black tomcat sleuth with his own fan newsletter. Douglas also wrote a pair of science fiction romantic thrillers featuring Minnesota psychiatrist Dr. Kevin Blake and his mysteriously gifted amnesiac patient Jane Doe. Douglas and her artist husband live in Fort Worth, Texas with their six cats and her large collection of cat shoes, cat purses and cat jewelry.

Irene Adler . . . Paris, France 19th century sleuth
- ❑ ❑ 1 - **Good Night, Mr. Holmes** (1990) *American Mystery Award winner* ★
- ❑ ❑ 2 - Good Morning, Irene (1990)
- ❑ ❑ 3 - Irene at Large (1992)
- ❑ ❑ 4 - Irene's Last Waltz (1994)

Kevin Blake, Dr. . . . psychiatrist in Minnesota
- ❑ ❑ 1 - Probe (1985)
- ❑ ❑ 2 - Counterprobe (1990)

Temple Barr & Midnight Louie . . . Las Vegas, Nevada public relations freelancer & tomcat sleuth
- ❑ ❑ 1 - Catnap (1992)
- ❑ ❑ 2 - Pussyfoot (1993)
- ❑ ❑ 3 - Cat on a Blue Monday (1994)
- ❑ ❑ 4 - Cat in a Crimson Haze (1995)
- ❑ ❑ 5 - Cat in a Diamond Dazzle (1996)

■ **Lauren Wright DOUGLAS** is the creator of lesbian private eye Caitlin Reece who works on Vancouver Island, British Columbia. The detective's strong supporting cast of independent professionals—Maggie the doctor, Sandy the cop, Gary the Vietnamese animal psychologist and Lester the electronics expert—are introduced in *The Always Anonymous Beast* (1988). As an investigator, Caitlin is primarily concerned with crimes against women, children and animals.

Caitlin Reece . . . Victoria, Canada lesbian detective
- ❑ ❑ 1 - The Always Anonymous Beast (1987)
- ❑ ❑ 2 - Ninth Life (1989)
- ❑ ❑ 3 - The Daughters of Artemis (1991)
- ❑ ❑ 4 - A Tiger's Heart (1992)
- ❑ ❑ 5 - Goblin Market (1993)
- ❑ ❑ 6 - A Rage of Maidens (1994)

■ **Alison DRAKE** is a pseudonym for T. J. MacGregor who also writes the St. James and McCleary series featuring a pair of south Florida private eyes. As Alison Drake, she is the creator of a police series featuring homicide detective Aline Scott on the fictional island of Tango Key—a tropical Florida paradise where her house is on stilts and she keeps a pet skunk named Wolfe. The series opener *Tango Key* (1988) is followed by *Fever* (1988), *Black Moon* (1989) and *High Strangeness* (1992), a tale of UFOs and a woman escaped from an exclusive psychiatric clinic. The author lives in south Florida.

Aline Scott . . . small resort town police detective in Tango Key, Florida
- ❑ ❑ 1 - Tango Key (1988)
- ❑ ❑ 2 - Fevered (1988)
- ❑ ❑ 3 - Black Moon (1989)
- ❑ ❑ 4 - High Strangeness (1992)

■ **Sarah DREHER** of Amherst, Massachusetts, is a clinical psychologist and prize-winning playwright who also writes mysteries featuring a lesbian sleuth. Introduced in 1985 with *Stoner McTavish*, Dreher's six-book series features a Boston-based travel agent, Stoner

McTavish, and her band of colorful friends and relatives. There's eccentric Aunt Hermione, Stoner's lover Gwen and her business partner Mary Lou—the travel agent who's afraid of flying. In book #5, the merry band accompanies Mary Lou's mother, the eminent Dr. Edith Kesselbaum, to a psychiatric convention at Disney World.

Stoner McTavish . . . lesbian travel agent in Boston, Massachusetts

- ❑ ❑ 1 - Stoner McTavish (1985)
- ❑ ❑ 2 - Something Shady (1986)
- ❑ ❑ 3 - Gray Magic (1987)
- ❑ ❑ 4 - A Captive in Time (1990)
- ❑ ❑ 5 - Otherworld (1993)
- ❑ ❑ 6 - Bad Company (1995)

■ **Margaret DUFFY**, born in Essex, England but currently living in Scotland, is the creator of an action-packed series featuring British government agents Ingrid Langley and Patrick Gillard. A former agent turned novelist, Ingrid gets called back to serve with her ex-husband Patrick. Together they make their sixth appearance in *Gallows Bird* (1993). One American reviewer aptly noted that Duffy's "wonderful sense of humor and frighteningly insightful view of male-female relationships" make these books "impossible to put down." Her new series character is Joanna McKenzie, former CID turned private detective, who finds herself working alongside her former colleague and old flame Inspector James Carrick. In their second appearance, *Prospect of Death* (1995), Joanna must clear the Chief Inspector's name after he is found intoxicated at the wheel of his crashed car with no recall of the accident.

Ingrid Langley & Patrick Gillard . . . novelist/British agent & British army major

- ❑ ❑ 1 - A Murder of Crows (1987)
- ❑ ❑ 2 - Death of a Raven (1988)
- ❑ ❑ 3 - Brass Eagle (1989)
- ❑ ❑ 4 - Who Killed Cock Robin? (1990)
- ❑ ❑ 5 - Rook-Shoot (1991)
- ❑ ❑ 6 - Gallows Bird (1993)

Joanna McKenzie . . . former CID turned P. I. in Bath, England

- ❑ ❑ 1 - Dressed to Kill (1994)
- ❑ ❑ 2 - Prospect of Death (1995)

■ **Sarah DUNANT**, British television journalist turned novelist, is the creator of Hannah Wolfe, contract private investigator for a London agency, and Marla Masterson, British professor of Anglo Saxon literature. Introduced in *Birth Marks* (1992) where she searches for a missing ballet dancer, Hannah returns in *Fat Lands* (1994) which was awarded the Silver Dagger by the British Crime Writers Association. So far there's only been one appearance of Marla Masterson who comes to America to aid a friend in *Snowstorms in a Hot Climate* (1988). In her public persona as a mystery writer and television host, Dunant appears in *Living Proof* (1995), John Harvey's latest entry in the Charlie Resnick eries, where inspector investigates the murder of a foul-mouthed American woman mystery writer at the Nottingham crime convention, *Shots on the Page*.

Hannah Wolfe . . . London P. I.

- ❑ ❑ 1 - Birth Marks (1992)
- ❑ ❑ 2 - **Fat Lands** (1993) *Silver Dagger* ★
- ❑ ❑ 3 - Under My Skin (1995)

Marla Masterson . . . young British professor of Anglo-Saxon literature in U.S.

- ❑ ❑ 1 - Snowstorms in a Hot Climate (1988)

■ **Sophie DUNBAR** is the creator of Claire and Dan Claiborne, a New Orleans hairdresser and her sleuthing husband, described by one reviewer as "delightfully irreverent, slightly wacky and sizzingly sexy." Introduced in *Behind Eclaire's Doors* (1994), their second adventure takes them to a Mississippi Gulf Coast resort in *Redneck Riviera* (1995). In book #3, they'll be having *A Bad Hair Day* (1996).

    Claire & Dan Claiborne . . . sleuthing pair in New Orleans, Louisiana
        ❑ ❑ 1 - Behind Eclaire's Doors (1993)
        ❑ ❑ 2 - Redneck Riviera (1995)
        ❑ ❑ 3 - A Bad Hair Day (1996)

■ **Susan DUNLAP** is the only American woman who writes a series in each of the three mystery types—police procedural, private eye and amateur sleuth. Jill Smith is a Berkeley, California, homicide detective with more than her share of unusual crimes, quirky suspects and police department politics to contend with. Kiernan O'Shaughnessy, who lives at the beach near La Jolla, is a former San Francisco medical examiner turned private investigator whose ex-football player houseman just happens to be a gourmet cook. And Vejay Haskell, whose adventures were re-released in paperback in 1994, reads meters for Pacific Gas & Electric in the picturesque Russian River region of northern California. Dunlap grew up in New York and attended Bucknell University and the University of North Carolina. She has been a teacher of Hatha Yoga and a social worker in New York City, Baltimore and Richmond, California. A founding member and past president of Sisters in Crime, she lives in northern California.

    Jill Smith . . . Berkeley, California homicide detective
        ❑ ❑ 1 - Karma (1981)
        ❑ ❑ 2 - As a Favor (1984)
        ❑ ❑ 3 - Not Exactly a Brahmin (1985)
        ❑ ❑ 4 - Too Close to the Edge (1987)
        ❑ ❑ 5 - A Dinner to Die For (1987)
        ❑ ❑ 6 - Diamond in the Buff (1990)
        ❑ ❑ 7 - Death and Taxes (1992)
        ❑ ❑ 8 - Time Expired (1993)
        ❑ ❑ 9 - Sudden Exposure (1996)

    Kiernan O'Shaughnessy . . . former San Francisco medical examiner turned P. I. in La Jolla, California
        ❑ ❑ 1 - Pious Deception (1989)
        ❑ ❑ 2 - Rogue Wave (1991)
        ❑ ❑ 3 - High Fall (1994)

    Vejay Haskell . . . northern California meter reader for Pacific Gas & Electric
        ❑ ❑ 1 - An Equal Opportunity Death (1983)
        ❑ ❑ 2 - The Bohemian Connection (1985)
        ❑ ❑ 3 - The Last Annual Slugfest (1986)

■ **Carola DUNN**, author of more than 30 Regency novels since 1980, is the creator of a new mystery series featuring Daisy Dalrymple, a young aristocratic woman of the 1920s, writing a series of magazine articles on English county homes. The daughter of a viscount, she chooses to earn her own living after the death of her father. Book #3 finds Daisy at the Royal Albert Hall when a murder occurs during a performance of Verdi's Requiem, hence the title, *Requiem for a Mezzo* (1996). In book #4, *Murder on the Flying Scotsman* (1997), Daisy's on her way to another stately home when a murder takes place on the express train from

London to Edinburgh. Born in London, Dunn came to the U.S. in 1968. She has traveled extensively in both eastern and western Europe and to Canada, Israel, Samoa and Fiji. After 17 years in San Diego she now lives in Oregon.

Daisy Dalrymple . . . young aristocratic woman writer in Chelsea
- ❏ ❏ 1 - Death at Wentwater Court (1994)
- ❏ ❏ 2 - The Winter Garden Mystery (1995)
- ❏ ❏ 3 - Requiem for a Mezzo (1996)
- ❏ ❏ 4 - Murder on the Flying Scotsman (1997)

■ **Dorothy DUNNETT** is the American byline of Scottish writer and portrait painter Dorothy Halliday, creator of a mystery series featuring portrait painter, yachtsman and British agent, Johnson Johnson. Johnson's yacht is named Dolly and each of his adventures (except the most recent) features a different female narrator or bird in the British title. *Dolly and the Singing Bird* (1968), set in Scotland, features operatic soprano Madame Tina Rossi, while blue-blooded chef and caterer Sarah Cassells tells the story of *Dolly and the Cookie Bird* (1970) set in Spain. Italy, the Bahamas and Morocco are other exotic locales used for this series of espionage thrillers. Dunnett is known for her historical novels including two series featuring the House of Niccolo and Francis Crawford of Lymond. A director of both Scottish television and the Edinburgh Book Festival, she lives in Edinburgh.

Johnson Johnson . . . portrait painter & British agent w/his yacht Dolly
- ❏ ❏ 1 - The Photogenic Soprano (1968)
      [Britain–Dolly and the Singing Bird]
- ❏ ❏ 2 - Murder in the Round (1970) [Britain–Dolly and the Cookie Bird]
- ❏ ❏ 3 - Match for a Murderer (1971) [Britain–Dolly and the Doctor Bird]
- ❏ ❏ 4 - Murder in Focus (1972) [Britain–Dolly and the Starry Bird]
- ❏ ❏ 5 - Split Code (1976) [Britain–Dolly and the Nanny Bird]
- ❏ ❏ 6 - Tropical Issue (1983) [Britain–Dolly and the Bird of Paradise]
- ❏ ❏ 7 - Moroccan Traffic (1992) [Britain–Send a Fax to the Kasbah]

■ **Michael Allen DYMMOCH** is the pseudonym of EM Grant, a professional driver who lives and works in the northern suburbs of Chicago. Her first novel, *The Man Who Understood Cats*, won the St. Martin's Press Malice Domestic award for best first traditional mystery in 1992 and was published the following year. John Thinnes and Jack Caleb, the Chicago cop and psychiatrist introduced earlier, will return in *The Death of Blue Mountain Cat* (1996).

John Thinnes & Jack Caleb, Dr. . . . cop & psychiatrist in Chicago, Illinois
- ❏ ❏ 1 - **The Man Who Understood Cats** (1993) *MD/SMP winner* ★
- ❏ ❏ 2 - The Death of Blue Mountain Cat (1995)

■ **Mignon G. EBERHART** published her 59th novel in 1988, exactly 59 years after her first mystery featuring nurse Sarah Keate, *The Patient in Room 18* (1929). The second title in this series, *While the Patient Slept* (1930), was awarded the Scotland Yard Prize. These two early titles from Nebraska native Eberhart were presented in new editions by the University of Nebraska Press in 1995. A graduate of Nebraska Wesleyan, she also wrote a four-book series featuring police detective Jacob Wait, published in the mid-1930s. Past president of the Mystery Writers of America, she also served on the faculty of the Famous Writers School. Her books have been translated into 16 languages and adapted for radio, television and film. When named Grand Master by the Mystery Writers of America in 1970, she was the first woman to be so honored since Agatha Christie in 1954. Eberhart also received a Lifetime Achievement Award from Malice Domestic in 1994.

Sarah Keate & Lance O'Leary . . . nurse & wealthy police detective in New York
 ❑ ❑ 1 - The Patient in Room 18 (1929)
 ❑ ❑ 2 - While the Patient Slept (1930)
 ❑ ❑ 3 - The Mystery of Hunting's End (1930)
 ❑ ❑ 4 - From This Dark Stairway (1931)
 ❑ ❑ 5 - Murder by an Aristocrat (1932)
 ❑ ❑ 6 - Wolf in Man's Clothing (1942)
 ❑ ❑ 7 - Man Missing (1954)

■ **Marjorie ECCLES** is the creator of a now eight-book police series featuring Detective Superintendent Gil Mayo and his assistant Detective Inspector Abigail Moon, introduced in *Cast a Cold Eye* (1988). A Yorkshire man transplanted to the Midlands, Mayo works from the divisional police headquarters across from the town hall in fictional Lavenstock. Before turning to crime writing, Eccles penned seven romantic suspense novels under the pseudonyms Judith Bordill and Jennifer Hyde. Born in Yorkshire, England where she spent much of her childhood, she later moved to the Midlands—the setting for her Inspector Mayo series—where she lived for 30 years. She currently lives in a picturesque village on the edge of the Chilterns in a Victorian house with a large garden which occupies most of her non-writing time.

 Gil Mayo . . . detective chief inspector in England
 ❑ ❑ 1 - Cast a Cold Eye (1988)
 ❑ ❑ 2 - Death of a Good Woman (1989)
 ❑ ❑ 3 - Requiem for a Dove (1990)
 ❑ ❑ 4 - More Deaths Than One (1990)
 ❑ ❑ 5 - Late of This Parish (1992)
 ❑ ❑ 6 - The Company She Kept (1993)
 ❑ ❑ 7 - An Accidental Shroud (1994)
 ❑ ❑ 8 - A Death of Distinction (1995)

■ **Rosemary EDGHILL** is the pseudonym of Eluki bes-Shahar, creator of a new mystery series featuring a contemporary witch named Karen Hightower. Also known as Bast the white witch, Hightower is a Manhattan graphics designer who first appears in *Speak Daggers to Her* (1994), followed by *Book of Moons* (1995).

 Karen Hightower . . . Manhattan graphic designer & white witch
 ❑ ❑ 1 - Speak Daggers to Her (1994)
 ❑ ❑ 2 - Book of Moons (1995)

■ **Ruth Dudley EDWARDS** is the creator of a laugh-out-loud funny mystery series featuring career civil servant Robert Amiss and his friend police Supt. James Milton. One reviewer described these adventures as well-plotted mysteries with a cast of characters straight out of a Pink Panther movie. After resigning his civil service appointment in disgust at the end of book #2, Amiss begins a series of temporary posts, thereby allowing Supt. Milton to make use of Amiss' investigative skills and Edwards to satirize a whole host of British institutions. In their most recent outing, *Murder at St. Martha's* (1995), no sacred cows are left unskewered in a truly hilarious take-off on stuffy British academia. In book #4, *Clubbed to Death* (1992), Amiss goes undercover as a waiter at a gentleman's club. In addition to her mystery writing, Edwards is a prize-winning biographer and historian who has written a history of *The Economist*. A former civil servant herself, Edwards was born and educated in Ireland but has lived in England since 1965.

James Milton & Robert Amiss . . . police superintendent & ex-civil servant in England

❑ ❑ 1 - Corridors of Death (1981)
❑ ❑ 2 - St. Valentine's Day Murders (1985)
❑ ❑ 3 - The English School of Murder (1990)
             [APA–The School of English Murder]
❑ ❑ 4 - Clubbed to Death (1992)
❑ ❑ 5 - Matricide at St. Martha's (1994)

■ **Lesley EGAN** is one of the pseudonyms of Elizabeth Linington who also wrote as Dell Shannon. As Lesley Egan she created Glendale cop Vic Varallo and Los Angeles attorney Jesse Falkenstein who are introduced together in *A Case for Appeal* (1961). At Varallo's request Falkenstein travels to the small southern California valley town of Contera to defend a woman accused of murder. At the end of the book, Varallo leaves Contera for the Glendale police force where his detective partner is a conflicted young woman officer named Delia Riordan, daughter of a disabled cop. By 1986 Egan produced a total of 26 books with Varallo and Falkenstein, while writing another 38 in her Luis Mendoza series as Dell Shannon and 13 more featuring Sgt. Ivor Maddox written as Elizabeth Linington. Her cops were always good guys and family issues were always important.

Jesse Falkenstein . . . lawyer in Los Angeles

❑ ❑ 1 - A Case for Appeal [includes Vic Varallo character] (1961)
❑ ❑ 2 - Against the Evidence (1962)
❑ ❑ 3 - My Name Is Death (1964)
❑ ❑ 4 - Some Avenger, Rise (1966)
❑ ❑ 5 - A Serious Investigation (1968)
❑ ❑ 6 - In the Death of a Man (1970)
❑ ❑ 7 - Paper Chase (1972)
❑ ❑ 8 - The Blind Search (1977)
❑ ❑ 9 - Back on Death (1978)
❑ ❑ 10 - Motive in Shadow (1980)
❑ ❑ 11 - The Miser (1981)
❑ ❑ 12 - Little Boy Lost (1983)
❑ ❑ 13 - The Wine of Life (1985)

Vic Varallo . . . small town cop moved to Glendale, California

❑ ❑ 1 - The Borrowed Alibi (1962)
❑ ❑ 2 - Run to Evil (1963)
❑ ❑ 3 - Detective's Due (1965)
❑ ❑ 4 - The Nameless Ones (1967)
❑ ❑ 5 - The Wine of Violence (1969)
❑ ❑ 6 - Malicious Mischief (1971)
❑ ❑ 7 - Scenes of Crime (1976)
o o 8 - A Dream Apart (1978)
❑ ❑ 9 - The Hunter and the Hunted (1979)
❑ ❑ 10 - A Choice of Crimes (1980)
❑ ❑ 11 - Random Death (1982)
❑ ❑ 12 - Crime for Christmas (1983)
❑ ❑ 13 - Chain of Violence (1985)

■ **Selma EICHLER** is the creator of Manhattan private eye Desiree Shapiro who makes her debut in *Murder Can Kill Your Social Life* (1994). The warm-hearted Desiree is a queen-sized 5' 2". Eichler is a freelance advertising copywriter and part-time interior designer in Manhattan.

Desiree Shapiro . . . 5' 2" queen-size Manhattan P. I. in New York
  ❑ ❑ 1 - Murder Can Kill Your Social Life (1994)
  ❑ ❑ 2 - Murder Can Ruin Your Looks (1995)
  ❑ ❑ 3 - Murder Can Stunt Your Growth (1996)
  ❑ ❑ 4 - Murder Can Wreck Your Reunion (1996)

■ **Charlotte ELKINS** was the American Art Librarian at the M. H. de Young Museum in San Francisco when husband Aaron sold his first mystery novel. Since then they have co-authored the Agatha award-winning short story "Nice Gorilla" and two entries in a new golf mystery series featuring LPGA pro Lee Ofsted and homicide detective Graham Sheldon. Charlotte has also written five pseudonymous romance novels. In addition to their joint efforts, Aaron Elkins writes two mystery series—one featuring anthropologist-detective Gideon Oliver and the other art curator and sleuth Chris Norgren. Published in six languages, Aaron's award-winning series have been filmed for series television. The writing duo recently moved from Washington state to the coast of Rhode Island.

Lee Ofsted & Graham Sheldon . . . golf pro & homicide detective in Washington
  ❑ ❑ 1 - A Wicked Slice (1989)
  ❑ ❑ 2 - Rotten Lies (1995)

■ **P. N. ELROD** is Patricia Nead Elrod of Richardson, Texas, creator of the six-part *Vampire Files* featuring Chicago's ace reporter Jack Fleming, a ladies' man transformed into a vampire by the lovely Maureen. Gunned down in a contract hit in the series opener, Jack returns in search of Maureen in book #2 only to discover that he is being stalked by a vampire hunter. Jack is philosophical about his situation—he'll never grow old or die, he sleeps all day and he gets to hunt down his own murderer.

Jack Fleming . . . reporter, ladies' man & vampire in Chicago, Illinois
  ❑ ❑ 1 - Bloodlust (1990)
  ❑ ❑ 2 - Lifeblood (1990)
  ❑ ❑ 3 - Bloodcircle (1990)
  ❑ ❑ 4 - Art in the Blood (1991)
  ❑ ❑ 5 - Fire in the Blood (1991)
  ❑ ❑ 6 - Blood on the Water (1992)

■ **Catherine ENNIS** is the creator of a lesbian mystery series featuring Dr. Bernadette Hebert, a crime lab expert in Louisiana. Following her debut in *Clearwater* (1991), Dr. Bernie returns in *Chataqua* (1993).

Dr. Bernadette Hebert . . . crime lab expert in Louisiana
  ❑ ❑ 1 - Clearwater (1991)
  ❑ ❑ 2 - Chatauqua (1993)

■ **Margaret ERSKINE** is the pseudonym of Margaret Wetherby Williams, Canadian born mystery writer who grew up in Devon, England. She is the creator of Scotland Yard Inspector Septimus Finch who appeared in 20 titles after his 1938 debut in *The Limping Man*. Fascinated by creepy old houses with secret rooms and strange artworks concealing criminal clues, Erskine was especially fond of large eccentric families and a number of her books feature a large cast of quirky characters. She died in 1984.

Septimus Finch . . . Scotland Yard Inspector in England
  ❑ ❑ 1 - And Being Dead (1938) [U.S.–The Limping Man]
     [APA–The Painted Mask]

❑ ❑ 2 - The Whispering House (1947) [U.S.–The Voice of the House]
❑ ❑ 3 - I Knew MacBean (1948) [APA–Caravan of Night]
❑ ❑ 4 - Give up the Ghost (1949)
❑ ❑ 5 - The Disappearing Bridegroom (1950) [U.S.–The Silver Ladies]
❑ ❑ 6 - Death of Our Dear One (1952) [U.S.–Look Behind You Lady]
             [APA–Don't Look Behind You]
❑ ❑ 7 - Dead by Now (1953)
❑ ❑ 8 - Fatal Relations (1955) [U.S.–Old Mrs. Ommanney Is Dead]
             [APA–The Dead Don't Speak]
❑ ❑ 9 - Sleep No More (1958)
❑ ❑ 10 - The House of the Enchantress (1959) [U.S.–A Graveyard Plot]
❑ ❑ 11 - The Woman at Belguardo (1961)
❑ ❑ 12 - The Case in Belmont Square (1963) [U.S.–No. 9 Belmont Square]
❑ ❑ 13 - Take a Dark Journey (1965) [U.S.–The Family at Tammerron]
❑ ❑ 14 - The Voice of Murder (1965)
❑ ❑ 15 - Case with Three Husbands (1967)
❑ ❑ 16 - The Ewe Lamb (1968)
❑ ❑ 17 - The Case of Mary Fielding (1970)
❑ ❑ 18 - The Brood of Folly (1971)
❑ ❑ 19 - Besides the Wench Is Dead (1973)
❑ ❑ 20 - Harriet Farewell (1975)
❑ ❑ 21 - The House in Hook Street (1978)

■ **Janet EVANOVICH** is the creator of a new series featuring lingerie buyer turned bounty hunter Stephanie Plum of Trenton, New Jersey. The rollicking series opener was nominated for four mystery awards as best first mystery and named Dilys Award winner by the Independent Mystery Booksellers Association as the book they most enjoyed selling in 1994. Before launching her funny mystery series, Evanovich wrote funny romance novels in the Loveswept series by Bantam. She says romance novels are particularly fun to write because they're like birthday cake in a peanut butter and jelly world. Evanovich, who currently lives in New Hampshire, earned a degree in art from Douglass College.

   Stephanie Plum . . . Trenton, New Jersey neophyte bounty hunter
   ❑ ❑ 1 - **One for the Money (1994)**
                 Agatha, Anthony, Edgar & Shamus nominee ☆ ☆ ☆ ☆
   ❑ ❑ 2 - Two for the Dough (1996)

■ **Elizabeth EYRE** is one of the pseudonyms used by Jill Staynes and Margaret Storey, former teachers and lifelong friends who are writing partners for two mystery series. As Elizabeth Eyre, they are creators of the historical series set in Renaissance Italy featuring Sigismondo, the Duke of Rocca's agent. Introduced in *Death of a Duchess* (1992), Sigismondo returns for his fifth adventure in *Axe for an Abbot* (1996). These stories are full of schemes and conspiracies with rich historical backgrounds. Staynes and Storey also write the Inspector Bone series as Susannah Stacey.

   Sigismondo . . . Italian agent of a Renaissance duke
   ❑ ❑ 1 - Death of a Duchess (1992)
   ❑ ❑ 2 - Curtains for the Cardinal (1993)
   ❑ ❑ 3 - Poison for the Prince (1994)
   ❑ ❑ 4 - Bravo for the Bride (1994)
   ❑ ❑ 5 - Axe for an Abbot (1996)

■ **Ann C. FALLON**, of Flushing, New York, is the creator of a contemporary Irish series featuring Dublin solicitor James Fleming introduced in *Blood is Thicker* (1990). Fleming is a comfortably well-off bachelor with an upper-middle class background and a love of railway travel whose law practice leads him to some unusual opportunities for legal sleuthing. Fleming's fifth appearance in *Hour of Our Death* (1995) involves a woman with a vision of the Blessed Virgin.

> **James Fleming** . . . Dublin solicitor
>   ❏ ❏ 1 - Blood Is Thicker (1990)
>   ❏ ❏ 2 - Where Death Lies (1991)
>   ❏ ❏ 3 - Dead Ends (1992)
>   ❏ ❏ 4 - Potter's Field (1993)
>   ❏ ❏ 5 - Hour of Our Death (1995)

■ **Gillian B. FARRELL**, actor and founder of the Byrdcliffe Actors' Theatre, worked as a detective before starting her Annie McGrogan series featuring a New York actress just returned from Los Angeles. Farrell once served papers on a Mafia Don during his divorce and helped Bernie Goetz with his defense. She brings her own intimate knowledge of both the theatre and P. I. world to this new series.

> **Annie McGrogan** . . . New York City P. I. & actor just back from Los Angeles
>   ❏ ❏ 1 - Alibi for an Actress (1992)
>   ❏ ❏ 2 - Murder and a Muse (1994)

■ **Quinn FAWCETT** is the joint pseudonym of Chelsea Quinn Yarbro and Bill Fawcett for their new historical series featuring Madame Victoire Vernet, the devoted wife of a young French policeman in the time of Napoleon. When her husband is wrongly accused of theft and murder, she singlemindedly sets out to clear his name with an investigation that leads from the relative safety of the boudoir into the treacherous eye of an assassination plot against the Emperor Napolean himself. A prolific writer of science fiction, horror, mystery and children's stories, Yarbro lives in Berkeley, California. Fawcett makes his home in Lake Zurich, Illinois.

> **Mme. Victoire Vernet** . . . French wife of Napoleonic gendarme
>   ❏ ❏ 1 - Napoleon Must Die (1993)
>   ❏ ❏ 2 - Death Wears a Crown (1993)

■ **Connie FEDDERSEN**, of Union City, Oklahoma, is the creator of a new series featuring CPA Amanda Hazard and country cop Dick Thorn of Vamoose, Oklahoma. They make their first appearance in *Dead in the Water* (1993) and have since been found in the cellar, the melon patch and the dirt.

> **Amanda Hazard** . . . Vamoose, Oklahoma CPA
>   ❏ ❏ 1 - Dead in the Water (1993)
>   ❏ ❏ 2 - Dead in the Cellar (1994)
>   ❏ ❏ 3 - Dead in the Melon Patch (1995)
>   ❏ ❏ 4 - Dead in the Dirt (1996)

■ **Jean FEMLING** is the creator of a southern California series featuring Orange County insurance claims investigator Martha Brant who first appears in *Hush, Money* (1989). Martha, who answers to the name Moz, is half-Filipino. Often mistaken for Mexican, she regularly encounters racial prejudice and discrimination.

Martha "Moz" Brant . . . southern California insurance claims investigator
- ❏ ❏ 1 - Hush, Money (1989)
- ❏ ❏ 2 - Getting Mine (1991)

■ **Ruth FENISONG** is the creator of New York City police Capt. Gridley Nelson, featured in a baker's dozen series titles from 1942 to 1962, starting with Murder *Needs a Face*. According to Ellen Nehr (*1001 Midnights*), these books enjoyed considerable popularity because Nelson had just about everything going for him in an era of uneducated but street-wise fictional cops. The olive-skinned, prematurely white-haired homicide detective had a Princeton education and the inherited wealth to hire Sammy, the honey-colored Harlem housekeeper from New Orleans, and support Kyrie, the beautiful ash-blonde wife, and their handsome young son. The housekeeper and her information pipeline to the servants of other wealthy families, are a tremendous help to Capt. Nelson. When Sammy gets herself hired as the new maid in a household under investigation in *The Butler Died in Brooklyn* (1943), it's her work behind the scenes that solves the case in time to prevent another murder.

Gridley Nelson . . . wealthy homicide detective with Harlem housekeeper in New York
- ❏ ❏ 1 - Murder Needs a Face (1942)
- ❏ ❏ 2 - Murder Needs a Name (1942)
- ❏ ❏ 3 - The Butler Died in Brooklyn (1943)
- ❏ ❏ 4 - Murder Runs a Fever (1943)
- ❏ ❏ 5 - Grim Rehearsal (1950)
- ❏ ❏ 6 - Dead Yesterday (1951)
- ❏ ❏ 7 - Deadlock (1952)
- ❏ ❏ 8 - The Wench Is Dead (1953)
- ❏ ❏ 9 - Miscast for Murder (1954) [APA–Too Lovely to Live]
- ❏ ❏ 10 - Bite the Hand (1956) [Britain–The Blackmailer]
- ❏ ❏ 11 - Death of the Party (1958)
- ❏ ❏ 12 - But Not Forgotten (1960) [Britain–Sinister Assignment]
- ❏ ❏ 13 - Dead Weight (1962)

■ **Tony FENNELLY** enjoyed careers as a go-go dancer, barmaid, welfare worker and Bourbon Street showgirl before turning to crime fiction. Her first novel, *The Glory Hole Murders* (1985) launched the Matt Sinclair series and earned her an Edgar nomination. This series about a gay epileptic ex-D. A. turned private eye in New Orleans has become a cult favorite, translated into German, Japanese, Danish and Czech. She has been a frequent guest on New York radio and invited guest speaker at the Tennessee Williams Festivals, the Semana Negra Festival in Gijon, Spain and The American Thriller Special in Cologne, Germany. Fennelly's latest series features Margo Fortier, ex-stripper turned columnist, who is introduced in *The Hippie in the Wall* (1994) followed by *1(900)D-E-A-D* (1996).

Margo Fortier . . . ex-stripper turned columnist in New Orleans, Louisiana
- ❏ ❏ 1 - The Hippie in the Wall (1994)
- ❏ ❏ 2 - 1(900)D-E-A-D (1996)

Matthew Arthur Sinclair . . . ex-D. A. turned P. I. in New Orleans, Louisiana
- ❏ ❏ 1 - **The Glory Hole Murders** (1985) *Edgar nominee* ☆
- ❏ ❏ 2 - The Closet Hanging (1987)
- ❏ ❏ 3 - Kiss Yourself Goodbye (1989)

■ **E. X. FERRARS** is the pseudonym of Morna Doris MacTaggart Brown (1907-1995), known in England as Elizabeth Ferrars. Born in what was then Rangoon, Burma, she earned a diploma in journalism from London's University College in 1928 and wrote her first mystery in 1940 at the age of 33. When her work crossed the Atlantic, Ferrars' American publisher insisted on initials to hide the fact the author was a woman. When they asked for a middle initial, she peevishly suggested an "X," never dreaming they were serious. For more than half a century, she produced one or two books each year, for a lifetime total of 66 novels. Her continuing characters include retired botany professor Andrew Basnett, introduced in *Something Wicked* (1983), and her much earlier amateur sleuth, Toby Dyke, who first appears in *Give a Corpse a Bad Name* (1940). Supt. Ditteridge appears only twice in the early 1970s and her longest running characters, Virginia and Felix Freer, are featured in nine installments from 1978 to 1992. Ferrars was a founding member of the British Crime Writers Association which she chaired in 1977-78. She received a special Silver Dagger in 1980 for 50 Outstanding Books.

Andrew Basnett . . . retired botany professor in England
❑ ❑ 1 - Something Wicked (1983)
❑ ❑ 2 - Root of All Evil (1984)
❑ ❑ 3 - The Crime and the Crystal (1985)
❑ ❑ 4 - The Other Devil's Name (1986)
❑ ❑ 5 - A Murder Too Many (1988)
❑ ❑ 6 - Smoke Without Fire (1990)
❑ ❑ 7 - A Hobby of Murder (1994)
❑ ❑ 8 - A Choice of Evils (1995)

Supt. Ditteridge . . . police superintendent in England
❑ ❑ 1 - A Stranger and Afraid (1971)
❑ ❑ 2 - Foot in the Grave (1973)

Toby Dyke . . . amateur sleuth in England
❑ ❑ 1 - Give a Corpse a Bad Name (1940) [U.S.–Rehearsals for Murder]
❑ ❑ 2 - Remove the Bodies (1940) [U.S.–Rehearsals for Murder]
❑ ❑ 3 - Death in Botanist's Bay (1941) [U.S.–Murder of a Suicide]
❑ ❑ 4 - Don't Monkey with Murder (1942) [U.S.–The Shape of a Stain]
❑ ❑ 5 - Your Neck in a Noose (1942) [U.S.–Neck in a Noose]

Virginia & Felix Freer . . . physiotherapist & businessman in England
❑ ❑ 1 - Last Will and Testament (1978)
❑ ❑ 2 - In at the Kill (1978)
❑ ❑ 3 - Frog in the Throat (1980)
❑ ❑ 4 - Thinner Than Water (1981)
❑ ❑ 5 - Death of a Minor Character (1983)
❑ ❑ 6 - I Met Murder (1985)
❑ ❑ 7 - Woman Slaughter (1989)
❑ ❑ 8 - Sleep of the Unjust (1990)
❑ ❑ 9 - Beware of the Dog (1992)

■ **G. G. FICKLING** is the shared pseudonym of Gloria and Forrest E. ("Skip") Fickling, creators of Honey West, billed as "the sexiest private eye ever to pull a trigger!" and introduced in *This Girl for Hire* (1957). Much is made of Honey's sex. Even her measurements (38-22-36) are printed on the back cover. But according to one reviewer "the plot is so confusing that the reader is unlikely to be convinced by its unraveling, which comes about more by accident that by good detective work." But Honey was a big success, and ended up with her own television series starring Anne Francis. The Ficklings also produced a three-book series featuring private eye Erik March, re-introduced in *Naughty but Dead* (1962) after his debut with Honey West in *This Girl for Hire* (1957). Erik appears for the last time, again with Honey, in *Stiff as a Broad* (1972).

Erik March . . . P. I. in California
- ❑ ❑ 1 - Naughty but Dead (1962)
- ❑ ❑ 2 - The Case of the Radioactive Redhead (1963)
- ❑ ❑ 3 - The Crazy Mixed-Up Nude (1964)

Honey West . . . sexiest P. I. ever to pull a trigger in California
- ❑ ❑ 1 - This Girl for Hire [Honey & Erik appear together] (1957)
- ❑ ❑ 2 - Girl on the Loose (1958)
- ❑ ❑ 3 - A Gun for Honey (1958)
- ❑ ❑ 4 - Girl on the Prowl (1959)
- ❑ ❑ 5 - Honey in the Flesh (1959)
- ❑ ❑ 6 - Dig a Dead Doll (1960)
- ❑ ❑ 7 - Kiss for a Killer (1960)
- ❑ ❑ 8 - Blood and Honey (1961)
- ❑ ❑ 9 - Bombshell (1964)
- ❑ ❑ 10 - Honey on Her Tail (1971)
- ❑ ❑ 11 - Stiff as a Broad [includes Erik March] (1972)

■ **Kate Clark FLORA** of Concord, Massachusetts, is the creator of two new series which she plans to alternate. One features Massachusetts educational consultant Thea Kozak and the other, Ross McIntyre, a small town high school biology teacher in Maine. Her first Thea Kozak title—a mystery about a law student involving legal questions of inheritance—was triggered by an anguished birth mother's letter to Ann Landers, but Flora says the idea first came to her during a romantic moonlight stroll on the beaches of Bermuda. *Silent Buddy*, the first Ross McIntyre, is the book she always wanted to write about drug smuggling and the hardscrabble life of a small Maine town. A graduate of Northeastern University law school and the daughter of a chicken farmer, Flora worked as a public sector attorney before turning to crime writing.

Ross McIntyre . . . small town high school biology teacher in Maine
- ❑ ❑ 1 - Silent Buddy (1995)

Thea Kozak . . . educational consultant in Massachusetts
- ❑ ❑ 1 - Chosen for Death (1994)
- ❑ ❑ 2 - Death in a Funhouse Mirror (1995)

■ **S. L. FLORIAN** is the creator of a new romantic mystery series featuring the Viscountess Delia Guilietta Ross-Merlani, Professor of Philosophy, Doctor of Letters and former dancer with the Monte Carlo Ballet. Delia is assisted in her first case—*Born to the Purple* (1992)—by Dr. Daniel Elliot, New York's Assistant Medical Examiner.

Viscountess Delia Ross-Merlani . . . English-Italian noblewoman in New York
- ❑ ❑ 1 - Born to the Purple (1992)

■ **Rae FOLEY** is the pseudonym of Elinore Denniston (1900-1978) who also wrote as Dennis Allan and Helen K. Maxwell. She produced a total of 47 crime novels, but only eleven feature her mild-mannered amateur sleuth Hiram Potter. In the series opener, *Death and Mr. Potter* (1955), his mother's funeral is concluding as a body plunges from an adjacent Gramercy Park rooftop into Potter's garden. He is forced to investigate when he suspects that one of her mourners may be the murderer. The series supporting cast includes Lt. O'Toole of homicide, playwright Graham Collinge and Potter's servants Tito and Antonia. One critic describes his mildness as his major detecting device—he makes things happen by "pottering around." Foley also produced a pair of mysteries featuring an almost invisible amateur sleuth John Harland, featured in *Girl From Nowhere* (1949) and *An Ape in Velvet*

(1951). Between 1936 and 1953, she wrote five nonseries novels as Dennis Allan. During the early 1970s she produced three using the byline Helen K. Maxwell.

Hiram Potter . . . mild-mannered amateur sleuth in NY City
- ❏ ❏ 1 - Death and Mr. Potter (1955) [APA–The Peacock Is a Bird of Prey]
- ❏ ❏ 2 - The Last Gamble (1956)
- ❏ ❏ 3 - Run for Your Life (1956)
- ❏ ❏ 4 - Where Is Mary Bostwick? (1958) [APA–Escape to Fear]
- ❏ ❏ 5 - Dangerous to Me (1959)
- ❏ ❏ 6 - It's Murder Mr. Potter (1961) [APA–Curtain Call]
- ❏ ❏ 7 - Repent at Leisure (1962) [Britain–The Deadly Noose]
- ❏ ❏ 8 - Back Door to Death (1963) [APA–Nightmare Honeymoon]
- ❏ ❏ 9 - Fatal Lady (1964)
- ❏ ❏ 10 - Call It Accident (1965)
- ❏ ❏ 11 - A Calculated Risk (1970)

■ **Leslie FORD** is the pseudonym of Zenith Jones Brown (1898-1983) who also wrote as Brenda Conrad and David Frome. Using the Ford byline she produced 16 titles in the Washington DC series featuring career soldier Col. John Primrose and attractive Georgetown widow Grace Latham. Ex-Army Intelligence, the Colonel and his military aide, the loyal Sgt. Buck, are introduced in 1934 with *The Strangled Witness* and later joined by Grace in book #2. The series concludes in 1953 with *Washington Whispers Murder*, one of the few mysteries to be written about McCarthyism. As Leslie Ford she also wrote a pair of early mysteries featuring Lt. Joseph Kelly—*Murder in Maryland* (1932) and *The Clue of the Judas Tree* (1933). As Brenda Conrad she wrote three nonseries novels featuring military nurses—*The Stars Give Warning* (1941), *Caribbean Conspiracy* (1942) and *Girl with a Golden Bar* (1944). Born in California, she served as a teaching assistant in the departments of English, Greek and Philosophy while a student at the University of Washington. She worked in New York as assistant to the editor and circulation manager for *Dial* magazine, and later served as a correspondent for the U.S. Air Force in England and the Pacific during the Second World War.

Col. John Primrose & Grace Latham . . . career soldier & attractive widow in Washington DC
- ❏ ❏ 1 - The Strangled Witness (1934)
- ❏ ❏ 2 - Ill-Met by Moonlight (1937)
- ❏ ❏ 3 - The Simple Way of Poison (1937)
- ❏ ❏ 4 - Three Bright Pebbles (1938)
- ❏ ❏ 5 - Reno Rendezvous (1939) [Britain–Mr. Cromwell is Dead]
- ❏ ❏ 6 - False to Any Man (1939) [Britain–Snow-White Murder]
- ❏ ❏ 7 - Old Lover's Ghost (1940)
- ❏ ❏ 8 - The Murder of a Fifth Columnist (1941) [Britain–A Capital Crime]
- ❏ ❏ 9 - Murder in the O.P.M. (1942) [Britain–The Priority Murder]
- ❏ ❏ 10 - Siren in the Night (1943)
- ❏ ❏ 11 - All for the Love of a Lady (1944) [Britain–Crack of Dawn]
- ❏ ❏ 12 - The Philadelphia Murder Story (1945)
- ❏ ❏ 13 - Honolulu Story (1946) [Britain–Honolulu Murder Story]
- ❏ ❏ 14 - The Woman in Black (1947)
- ❏ ❏ 15 - The Devil's Stronghold (1948)
- ❏ ❏ 16 - Washington Whispers Murder (1953) [Britain–The Lying Jade]

■ **Katherine V. FORREST**, of San Francisco, California, is the creator of a series featuring lesbian homicide detective Kate Delafield of the LAPD introduced in *Amateur City* (1984). The second installment of this two-time Lambda award winning series, *The Beverly Malibu* (1989), has been optioned by Hollywood film director Tim Hunter. In addition to her mystery series work, Forrest is the author of *Curious Wine*, the all-time best-selling love story published by Naiad Press where Forrest also works as an editor. She also wrote a fantasy science fiction lesbian romance titled *Daughters of a Coral Dawn*.

    Kate Delafield . . . LAPD lesbian homicide detective

        ❑ ❑ 1 - Amateur City (1984)
        ❑ ❑ 2 - Murder at the Nightwood Bar (1986)
        ❑ ❑ 3 - **The Beverly Malibu (1989)** *Lambda winner* ★
        ❑ ❑ 4 - **Murder by Tradition (1991)** *Lambda winner* ★

■ **Earlene FOWLER** is a native Californian, raised in La Puente, who says her Southern mother and Western father account for the appearance of quilts, cattle, smart-mouthed women, cowboys and a sexy Latino cop in her new mystery series starring Benni Harper, ex-rancher and folk art museum curator. The series is set in San Celina, an artistic and ranching community on the central California coast with a supporting cast that includes her immensely likable grandmother Dove. Armed with a list of several thousand quilt patterns, Fowler doesn't expect to run out of titles for future mystery installments anytime soon. She lives in Fountain Valley with her ten pairs of cowboy boots and prodigious collection of Patsy Cline tapes.

    Albenia "Benni" Harper . . . San Celina, California ex-rancher & folk art museum curator

        ❑ ❑ 1 - **Fool's Puzzle (1994)** *Agatha nominee* ☆
        ❑ ❑ 2 - Irish Chain (1995)
        ❑ ❑ 3 - Kansas Troubles (1996)

■ **Valerie FRANKEL** is an editor at *Mademoiselle* and creator of a New York series featuring Times Square private eye and smart-mouth Wanda Mallory introduced in *Deadline for Murder* (1991). A graduate of Dartmouth College where she wrote a weekly column for the school paper, Frankel got her first magazine job as a fact checker for *New York Woman* in 1987.

    Wanda Mallory . . . New York City detective agency owner

        ❑ ❑ 1 - A Deadline for Murder (1991)
        ❑ ❑ 2 - Murder on Wheels (1992)
        ❑ ❑ 3 - Prime Time for Murder (1994)
        ❑ ❑ 4 - A Body to Die For (1995)

■ **Anthea FRASER** is the author of more than 29 novels including her 13-book police series featuring Detective Chief Inspector David Webb, introduced in *A Shroud for Delilah* (1984). Beginning with the title of book #5 (*The Nine Bright Shiners*) she started working her way through the verses of "Green Grow the Rushes-O," although not in order. Fraser began her writing career with short stories and then moved to romantic fiction and later paranormal fiction, before settling in crime fiction with DCI Webb who eventually becomes her consistent point of view. She created not just a town (Shillingham) but an entire fictional county (Broadshire) and put it in one of her favorite parts of England—the southwest where the northern half of Wiltshire is actually located. Her work has been translated into seven languages. Secretary of the British Crime Writers Association since 1986, she lives in Hertfordshire, England.

    David Webb . . . British police inspector

        ❑ ❑ 1 - A Shroud for Delilah (1984)
        ❑ ❑ 2 - A Necessary End (1985)
        ❑ ❑ 3 - Pretty Maids All in a Row (1986)

  ❑ ❑ 4 - Death Speaks Softly (1987)
  ❑ ❑ 5 - The Nine Bright Shiners (1987)
  ❑ ❑ 6 - Six Proud Walkers (1988)
  ❑ ❑ 7 - The April Rainers (1989)
  ❑ ❑ 8 - Symbols at Your Door (1990)
  ❑ ❑ 9 - The Lily-White Boys (1991)
  ❑ ❑ 10 - Three, Three the Rivals (1992)
  ❑ ❑ 11 - The Gospel Makers (1994)
  ❑ ❑ 12 - Seven Stars (1995)
  ❑ ❑ 13 - One is One and All Alone (1996)

■ **Lady Antonia FRASER**, born in London, the daughter of Lord Longford, who was himself a writer, earned her BA and MA in history at Oxford. She is the author of a long-running mystery series featuring glamorous British television personality and investigative journalist Jemima Shore, introduced in 1977 with *Quiet as a Nun*. In addition to serving as editor of the Kings and Queens of England biography series, Fraser has written a number of critically-acclaimed historical biographies including Mary, Queen of Scots, Cromwell and The Wives of Henry VIII. A past chairman of the British Crime Writers Association, she lives in London with her husband, dramatist Harold Pinter.

Jemima Shore . . . British TV interviewer
  ❑ ❑ 1 - Quiet as a Nun (1977)
  ❑ ❑ 2 - The Wild Island (1978)
  ❑ ❑ 3 - A Splash of Red (1981)
  ❑ ❑ 4 - Cool Repentance (1982)
  ❑ ❑ 5 - Oxford Blood (1985)
  ❑ ❑ 6 - Jemima Shore's First Case & Other Stories (1986)
  ❑ ❑ 7 - Your Royal Hostage (1987)
  ❑ ❑ 8 - The Cavalier Case (1991)
  ❑ ❑ - Jemima Shore at the Sunny Grave [9 stories] (1993)
  ❑ ❑ 9 - Political Death (1994)

■ **Margaret FRAZER** is the shared pseudonym of Mary Pulver Kuhfeld and Gail Bacon for their medieval mystery series featuring Sister Frevisse, hosteler of the priory at St. Frideswide. A niece of Thomas Chaucer and great-niece of Geoffrey Chaucer, Sister Frevisse first appears in *The Novice's Tale* (1992), followed by the Edgar-nominated *The Servant's Tale* (1993). Kuhfeld and Bacon live about five miles apart in the Minneapolis area and decide together on plot before one begins writing the manuscript which they continue sending back and forth until it is finished. At deadline they've been known to sit shoulder to shoulder fussing over every paragraph. Kuhfeld is also the creator of a series featuring Peter and Kori Price Brichter which she writes as Mary Monica Pulver.

Sister Frevisse . . . medieval nun in Oxfordshire, England
  ❑ ❑ 1 - The Novice's Tale (1992)
  ❑ ❑ 2 - **The Servant's Tale** (1993) *Edgar nominee* ☆
  ❑ ❑ 3 - The Outlaw's Tale (1994)
  ❑ ❑ 4 - The Bishop's Tale (1994)
  ❑ ❑ 5 - The Boy's Tale (1995)
  ❑ ❑ 6 - The Murderer's Tale (1996)

■ **Mickey FRIEDMAN** is Michaele Thompson Friedman, creator of pair of mysteries featuring American expatriate journalist Georgia Lee Maxwell. A Paris-based freelance writer, Maxwell is introduced in *Magic Mirror* (1988) and returns in *A Temporary Ghost* (1989).

Friedman's nonseries mysteries include *Hurricane Season* (1983), *The Fault Tree* (1984), *Paper Phoenix* (1986), *Venetian Mask* (1987) and *Riptide*. As publications chair of Mystery Writers of America (MWA), she compiled the top 100 mystery novels of all time (selected by MWA members). This list, with annotations by Otto Penzler, was published as *The Crown Crime Companion* (1995).

Georgia Lee Maxwell . . . Paris-based freelance writer
    ❏ ❏ 1 - Magic Mirror (1988) [Britain–Deadly Reflections]
    ❏ ❏ 2 - A Temporary Ghost (1989)

■ **Susan FROETSCHEL** is the creator of a new Alaska mystery series featuring Jane McBride, who makes her first appearance in *Alaska Gray* (1994). Leaving Boston and bad memories behind, McBride arrives in Sitka to take a job as finance director, only to find the position no longer exists. This is Froetschel's first novel.

Jane McBride . . . finance director in Sitka, Alaska
    ❏ ❏ 1 - Alaska Gray (1994)

■ **David FROME** is the earliest pseudonym of Zenith Jones Brown (1898-1983) and the one she used for her first novel, *The Murder of an Old Man* (1929), featuring Maj. Gregory Lewis who reappears only once in *The Strange Death of Martin Green* (1931), published in London as *The Murder on the Sixth Hole* (1931). Her longer Frome series features the rabbity Mr. Pinkerton who stumbles over bodies with his friend Sgt. Bull in eleven installments from 1930 to 1950, starting with *The Hammersmith Murders*. Her early mysteries were written while her husband was doing research at Oxford, leaving her plenty of time to devote to her writing. According to Ellery Queen, "She soaked in so much local color and acquired so much familiarity with the English idiom that...no one dreamed she was an American." After the Browns returned to the U.S. she began writing American mystery backgrounds and chose a second pseudonym (Leslie Ford) which eventually became better known than the first (David Frome). Born in California, she served as a teaching assistant in the departments of English, Greek and Philosophy while a student at the University of Washington. She worked in New York as assistant to the editor and circulation manager for *Dial* magazine, and later served as a correspondent for the U.S. Air Force in England and the Pacific during the Second World War.

Evan Pinkerton . . . Welshman in England
    ❏ ❏ 1 - The Hammersmith Murders (1930)
    ❏ ❏ 2 - Two Against Scotland Yard (1931) [Britain–The By-Pass Murder]
    ❏ ❏ 3 - The Man from Scotland Yard (1932)
           [Britain–Mr. Simpson Finds a Body]
    ❏ ❏ 4 - The Eel Pie Murders (1933) [Britain–The Eel Pie Mystery]
    ❏ ❏ 5 - Mr. Pinkerton Goes to Scotland Yard (1934)
           [Britain–Arsenic in Richmond]
    ❏ ❏ 6 - Mr. Pinkerton Finds a Body (1934) [Britain–The Body in the Turl]
    ❏ ❏ 7 - Mr. Pinkerton Grows a Beard (1935)
           [Britain–The Body in Bedford Square]
    ❏ ❏ 8 - Mr. Pinkerton Has the Clue (1936)
    ❏ ❏ 9 - The Black Envelope (1937) [Britain–The Guilt is Plain]
    ❏ ❏ 10 - Mr. Pinkerton at the Old Angel (1939)
           [Britain–Mr. Pinkerton and the Old Angel]
    ❏ ❏ 11 - Homicide House (1950) [Britain–Murder on the Square]

■ **Margot J. FROMER**, of Silver Spring, Maryland brings her background as a medical writer and 20 years of nursing experience to her mystery series featuring Amanda Knight, RN, director of nursing at the fictional JFK Memorial Hospital in Washington DC. Some of her best ideas for poisonings have come while doing research for serious medical articles and with life becoming more and more bizarre, so are her ideas for fiction, she says.

    Amanda Knight . . . hospital director of nursing in Washington DC
- ❏ ❏   1 - Scalpel's Edge (1991)
- ❏ ❏   2 - Night Shift (1993)

■ **Sara Hoskinson FROMMER** is the creator of a mystery series featuring music and quilts, starring symphony orchestra manager Joan Spencer who makes her first appearance in *Murder in C Major* (1993) followed by *Buried in Quilts* (1994). Both are set in the fictional college town of Oliver, Indiana, smaller than the better-know Bloomington where Frommer currently resides. Born in Chicago to Hoosier parents, she grew up in Hawaii and Illinois, graduated from Oberlin College and Brown University and has lived in Indiana most of her adult life. An experienced quilter, she plays viola in the Bloomington Symphony Orchestra.

    Joan Spencer . . . symphony orchestra manager in Oliver, Indiana
- ❏ ❏   1 - Murder in C Major (1993)
- ❏ ❏   2 - Buried in Quilts (1994)

■ **Eileen FULTON**, star of the CBS daytime drama "As the World Turns," is the creator of a mystery series featuring glamorous television soap star Nina McFall and Lt. Dino Rossi NYPD cop, introduced in *Take One for Murder* (1988).

    Nina McFall & Dino Rossi, Lt. . . . glamorous TV soap star & NYPD cop in New York
- ❏ ❏   1 - Take One for Murder (1988)
- ❏ ❏   2 - Death of a Golden Girl (1988)
- ❏ ❏   3 - Dying for Stardom (1988)
- ❏ ❏   4 - Lights, Camera, Death (1988)
- ❏ ❏   5 - A Setting for Murder (1988)
- ❏ ❏   6 - Fatal Flashback (1989)

■ **Ruthe FURIE** worked as a journalist, artist and teacher before turning her hand to mysteries and launching her series detective Fran Kirk, introduced in *If Looks Could Kill* (1995). A former battered wife, Fran is "plain and earnest, just like Buffalo," says her creator. Fran's second adventure takes her to a natural food farm in Wyoming County, New York, where the only thing non-toxic is the food. Furie did her research for book #3, *A Deadly Paté* (1996), while visiting her daughter who lives in France. Reared in Brooklyn, Furie earned her degrees in Buffalo where she currently resides. She worked previously at *The New York Daily News*, *The Buffalo News*, and *The Hackensack Record* and with her former husband, co-authored a mystery novel (*Hell Gate*) under her former name Ruth Stout.

    Fran Kirk . . . former battered wife & P. I. in training in Cheektowaga, New York
- ❏ ❏   1 - If Looks Could Kill (1995)
- ❏ ❏   2 - Natural Death (1996)
- ❏ ❏   3 - A Deadly Paté (1997)

■ **Frances FYFIELD** is the pseudonym of Frances Hegarty, a solicitor specializing in criminal law and creator of two British legal series. The longer series features London Crown Prosecutor Helen West and Detective Superintendent Geoffrey Bailey whose first outing, *A Question of Guilt* (1988), was nominated for an Agatha, Edgar and Anthony. The shorter series features Sarah Fortune, solicitor with a prestigious British firm. Under her own name, Hegarty has also written several psychological novels.

Helen West . . . London Crown Prosecutor
- ❏ ❏ 1 - **A Question of Guilt** (1988)
    Agatha, Anthony & Edgar nominee ☆ ☆ ☆
- ❏ ❏ 2 - Not That Kind of Place (1990) [Britain–Trial by Fire]
- ❏ ❏ 3 - Deep Sleep (1991)
- ❏ ❏ 4 - Shadow Play (1993)
- ❏ ❏ 5 - A Clear Conscience (1994)

Sarah Fortune . . . lawyer in prestigious British firm
- ❏ ❏ 1 - Shadows on the Mirror (1989)
- ❏ ❏ 2 - Perfectly Pure and Good (1994)

■ **Kate GALLISON** is the creator of two mystery series, one featuring a Trenton private eye and the other an Episcopalian parish priest. The Trenton P. I. Nick Magaracz is introduced in *Unbalanced Accounts* (1986) and bows out in *The Jersey Monkey* (1992). Mother Lavinia Grey, who debuts in *Bury the Bishop* (1995) returns in *Devil's Worshop* (1996). At various times in her career, Gallison has worked as a store clerk, bill collector and computer specialist. A native of Philadelphia, she currently lives in Lambertville, New Jersey.

Mother Lavinia Grey . . . Episcopal vicar & practicing therapist in Fishersville, New Jersey
- ❏ ❏ 1 - Bury the Bishop (1995)
- ❏ ❏ 2 - The Devil's Workshop (1996)

Nick Magaracz . . . private eye in Trenton, New Jersey
- ❏ ❏ 1 - Unbalanced Accounts (1986)
- ❏ ❏ 2 - The Death Tape (1987)
- ❏ ❏ 3 - The Jersey Monkey (1992)

■ **Dorothy GARDINER** (1894-1979) was an American, born in Naples, Italy and educated at the University of Colorado. She was the creator of one of the earliest regional mysteries with her Colorado sheriff Moss Magill, an easy going but shrewd country lawman of the West. Gardiner takes him to the Scottish Highlands in *The Seventh Mourner* (1958) for what some say is her best work, providing wonderful impressions of the sheriff's comparison of the Rocky Mountains to the Scottish Highlands. Gardiner also wrote a pair of mysteries in the early '30s featuring an amateur sleuth, Mr. Watson. She is perhaps best known among mystery writers for her contribution to the field as Executive Secretary of the MWA from 1950 to 1957. She also assisted John Creasey in the initiation of the British Crime Writers Association and co-edited the first writings of Raymond Chandler to be published after his death, *Raymond Chandler Speaking* (1962).

Moss Magill . . . sheriff in Notlaw, Colorado
- ❏ ❏ 1 - What Crime Is It? (1956) [Britain–The Case of the Hula Clock]
- ❏ ❏ 2 - The Seventh Mourner (1958)
- ❏ ❏ 3 - Lion in Wait (1963) [Britain–Lion? or Murderer?]

Mr. Watson . . . amateur sleuth in California
- ❏ ❏ 1 - The Transatlantic Ghost (1933)
- ❏ ❏ 2 - A Drink for Mr. Cherry (1934) [Britain–Mr. Watson Intervenes]

■ **Susan GEASON** is the creator of a new mystery series set in Sydney, Australia, featuring a failed journalist, sacked political minder and fledgling P. I. named Syd Fish, who makes his first appearance in *Shaved Fish* (1993). Geason says her detective comes to his present job via the yellow press and politics, both areas demanding moral flexibility and a strong stomach. Politically incorrect on any number of grounds, Syd gets on well with losers and low lifes and is no stranger to sleaze. Born in Tasmania, Geason has lived in Brisbane, Canberra and Toronto where she earned an MA in political theory from the University of Toronto. She has worked as a journalist with the *National Times* and as a policy adviser in Parliament House (Canberra) and the New South Wales Premier's Department. She is currently a freelance researcher, writer, speechwriter and book reviewer in Sydney.

    Syd Fish . . . Sydney, Australia P. I.
- ❑ ❑ 1 - Shaved Fish (1993)
- ❑ ❑ 2 - Dogfish (1993)
- ❑ ❑ 3 - Sharkbait (1993)

■ **Elizabeth GEORGE** is really Susan Elizabeth George, creator of a best-selling series featuring Scotland Yard Inspector and eighth earl of Asherton Thomas Lynley and his working class partner Sgt. Barbara Havers. The supporting cast includes the crippled forensic pathologist Simon Allcourt-St. James, who is Lynley's best friend, now married to the photographer Deborah who was once Lynley's girlfriend. Lynley has an off-again on-again relationship with the often bristly Lady Helen Clyde who is Simon's laboratory assistant and his former lover. The first installment in this intense psychological series, *A Great Deliverance* (1988), won the Anthony and Agatha awards for best first novel and received nominations for the Edgar and Macavity awards that year. An American born in Warren, Ohio and raised in northern California, George earned degrees in English and counseling before teaching high school English in Orange County for 13 years. While still teaching she wrote her books during summer breaks. In fact, her first book was written in the six weeks between the end of a research trip to England and the beginning of the new school year. She says she first fell in love with England when she visited as a teenager on a Shakespeare study tour. She lives in Huntington Beach where she writes full time and teaches in-home writing classes.

    Thomas Lynley & Barbara Havers . . . Scotland Yard inspector & detective sergeant
- ❑ ❑ 1 - **A Great Deliverance (1988)** *Agatha & Anthony winner* ★ ★
   Edgar & Macavity nominee ☆ ☆
- ❑ ❑ 2 - Payment in Blood (1989)
- ❑ ❑ 3 - Well-Schooled in Murder (1990)
- ❑ ❑ 4 - A Suitable Vengeance (1991)
- ❑ ❑ 5 - For the Sake of Elena (1992)
- ❑ ❑ 6 - Missing Joseph (1993)
- ❑ ❑ 7 - Playing for the Ashes (1994)
- ❑ ❑ 8 - In the Presence of the Enemy (1996)

■ **Anthony GILBERT** is the pseudonym of Lucy Beatrice Malleson (1899-1973) who also wrote as Anne Meredith and J. Kilmeny Keith. She is best known for her creation of Arthur G. Crook, that perpetually brown-suited lawyer-detective who was billed as "The Criminals' Hope and The Judges' Despair." Thought by some to be the most interesting fictional detective ever to solve a case, Crook was featured in 50 books starting with *Murder by Experts* (1936) and finishing with *A Nice Little Killing (1974).* The ebullient Cockney was a lover of automobiles and his own car (the Scourge and later the Superb) starred in some wonderful chases. Before launching her Crook series, Gilbert wrote nine mysteries featuring Scott Egerton, Liberal Member of Parliament and man about town, introduced in *The Tragedy at Freyne (1927).* Born in London, she was a founding member of the Detection Club and served as General Secretary. In addition to her autobiography, *Three-a-Penny* (1940), she wrote 20 nonseries novels as Anne Meredith between 1934 and 1962. She also wrote 27 original radio plays and another adapted from one of her own novels along with at least 30 uncollected short stories.

Arthur G. Crook . . . Cockney lawyer-detective in England

❑ ❑ 1 - Murder by Experts (1936)
❑ ❑ 2 - The Man Who Wasn't There (1937)
❑ ❑ 3 - Murder Has No Tongue (1937)
❑ ❑ 4 - Treason in My Breast (1938)
❑ ❑ 5 - The Bell of Death (1939)
❑ ❑ 6 - The Clock in the Hatbox (1939)
❑ ❑ 7 - Dear Dead Woman (1940) [U.S.–Death Takes a Redhead]
❑ ❑ 8 - The Vanishing Corpse (1941) [U.S.–She Vanished in the Dawn]
❑ ❑ 9 - The Woman in Red (1941) [APA–The Mystery of the Woman in Red]
❑ ❑ 10 - Something Nasty in the Woodshed (1942)
             [U.S.–Mystery in the Woodshed]
❑ ❑ 11 - The Case of the Tea-Cosy's Aunt (1942)
             [U.S.–Death in the Blackout]
❑ ❑ 12 - The Mouse Who Wouldn't Play Ball (1943) [U.S.–30 Days to Live]
❑ ❑ 13 - He Came by Night (1944) [U.S.–Death at the Door]
❑ ❑ 14 - The Scarlet Button (1944) [APA–Murder is Cheap]
❑ ❑ 15 - Don't Open the Door! (1945) [U.S.–Death Lifts the Latch]
❑ ❑ 16 - Lift up the Lid (1945) [U.S.–The Innocent Bottle]
❑ ❑ 17 - The Black Stage (1945) [U.S.–Murder Cheats the Bride]
❑ ❑ 18 - The Spinster's Secret (1946) [U.S.–By Hook or By Crook]
❑ ❑ 19 - Death in the Wrong Room (1947)
❑ ❑ 20 - Die in the Dark (1947) [U.S.–The Missing Widow]
❑ ❑ 21 - Death Knocks Three Times (1949)
❑ ❑ 22 - A Nice Cup of Tea (1950) [U.S.–The Wrong Body]
❑ ❑ 23 - Murder Comes Home (1950)
❑ ❑ 24 - Lady Killer (1951)
❑ ❑ 25 - And Death Came Too (1952)
❑ ❑ 26 - Miss Pinnegar Disappears (1952) [U.S.–A Case For Mr. Crook]
❑ ❑ 27 - Footsteps Behind Me (1953) [U.S.–Black Death] [APA–Dark Death]
❑ ❑ 28 - Snake in the Grass (1954) [U.S.–Death Won't Wait]
❑ ❑ 29 - Is She Dead Too? (1955) [U.S.–A Question of Murder]
❑ ❑ 30 - Riddle of a Lady (1956)
❑ ❑ 31 - Give Death a Name (1957)
❑ ❑ 32 - Death Against the Clock (1958)
❑ ❑ 33 - Death Takes a Wife (1959) [U.S.–Death Casts a Long Shadow]
❑ ❑ 34 - Third Crime Lucky (1959) [U.S.–Prelude to Murder]
❑ ❑ 35 - Out for the Kill (1960)
❑ ❑ 36 - She Shall Die (1961) [U.S.–After the Verdict]
❑ ❑ 37 - Uncertain Death (1961)
❑ ❑ 38 - No Dust in the Attic (1962)
❑ ❑ 39 - Ring for a Noose (1963)
❑ ❑ 40 - Knock, Knock, Who's There? (1964) [U.S.–The Voice]
❑ ❑ 41 - The Fingerprint (1964)
❑ ❑ 42 - Passenger to Nowhere (1965)
❑ ❑ 43 - The Looking Glass Murder (1966)
❑ ❑ 44 - The Visitor (1967)
❑ ❑ 45 - Night Encounter (1968) [U.S.–Murder Anonymous]
❑ ❑ 46 - Missing from Her Home (1969)
❑ ❑ 47 - Death Wears a Mask (1970) [U.S.–Mr. Crook Lifts the Mask]
❑ ❑ 48 - Tenant for the Tomb (1971)

  ❑ ❑ 49 - Murder's a Waiting Game (1972)
  ❑ ❑ 50 - A Nice Little Killing (1974)

Scott Egerton . . . Liberal M. P. & man about town in England

  ❑ ❑ 1 - The Tragedy at Freyne (1927)
  ❑ ❑ 2 - The Murder of Mrs. Davenport (1928)
  ❑ ❑ 3 - Death at Four Corners (1929)
  ❑ ❑ 4 - The Mystery of the Open Window (1929)
  ❑ ❑ 5 - The Night of the Fog (1930)
  ❑ ❑ 6 - The Body on the Beam (1932)
  ❑ ❑ 7 - The Long Shadow (1932)
  ❑ ❑ 8 - An Old Lady Dies (1934)
  ❑ ❑ 9 - The Man Who Was Too Clever (1935)

■ **B. M. GILL** is the pseudonym of Welsh novelist Barbara Margaret Trimble who writes romantic thrillers under the names Margaret Blake and Barbara Gilmour. Her series character, police inspector Tom Maybridge, introduced in *Victims* (1980), returns in *Seminar for Murder* (1985) and *The Fifth Rapunzel* (1990). Gill won a Gold Dagger in 1984 for her nonseries novel *The Twelfth Juror*.

Tom Maybridge . . . police inspector in England

  ❑ ❑ 1 - Victims (1980) [U.S.–Suspect]
  ❑ ❑ 2 - Seminar for Murder (1985)
  ❑ ❑ 3 - The Fifth Rapunzel (1990)

■ **Dorothy GILMAN** wrote a dozen children's books under her married name of Dorothy Gilman Butters before launching her series featuring the CIA's most unlikely agent, New Jersey grandmother Emily Pollifax. Mrs. Pollifax travels the globe narrowly escaping danger, often one quick step ahead of her pursuers. In addition to the Mrs. Pollifax titles, Gilman has written five other novels of adventure and suspense along with numerous short stories. She has also been a teacher of drawing and creative writing.

Emily Pollifax . . . New Jersey grandmother & CIA agent

  ❑ ❑ 1 - The Unexpected Mrs. Pollifax (1966)
  ❑ ❑ 2 - The Amazing Mrs. Pollifax (1970)
  ❑ ❑ 3 - The Elusive Mrs. Pollifax (1971)
  ❑ ❑ 4 - A Palm for Mrs. Pollifax (1973)
  ❑ ❑ 5 - Mrs. Pollifax on Safari (1976)
  ❑ ❑ 6 - Mrs. Pollifax on the China Station (1983)
  ❑ ❑ 7 - Mrs. Pollifax and the Hong Kong Buddha (1985)
  ❑ ❑ 8 - Mrs. Pollifax and the Golden Triangle (1988)
  ❑ ❑ 9 - Mrs. Pollifax and the Whirling Dervish (1990)
  ❑ ❑ 10 - Mrs. Pollifax and the Second Thief (1993)
  ❑ ❑ 11 - Mrs. Pollifax Pursued (1995)
  ❑ ❑ 12 - Mrs. Pollifax and the Lion Killer (1996)

■ **Noreen GILPATRICK** is the creator of a new police series featuring Seattle police detective Kate McLean introduced in *Final Design* (1993). Returning in *Shadow of Death* (1995), Kate misses her ex-partner Sam who has taken a desk job and is attempting a reconciliation with his wife. Prior to starting her mystery writing career, Gilpatrick worked in both the print and broadcast media, including a stint on the staff of *Psychology Today*. She once owned her own advertising agency in Seattle and lived on an island in Puget Sound. She has worked as a press aide for a gubernatorial candidate, and as producer and program specialist for a PBS affiliate in Kentucky. Her first novel, *The Piano Man* (1991), won the Malice

Domestic award for best first traditional mystery and in its review *The New York Times* said, "Ms. Gilpatrick knows exactly how to raise goose flesh."

> **Kate McLean** . . . Seattle, Washington police detective
> ❑ ❑ 1 - Final Design (1993)
> ❑ ❑ 2 - Shadow of Death (1995)

■ **Jaqueline GIRDNER** lives in Marin County, California where she has been a psychiatric aide, family law attorney and business owner, before launching her mystery series featuring Kate Jasper, gag gift wholesaler, introduced in *Adjusted to Death* (1991) which involves murder in a chiropractic office. Among Girdner's own entrepreneurial ventures were a pinball refurbishing business, a mill-end yarn emporium and a greeting card company. In addition to her writing, she practices tai chi and keeps the books for her husband's computer business.

> **Kate Jasper** . . . Marin County, California gag gift wholesaler
> ❑ ❑ 1 - Adjusted to Death (1991)
> ❑ ❑ 2 - The Last Resort (1991)
> ❑ ❑ 3 - Murder Most Mellow (1992)
> ❑ ❑ 4 - Fat-Free and Fatal (1993)
> ❑ ❑ 5 - Tea-Totally Dead (1994)
> ❑ ❑ 6 - A Stiff Critique (1995)
> ❑ ❑ 7 - Most Likely to Die (1996)

■ **E. X. GIROUX** is the pseudonym of Canadian author Doris Shannon for her English mystery series featuring barrister Robert Forsythe and his secretary Abigail Sanderson who sometimes does the larger share of detecting in their partnership. Giroux lives in British Columbia, not far from the Washington State border.

> **Robert Forsythe & Abigail Sanderson** . . . London barrister & his secretary
> ❑ ❑ 1 - A Death for Adonis (1984)
> ❑ ❑ 2 - A Death for a Darling (1985)
> ❑ ❑ 3 - A Death for a Dancer (1986)
> ❑ ❑ 4 - A Death for a Doctor (1986)
> ❑ ❑ 5 - A Death for a Dilletante (1987)
> ❑ ❑ 6 - A Death for a Dietician (1988)
> ❑ ❑ 7 - A Death for a Dreamer (1989)
> ❑ ❑ 8 - A Death for a Double (1990)
> ❑ ❑ 9 - A Death for a Dancing Doll (1991)
> ❑ ❑ 10 - A Death for a Dodo (1993)

■ **Leslie GLASS**, playwright and author of three previous nonseries novels, is the creator of a new series featuring police detective April Woo of the NYPD. The opening installment has been described as a police procedural with the insights of an analyst's couch. Glass is actively involved with a number of forensic and psychologic projects as an advisor to the John Jay College of Criminal Justice. The married mother of two teenagers divides her time among New York City, Martha's Vineyard and Sarasota, Florida.

> **April Woo** . . . New York City police detective
> ❑ ❑ 1 - Burning Time (1993)
> ❑ ❑ 2 - Hanging Time (1995)

■ **Alison GLEN** is the shared pseudonym of writing partners Cheryl Meredith Lowry and Louise Vetter of Columbus, Ohio, for their new series featuring Columbus freelance writer Charlotte Sams, introduced in *Showcase* (1992). Lowry is currently the training coordinator for Community Mediation Services in Columbus, but murder is not one of the conflict resolution techniques she recommends to her trainees. Vetter is senior research specialist emeritus at Ohio State University and an enthusiastic Earthwatch volunteer, digging up mammoth bones near Oxford, in search of the Saxon church that predated the Norman cathedral in St. Albans in England.

Charlotte Sams . . . Columbus, Ohio freelance writer
- ❑ ❑ 1 - Showcase (1992)
- ❑ ❑ 2 - Trunk Show (1995)

■ **Alison GORDON** was the first woman journalist to cover major league baseball when she wrote about the Toronto Blue Jays during the 1980s. It's no surprise that her woman sleuth is sportswriter Kate Henry who covers the fictional Toronto Titans. If you like to read about writers at work, you'll enjoy this series. If you're also a baseball fan, you'll be in heaven.

Kate Henry . . . Toronto, Canada baseball newswriter
- ❑ ❑ 1 - The Dead Pull Hitter (1989)
- ❑ ❑ 2 - Safe at Home (1991)
- ❑ ❑ 3 - Night Game (1993)
- ❑ ❑ 4 - Striking Out (1995)

■ **Paula GOSLING** was born and raised in Detroit where she worked in advertising before moving to England and writing *A Running Duck* (renamed *Fair Game* in the U.S.) which won the Creasey award for best first novel and was later made into the Sylvester Stallone film *Cobra*. The book was turned into yet another Hollywood film in 1995 starring Cindy Crawford. The first title in the Jack Stryker and Kate Trevorne series, *Monkey Puzzle*, set in the American Midwest, was awarded the coveted Gold Dagger for best novel in 1985. Three years later Gosling became chairman of the British Crime Writers Association, a title previously held by Lady Antonia Fraser and Simon Brett. Gosling's 1994 title *A Few Dying Words* returns to Blackwater Bay (the setting of Jack and Kate's previous outing) but features different characters who return in book #2 of the Blackwater Bay series, *The Dead of Winter*. Gosling recently announced her intention to abandon her series for awhile and write one-offs instead. A mystery set in Detroit's General Motors Building is one of the novels on her drawing board.

Blackwater Bay mystery . . . police series with a Great Lakes setting
- ❑ ❑ 1 - A Few Dying Words (1994)
- ❑ ❑ 2 - The Dead of Winter (1995)

Jack Stryker & Kate Trevorne . . . Grantham, Ohio homicide cop & English professor
- ❑ ❑ 1 - **Monkey Puzzle** (1985) *Gold Dagger* ★
- ❑ ❑ 2 - Backlash (1989)
- ❑ ❑ 3 - The Body in Blackwater Bay (1992)

Luke Abbott . . . English cop
- ❑ ❑ 1 - The Wychford Murders (1986)
- ❑ ❑ 2 - Death Penalties (1991)

■ **Sue GRAFTON** is the creator of the Kinsey Millhone private eye series, often referred to as the alphabet mysteries, launched in 1982 with *"A" is for Alibi*, followed in 1985 by *"B" is for Burglar*. Grafton added a book each year, typically in early May to celebrate Kinsey's birthday, until 1995 when she shifted to late summer for her newest release. If the series continues at the book-a-year rate, *"Z" is for Zero* [most likely] will be Grafton's 2009 release, at which time the author will be 69 and thanks to the marvels of fictional time, Kinsey will celebrate her 40th birthday. That smart-mouthed P. I. from Santa Teresa will probably still be eating peanut butter and pickle sandwiches. In her Hollywood days, Grafton wrote a number of screenplays and television scripts, including a 1975 episode of the sitcom *Rhoda*. Recipient of four Anthonys and a Shamus for her Kinsey novels, she is widely recognized as one of the Big Three in contemporary P. I. fiction, along with Sara Paretsky and Marcia Muller. Grafton is the daughter of Louisville, Kentucky, attorney and mystery writer C. W. Grafton who started his own legal mystery series with *The Rat Began to Knaw the Rope* (1943). Despite plans to produce a ten-book series titled with lines from a classic nursery rhyme, he published only two series titles and the better-known nonseries novel, *Beyond a Reasonable Doubt* (1950).

      Kinsey Millhone . . . Santa Teresa, California ex-cop P. I.

❑	❑	1	-	**"A" is for Alibi** (1982) *Anthony winner* ★ *Shamus nominee* ☆
❑	❑	2	-	**"B" is for Burglar** (1985) *Anthony & Shamus winner* ★ ★
❑	❑	3	-	**"C" is for Corpse** (1986) *Anthony winner* ★ *Shamus nominee* ☆
❑	❑	4	-	**"D" is for Deadbeat** (1987)
❑	❑	5	-	**"E" is for Evidence** (1988)
❑	❑	6	-	**"F" is for Fugitive** (1989)
❑	❑	7	-	**"G" is for Gumshoe** (1990) *Anthony & Shamus winner* ★ ★
❑	❑	8	-	**"H" is for Homicide** (1991)
❑	❑	9	-	**"I" is for Innocent** (1992) *American Mystery Award winner* ★
❑	❑	10	-	**"J" is for Judgment** (1993)
❑	❑	11	-	**"K" is for Killer** (1994) *Shamus winner* ★ *Anthony nominee* ☆
❑	❑	12	-	**"L" is for Lawless** (1995)

■ **Caroline GRAHAM**, of Birmingham, England, is the creator of the police series featuring Chief Inspector Tom Barnaby whose first outing, *The Killings at Badger's Drift* (1987), was awarded a Macavity for best first mystery and nominated for an Agatha award. Graham is also a playwright with experience in both stage and television and the author of several children's books.

      Tom Barnaby . . . chief inspector in England

❑	❑	1	-	**The Killings at Badger's Drift** (1987) *Macavity winner* ★ *Agatha nominee* ☆
❑	❑	2	-	Death of a Hollow Man (1989)
❑	❑	3	-	Death in Disguise (1993)
❑	❑	4	-	Written in Blood (1995)

■ **Ann GRANGER** lives in Bicester, England near the city of Oxford and has worked in the diplomatic service in various parts of the world, much like her series protagonist, foreign service officer Meredith Mitchell. A 30-something Foreign Office employee, Mitchell works in London, commuting by train each day from her terraced Bamford cottage in the Cotswolds. The series cast prominently features Chief Inspector Alan Markby who would like nothing better than to see Meredith retire from the service and join him in Bamford. She has reservations about police work but can never resist the temptation to sleuth, which often gets her into tight corners.

Inspector Alan Markby & Meredith Mitchell . . . detective inspector & Foreign Service officer in Cotswolds, England

    ❏ ❏   1   -   Say It with Poison (1991)
    ❏ ❏   2   -   A Season for Murder (1992)
    ❏ ❏   3   -   Cold in the Earth (1993)
    ❏ ❏   4   -   Murder Among Us (1993)
    ❏ ❏   5   -   Where Old Bones Lie (1993)
    ❏ ❏   6   -   Flowers for His Funeral (1994)
    ❏ ❏   7   -   A Fine Place for Death (1995)
    ❏ ❏   8   -   Candle for a Corpse (1995)
    ❏ ❏   9   -   A Touch of Mortality (1996)

■ **Linda GRANT** is the pseudonym of Linda V. Williams, creator of San Francisco P. I. Catherine Sayler, private investigator and corporate crime specialist. Catherine's assistant Jesse, the young computer whiz who later becomes her partner, adds a convincing technical dimension to their cases. The fourth installment of this two-time Anthony-nominated series, *A Woman's Place* (1994), is a not-to-be-missed case of sexual harassment that turns to murder. Before launching her mystery writing career, Grant spent two years in Ethiopia with the Peace Corps, worked as a high school English teacher, wrote training materials for community action agencies, taught computer classes and trained teachers. A past president of Sisters in Crime, she lives in Berkeley, California.

Catherine Sayler . . . San Francisco, California private investigator

    ❏ ❏   1   -   **Random Access Murder** (1988) *Anthony nominee* ☆
    ❏ ❏   2   -   Blind Trust (1990)
    ❏ ❏   3   -   **Love nor Money** (1991) *Anthony nominee* ☆
    ❏ ❏   4   -   A Woman's Place (1994)
    ❏ ❏   5   -   Lethal Genes (1996)

■ **Lesley GRANT-ADAMSON** is the creator of three mystery series set in London, including her earliest series with newspaper reporter and gossip columnist Rain Morgan featured in five books beginning with *Death on Widow's Walk* (1985). London Irish private eye Laura Flynn debuts in *Too Many Questions* (1991) and Jim Rush is introduced in *A Life of Adventure* (1992). An incompetent con man, Rush is a young American inveigling his way into English society. The author has been a feature writer on the *Guardian*, one of England's leading national newspapers, and a freelance writer of television documentaries and fiction. She and her journalist husband Andrew Grant-Adamson lived for several years in an olive grove in the Alpujarra region of Andalusia and recently wrote a portrait of the area, *A Season in Spain* (1995).

Jim Rush . . . American on the run from British police in England

    ❏ ❏   1   -   A Life of Adventure (1992)
    ❏ ❏   2   -   Dangerous Games (1994)

Laura Flynn . . . London private investigator

    ❏ ❏   1   -   Too Many Questions (1991) [Britain–Flynn]
    ❏ ❏   2   -   The Dangerous Edge (1994)

Rain Morgan . . . newspaper reporter in London

    ❏ ❏   1   -   Death on Widow's Walk (1985) [Britain–Patterns in the Dust]
    ❏ ❏   2   -   The Face of Death (1985)
    ❏ ❏   3   -   Guilty Knowledge (1986)
    ❏ ❏   4   -   Wild Justice (1987)
    ❏ ❏   5   -   Curse the Darkness (1990)

■ **Dulcie GRAY** is the pseudonym of Dulcie Winifred Catherine Dennison, a star of the London stage, film, radio and television, who wrote 17 novels, a collection of short stories and several plays while managing a successful acting career. Her series character, Inspector Superintendent Cardiff appears only twice—in *Epitaph for a Dead Actor* (1960) and *Died in the Red* (1968). Although most of her books are set in England she produced at least three titles with more exotic locales—Morocco, South Africa and Australia. Born in Kuala Lumpur, Malaya, she was educated in England and Malaya and at London's Academy des Beaux Arts. She received the Queen's Silver Jubilee Medal in 1977 and in 1983 the C.B.E., Commander, Order of the British Empire.

> **Inspector Supt. Cardiff** . . . police inspector in England
> ❑ ❑ 1 - Epitaph for a Dead Actor (1960)
> ❑ ❑ 2 - Died in the Red (1968)

■ **Gallagher GRAY** is the pseudonym of Katy Munger, a North Carolina native and graduate of the University of North Carolina at Chapel Hill who once worked in the personnel department of a private bank on Wall Street. She is now a New York-based writer and creator of the mystery series featuring 50-something T. S. Hubbert and his 80-something Auntie Lil, a former dress designer. Shortly after his retirement from 35 years in personnel with a New York City law firm, T. S. is drafted as a reluctant sleuthing partner by the feisty Lillian, who is determined that her nephew give up his new-found habit of watching TV soap operas.

> **Theodore S. Hubbert & Auntie Lil** . . . 60-something retired personnel manager & 80-something dress designer in New York
> ❑ ❑ 1 - Partners in Crime (1991)
> ❑ ❑ 2 - A Cast of Killers (1992)
> ❑ ❑ 3 - Death of a Dream Maker (1995)

■ **Anna Katherine GREEN** (1846-1935), often referred to as the "mother of the detective story," is the creator of Ebenezer Gryce, the first series detective developed by an American writer. Unfortunately she is also a prime example of an author who for much of her career was a household word, but today is known only to scholars and serious students of the genre. *The Leavenworth Case* (1878), published nine years ahead of the first Sherlock Holmes, was not the first American novel of detection, but it was the first American detection bestseller—more than a million copies in its day. It contained all the elements of the traditional cozy—a body in the library, a stealthy butler, a diagram of the crime scene and a portly detective. It also contained one of the first literary uses of ballistics testimony, a coroner's inquest and plenty of legal jargon, no doubt picked up from her prominent attorney father. Green also gets credit for one of the earliest little old lady snoops, Miss Amelia Butterworth, featured in at least three of the later Gryce novels. Caleb Sweetwater, Green's second series policeman, appears in three novels starting with *Agatha Webb* in 1899. And Green broke new ground yet again with her creation of Violet Strange—an upper class New York Nancy Drew who solves cases for fees while keeping her activities hidden from her father. Violet didn't get a book series of her own, but is featured in nine short stories (one including Ebenezer Gryce) printed as *The Golden Slipper and Other Problems for Violet Strange* (1915). Born in Brooklyn and educated in Vermont at Ripley Female College, Green lived most of her life in Buffalo as the wife of furniture tycoon Charles Rohlfs.

> **Caleb Sweetwater** . . . policeman in New York
> ❑ ❑ 1 - Agatha Webb (1899)
> ❑ ❑ 2 - The Woman in the Alcove (1906)
> ❑ ❑ 3 - The House of the Whispering Pines (1910)

Ebenezer Gryce . . . portly policeman in New York
- ❑ ❑ 1 - The Leavenworth Case (1878)
- ❑ ❑ 2 - A Strange Disappearance (1880)
- ❑ ❑ 3 - Hand and Ring (1883)
- ❑ ❑ 4 - Behind Closed Doors (1888)
- ❑ ❑ 5 - A Matter of Millions (1890)
- ❑ ❑ 6 - The Doctor, His Wife, and the Clock (1895)
- ❑ ❑ 7 - That Affair Next Door [incl Mrs. Amelia Butterworth] (1897)
- ❑ ❑ 8 - Lost Man's Lane [incl Mrs. Amelia Butterworth] (1898)
- ❑ ❑ 9 - The Circular Study [incl Mrs. Amelia Butterworth] (1900)
- ❑ ❑ 10 - One of My Sons (1901)
- ❑ ❑ 11 - Initials Only [incl Caleb Sweetwater] (1911)
- ❑ ❑ 12 - The Mystery of the Hasty Arrow [incl Caleb Sweetwater] (1911)

■ **Christine GREEN** is the creator of a new English mystery series featuring nurse and medical investigator Kate Kinsella, introduced in *Deadly Errand* (1991) and an even newer series featuring a boozy Irishman and young policewoman, Chief Inspector Connor O'Neill and Detective Sgt. Fran Wilson, introduced in *Death in the Country* (1994). Green lives in Northhampton where she works part-time at a charity-run nursing home.

Chief Inspector Connor O'Neill & Detective Sergeant Fran Wilson . . . village inspector & new policewoman in Fowchester England
- ❑ ❑ 1 - Death in the Country (1994)
- ❑ ❑ 2 - Die in My Dreams (1995)
- ❑ ❑ 3 - Fatal Cut (1996)

Kate Kinsella . . . British nurse & medical investigator
- ❑ ❑ 1 - Deadly Errand (1991)
- ❑ ❑ 2 - Deadly Admirer (1992)
- ❑ ❑ 3 - Deadly Practice (1994)

■ **Edith Pinero GREEN** is the creator of Dearborn V. Pinch, a charming and enterprising old gentleman who still has a sharp eye for the ladies. The 70-something Mr. Pinch, known to help out friends with problems they do not wish to take to the police, is visited by an old flame in the series opener, *Rotten Apples* (1977). It seems that Antoinette Ormach is a member of the Rotten Apple Corps, formed some 40 years earlier by eleven people who had each committed a minor crime. As members start dying under suspicious circumstances, Antoinette fears she may be next. And when she is murdered, Pinch feels obligated to root out the rotten apple. Green's publishers called Mr. Pinch "the world's oldest and cleverest detective." Others have called him "the horniest old man in mystery fiction." A native of New Jersey, Green earned her BA at the New School for Social Research and worked for seven years at a New York advertising agency.

Dearborn V. Pinch . . . 70-something ladies man in New York
- ❑ ❑ 1 - Rotten Apples (1977)
- ❑ ❑ 2 - Sneaks (1979)
- ❑ ❑ 3 - Perfect Fools (1982)

■ **Kate GREEN** teaches a graduate course in writing at Hamline University and is a published poet and author of six children's books, including *Fossil Family Tales* and *A Number of Animals*, her collaboration with British engraver Christopher Wormell. She is the creator of professional psychic Theresa Fortunato who assists LAPD homicide detective Oliver Jardino in the Edgar-nominated *Shattered Moon*. The second installment of this series, *Black Dreams*, received the 1993 Minnesota Book Award. Green has also written two nonseries mystery-suspense thrillers—*Night Angel* and *Shooting Star*. Her undergraduate degree is from the University of Minnesota and her MA from Boston University.

Theresa Fortunato & Oliver Jardino . . . professional psychic & LAPD detective
- ❑ ❑ 1 - **Shattered Moon** (1986) *Edgar nominee* ☆
- ❑ ❑ 2 - Black Dreams (1993)

■ **Diane M. GREENWOOD**, who describes herself as an ecclesiastical civil servant, is the creator of a mystery series featuring the Reverend Theodora Braithwaite, British deaconess, introduced in *Clerical Errors* (1991). The author holds degrees from Oxford (classics) and London University (theology) and works for the diocese of Rochester in Greenwich, England.

Rev. Theodora Braithwaite . . . British deaconess
- ❑ ❑ 1 - Clerical Errors (1991)
- ❑ ❑ 2 - Unholy Ghosts (1992)
- ❑ ❑ 3 - Idol Bones (1993)
- ❑ ❑ 4 - Holy Terrors (1994)
- ❑ ❑ 5 - Every Deadly Sin (1995)
- ❑ ❑ 6 - Mortal Spoils (1996)

■ **Kerry GREENWOOD** is the creator of a series set in 1920s Australia featuring Phryne (pronounced FREE-nee) Fisher, jejune Londoner who moves to Melbourne and takes up a bit of detection. Her prized possession is a gigantic fire engine red Hispano-Suiza which she typically drives herself. And she never travels without her Beretta .32. Greenwood says Phryne's name comes from Herodotus' histories where Phryne was the courtesan of ancient Thebes—a woman so rich she offered to rebuild the city's walls if she could put a sign on them saying "The Walls of Thebes, Ruined by Time, Rebuilt by Phryne the Courtesan." The Thebans refused her offer. During her subsequent trial for impersonating a goddess (a capital crime in ancient Greece), her counsel had run out of arguments when he ripped off her garment, displaying her naked form to the jury, saying, "Could anyone this beautiful have done anything wrong?" And being Greeks, they acquitted her. A playwright, singer and qualified solicitor, Greenwood works part-time as a public defender for Sunshine Legal Aid in Melbourne. She has also worked as a factory hand, director, producer, translator, costume maker and cook. She lives in suburban Footscray with a registered wizard, five cats and a duck named Quark. With Jenny Pausacker she is the author of *Recipes for Crime (1995)* with recipes and stories in the style of nine crime fiction writers (see *Chapter 10, Other Resources*, for more information).

Phryne Fisher . . . 1920s Melbourne, Australian sleuth
- ❑ ❑ 1 - Cocaine Blues (1989) [U.S.–Death by Misadventure]
- ❑ ❑ 2 - Flying Too High (1990)
- ❑ ❑ 3 - Murder on the Ballarat Train (1991)
- ❑ ❑ 4 - Death at Victoria Dock (1992)
- ❑ ❑ 5 - The Green Mill Murder (1993)
- ❑ ❑ 6 - Blood and Circuses (1994)
- ❑ ❑ 7 - Ruddy Gore (1995)
- ❑ ❑ 8 - Urn Burial (1996)

■ **Roma GRETH** is the creator of a pair of mystery novels featuring Hana Shaner, a carpet company heiress in the Pennsylvania Dutch town of Conover, Pennsylvania. Hana makes her debut in *Now You Don't* (1988) and returns later in *Plain Murder* (1989).

Hana Shaner . . . carpet company heiress in Pennsylvania Dutch country in Conover, Pennsylvania

> ❏ ❏ 1 - Now You Don't (1988)
> ❏ ❏ 2 - Plain Murder (1989)

■ **Martha GRIMES**, a native of Garrett County Maryland, writes a popular mystery series featuring Inspector Richard Jury of Scotland Yard. Each title in the now 13-book series takes its name from an English pub, starting with the first installment *The Man with a Load of Mischief* (1981), which takes the Inspector to the village of Long Piddleton. Along with his hypochondriac sergeant, Jury is assisted in the investigation by Melrose Plant, a professor of French romantic poetry who becomes a recurring character in the series. Grimes earned both her BA and MA degrees from the University of Maryland and teaches English at Montgomery College in Tacoma Park, Maryland. She occasionally teaches detective fiction at Johns Hopkins and makes an annual visit to England for book research. Her 1992 novel *End of the Pier* is a nonseries mystery set in the U.S.

Inspector Richard Jury . . . Scotland Yard investigator

> ❏ ❏ 1 - The Man with a Load of Mischief (1981)
> ❏ ❏ 2 - The Old Fox Deceived (1982)
> ❏ ❏ 3 - The Anodyne Necklace (1983)
> ❏ ❏ 4 - The Dirty Duck (1984)
> ❏ ❏ 5 - Jerusalem Inn (1984)
> ❏ ❏ 6 - Help the Poor Struggler (1985)
> ❏ ❏ 7 - The Deer Leap (1985)
> ❏ ❏ 8 - I Am the Only Running Footman (1986)
> ❏ ❏ 9 - The Five Bells and Bladebone (1987)
> ❏ ❏ 10 - The Old Silent (1989)
> ❏ ❏ 11 - The Old Contemptibles (1990)
> ❏ ❏ 12 - The Horse You Came in On (1993)
> ❏ ❏ 13 - Rainbow's End (1995)

■ **Lucretia GRINDLE** is the creator of a new English mystery series featuring Detective Superintendent Inspector H. W. Ross who debuts in *The Killing of Ellis Martin* (1993).

Inspector H. W. Ross . . . detective superintendent in England

> ❏ ❏ 1 - The Killing of Ellis Martin (1993)
> ❏ ❏ 2 - So Little to Die For (1994)

■ **Sally GUNNING** lives and works on Cape Cod where her family roots go back many generations. She is the creator of the Peter Bartholomew series set on the fictional island of Nashtoba—a mixture of Cape Cod past and present. Peter, who owns an odd-job company, is introduced in *Hot Water* (1990) and each subsequent title finds him dealing with water of another sort—under, ice, troubled, rough and still. Gunning has a degree in sociology from the University of Rhode Island and works full time as the office manager for a small town medical office.

Peter Bartholomew . . . Cape Cod, Massachusetts small business owner

> ❏ ❏ 1 - Hot Water (1990)
> ❏ ❏ 2 - Under Water (1992)
> ❏ ❏ 3 - Ice Water (1993)
> ❏ ❏ 4 - Troubled Water (1993)
> ❏ ❏ 5 - Rough Water (1994)
> ❏ ❏ 6 - Still Water (1996)

■ **Batya GUR** is the author of what is probably the first mystery novel by an Israeli writer to reach American readers—*Saturday Morning Murder: A Psychoanalytic Case* (1988), translated from the Hebrew by Dalya Bilu and published in the U.S. in 1992. A senior analyst at the Jerusalem Psychoanalytic Institute is murdered and Chief Inspector Michael Ohayon, deputy head of the Investigations Division of the Jerusalem Subdistrict, soon deduces that each member of the Institute staff is a probable suspect. The psychiatric professionals do not immediately recognize the abilities of the tall chief inspector, who majored in medieval history and was reputed to have aroused the envy of his fellow students by his ability to remember the names of all the popes and royal dynasties of Europe. His finely tuned memory was a gift Ohayan found useful to keep to himself. Two more installments in the Ohayan series follow—*Literary Murder* (1993) and *Murder on the Kibbutz: A Communal Case* (1994). All three have been bestsellers in Israel, each bigger than the one before. Gur teaches literature in Jerusalem.

Michael Ohayon . . . chief inspector in Jerusalem, Israel
❑ ❑ 1 - Saturday Morning Murder (1988)
❑ ❑ 2 - Literary Murder (1993)
❑ ❑ 3 - **Murder on the Kibbutz: A Communal Case** (1994)
Anthony nominee ☆

■ **Carolyn A. HADDAD** is the creator of Becky Belski, a Chicago computer investigator introduced in *Caught in the Shadows* (1992). Haddad is the author of four earlier novels written as C. A. Haddad, including two featuring David Haham—*Bloody September* (1976) and *Operation Apricot* (1988)—set in the Middle East. Haddad lives in Chicago.

Becky Belski . . . Chicago, Illinois computer investigator
❑ ❑ 1 - Caught in the Shadows (1992)

■ **Jane HADDAM** (rhymes with Adam) is the pseudonym of Orania Papazoglou for her holiday series featuring retired FBI agent Gregor Demarkian. Under the Papazoglou name she is the creator of a five-book series featuring Patience Campbell McKenna—romance novelist turned crime writer. Before turning to mystery writing Papazoglou was editor of *Greek Accent* magazine and freelanced for *Glamour*, *Mademoiselle* and *Working Woman*. She also wrote two psychological thrillers under the Papazoglou name, but remains best known for her work as Jane Haddam which has been nominated for an Edgar and an Anthony. Under the name Ann Paris she wrote two other titles—*Graven Image* (1987) set in Greece and *Arrowheart* (1988) set in France. A graduate of Vassar College, she is married to award-winning mystery writer and columnist William DeAndrea. After several years in London, they have returned to New York.

Gregor Demarkian . . . Philadelphia, Pennsylvania former FBI department head
❑ ❑ 1 - **Not a Creature Was Stirring** (1990) *Edgar & Anthony nominee* ☆ ☆
❑ ❑ 2 - Precious Blood (1991)
❑ ❑ 3 - Act of Darkness (1991)
❑ ❑ 4 - Quoth the Raven (1991)
❑ ❑ 5 - A Great Day for the Deadly (1992)
❑ ❑ 6 - Feast of Murder (1992)
❑ ❑ 7 - A Stillness in Bethlehem (1992)
❑ ❑ 8 - Murder Superior (1993)
❑ ❑ 9 - Festival of Deaths (1993)
❑ ❑ 10 - Bleeding Hearts (1994)
❑ ❑ 11 - Dear Old Dead (1994)
❑ ❑ 12 - Fountain of Death (1995)

■ **Lisa HADDOCK** is the creator of a new lesbian mystery series featuring newspaper copy editor Carmen Ramirez, introduced in *Edited Out* (1994) followed by *Final Cut* (1995). The series is set in Frontier City, Oklahoma.

    Carmen Ramirez . . . lesbian newspaper copy editor in Frontier City, Oklahoma
- ❏ ❏ 1 - Edited Out (1994)
- ❏ ❏ 2 - Final Cut (1995)

■ **Jean HAGER** is the creator of three ongoing mystery series. including two about contemporary Cherokee life in Oklahoma. The first features Mitch Bushyhead, a half-Cherokee police chief who grew up and married outside the tribe. After his wife's death he has to cope with raising a teenage daughter alone. The second Cherokee series spotlights Molly Bearpaw, civil rights investigator for the Native American Advocacy Council. Hager's newest series features Tess Darcy, proprietor of Iris House, an elegant bed and breakfast in Victoria Springs, Missouri. Hager's first book was a children's mystery published in 1970. Since then she has produced more than 45 novels, including several for Playboy which appeared under Playboy house names, Amanda McAllister and Sara North, also used by others. Under the North byline she wrote *Evil Side of Eden* (1976) and *Shadow of the Tamaracks* (1979). As McAllister she is credited with *Terror in the Sunlight* (1977) and *Death Comes to a Party* (1977). One-sixteenth Cherokee herself, Hager is a former high school English teacher who has been writing full time since 1975. She lives in Tulsa, Oklahoma.

    Mitch Bushyhead . . . Buckskin, Oklahoma police chief of Cherokee descent
- ❏ ❏ 1 - The Grandfather Medicine (1989)
- ❏ ❏ 2 - Night Walker (1990)
- ❏ ❏ 3 - Ghostland (1992)
- ❏ ❏ 4 - The Fire Carrier (1996)

    Molly Bearpaw . . . Tahlequah, Oklahoma Cherokee civil rights investigator
- ❏ ❏ 1 - Ravenmocker (1992)
- ❏ ❏ 2 - The Redbird's Cry (1994)
- ❏ ❏ 3 - Seven Black Stones (1995)

    Tess Darcy . . . Ozarks bed & breakfast owner in Victoria Springs, Missouri
- ❏ ❏ 1 - Blooming Murder (1994)
- ❏ ❏ 2 - Dead and Buried (1995)
- ❏ ❏ 3 - Death on the Drunkard's Path (1996)

■ **Mary Bowen HALL** (1932-1994) once described her series featuring the fiercely independent part-time salvage dealer Emma Chizzit as "California cozies." Set in Sacramento, the four-book series features a ruggedly enterprising older woman sleuth. Hall made a significant contribution to the field with her ambitious survey on women protagonists in mystery fiction, jointly sponsored by Sisters in Crime and the National Women's History Project. One of her books for young adults, *Some Reasons for War*, co-authored with historian Sue Mansfield, won the publishing industry's Olive Branch Award in 1989. Shortly before her death in 1994, she allowed her losing battle with breast cancer to be the subject of an inspirational feature for *People* magazine.

    Emma Chizzit . . . Sacramento, California salvage dealer
- ❏ ❏ 1 - Emma Chizzit and the Queen Anne Killer (1989)
- ❏ ❏ 2 - Emma Chizzit and the Sacramento Stalker (1990)
- ❏ ❏ 3 - Emma Chizzit and the Napa Nemesis (1992)
- ❏ ❏ 4 - Emma Chizzit and the Mother Lode Marauder (1993)

■ **Patricia HALL** is the creator of two new British mystery series, the first of which features Inspector Alex Sinclair and social worker Kate Weston, introduced in *The Poison Pool* (1993). The second series features Yorkshire reporter Laura Ackroyd and local policeman Michael Thackeray, introduced in *Death by Election* (1994). Laura and her ex-boyfriend Vince, a fellow reporter and expert muckraker, are at odds over almost everything. The cop with the stiff upper lip is interested in Laura but doesn't do anything about it. Stay tuned.

> **Alex Sinclair & Kate Weston** . . . British Inspector & social worker
> ❏ ❏ 1 - The Poison Pool (1993)

> **Laura Ackroyd & Michael Thackeray** . . . reporter & police inspector in Yorkshire, England
> ❏ ❏ 1 - Death by Election (1994)
> ❏ ❏ 2 - Dying Fall (1995)
> ❏ ❏ 3 - In the Bleak Midwinter (1996)

■ **Barbara HAMBLY** is the creator of a new cross-genre series featuring professor James Asher, a part-time spy in London at the time of Sherlock Holmes. Introduced in *Those Who Hunt the Night* (1988), Asher and his detecting skills are wanted by Simon Ysidro, London's oldest vampire. Think history-mystery vampire story. Hambly is a well-known fantasy writer, with more than a dozen titles to her credit, including *The Darwath Trilogy*, *The Windrose Chronicles*, the Sunwolf and Starhawk series and the Sun-Cross novels. A San Diego native, Hambly holds a master's degree in medieval history and has studied in France and New South Wales, Australia. She earned a Black Belt in karate in 1978 and has worked as a karate instructor and competed in several national tournaments.

> **James Asher** . . . professor & one-time spy in London
> ❏ ❏ 1 - Those Who Hunt the Night (1988)
> ❏ ❏ 2 - Traveling with the Dead (1995)

■ **Laurell K. HAMILTON** is the creator of a fictional alternate world where vampires are legal citizens in her cross-genre series featuring Anita Blake, reanimator and vampire hunter in St. Louis, Missouri. Introduced in *Deadly Pleasures* (1993), Anita is an investigator for Animators, Inc. and an expert on creatures of the night. She is a sassy, savvy private eye cast in a romantic vampire series—lots of fun, even for people who wouldn't be caught dead (pardon the expression) reading a vampire novel.

> **Anita Blake** . . . reanimator & vampire hunter in St. Louis, Missouri
> ❏ ❏ 1 - Guilty Pleasures (1993)
> ❏ ❏ 2 - The Laughing Corpse (1994)
> ❏ ❏ 3 - Circus of the Damned (1995)
> ❏ ❏ 4 - The Lunatic Cafe (1996)

■ **Mollie HARDWICK** is the creator of Doran Fairweather, owner of an antiques business and soon-to-be-wife of local vicar Rodney Chelmarsh, who has a quote from literature or Scripture for absolutely everything. Art, antiques, religion and literature figure prominently in these perfect cozies, starting with *Malice Domestic* (1986). Hardwick also writes historical novels and is best known for her *Upstairs, Downstairs* series which was brought to life on public television. In the early 80s she produced several short story collections featuring Inspector Jean Darblay from the Juliet Bravo series on BBC television—*Juliet Bravo 1 and 2* (1980) and *Calling Juliet Bravo* (1981).

Doran Fairweather . . . British antiques dealer in Kent, England
- ❏ ❏ 1 - Malice Domestic (1986)
- ❏ ❏ 2 - Parson's Pleasure (1987)
- ❏ ❏ 3 - Uneaseful Death (1988)
- ❏ ❏ 4 - The Bandersnatch (1989)
- ❏ ❏ 5 - Perish in July (1989)
- ❏ ❏ 6 - The Dreaming Damozel (1990)

■ **Charlaine HARRIS** is the author of the Aurora "Roe" Teagarden series featuring a 20-something librarian whose first adventure, *Real Murders* (1990), was nominated for an Agatha. In later installments Roe joins her mother's real estate firm and tries her hand at selling houses. Harris has written several nonseries mysteries also set in the South with strong, independent women protagonists. In 1996 she introduces a new series featuring Lily Bard of Shakespeare, Arkansas. A rape survivor and beginning student of karate, Lily debuts in *Shakespeare's Landlord*, a much grittier series opener than *Real Murders*. A native of Mississippi and graduate of Rhodes College in Memphis, Tennessee, with degrees in English and communication arts, Harris lives in Arkansas where she is a student of goju karate.

Aurora Teagarden . . . Georgia librarian turned real estate agent
- ❏ ❏ 1 - **Real Murders** (1990) *Agatha nominee* ☆
- ❏ ❏ 2 - A Bone to Pick (1992)
- ❏ ❏ 3 - Three Bedrooms, One Corpse (1994)
- ❏ ❏ 4 - The Julius House (1995)
- ❏ ❏ 5 - Dead Over Heels (1996)

■ **Lee HARRIS** is the pseudonym of Syrell Rogovin Leahy, creator of the Edgar-nominated mystery series featuring former nun Christine Bennett, who lives in a suburb of New York and investigates crimes with answers buried in the past. Each title, beginning with *The Good Friday Murder* (1992), represents a holiday murder, typically one involving the church. The 30-something Bennett takes her name from the Buffalo high school (Bennett High) that proudly claims two mystery writers among its 1956 graduates—Lee Harris and Lawrence Block. During the '70s and '80s, Harris wrote a dozen mainstream novels under her own name, including her first novel *A Book of Ruth* (1975). A graduate of Cornell University, she later studied in Germany as a Fulbright scholar. She lives in Tenafly, New Jersey.

Christine Bennett . . . New York ex-nun
- ❏ ❏ 1 - **The Good Friday Murder** (1992) *Edgar nominee* ☆
- ❏ ❏ 2 - The Yom Kippur Murder (1992)
- ❏ ❏ 3 - The Christening Day Murder (1993)
- ❏ ❏ 4 - The St. Patrick's Day Murder (1994)
- ❏ ❏ 5 - The Christmas Night Murder (1994)
- ❏ ❏ 6 - The Thanksgiving Day Murder (1995)
- ❏ ❏ 7 - The Passover Murder (1996)

■ **Jamie HARRISON** is the creator of a critically-acclaimed new series featuring Jules Clement, a 30-something archaeologist turned sheriff in Blue Deer, Montana, where his father was county sheriff when Jules was a high schooler. *The Edge of the Crazies* (1995) refers to Montana's Crazy Mountains and to the zany cast assembled for this psychological thriller disguised as a humorous police mystery. The daughter of novelist Jim Harrison, the author lives in Montana where she is working on Sheriff Clement's next case.

Jules Clement . . . 30-something archaeologist turned sheriff in Blue Deer, Montana
- ❏ ❏ 1 - The Edge of the Crazies (1995)

■ **Cynthia HARROD-EAGLES**, well-known British historical novelist, is the creator of a mystery series she never intended to write. The first Bill Slider novel, *Orchestrated Death* (1991) was actually a gift for her sister, after one too many lamentations that "no one writes mysteries anymore like Dorothy L. Sayers." Her sister loved the story and so did everyone else who read it and before long, Harrod-Eagles was gaining new fans as a mystery writer. She is the author of more than 30 historical, fantasy and romance novels, including more than 15 titles in the Dynasty series and another ten published under the pseudonyms Emma Woodhouse and Elizabeth Bennett. Born in London, she studied at the University of Edinburgh and University College, London, where she received her BA (with honors) in English. Her passions are music, gardening, history, horses, architecture and the English countryside. In addition to her writing, she finds time to play in several amateur orchestras.

    Bill Slider . . . detective inspector in England
- ❏ ❏ 1 - Orchestrated Death (1991)
- ❏ ❏ 2 - Death Watch (1992)
- ❏ ❏ 3 - Death To Go (1993) [APA–Necrochip]
- ❏ ❏ 4 - Grave Music (1994) [Britain–Dead End]
- ❏ ❏ 5 - Blood Lines (1996)

■ **Carolyn G. HART** is perhaps best known for her Death on Demand series featuring South Carolina mystery bookstore owner Annie Laurance and her sleuthing partner Max Darling. This series is chock full of mystery personalities and crime fiction lore and has won a virtual trophy case of awards and nominations. Hart recently introduced a series featuring veteran Oklahoma journalist Henrietta O'Dwyer Collins, known to her friends as Henrie O, brought to life by Barbara Eden in a television movie co-starring William Shatner. In addition to her adult mystery series, Hart has written five juvenile mysteries, including her first book, *The Secret of the Cellars* (1964), and numerous short stories. An Oklahoma native, she is a former assistant professor of professional writing at her alma mater, the University of Oklahoma, where she earned a degree in journalism. A past president of Sisters in Crime, Hart lives in Oklahoma City.

    Annie Laurance & Max Darling . . . South Carolina bookstore owner & investigator
- ❏ ❏ 1 - **Death on Demand** (1987) *Anthony & Macavity nominee* ☆ ☆
- ❏ ❏ 2 - Design for Murder (1987)
- ❏ ❏ 3 - **Something Wicked** (1988) *Agatha & Anthony winner* ★ ★
- ❏ ❏ 4 - **Honeymoon with Murder** (1988) Anthony winner ★
- ❏ ❏ 5 - **A Little Class on Murder** (1989) *Macavity winner* ★
      Agatha & Anthony nominee ☆ ☆
- ❏ ❏ 6 - **Deadly Valentine** (1990) *Agatha & Macavity nominee* ☆ ☆
- ❏ ❏ 7 - **The Christie Caper** (1991)
      Agatha, Anthony & Macavity nominee ☆ ☆ ☆
- ❏ ❏ 8 - **Southern Ghost** (1992) *Agatha & Anthony nominee* ☆ ☆
- ❏ ❏ 9 - The Mint Julep Murder (1995)

    Henrietta O'Dwyer Collins . . . South Carolina 70-something reporter
- ❏ ❏ 1 - **Dead Man's Island** (1993) *Agatha winner* ★
- ❏ ❏ 2 - **Scandal in Fair Haven** (1994) *Agatha nominee* ☆
- ❏ ❏ 3 - **Death in Lovers' Lane** (1996)

■ **Ellen HART** is the pseudonym of Patricia Boenhardt, who claims that her twelve years as a sorority house kitchen manager at the University of Minnesota were more than sufficient inspiration to commit murder—but strictly on paper. She is the creator of the Jane Lawless series featuring a lesbian Minneapolis restaurant owner and her college friend Cordelia Thorn, artistic director of a St. Paul theatre, introduced in the Lambda-nominated *Hal-*

lowed Murder (1989). Jane's father, prominent criminal attorney Raymond Lawless, is a continuing cast member in this series and his influence changes along with the story. Book #5 ihe Lawless won the Lambda Literary Award and book #2 was named one of the five best mysteries of the year by the *Minneaplis Star Tribune*. Hart recently introduced a gourmet journalism series featuring Sophie Greenway, magazine editor and part-time food critic for a Minneapolis newspaper, married to Bram Baldric, Minneapolis radio talk-show host. Sophie and Bram make their first appearance in *This Little Piggy Went to Murder* (1994).

Jane Lawless . . . Minneapolis, Minnesota lesbian restaurateur
- ❑ ❑ 1 - **Hallowed Murder** (1989) *Lambda nominee* ☆
- ❑ ❑ 2 - Vital Lies (1991)
- ❑ ❑ 3 - Stage Fright (1992)
- ❑ ❑ 4 - A Killing Cure (1993)
- ❑ ❑ 5 - **A Small Sacrifice** (1994) *Lambda winner* ★
- ❑ ❑ 6 - Faint Praise (1995)
- ❑ ❑ 7 - Robber's Wine (1996)

Sophie Greenway . . . magazine editor & food critic for Minneapolis, Minnesota newspaper
- ❑ ❑ 1 - This Little Piggy Went to Murder (1994)
- ❑ ❑ 2 - For Every Evil (1995)
- ❑ ❑ 3 - The Oldest Sin (1997)

■ **Jeanne HART** (1919-1990) is the creator of a mystery trilogy featuring homicide detective Carl Pedersen and his wife Freda of fictional Bay Cove (read Santa Cruz), California. *Fetish* (1987), which earned a Macavity nomination for best first mystery, tells the story of three unmarried middle-aged women whose lives are changed after they run a local newspaper ad seeking a shared escort. Following the author's sudden death in the summer of 1990, family friend and mystery writer Lia Matera prepared Hart's last completed manuscript for publication.

Carl & Freda Pedersen . . . Bay Cove, California police lieutenant & wife
- ❑ ❑ 1 - **Fetish** (1987) [Britain–**A Personal Possession**] *Macavity nominee* ☆
- ❑ ❑ 2 - Some Die Young (1990)
- ❑ ❑ 3 - Threnody for Two (1991) [Britain–Lament for Two Ladies]

■ **Gini HARTZMARK** attended the law and business schools of the University of Chicago and wrote business and economics textbooks before turning to novel writing. She also produced articles on a variety of topics for Chicago newspapers and national magazines. Her Edgar-nominated series features Katherine Prescott Milholland, a Chicago attorney specializing in mergers and acquisitions, introduced in *Principal Defense* (1992). After two adventures in paperback, Milholland moved to hardcover with *Bitter Business* (1995). Hartzmark currently lives in Arizona.

Katherine Prescott Milholland . . . Chicago, Illinois corporate attorney
- ❑ ❑ 1 - **Principal Defense** (1992) *Edgar nominee* ☆
- ❑ ❑ 2 - Final Option (1994)
- ❑ ❑ 3 - Bitter Business (1995)

■ **S. T. HAYMON** is Sylvia Theresa Haymon, creator of the award-winning police series featuring Benjamin Jurnet, introduced in *Death and the Pregnant Virgin* (1980). After winning the Silver Dagger for book #2 *Ritual Murder* (1982), Haymon turned up the heat in book #3 *Stately Homicide* (1984) where Jurnet finds himself taking a stately home tour of Bullen Hall. Lost love letters from Anne Boleyn to her brother George Bullen have been sequestered by the Trust's incoming curator when he discovers his predecessor plans to write a book about the incestuous relationship. Guess which curator ends up dead in the Bullen Hall moat—attacked and partially eaten by giant eels? The *Washington Post* has said "it can only be a matter of time before the critics discover S. T. Haymon and recognize a serious novelist who just happens to write mysteries." Her work is often mentioned along with other British greats Dorothy L. Sayers and P. D. James. Born in Norwich, Haymon lives in London.

Inspector Benjamin Jurnet . . . detective inspector in Norwich, England
- ❑ ❑ 1 - Death and the Pregnant Virgin (1980)
- ❑ ❑ 2 - **Ritual Murder** (1982) *Silver Dagger* ★
- ❑ ❑ 3 - Stately Homicide (1984)
- ❑ ❑ 4 - Death of a God (1987)
- ❑ ❑ 5 - A Very Particular Murder (1989)
- ❑ ❑ 6 - Death of a Warrior Queen (1991)
- ❑ ❑ 7 - A Beautiful Death (1994)

■ **Sparkle HAYTER** is the creator of an award-winning new series featuring New York City cable news reporter Robin Hudson, introduced in the fast-paced funny mystery *What's a Girl Gotta Do?* (1994). Born and raised in western Canada, Hayter moved to New York City in 1980 to complete a degree in film at NYU. She went directly to CNN where she worked as an intern, assignment editor, producer, field producer and writer both in New York and Atlanta. After her working papers expired in 1986 (she's a card-carrying alien), Hayter spent six months backpacking alone across Europe and Asia and another four months in India and Pakistan. While riding trains around India she ran out of reading material and wrote the first draft of *What's a Girl Gotta Do?* The manuscript spent several years languishing in a drawer before she rewrote it and won the Ellis Award for best first mystery for her efforts. Working as a freelance television correspondent she spent twelve months covering the Afghan war and returned to New York to work for two years doing stand-up comedy. A Bugs Bunny fanatic who collects fish, eyeballs, pen and pencil boxes and Dana Girls mysteries, she swears Sparkle Hayter is the one-and-only real name her parents gave her.

Robin Hudson . . . New York City cable news reporter
- ❑ ❑ 1 - **What's a Girl Gotta Do?** (1994) *Ellis winner* ★
- ❑ ❑ 2 - Nice Girls Finish Last (1996)

■ **M. V. HEBERDEN**, Mary Violet Heberden (1906-1965), wrote more than 30 high-action private eye novels under her own name and a pseudonym between 1939 and 1953. She was one of only four women to appear on mystery critic James Sandoe's personal checklist of 31 authors of tough-guy detective stories, *The Hard-Boiled Dick*. Her private eyes include Desmond Shannon, a high-priced Irish-American in New York City, featured in 17 titles beginning with *Death on the Door Mat* (1939) and former Naval Intelligence officer Rick Vanner who made two return appearances after *Murder Cancels All Debts* (1946). Under the pseudonym Charles L. Leonard she wrote eleven titles in a series featuring Washington DC private eye Paul Kilgerrin, a ruthless espionage expert introduced in *Deadline for Destruction* (1942). Born in England, she was a world traveler, office manager and timber importer.

Desmond Shannon . . . high-priced Irish-American P. I. in New York
- ❑ ❑ 1 - Death on the Door Mat (1939)
- ❑ ❑ 2 - Fugitive from Murder (1940)
- ❑ ❑ 3 - Subscription to Murder (1940)
- ❑ ❑ 4 - Aces, Eights and Murder (1940)
- ❑ ❑ 5 - The Lobster Pick Murder (1940)
- ❑ ❑ 6 - Murder Follows Desmond Shannon (1942)
- ❑ ❑ 7 - Murder Makes a Racket (1942)
- ❑ ❑ 8 - Murder Goes Astray (1943)

❑ ❑ 9 - Murder of a Stuffed Shirt (1944)
❑ ❑ 10 - Vicious Pattern (1945)
❑ ❑ 11 - Drinks on the Victim (1947)
❑ ❑ 12 - They Can't All Be Guilty (1947)
❑ ❑ 13 - The Case of the Eight Brothers (1947)
❑ ❑ 14 - Exit This Way (1950) [APA–You'll Fry Tomorrow]
❑ ❑ 15 - That's the Spirit (1950) [Britain–Ghosts Can't Kill]
❑ ❑ 16 - Tragic Target (1952)
❑ ❑ 17 - Murder Unlimited (1953)

Rick Vanner . . . former Naval Intelligence officer in New York
❑ ❑ 1 - Murder Cancels All Debts (1946)
❑ ❑ 2 - Engaged to Murder (1949)
❑ ❑ 3 - The Sleeping Witness (1951)

■ **Louise HENDRICKSEN**, who worked in the medical field prior to writing full time, shares her keen interest in forensic science with her protagonist, Dr. Amy Prescott of the Western Washington Crime Laboratory in Seattle. Amy's father, who sometimes consults with her on unusual cases, is the medical examiner on Lomitas Island in Puget Sound. The series opener featuring this likable pair of forensic investigators is *With Deadly Intent* (1993). Hendricksen lives with her husband Gene in Renton, Washington.

Dr. Amy Prescott . . . Seattle, Washington crime lab physician
❑ ❑ 1 - With Deadly Intent (1993)
❑ ❑ 2 - Grave Secrets (1994)
❑ ❑ 3 - Lethal Legacy (1995)

■ **Sue HENRY** lives and writes in Anchorage, Alaska, the setting for her mystery series featuring Alaska State Trooper Alex Jensen and his musher friend Jessie Arnold. Their first adventure, *Murder on the Iditarod Trail* (1991), won both the Anthony and Macavity for best first novel. It also became the subject of a CBS-TV movie starring Corbin Bernsen (Arnie Becker of *L. A. Law*), Kate Jackson (best known for her role in *Charlie's Angels*) and Michael Damian (Danny Romalotti from *The Young & the Restless*). Expected to air in early 1996, the retitled suspense thriller, *The Cold Heart of a Killer*, was filmed (in part) in Alaska. Book #2 in this series, *Termination Dust* (1995), is set in Klondike Gold Rush country with a 100-year-old mystery complicating a modern murder. Book #3 promises a threatening tangle of murder, big-game poachers and small planes in the Alaskan wilderness. Henry is editor of *Books-in-Print* for Sisters in Crime and recently retired from her administrative position at the University of Alaska to write full time.

Jessie Arnold & Sergeant Alex Jensen . . . Anchorage, Alaska sled dog racer & state trooper
❑ ❑ 1 - **Murder on the Iditarod Trail** (1991)
       Anthony & Macavity winner ★ ★
❑ ❑ 2 - Termination Dust (1995)
❑ ❑ 3 - Sleeping Lady (1996)

■ **Nancy HERNDON** is the creator of a new mystery series featuring detective sergeant Elena Jarvis with the Crimes Against Persons unit of the Los Santos, Texas, police department, introduced in *Acid Bath* (1995). Three chapters of the series opener were first published as short stories in *The Third (and Fourth) WomanSleuth Anthologies*. Herndon is a former college English instructor whose first novel *Wanton Angel* was published under the pen-name Elizabeth Chadwick. Her short stories have appeared in *Lighthouse*, *The West Texas Sun* and *Women of the West*. She lives in El Paso.

Elena Jarvis . . . detective with the Crimes Against Persons unit in Los Santos, Texas

❏ ❏ 1 - Acid Bath (1995)
❏ ❏ 2 - Widows' Watch (1995)

■ **Joan HESS** is the creator of two Anthony-nominated series detectives who live and work in small Arkansas towns. Police chief Arly Hanks, introduced in *Malice in Maggody* (1987), heads a cast of vintage Southern characters, including the good old boy who watches TV with his pet pig. The second series features Claire Malloy, bookstore owner in a small college town, and the mother of an annoying teenage daughter, first seen in *Strangled Prose* (1986), chosen as best first novel by a *Drood Review* readers poll and nominated for an Anthony award. Under the name Joan Hadley, she wrote two novels featuring Theo Bloomer, a plant-loving retiree with a nose for crime detection—*Night-Blooming Cereus* (1986) and *Deadly Ackee* (1990). A fifth-generation resident of Fayetteville, Arkansas, Hess has won a number of awards and nominations for her short stories. She holds a BA in art from the University of Arkansas and an MA in education from Long Island University and once taught art to three- and four-year-olds in a private preschool.

Arly Hanks . . . Maggody, Arkansas small-town police chief

❏ ❏ 1 - Malice in Maggody (1987)
❏ ❏ 2 - **Mischief in Maggody** (1988) *Agatha nominee* ☆
❏ ❏ 3 - Much Ado in Maggody (1989)
❏ ❏ 4 - Mortal Remains in Maggody (1991)
❏ ❏ 5 - Madness in Maggody (1991)
❏ ❏ 6 - Maggody in Manhattan (1992)
❏ ❏ 7 - **O Little Town of Maggody** (1993)
              Agatha & Anthony nominee ☆ ☆
❏ ❏ 8 - Martians in Maggody (1994)
❏ ❏ 9 - Miracles in Maggody (1995)

Claire Malloy . . . small-town bookstore owner in Farberville, Arkansas

❏ ❏ 1 - **Strangled Prose** (1986) *Anthony nominee* ☆
❏ ❏ 2 - The Murder at the Murder at the Mimosa Inn (1986)
❏ ❏ 3 - Dear Miss Demeanor (1987)
❏ ❏ 4 - A Really Cute Corpse (1988)
❏ ❏ 5 - **A Diet to Die For** (1989) *American Mystery Award winner* ★
❏ ❏ 6 - Roll Over and Play Dead (1991)
❏ ❏ 7 - Death by the Light of the Moon (1992)
❏ ❏ 8 - Poisoned Pins (1993)
❏ ❏ 9 - Tickled to Death (1994)
❏ ❏ 10 - Busy Bodies (1995)

■ **Georgette HEYER** (1902-1974), is perhaps best known as an English historical writer and undisputed queen of the Regency novel (she wrote more than 40). She is also the author of twelve mysteries, including two four-book police series. Supt. Hannasyde is introduced in *Death in the Stocks* (1935) and his one-time assistant, Inspector Hemingway, returns in 1939 to start a series of his own, beginning with *No Wind of Blame*. Heyer, who lived in east Africa and Yugoslavia from 1925 to 1929, also wrote as Stella Martin.

Superintendent Hannasyde . . . police superintendent in England

❏ ❏ 1 - Death in the Stocks (1935) [U.S.–Merely Murder]
❏ ❏ 2 - Behold, Here's Poison (1936)
❏ ❏ 3 - They Found Him Dead (1937)
❏ ❏ 4 - A Blunt Instrument (1938)

Inspector Hemingway . . . one-time assistant to Superintendent Hannasyde in England
- ❏ ❏ 1 - No Wind of Blame (1939)
- ❏ ❏ 2 - Envious Casca (1941)
- ❏ ❏ 3 - Duplicate Death (1951)
- ❏ ❏ 4 - Detection Unlimited (1953)

■ **Domini HIGHSMITH** is the creator of a new historical mystery series set in East Yorkshire, England in 1180. A medieval priest and nurse, Father Simeon and Elvira, who serve as child guardians, are introduced in *Keeper at the Shrine* (1995). Reviewers have described this series opener as full of graphic sex and violence.

Father Simeon & Elvira . . . medieval priest & nurse in East Yorkshire England
- ❏ ❏ 1 - Keeper at the Shrine (1995)

■ **Patricia HIGHSMITH** (1921-1995) is the author name of Mary Patricia Plangman, who borrowed "Highsmith" from her stepfather. Born in Fort Worth, Texas and educated in New York City, she lived much of her life in Switzerland. Her first novel, the suspense classic *Strangers on a Train* (1950), was filmed and made famous by Alfred Hitchcock. In addition to her 20 novels, she produced seven highly-acclaimed short story collections, including *The Animal-Lover's Book of Beastly Murder* (1986). In the early 1950s she wrote a novel about lesbian relationships, *The Price of Salt*, under the pseudonym Claire Morgan. Her series character, the charming psychopath and successful forger-impersonator Tom Ripley, is introduced in *The Talented Mr. Ripley* (1955) which was nominated for an Edgar award. Highsmith was awarded a Silver Dagger for *Two Faces of January* in 1964 and also received the O Henry Memorial Award and Le Grand Prix de Litterature Policiere. While the *New Yorker* called her novels "peerlessly disturbing," Gore Vidal said "she is certainly one of the most interesting writers of this dismal century."

Tom Ripley . . . charming forger & psychopath in England
- ❏ ❏ 1 - **The Talented Mr. Ripley** (1955) *Edgar nominee* ☆
- ❏ ❏ 2 - Ripley Underground (1970)
- ❏ ❏ 3 - Ripley's Game (1974)
- ❏ ❏ 4 - The Boy Who Followed Ripley (1980)
- ❏ ❏ 5 - Ripley Under Water (1992)

■ **Lynn S. HIGHTOWER** is the creator of a futuristic police series starring homicide detective David Silver and his Elaki partner, String, a seven-foot stingray who smells like fresh limes, introduced in *Alien Blues* (1992). Nancy Pickard called this series brilliantly entertaining. Hightower's 1993 novel, *Satan's Lambs*, introduced Lexington private eye Lena Padget and won the Shamus award for best first P. I. novel. Her 1995 suspense thriller, *Flashpoint*, features a female cop and a female serial killer in a deadly cat and mouse game starring detective Sonora Blair of the Cincinnati Police Department Homicide Division. Born in Chattanooga, Tennessee, Hightower lives in Lexington where she shares an office with her Golden Retriever Griffin. During a 1994 visit to Singapore, she was careful not to commit any acts of delinquency.

David Silver & String . . . homicide cop & alien Elaki partner in USA
- ❏ ❏ 1 - Alien Blues (1992)
- ❏ ❏ 2 - Alien Eyes (1993)
- ❏ ❏ 3 - Alien Heat (1994)
- ❏ ❏ 4 - Alien Rites (1995)

Lena Padget . . . Lexington, Kentucky P. I.
❑ ❑ 1 - **Satan's Lambs** (1993) *Shamus winner* ★

Sonora Blair . . . homicide detective in Cincinnati, Ohio
❑ ❑ 1 - Flashpoint (1995)

■ **Dolores HITCHENS** (1907-1973) was a remarkably versatile writer who created first-rate novels over a wide range of crime fiction—straight and psychological suspense, whodunit, private eye, police procedural and neo-Gothic. She even wrote a darn good western. But her 1940s cat books with little old lady sleuth Rachel Murdock (written as D. B. Olsen) seem to be what readers remember. Much the pity according to Bill Pronzini (*1001 Midnights*), who claims her *Sleep with Slander* (1960), featuring Long Beach P. I. Jim Sader, is the best hard-boiled private eye novel ever written by a woman—and one of the best written by anybody. With her railroad detective husband Bert, she wrote five novels about a fictional group of southern California railroad cops beginning with *F.O.B. Murder* (1955). One of these cops, John Farrel, is featured in three titles—*End of the Line* (1957), *The Man Who Followed Women* (1959) and *The Grudge* (1963).

Jim Sader . . . P. I. in Long Beach, California
❑ ❑ 1 - Sleep with Strangers (1957)
❑ ❑ 2 - Sleep with Slander (1960)

■ **Teri HOLBROOK** is the creator of a new mystery series featuring Southern historian and American expatriate, Gale Grayson, an Atlanta native living in Fetherbridge, England. A very pregnant Gale is introduced in *A Far and Deadly Cry* (1995) shortly after the death of her ecoterrorist husband, Tom, an English poet. When the babysitter is killed on her way to Gale's home, Scotland Yard has lots of questions, forcing Gale to investigate on her own behalf when the village turns against her. After earning a degree in anthropology and linguistics from The College of William and Mary, Holbrook worked as a journalist for five years before giving birth to the inspiration for Katie Pru. Along with her husband, syndicated cartoonist Bill Holbrook (*On the Fastrack* and *Safe Havens*), she shares child-rearing duties in a complicated schedule that allows both of them to work full time from home offices in Atlanta and keep up with two young daughters. Like her character, Holbrook is a native of Atlanta—fifth generation, in fact.

Gale Grayson . . . American expatriate historian in Fetherbridge, England
❑ ❑ 1 - A Far and Deadly Cry (1995)
❑ ❑ 2 - The Grass Widow (1996)

■ **Isabelle HOLLAND** is the creator of a mystery series featuring the Reverend Claire Aldington, psychologist and priest at St. Anselm's Episcopal Church in Manhattan—a wealthy congregation in an inner-city neighborhood. A widow with a problem teenage stepdaughter, Rev. Aldington makes her first appearance in *The Lost Madonna* (1983). Born in Basel, Switzerland where her father was American consul, Holland moved to Guatemala City at the age of three and from there to Liverpool when she was seven. She graduated from Tulane University in New Orleans and later moved to New York City where currently lives. Her first story was published when she was 13, in *Tiger Tim*, an English children's magazine. While working in magazine and book publishing for many years, she has written more than 50 novels for children and adults. Her books for young adults in particular have been internationally recognized, beginning with her first published novel, the semi-autobiographical *Cecily* (1967). *Of Love and Death and Other Journeys* (1976) was nominated for a National Book Award.

Reverend Claire Aldington . . . New York Episcopal priest
- ❑ ❑ 1 - The Lost Madonna (1983)
- ❑ ❑ 2 - A Death at St. Anselm's (1984)
- ❑ ❑ 3 - Flight of the Archangel (1985)
- ❑ ❑ 4 - A Lover Scorned (1986)
- ❑ ❑ 5 - A Fatal Advent (1989)
- ❑ ❑ 6 - The Long Search (1990)

■ **Gerelyn HOLLINGSWORTH** is the creator of a new mystery series featuring Kansas City P. I. Frances Finn, introduced in *Murder at St. Adelaide's* (1995). Having taken over the family agency after the death of her father, Frances is called back to the Kansas convent of St. Adelaide's where she attended school. The dying Mother Superior wants her to investigate the 30-year-old murder of a nun who was thought to have died from an illness contracted on a mission to Guatemala. Hollingsworth says the archives of the religious orders and local parishes hold many stories. A native of Kansas City, Hollingsworth lives in St. Louis, Missouri.

Frances Finn . . . Kansas City P. I.
- ❑ ❑ 1 - Murder at St. Adelaide's (1995)

■ **Hazel HOLT** lives in Somerset, England where she writes the Mrs. Malory series featuring a 50-something widowed literary magazine writer from the seaside village of Taviscombe, first appearing in *Mrs. Malory Investigates* (1989). She is a former television critic and feature writer and official biographer and literary executor of English novelist Barbara Pym. Her son is the writer Tom Holt.

Sheila Malory . . . British literary magazine writer in Devon, England
- ❑ ❑ 1 - Mrs. Malory Investigates (1989) [Britain–Gone Away]
- ❑ ❑ 2 - The Cruellest Month (1991)
- ❑ ❑ 3 - The Shortest Journey (1992)
- ❑ ❑ 4 - Mrs. Malory and the Festival Murders (1993) [Britain–Uncertain Death]
- ❑ ❑ 5 - Mrs. Malory: Detective in Residence (1994) [Britain–Murder on Campus]
- ❑ ❑ 6 - Mrs. Malory Wonders Why (1995) [Britain–Superfluous Death]
- ❑ ❑ 7 - Death of a Dean (1996)

■ **Susan HOLTZER** spent most of her life in Ann Arbor, Michigan, the setting for *Something To Kill For* (1994), winner of the St. Martin's Press award for best first traditional mystery. The series opener, introducing computer programmer Anneke Haagen, shows how Ann Arbor earned its reputation for the best garage sales in the country and Holtzer has the Rolex and pearls to prove it. She earned a master's degree in journalism from the University of Michigan, where she worked on *The Michigan Daily* as an undergraduate. First among her passions is football which may be why her series cop, Karl Genesko, is a former linebacker. It gives her license to talk football in her mysteries. In fact, book #3 will feature a murder in the Michigan stadium. Holtzer lives in San Francisco, where she and her husband own and operate a small educational publishing company.

Anneke Haagen . . . Ann Arbor, Michigan computer consultant
- ❑ ❑ 1 - **Something To Kill For** (1994) *Malice Domestic/SMP winner* ★
- ❑ ❑ 2 - Curly Smoke (1995)

■ **Kay HOOPER** is the author of 57 paperback titles with four million copies in print, including two mystery novels featuring Lane Montana, finder of lost things and Trey Fortier, Atlanta homicide detective, first appearing in *Crime of Passion* (1991). Their supporting cast includes Lane's twin brother the artist and her Siamese cat Choo. In the Shamus-nominated sequel, *House of Cards* (1991), she takes the lieutenant to meet her family, but a murder takes center stage at the reunion. Hooper wrote eleven titles featuring Hagen, government agent, opening with *In Serena's Web* (1987). She has written a number of Southern gothic suspense novels, including her first hardcover title, *Amanda* (1995), where according to one reviewer, the family mansion (Glory) makes Southfork look like a convent. When Amanda returns to Glory, all hell breaks loose. A California native, Hooper lives in North Carolina. She also writes romance novels under the name Kay Robbins.

Hagen . . . government agent in USA

❑ ❑ 1 - In Serena's Web (1987)
❑ ❑ 2 - Raven on the Wing (1987)
❑ ❑ 3 - Rafferty's Wife (1987)
❑ ❑ 4 - Zach's Law (1987)
❑ ❑ 5 - Captain's Paradise (1988)
❑ ❑ 6 - Outlaw Derek (1988)
❑ ❑ 7 - Shades of Gray (1988)
❑ ❑ 8 - The Fall of Lucas Kendrick (1988)
❑ ❑ 9 - Unmasking Kelsey (1988)
❑ ❑ 10 - Aces High (1989)
❑ ❑ 11 - It Takes a Thief (1989)

Lane Montana & Trey Fortier . . . finder of lost things & Atlanta homicide detective

❑ ❑ 1 - Crime of Passion (1991)
❑ ❑ 2 - **House of Cards** (1991) *Shamus nominee* ☆

■ **Ruby HORANSKY** is the pseudonym of Rebecca Holland of Brooklyn, New York, creator of a new police series featuring NYPD homicide detective Nikki Trakos introduced in *Dead Ahead* (1990).

Nikki Trakos . . . New York City homicide detective

❑ ❑ 1 - Dead Ahead (1990)
❑ ❑ 2 - Dead Center (1994)

■ **Wendy HORNSBY** is a southern California native with graduate degrees in ancient and medieval history who teaches at California State University at Long Beach. She also writes sizzling California mysteries and award-winning short stories. Her 1991 story, "Nine Sons," won an Edgar award. Her first full-length series features history professor Kate Teague and homicide detective Roger Tejeda, introduced in *No Harm* (1987). And her more recent and longer-running series stars documentary film maker Maggie MacGowen, first appearing in *Telling Lies* (1992). Maggie's supporting cast includes her teenage daughter, a stalwart neighbor and a handsome homicide detective Mike Flint with his teenage son. Maggie's latest film project, *77th Street Requiem* (1995), involves an 20-year-old unsolved case where Mike was a close friend of the murdered police officer. Hornsby's latest work of fiction, which earned her a starred review in *Publisher's Weekly*, is based on an actual LAPD case.

Kate Teague & Roger Tejeda . . . southern California college professor & homicide detective

❑ ❑ 1 - No Harm (1987)
❑ ❑ 2 - Half a Mind (1990)

Maggie MacGowen . . . California investigative film maker
    ❏ ❏ 1 - Telling Lies (1992)
    ❏ ❏ 2 - Midnight Baby (1993)
    ❏ ❏ 3 - Bad Intent (1994)
    ❏ ❏ 4 - 77th Street Requiem (1995)

■ **Melodie Johnson HOWE** is a Los Angeles native who dreamed of becoming a movie star and novelist. After attending Stephens College in Columbia, Missouri and the University of Southern California, she was discovered by Universal Studios and signed her first acting contract. While working in television, movies and commercials, she studied writing at UCLA and produced *The Mother Shadow* (1989), which was nominated for three mystery awards as best first novel. Private eye Claire Conrad and Maggie Hill return for their second adventure in *Beauty Dies* (1994).

Claire Conrad & Maggie Hill . . . southern California P. I. & secretary
    ❏ ❏ 1 - **The Mother Shadow** (1989)
         Edgar, Anthony & Agatha nominee ☆ ☆ ☆
    ❏ ❏ 2 - Beauty Dies (1994)

■ **Tanya HUFF** is the creator of a cross-genre series featuring ex-cop Vicki Nelson, now a Toronto private eye, introduced in *Blood Price* (1992). This P. I. is no Canadian Kinsey Millhone. Her significant other (and she has one) is a vampire. Born in Halifax, Nova Scotia, Huff earned a BAA in radio and television arts from Ryerson Polytechnical Institute. She has been a contributor, sometimes under the name T. S. Huff or the pseudonym Terri Hanover, of short stories and novellas, including the space opera "The Chase Is On." Her continuing humorous series about Magdelene—the most powerful wizard in the world—is seen in "Third Time Lucky," "And Who Is Joah?" (nominated for a CASPER award in 1987) and "*The Last Lesson*," all featured in *Amazing Short Stories*. Huff, who once managed a science fiction bookstore in Toronto and served three years in the Canadian Naval Reserve, says her work has a sneaky feminism. She lives in Toronto.

Vicki Nelson . . . ex-cop turned P. I. in Toronto, Canada
    ❏ ❏ 1 - Blood Price (1992)
    ❏ ❏ 2 - Blood Trail (1992)
    ❏ ❏ 3 - Blood Lines (1993)
    ❏ ❏ 4 - Blood Pact (1993)

■ **Elspeth HUXLEY** lived in Kenya from the age of five until she was 18 and although she wrote mainstream novels, travel books and biography, she is best known for *The Flame Trees of Thika: Memories of an African Childhood* (1959). Her African mystery series features Superintendent Vachell of the Chania CID, a young Scot who learned his trade in the Royal Canadian Mounted Police. Introduced in Murder at *Government House* (1937), Vachell loves Africa and police work and loves the chase. Reviewers praised Huxley for her exotic, authentic settings, her understanding of Kenya's people and her ability to mix comedy and satire with mystery. A member of the BBC Advisory Council from 1954 to 1960, Huxley served as Wiltshire's Justice of the Peace for 30 years and was named Commander, Order of the British Empire, in 1962.

Superintendent Vachell . . . young Scotsman trained by the RCMP in Kenya
    ❏ ❏ 1 - Murder at Government House (1937)
    ❏ ❏ 2 - Murder on Safari (1938)
    ❏ ❏ 3 - The African Poison Murders (1939) [Britain–Death of an Aryan]

■ **Eleanor HYDE** is the creator of a new mystery series featuring 30-something New York fashion magazine editor Lydia Miller, first appearing in *In Murder We Trust* (1995). During a holiday weekend in the Hamptons, she finds her millionaire host dead in his swimming pool. No sooner does she learn she's the chief beneficiary of his will, she becomes the chief suspect in his murder. A playwright who has written for *Cosmopolitan*, *Redbook*, *Ladies Home Journal* and *McCall's*, Hyde lives in New York City where she heads the mentor program for the New York chapter of MWA.

> **Lydia Miller** . . . 30-something fashion editor in New York
> ❑ ❑ 1 - In Murder We Trust (1995)
> ❑ ❑ 2 - Animal Instincts (1996)

■ **Marian J. A. JACKSON** is the creator a of historical mystery series set at the turn of the century, featuring American heiress Abigail Patience Danforth who wants to become the world's first female consulting detective. She asks the advice of Sir Arthur Conan Doyle who is less than enthusiastic about her plans. When Mark Twain gives his approval, the die is cast. Much of the first installment takes place in England, but book #2 sends Abigail back to New York where she and her companion Maude Cunningham board a train for their adventure out West. *The Sunken Treasure* (1994) finds Abigail and Maude on a yacht sailing from Panama to New Orleans, with Abigail wondering how she'll unlock the secrets of Houdini. For eight years Jackson was manager of the technical services department of the Institute of Electrical and Electronics Engineers in New York City where she still lives. Born in Birmingham, Alabama, she attended New York University.

> **Abigail Patience Danforth** . . . turn-of-the century consulting detective
> ❑ ❑ 1 - The Punjat's Ruby (1990)
> ❑ ❑ 2 - The Arabian Pearl (1990)
> ❑ ❑ 3 - Cat's Eye (1991)
> ❑ ❑ 4 - Diamond Head (1992)
> ❑ ❑ 5 - The Sunken Treasure (1994)

■ **Muriel Resnick JACKSON** is the creator of a new mystery series featuring Merrie Lee Spencer, a New Yorker transplanted to North Carolina, introduced in *The Garden Club* (1992).

> **Merrie Lee Spencer** . . . Manhattan transplant in North Carolina
> ❑ ❑ 1 - The Garden Club (1992)

■ **Jonnie JACOBS** was a high school English teacher and counselor and later an attorney with a large San Francisco law firm before writing her first mystery. Amateur sleuth and suburban mom Kate Austen, first appears in *Murder Among Neighbors* (1994) and later *Murder Among Friends* (1995). Not content with just one series, Jacobs has created California attorney Kali O'Brien, making her debut in *Shadow of Doubt* (1996). Jacobs lives with her husband and two sons in northern California.

> **Kali O'Brien** . . . attorney in Gold Country, California
> ❑ ❑ 1 - Shadow of Doubt (1996)

> **Kate Austen** . . . Bay area single mother in Walnut Hills, California
> ❑ ❑ 1 - Murder Among Neighbors (1994)
> ❑ ❑ 2 - Murder Among Friends (1995)

■ **Nancy Baker JACOBS** is a one of the few private eye writers who can claim actual experience as working private investigator. She is the author of four suspense novels, six nonfiction books and a "colorful" mystery series featuring Minneapolis P. I. Devon MacDonald, introduced in *The Turquoise Tatoo* (1991). In this series opener, Devon is hired by a Jewish doctor who once donated his sperm to a local sperm bank and now must find a half-sibling for a possible bone marrow donation before his son dies of leukemia. When Devon locates a potential donor, he turns out to be the son of an Aryan supremacist. Three of Jacobs' suspense titles—*Daddy's Gone A-Hunting*, *See Mommy Run* and *Deadly Companion*—have been optioned for motion pictures. A former Minnesotan, she now lives in California.

Devon MacDonald . . . Minneapolis, Minnesota ex-teacher P. I.
- ❑ ❑ 1 - The Turquoise Tattoo (1991)
- ❑ ❑ 2 - A Slash of Scarlet (1992)
- ❑ ❑ 3 - The Silver Scalpel (1993)

■ **Jody JAFFE** is the creator of an equestrian mystery series featuring Natalie Gold, newspaper reporter on the horse show circuit in Charlotte, North Carolina. Dying to get off the fashion beat, Nattie makes her first appearance in *Horse of a Different Killer* (1995). Despite the fact that she's a Yankee from Philadelphia, Nattie knows horses, having scrimped and saved to buy her own hunter, the aptly-named Brenda Starr. Jaffee wrote her book about killing horses for insurance money before 23 arrests were made for such crimes in 1994. She has been riding and showing hunters for the past 24 years and spent 10 years as a reporter on *The Charlotte Observer*, where she once out-ranked co-worker Patricia Cornwell. A Cornell University graduate, Jaffe is married to Charlie Shepard, who won a Pulitzer for his work uncovering the PTL scandal. They live in Chevy Chase, Maryland.

Natalie Gold . . . reporter on the horse show circuit in Charlotte, North Carolina
- ❑ ❑ 1 - Horse of a Different Killer (1995)
- ❑ ❑ 2 - Chestnut Mare, Beware (1996)

■ **P. D. JAMES** is Phyllis Dorothy James White, who spent 30 years in British Civil Service, including the Police and Criminal Law Departments of the Home Office. She is the recipient of numerous prizes and honors, including the Order of the British Empire and three Silver Daggers, in addition to a Diamond Dagger for lifetime achievement. Six of her novels have been filmed and broadcast on British and American television. She has served as a magistrate and governor of the BBC. Her well-known series characters are police commander and published poet Adam Dalgleish and Cordelia Gray, who each make appearances in the other's books. Cordelia is introduced in 1972 when she inherits a private enquiry firm from her former partner in *An Unsuitable Job for a Woman*, nominated for an Edgar award. The book was hailed at the time as a landmark for no-nonsense women investigators.

Adam Dalgleish . . . published poet of Scotland Yard
- ❑ ❑ 1 - Cover Her Face (1962)
- ❑ ❑ 2 - A Mind to Murder (1963)
- ❑ ❑ 3 - Unnatural Causes (1967)
- ❑ ❑ 4 - **Shroud for a Nightingale** (1971) *Silver Dagger* ★
  Edgar nominee ☆
- ❑ ❑ 5 - **The Black Tower** (1975) *Silver Dagger* ★
- ❑ ❑ 6 - Death of an Expert Witness (1977)
- ❑ ❑ 7 - **A Taste for Death** (1986) *Macavity & Silver Dagger winner* ★ ★
- ❑ ❑ 8 - Devices and Desires (1989)
- ❑ ❑ 9 - Original Sin (1994)

Cordelia Gray . . . fledgling P. I. in London
- ❑ ❑ 1 - **An Unsuitable Job for a Woman** (1972) *Edgar nominee* ☆
- ❑ ❑ 2 - The Skull Beneath the Skin (1982)

■ **J. A. JANCE** is Judith A. Jance, creator of the well-known, much-loved, award-winning Seattle series featuring J. P. Beaumont, introduced in *Until Proven Guilty* (1985). The once hard-drinking Seattle homicide cop with the high-rise condo and fast car makes his 13th appearance in *Name Withheld* (1995). Jance is also the creator of a new law enforcement series featuring Joanna Brady, who first appears in *Desert Heat* (1993), where she faces some tough decisions after the death of her husband in Cochise County, Arizona. Before she began telling stories for a living, Jance spent two years teaching high school English, five years as a school librarian on an Arizona Indian reservation and ten years selling life insurance. A graduate of the University of Arizona, she is also the author of a psychological thriller, *Hour of the Hunter*.

    J. P. Beaumont . . . Seattle, Washington homicide detective
        ❏ ❏   1 - Until Proven Guilty (1985)
        ❏ ❏   2 - Injustice for All (1986)
        ❏ ❏   3 - Trial by Fury (1986)
        ❏ ❏   4 - Taking the Fifth (1987)
        ❏ ❏   5 - Improbable Cause (1988)
        ❏ ❏   6 - A More Perfect Union (1988)
        ❏ ❏   7 - Dismissed with Prejudice (1989)
        ❏ ❏   8 - Minor in Possession (1990)
        ❏ ❏   9 - Payment in Kind (1991)
        ❏ ❏   10 - **Without Due Process** (1992) *American Mystery Award winner* ★
        ❏ ❏   11 - **Failure to Appear** (1993) *American Mystery Award winner* ★
        ❏ ❏   12 - Lying in Wait (1994)
        ❏ ❏   13 - Name Withheld (1995)

    Joanna Brady . . . deputy sheriff's widow turned sheriff in Cochise County, Arizona
        ❏ ❏   1 - Desert Heat (1993)
        ❏ ❏   2 - Tombstone Courage (1994)
        ❏ ❏   3 - Shoot, Don't Shoot (1995)

■ **Veronica Parker JOHNS** (1907-1988) was the creator of two mystery series from the '40s and '50s, including the first believable, dignified black detective in mystery fiction, Webster Flagg, 60-something Harlem actor, butler and houseman, semi-retired from opera and the stage. A man of considerable talents, Flagg learns the fine points of Italian cooking from Caruso when they are cast-mates in *Aida*. And he solves his first crime while serving lobster thermidor (which he prepared himself) in *Murder by the Day* (1953). In *Hush, Gabriel!* (1940) Agatha Welch meets a judge, finds a husband and solves a crime while visiting her sister in the Virgin Islands. In her autobiographical book, *She Sells Sea Shells*, Johns tells all about a shell shop she owned and operated in New York City, but gives short shrift (two sentences) to her mystery novels. Born in New York City, she attended Columbia School of Journalism and was actively involved in MWA during its formative years.

    Agatha Welch . . . middle-aged woman sleuth in Connecticut
        ❏ ❏   1 - Hush, Gabriel! (1940)
        ❏ ❏   2 - Shady Doings (1941)

    Webster Flagg . . . 60-something Harlem actor/butler/houseman in New York
        ❏ ❏   1 - Murder by the Day (1953)
        ❏ ❏   2 - Servant's Problem (1958)

■ **Hazel Wynn JONES** was the creator of a pair of novels featuring documentary film director Emma Shaw, who first appeared in *Death and the Trumpets of Tuscany* (1988), followed by *Shot on Location* (1990). Both books are set in Italy. Jones also wrote a nonseries mystery titled *Murder in a Manner of Speaking* (1989). She worked as both a scriptwriter and documentary film director before her death in 1990.

Emma Shaw . . . documentary film director in Italy
- ❏ ❏ 1 - Death and the Trumpets of Tuscany (1988)
- ❏ ❏ 2 - Shot on Location (1990)

■ **Jennifer JORDAN** is the creator of two contemporary British mystery series, including three novels featuring Barry and Dee Vaughn, a sleuthing couple from the London suburb of Woodfield, introduced in *A Good Weekend for Murder* (1987). Barry is a history lecturer at Woodfield Tech and the author of spoofy crime novels, while Dee is a former roving reporter for the magazine *Trends* turned part-time office temp. A third family member is their Schnauzer dog, Bella. Jordan's more recent amateur sleuth is Kristin Ashe, who makes her debut in *A Safe Place to Sleep* (1992).

Barry & Dee Vaughan . . . sleuthing couple in Woodfield, England
- ❏ ❏ 1 - A Good Weekend for Murder (1987)
- ❏ ❏ 2 - Murder Under the Mistletoe (1988)
- ❏ ❏ 3 - Book Early for Murder (1990)

Kristin Ashe . . . amateur sleuth in England
- ❏ ❏ 1 - A Safe Place to Sleep (1992)
- ❏ ❏ 2 - Existing Solutions (1993)

■ **Christine T. JORGENSEN** is the creator of Stella the Stargazer, astrologer and advice columnist to the lovelorn, introduced in *A Love To Die For* (1994). Stella is really the former Jane Smith, a Denver accountant with a penchant for handmade lingerie and a yen for change. It's no surprise then that her pet of choice is Fluffy the chameleon (anole actually). In *You Bet Your Life* (1995), Stella and Fluffy head for Silverado and a weekend of bridge and one-armed bandits. Formerly a Denver social worker, Jorgensen owns two little Fluffies of her own and has first-hand experience traveling with chameleons (anoles actually).

Stella the Stargazer . . . accountant turned astrologer & lovelorn columnist in Denver, Colorado
- ❏ ❏ 1 - A Love to Die For (1994)
- ❏ ❏ 2 - You Bet Your Life (1995)
- ❏ ❏ 3 - Curl Up and Die (1996)

■ **Lucille KALLEN** wrote for television and the theatre in addition to creating the mystery series featuring small-town newspaper editor C. B. Greenfield and reporter Maggie Rome, who plays Archie to his Nero Wolfe. Their first adventure, *Introducing C. B. Greenfield* (1979), was an American Book Award nominee. Kallen's writing career began with her comedy material for Sid Caesar and Imogene Coca, who appeared together on "Your Show of Shows." During her five-year stint at NBC, Kallen was part of the team that headed up a group of writers which included none other than Mel Brooks. When the television industry moved from New York to California, she stayed in New York and turned to writing novels.

Maggie Rome & C. B. Greenfield . . . Connecticut reporter & editor/publisher
- ❏ ❏ 1 - Introducing C. B. Greenfield (1979)
- ❏ ❏ 2 - The Tanglewood Murder (1980)
- ❏ ❏ 3 - No Lady in the House (1982)
- ❏ ❏ 4 - The Piano Bird (1984)
- ❏ ❏ 5 - A Little Madness (1986)

■ **Leona KARR** is the author of several gothic and romantic suspense novels, including the best-selling title *Stranger in the Mist*. She is also the creator of a new mystery series featuring Addie Devore, newspaper owner in a small Colorado town, introduced in *Murder in Bandora* (1993). Karr lives in Denver.

   Addie Devore . . . Colorado small-town newspaper owner
   ❑ ❑ 1 - Murder in Bandora (1993)

■ **Faye KELLERMAN** is the creator of an award-winning mystery series featuring LAPD detective Peter Decker, an ethnic Jew reared as a Baptist by his adoptive parents, and Rina Lazarus, an Orthodox Jewish widow with two young sons. Their first appearance, *The Ritual Bath* (1986), was a Macavity winner. In seven subsequent novels, Rina has assisted in several cases and Peter has worked with his cop partner Marge Dunn and even his daughter Cindy. But Marge is on vacation, Cindy's away at college and Rina is occupied with her wife and mother role, and as a result, Det. Sgt. Decker does most of his work solo in *Justice* (1995), described by some as Kellerman's most powerful book yet. She is also the author of *The Quality of Mercy*, a novel of intrigue set in Elizabethan England, where the daughter of the queen's own physician has a passionate and dangerous adventure with fledgling dramatist William Shakespeare. Born in St. Louis, Kellerman earned a BA in mathematics and her DDS degree at UCLA, where she met her husband Jonathan Kellerman, a clinical children's psychologist and mystery writer.

   Peter Decker & Rina Lazarus . . . LAPD detective & wife
   ❑ ❑ 1 - **The Ritual Bath** (1986) *Macavity winner* ★
   ❑ ❑ 2 - Sacred and Profane (1987)
   ❑ ❑ 3 - Milk and Honey (1990)
   ❑ ❑ 4 - Day of Atonement (1992)
   ❑ ❑ 5 - False Prophet (1992)
   ❑ ❑ 6 - Grievous Sin (1993)
   ❑ ❑ 7 - Sanctuary (1994)
   ❑ ❑ 8 - Justice (1995)

■ **Mary KELLY** is the creator of two mystery series from the '50s and '60s. The earlier series features Scottish Inspector Brett Nightingale who first appears in A Cold Coming. But it was private eye Hedley Nicholson's first case, *The Spoilt Kill* (1961), that won a Gold Dagger from the British Crime Writers Association for best crime novel of the year. Her nonseries novels include *March to the Gallows* (1964), *Dead Corse* (1966), *Write on Both Sides of the Paper* (1969), *The Twenty-Fifth Hour* (1971) and *The Girl in the Alley* (1974). Born in London, Kelly was educated at the University of Edinburgh where she earned a master's degree. She taught briefly in a private school and later in Surrey County Council schools.

   Brett Nightingale . . . Scottish Inspector in Edinburgh
   ❑ ❑ 1 - A Cold Coming (1956)
   ❑ ❑ 2 - Dead Man's Riddle (1957)
   ❑ ❑ 3 - The Christmas Egg (1958)

   Hedley Nicholson . . . P. I. in England
   ❑ ❑ 1 - **The Spoilt Kill** (1961) *Gold Dagger* ★
   ❑ ❑ 2 - Due to a Death (1962) [U.S.–The Dead of Summer]

■ **Mary Ann KELLY**, a former model and song lyricist, is the creator of a mystery series featuring photographer Claire Breslinsky, recently returned to her childhood neighborhood in Queens after ten years abroad. The series cast, introduced in *Park Lane South, Queens* (1990), includes Claire's two sisters—Zinnie the police officer and Carmela the fashion columnist—her Polish father and Irish mother and one gay ex-brother-in-law. Kelly, who has lived in Europe and India, is now back in her native Queens where she lives with her husband and young son.

    Claire Breslinsky . . . New York City freelance photographer
- ❑ ❑ 1 - Parklane South, Queens (1990)
- ❑ ❑ 2 - Foxglove (1992)
- ❑ ❑ 3 - Keeper of the Mill (1995)

■ **Nora KELLY** is the creator of history professor Gillian Adams who during the first installment, *In the Shadow of King's* (1984), travels to Cambridge where she assists Scotland Yard in solving the murder of another professor. In book #2, *My Sister's Keeper* (1992), she returns to Vancouver where she chairs the history department at the University of the Pacific Northwest. Book #3, *Bad Chemistry* (1993) sends her back to England and another murder among academics. Like her series protagonist, Kelly is a professor of history. She lives in Vancouver, British Columbia.

    Gillian Adams . . . University of the Pacific Northwest (Canada) history chair
- ❑ ❑ 1 - In the Shadow of King's (1984)
- ❑ ❑ 2 - My Sister's Keeper (1992)
- ❑ ❑ 3 - Bad Chemistry (1993)

■ **Susan KELLY** is the creator of Liz Connors, Cambridge freelance magazine writer and former English professor. The first book in this series, *The Gemini Man* (1985), was nominated for an Anthony as best first novel. It was also voted one of the top ten books of the year by the National Mystery Readers Poll. Kelly has a doctorate in medieval literature from the University of Edinburgh and has been a consultant to the Massachusetts Criminal Justice Training Council as well as a teacher of crime-report writing at the Cambridge Police Academy. Like her immensely likable series protagonist, Kelly is a former English professor who lives and works in Cambridge, Massachusetts.

    Liz Connors . . . Cambridge, Massachusetts freelance crime writer
- ❑ ❑ 1 - **The Gemini Man** (1985) *Anthony nominee* ☆
- ❑ ❑ 2 - The Summertime Soldiers (1986)
- ❑ ❑ 3 - Trail of the Dragon (1988)
- ❑ ❑ 4 - Until Proven Innocent (1990)
- ❑ ❑ 5 - And Soon I'll Come to Kill You (1991)
- ❑ ❑ 6 - Out of the Darkness (1992)

■ **Susan B. KELLY**, creator of the Hop Valley series with Detective Inspector Nick Trevellyan and Alison Hope, was born in the Thames Valley region of England and worked for twelve years as a computer programmer before writing full time. When her novels crossed the Atlantic, her U.S. publisher added the B to distinguish her from the American Susan Kelly. Alison Hope is the savvy and successful owner of a London software company that relocates to the Hop Valley in the first installment where Alison is also a suspect in the death of her cousin and former business partner.

    Alison Hope & Nick Trevellyan . . . Hop Valley, England software designer & detective inspector
- ❑ ❑ 1 - Hope Against Hope (1990)
- ❑ ❑ 2 - Time of Hope (1990)
- ❑ ❑ 3 - Hope Will Answer (1993)
- ❑ ❑ 4 - Kid's Stuff (1994)
- ❑ ❑ 5 - Death is Sweet (1996)

■ **Toni L. P. KELNER** is the creator of a new mystery series featuring Laura Fleming, a small-town North Carolina sleuth who moves from Byerly to Boston before making her debut in *Down Home Murder* (1993). Laura's "home" again in book #2 when Aunt Daphine must be rescued from a blackmailer. And in book #3 it's cousin Ilene who must get out of jail in time for Aunt Ruby Dee's wedding (her second marriage to her third husband). Like her series character, Kelner grew up in North Carolina and later moved to Boston where she now lives. Kelner also writes software documentation which she says is ideal training for mystery writing—how software works is always a mystery, programmers (like suspects) never tell the whole story, and the result is usually fiction.

    Laura Fleming . . . Byerly, North Carolina small-town detective
- ❏ ❏ 1 - Down Home Murder (1993)
- ❏ ❏ 2 - Dead Ringer (1994)
- ❏ ❏ 3 - Trouble Looking for a Place to Happen (1995)

■ **Susan KENNEY** teaches English at Colby College in Maine where she received a creative writing grant from the National Endowment for the Arts after winning the 1982 O. Henry Prize for a short story. Her mystery series features English professor Roz Howard and British artist and painter Alan Stewart, introduced in *Garden of Malice* (1983). Sailing fans will be in heaven with book #3, *One Fell Sloop* (1990).

    Roz Howard & Alan Stewart . . . American professor & British painter in Maine
- ❏ ❏ 1 - Garden of Malice (1983)
- ❏ ❏ 2 - Graves of Academe (1985)
- ❏ ❏ 3 - One Fell Sloop (1990)

■ **Karen KIJEWSKI** (pronounced key-EFF-ski) is the creator of the triple-award-winning Kat Colorado series, featuring a sometimes bar-tending Sacramento private eye introduced in *Katwalk* (1988), winner of Shamus and Anthony awards as well as the St. Martin's Press award for best first private eye novel. The supporting cast includes her best friend Charity Collins, hotshot dessert-loving advice columnist and cutting horse-owner; Kat's 80-something adopted grandmother Alma; handsome Las Vegas cop Hank; Kat's dog Ranger (blue and brown-eyed Australian sheepdog) and Hank's dog Mars (mostly black Lab). The kitten who arrives at the conclusion of book #2 is still without a name at the end of book #3. Kijewski is a former high school English teacher and bartender. Like her character, she lives in Sacramento, California.

    Kat Colorado . . . Sacramento, California P. I.
- ❏ ❏ 1 - Katwalk (1988) *SMP/PWA, Shamus & Anthony winner* ★ ★ ★
- ❏ ❏ 2 - Katapult (1990)
- ❏ ❏ 3 - Kat's Cradle (1991)
- ❏ ❏ 4 - Copy Kat (1992)
- ❏ ❏ 5 - Wild Kat (1994)
- ❏ ❏ 6 - Alley Cat Blues (1995)

■ **Laurie R. KING** is a third-generation native of the San Francisco area who has lived briefly in 20 countries on five continents since her marriage to an Anglo-Indian professor of religious studies. Her series opener with San Francisco homicide detectives Kate Martinelli and Alonzo Hawkin, *A Grave Talent* (1993), won an Edgar and was nominated for an Anthony award. You'll want to read *To Play the Fool* (1995) for the sheer pleasure of meeting Brother Erasmus—unofficial leader of the Berkeley homeless and a Holy Fool who speaks only in quotations (Biblical and Shakespearean). But do yourself the favor of starting at the beginning. Read *A Grave Talent* first. King is also the creator of Mary Russell, a teenage student of Sherlock Holmes, who debuts in *The Beekeeper's Apprentice* (1994), nominated for an Agatha award. In book #2, *A Monstrous Regiment of Women* (1995), Mary has come into her inheritance and sets out for London to visit the retired beekeeper Holmes. This time the compelling character is a feminist preacher surrounded by intrigue and not a few suspicious deaths. Don't miss it.

Kate Martinelli & Alonzo Hawkin . . . homicide detectives in San Francisco
  ❑ ❑ 1 - **A Grave Talent** (1993) *Edgar winner* ★ *Anthony nominee* ☆
  ❑ ❑ 2 - To Play the Fool (1995)
  ❑ ❑ 3 - With Child (1996)

Mary Russell . . . teenage student of Sherlock Holmes in LOCATION??
  ❑ ❑ 1 - **The Beekeeper's Apprentice** (1994) *Agatha nominee* ☆
  ❑ ❑ 2 - A Monstrous Regiment of Women (1995)

■ **Kate KINGSBURY** is the pseudonym of Doreen Roberts for her new Edwardian mystery series featuring Pennyfoot Hotel owner and manager Cecily Sinclair, introduced in *Room with a Clue* (1993). Beginning in 1905, each book advances in time three months, changing the seasons as well as the fortunes and misfortunes of the characters. British-born Roberts is the author of more than a dozen novels of romantic suspense, including *Hot Pursuit* (1990), written as Roberta Kent, another of her pseudonyms. A resident of the United States for more than 30 years, she lives in Vancouver, Washington.

Cecily Sinclair . . . Edwardian hotel owner in Badger's End, England
  ❑ ❑ 1 - Room with a Clue (1993)
  ❑ ❑ 2 - Do Not Disturb (1994)
  ❑ ❑ 3 - Service for Two (1994)
  ❑ ❑ 4 - Eat, Drink, and Be Buried (1994)
  ❑ ❑ 5 - Check-out Time (1995)
  ❑ ❑ 6 - Grounds for Murder (1995)
  ❑ ❑ 7 - Pay the Piper (1996)

■ **Mary KITTREDGE** was once a respiratory therapist for a major city hospital in the state of Connecticut, the setting for her two mystery series with medical backgrounds. Witty and resourceful freelance writer Charlotte Kent makes her first appearance in California with *Murder in Mendocino* (1987), but returns to Connecticut in book #2 accompanied by the boy she later adopts. Her love interest is a surgeon. Kittredge's longer-running series features independently wealthy Edwina Crusoe, a registered nurse who becomes a medical consultant, working on only those cases that intrigue her. Edwina's mother, a successful romance novelist, and wealthy in her own right, gets into a writing slump in *Kill or Cure* (1995) but recovers with typical flair. Edwina marries Martin (the cop) and by book #6 they are parents of hell-raising twin boys.

Charlotte Kent . . . Connecticut freelance writer
  ❑ ❑ 1 - Murder in Mendocino (1987)
  ❑ ❑ 2 - Dead and Gone (1989)
  ❑ ❑ 3 - Poison Pen (1990)

Edwina Crusoe . . . New Haven, Connecticut RN & medical consultant
  ❑ ❑ 1 - Fatal Diagnosis (1990)
  ❑ ❑ 2 - Rigor Mortis (1991)
  ❑ ❑ 3 - Cadaver (1992)
  ❑ ❑ 4 - Walking Dead Man (1992)
  ❑ ❑ 5 - Desperate Remedy (1993)
  ❑ ❑ 6 - Kill or Cure (1995)

■ **Alanna KNIGHT**, a historical novelist and expert on Robert Louis Stevenson, is also the creator of a mystery series set in Victorian Edinburgh featuring police inspector Jeremy Faro. The inspector is a widower whose two young daughters live with their grandmother in Orkney, but a grown stepson, Dr. Vincent Laurie, is frequently on hand to assist unofficially. Now in its 9th installment, this series begins with *Enter Second Murderer* (1988).

Jeremy Faro . . . Victorian detective inspector in Edinburgh, Scotland
- ❏ ❏ 1 - Enter Second Murderer (1988)
- ❏ ❏ 2 - Bloodline (1989)
- ❏ ❏ 3 - Deadly Beloved (1989)
- ❏ ❏ 4 - Killing Cousins (1990)
- ❏ ❏ 5 - A Quiet Death (1991)
- ❏ ❏ 6 - To Kill a Queen (1992)
- ❏ ❏ 7 - The Evil That Men Do (1993)
- ❏ ❏ 8 - The Missing Duchess (1994)
- ❏ ❏ 9 - The Bull Slayers (1995)

■ **Kathleen Moore KNIGHT** (1890-1984) wrote more than 36 mysteries between 1935 and 1960, but she is best known for her series featuring fish market owner, Elisha Macomber, chairman of the Board of Selectman of Penberthy Township (read Cape Cod or Martha's Vineyard), Massachusetts. Although the 16-book series spans 25 years, the 70-something Macomber never ages, nor is he bothered by any physical ailments. Fulfilling a lifelong dream, he travels to Panama for three adventures involving young American expatriates. Mexico and Panama are also the setting for several nonseries books Knight wrote under the name Alan Amos. Often overlooked is her four-book series starring 30-something Margot Blair, partner in the New York public relations firm of Norman and Blair. Margot's cases are typically tied to the difficulties of daily life during the Second World War but the series finale takes her to Mexico City in search of the daughter of a dead client.

Elisha Macomber . . . selectman & owner of a fish market in Cape Cod, Massachusetts
- ❏ ❏ 1 - Death Blew Out the Match (1935)
- ❏ ❏ 2 - The Clue of the Poor Man's Shilling (1936) [Britain–The Poor Man's Shilling]
- ❏ ❏ 3 - The Wheel That Turned (1936) [APA–Murder Greets Jean Holton]
- ❏ ❏ 4 - Seven Were Veiled (1937) [Britain–Seven Were Suspect] [APA–Death Wears a (Bridal) Veil]
- ❏ ❏ 5 - The Tainted Token (1938) [APA–The Case of the Tainted Token]
- ❏ ❏ 6 - Acts of Black Night (1938)
- ❏ ❏ 7 - Death Came Dancing (1940)
- ❏ ❏ 8 - The Trouble at Turkey Hill (1946)
- ❏ ❏ 9 - Footbridge to Death (1947)
- ❏ ❏ 10 - Bait for Murder (1948)
- ❏ ❏ 11 - The Bass Derby Murder (1949)
- ❏ ❏ 12 - Death Goes to a Reunion (1952)
- ❏ ❏ 13 - Valse Macabre (1952)
- ❏ ❏ 14 - Akin to Murder (1953)
- ❏ ❏ 15 - Three of Diamonds (1953)
- ❏ ❏ 16 - Beauty Is a Beast (1959)

Margot Blair . . . partner in a PR agency in New York
- ❏ ❏ 1 - Rendezvous with the Past (1940)
- ❏ ❏ 2 - Exit a Star (1941)
- ❏ ❏ 3 - Terror by Twilight (1942)
- ❏ ❏ 4 - Design in Diamonds (1944)

■ **Kathryn Lasky KNIGHT** is the author of numerous children's books under the name Kathryn Lasky. Her first adult novel is *Trace Elements* (1986), the opening title of her mystery series featuring Calista Jacobs, an illustrator of children's books in Cambridge, Massachusetts, who starts a sleuthing career with the hunt for her husband's killer. Other regulars in this cast are Calista's son Charley, the computer wizard, and Archie Baldwin, an archaeologist from the Smithsonian Institute.

> **Calista Jacobs** . . . award-winning illustrator of children's books in Cambridge, Massachusetts
> ❑ ❑ 1 - Trace Elements (1986)
> ❑ ❑ 2 - Mortal Words (1990)
> ❑ ❑ 3 - Mumbo Jumbo (1991)
> ❑ ❑ 4 - Dark Swain (1994)

■ **Phyllis KNIGHT** is the creator of ex-rocker, gay woman P. I. Lil Ritchie, who moves from the coast of Maine to the Virginia Blue Ridge in the series opener, *Switching the Odds* (1992), nominated for a Shamus award as best first private eye novel. Throughout the series Lil travels to places the author knows well, including Downeast Maine; Austin, Texas; Charlottesville, Virginia; and Montreal, Quebec. Music is Lil's driving force, a rich inheritance from Knight's ancestors. While her father's people were mostly mountain dwellers and musicians, her mother is a direct descendent of Francis Scott Key. As a child, Knight and her sister sang all over Virginia in the family dance band and appeared weekly on TV and radio programs broadcast to 26 states. Starting in high school she was a regular on the folk music/coffee house circuit, alone and with her bands—Possum Delight, Violet Crown and later Dulces Suenos (Sweet Dreams). She lives in Charlottesville, Virginia after moving home from Downeast Maine. On warm evenings she can be found on the front porch playing her twelve-string guitar. Hidden by the trees and overgrown shrubs, she can be heard by passersby, but not seen.

> **Lil Ritchie** . . . ex-rocker & gay woman P. I. in coastal Maine
> ❑ ❑ 1 - **Switching the Odds** (1992) *Shamus nominee* ☆
> ❑ ❑ 2 - Shattered Rhythms (1994)
> ❑ ❑ 3 - Lost to Sight (1996)

■ **Dolores KOMO** is the creator of Clio Browne, the first black woman private eye in mystery fiction. Clio is a cop's widow and owner of her own agency in St. Louis, Missouri. Komo is at work on Clio's next case, to be titled *Affairs of Death*.

> **Clio Browne** . . . cop's widow & P. I. agency owner in St. Louis, Missouri
> ❑ ❑ 1 - Clio Browne: Private Investigator (1988)

■ **Gabrielle KRAFT** is a former executive story editor and story analyst at major Hollywood film studios. She is also the creator of a four-book mystery series featuring Jerry Zalman, Beverly Hills attorney and deal maker, whose first adventure, *Bullshot* (1987), was nominated for an Edgar award. This series has been described as smart and snappy and full of sarcastic commentary on the Looney Tunes of LaLa Land.

> **Jerry Zalman** . . . Beverly Hills, California deal maker
> ❑ ❑ 1 - **Bullshot** (1987) *Edgar nominee* ☆
> ❑ ❑ 2 - Screwdriver (1988)
> ❑ ❑ 3 - Let's Rob Roy (1989)
> ❑ ❑ 4 - Bloody Mary (1990)

■ **Katherine E. KREUTER** is the creator of a new mystery series featuring mystery writer and private eye Paige Taylor, who makes her debut in Fool *Me Once* (1994).

> **Paige Taylor** . . . mystery writer & P. I.
> ❏ ❏ 1 - Fool Me Once (1994)

■ **Rochelle Majer KRICH** is the creator of LAPD homicide detective Jessie Drake, whose first installment, *Fair Game* (1993), was nominated for an Agatha award. Krich's first mystery, the Anthony award-winning *Where's Mommy Now?* has been retitled *Perfect Alibi* for the Hollywood movie starring Teri Garr and Hector Elizondo. The novel is being re-issued under its new title to coincide with the release of the film. The daughter of Holocaust survivors, Krich has chosen a number of Holocaust survivors for her lead characters in *Angel of Death* (1994), another Agatha nominee. Krich chairs the English department at a private high school and serves on the national board of Mystery Writers of America. Born in Germany, she lived in New York and New Jersey until moving to California in 1960. A former national newsletter editor for Sisters in Crime, she lives in Los Angeles with her husband and their six children.

> **Jessie Drake** . . . Los Angeles, California police detective
> ❏ ❏ 1 - **Fair Game** (1993) *Agatha nominee* ☆
> ❏ ❏ 2 - Angel of Death (1994) *Agatha nominee* ☆

■ **Mary KRUGER** is the creator of a series of Gilded Age (1890s) mysteries featuring amateur sleuth Brooke Cassidy and private eye Matt Devlin in Newport, Rhode Island, introduced in *Death on the Cliff Walk* (1994). Kruger lives in Massachusetts.

> **Brooke Cassidy & Matt Devlin** . . . mystery writer & P. I. in Newport RI
> ❏ ❏ 1 - Death on the Cliff Walk (1994)
> ❏ ❏ 2 - No Honeymoon for Death (1995)

■ **Kathleen KUNZ** is the creator of mystery fiction's first professional genealogist sleuth, Terry Girard, who makes her debut in *Murder Once Removed* (1993). Terry is a partner with her Aunt Cecile in their research business, The Family Album, and when CeCe dies suspiciously, Terry must find who has the family secret to kill for. Like her protagonist, Kunz is a native of St. Louis with a keen interest in matters genealogical. Her 4th great-grandfather Jean Baptiste and his son Auguste arrived with Chouteau from New Orleans and staked their claim on the St. Louis riverbank. Kunz teaches professional writing at the University of Oklahoma and has published articles and short fiction in *Ellery Queen Mystery Magazine*, *Good Housekeeping* and *Parents*. Her late brother, Chris King, was co-owner of Big Sleep Books in the Central West End of St. Louis.

> **Terry Girard** . . . St. Louis, Missouri genealogist for hire
> ❏ ❏ 1 - Murder Once Removed (1993)
> ❏ ❏ 2 - Death in a Private Place (1996)

■ **Sarah LACEY** is the pseudonym of Kay Mitchell for her series featuring 25-year-old tax inspector Leah Hunter, first appearing in *File Under: Deceased* (1992). Leah likes her freedom too much to be anything but single and says living solo is an unbeatable way to keep down household chores. She describes Bramfield, the Yorkshire town where she lives and works, as the kind of place where pubs still sport dart boards and beer-bellied males are more common than litter bins. Under her own name Mitchell writes a police series featuring Malminster Chief Inspector John Morrissey, a married father of two teenagers. Born in Wakefield, England, she earned an honors degree in English at Leeds University and later trained as a nurse. She has worked as a night sister and theater sister and in a hospital casualty department. After becoming a midwife, Mitchell also worked as a health visitor. She lives in Wakefield where she writes full time.

Leah Hunter . . . Yorkshire, England tax inspector
 ❑ ❑ 1 - File Under: Deceased (1992)
 ❑ ❑ 2 - File Under: Missing (1993)
 ❑ ❑ 3 - File Under: Arson (1994)
 ❑ ❑ 4 - File Under: Jeopardy (1995)

■ **Carroll LACHNIT** is the creator of a new mystery series featuring ex-cop turned law student Hannah Barlow, introduced in *Murder in Brief* (1995). Hannah and her moot court partner—golden boy of the second year class—are accused of plagiarism. But before he can prove their innocence, he's run down by a train and Hannah is left to refute the charges. Lachnit admits that Hannah's law school is suspiciously similar to Chapman University in Orange County, but says she got her first glimpse of the fierce competition of law schools when her husband entered Southwestern University School of Law in the mid-'80s. A former court reporter, Lachnit spent almost nine years at the Orange County *Register* where she covered a wide range of stories, including the 1984 Olympics and the trial in Yugoslavia of an Orange County resident charged with Nazi-era war crimes.

Hannah Barlow . . . ex-cop turned law student in Orange County, California
 ❑ ❑ 1 - Murder in Brief (1995)
 ❑ ❑ 2 - A Blessed Death (1996)

■ **Mercedes LACKEY** is the creator of a cross-genre series featuring Diana Tregarde, freelance investigator of unnatural events and romance novelist from Hartford, Connecticut. Refusing compensation for her occult work, Diana earns her living writing romance novels, including the occasional Regency. In the series opener, *Burning Water* (1989), Di heads for Dallas to assist her college friend-turned-police-detective Mark Valdez with a case involving a serial killer. Author of *The Heralds of Valdemar* fantasy series, Lackey has written and recorded more than 50 songs for a small recording company specializing in science fiction music (Off-Centaur). A Chicago native and graduate of Purdue University, she has worked as an artist's model, computer programmer, surveyor, layout designer and data processing analyst. She now lives in Tulsa, Oklahoma.

Diana Tregarde . . . romance author & practicing witch in Hartford, Connecticut
 ❑ ❑ 1 - Burning Water (1989)
 ❑ ❑ 2 - Children of the Night (1990)
 ❑ ❑ 3 - Jinx High (1991)

■ **J. Dayne LAMB** is the creator of a new mystery series featuring 30-something Teal Stewart, savvy CPA from Boston's Beacon Hill, introduced in *Questionable Behavior* (1993). A frequent traveler, Teal heads for a trendy California spa—"The Ranch" in Baja—in *A Question of Preference* (1994) and then to Michigan's Upper Peninsula in *Unquestioned Loyalty* (1995). Born in San Francisco but raised in Brookline, Massachusetts, Lamb is a former CPA with a BA in philosophy from Hope College in Michigan and an MS in accounting from Northeastern University. President of the New England Chapter of Sisters in Crime, she teaches mystery writing at the Boston Center for Adult Education.

Teal Stewart . . . Boston, Massachusetts Certified Public Accountant
 ❑ ❑ 1 - Questionable Behavior (1993)
 ❑ ❑ 2 - A Question of Preference (1994)
 ❑ ❑ 3 - Unquestioned Loyalty (1995)

■ **Mercedes LAMBERT** is the creator of Whitney Logan, 20-something Los Angeles attorney and her street smart sometimes partner, Lupe, a Chicana prostitute, introduced in *Dogtown* (1991). Lambert lives in Montebello, California with her two children, where she is working on her second novel.

    Whitney Logan . . . 20-something Los Angeles attorney
       ❑ ❑ 1 - Dogtown (1991)

■ **Marsha LANDRETH** is the creator of a medical mystery series featuring Dr. Samantha Turner, medical examiner of Sheridan, Wyoming, introduced in *The Holiday Murders* (1992). Sam determines smallpox was the cause of death in *Vial Murders* (1994)—a disease that was declared eradicated in 1977. Small wonder that no one believes her. Under the pseudonym Tyler Cortland she writes mainstream medical sagas, including *The Healers*, *The Hospital* and *The Doctors* (1995). Author of *William T. Sherman*, a civil war biography of the famous general, she has also written a western titled *French Creek*. A native of Denver with a degree in theatre arts from the University of Northern Colorado, Landreth once lived in Sheridan, Wyoming. She now lives in southern California where she also writes screenplays, including the one for *The Holiday Murders*, previously optioned for a TV movie starring Suzanne Pleshette.

    Dr. Samantha Turner . . . Sheridan, Wyoming medical examiner
       ❑ ❑ 1 - The Holiday Murders (1992)
       ❑ ❑ 2 - A Clinic for Murder (1993)
       ❑ ❑ 3 - Vial Murders (1995)

■ **Jane LANGTON** is the creator of the Edgar-nominated Homer Kelly series featuring a Thoreau scholar-attorney-ex-cop living and loving the rich New England history of Boston and Concord. The series begins with *The Transcendental Murder* (1964), later reissued as *The Minuteman Murder* (1976) in celebration of the Bicentennial. A former Middlesex County (Massachusetts) police lieutenant, Homer Kelly is an expert on the works of Emerson and Thoreau, and as a result, these mysteries are both literate and literary with a rich background of academia, prose, poetry and cultural and natural history. Langton's many devoted readers look forward to her wonderful pen and ink sketches which illustrate each book, almost as much as the stories themselves. Langton earned master's degrees from both Radcliffe College and the University of Michigan, where she was Phi Beta Kappa. A student at the Boston Museum School of Art and a one-time teacher of children's literature, she has written a number of works of fiction for children. Her experience with the seamy side of life comes, she says, from teaching Sunday School.

    Homer Kelly . . . Harvard professor & retired detective in Cambridge, Massachusetts
       ❑ ❑ 1 - The Transcendental Murder (1964)
                 [APA–The Minuteman Murder ('76)]
       ❑ ❑ 2 - Dark Nantucket Noon (1975)
       ❑ ❑ 3 - The Memorial Hall Murder (1978)
       ❑ ❑ 4 - Natural Enemy (1982)
       ❑ ❑ 5 - **Emily Dickinson Is Dead** (1984) *Edgar nominee* ☆
       ❑ ❑ 6 - Good and Dead (1986)
       ❑ ❑ 7 - Murder at the Gardner (1988)
       ❑ ❑ 8 - The Dante Game (1991)
       ❑ ❑ 9 - God in Concord (1992)
       ❑ ❑ 10 - Divine Inspiration (1993)
       ❑ ❑ 11 - The Shortest Day (1995)

■ **Janet LA PIERRE** is a former high school English teacher who writes novels of mystery and suspense, typically set on the chilly, foggy, sparsely-populated northern coast of California. Her series detectives are Vince Gutierrez, police chief of Port Silva, and Meg Halloran, teacher and single mother, first appearing in *Unquiet Grave* (1987), nominated for a Macavity award. Later in the series another cop & single mother pair take the lead roles while Vince and Meg become supporting characters. Born in Iowa and educated at the University of Arizona-Tucson, La Pierre helped run a large co-op nursery school where she says she learned small children have no conscience, much cunning, and will do anything.

Vince Gutierrez & Meg Halloran . . . police chief & school teacher in Port Silva, California
  ❏ ❏ 1 - **Unquiet Grave** (1987) *Macavity nominee* ☆
  ❏ ❏ 2 - Children's Games (1989)
  ❏ ❏ 3 - Cruel Mother (1990)
  ❏ ❏ 4 - Grandmother's House (1991)
  ❏ ❏ 5 - **Old Enemies** (1993) *Anthony nominee* ☆

■ **Lynda LA PLANTE** was the original writer for the television series featuring London's Detective Chief Inspector Jane Tennison, star of PBS *Mystery!*, later novelized as *Prime Suspect 1, 2,* and *3*. In late 1995 it was announced that a different writer will produce each of the episodes in *Prime Suspect 4*. La Plante trained for the stage at the Royal Academy of Dramatic Arts and later became a successful television actress after extensive work in repertory theatre and seasons with the National Theatre and the Royal Shakespeare Theatre. She turned to writing full time after phenomenal success with her TV series *Widows* which sold in 26 countries worldwide. Her first novel, *Legacy*, was an international bestseller, followed by *Bella Mafia* and *Entwined* (1993).

Dolly Rawlins . . . young English widow
  ❏ ❏ 1 - The Widows (1983)
  ❏ ❏ 2 - The Widows II (1985)

Jane Tennison . . . London detective chief inspector
  ❏ ❏ 1 - Prime Suspect (1993)
  ❏ ❏ 2 - Prime Suspect 2 (1993)
  ❏ ❏ 3 - Prime Suspect 3 (1994)

■ **Emma LATHEN** is the pseudonym of Mary J. Latsis and Martha Henissart for their more than 20 installments in the John Putnam Thatcher series—winner of both a Gold and Silver Dagger, an Ellery Queen award and an Edgar nomination. Lathen has been called America's Agatha Christie, but some think she's better. A reserved and dignified widower, Thatcher is senior vice president of Sloan Guaranty Trust in New York City, ably assisted in his business and financial detecting by his stalwart secretary Miss Corsa, other banking colleagues and the fussy Everett Gabler, whose attention to detail extends even to dog shows and kennel owners (*A Place for Murder*). Different aspects of commerce and finance are central to each book, ranging from Russian wheat deals (in the Gold Dagger winner *Murder Against the Grain*) to the garment industry (*The Longer the Thread*) and even the Lake Placid Winter Olympics (*Going for the Gold*). These two authors also write a Congressional series under another shared pseudonym, R. B. Dominic. Their rumpled Ohio Congressman, Ben Safford, has been described as astute but unassuming, beginning with *Murder Sunny Side Up* (1968). Educated at Wellesley and Harvard, after growing up in Forest Park, Illinois, Latsis worked for a number of years as an economist, including a stint at the UN Food and Agricultural Organization in Rome. A native of New York City, Hennisart worked as an attorney in corporate finance and banking for many years. Known to jealously guard their personal privacy, Latsis and Henissart are known to be living in Massachusetts.

John Putnam Thatcher . . . New York City Wall Street financial whiz
- ❑ ❑ 1 - Banking on Death (1961)
- ❑ ❑ 2 - A Place for Murder (1963)
- ❑ ❑ 3 - **Accounting for Murder** (1964) *Silver Dagger* ★
- ❑ ❑ 4 - Murder Makes the Wheels Go 'Round (1966)
- ❑ ❑ 5 - Death Shall Overcome (1966)
- ❑ ❑ 6 - **Murder Against the Grain** (1967) *Gold Dagger* ★
- ❑ ❑ 7 - A Stitch in Time (1968)
- ❑ ❑ 8 - Come to Dust (1968)
- ❑ ❑ 9 - **When in Greece** (1969) *Edgar nominee* ☆
- ❑ ❑ 10 - Murder To Go (1969)
- ❑ ❑ 11 - Pick up Sticks (1970)
- ❑ ❑ 12 - Ashes to Ashes (1971)
- ❑ ❑ 13 - The Longer the Thread (1971)
- ❑ ❑ 14 - Murder Without Icing (1972)
- ❑ ❑ 15 - Sweet and Low (1974)
- ❑ ❑ 16 - By Hook or by Crook (1975)
- ❑ ❑ 17 - Double, Double, Oil and Trouble (1978)
- ❑ ❑ 18 - Going for the Gold (1981)
- ❑ ❑ 19 - **Green Grow the Dollars** (1982) *Ellery Queen Award* ★
- ❑ ❑ 20 - Something in the Air (1988)
- ❑ ❑ 21 - East Is East (1991)
- ❑ ❑ 22 - Right on the Money (1993)

■ **Janet LAURENCE** brings both cooking and writing experience to her mystery series featuring British caterer, chef & food writer Darina Lisle, introduced in *A Deepe Coffyn* (1989). This book-a-year series (soon to be eight adventures for Darina) offers a superabundance of glorious food descriptions, but no actual recipes. In addition to her cooking experience, Laurence has been a contributing writer for the *Daily Telegraph* and *Country Life* in England.

Darina Lisle . . . British caterer, chef & food writer
- ❑ ❑ 1 - A Deepe Coffyn (1989)
- ❑ ❑ 2 - A Tasty Way to Die (1990)
- ❑ ❑ 3 - Hotel Morgue (1991)
- ❑ ❑ 4 - Recipe for Death (1992)
- ❑ ❑ 5 - Death and the Epicure (1993)
- ❑ ❑ 6 - Death at the Table (1994)
- ❑ ❑ 7 - Death a la Provencale (1995)
- ❑ ❑ 8 - Diet for Death (1996)

■ **Janice LAW** is the creator of the Anna Peters series featuring a Washington DC private eye skilled in corporate blackmail, first appearing in *The Big Pay-off* (1976). Nominated for an Edgar, the series opener features business intrigue mixed with oil exploration in the North Sea. Long out of print, this book will not be easy to find (try inter-library loan), but you'll be rewarded for your effort. The enterprising and likable Anna is one tough cookie and if you've ever dreamed of blackmailing a jerk-of-a-boss, you'll cheer out loud as you rip through these 179 pages. Golf enthusiasts will especially enjoy book #5, *Death Under Par* (1981), where Anna accompanies her sports illustrator husband Harry to the British Open.

Anna Peters . . . international oil company secretary turned P. I. in Washington DC

❑ ❑ 1 - **The Big Pay-off** (1976) *Edgar nominee* ☆
❑ ❑ 2 - Gemini Trip (1977)
❑ ❑ 3 - Under Orion (1978)
❑ ❑ 4 - The Shadow of the Palms (1980)
❑ ❑ 5 - Death Under Par (1981)
❑ ❑ 6 - Time Lapse (1992)
❑ ❑ 7 - A Safe Place to Die (1993)
❑ ❑ 8 - Backfire (1994)

■ **Hilda LAWRENCE** wrote a three-book series in the mid 1940s featuring Manhattan private eye Mark East and two spinster sleuths, Bessie Petty and Beulah Pond. This series, beginning with *Blood Upon the Snow* (1944), has been described as an interesting juxtaposition of the hard-boiled vs. the little old lady school of detection, the mores of Manhattan vs. life in a small New England village. According to Michele Slung, Lawrence's masterpiece is *Death of a Doll* (1947), set in a New York boarding house for women. Miss Beulah and Miss Bessie go undercover, as it were, at Hope House and, aided and abetted by Mark, end up solving the crime. Lawrence also produced a novel of suspense titled *The Deadly Pavilion* (1948) and two novellas published together as *Duet of Death* (1949). Her varied career included grading papers at Johns Hopkins, working at *Publishers Weekly* and churning out radio scripts for *The Rudy Vallee Show*.

Mark East, Bessie Petty & Beulah Pond . . . Manhattan P. I. & two little old ladies from New England

❑ ❑ 1 - Blood Upon the Snow (1944)
❑ ❑ 2 - A Time to Die (1944)
❑ ❑ 3 - Death of a Doll (1947)

■ **Martha LAWRENCE** is the creator of a new mystery series featuring Dr. Elizabeth Chase, a Stanford-trained parapsychologist turned private eye. Armed with a double-PhD and her "gift," Dr. Chase takes on the skeptics, including San Diego police officer Tom McGowan who asks for her help. *Murder in Scorpio* (1995) is Lawrence's debut novel.

Dr. Elizabeth Chase . . . Stanford-trained parapsychologist turned P. I. in San Diego, California

❑ ❑ 1 - Murder in Scorpio (1995)

■ **Barbara LEE**'s first mystery, *Death in Still Waters*, won the Malice Domestic Best First Mystery award in 1994 and was published by St. Martin's in 1995. She is the founder of a writing services company and one of the organizers of the Chesapeake Chapter of Sisters in Crime. A born and bred New Yorker—both city and state—she was born in the Adirondacks, grew up in Cooperstown and lived for many years in New York City. She currently lives in Columbia, Maryland, where she is at work on her second novel.

Eve Elliott . . . ex-New York advertising exec turned realtor in Anne Arundel County, Maryland

❑ ❑ 1 - **Death in Still Waters** (1995) *MD/SMP best first mystery* ★

■ **Marie LEE** is the creator of a new mystery series featuring Marguerite Smith, a retired Massachusetts science teacher, who first appears in *The Curious Cape Cod Skull* (1995).

Marguerite Smith . . . retired science teacher in Cape Cod, Massachusetts

❑ ❑ 1 - The Curious Cape Cod Skull (1995)

■ **Wendi LEE** is the creator of a new mystery series featuring Angela Matelli, a good Italian girl from East Boston, who also happens to be an ex-Marine turned P. I. Although she appeared earlier in a number of short stories, including ones in *Noir* magazine and several mystery anthologies, Angela's debut novel is *The Good Daughter* (1994). Her first client is an ex-cop who ends up dead after hiring Angela to check out his daughter's boyfriend. Under the W. W. Lee byline, she is the author of a six-book series starring Jefferson Birch, P. I. in the Old West, introduced in *Rogue's Gold*. A one-time resident of Boston, she now lives in Muscatine, Iowa where she works as associate editor of *Mystery Scene* magazine.

Angela Matelli . . . ex-Marine turned P. I. in Boston, Massachusetts
- ❑ ❑ 1 - The Good Daughter (1994)
- ❑ ❑ 2 - Missing Eden (1996)

Jefferson Birch . . . Old West P. I.
- ❑ ❑ 1 - Rogue's Gold (1989)
- ❑ ❑ 2 - Rustler's Venom (1990)
- ❑ ❑ 3 - Rancher's Blood (1991)
- ❑ ❑ 4 - Robber's Trail (1992)
- ❑ ❑ 5 - Outlaw's Fortune (1993)
- ❑ ❑ 6 - Cannon's Revenge (1995)

■ **Margaret LEEK** is one of the pseudonyms of Sara Hutton Bowen-Judd (1922-1985) who wrote more than 50 mystery novels over a 25-year period, primarily as Sara Woods. Making good use of her working experience in a solicitor's office, she constructs a legal background for most of her work. Her best known character, Antony Maitland, is often called the British Perry Mason, but she was no Erle Stanley Gardner. Refraining from courtroom tricks, she seldom produced mystery witnesses or spontaneous confessions. Under the Leek byline, she wrote a three-book series with attorney Stephen Marryat, starting with *We Must Have a Trial* (1980). Born and educated in England, she didn't start writing seriously until moving to Nova Scotia. Although her setting and character are distinctly British, she is considered Canada's most successful writer of mystery fiction. She also wrote as Anne Burton and Mary Challis.

Stephen Marryat . . . attorney in England
- ❑ ❑ 1 - We Must Have a Trial (1980)
- ❑ ❑ 2 - The Healthy Grave (1980)
- ❑ ❑ 3 - Voice of the Past (1981)

■ **Elizabeth LEMARCHAND** was for 20 years (1940-1960) Deputy Headmistress of Godolphin School, the alma mater of Josephine Bell and Dorothy L. Sayers among others. Forced to retire early because of a serious illness, she began writing as a hobby during convalescence and saw her first mystery published at the age of 61. She produced a total of 17 novels featuring Scotland Yard investigators Tom Pollard and Gregory Toye, introduced in *Death of an Old Girl* (1967). In each of her well-constructed and frequently ingenious books, readers are treated to maps, timetables, floor plans and printed casts of characters— standard fare during the earlier Golden Age of Detection. Lemarchand's detectives are old-fashioned family men. Pollard's wife Jane, a red-headed art teacher, presents her husband with twins in book #2, *The Affacombe Affair* (1968). Toye has a weakness for Western movies and a vast knowledge of automobiles. Born in Devon and educated at the Ursuline Convent, Lemarchand earned a master's degree at the University of Exeter in 1929.

Tom Pollard & Gregory Toye . . . Scotland Yard detectives in England
- ❑ ❑ 1 - Death of an Old Girl (1967)
- ❑ ❑ 2 - The Affacombe Affair (1968)

❏	❏	3	-	Alibi for a Corpse (1969)
❏	❏	4	-	Death on Doomsday (1971)
❏	❏	5	-	Cyanide with Compliments (1972)
❏	❏	6	-	Let or Hindrance (1973) [U.S.–No Vacation from Murder]
❏	❏	7	-	Buried in the Past (1974)
❏	❏	8	-	Step in the Dark (1976)
❏	❏	9	-	Unhappy Returns (1977)
❏	❏	10	-	Suddenly While Gardening (1978)
❏	❏	11	-	Change for the Worse (1980)
❏	❏	12	-	Nothing To Do with the Case (1981)
❏	❏	13	-	Troubled Waters (1982)
❏	❏	14	-	The Wheel Turns (1983)
❏	❏	15	-	Light through the Glass (1984)
❏	❏	16	-	Who Goes Home? (1986)
❏	❏	17	-	The Glade Manor Murder (1988)

■ **Donna LEON** is an American expatriate living in Venice, the setting for her mystery series involving Italian police officer Guido Brunetti and his wealthy wife Paola, a professor of English literature. Their two teenage children and her parents round out the continuing cast of characters introduced in *Death at la Fenice* (1992), which won Japan's Suntory prize for best suspense novel. Leon teaches English at the University of Maryland extension in Venice and is familiar with the local U.S. military installation which she uses in book #2, *Death in a Strange Country* (1993).

Guido Brunetti . . . police commissario in Venice, Italy

❏	❏	1	-	Death at la Fenice (1992)
❏	❏	2	-	Death in a Strange Country (1993)
❏	❏	3	-	Dressed for Death (1994) [Britain–The Anonymous Venetian]
❏	❏	4	-	Death and Judgment (1995) [APA–A Venetian Reckoning]
❏	❏	5	-	Acqua Alta (1996)

■ **Charles L. LEONARD** is the pseudonym of Mary Violet Heberden (1906-1965) who wrote more than 30 high-action private eye novels under her own name and a pseudonym between 1939 and 1953. Her two private eye series as M. V. Heberden include 17 books with Irish-American Desmond Shannon and three with ex-Naval Intelligence officer Rick Vanner. Under the Charles Leonard byline she wrote eleven titles featuring Washington DC private eye and spy Paul Kilgerrin introduced in *The Stolen Squadron* (1942). Ruthless and amoral, Kilgerrin uses any method necessary to get results, including cold-blooded murder (he commits two in *The Stolen Squadron*). The Kilgerrin series contains some great action scenes and lots of gangsters whose dialogue is "so bad it's almost painful to read," according to Bill Pronzini (*1001 Midnights*). *The Stolen Squadron* also introduces test pilot Gerry Cordent, one of the early "liberated" women of modern crime fiction. She is an associate of Kilgerrin's in the series opener and later installments. Born in England, Heberden was a world traveler, office manager and timber importer.

Paul Kilgerrin . . . P. I. spy in Washington DC

❏	❏	1	-	The Stolen Squadron (1942)
❏	❏	2	-	Deadline for Destruction (1942)
❏	❏	3	-	The Fanatic of Fez (1943) [APA–Assignment to Death]
❏	❏	4	-	The Secret of the Spa (1944)
❏	❏	5	-	Expert in Murder (1945)
❏	❏	6	-	Pursuit in Peru (1946)
❏	❏	7	-	Search for a Scientist (1948)
❏	❏	8	-	The Fourth Funeral (1948)

❑ ❑ 9 - Sinister Shelter (1949)
❑ ❑ 10 - Secrets for Sale (1950)
❑ ❑ 11 - Treachery in Trieste (1951)

■ **Sherry LEWIS** is the creator of senior sleuth, Fred Vickery, a 70-something retiree in Cutler, Colorado, introduced in *No Place for Secrets* (1995), and scheduled to return in *No Place Like Home* (1996).

Fred Vickery . . . 70-something retiree in Cutler, Colorado
❑ ❑ 1 - No Place for Secrets (1995)
❑ ❑ 2 - No Place Like Home (1996)

■ **Elizabeth LININGTON** was Barbara Elizabeth Linington (1921-1988), whose prolific writing career produced mysteries, historical novels and romantic suspense. Because she wrote so many police procedurals, she was often called the "Queen of the Procedurals." For more than 20 years she completed an average of three books a year for a lifetime total of 88 novels. When she launched her Sgt. Maddox series as Elizabeth Linington, it was her fourth police series in as many years. She led with the Luis Mendoza series (her longest and best known) in 1960, followed by two series she wrote as Lesley Egan (the Jesse Falkenstein and Vic Varallo series in 1961 and 1962) and then the Ivor Maddox series beginning in 1964. Sgt. Ivor Maddox of the Wilcox Street station in Hollywood comes with a made-for-TV supporting cast—one cop who always falls for the wrong girl, one serious and sarcastic one, a philosopher cop, a friendly one, a grandmotherly one, and the young, attractive and competent woman officer (Sue Carstairs) that the sergeant later marries. Linington maintained that she always tried to keep her police techniques authentic and she often based her books on real crime cases while making sure they stayed interesting. Linington also wrote as Anne Blaisdell, Lesley Egan, Egan O'Neill and Dell Shannon.

Sergeant Ivor Maddox . . . book collecting mystery addict cop in Hollywood, California
❑ ❑ 1 - Greenmask! (1964)
❑ ❑ 2 - No Evil Angel (1964)
❑ ❑ 3 - Date with Death (1966)
❑ ❑ 4 - Something Wrong (1967)
❑ ❑ 5 - Policeman's Lot (1968)
❑ ❑ 6 - Practice to Deceive (1971)
❑ ❑ 7 - Crime by Chance (1973)
❑ ❑ 8 - Perchance of Death (1977)
❑ ❑ 9 - No Villian Need Be (1979)
❑ ❑ 10 - Consequence of Crime (1980)
❑ ❑ 11 - Skeletons in the Closet (1982)
❑ ❑ 12 - Felony Report (1984)
❑ ❑ 13 - Strange Felony (1986)

■ **Gillian LINSCOTT** is a former Parliamentary reporter for the BBC and creator of two mystery series, including her ongoing Edwardian novels featuring Nell Bray, radical suffragette, follower of Emmeline Pankhurst and member of the Women's Social and Political Union. Nell first deals with murder in the high-fashion resort town of Biarritz in *Sister Beneath the Sheet* (1991) and then moves into a World War I military hospital for *Hanging on the Wire* (1992). In her latest adventure, *Crown Witness* (1995), Nell is recruited to watch for trouble during a procession of suffragettes and their sympathizers to honor the upcoming coronation of King George V. Her earlier series features Birdie Linnet, an ex-cop working as a fitness trainer, involved with a much younger woman who happens to be a travel agent.

On holiday in France, Birdie finds himself the prime suspect in the murder of his ex-wife's lover. Linscott says Birdie is remarkable chiefly for getting the point later than anybody else on the page. He's well-meaning but none too intelligent and frequently gets hit on the head. Linscott is also the author of a historical mystery set in Africa, *Murder, I Presume*.

Birdie Linnet . . . ex-cop fitness trainer in England
- ❏ ❏ 1 - A Healthy Body (1984)
- ❏ ❏ 2 - Murder Makes Tracks (1985)
- ❏ ❏ 3 - A Whiff of Sulphur (1987)

Nell Bray . . . British suffragette
- ❏ ❏ 1 - Sister Beneath the Sheet (1991)
- ❏ ❏ 2 - Hanging on the Wire (1992)
- ❏ ❏ 3 - Stage Fright (1993)
- ❏ ❏ 4 - An Easy Day for a Lady (1994) [Britain–Widow's Peak]
- ❏ ❏ 5 - Crown Witness (1995)

■ **Nancy LIVINGSTON** (1935-1995) was the creator of a delightful series featuring retired English tax inspector G. D. H. Pringle and his lady friend Mavis Bignell, first appearing in *The Trouble at Aquitaine* (1985), which won the Crime Writers Association Poisoned Chalice Award. Book #4 in the series, *Death in a Distant Land*, won the Punch Prize for the funniest British crime novel of 1988 and Book of the Year from the London *Sunday Times*. Livingston worked as an actress, flight attendant and television production assistant before becoming a writer. In addition to her mysteries, she wrote four historical novels and her radio plays have been broadcast in both the United States and Britain.

G. D. H. Pringle . . . retired tax inspector in England
- ❏ ❏ 1 - The Trouble at Aquitaine (1985)
- ❏ ❏ 2 - Fatality at Bath & Wells (1986)
- ❏ ❏ 3 - Incident at Parga (1987)
- ❏ ❏ 4 - Death in a Distant Land (1988)
- ❏ ❏ 5 - Death in Close-Up (1989)
- ❏ ❏ 6 - Mayhem in Parva (1990)
- ❏ ❏ 7 - Unwilling to Vegas (1991)
- ❏ ❏ 8 - Quiet Murder (1992)

■ **Frances & Richard LOCKRIDGE**, beginning in the 1940s, produced dozens of rollicking mysteries in books, movies and a successful TV series. Their best-known creation (still in print more than 50 years later) is the popular series featuring Pam and Jerry North, who debut in *The Norths Meet Murder* (1940). Nearly all the Lockridge novels are part of a vast network of inter-connected series where numerous characters pop in and out of each other's novels. Inspector Merton Heimrich of the New York State Police, first introduced as a character in the North series, moved out on his own in 1947 for a run that lasted 22 books. Police officers Bill Weigand and Nathan Shapiro also appear with the Norths and later in several books of their own. Born in St. Joseph and educated at the University of Missouri, Richard Lockridge (1898-1982) was a Kansas City newspaper reporter when he married Frances (1896-1963), a reporter and music critic for the Kansas City *Post*. After their move to New York, he wrote for the *New York Sun* and the *New Yorker* before they launched the Norths with her story line, his characters and his text. After her death in 1963, Richard wrote only two more Mr. and Mrs. North titles, although he continued with nonseries mysteries and several suspense novels. In 1965 he married New York freelance writer Hildegarde Dolson who created a mystery series of her own during the 1970s.

Insp. Merton Heimrich . . . State Police Bureau of Criminal Investigation in New York

❑ ❑ 1 - Think of Death (1947)
❑ ❑ 2 - I Want to Go Home (1948)
❑ ❑ 3 - Spin Your Web, Lady! (1949)
❑ ❑ 4 - Foggy, Foggy Death (1950)
❑ ❑ 5 - A Client Is Cancelled (1951)
❑ ❑ 6 - Death by Association (1952)
❑ ❑ 7 - Stand up and Die (1952)
❑ ❑ 8 - Death and the Gentle Bull (1954)
❑ ❑ 9 - Burnt Offering (1955)
❑ ❑ 10 - Let Dead Enough Alone (1956)
❑ ❑ 11 - Practice to Deceive (1957)
❑ ❑ 12 - Accent on Murder (1958)
❑ ❑ 13 - Show Red for Danger (1960)
❑ ❑ 14 - With One Stone (1961)
❑ ❑ 15 - First Come, First Kill (1962)
❑ ❑ 16 - The Distant Clue (1963)
❑ ❑ 17 - Murder Can't Wait (1964)
❑ ❑ 18 - Murder Roundabout (1966)
❑ ❑ 19 - With Option to Die (1967)
❑ ❑ 20 - A Risky Way to Kill (1969)
❑ ❑ 21 - Inspector's Holiday (1971)
❑ ❑ 22 - Not I, Said the Sparrow (1973)
❑ ❑ 23 - Dead Run (1976)
❑ ❑ 24 - The Tenth Life (1977)

Pam & Jerry North . . . New York City book publisher & wife

❑ ❑ 1 - The Norths Meet Murder (1940)
❑ ❑ 2 - Murder Out of Turn (1941)
❑ ❑ 3 - A Pinch of Poison (1941)
❑ ❑ 4 - Death on the Aisle (1942)
❑ ❑ 5 - Hanged for a Sheep (1942)
❑ ❑ 6 - Death Takes a Bow (1943)
❑ ❑ 7 - Killing the Goose (1944)
❑ ❑ 8 - Payoff for the Banker (1945)
❑ ❑ 9 - Death of a Tall Man (1946)
❑ ❑ 10 - Murder Within Murder (1946)
❑ ❑ 11 - Untidy Murder (1947)
❑ ❑ 12 - Murder Is Served (1948)
❑ ❑ 13 - The Dishonest Murder (1949)
❑ ❑ 14 - Murder in a Hurry (1950)
❑ ❑ 15 - Murder Comes First (1951)
❑ ❑ 16 - Dead as a Dinosaur (1952)
❑ ❑ 17 - Death Has a Small Voice (1953)
❑ ❑ 18 - Curtain for a Jester (1953)
❑ ❑ 19 - A Key to Death (1954)
❑ ❑ 20 - Death of an Angel (1955)
❑ ❑ 21 - Voyage into Violence (1956)
❑ ❑ 22 - The Long Skeleton (1958)
❑ ❑ 23 - Murder Is Suggested (1959)
❑ ❑ 24 - The Judge Is Reversed (1960)
❑ ❑ 25 - Murder Has Its Points (1961)
❑ ❑ 26 - Murder by the Book (1963)

■ **Margaret LOGAN** is the author of a travel memoir, numerous travel articles and several nonseries mysteries, including *Deathampton Summer* (1988), *A Killing in Venture Capital* (1989) and *C.A.T. Caper* (1990), inspired by grading essays on English composition achievement tests. She recently introduced amateur sleuth and Boston interior decorator Olivia Chapman in the 1994 series debut *The End of an Altruist*. Logan was born in China, where all four of her grandparents were missionaries and her parents worked for the missions there. A graduate of the University of Richmond, she has an MA in creative writing from Boston University, and has taught travel writing at the Harvard Extension School. She currently makes her home in Southampton, New York, where she has learned that living with renovation is harder than writing about it.

  Olivia Chapman . . . interior decorator in Boston, Massachusetts
    ❑ ❑ 1 - The End of an Altruist (1994)
    ❑ ❑ 2 - Never Let a Stranger in Your House (1995)

■ **Mary LOGUE** is the creator of a new mystery series featuring Minneapolis journalist Laura Malloy, introduced in *Still Explosion* (1993).

  Laura Malloy . . . Minneapolis, Minnesota journalist
    ❑ ❑ 1 - Still Explosion (1993)

■ **Randye LORDEN**, born and raised in Chicago, has lived in New York for a number of years. Her short fiction has been published in *Ellery Queen Mystery Magazine* and *New Mystery*. The first installment of her new mystery series featuring Sydney Sloane, *Brotherly Love* (1993), was nominated for a Shamus award for best first P. I. novel.

  Sydney Sloane . . . New York City upper west side P. I.
    ❑ ❑ 1 - **Brotherly Love** (1993) *Shamus nominee* ☆
    ❑ ❑ 2 - Sister's Keeper (1994)

■ **M. K. LORENS** is Margaret Keilstrup Lorens of Fremont, Nebraska, creator of a mystery series featuring Shakespearean scholar Winston Marlowe Sherman. In addition to Sherman's college teaching, he writes mystery novels as a woman. The professor is also the pseudonymous Henrietta Slocum, whose series sleuth just happens to be a man named Winchester Hyde. The professor's lady-love is concert pianist Sarah Cromwell, whose younger brother David the actor lives with them—along with the professor's retired colleague Edward Merriman—in the family mansion. Sarah's, that is. Just keeping track of who's on first will keep your little grey cells busy.

  Winston Marlowe Sherman . . . Shakespeare professor & mystery writer in New York
    ❑ ❑ 1 - Sweet Narcissus (1990)
    ❑ ❑ 2 - Ropedancer's Fall (1990)
    ❑ ❑ 3 - Deception Island (1991)
    ❑ ❑ 4 - Dreamland (1992)
    ❑ ❑ 5 - Sorrowheart (1993)

■ **Sarah LOVETT** is the creator of a new forensic series featuring Sante Fe psychologist Dr. Sylvia Strange, introduced in *Dangerous Attachments* (1995). Published in seven countries simultaneously, this debut novel is under active development as a television movie. As a freelance paralegal and legal researcher, Lovett learned about the prison system first-hand working for the New Mexico Office of the Attorney General. With her degree in criminal justice, she is a member of the national law enforcement fraternity. She is also working towards a degree in criminology and attends conferences of the American Academy of Forensic Psychology. She is the author of 23 nonfiction science and travel titles for adults and children, including the Extremely Weird series for kids which had her raising tadpoles for *Extremely Weird Frogs*. She has danced professionally and managed a non-profit theater. Her less glamorous jobs include gas station attendant, motel maid, upholstery assistant and cocktail waitress. Raised in California, she now lives in passive solar adobe house in Sante Fe, New Mexico, with four-legged friends Big Mac and Little Lulu.

Dr. Sylvia Strange . . . forensic psychologist in Sante Fe, New Mexico
- ❏ ❏ 1 - Dangerous Attachments (1995)
- ❏ ❏ 2 - Acquired Motive (1996)

■ **Margaret LUCKE** is a native of Washington DC who currently lives near San Francisco where she works as a journalist, editor and business writer. Her first mystery featuring San Francisco private eye Jessica Randolph, *A Relative Stranger* (1991), was nominated for an Anthony award for best first novel.

Jessica Randolph . . . artist working as a P. I. in San Francisco, California
- ❏ ❏ 1 - **A Relative Stranger** (1991) *Anthony nominee* ☆
- ❏ ❏ 2 - Bridge to Nowhere (1996)

■ **Nan & Ivan LYONS** are authors of the comedy classic *Someone is Killing the Great Chefs of Europe*, featuring chef Natasha O'Brien. The 1978 film starred Jacqueline Bisset as chef Natasha O'Brien and Robert Morley as one of the unluckier chefs.

Natasha O'Brien & Millie Ogden . . . pair of culinary artists
- ❏ ❏ 1 - Someone Is Killing the Great Chefs of Europe (1976)
- ❏ ❏ 2 - Someone Is Killing the Great Chefs of America (1993)

■ **T. J. MACGREGOR** is Trish Janeshutz MacGregor, creator of the action-packed south Florida P. I. series starring Quin St. James and Mike McCleary, owners of the husband-and-wife investigations firm which they founded. Following their Shamus-nominated introduction in *Dark Fields* (1986), Quin and Mike have now appeared in a total of ten novels, most recently, *Mistress of the Bones* (1995). As Trish Janeshutz, MacGregor has published several nonseries suspense thrillers and as Alison Drake she writes the Aline Scott series and an occasional horror novel. She lives in Florida.

Quin St. James & Mike McCleary . . . south Florida P. I. & cop
- ❏ ❏ 1 - **Dark Fields** (1986) *Shamus nominee* ☆
- ❏ ❏ 2 - Kill Flash (1987)
- ❏ ❏ 3 - Death Sweet (1988)
- ❏ ❏ 4 - On Ice (1989)
- ❏ ❏ 5 - Kin Dread (1990)
- ❏ ❏ 6 - Death Flats (1991)
- ❏ ❏ 7 - Spree (1992)
- ❏ ❏ 8 - Storm Surge (1993)
- ❏ ❏ 9 - Blue Pearl (1994)
- ❏ ❏ 10 - Mistress of the Bones (1995)

■ **Amanda MACKAY** is the creator of two mysteries featuring Hannah Land, a mildly bookish sleuth introduced in *Murder is Academic* (1976). Armed with her recent PhD in political science, the divorced Hannah leaves New York for Duke University, where her amateur sleuthing is complemented by the professional charm of Durham police lieutenant

Bobby Gene Jenkins. Hannah's situation in *Death on the Eno* (1981) gives new meaning to the term "armchair detective." After a suspicious boating accident, she spends much of book #2 in a body cast (to the waist). A native of Virginia, Mackay lives in North Carolina.

Hannah Land . . . divorced New York PhD at Duke University in Durham, North Carolina

    ❏ ❏ 1 - Murder Is Academic (1976)
    ❏ ❏ 2 - Death on the Eno (1981)

■ **Charlotte MACLEOD** is the creator of two series under her own name, both with charming New England settings. The Peter Shandy series, nominated for both an Edgar and an Agatha award, features the professor and his librarian wife Helen at an agricultural college in rural Massachusetts, beginning with *Rest You Merry* (1978). The Sarah Kelling series, featuring blue-blooded Sarah and her quirky Boston family, along with Sarah's investigator husband Max, opens with *The Family Vault* (1979). Under the name Alisa Craig, MacLeod writes two series set in Canada. She is also the author of a biography of Mary Roberts Rineheart. Born in Bath, New Brunswick, she has spent much of her life in the Boston area, but now lives in Maine.

Peter Shandy & Helen Marsh Shandy . . . Balaclava County, Massachusetts college botany professor & librarian wife

    ❏ ❏ 1 - Rest You Merry (1978)
    ❏ ❏ 2 - The Luck Runs Out (1979)
    ❏ ❏ 3 - Wrack and Rune (1982)
    ❏ ❏ 4 - Something the Cat Dragged In (1983)
    ❏ ❏ 5 - The Curse of the Giant Hogweed (1985)
    ❏ ❏ 6 - **The Corpse in Oozak's Pond** (1986) *Edgar nominee* ☆
    ❏ ❏ 7 - Vane Pursuit (1989)
    ❏ ❏ 8 - **An Owl Too Many** (1991) *Agatha nominee* ☆
    ❏ ❏ 9 - Something in the Water (1994)

Sarah Kelling & Max Bittersohn . . . Boston, Massachusetts investigative couple

    ❏ ❏ 1 - The Family Vault (1979)
    ❏ ❏ 2 - The Withdrawing Room (1980)
    ❏ ❏ 3 - The Palace Guard (1981)
    ❏ ❏ 4 - The Bilbao Looking Glass (1983)
    ❏ ❏ 5 - The Convivial Codfish (1984)
    ❏ ❏ 6 - The Plain Old Man (1985)
    ❏ ❏ 7 - The Silver Ghost (1987)
    ❏ ❏ 8 - The Recycled Citizen (1987)
    ❏ ❏ 9 - The Gladstone Bag (1989)
    ❏ ❏ 10 - The Resurrection Man (1992)
    ❏ ❏ 11 - The Odd Job (1995)

■ **Jaye MAIMAN** is the creator of a new lesbian mystery series featuring Robin Miller, travel and romance writer turned private eye in New York City. The series opens with *I Left My Heart* (1991), followed by *Crazy for Loving* (1992), winner of the Lambda Award for best lesbian mystery.

Robin Miller . . . travel & romance writer turned P. I. in New York

    ❏ ❏ 1 - I Left My Heart (1991)
    ❏ ❏ 2 - **Crazy for Loving** (1992) *Lambda winner* ★
    ❏ ❏ 3 - Under My Skin (1993)
    ❏ ❏ 4 - Someone to Watch (1995)

■ **Valerie S. MALMONT** is the creator of a new mystery series featuring ex-New York crime writer Tori Miracle, who gets involved with murder while visiting a small Pennsylvania town in *Death Pays the Rose Rent* (1994). The second title in this series is scheduled for publication in 1996 and Malmont is at work on the third. After working as a librarian in Washington, Virginia, Pennsylvania and Taiwan, Malmont now lives in rural Pennsylvania, much like her amateur sleuth. She grew up on Okinawa where her father reorganized the local police force after World War II and later lived in Laos and Taiwan. She has a degree in anthropology from the University of New Mexico and a master's in library science from the University of Washington.

    Tori Miracle . . . ex-NYC crime writer turned Pennsylvania novelist
      ❏ ❏ 1 - Death Pays the Rose Rent (1994)

■ **Mabel MANEY** is the creator of a series of lesbian parodies of Nancy Drew, Cherry Ames and most recently the Hardy Boys. Along with Cherry Aimless (the not-so-nice nurse) and the Hardly Boys (the ghost in the closet), Nancy Clue has been described as "whitegirl '50s meets the oh-so-queer '90s."

    Nancy Clue . . . gay-lesbian parody of Nancy Drew, Girl Sleuth in River Depths, Illinois
      ❏ ❏ 1 - The Case of the Not-So-Nice Nurse (1993)
      ❏ ❏ 2 - The Case of the Good-for-Nothing Girlfriend (1994)
      ❏ ❏ 3 - The Ghost in the Closet (1995)

■ **Jessica MANN** was educated at Cambridge where she studied archaeology and Anglo-Saxon. Her series detectives are both archaeologists, Professor Thea Crawford and her student Tamara Hoyland. Hoyland is later recruited to work as a Department E spy, using her archaeological work as a convenient cover. Mann, a respected critic for *British Book News* and the BBC, is also the author of the 1981 critical study of English women mystery authors, *Deadlier Than the Male*.

    Tamara Hoyland . . . British secret agent & archaeologist
      ❏ ❏ 1 - Funeral Sites (1982)
      ❏ ❏ 2 - No Man's Island (1983)
      ❏ ❏ 3 - Grave Goods (1984)
      ❏ ❏ 4 - A Kind of Healthy Grave (1986)
      ❏ ❏ 5 - Death Beyond the Nile (1988)
      ❏ ❏ 6 - Faith, Hope and Homicide (1991)

    Thea Crawford . . . archaeology professor in England
      ❏ ❏ 1 - The Only Security (1972) [U.S.–Troublecross]
      ❏ ❏ 2 - Captive Audience (1975)

■ **Jackie MANTHORNE** is the creator of a new lesbian mystery series featuring Harriett Hubley of Montreal, Canada, introduced in *Ghost Motel* (1994) and later in *Deadly Reunion* (1995) and *Last Resort* (1995). Manthorne lives in Toronto, Ontario.

    Harriett Hubley . . . intrepid lesbian sleuth in Montreal, Canada
      ❏ ❏ 1 - Ghost Motel (1994)
      ❏ ❏ 2 - Deadly Reunion (1995)
      ❏ ❏ 3 - Last Resort (1995)

■ **Linda MARIZ** is the author of a new mystery series featuring Laura Ireland, former Olympic volleyball star and graduate student in Bellingham, Washington. Mariz is currently writing a trilogy featuring a pair of sister sleuths—one a historian, the other a wrestler. Born in New Orleans and raised in Atlanta, Mariz is a nationally-ranked butterfly swimmer with degrees in history from the University of Missouri at Columbia and Western Washington University. She lives in Bellingham, Washington, also home to mystery writers Audrey Peterson and Jo Dereske.

    Laura Ireland . . .former Olympic volleyball star in Bellingham, Washington
- ❑ ❑ 1 - Body English (1992)
- ❑ ❑ 2 - Snake Dance (1992)

■ **Margaret MARON** is the creator of a dozen novels featuring two very different series characters—New York cop Sigrid Harald and North Carolina judge Deborah Knott. After winning an Agatha for best short story with "Deborah's Judgment," Maron swept the mystery awards the following year with her new series opener, *Bootlegger's Daughter* (1992), winner of the Agatha, Anthony, Edgar and Macavity awards for best novel. Book #2 in this Southern series earned the author Agatha and Anthony nominations, again for best novel. After a four-year absence, Maron's New York cop returns in *Fugitive Colors* (1995). Although 14 years and seven novels precede Sigrid's latest appearance, only one incredible year has passed in the life of the awkward duckling who has turned into a swan. Read *Fugitive Colors* and then return to *One Coffee With* (1981) and work your way back to the present. Three of the first five Sigrid titles have been re-released in paperback, with more to follow. A past president of Sisters in Crime, Maron lives on a farm outside Raleigh, North Carolina.

    Deborah Knott . . . North Carolina district judge
- ❑ ❑ 1 - **Bootlegger's Daughter** (1992) *Agatha, Anthony, Edgar & Macavity winner* ★ ★ ★
- ❑ ❑ 2 - **Southern Discomfort** (1993) *Agatha & Anthony nominee* ☆ ☆
- ❑ ❑ 3 - Shooting at Loons (1994)
- ❑ ❑ 4 - Up Jumps the Devil (1996)

    Sigrid Harald . . . New York City police lieutenant
- ❑ ❑ 1 - One Coffee With (1981)
- ❑ ❑ 2 - Death of a Butterfly (1984)
- ❑ ❑ 3 - Death in Blue Folders (1985)
- ❑ ❑ 4 - The Right Jack (1987)
- ❑ ❑ 5 - Baby Doll Games (1988)
- ❑ ❑ 6 - **Corpus Christmas** (1989) *Agatha & American Mystery Award nominee* ☆ ☆
- ❑ ❑ 7 - Past Imperfect (1991)
- ❑ ❑ 8 - Fugitive Colors (1995)

■ **Ngaio MARSH** (1895-1982), a native of New Zealand, was working as an interior decorator in London when she wrote her first of 32 mysteries featuring aristocratic police inspector, Roderick Alleyn, second son of a baronet, whose 18th adventure won a Silver Dagger. His social connections were especially useful in crime-solving among the upper classes during his 48-year detecting career. As founder of the British Commonwealth Theatre Company, Nagio (pronounced NYE-oh) Marsh's interest in theatre featured prominently in her mystery plots and settings. She was named to the Order of the British Empire in 1948 and Dame Commander in 1966, both honors for her theatre activities rather than mystery writing. In 1977 she was named Grand Master by the Mystery Writers of America, having twice been Edgar nominated.

Roderick Alleyn . . . inspector son of a baronet in London

- ❑ ❑ 1 - A Man Lay Dead (1934)
- ❑ ❑ 2 - Enter a Murderer (1935)
- ❑ ❑ 3 - The Nursing-Home Murder (1935)
- ❑ ❑ 4 - Death in Ecstasy (1936)
- ❑ ❑ 5 - Vintage Murder (1937)
- ❑ ❑ 6 - Artists in Crime (1938)
- ❑ ❑ 7 - Death in a White Tie (1938)
- ❑ ❑ 8 - Overture to Death (1939)
- ❑ ❑ 9 - Death at the Bar (1940)
- ❑ ❑ 10 - Death of a Peer (1940) [Britain–Surfeit of Lampreys]
- ❑ ❑ 11 - Death and the Dancing Footman (1941)
- ❑ ❑ 12 - Colour Scheme (1943)
- ❑ ❑ 13 - Died in the Wool (1945)
- ❑ ❑ 14 - Final Curtain (1947)
- ❑ ❑ 15 - Swing, Brother, Swing (1949) [U.S.–A Wreath for Rivera]
- ❑ ❑ 16 - Opening Night (1951) [U.S.–Night at the Vulcan]
- ❑ ❑ 17 - Spinsters in Jeopardy (1953) [APA–The Bride of Death]
- ❑ ❑ 18 - **Scales of Justice** (1955) *Silver Dagger* ★
- ❑ ❑ 19 - Death of a Fool (1956) [Britain–Off with His Head]
- ❑ ❑ 20 - Singing in the Shrouds (1958)
- ❑ ❑ 21 - False Scent (1959)
- ❑ ❑ 22 - Hand in Glove (1962)
- ❑ ❑ 23 - Dead Water (1963)
- ❑ ❑ 24 - **Killer Dolphin** (1966) [Britain–**Death at the Dolphin**] *Edgar nominee* ☆
- ❑ ❑ 25 - Clutch of Constables (1968)
- ❑ ❑ 26 - When in Rome (1970)
- ❑ ❑ 27 - **Tied up in Tinsel** (1972) *Edgar nominee* ☆
- ❑ ❑ 28 - Black as He's Painted (1974)
- ❑ ❑ 29 - Last Ditch (1977)
- ❑ ❑ 30 - Grave Mistake (1978)
- ❑ ❑ 31 - Photo-Finish (1980)
- ❑ ❑ 32 - Light Thickens (1982)

■ **Lee MARTIN** is the pseudonym of Ft. Worth police veteran Anne Wingate who holds a PhD in English and has authored mystery novels as Lee Martin, Anne Wingate and Martha G. Webb. The author's eight years of police experience, much of it with the major crime scene unit, give the Deb Ralston series a realistic punch. Ralston manages to juggle a trio of adopted children, each with a different ethnic heritage, and a husband who works full time while completing a graduate degree. Wingate lives in Salt Lake City, Utah.

Deb Ralston . . . Ft. Worth, Texas police detective & mother

- ❑ ❑ 1 - Too Sane a Murder (1984)
- ❑ ❑ 2 - A Conspiracy of Strangers (1986)
- ❑ ❑ 3 - Death Warmed Over (1988)
- ❑ ❑ 4 - Murder at the Blue Owl (1988)
- ❑ ❑ 5 - Hal's Own Murder Case (1989)
- ❑ ❑ 6 - Deficit Ending (1990)
- ❑ ❑ 7 - The Mensa Murders (1990)
- ❑ ❑ 8 - Hacker (1992)
- ❑ ❑ 9 - The Day That Dusty Died (1993)
- ❑ ❑ 10 - Inherited Murder (1994)
- ❑ ❑ 11 - Bird in a Cage (1995)

■ **Sarah Jill MASON** is perhaps best known as Hamilton Crane, current author of the Miss Seeton series originated by Heron Carvic, which Mason took over starting with book #9, *Miss Seeton Cracks the Case* (1991). Mason is the creator of another English village series featuring Detective Superintendent Trewley and his female partner Sergeant Stone, judo black belt and former medical student. Trewley and Stone first appear in *Murder in the Maze* (1993).

      D. S. Trewley & Sergeant Stone . . . Allshire, English village detective partners
- ❑ ❑ 1 - Murder in the Maze (1993)
- ❑ ❑ 2 - Frozen Stiff (1993)
- ❑ ❑ 3 - Corpse in the Kitchen (1994)
- ❑ ❑ 4 - Dying Breath (1994)

■ **Lia MATERA**, former teaching fellow at Stanford University Law School, is the author of two San Francisco attorney series. The daughter of aging-but-still-active Berkeley radicals, Willa Jansson is the star of a thrice-nominated series described by the *New York Times* as "among the most articulate and surely the wittiest of amateur sleuths." Willa starts the series as a law student and returns in *Last Chants* (1996) after a five-year absence. The brilliant Laura Di Palma is darker by comparison. The dragon defense attorney with a paid-for Mercedes and a high-profile life is on a collision course with one ex-husband and two former lovers making new demands.

      Laura Di Palma . . . San Francisco, California attorney
- ❑ ❑ 1 - The Smart Money (1988)
- ❑ ❑ 2 - The Good Fight (1990)
- ❑ ❑ 3 - A Hard Bargain (1992)
- ❑ ❑ 4 - Face Value (1994)
- ❑ ❑ 5 - Designer Crimes (1995)

      Willa Jansson . . . San Francisco, California law student turned attorney
- ❑ ❑ 1 - **Where Lawyers Fear to Tread (1986)** *Anthony nominee* ☆
- ❑ ❑ 2 - **A Radical Departure (1987)** *Edgar nominee* ☆
- ❑ ❑ 3 - **Hidden Agenda (1989)**
- ❑ ❑ 4 - **Prior Convictions (1991)** *Edgar nominee* ☆
- ❑ ❑ 5 - Last Chants (1996)

■ **Linda MATHER** is the creator of a new mystery series featuring professional astrologer Jo Hughes introduced in *Blood of an Aries* (1994).

      Jo Hughes . . . professional astrologer
- ❑ ❑ 1 - Blood of an Aries (1994)
- ❑ ❑ 2 - Beware Taurus (1994)
- ❑ ❑ 3 - Gemini Doublecross (1995)

■ **Francine MATHEWS** is the creator of a new mystery series featuring Nantucket police detective Meredith "Merry" Folger, introduced in *Death in the Off-Season* (1994). The daughter of the Nantucket police chief, Merry spent much of her first case proving to her father and herself that she has what it takes to solve a murder. She's more savvy and experienced in *Death in Rough Water* (1995) but this time one of her childhood friends is involved. A graduate of Princeton and Stanford universities, Mathews is the recipient of a Mellon Foundation Fellowship and has worked as a journalist and intelligence officer for the CIA. She currently lives in Evergreen, Colorado, where she writes full time.

Meredith "Merry" Folger . . . Nantucket, Massachusetts P. I.
- ❑ ❑ 1 - Death in the Off-Season (1994)
- ❑ ❑ 2 - Death in Rough Water (1995)

■ **Stefanie MATTESON**, of Montclair, New Jersey, is the creator of a mystery series starring Charlotte Graham, Oscar-winning actress of film and stage. Although these novels do not feature actual theatre settings, they are rich in background chosen for each story, starting with the chic New York spa in book #1. Charlotte's newest adventure (#7) is *Murder Among the Angels* (1996). Matteson graduated from Skidmore College and later attended graduate school at Boston University.

Charlotte Graham . . . New York City Oscar-winning actress
- ❑ ❑ 1 - Murder at the Spa (1990)
- ❑ ❑ 2 - Murder at Teatime (1991)
- ❑ ❑ 3 - Murder on the Cliff (1991)
- ❑ ❑ 4 - Murder on the Silk Road (1992)
- ❑ ❑ 5 - Murder at the Falls (1993)
- ❑ ❑ 6 - Murder on High (1994)
- ❑ ❑ 7 - Murder Among the Angels (1996)

■ **Alex MATTHEWS** is the creator of a new mystery series scheduled to debut with *Secret's Shadow* (1996), featuring thirty-something psychotherapist Cassidy McCabe from Oak Park, Illinois, who finds a calico cat and romance with a client's brother in the series opener. Like her protagonist, Matthews is a practicing psychotherapist with a home office in Oak Park, Illinois. But in Matthews' case, the therapy practice is a partnership with her husband.

Cassidy McCabe . . . psychotherapist in Oak Park, Illinois
- ❑ ❑ 1 - Secret's Shadow (1996)
- ❑ ❑ 2 - Satan's Silence (1997)

■ **A. E. MAXWELL** is a pseudonym of the wife-and-husband writing team of Ann and Evan Maxwell, creators of the Fiddler and Fiora series. Fiddler is independently wealthy, thanks to his Uncle Jake's ill-gotten gains and ex-wife Fiora's investment banking genius. He's also something of a knight-errant, a throwback to earlier times when a knight might travel widely in search of adventure, to show off his military skills or engage in deeds of chivalry. In Fiddler's case, those opportunities always find him. Fiddler's buddy Benny, the Ice Cream King of Saigon, provides electronics wizardry for many of their high action capers, beginning with *Just Another Day in Paradise* (1985). As A. E. Maxwell they also wrote a nonseries novel set in World War II New Mexico, *Steal the Sun* (1982). In addition to the Fiddler and Fiora series, Ann has written more than 35 other titles—science fiction and romantic suspense as Ann Maxwell and romance as Elizabeth Lowell, including *Tell Me No Lies* (1986). Evan is a former reporter for the *Los Angeles Times*. The Maxwells currently live in the San Juan Islands of Washington state.

Fiddler & Fiora Flynn (ex-husband & wife) . . . southern California detective & investment banker
- ❑ ❑ 1 - Just Another Day in Paradise (1985)
- ❑ ❑ 2 - The Frog and the Scorpion (1986)
- ❑ ❑ 3 - Gatsby's Vineyard (1987)
- ❑ ❑ 4 - Just Enough Light to Kill (1988)
- ❑ ❑ 5 - The Art of Survival (1989)
- ❑ ❑ 6 - Money Burns (1991)
- ❑ ❑ 7 - The King of Nothing (1992)
- ❑ ❑ 8 - Murder Hurts (1993)

■ **Melanie MCALLESTER** is the creator of a new police series featuring lesbian homicide detectives Elizabeth Mendoza and Ashley Johnson, introduced in *The Lessons* (1994).

    Elizabeth Mendoza & Ashley Johnson . . . lesbian homicide detectives
       ❏ ❏   1 -   The Lessons (1994)

■ **Taylor MCCAFFERTY** is Barbara Taylor McCafferty, an identical twin, born and raised in Louisville, Kentucky. Having set her sights on a writing career at the age of eight, she graduated magna cum laude with a degree in fine art from the University of Louisville and worked as an art director and advertising copywriter for a Louisville ad agency. She currently writes two mystery series set in Kentucky, one with a male private eye, the other a woman selling real estate. Haskell Blevins, the only P. I. in Pigeon Fork, Kentucky, first appears in *Pet Peeves* (1990) which reviewers called "wickedly delightful" and "downright hilarious." The real estate series, written under her pseudonym Tierney McClellan, features 40-something Schuyler Ridgway of Louisville, Kentucky, introduced in *Heir Condition* (1995). McCafferty and her attorney sister Beverly are collaborating on a novel that promises to be the first twin sister act in crime fiction.

    Haskell Blevins . . . Pigeon Fork, Kentucky small-town P. I.
       ❏ ❏   1 -   Pet Peeves (1990)
       ❏ ❏   2 -   Ruffled Feathers (1992)
       ❏ ❏   3 -   Bed Bugs (1992)
       ❏ ❏   4 -   Thin Skins (1994)
       ❏ ❏   5 -   Hanky Panky (1995)

■ **Tierney MCCLELLAN** is the pseudonym of Barbara Taylor McCafferty for her new series featuring Schuyler (pronounced SKY-ler) Ridgway, 40-something real estate agent in Louisville, Kentucky and divorced mother two 20-something sons. In her debut adventure, *Heir Condition* (1995), Schuyler is suspected of having an affair with a rich old man who names her in his will. Schuyler claims she barely knew him. What she does know is that selling houses in a dead market can be murder. Under her own name, McCafferty writes the Haskell Blevins series, featuring Pigeon Fork's only private eye, whose fifth case is *Hanky Panky* (1995). McCafferty lives on eleven wooded acres in Lebanon Junction, Kentucky, and is collaborating on a mystery with her attorney sister and identical twin, Beverly.

    Schuyler Ridgway . . . 40-something real estate agent in Louisville, Kentucky
       ❏ ❏   1 -   Heir Condition (1995)
       ❏ ❏   2 -   Closing Statement (1995)
       ❏ ❏   3 -   A Killing in Real Estate (1996)

■ **Lise MCCLENDON** is the creator of a new mystery series featuring gallery owner and art forgery expert Alix Thorssen introduced in *The Bluejay Shaman* (1994). In her own words, Alix is a "semi-prosperous art dealer, so-so kayaker, single girl, thirty-something." After her first adventure in Montana, Alix returns home to the Jackson, Wyoming art gallery she co-owns with the oh-so appealing Paolo Segundo in book #2. Both the gallery and her partnership are at a crossroads when her appraisal skills are sought in the fire investigation at a neighboring gallery where a local artist has died in the fire. *Publishers Weekly* credited *Painted Truth* (1995) with "lightening-fast adventure" and "enough false trails to stock a national park." A former broadcasting instructor and public relations hack (her words), McClendon once owned a video production business. She lives in Montana.

    Alix Thorssen . . . Jackson, Wyoming gallery owner & art forgery expert
       ❏ ❏   1 -   The Bluejay Shaman (1994)
       ❏ ❏   2 -   Painted Truth (1995)

■ **Helen MCCLOY** (1904-1993) was the author of 13 books featuring Dr. Basil Willing, perhaps the first American psychiatrist detective and no doubt the first to use psychiatry in detecting clues and analyzing the criminal mind. He came from Baltimore but had a Russian mother, which made it plausible for him to be fluent in several languages and study in Paris and Vienna after being at Johns Hopkins. McCloy was one of the founders of the Mystery Writers of America in 1945 and became its first woman president in 1950. After studying at the Sorbonne in the early 1920s, she later served as foreign art critic for several American publications in Europe, before returning to the U.S. in 1932. She wrote at least 15 nonseries novels, in addition to the mystery criticism which earned her an Edgar in 1953, shared with her husband, mystery writer Brett Halliday. Together they wrote a review column during the '50s and '60s in the Westport, Connecticut *Town Crier* and a short story which earned them an Edgar nomination in 1961—the same year they were divorced. Earlier they founded a publishing company and the literary agency Halliday and McCloy. She was named Grand Master by the Mystery Writers of America in 1989, one of only eight women to be so honored since Agatha Christie in 1954.

Dr. Basil Willing . . . psychiatrist & FBI consultant in New York

❑ ❑ 1 - Dance of Death (1938) [APA–Design for Dying]
❑ ❑ 2 - The Man in the Moonlight (1940)
❑ ❑ 3 - The Deadly Truth (1941)
❑ ❑ 4 - Who's Calling? (1942)
❑ ❑ 5 - Cue for Murder (1942)
❑ ❑ 6 - The Goblin Market (1943)
❑ ❑ 7 - The One That Got Away (1945)
❑ ❑ 8 - Through a Glass Darkly (1950)
❑ ❑ 9 - Alias Basil Willing (1951)
❑ ❑ 10 - The Long Body (1955)
❑ ❑ 11 - Two-thirds of a Ghost (1956)
❑ ❑ 12 - Mr. Splitfoot (1968)
❑ ❑ 13 - Burn This (1980)

■ **Vickie P. MCCONNELL** is the creator of a 1980s lesbian mystery series featuring Denver journalist Nyla Wade, introduced in *Mrs. Porter's Letter* (1982), followed by *The Burnton Widows* (1984) and *Double Daughter* (1988).

Nyla Wade . . . lesbian journalist in Denver, Colorado

❑ ❑ 1 - Mrs. Porter's Letter (1982)
❑ ❑ 2 - The Burnton Widows (1984)
❑ ❑ 3 - Double Daughter (1988)

■ **Sharyn MCCRUMB** has created popular characters in mystery, science fiction and folklore and is a recognized voice of Appalachian culture and mythology. In 1995 she became the first mystery writer to win an Anthony in two categories the same year, when she took home awards for best novel and best short story with *She Walks These Hills* (1994) and *Monster of Glamis* (1994). Her primary mystery character is Elizabeth MacPherson, forensic anthropologist and cousin of the disappearing bride in the series opener, *Sick of Shadows* (1984). Her award-winning science fiction satire, *Bimbos of the Death Sun* (1988), has college professor James Owens Mega exploring the zany world of sci-fi fandom as author Jay Omega. Her latest and now best-known series features Appalachian sheriff Spencer Arrowood first appearing in the charmed title, *If Ever I Return, Pretty Peggy-O* (1990), which won a Macavity award and an Anthony nomination. McCrumb says she gets her storytelling gift and her love of the Appalachian Mountains from her great-grandfathers who were circuit preachers in North Carolina 100 years ago.

Elizabeth MacPherson . . . forensic anthropologist in Southern U.S.
- ❏ ❏ 1 - Sick of Shadows (1984)
- ❏ ❏ 2 - Lovely in Her Bones (1985)
- ❏ ❏ 3 - Highland Laddie Gone (1986)
- ❏ ❏ 4 - **Paying the Piper** (1988) *Agatha & Anthony nominee* ☆ ☆
- ❏ ❏ 5 - The Windsor Knot (1990)
- ❏ ❏ 6 - Missing Susan (1991)
- ❏ ❏ 7 - MacPherson's Lament (1992)
- ❏ ❏ 8 - If I'd Killed Him When I Met Him (1995)

Dr. James Owens Mega . . . college professor & science-fiction author
- ❏ ❏ 1 - **Bimbos of the Death Sun** (1988) *Edgar winner* ★ *Anthony nominee* ☆
- ❏ ❏ 2 - Zombies of the Gene Pool (1992)

Spencer Arrowood . . . Appalachian sheriff
- ❏ ❏ 1 - **If Ever I Return, Pretty Peggy-O** (1990) *Macavity winner* ★ *Anthony nominee* ☆
- ❏ ❏ 2 - **The Hangman's Beautiful Daughter** (1992) *Agatha & Anthony nominee* ☆ ☆
- ❏ ❏ 3 - **She Walks These Hills** (1994) *Agatha, Anthony & Macavity winner* ★ ★ ★
- ❏ ❏ 4 - The Rosewood Casket (1996)

■ **Val MCDERMID** is the creator of two mystery series—private eye Kate Brannigan and journalist Lindsay Gordon. Kate is the junior partner in the Manchester firm of Mortensen and Brannigan, introduced in *Dead Beat* (1992). She and computer wizard Bill Mortensen handle surveillance and security systems and all aspects of computer fraud. Kate lives next door to rock music journalist Richard Barclay, also her lover, in a pair of cottages joined by a shared greenhouse. Lindsay Gordon, first appearing in *Report for Murder* (1987), is a self-described cynical socialist lesbian feminist. McDermid grew up in a Scottish mining community and later read English at Oxford. She worked as a journalist on local and national newspapers, ending with a three-year stint as Northern Bureau Chief of a national Sunday tabloid. During much of 1994, McDermid traveled throughout the United States interviewing working women private eyes for her work of nonfiction *A Suitable Job for a Woman*, published in Britain in 1995.

Kate Brannigan . . . Manchester, England P. I.
- ❏ ❏ 1 - Dead Beat (1992)
- ❏ ❏ 2 - Kick Back (1993)
- ❏ ❏ 3 - **Crack Down** (1994) *Anthony nominee* ☆
- ❏ ❏ 4 - Clean Break (1995)
- ❏ ❏ 5 - Blue Genes (1996)

Lindsay Gordon . . . lesbian journalist & socialist in Glasgow, Scotland
- ❏ ❏ 1 - Report for Murder (1987)
- ❏ ❏ 2 - Common Murder (1989)
- ❏ ❏ 3 - Final Option (1991)
- ❏ ❏ 4 - Union Jack (1993)

■ **Patricia MCFALL**, of Orange County, California, is a university writing instructor and active member of several mystery organizations. She has traveled extensively in Europe and Asia and lived for a year in Sapporo and Kyoto, Japan, the setting for her first novel *Night Butterfly*, named one of the ten best mysteries of 1992 by the *Los Angeles Times*.

Nora James . . . American linguistics grad student working in Japan
    ❑ ❑ 1 - Night Butterfly (1992)

■ **Patricia MCGERR** (1917-1985), a native of Nebraska, earned a BA from the University of Nebraska and an MA in journalism from Columbia by the age of 20. She spent six years in Washington DC as public relations director for the American Road Builders Association and later edited a construction industry magazine before going freelance in 1948. Her first novel *Pick Your Victim* (1946) was called a masterpiece by critic Jacques Barzun. Her only series detective, Selena Mead, widowed Washington magazine writer and counterspy, appears in numerous short stories, several novelettes and two novels. McGerr wrote eleven other nonseries novels between 1947 and 1975.

Selena Mead . . . British government agent
    ❑ ❑ 1 - Is There a Traitor in the House (1964)
    ❑ ❑ 2 - Legacy of Danger (1970)

■ **Janet MCGIFFIN** is the creator of a medical mystery series featuring Dr. Maxene St. Clair, emergency room physician at an inner city hospital in Milwaukee, Wisconsin. In her third appearance, *Elective Murder* (1995), Dr. St. Clair is appointed to interim office in the Wisconsin legislature and finds herself thinking about running for election after her latest case is closed. McGiffin knows Milwaukee well but currently resides in Tel Aviv, Israel.

Dr. Maxene St. Clair . . . Milwaukee, Wisconsin emergency room physician
    ❑ ❑ 1 - Emergency Murder (1992)
    ❑ ❑ 2 - Prescription for Death (1993)
    ❑ ❑ 3 - Elective Murder (1995)

■ **Jill MCGOWN** is the creator of a popular and highly-regarded police series featuring Chief Inspector Lloyd (whose first name is a series mystery) and his partner and lover, Inspector Judy Hill, first appearing in *A Perfect Match* (1983). McGown tells her stories from multiple points of view, frequently shifting back and forth between the detectives and the detected. McGown also writes nonseries puzzle and suspense novels under her own name and as Elizabeth Chaplin.

Chief Inspector Lloyd & Judy Hill . . . detective inspectors in East Anglia England
    ❑ ❑ 1 - A Perfect Match (1983)
    ❑ ❑ 2 - Redemption (1988) [U.S.–Murder at the Old Vicarage 1989]
    ❑ ❑ 3 - Death of a Dancer (1989) [U.S.–Gone to Her Death 1990]
    ❑ ❑ 4 - The Murders of Mrs. Austin & Mrs. Beale (1991)
    ❑ ❑ 5 - The Other Woman (1992)
    ❑ ❑ 6 - Murder Now and Then (1993)
    ❑ ❑ 7 - A Shred of Evidence (1995)

■ **Christine MCGUIRE** is a prosecutor in a northern California district attorney's office where she heads the Special Prosecutions Unit. She also teaches at the FBI academy in Quantico, Virginia. Her first book, *Perfect Victim*, was a nonfiction account of a sexual enslavement case and a #1 *New York Times* bestseller which sold over one million copies. McGuire's new mystery series features Kathryn Mackay, a northern California prosecuting attorney, introduced in *Until Proven Guilty* (1993).

Kathryn Mackay . . . northern California prosecuting attorney
    ❑ ❑ 1 - Until Proven Guilty (1993)
    ❑ ❑ 2 - Until Justice is Done (1994)

■ **Bridget MCKENNA** is the author of the Caley Burke P. I. series set in northern California, beginning with *Murder Beach* (1993) and followed by *Dead Ahead* (1994) which was nominated for a Shamus award. McKenna also writes science fiction and fantasy and was nominated for awards (Nebula and Hugo) in both genres in 1994. She is currently collaborating on a San Francisco mystery with Marti McKenna.

   Caley Burke . . . 30-something northern California P. I.
    ❏ ❏ 1 - Murder Beach (1993)
    ❏ ❏ 2 - **Dead Ahead** (1994) *Shamus nominee* ☆
    ❏ ❏ 3 - Caught Dead (1995)

■ **Victoria MCKERNAN** is the creator of amateur sleuth Chicago Nordejoong, a professional scuba diver in Florida. After the death of her Tobago island mother, Chicago grew up at sea on merchant ships with her Norwegian father. While working as a diving instructor and preparing her boat for a two-year sail, she crosses paths with a former lover—an island-hopping charter pilot named Alex who happens to be a former government agent. In addition to the flowers he brings as a peace offering, Alex arrives with a guinea pig for Lassie, Chicago's eight-foot boa constrictor. A scuba instructor herself, the author has dived around the world from the Coral Sea to the Blue Hole. When not diving she lives and writes in Washington DC.

   Chicago Nordejoong . . . professional scuba diver in Florida
    ❏ ❏ 1 - Osprey Reef (1990)
    ❏ ❏ 2 - Point Deception (1992)
    ❏ ❏ 3 - Crooked Island (1994)

■ **G. A. MCKEVETT** is the creator of a new mystery series featuring Savannah Reid, an ex-cop who now owns a California detective agency. Having been dropped from the force for a weight problem, Savannah launches a new career beginning with *Just Desserts* (1995).

   Savannah Reid . . . southern California ex-cop & owner of a new detective agency
    ❏ ❏ 1 - Just Desserts (1995)
    ❏ ❏ 2 - Bitter Sweets (1996)

■ **Claire MCNAB** is the creator of an Australian police series featuring Carol Ashton, a blond and beautiful Detective Inspector and single mother in Sydney who makes her first appearance in *Lessons in Murder* (1988), published again in 1990 as *Silver Moon*. The series is now in its seventh installment with *Double Bluff* (1995). McNab worked in television and spent twelve years as a teacher before she started writing comedy plays and textbooks for English, with the idea that these writing ventures would help support her fiction writing.

   Carol Ashton . . . Detective Inspector & single mother in Sydney Australia
    ❏ ❏ 1 - Lessons in Murder (1988) [APA–Silver Moon ('90)]
    ❏ ❏ 2 - Fatal Reunion (1989)
    ❏ ❏ 3 - Death Down Under (1990)
    ❏ ❏ 4 - Cop Out (1991)
    ❏ ❏ 5 - Dead Certain (1992) [APA–Off Key]
    ❏ ❏ 6 - Body Guard (1994)
    ❏ ❏ 7 - Double Bluff (1995)

■ **Karin MCQUILLAN** arrived in east Africa as a Peace Corps volunteer just three weeks out of college. Visiting remote villages by dugout canoe through croc-infested waters, she was often the first white woman natives had ever seen. She witnessed devil dancing and female circumcision, consulted a witch doctor and visited urban shantytowns and homes of the elite. On return trips to Kenya, her studies of elephants, lions and cheetahs have given her an intimate knowledge of both man and animal behavior. McQuillan and her series detective Jazz Jasper, independent safari leader in Kenya, are passionate about conservation issues and the land, the animals and the people of Africa. Jazz debuts in *Deadly Safari* (1990) and returns in *Elephants' Graveyard* (1993) and *The Cheetah Chase* (1994). McQuillan lives in Cambridge, Massachusetts.

Jazz Jasper . . . American safari guide in Kenya
- ❏ ❏ 1 - Deadly Safari (1990)
- ❏ ❏ 2 - Elephants' Graveyard (1993)
- ❏ ❏ 3 - The Cheetah Chase (1994)

■ **Susanna Hofmann MCSHEA** is the creator of New York City divorcee Mildred Bennett who retires to Raven's Wing, Connecticut where she joins forces with several of the locals in their debut appearance as the *Hometown Heroes* (1990).

Mildred Bennett & friends . . . a quartet of senior sleuths in Raven's Wing, Connecticut
- ❏ ❏ 1 - Hometown Heroes (1990)
- ❏ ❏ 2 - The Pumpkin Shell Wife (1992)
- ❏ ❏ 3 - Ladybug, Ladybug (1994)

■ **M. R. D. MEEK** is Margaret Reid Duncan Meek of Cornwall, England, who began writing detective fiction in 1980 after a varied life as a wife, mother and solicitor. Her honors Law Degree is from London University where she enrolled after the death of her first husband. Her legal background provides authentic detail for her series detective, solicitor Lennox Kemp, introduced in *With Flowers That Fell* (1983).

Lennox Kemp . . . London solicitor detective
- ❏ ❏ 1 - With Flowers That Fell (1983)
- ❏ ❏ 2 - Hang the Consequences (1984)
- ❏ ❏ 3 - The Split Second (1985)
- ❏ ❏ 4 - In Remembrance of Rose (1986)
- ❏ ❏ 5 - A Worm of Doubt (1987)
- ❏ ❏ 6 - A Mouthful of Sand (1988)
- ❏ ❏ 7 - A Loose Connection (1989)
- ❏ ❏ 8 - This Blessed Plot (1990)
- ❏ ❏ 9 - Touch & Go (1993)
- ❏ ❏ 10 - Postscript to Murder (1996)

■ **Leslie MEIER** is the creator of a new series featuring amateur sleuth Lucy Stone who lives in a small New England town. The series opener, *Mail Order Murder* (1993) is followed by *Tippy-Toe Murder* (1994).

Lucy Stone . . . small-town New England sleuth in Maine
- ❏ ❏ 1 - Mail-Order Murder (1993)
- ❏ ❏ 2 - Tippy-Toe Murder (1994)

■ **Jennie MELVILLE** is the pseudonym of Gwendoline Butler for her English mystery series featuring constable Charmian Daniels of the suburban Deerham Hills police department. Under the Melville name, Butler has also written 15 nonseries novels, including historical and romantic suspense.

Charmian Daniels . . . Deerham Hills, England police detective
- ❑ ❑ 1 - Come Home and Be Killed (1962)
- ❑ ❑ 2 - Burning Is a Substitute for Loving (1963)
- ❑ ❑ 3 - Murderer's Houses (1964)
- ❑ ❑ 4 - There Lies Your Love (1965)
- ❑ ❑ 5 - Nell Alone (1966)
- ❑ ❑ 6 - A Different Kind of Summer (1967)
- ❑ ❑ 7 - A New Kind of Killer (1970)
- ❑ ❑ 8 - Murder Has a Pretty Face (1981)
- ❑ ❑ 9 - Windsor Red (1988)
- ❑ ❑ 10 - Murder in the Garden (1989)
- ❑ ❑ 11 - Making Good Blood (1989)
- ❑ ❑ 12 - Witching Murder (1990)
- ❑ ❑ 13 - Dead Set (1993)
- ❑ ❑ 14 - Footsteps in the Blood (1993)
- ❑ ❑ 15 - Death in the Family (1994) [Britain–Baby Drop]
- ❑ ❑ 16 - The Morbid Kitchen (1995)
- ❑ ❑ 17 - The Woman Who Was Not There (1996)

■ **D. R. MEREDITH** is Doris Meredith, a former librarian and bookseller, now better known as the creator of two continuing series set in the Texas Panhandle. The first features honest and courageous Sheriff Charles Matthews of fictional Crawford County, Texas. The second is set in the real Texas town of Canadian with its lovely Victorian homes, brick streets and giant cottonwood trees. This is the venue of John Lloyd Branson, wise and good defense attorney, and his smart and lovely assistant, Lydia Fairchild, a law student from Southern Methodist University in Dallas. She calls him John Lloyd and he calls her Miss Fairchild as they struggle to keep their personal attraction under wraps. A resident of Amarillo, Meredith has been a junior high school English teacher and a bookkeeper.

Charles Matthews . . . west Texas sheriff
- ❑ ❑ 1 - The Sheriff & the Panhandle Murders (1984)
- ❑ ❑ 2 - The Sheriff & the Branding Iron Murders (1985)
- ❑ ❑ 3 - The Sheriff & the Folsom Man Murders (1987)
- ❑ ❑ 4 - The Sheriff & the Pheasant Hunt Murders (1993)
- ❑ ❑ 5 - The Homefront Murders (1995)

John Lloyd Branson & Lydia Fairchild . . . Canadian, Texas defense attorney & assistant
- ❑ ❑ 1 - **Murder by Impulse** (1988) *Anthony nominee* ☆
- ❑ ❑ 2 - **Murder by Deception** (1989) *Anthony nominee* ☆
- ❑ ❑ 3 - Murder by Masquerade (1990)
- ❑ ❑ 4 - Murder by Reference (1991)
- ❑ ❑ 5 - Murder by Sacrilege (1993)

■ **Annette MEYERS** is currently senior vice president of an executive search firm specializing in the brokerage industry and she was previously assistant to theatre producer and director Hal Prince. So it's only natural that her Smith & Wetzon series has one foot on Wall Street and the other on Broadway. Former dancer Leslie Wetzon and her pretentious partner Xenia Smith make their first appearance in *The Big Killing* (1989). In *These Bones Were Made for Dancin'* (1995), Leslie and her best friend Carlos co-produce and dance in two benefit performances of a show they did together 18 years earlier. Meyers is working on a psychological novel titled *Tracing Colors* and with her husband Martin also writes a 17th century historical series as Maan Meyers. A resident of New York City, she serves as secretary of Sisters in Crime International.

Xenia Smith & Leslie Wetzon . . . Wall Street headhunters
  ❑ ❑ 1 - The Big Killing (1989)
  ❑ ❑ 2 - Tender Death (1990)
  ❑ ❑ 3 - The Deadliest Option (1991)
  ❑ ❑ 4 - Blood on the Street (1992)
  ❑ ❑ 5 - Murder: The Musical (1993)
  ❑ ❑ 6 - These Bones Were Made for Dancin' (1995)
  ❑ ❑ 7 - The Groaning Board (1997)

■ **Maan MEYERS** is the shared pseudonym of MArtin and ANnette Meyers for their New Amsterdam historical series featuring the Tonnemans, who first appear in *The Dutchman* (1992). Author of five books in the Patrick Hardy detective series, Martin is an actor who novelized the Cher movie *Suspect* and wrote the television song lyrics for *Captain Kangaroo*. Annette is senior vice president of an executive search firm specializing in Wall Street placements and writes the Smith and Wetzon series starring two women who run their own placement firm.

The Tonnemans . . . New Amsterdam historical series (1664-1808) in New York
  ❑ ❑ 1 - The Dutchman (1992)
  ❑ ❑ 2 - The Kingsbridge Plot (1993)
  ❑ ❑ 3 - The High Constable (1994)
  ❑ ❑ 4 - The Dutchman's Dilemma (1995)

■ **Barbara MICHAELS** is one of the pseudonyms of Dr. Barbara Mertz, who trained as an archaeologist and holds a PhD from the University of Chicago's Oriental Institute. As Dr. Mertz she is the author of two popular nonfiction books on ancient Egypt. Under her two pseudonyms she has published more than 50 novels of mystery and suspense, including three series written as Elizabeth Peters. These include the Amelia Peabody series featuring a Victorian Egyptologist, the Vicky Bliss series starring a sexy art historian and the Jacqueline Kirby series with a librarian turned romance writer. As Barbara Michaels she writes bestselling suspense novels, often with historical and supernatural aspects. A recent Michaels novel, *Stitches in Time* (1995), is the third in a trilogy featuring the historic Georgetown house which made its first fictional appearance in *Ammie, Come Home* (1968) more than 25 years ago.

Georgetown house . . . historic home in Washington DC
  ❑ ❑ 1 - Ammie, Come Home (1968)
  ❑ ❑ 2 - Shattered Silk (1986)
  ❑ ❑ 3 - Stitches in Time (1995)

■ **Penny MICKELBURY** is a former Washington DC reporter who has chased stories in print, radio and television in New York, Illinois and California. She is back in Washington where she teaches and writes historical fiction and short stories, in addition to her lesbian mystery series starring Gianna Maglione and Mimi Patterson. Lt. Maglione is head of Washington's Hate Crimes Unit. Her lover, Mimi Patterson, is a black investigative reporter whose work often puts them in conflict.

Gianna Maglione & Mimi Patterson . . . lesbian police lieutenant & reporter in Washington DC
  ❑ ❑ 1 - Keeping Secrets (1994)
  ❑ ❑ 2 - Night Songs (1995)

■ **Margaret MILLAR** (1915-1994) might have been better known in her own right had she not been married to Kenneth Millar, who as Ross Macdonald was critically acclaimed for his Lew Archer series. Born in Kitchener, Ontario, she wrote her first mystery while confined to bed with a heart ailment at the age of 26, while her husband was a graduate student at the University of Michigan. Her earliest series detective was psychiatrist Paul Prye, whose police contact, Inspector Sands of the Toronto Police Department, was given his own series beginning in 1943. After her daughter's death in 1970, Millar stopped writing for six years, until introducing attorney Tom Aragon in 1976. One of her nonseries works, *A Beast in View*, won the Edgar for best novel in 1955. President of the Mystery Writers of America in 1957 and 1958, she was later named Grand Master in 1982, one of only eight women to be so honored since Agatha Christie in 1954.

Inspector Sands . . . police detective in Toronto, Canada
- ❑ ❑ 1 - Wall of Eyes (1943)
- ❑ ❑ 2 - The Iron Gates (1945)

Dr. Paul Prye . . . psychiatrist in Toronto, Canada
- ❑ ❑ 1 - The Invisible Worm (1941)
- ❑ ❑ 2 - The Weak-Eyed Bat (1942)
- ❑ ❑ 3 - The Devil Loves Me (1942)

Tom Aragon . . . California attorney
- ❑ ❑ 1 - Ask Me for Tomorrow (1976)
- ❑ ❑ 2 - The Murder of Miranda (1979)
- ❑ ❑ 3 - Mermaid (1982)

■ **Marlys MILLHISER**, of Boulder, Colorado, is the creator of a mystery series featuring Charlie Greene, Hollywood literary agent, single mother and reluctant sleuth, who first appears in *Murder at Moot Point* (1992), set on the Oregon coast. In *Death of the Office Witch* (1993) Charlie's back in Hollywood where she lives and works, but *Murder in a Hot Flash* (1995) takes her to the Canyonlands of Utah. The author's short stories and feature articles appear in numerous mystery publications. She has also written several nonseries novels, including *Willing Hostage* (1976), *The Mirror* (1978), *Nightmare Country* (1981) and *The Threshold* (1984).

Charlie Greene . . . Hollywood literary agent
- ❑ ❑ 1 - Murder at Moot Point (1992)
- ❑ ❑ 2 - Death of the Office Witch (1993)
- ❑ ❑ 3 - Murder in a Hot Flash (1995)

■ **Gladys MITCHELL** (1901-1983) was born in Cowley, Oxfordshire and earned a diploma in history at University College, London in 1926, after starting a teaching career that was to last 40 years. Her 66-book series features psychologist Beatrice Adela Lestrange Bradley who runs a clinic and acts as a consultant to the Home Office. The books are chock full of the author's two favorite subjects—Freudian psychology and the supernatural. And in the best tradition of the village witch, Mrs. Bradley mesmerizes children and animals who, in turn, adore her. The shriveled old woman is described as a "sinister pterodactyl with a Cheshire cat smile." Although she is an institution in Britain, only a few of these titles were published in the United States. Mitchell also wrote mystery and nonmystery novels under two male pseudonyms. As Stephen Hockaby she wrote five nonmystery novels and as Malcolm Torrie she produced a six-book series featuring Timothy Herring, director of the Society for the Preservation of Buildings of Historic Interest. An early member of the London Detection Club, along with Dorothy L. Sayers and Agatha Christie, Mitchell received a special award from the British Crime Writers Association in 1975 in honor of 50 outstanding books.

Beatrice Lestrange Bradley . . . London psychiatrist & consultant to Home Office

❑ ❑ 1 - Speedy Death (1929)
❑ ❑ 2 - The Mystery of a Butcher's Shop (1929)
❑ ❑ 3 - The Longer Bodies (1930)
❑ ❑ 4 - The Saltmarsh Murders (1932)
❑ ❑ 5 - Death at the Opera (1934) [Britain–Death in the Wet]
❑ ❑ 6 - The Devil at Saxon Wall (1935)
❑ ❑ 7 - Dead Men's Morris (1936)
❑ ❑ 8 - Come Away, Death (1937)
❑ ❑ 9 - St. Peter's Finger (1938)
❑ ❑ 10 - Printer's Error (1939)
❑ ❑ 11 - Brazen Tongue (1940)
❑ ❑ 12 - When Last I Died (1941)
❑ ❑ 13 - Hangman's Curfew (1941)
❑ ❑ 14 - Laurels are Poison (1942)
❑ ❑ 15 - The Worsted Viper (1943)
❑ ❑ 16 - Sunset Over Soho (1943)
❑ ❑ 17 - The Rising of the Moon (1945)
❑ ❑ 18 - Here Comes a Chopper (1946)
❑ ❑ 19 - Death and the Maiden (1947)
❑ ❑ 20 - The Dancing Druids (1948)
❑ ❑ 21 - Tom Brown's Body (1949)
❑ ❑ 22 - Groaning Spinney (1950)
❑ ❑ 23 - The Devil's Elbow (1951)
❑ ❑ 24 - The Echoing Strangers (1952)
❑ ❑ 25 - Merlin's Furlong (1953)
❑ ❑ 26 - Faintly Speaking (1954)
❑ ❑ 27 - Watson's Choice (1955)
❑ ❑ 28 - Twelve Horses and the Hangman's Noose (1956)
❑ ❑ 29 - The Twenty-Third Man (1957)
❑ ❑ 30 - Spotted Hemlock (1958)
❑ ❑ 31 - The Man Who Grew Tomatoes (1959)
❑ ❑ 32 - Say It with Flowers (1960)
❑ ❑ 33 - Nodding Canaries (1961)
❑ ❑ 34 - My Bones Will Keep (1962)
❑ ❑ 35 - Adders on the Heath (1963)
❑ ❑ 36 - Death of a Delft Blue (1964)
❑ ❑ 37 - Pageant of Murder (1965)
❑ ❑ 38 - Skeleton Island (1967)
❑ ❑ 39 - Three Quick and Five Dead (1968)
❑ ❑ 40 - Dance to Your Daddy (1969)
❑ ❑ 41 - Gory Dew (1970)
❑ ❑ 42 - Lament for Leto (1971)
❑ ❑ 43 - A Hearse in May-Day (1972)
❑ ❑ 44 - The Murder of Busy Lizzie (1973)
❑ ❑ 45 - Winking at the Brim (1974)
❑ ❑ 46 - A Javelin for Jonah (1974)
❑ ❑ 47 - My Father Sleeps (1974)
❑ ❑ 48 - Mingled with Venom (1974)
❑ ❑ 49 - Convent on Styx (1975)
❑ ❑ 50 - The Croaking Raven (1975)
❑ ❑ 51 - Late, Late in the Evening (1976)
❑ ❑ 52 - Fault in the Structure (1977)
❑ ❑ 53 - Noonday and Night (1977)

❏ ❏ 54 - Wraiths and Changelings (1978)
❏ ❏ 55 - Nest of Vipers (1979)
❏ ❏ 56 - The Mudflats of the Dead (1979)
❏ ❏ 57 - The Whispering Knights (1980)
❏ ❏ 58 - Uncoffin'd Clay (1980)
❏ ❏ 59 - The Death-Cap Dancers (1981)
❏ ❏ 60 - Lovers, Make Moan (1981)
❏ ❏ 61 - Death of a Burrowing Mole (1982)
❏ ❏ 62 - Here Lies Gloria Mundy (1982)
❏ ❏ 63 - Cold, Lone and Still (1983)
❏ ❏ 64 - The Greenstone Griffins (1983)
❏ ❏ 65 - The Crozier Pharaohs (1984)
❏ ❏ 66 - No Winding-Sheet (1984)

■ **Kay MITCHELL** gave herself six months to sell her first short story in 1985. When it sold in three she started work on her first novel, which she completed four years later. *A Lively Form of Death* (1990) introduces Malminster Chief Inspector John Morrissey, a married father of two teenagers, who has since appeared in four additional installments with his likable and well-drawn colleagues. Under the pseudonym Sarah Lacey, she writes a series featuring 25-year-old Yorkshire tax inspector Leah Hunter, introduced in *File Under: Deceased* (1992). Born in Wakefield, England, Mitchell earned an honors degree in English at Leeds University and later trained as a nurse. She has worked as a night sister and a theater sister and in a hospital casualty department. After becoming a midwife, she also worked as a health visitor. She lives in Wakefield where she writes full time.

John Morrissey . . . Chief Inspector in Malminster England
❏ ❏ 1 - A Lively Form of Death (1990)
❏ ❏ 2 - In Stony Places (1991)
❏ ❏ 3 - A Strange Desire (1994) [U.S.–Roots of Evil]
❏ ❏ 4 - A Portion for Foxes (1995)
❏ ❏ 5 - A Rage of Innocence (1996)

■ **Gwen MOFFAT** is an experienced mountain climber, youth hostel director, journalist, novelist, and the first woman ever to become a professional rock climbing guide. For 20 years she was a member of rescue teams in Britain and the Swiss Alps. And she has given her sleuth Melinda Pink many of her own proficiencies, including mountain climbing and novel-writing. Miss Pink is a middle-aged Utah Justice of the Peace with incipient arthritis and a weight problem, but she is definitely not cozy. Moffat freely admits to exploiting her personal interests in the books she writes—wildlife, good food, wine, organic living, prehistory, the supernatural and cats. In addition to her series featuring Miss Pink, she has authored several nonfiction titles, including *Two Star Red: A Book about R.A.F Mountain Rescue* (1964) and *Hard Road West: Alone on the California Trail* (1981), an account of her journey across America. She also wrote a historical novel, *The Buckskin Girl* (1982), based on that same adventure. Moffat lives in North Wales.

Melinda Pink . . . Utah writer & mountain climber
❏ ❏ 1 - Lady with a Cool Eye (1973)
❏ ❏ 2 - Miss Pink at the Edge of the World (1975)
❏ ❏ 3 - Over the Sea to Death (1976)
❏ ❏ 4 - A Short Time to Live (1976)
❏ ❏ 5 - Persons Unknown (1978)
❏ ❏ 6 - The Buckskin Girl (1982)
❏ ❏ 7 - Miss Pink's Mistake (1982)
❏ ❏ 8 - Die Like a Dog (1982)

   ❑ ❑ 9 - Last Chance Country (1983)
   ❑ ❑ 10 - Grizzly Trail (1984)
   ❑ ❑ 11 - Snare (1987)
   ❑ ❑ 12 - The Stone Hawk (1989)
   ❑ ❑ 13 - Rage (1990)
   ❑ ❑ 14 - Veronica's Sisters (1992)

■ **Miriam Grace MONFREDO** is the creator of Glynis Tryon, town librarian and fiercely independent woman of Seneca Falls, New York. Outcast from her Rochester family for her staunch refusal to marry, Glynis meets Elizabeth Cady Stanton at a historic 1848 meeting on women's rights. Their story, nominated for Agatha and Macavity awards, is the one told in *Seneca Falls Inheritance* (1992). By 1854 (in book #2), Glynis is involved with the Underground Railway and the town constable, Cullen Stuart, who wants to marry her. But Glynis and the deputy, Jacques Sundown (who is part Seneca Indian), are on their own in *North Star Conspiracy* (1993), preparing to violate the Fugitive Slave Law. Other continuing players include Jeremiah Merrycoyf, Esq., fine upstanding servant of the law and good friend to Glynis and the constable, hardware store owner Abraham Levy and Glynis's landlady Harriet Peartree. Director of a legal and historical research firm, Monfredo has been a newspaper columnist and feature writer with a specialty in women's history. Her mysteries are part of a thoughtfully planned body of work to tell the story of minority and women's rights. She holds degrees in history and library and information science and conducts writer's workshops for the New York State Council of the Arts.

  Glynis Tryon . . . librarian & suffragette in Seneca Falls, New York
   ❑ ❑ 1 - **Seneca Falls Inheritance** (1992) *Agatha & Macavity nominee* ☆ ☆
   ❑ ❑ 2 - North Star Conspiracy (1993)
   ❑ ❑ 3 - Blackwater Spirits (1995)
   ❑ ❑ 4 - Through a Gold Eagle (1996)

■ **Yvonne E. MONTGOMERY** is the creator of Denver stockbroker Finny Aletter whose boss is murdered in the first installment, *Scavengers* (1987). *Publisher's Weekly* called this series "Nancy Drew with an MBA and a sex life." With M. J. Adamson she writes historical romance (*Bridey's Mountain*) as Yvonne Adamson. Like Finny Aletter, Montgomery lives in Denver.

  Finny Aletter . . . Denver, Colorado stockbroker turned carpenter
   ❑ ❑ 1 - Scavengers (1987)
   ❑ ❑ 2 - Obstacle Course (1990)

■ **Susan MOODY** is a past chairman of the British Crime Writers Association and the creator of two mystery series with unusual women protagonists. The first features Penelope Wanawake, beautiful, black, six-foot daughter of Englishwoman Lady Helena Hurley and Dr. Benjamin Wanawake, African ambassador to the United Nations. Educated in England, France, Switzerland and the United States, Penny travels the globe as a freelance photographer. Her love interest is antiques dealer and jewel thief Barnaby Midas, who steals from the rich to aid her fund-raising efforts for world famine relief. Moody's newer series features British biology teacher turned bridge professional Cassandra Swann, who has now made four appearances in Britain. Moody, who spent ten years living in Tennessee during the 1960s, writes nonmysteries under the name Susannah James. She also penned the notorious romantic suspense novel inspired by Nescafé Gold Blend advertising in Britain—clearly the forerunner of American television commercials for Taster's Choice. A native of Oxford, she now lives in Bedford, England.

Cassandra Swann . . . British biology teacher turned bridge professional Cotswolds, England

      ❑ ❑ 1 - Death Takes a Hand (1993) [Britain–Takeout Double]
      ❑ ❑ 2 - Grand Slam (1994)
      ❑ ❑ 3 - King of Hearts (1995)
      ❑ ❑ 4 - Doubled in Spades (1996)

Penny Wanawake . . . 6-ft. photographer daughter of black UN diplomat in England

      ❑ ❑ 1 - Penny Black (1984)
      ❑ ❑ 2 - Penny Dreadful (1984)
      ❑ ❑ 3 - Penny Post (1985)
      ❑ ❑ 4 - Penny Royal (1986)
      ❑ ❑ 5 - Penny Wise (1988)
      ❑ ❑ 6 - Penny Pinching (1989)
      ❑ ❑ 7 - Penny Saving (1993)

■ **Barbara MOORE** is the creator of two wonderful mysteries featuring Dr. Gordon Christy, a New Mexico veterinarian introduced in *The Doberman Wore Black* (1983). Along with a chameleon and a couple of cockatoos, Christy is on his way to Vail, Colorado, to babysit the practice of a fellow vet when he is run off the road by a black MG. Next to the driver sits a grinning Doberman named Gala, who later joins forces with the doc. Lots of interesting animal lore deftly woven into the mystery.

    Dr. Gordon Christy . . . veterinarian in New Mexico

      ❑ ❑ 1 - The Doberman Wore Black (1983)
      ❑ ❑ 2 - The Wolf Whispered Death (1986)

■ **Mary MORELL** is the creator of the first Hispanic lesbian mystery series which stars Lucia Ramos, a San Antonio homicide detective. Lucy is introduced in *Final Session* (1991), winner of the 1990 lesbian fiction contest sponsored by Spinsters Ink. She returns in *Final Rest* (1993) and travels to Alabama to help a friend. After several decades in Texas, the author now lives in New Mexico where she is co-owner, along with her partner, of a Full Circle, a feminist bookstore in Albuquerque. She has worked as a counselor, an English teacher and a travel agency manager.

    Lucia Ramos . . . lesbian police detective in San Antonio, Texas

      ❑ ❑ 1 - Final Session (1991)
      ❑ ❑ 2 - Final Rest (1993)

■ **Kate MORGAN** is the pseudonym of Ann Hamilton Whitman for her Dewey James series featuring a 60-something small-town librarian who is also the widow of a police chief. The series opens with *A Slay at the Races* (1990). Dewey's hometown knows her as slightly eccentric and given to quoting often from the literary classics.

    Dewey James . . . 60-something small-town librarian in New York

      ❑ ❑ 1 - A Slay at the Races (1990)
      ❑ ❑ 2 - Murder Most Fowl (1991)
      ❑ ❑ 3 - Home Sweet Homicide (1992)
      ❑ ❑ 4 - Mystery Loves Company (1992)
      ❑ ❑ 5 - Days of Crime and Roses (1992)
      ❑ ❑ 6 - Wanted Dude or Alive (1994)

■ **Anne MORICE** is the author name used by Felicity Anne Morice Worthington Shaw (1918-1989), creator of a 23-book series featuring English actress Theresa "Tessa" Crichton, introduced in *Death in the Grand Manor* (1970). As an actress, Tessa is a master of dramatic exaggeration and brilliant exit lines. Although sometimes caustic, she is always upbeat, confident and often wickedly funny. The supporting cast includes Tessa's cousin, play-wright Toby Crichton, Toby's daughter Ellen and detective inspector Robin Price who be-comes Tessa's husband in *Murder in Married Life* (1971). Although Tessa looks to her hus-band for professional expertise and support, it is cousin Toby who is always ready to join in her schemes. Eccentric but lovable, he is her playmate and sleuthing confidant. He's also a great dialogue partner as Tessa sorts through events and tries out solutions. While married to her film director husband, Morice also wrote several plays and four nonseries novels. Owing in part to her husband's work with UNESCO and the World Bank, she lived in Egypt, Kenya, Cyprus, Sudan, Tunisia, Uganda, India, France, Taiwan and the United States. Her first Tessa novel was written in Paris.

Tessa Crichton . . . English actress sleuth
- ❏ ❏ 1 - Death in the Grand Manor (1970)
- ❏ ❏ 2 - Murder in Married Life (1971)
- ❏ ❏ 3 - Death of a Gay Dog (1973)
- ❏ ❏ 4 - Murder on French Leave (1973)
- ❏ ❏ 5 - Death and the Dutiful Daughter (1974)
- ❏ ❏ 6 - Death of a Heavenly Twin (1974)
- ❏ ❏ 7 - Killing with Kindness (1975)
- ❏ ❏ 8 - Nursery Tea and Poison (1975)
- ❏ ❏ 9 - Death of a Wedding Guest (1976)
- ❏ ❏ 10 - Murder in Mimicry (1977)
- ❏ ❏ 11 - Scared to Death (1977)
- ❏ ❏ 12 - Murder by Proxy (1978)
- ❏ ❏ 13 - Murder in Outline (1979)
- ❏ ❏ 14 - Death in the Round (1980)
- ❏ ❏ 15 - The Men in Her Death (1981)
- ❏ ❏ 16 - Sleep of Death (1982)
- ❏ ❏ 17 - Hollow Vengeance (1982)
- ❏ ❏ 18 - Murder Post-Dated (1983)
- ❏ ❏ 19 - Getting Away with Murder (1984)
- ❏ ❏ 20 - Dead on Cue (1985)
- ❏ ❏ 21 - Publish and Be Killed (1986)
- ❏ ❏ 22 - Treble Exposure (1987)
- ❏ ❏ 23 - Fatal Charm (1988)

■ **B. J. MORISON** is Betty Jane Morison, creator of Elizabeth Lamb Worthington and the mystery series starring this pre-teenager in '70s coastal Maine. Only eight years old in *Champagne and a Gardener* (1982), Elizabeth ages to 13 by the time her fifth case rolls around in *The Martini Effect* (1992). These books are set in real time, but take place a decade earlier than they were written.

Elizabeth Lamb Worthington . . . pre-teenager in the 1970s in coastal, Maine
- ❏ ❏ 1 - Champagne and a Gardener (1982)
- ❏ ❏ 2 - Port and a Star Border (1984)
- ❏ ❏ 3 - Beer and Skittles (1985)
- ❏ ❏ 4 - The Voyage of the Chianti (1987)
- ❏ ❏ 5 - The Martini Effect (1992)

■ **Patricia MOYES** is the author of a long-running series featuring globe-trotting Scotland Yard Chief Superintendent Henry Tibbett and his wife Emmy, introduced in *Dead Men Don't Ski* (1959) where a corpse is discovered in a ski lift in the Italian Tirol. Another skiing adventure, *Season of Snows and Sins* (1971) was an Edgar award winner. The Tibbetts' travels reflect the author's varied residences—Switzerland, The Netherlands, Washington DC and the British Virgin Islands as well as her favorite sports—skiing and sailing. Born in Ireland and educated in England, Moyes launched her writing career with a World War II documentary script on radar. Following her war-time service in the Women's Auxiliary Air Force (background for book #6 *Johnny Underground*), she spent eight years as company secretary for Peter Ustinov Productions in London (background for book #5 *Falling Star*), followed by five years as assistant editor for *Vogue* magazine, also in London (background for book #4 *Murder a la Mode*). She has written at least one stage play, screenplay and radio play, in addition to the nonfiction title *How to Talk to Your Cat* (1978). Known to her friends as Penny Haszard, Moyes lives on Virgin Gorda in the Caribbean.

    Henry & Emmy Tibbett . . . Scotland Yard Inspector & wife

      ❑ ❑   1 - Dead Men Don't Ski (1959)
      ❑ ❑   2 - Down Among the Dead Men (1961)
      ❑ ❑   3 - Death on the Agenda (1962)
      ❑ ❑   4 - Murder a la Mode (1963)
      ❑ ❑   5 - Falling Star (1964)
      ❑ ❑   6 - Johnny Underground (1965)
      ❑ ❑   7 - Murder Fantastical (1967)
      ❑ ❑   8 - Death and the Dutch Uncle (1968)
      ❑ ❑   9 - **Many Deadly Returns** (1970) [Britain–**Who Saw Her Die?**]
                        Edgar nominee ☆
      ❑ ❑ 10 - **Season of Snows and Sins** (1971) *Edgar winner* ★
      ❑ ❑ 11 - The Curious Affair of the Third Dog (1973)
      ❑ ❑ 12 - Black Widower (1975)
      ❑ ❑ 13 - The Coconut Killings (1977)
      ❑ ❑ 14 - Who Is Simon Warwick? (1979)
      ❑ ❑ 15 - Angel Death (1980)
      ❑ ❑ 16 - A Six-Letter Word for Death (1983)
      ❑ ❑ 17 - Night Ferry to Death (1985)
      ❑ ❑ 18 - Black Girl, White Girl (1989)
      ❑ ❑ 19 - Twice in a Blue Moon (1993)

■ **Marcia MULLER** is widely credited as the first American author to write a detective series starring a woman private eye. In 1977 *Edwin of the Iron Shoes* launched the career of Sharon McCone, investigator for All Souls Legal Cooperative in San Francisco. After 14 books at All Souls, Sharon forms her own McCone Investigations and learns to fly (literally). In *Double* (1984) she teams up with Bill Pronzini's Nameless Detective to solve a murder at a San Diego convention of investigators. McCone narrates the odd-numbered chapters and Nameless the even ones, in a she-said-he-said routine that has more well-placed shots than a professional tennis match. Muller and Pronzini have also collaborated on numerous short story anthologies in addition to their wonderful 1986 reference work, *1001 Midnights: The Aficionado's Guide to Mystery and Detective Fiction*. Muller's other series characters were intended to make only three appearances—Elena Oliverez, Santa Barbara museum curator of Mexican arts; and Joanna Stark, Napa Valley international art investigator. As a result of her interest in building miniature houses and furniture, Muller has constructed built-to-scale models of all the rooms at All Souls, right down to the light over the kitchen sink which she wired herself. Photos of these miniatures were printed in the 1994 program book for Bouchercon 25 where Muller was the Author Guest of Honor. A Detroit native and University of Michigan graduate (BA in English, MA in journalism), Muller moved to the Bay area after college, where she has lived and worked since. In 1993 she was honored with a Life Achievement award by the Private Eye Writers of America.

Elena Oliverez . . . Mexican arts museum curator in Santa Barbara, California
- ❑ ❑   1   -   The Tree of Death (1983)
- ❑ ❑   2   -   The Legend of the Slain Soldiers (1985)
- ❑ ❑   3   -   Beyond the Grave (1986)

Joanna Stark . . . Napa Valley, California international art investigator
- ❑ ❑   1   -   The Cavalier in White (1986)
- ❑ ❑   2   -   There Hangs the Knife (1988)
- ❑ ❑   3   -   Dark Star (1989)

Sharon McCone . . . San Francisco legal investigator turned P. I.
- ❑ ❑   1   -   Edwin of the Iron Shoes (1977)
- ❑ ❑   2   -   Ask the Cards a Question (1982)
- ❑ ❑   3   -   The Cheshire Cat's Eye (1983)
- ❑ ❑   4   -   Games to Keep the Dark Away (1984)
- ❑ ❑   5   -   Leave a Message for Willie (1984)
- ❑ ❑   6   -   Double [with Bill Pronzini] (1984)
- ❑ ❑   7   -   There's Nothing To Be Afraid Of (1985)
- ❑ ❑   8   -   Eye of the Storm (1988)
- ❑ ❑   9   -   There's Something in a Sunday (1989)
- ❑ ❑ 10 -   **The Shape of Dread** (1989) *American Mystery Award winner* ★
  Shamus nominee ☆
- ❑ ❑ 11 -   Trophies and Dead Things (1990)
- ❑ ❑ 12 -   **Where Echoes Live** (1991) *Shamus nominee* ☆
- ❑ ❑ 13 -   Pennies on a Dead Woman's Eyes (1992)
- ❑ ❑ 14 -   **Wolf in the Shadows** (1993) *Anthony winner* ★
  Shamus & Edgar nominee ☆ ☆
- ❑ ❑ 15 -   Till the Butchers Cut Him Down (1994)
- ❑ ❑   -   The McCone Files [15 short stories] (1995)
- ❑ ❑ 16 -   A Wild and Lonely Place (1995)
- ❑ ❑ 17 -   The Broken Promise Land (1996)

■ **Donna Huston MURRAY** is the creator of a new mystery series featuring Ginger Struve Barnes, who, like the author, is a transplant from the other side of the Schuykill, married to the head of a small Main Line private school. There is no shortage of pretentiousness (fictionally speaking) on the Main Line—that string of upscale real estate to the west of Philadelphia. Ginger, her husband and the Bryn Derwyn Academy are introduced in *The Main Line is Murder* (1995), described by one reviewer as "Spenser as a housewife." Ginger's next adventure, *Final Arrangements* (1996), takes place against the backdrop of the Philadelphia Flower Show.

Ginger Struve Barnes . . . amateur sleuth in Philadelphia, Pennsylvania
- ❑ ❑   1   -   The Main Line Is Murder (1995)
- ❑ ❑   2   -   Final Arrangements (1996)

■ **Amy MYERS** is the creator of a Victorian mystery series featuring master chef Auguste Didier who is both British and French, first appearing in *Murder in a Pug's Parlor* (1987).

Auguste Didier . . . British-French Victorian master chef in England
- ❑ ❑   1   -   Murder in a Pug's Parlour (1987)
- ❑ ❑   2   -   Murder in the Limelight (1987)

❑ ❑ 3 - Murder at Plum's (1989)
❑ ❑ 4 - Murder at the Masque (1991)
❑ ❑ 5 - Murder Makes an Entree (1992)
❑ ❑ 6 - Murder Under the Kissing Bough (1992)
❑ ❑ 7 - Murder in the Smokehouse (1994)
❑ ❑ 8 - Murder at the Music Hall (1995)

■ **Tamar MYERS** is the creator of a new mystery series featuring Magdalena Yoder, owner and operator of a Mennonite inn in Pennsylvania, introduced in *Too Many Crooks Spoil the Broth* (1994). The daughter of Mennonite missionaries, Myers was born and raised in a remote region of the Belgian Congo (now Zaire). She wrote her first book at the age of ten after reading all the books her parents had brought to their rain forest post. A resident of South Carolina, she is the author of hundred of articles on topics of horticultural interest.

Magdalena Yoder . . . Mennonite inn owner & operator in Hernia, Pennsylvania
❑ ❑ 1 - Too Many Crooks Spoil the Broth (1994)
❑ ❑ 2 - Parsley, Sage, Rosemary and Crime (1995)
❑ ❑ 3 - No Use Dying Over Spilled Milk (1996)

■ **Magdalen NABB** is an Englishwoman who has lived in Florence since 1975, the setting for her mystery series featuring the very appealing Marshal Salvatore Guarnaccia who has now appeared in 10 installments since his series debut in *Death of an Englishmen* (1981). Nabb was originally a potter, but now paints exquisite portraits of the city of Florence and the people who live there. In addition to her Guarnaccia series she has written a novel, one play and three novels for juveniles featuring a young girl named Josie Smith.

Salvatore Guarnaccia . . . Italian police marshal in Florence
❑ ❑ 1 - Death of an Englishman (1981)
❑ ❑ 2 - Death of a Dutchman (1982)
❑ ❑ 3 - Death in Springtime (1983)
❑ ❑ 4 - Death in Autumn (1984)
❑ ❑ 5 - The Marshal and the Murderer (1987)
❑ ❑ 6 - The Marshal and the Madwoman (1988)
❑ ❑ 7 - The Marshal's Own Case (1990)
❑ ❑ 8 - The Marshal Makes His Report (1991)
❑ ❑ 9 - The Marshal at the Villa Torrini (1994)
❑ ❑ 10 - The Marshal and the Forgery (1995)

■ **Janet NEEL** is the pseudonym used by Janet Cohen for her series featuring John McLeish of Scotland Yard and civil servant Francesca Wilson, whose first adventure won the John Creasey first novel prize from the British Crime Writers Association. This series has lots of wonderful music background thanks to Francesca's four brothers, one of whom is a rock star. The author, like her female protagonist, was once an administrator in Britain's Department of Trade and Industry, but now works in London's financial district. As Janet Cohen she wrote a 1992 legal thriller, *The Highest Bidder*.

John McLeish & Francesca Wilson . . . detective inspector & civil servant in England
❑ ❑ 1 - **Death's Bright Angel** (1988) *Creasey winner* ★
❑ ❑ 2 - Death on Site (1989)
❑ ❑ 3 - Death of a Partner (1991)
❑ ❑ 4 - Death Among the Dons (1993)

■ **Barbara NEELY** is the creator of Blanche White, a middle-aged black domestic in North Carolina, whose first outing, *Blanche on the Lam* (1992), was awarded three mystery prizes for best first novel—the Agatha, Anthony and Macavity awards. Feisty, funny, feminist Blanche flees the courthouse after being sentenced to 30 days in jail for writing $42.50 worth of bad checks after four of her employers left town without paying Blanche's wages. She ends up at the summer house of a wealthy family keeping their own secrets—including a dead body. When she becomes a suspect, Blanche has no choice but to find the real killer. Neely's short fiction has been published in various anthologies. She lives in Jamaica Plain, Massachusetts.

> **Blanche White** . . . middle-aged black domestic in North Carolina
> ❑ ❑ 1 - **Blanche on the Lam** (1992) *Agatha, Anthony & Macavity winner* ★ ★ ★
> ❑ ❑ 2 - Blanche Among the Talented Tenth (1994)

■ **Sharan NEWMAN** is the creator of a historical series featuring novice and scholar Catherine LeVendeur in 12th century France. Catherine's first adventure, *Death Comes as Epiphany* (1993) won the Macavity and received Agatha and Anthony nominations for best first mystery. Herself a medievalist, Newman is completing a PhD in history at the University of California, Santa Barbara. A member of the Medieval Academy, she has also written an Arthurian trilogy from the point of view of Guinevere (*Guinevere, The Chessboard Queen,* and *Guinevere Evermore*), science fiction short stories and numerous academic papers.

> **Catherine LeVendeur** . . . novice & scholar in 12th century France
> ❑ ❑ 1 - **Death Comes as Epiphany** (1993) *Macavity winner* ★ *Agatha & Anthony nominee* ☆ ☆
> ❑ ❑ 2 - The Devil's Door (1994)
> ❑ ❑ 3 - The Wandering Arm (1995)

■ **Helen NIELSEN** is the creator of Chicago attorney Simon Drake who is transplanted to southern California during the legal mystery series which ran from 1951 to 1976. The first title, set in Chicago, was *Gold Coast Nocturne*, published in Britain as *Murder by Proxy*.

> **Simon Drake** . . . Chicago attorney transplanted to southern California in California
> ❑ ❑ 1 - Gold Coast Nocturne (1951) [Britain–Murder by Proxy]
> ❑ ❑ 2 - After Midnight (1966)
> ❑ ❑ 3 - A Killer in the Street (1967)
> ❑ ❑ 4 - Darkest Hour (1969)
> ❑ ❑ 5 - The Severed Key (1973)
> ❑ ❑ 6 - The Brink of Murder (1976)

■ **Suzanne NORTH** of Saskatoon, Saskatchewan, is the creator of a new mystery series featuring Phoebe Fairfax, TV video photographer from Calgary, Alberta, introduced in *Healthy, Wealthy and Dead* (1994). This series debut of the indomitable Phoebe was nominated for an Ellis award from the Crime Writers of Canada as best first mystery novel.

> **Phoebe Fairfax** . . . TV video photographer from Calgary, Canada
> ❑ ❑ 1 - **Healthy, Wealthy & Dead** (1994) *Ellis nominee* ☆

■ **Meg O'BRIEN** is the creator of a four-book series with smart-mouthed Jessica James, investigative reporter and recovering alcoholic from Rochester, New York, first appearing in *The Daphne Decisions* (1990). Jesse's sometimes lover is mobster Marcus Andrelli from the elite branch of the New York mob where everybody went to Harvard and drugs and prostitution are out. O'Brien once lived in Rochester, but is now a resident of Redondo Beach, California. She is the author of three recent suspense novels including *The Keeper* (1992), *Thin Ice* (1993), and *I'll Love You Till I Die* (1995). *Thin Ice* features two PhD sisters from Georgetown University—one a quiet scholar of mythology and comparative religion, the other a research biochemist. After Mary Clare's car plunges into the Potomac, Nicole takes her dead sister's place at a scientific conference, only to learn Mary Clare had gone to great lengths to conceal a recent discovery. And when Nicole stumbles onto the connection between a ruthless pharmaceutical conglomerate and a political powerhouse back in Washington, her life is in danger too.

Jessica James . . . Rochester, New York newspaper reporter
- ❏ ❏ 1 - The Daphne Decisions (1990)
- ❏ ❏ 2 - Salmon in the Soup (1990)
- ❏ ❏ 3 - Hare Today, Gone Tomorrow (1991)
- ❏ ❏ 4 - Eagles Die Too (1992)

■ **Maxine O'CALLAGHAN** is the author of a dozen novels of horror and dark suspense, romance and mystery. Her five titles in the Delilah West series feature an Orange County private eye introduced in *Death is Forever* (1980). No matter that Delilah got where she is the same way Margaret Chase Smith became the first woman United States senator or Katherine Graham editor and publisher of *The Washington Post*—her husband died and left her the business. Independent, realistic and stubborn as a mule (characteristics O'Callaghan says she shares), Delilah is sometimes cited as the first contemporary American woman private eye, based on her 1974 introduction in an *Alfred Hitchcock Mystery Magazine* short story titled *A Change of Clients*. O'Callaghan is currently writing a second series starring Dr. Anne Menlo, a Phoenix child psychologist, who will first appear in *Shadow of a Child* (1996). A native of Tennessee, O'Callaghan lives in Mission Viejo, California. Her nonmystery titles include *The Bogeyman* (1986), *Dark Visions* (1988), *Something's Calling Me Home* (1991), *Dark Time* (1992) and *Dangerous Charade* (1985), a romance written pseudonymously as Marissa Owens.

Dr. Anne Menlo . . . child psychologist in Phoenix, Arizona
- ❏ ❏ 1 - Shadow of a Child (1996)
- ❏ ❏ 2 - Ashes to Ashes (1997)

Delilah West . . . Orange County, California P. I.
- ❏ ❏ 1 - Death Is Forever (1980)
- ❏ ❏ 2 - Run from Nightmare (1981)
- ❏ ❏ 3 - Hit and Run (1989)
- ❏ ❏ 4 - Set-Up (1991)
- ❏ ❏ 5 - Trade-Off (1994)

■ **Carol O'CONNELL** is the creator of a new police series featuring Kathleen Mallory, NYPD cop raised by a police inspector and his wife after a youth of crime that lasted into her teens on the streets of Manhattan. Quirky, brilliant and beautiful, Mallory gives new meaning to the terms "borderline sociopath" and "lone-wolf investigation." One reviewer called her a "gun-packing Alice" in a "world of characters as clever and without conscience as she." The series opener, *Mallory's Oracle*, was nominated for both an Edgar and Anthony award for best first mystery of 1994.

Kathleen Mallory . . . NYPD cop
- ❏ ❏ 1 - **Mallory's Oracle** (1994) *Anthony & Edgar nominee* ☆ ☆
- ❏ ❏ 2 - The Man Who Cast Two Shadows (1995)
- ❏ ❏ 3 - Killing Critics (1996)

■ **Catherine O'CONNELL** is the creator of a new series featuring NYPD homicide detective Karen Levinson introduced in *Skins* (1993).

> **Karen Levinson** . . . NYPD homicide detective
> ❏ ❏ 1 - Skins (1993)

■ **Lillian O'DONNELL** is best known for Norah Mulcahaney, NYPD star of crime fiction's longest-running police series (approaching 25 years) starring a woman officer. The 28-year-old rookie makes her first appearance in *The Phone Calls* (1972) which was later used as the basis for a French film, *The Night Caller*, starring Jean Paul Belmando. Several of her continuing cast-mates—Jim Felix, Roy Brennan, Dr. Asa Osterman and the handsome Joseph Capretto whom she later married—are featured in two pre-Norah books—*Death of a Player* (1964) and *The Face of the Crime* (1968). O'Donnell wrote a three-book series featuring Mici (pronounced MIT-zi) Anhalt, a Hungarian-American (like O'Donnell) caseworker with the Crime Victim's Compensation Board, starting with *Aftershock* (1977). The Gwenn Ramadge series, O'Donnell's newest, opening with *A Wreath for the Bride* (1990), features a young woman P. I. some think reminiscent of Cordelia Gray. O'Donnell's pre-mystery-writing careers include her work as an actress, a dancer and the first woman stage manager in the history of the New York theater. After training at the American Academy of Dramatic Arts in New York, she appeared in the 1941 Broadway production of *Pal Joey* and two years later was named stage manager for *Private Lives*. During the '40s and early '50s she worked as a director for the Schubert Organization and performed in live television on numerous shows.

> **Gwenn Ramadge** . . . New York City P. I. for corporate investigations
> ❏ ❏ 1 - A Wreath for the Bride (1990)
> ❏ ❏ 2 - Used to Kill (1993)
> ❏ ❏ 3 - Raggedy Man (1995)

> **Mici Anhalt** . . . New York City criminal justice investigator
> ❏ ❏ 1 - Aftershock (1977)
> ❏ ❏ 2 - Falling Star (1979)
> ❏ ❏ 3 - Wicked Designs (1980)

> **Norah Mulcahaney** . . . NYPD detective
> ❏ ❏ 1 - The Phone Calls (1972)
> ❏ ❏ 2 - Don't Wear Your Wedding Ring (1973)
> ❏ ❏ 3 - Dial 557 R-A-P-E (1974)
> ❏ ❏ 4 - The Baby Merchants (1975)
> ❏ ❏ 5 - Leisure Dying (1976)
> ❏ ❏ 6 - No Business Being a Cop (1979)
> ❏ ❏ 7 - The Children's Zoo (1981)
> ❏ ❏ 8 - Cop Without a Shield (1983)
> ❏ ❏ 9 - Ladykiller (1984)
> ❏ ❏ 10 - Casual Affairs (1985)
> ❏ ❏ 11 - The Other Side of the Door (1987)
> ❏ ❏ 12 - **A Good Night to Kill** (1989) *American Mystery Award winner* ★
> ❏ ❏ 13 - A Private Crime (1991)
> ❏ ❏ 14 - Pushover (1992)
> ❏ ❏ 15 - Lockout (1994)

■ **Sister Carol Anne O'MARIE**, CSJ, of San Francisco, entered the convent right out of high school in 1951. O'Marie (pronounced Oh-MARY) taught Catholic school in Arizona and California for 20 years before becoming director of an Oakland walk-in shelter for homeless women. Her series character, Sister Mary Helen, is a 70-something San Francisco nun with a talent for running into murder.

Sister Mary Helen . . . San Francisco, California 70-something nun
- ❑ ❑ 1 - A Novena for Murder (1984)
- ❑ ❑ 2 - Advent of Dying (1986)
- ❑ ❑ 3 - The Missing Madonna (1988)
- ❑ ❑ 4 - Murder in Ordinary Time (1991)
- ❑ ❑ 5 - Murder Makes a Pilgrimmage (1993)
- ❑ ❑ 6 - Death Goes on Retreat (1995)

■ **Shannon OCORK** of New York City is the author of a three-book series from the early '80s featuring Theresa Tracy "T. T." Baldwin, a 20-something sports photographer for the daily newspaper *New York Graphic*. OCork is also the author of *Death of a Murder Maven* (1990) which features the demise of a bestselling mystery author, crushed by an avalanche of falling books at a Writers of Mystery convention. OCork is married to MWA Grand Master Hillary Waugh.

Theresa Tracy Baldwin . . . sports photographer for New York daily
- ❑ ❑ 1 - Sports Freak (1980)
- ❑ ❑ 2 - End of the Line (1981)
- ❑ ❑ 3 - Hell Bent for Heaven (1983)

■ **Lenore Glen OFFORD** (1905-1991) was the Mystery Book Critic at the *San Francisco Chronicle* from 1950 until 1982. Earlier she wrote two mystery series, each featuring a pair of Bay Area sleuths—Bill and Coco Hastings of San Francisco and Todd McKinnon and Georgine Wyeth of Berkeley. Born in Spokane, Washington, Offord was a graduate of Mills College and a resident of Berkeley.

Bill & Coco Hastings . . . San Francisco, California sleuthing pair
- ❑ ❑ 1 - Murder on Russian Hill (1938) [Britain–Murder Before Breakfast]
- ❑ ❑ 2 - Clues to Burn (1942)

Todd McKinnon & Georgine Wyeth . . . pulp writer & single working mother in Berkeley, California
- ❑ ❑ 1 - Skeleton Key (1943)
- ❑ ❑ 2 - The Glass Mask (1944)
- ❑ ❑ 3 - The Smiling Tiger (1949)
- ❑ ❑ 4 - Walking Shadow (1959)

■ **Susan OLEKSIW** (pronounced oh-LECK-see) is the creator of a Massachusetts police series featuring Mellingham chief Joe Silva introduced in *Murder in Mellingham* (1993). She is also editor of the *Reader's Guide to the Classic British Mystery*, which provides short synopses of the works of 121 authors up to 1985. Within the almost 600 pages of this ambitious work, she provides helpful information about the British class system and structure of the metropolitan and local police forces. Having read most of the 1,440 British mysteries cited in her work, Oleksiw started the book as guide for her husband's leisure reading. She holds a PhD in Sanskrit from the University of Pennsylvania and has lived and travelled extensively in India. She currently lives in the Boston area where she teaches literature and writing at various colleges.

Joe Silva . . . chief of police in Mellingham, Massachusetts
- ❑ ❑ 1 - Murder in Mellingham (1993)
- ❑ ❑ 2 - Double Take (1994)
- ❑ ❑ 3 - Family Album (1995)

■ **B. J. OLIPHANT** is one of the pseudonyms of Sheri S. Tepper, a popular science fiction author who writes mysteries under two different names. As B. J. Oliphant, Tepper writes a series featuring 50-something Washington DC career woman Shirley McClintock. In the Edgar-nominated series opener, *Dead in the Scrub* (1990), Shirley returns to Colorado to manage the family ranch after the death of her parents. As A. J. Orde, Tepper is the creator of Jason Lynx, Denver antiques dealer and compulsive puzzle-solver whose romantic inter-est is a Denver cop, making this series a charming reversal of the female amateur detective with a male-cop-as-love-interest. Tepper lives in Santa Fe, New Mexico.

Shirley McClintock . . . 50-something rancher in Colorado
 ❏ ❏ 1 - **Dead in the Scrub** (1990) *Edgar nominee* ☆
 ❏ ❏ 2 - The Unexpected Corpse (1990)
 ❏ ❏ 3 - Deservedly Dead (1992)
 ❏ ❏ 4 - Death and the Delinquent (1992)
 ❏ ❏ 5 - Death Served up Cold (1994)
 ❏ ❏ 6 - A Ceremonial Death (1996)

■ **Maria Antonia OLIVER**, born in Manacor, Majorca, Spain, is a leading Catalan writer who is also well known as a translator of English and American classics into her native language. Her first mystery featuring Catalan investigator Lonia Guiu was well received in Europe and North America.

Lonia Guiu . . . Catalan, Spain P. I.
 ❏ ❏ 1 - A Study in Lilac (1987)
 ❏ ❏ 2 - Antipodes (1989)

■ **D. B. OLSEN** is the pseudonym and (then) married name used by Dolores Hitchens (1907-1973) early in her mystery-writing career. She created several Los Angeles series characters during the 1930s and 1940s, including Prof. A. Pennyfather, teacher of English literature at Clarendon College, and Miss Rachel Murdock, spinster sleuth. Miss Rachel is assisted by her sister, Miss Jennifer, her cat Samantha, and police detective Lt. Stephen Mayhew, introduced in *The Cat Saw Murder* (1939). Mayhew is also featured in two titles of his own. More than 25 years before Lilian Jackson Braun launched the "Cat Who" craze, Olsen introduced the first mystery series with a "Cat" in every title. But according to Bill Pronzini in *1001 Midnights*, this author produced her best work as Dolores Hitchens, par-ticularly *Sleep with Slander* (1960) which he calls the best hard-boiled private eye novel written by a woman. As Hitchens she also wrote five novels with her railroad detective husband about a fictional group of railroad cops in southern California.

Professor A. Pennyfather . . . professor at Clarendon College in Los Angeles
 ❏ ❏ 1 - Bring the Bride a Shroud (1945) [APA–A Shroud for the Bride]
 ❏ ❏ 2 - Gallows for the Groom (1947)
 ❏ ❏ 3 - Devious Design (1948)
 ❏ ❏ 4 - Something About Midnight (1950)
 ❏ ❏ 5 - Love Me in Death (1951)
 ❏ ❏ 6 - Enrollment Cancelled (1952) [APA–Dead Babes in the Wood]

Rachel & Jennifer Murdock . . . sister sleuths in Los Angeles
 ❏ ❏ 1 - The Cat Saw Murder (1939)
 ❏ ❏ 2 - The Alarm of the Black Cat (1942)
 ❏ ❏ 3 - Cat's Claw (1943)
 ❏ ❏ 4 - Catspaw for Murder (1943)
 ❏ ❏ 5 - The Cat Wears a Noose (1944)
 ❏ ❏ 6 - Cats Don't Smile (1945)

❏ ❏ 7 - Cats Don't Need Coffins (1946)
❏ ❏ 8 - Cats Have Tall Shadows (1948)
❏ ❏ 9 - The Cat Wears a Mask (1949)
❏ ❏ 10 - Death Wears Cat's Eyes (1950)
❏ ❏ 11 - The Cat and Capricorn (1951)
❏ ❏ 12 - The Cat Walk (1953)
❏ ❏ 13 - Death Walks on Cat Feet (1956)

Lt. Stephen Mayhew . . . police detective in Los Angeles
❏ ❏ 1 - The Ticking Heart (1940)
❏ ❏ 2 - The Clue in the Clay (1948)

■ **A. J. ORDE** is one of the pseudonyms of bestselling science fiction author Sheri S. Tepper, who writes mysteries under two different names. As A. J. Orde she's the creator of Jason Lynx, Denver antiques dealer and compulsive puzzle solver. His romantic interest, Grace Willis, just happens to be a Denver cop, making this series a charming reversal of the female amateur detective with a male-cop-as-love-interest. Their supporting cast includes Grace's troubled brother, Mark and Eugenia from Jason Lynx Interiors and the delightful animal trio of Bela, Schnitz and Critter. Bela is Jason's 120-lb. white Kuvasz dog and Schnitz his 12-lb. Maine Coon kitten, whose daddy just happens to be Grace's 29-lb. tomcat Critter. Be sure to start this series at the beginning so you don't miss any of the continuing story about Jason's mysterious family origins. As B. J. Oliphant, Tepper writes the Edgar-nominated Shirley McClintock series about a 50-something Washington DC career woman who returns to manage the family ranch in Colorado after the death of her parents. Tepper lives in Santa Fe, New Mexico.

Jason Lynx . . . Denver, Colorado antiques dealer & interior decorator
❏ ❏ 1 - A Little Neighborhood Murder (1989)
❏ ❏ 2 - Death and the Dogwalker (1990)
❏ ❏ 3 - Death for Old Times' Sake (1992)
❏ ❏ 4 - Looking for the Aardvark (1993) [APA–Dead on Sunday]
❏ ❏ 5 - A Long Time Dead (1995)

■ **Denise OSBORNE**, of Capitola, California, has won awards for her screenplays and short films. Her new mystery series features Queenie Davilow, struggling screenwriter, who moonlights doing security checks in the Hollywood film community. Introduced in *Murder Offscreen* (1994), Queenie returns in *Cut to: Murder* (1995).

Queenie Davilow . . . Hollywood screenwriter
❏ ❏ 1 - Murder Offscreen (1994)
❏ ❏ 2 - Cut to: Murder (1995)

■ **Abigail PADGETT** is a former court investigator in San Diego who works as an advocate for the mentally ill. Her avid interest in desert preservation and Native American culture is showcased brilliantly in her new mystery series featuring 40-year-old Barbara Joan "Bo" Bradley, a San Diego child abuse investigator first appearing in *Child of Silence* (1993). Her critically-acclaimed debut novel, nominated for Agatha and Anthony awards, was the first to introduce a working professional living with manic depression. This powerful and informative series has a wonderful supporting cast—Bo's elderly fox terrier Mildred, her best friend and office mate Estrella "Es" Benedict, their sullen supervisor Madge Aldenhoven (the shining light of bureaucracies everywhere), the wise and caring Dr. Eva Broussard and that dashing French-speaking Dr. Andrew LaMarche, San Diego pediatrician and international authority on child abuse, who falls for Bo in the first installment.

Barbara Joan "Bo" Bradley . . . San Diego, California child abuse investigator

- ❑ ❑ 1 - **Child of Silence** (1993) *Agatha & Anthony nominee* ☆ ☆
- ❑ ❑ 2 - Strawgirl (1994)
- ❑ ❑ 3 - Turtle Baby (1995)

■ **Emma PAGE** is the pseudonym of Honoria Tirbutt, creator of seven mystery titles from the 1980s featuring British police Inspector Kelsey. She also produced four nonseries mysteries in the early 1970s, including *A Fortnight by the Sea* (1973) renamed *Add a Pinch of Cyanide* when it was published later that same year in the U.S.

Inspector Kelsey . . . police inspector in England

- ❑ ❑ 1 - Missing Woman (1980)
- ❑ ❑ 2 - Every Second Thursday (1981)
- ❑ ❑ 3 - Last Walk Home (1982)
- ❑ ❑ 4 - Cold Light of Day (1983)
- ❑ ❑ 5 - Scent of Death (1985)
- ❑ ❑ 6 - Final Moments (1987)
- ❑ ❑ 7 - A Violent End (1988)
- ❑ ❑ 8 - Murder Comes Caller (1995)

■ **Katherine Hall PAGE** won the Agatha for best first novel with her opening title in the Faith Sibley Fairchild series in 1990. Daughter of a minister and wife of a minister, this catering detective is surrounded by classic church characters and small-town New England. Page, who holds a doctorate in education, is also working on a juvenile series, *Christie and Company*.

Faith Sibley Fairchild . . . Massachusetts minister's wife & culinary artist

- ❑ ❑ 1 - **The Body in the Belfry** (1990) *Agatha winner* ★
- ❑ ❑ 2 - The Body in the Kelp (1991)
- ❑ ❑ 3 - The Body in the Bouillon (1991)
- ❑ ❑ 4 - The Body in the Vestibule (1992)
- ❑ ❑ 5 - The Body in the Cast (1993)
- ❑ ❑ 6 - The Body in the Basement (1994)
- ❑ ❑ 7 - The Body in the Bog (1996)

■ **Robin PAIGE** is the pseudonym used by Susan Wittig Albert and her husband Bill for their charming new Victorian series set in England with an American amateur detective. She is Kathryn Ardleigh, 25-year-old self-supporting writer of penny dreadfuls who gets called to England to act as secretary to an aunt she didn't know she had. In her second adventure she meets the real life Beatrix Potter. Under her own name, Albert writes the China Bayles mystery series featuring an ex-attorney herb shop owner in Pecan Springs, Texas.

Kathryn Ardleigh . . . 25-year-old American author who travels to Victorian Dedham, England

- ❑ ❑ 1 - Death at Bishop's Keep (1994)
- ❑ ❑ 2 - Death at Gallows Green (1995)

■ **Orania PAPAZOGLOU** is the creator of the Patience Campbell McKenna series featuring a romance novelist turned crime writer. A never-published magazine exposé on the romance publishing business became fodder for this humorous series. Before turning to mystery writing, Papazoglou was editor of *Greek Accent* magazine and freelanced for *Glam-*

our, *Mademoiselle* and *Working Woman*. She also wrote two psychological thrillers as Papazoglou, but remains best known for her Gregor Demarkian series written as Jane Haddam, nominated for an Edgar and an Anthony. Under the name Ann Paris she wrote two other titles—*Graven Image* (1987) set in Greece and *Arrowheart* (1988) set in France. A graduate of Vassar College, she is married to award-winning mystery writer and columnist William DeAndrea. After several years in London, they have returned to New York.

Patience Campbell McKenna . . . 6-ft romance novelist turned crime writer in New York

- ❏ ❏ 1 - **Sweet, Savage Death** (1984) *Edgar nominee* ☆
- ❏ ❏ 2 - Wicked, Loving Murder (1985)
- ❏ ❏ 3 - Death's Savage Passion (1986)
- ❏ ❏ 4 - Rich, Radiant Slaughter (1988)
- ❏ ❏ 5 - Once and Always Murder (1990)

■ **Sara PARETSKY** grew up in Kansas where she earned her BA in political science summa cum laude at the University of Kansas. She has a PhD in medieval history and an MBA from the University of Chicago. One of the founding members of Sisters in Crime, she served as its first president in 1986. Before turning to mystery writing full time, she was a freelance business writer and later a marketing manager for a major insurance company. Paretsky's series detective is V. I. Warshawski, one of the toughest and bestselling private eyes in contemporary fiction. V. I. (Victoria Iphegenia) is the daughter of a Polish cop and an Italian-Jewish opera singer. A former public defender, this P. I. has a nose for white collar crime, a fondness for silk shirts and a strong attachment to the red Bruno Magli pumps that bring her luck. In addition to a Silver Dagger in 1988, Paretsky won a 1991 Anthony for *A Woman's Eye*, a collection of 21 short stories by well-known women crime writers, to be followed by another such anthology in 1996. A collection of V. I. short stories titled *Windy City Blues* (1995) is the most recent appearance of Paretsky's popular private eye. Written especially for this collection, the lead story "*Grace Notes*" concerns a musical composition given to V. I.'s mother Gabriella, by the famous Italian singer who composed it, when she left Italy during the Second World War. This story fills in many of the details about the mother who died when V. I. was a young girl. Paretsky is a resident of Chicago. And like V. I., her dog of choice is a golden labrador.

V. I. Warshawski . . . Chicago, Illinois attorney turned P. I.

- ❏ ❏ 1 - Indemnity Only (1982)
- ❏ ❏ 2 - Deadlock (1984)
- ❏ ❏ 3 - Killing Orders (1985)
- ❏ ❏ 4 - Bitter Medicine (1987)
- ❏ ❏ 5 - **Blood Shot** (1988) [Britain–Toxic Shock]
      Silver Dagger ★ ***Anthony & Shamus nominee*** ☆ ☆
- ❏ ❏ 6 - Burn Marks (1990)
- ❏ ❏ 7 - Guardian Angel (1991)
- ❏ ❏ 8 - Tunnel Vision (1994)
- ❏ ❏   - Windy City Blues [short stories] (1995)

■ **Barbara PARKER** of Ft. Lauderdale, Florida is the creator of a new legal mystery series featuring Miami corporate attorney Gail Connor, introduced in the Edgar-nominated Suspicion of Innocence (1994).

Gail Connor . . . corporate attorney in Miami, Florida

- ❏ ❏ 1 - **Suspicion of Innocence** (1994) *Edgar nominee* ☆
- ❏ ❏ 2 - Suspicion of Guilt (1995)

■ **Barbara PAUL** of Pittsburgh is a former English and drama teacher with a working theatre background. A native of Kentucky, she earned a B.A. from Bowling Green State University before studying in Norway and Austria. She holds an M.A. from the University of Redlands
in California and a PhD from the University of Pittsburgh. Her historical mystery series
features opera stars Enrico Caruso and Geraldine Farrar as amateur sleuths. Paul also
writes a police series featuring NYPD officer Marian Larch and her friend Kelly Ingram,
television actress.

    Enrico Caruso . . . Italian tenor in New York
- ❑ ❑ 1 - A Cadenza for Caruso (1984)
- ❑ ❑ 2 - Prima Donna at Large (1985)
- ❑ ❑ 3 - A Chorus of Detectives (1987)

    Marian Larch . . . NYPD officer
- ❑ ❑ 1 - The Renewable Virgin (1984)
- ❑ ❑ 2 - He Huffed and He Puffed (1989)
- ❑ ❑ 3 - Good King Sauerkraut (1989)
- ❑ ❑ 4 - You Have the Right to Remain Silent (1992)
- ❑ ❑ 5 - The Apostrophe Thief (1993)
- ❑ ❑ 6 - Fare Play (1995)

■ **Joanne PENCE** is a San Francisco native and manager with the Social Security Admin-
istration. In her romantic mystery series, freelance cooking writer Angelina Amalfi gets involved with San Francisco homicide detective Paavo Smith, much to the dissatisfaction of
Angelina's wealthy father and Paavo's colleagues. The series opening title was nominated
for "Best Romantic Suspense of 1993" by the Romance Writers of America and will return in
1996 with *Cooking Most Deadly*.

    Angelina Amalfi . . . food columnist & restaurant reviewer in San Francisco, California
- ❑ ❑ 1 - Something's Cooking (1993)
- ❑ ❑ 2 - Too Many Cooks (1994)
- ❑ ❑ 3 - Cooking up Trouble (1995)
- ❑ ❑ 4 - Cooking Most Deadly (1996)

■ **Anne PERRY**, born in London, is the creator of two historical mystery series set in Victorian England. The longer-running series (set in the late 1880s) features Inspector Thomas
Pitt and his wife Charlotte who leaves her upper-middle-class home to marry the policeman
after assisting him with the case featured in book #1. Meanwhile her sister Emily marries
"up" the social ladder, and she and Charlotte work together "assisting" Thomas with future
investigations. Writing in *1001 Midnights*, reviewer Karol Kay Hope observed that if you ever
wondered "why women began to rebel against social constriction at the turn of the 20th
century, these books will clear up that mystery." Pitt's 16th case will be titled *Pentecost
Alley* (1996). Perry's second series features Inspector William Monk who wakes up in a
hospital during the mid-1850s with no recall of his identity. Lucky for Monk, capable nurse
Hester Latterly is on the job. Prior to launching her mystery-writing career, Perry worked as
a flight attendant, store buyer and property underwriter in Los Angeles where she lived from
1967 to 1972. She now lives in a twelve-room converted barn in Scotland.

    Thomas & Charlotte Pitt . . . Victorian police inspector & wife in London
- ❑ ❑ 1 - The Cater Street Hangman (1979)
- ❑ ❑ 2 - Callander Square (1980)
- ❑ ❑ 3 - Paragon Walk (1981)
- ❑ ❑ 4 - Resurrection Row (1981)
- ❑ ❑ 5 - Rutland Place (1983)

❑ ❑ 6 - Bluegate Fields (1984)
❑ ❑ 7 - Death in Devil's Acre (1985)
❑ ❑ 8 - Cardington Crescent (1987)
❑ ❑ 9 - Silence in Hanover Close (1988)
❑ ❑ 10 - Bethlehem Road (1990)
❑ ❑ 11 - Highgate Rise (1991)
❑ ❑ 12 - Belgrave Square (1992)
❑ ❑ 13 - Farrier's Lane (1993)
❑ ❑ 14 - The Hyde Park Headsman (1994)
❑ ❑ 15 - Traitor's Gate (1995)
❑ ❑ 16 - Pentecost Alley (1996)

Inspector William Monk . . . amnesiac Victorian police inspector
❑ ❑ 1 - **The Face of a Stranger** (1990) *Agatha nominee* ☆
❑ ❑ 2 - A Dangerous Mourning (1991)
❑ ❑ 3 - **Defend and Betray** (1992) *American Mystery Award winner* ★
    Agatha nominee ☆
❑ ❑ 4 - A Sudden, Fearful Death (1993)
❑ ❑ 5 - Sins of the Wolf (1994)
❑ ❑ 6 - Cain His Brother (1995)

■ **Elizabeth PETERS** is only one of the pseudonyms of the talented and prolific Barbara Mertz who holds a PhD in Egyptology from the University of Chicago and has written more than 50 novels of mystery and suspense. As Elizabeth Peters she is the creator of three mystery series, the best-known featuring Amelia Peabody, brilliant Victorian archaeologist. Amelia's adventures include her Egyptologist husband Radcliffe Emerson and their precocious son Ramses. Peters' other series stars are Jacqueline Kirby, middle-aged librarian romance novelist and Vicky Bliss, tall, voluptuous and clever art historian. As Barbara Michaels, she is the author of six consecutive *New York Times* best sellers and in 1987 was awarded the Anthony Grand Master for her suspense thrillers. As Barbara Mertz, she is the author of nonfiction books on Egyptology, including *Temples, Tombs and Hieroglyphs* and *Red Land, Black Land...Life in Ancient Egypt*. The author lives in a historic farmhouse in Frederick, Maryland with two dogs and six cats.

Amelia Peabody . . . Victorian feminist archaeologist in Kent, England
❑ ❑ 1 - Crocodile on the Sandbank (1975)
❑ ❑ 2 - The Curse of the Pharaohs (1981)
❑ ❑ 3 - The Mummy Case (1985)
❑ ❑ 4 - Lion in the Valley (1986)
❑ ❑ 5 - The Deeds of the Disturber (1988)
❑ ❑ 6 - **The Last Camel Died at Noon** (1991) *Agatha nominee* ☆
❑ ❑ 7 - **The Snake, the Crocodile and the Dog** (1992) *Agatha nominee* ☆

Jacqueline Kirby . . . librarian turned romance novelist in New York
❑ ❑ 1 - The Seventh Sinner (1972)
❑ ❑ 2 - The Murders of Richard III (1974)
❑ ❑ 3 - Die for Love (1984)
❑ ❑ 4 - **Naked Once More** (1989)
    Agatha & American Mystery Award winner ★ ★

Vicky Bliss . . . art historian in Bavaria, Germany
❑ ❑ 1 - Borrower of the Night (1973)
❑ ❑ 2 - Street of the Five Moons (1978)
❑ ❑ 3 - Silhouette in Scarlet (1983)
❑ ❑ 4 - Trojan Gold (1987)
❑ ❑ 5 - **Night Train to Memphis** (1994) *Agatha nominee* ☆

■ **Ellis PETERS** (1913-1995) is the pseudonym of Edith Mary Pargeter, English novelist and mystery writer, widely known as the creator of Brother Cadfael, a 12th century Welshman and herbalist at the Benedictine monastery of St. Peter and St. Paul in Shrewsbury, England. Translated into 20 languages, the Cadfael books are now a television series featuring Sir Derek Jakobi as the late-in-life monk. The author once worked as a chemist's assistant and served in the Royal Navy where she received the British Empire Medal in 1944. She began her publishing career with historical and straight novels written as Edith Pargeter before launching her mystery career with the Felse Family series, also under her own name. To avoid confusing her readers, she adopted the Ellis Peters pseudonym with her second Felse novel and continued using it for her mysteries. The professional detective in the Felse family is George who rises to the rank of Detective Chief Inspector, ably assisted by his wife Bunty, a concert contralto before her marriage. The music world and their sleuthing son Dominic are recurring threads in this series. In addition to her work as Peters and Pargeter, she published two mysteries as Joylon Carr—Murder in the Dispensary (1938) and Death Comes by Post (1940) and one title as John Redfern (The Victim Needs a Nurse, 1940). She also translated numerous English works of fiction and nonfiction into Czech. The winner of an Edgar, Silver Dagger, Diamond Dagger, and in 1994 the Order of the British Empire, she died in October 1995 at the age of 82.

Brother Cadfael . . . Shrewsbury, England medieval monk & herbalist

- ❑ ❑ 1 - A Morbid Taste for Bones (1977)
- ❑ ❑ 2 - One Corpse Too Many (1979)
- ❑ ❑ 3 - **Monk's Hood** (1980) *Silver Dagger* ★
- ❑ ❑ 4 - St. Peter's Fair (1981)
- ❑ ❑ 5 - The Leper of St. Giles (1981)
- ❑ ❑ 6 - The Virgin in the Ice (1982)
- ❑ ❑ 7 - The Sanctuary Sparrow (1983)
- ❑ ❑ 8 - The Devil's Novice (1983)
- ❑ ❑ 9 - The Dead Man's Ransom (1984)
- ❑ ❑ 10 - The Pilgrim of Hate (1984)
- ❑ ❑ 11 - An Excellent Mystery (1985)
- ❑ ❑ 12 - The Raven in the Foregate (1986)
- ❑ ❑ 13 - The Rose Rent (1986)
- ❑ ❑ 14 - The Hermit of Eyton Forest (1987)
- ❑ ❑ 15 - The Confession of Brother Haluin (1988)
- ❑ ❑ 16 - The Heretic's Apprentice (1989)
- ❑ ❑ 17 - **The Potter's Field** (1989) *Agatha nominee* ☆
- ❑ ❑ 18 - Summer of the Danes (1991)
- ❑ ❑ 19 - The Holy Thief (1992)
- ❑ ❑ 20 - Brother Cadfael's Penance (1994)

George, Bunty & Dominic Felse . . . family of detectives in Comerford, Shropshire, England

- ❑ ❑ 1 - Fallen into the Pit (1951)
- ❑ ❑ 2 - **Death and the Joyful Woman** (1962) *Edgar winner* ★
- ❑ ❑ 3 - Flight of a Witch (1964)
- ❑ ❑ 4 - A Nice Derangement of Epitaphs (1965) [U.S.–Who Lies Here?]
- ❑ ❑ 5 - The Piper on the Mountain (1966)
- ❑ ❑ 6 - Black Is the Colour of My True Love's Heart (1967)
- ❑ ❑ 7 - The Grass-Widow's Tale (1968)
- ❑ ❑ 8 - The House of Green Turf (1969)
- ❑ ❑ 9 - Morning Raga (1969)
- ❑ ❑ 10 - The Knocker on Death's Door (1970)
- ❑ ❑ 11 - Death To the Landlords! (1972)
- ❑ ❑ 12 - City of Gold and Shadows (1973)
- ❑ ❑ 13 - Rainbow's End (1978)

■ **Audrey PETERSON** has, like her series character Claire Camden, been an English professor and traveled to England for academic research. A California native, Peterson once taught English literature in Long Beach but now makes her home in the state of Washington. Her earlier mystery series, also set in England, feature music professor Andrew Quentin and his former graduate student Jane Winfield. Peterson is the author of *Victorian Masters of Mystery*, a study of 19th century writers from Wilkie Collins to Conan Doyle.

Claire Camden . . . California English professor in Britain
- ❑ ❑ 1 - Dartmoor Burial (1992)
- ❑ ❑ 2 - Death Too Soon (1994)
- ❑ ❑ 3 - Shroud for a Scholar (1995)

Jane Winfield . . . British journalist & music writer
- ❑ ❑ 1 - The Nocturne Murder (1988)
- ❑ ❑ 2 - Death in Wessex (1989)
- ❑ ❑ 3 - Murder in Burgundy (1989)
- ❑ ❑ 4 - Deadly Rehearsal (1990)
- ❑ ❑ 5 - Elegy in a Country Graveyard (1990)
- ❑ ❑ 6 - Lament for Christabel (1991)

■ **Rhona PETRIE** is one of the pseudonyms of Eileen-Marie Duell Buchanan who also writes as Clare Curzon and Marie Buchanan. Born in Sussex and educated at the University of London, she has worked as an interpreter, translator, teacher and secretary. Her five novels featuring Inspector MacLurg are classic whodunnits. Also published under the Petrie pseudonym are a pair of novels—*Foreign Bodies* (1967) and *Despatch of a Dove* (1969)—featuring the urbane Dr. Nassim Pride, Anglo-Sudanese scientist with a love for all things British.

Marcus MacLurg . . . British police Inspector
- ❑ ❑ 1 - Death in Deakins Wood (1963)
- ❑ ❑ 2 - Murder by Precedent (1964)
- ❑ ❑ 3 - Running Deep (1965)
- ❑ ❑ 4 - Dead Loss (1966)
- ❑ ❑ 5 - MacLurg Goes West (1968)

■ **Nancy PICKARD** (pronounced Pi-CARD) is a ten-time nominee and five-time winner of Agatha, Anthony, Edgar and Macavity awards for her ten-book Jenny Cain mystery series. Past director of the Port Frederick Civic Foundation, Jenny is now director of her own charitable foundation in the seaport town of Port Frederick, Massachusetts, where the bygone Cain Clams was once the town's largest employer. Married to a handsome police lieutenant named Geof, Jenny has solved enough crimes to qualify as a pro herself. Pickard is past president of Sisters in Crime and author of *The 27-Ingredient Chili Con Carne Murders*, a Eugenia Potter mystery based on an unfinished manuscript left by Virginia Rich at the time of her death. Winner of numerous short story awards, Pickard says her first peak experience was being elected student council president in the seventh grade. She lives in a suburb of Kansas City not far from Jill Churchill.

Jenny Cain . . . Port Frederick, Massachusetts foundation director
- ❑ ❑ 1 - Generous Death (1984)
- ❑ ❑ 2 - **Say No to Murder** (1985) *Anthony winner* ★
- ❑ ❑ 3 - **No Body** (1986) *Anthony nominee* ☆
- ❑ ❑ 4 - **Marriage Is Murder** (1987) *Macavity winner* ★ *Anthony nominee* ☆
- ❑ ❑ 5 - **Dead Crazy** (1988) *Anthony & Agatha nominee* ☆ ☆
- ❑ ❑ 6 - **Bum Steer** (1989) *Agatha winner* ★

❑ ❑ 7 - I. O. U. (1991) *Agatha & Macavity winner* ★ ★ *Edgar nominee* ☆
❑ ❑ 8 - But I Wouldn't Want to Die There (1993)
❑ ❑ 9 - Confession (1994)
❑ ❑ 10 - Twilight (1995)

■ **Marissa PIESMAN** is a prosecuting attorney in Manhattan who launched her writing career as co-author of *The Yuppie Handbook*. Piesman is the creator of detective Nina Fischman, neurotic New York attorney for the Legal Services Project for Seniors. Nina and her energetic mother Ida obsess in style about money, men, fashion, crime, religion and more.

Nina Fischman . . . New York City legal services attorney
❑ ❑ 1 - Unorthodox Practices (1989)
❑ ❑ 2 - Personal Effects (1991)
❑ ❑ 3 - Heading Uptown (1993)
❑ ❑ 4 - Close Quarters (1994)
❑ ❑ 5 - Alternate Sides (1995)

■ **Elizabeth PINCUS** is a San Francisco film editor, freelance writer and former private eye. Her writing has appeared in numerous publications, including *SF Weekly*, the *San Francisco Chronicle* and the *San Francisco Review of Books* and the WomanSleuth Anthologies. Pincus' Lambda award-winning series features Nell Fury, a lesbian P. I. working in San Francisco.

Nell Fury . . . San Francisco, California lesbian P. I.
❑ ❑ 1 - The Two-Bit Tango (1992)
❑ ❑ 2 - The Solitary Twist (1993)
❑ ❑ 3 - The Hangdog Hustle (1995)

■ **Zelda POPKIN** (1898-1983), a native of Brooklyn, was the creator of a five-book series from the early 1940s featuring former department store detective Mary Carner. At the age of 17 Popkin became the first female general assignment reporter for the *Wilkes-Barre Times Leader* and later attended Columbia University and New York University Law School. For almost 25 years she was a partner with her husband in a New York City public relations bureau. In addition to the Carner series she published two nonseries novels set in New York—*So Much Blood* (1944) and *A Death of Innocence* (1971).

Mary Carner . . . former department store detective in New York city
❑ ❑ 1 - Death Wears a White Gardenia (1938)
❑ ❑ 2 - Murder in the Mist (1940)
❑ ❑ 3 - Time Off for Murder (1940)
❑ ❑ 4 - Dead Man's Gift (1941)
❑ ❑ 5 - No Crime for a Lady (1942)

■ **Sharon PORATH** is the creator of a new mystery series featuring amateur sleuth Kendra MacFarlane who is introduced in the 1995 title *Dead File*.

Kendra MacFarlane . . . amateur sleuth
❑ ❑ 1 - Dead File (1995)

■ **Anna PORTER** has had a highly successful career in Canadian publishing, as editor-in-chief of McClelland and Stewart, president of Seal Books, publisher of Key Porter Books, chairman of Doubleday Canada and author of mystery thrillers. Porter's first-hand experience with the international publishing world adds a special dimension to her character Judith Hayes, freelance journalist and mother of two teenagers introduced in *Hidden Agenda* (1985).

> **Judith Hayes** . . . journalist in Toronto
> ❑ ❑ 1 - Hidden Agenda (1985)
> ❑ ❑ 2 - Mortal Sins (1987)

■ **Joyce PORTER** (1924-1990) wrote 30 series mystery novels using three different comic characters, each a spoof of one form or another. Her Hon-Con series features the Honorable Constance Ethel Morrison Burke, a gentlewoman of independent means who turns her considerable energy to sleuthing in five novels from the 1970s. The Eddie Brown series features a reluctant and cowardly foreign agent who is sent to Russia in the opening title, *Sour Cream with Everything* (1966). And last but not least are her 21 novels with that "oaf of Scotland Yard," Inspector Wilfred Dover, grossly overweight and unfailingly surly. He frequently arrives at crime scenes just in time to quit for lunch, but not before insulting everyone around him, including his assistant Sgt. MacGregor, whose elegance is exceeded only by his patience. According to Porter, the lazy policeman's career endures because most criminals are even more inept and stupid than Inspector Dover, who is said to be so unlikable that he's likable. Eleven of her previously uncollected Dover short stories are now available in *Dover: The Collected Short Stories* (1995). Born in Marple, Cheshire, and educated at King's College in London where she earned a BA with honors in 1945, Porter served in the Women's Royal Air Force as a flight officer from 1949 to 1963.

> **Eddie Brown** . . . comic spy in England
> ❑ ❑ 1 - Sour Cream with Everything (1966)
> ❑ ❑ 2 - The Chinks in the Curtain (1967)
> ❑ ❑ 3 - Neither a Candle nor a Pitchfork (1969)
> ❑ ❑ 4 - Only with a Bargepole (1971)

> **Honorable Constance Ethel Morrison Burke** . . . comic senior sleuth in England
> ❑ ❑ 1 - Rather a Common Sort of Crime (1970)
> ❑ ❑ 2 - A Meddler and Her Murder (1972)
> ❑ ❑ 3 - The Package Included Murder (1975)
> ❑ ❑ 4 - Who the Heck Is Sylvia? (1977)
> ❑ ❑ 5 - The Cart Before the Crime (1979)

> **Wilfred Dover** . . . a fat lout of a Chief Inspector in England
> ❑ ❑ 1 - Dover One (1964)
> ❑ ❑ 2 - Dover Two (1965)
> ❑ ❑ 3 - Dover Three (1965)
> ❑ ❑ 4 - Dover and the Unkindest Cut of All (1967)
> ❑ ❑ 5 - Dover and the Sense of Justice (1968)
> ❑ ❑ 6 - Dover Goes to Pott (1968)
> ❑ ❑ 7 - Dover Pulls a Rabbit (1969)
> ❑ ❑ 8 - Dover Fails to Make His Mark (1970)
> ❑ ❑ 9 - Dover Strikes Again (1970)
> ❑ ❑ 10 - A Terrible Drag for Dover (1971)
> ❑ ❑ 11 - Dover and the Dark Lady (1972)
> ❑ ❑ 12 - It's Murder with Dover (1973)
> ❑ ❑ 13 - Dover Tangles with High Finance (1975)
> ❑ ❑ 14 - Dover and the Claret Tappers (1976)

❑ ❑ 15 - Dover Does Some Spadework (1977)
❑ ❑ 16 - When Dover Gets Knotted (1977)
❑ ❑ 17 - Dover Without Perks (1978)
❑ ❑ 18 - Dover Doesn't Dilly-Dally (1978)
❑ ❑ 19 - Dead Easy for Dover (1978)
❑ ❑ 20 - Dover Goes to School (1978)
❑ ❑ 21 - Dover Beats the Band (1980)

■ **Deborah POWELL** is the creator of a Texas series featuring Hollis Carpenter, a gay woman crime reporter in 1930s Houston who appears in a pair of novels from 1991 and 1992.

Hollis Carpenter . . . gay woman crime reporter in Houston, Texas
❑ ❑ 1 - Bayou City Streets (1991)
❑ ❑ 2 - Houston Town (1992)

■ **Sandra West PROWELL** is a fourth-generation Montanan and great granddaughter of early pioneers. Cofounder of the Montana Authors Coalition and coproducer of the literary heritage map of Montana, she is also creator of the Shamus-nominated series featuring Montana P. I. Phoebe Siegel. When Prowell isn't writing, she enjoys fishing, beading and researching herbal and medicinal plants native to Montana.

Phoebe Siegel . . . Billings, Montana ex-cop P. I.
❑ ❑ 1 - **By Evil Means** (1993) *Shamus nominee* ☆
❑ ❑ 2 - **The Killing of Monday Brown** (1994) *Shamus nominee* ☆
❑ ❑ 3 - Death of a Wallflower (1995)

■ **Dianne G. PUGH**, a Los Angeles native and UCLA graduate, currently works as a marketing director for a California computer company. She has a BA in philosophy and an MBA in marketing and finance. Her series detective Iris Thorne is a 30-something Los Angeles investment counselor, first seen in *Cold Call* (1993).

Iris Thorne . . . Los Angeles investment counselor
❑ ❑ 1 - Cold Call (1993)
❑ ❑ 2 - Slow Squeeze (1994)

■ **Mary Monica PULVER** is the author name used by Mary Pulver Kuhfeld of St. Louis Park, Minnesota for her series featuring Illinois police detective Peter Brichter and his horse breeder wife Kori Price. Horse loving fans of police procedurals will enjoy this series where the second installment actually begins the story. Kuhfeld also writes an Oxfordshire medieval mystery series with Gail Bacon under the shared pseudonym of Margaret Frazer. A veteran of the U.S. Navy and a lover of Arabian horses herself, the author is married to museum curator, Dr. Albert Kuhfeld, who sometimes collaborates with her on short stories. They live in Minnesota.

Peter & Kori Price Brichter . . . Illinois police detective & horse breeder
❑ ❑ 1 - Murder at the War (1987) [APA–Knight Fall]
❑ ❑ 2 - The Unforgiving Minutes [prequel] (1988)
❑ ❑ 3 - Ashes to Ashes (1988)
❑ ❑ 4 - Original Sin (1991)
❑ ❑ 5 - Show Stopper (1992)

■ **Erica QUEST** is the joint pseudonym of Nancy Buckingham Sawyer and her husband John Sawyer for their mystery series set in the Cotswolds featuring Detective Chief Inspector Kate Maddox, first appearing in *Death Walk* (1988). They also share the pseudonym Nancy Buckingham for more than 16 historical and romantic suspense novels. Before writing fiction full time she was a medical social worker and he was an advertising executive.

    Kate Maddox . . . Detective Chief Inspector in the Cotswolds, England
       ❏ ❏ 1 - Death Walk (1988)
       ❏ ❏ 2 - Cold Coffin (1990)
       ❏ ❏ 3 - Model Murder (1991)

■ **Elizabeth QUINN** is Elizabeth Quinn Barnard, skiier, hiker, mountain biker, river rafter and mother of a two in Grant's Pass, Oregon, where she teaches creative writing at Rogue Community College and fine-tunes her personal homepage on the World Wide Web. A native of upstate New York, she is the creator of a new mystery series featuring Lauren Maxwell, PhD, widowed mother of two and Anchorage-based naturalist-investigator for the Wild American Society, introduced in *Murder Most Grizzly* (1993). Lauren's adventures feature a different animal in each title—grizzlies, wolves and lambs so far, with killer whales expected in book #4. After completing a master's degree in journalism from Boston University, Quinn worked for several small dailies in Massachusetts and later taught in the journalism school at the University of Rhode Island before moving west with her husband, an Associated Press correspondent.

    Lauren Maxwell . . . Alaska wildlife investigator PhD
       ❏ ❏ 1 - Murder Most Grizzly (1993)
       ❏ ❏ 2 - A Wolf in Death's Clothing (1995)
       ❏ ❏ 3 - Lamb to the Slaughter (1996)

■ **Sheila RADLEY** is the name used by Sheila Robinson for her series introduced in 1978 with Inspector Douglas Quantrill, English village police detective and family man. He is joined by a woman partner, Sergeant Hilary Lloyd, in book #4 of this continuing series now in its ninth installment. Robinson earned a B.A. in history from the University of London and later worked as a teacher and in advertising, in addition to nine years in the Women's Royal Air Force. After moving to the country in 1964, she worked for 14 years running a village store and post office. In her spare time she started writing the series that debuted just months before her 50th birthday. Under the name Hester Rowan she also wrote a trio of romantic thrillers in the late 1970s.

    Douglas Quantrill & Hilary Lloyd . . . Suffolk, England detective chief inspector & sergeant partner
       ❏ ❏ 1 - Death and the Maiden (1978) [U.S.–Death in the Morning]
       ❏ ❏ 2 - The Chief Inspector's Daughter (1980)
       ❏ ❏ 3 - A Talent for Destruction (1982)
       ❏ ❏ 4 - Blood on the Happy Highway (1983)
             [U.S.–The Quiet Road to Death]
       ❏ ❏ 5 - Fate Worse Than Death (1985)
       ❏ ❏ 6 - Who Saw Him Die? (1987)
       ❏ ❏ 7 - This Way Out (1989)
       ❏ ❏ 8 - Cross My Heart and Hope to Die (1992)
       ❏ ❏ 9 - Fair Game (1994)

■ **J. M. REDMANN** is the author of three novels in a new series featuring Michelle "Micky" Knight, a proudly gay woman private eye in New Orleans, who makes her first appearance in *Death by the Riverside* (1990). Book #2 in this series was nominated for a Lambda award as the best lesbian mystery of 1993. Redmann grew up in Ocean Springs, Mississippi, a small town on the Gulf of Mexico and after living in New York City for a number of years has returned to the South. Like her character, Redmann lives in New Orleans.

Michelle "Micky" Knight . . . lesbian P. I. in New Orleans LA
- ❑ ❑ 1 - Death by the Riverside (1990)
- ❑ ❑ 2 - **Deaths of Jocasta** (1993) *Lambda nominee* ☆
- ❑ ❑ 3 - The Intersection of Law and Desire (1995)

■ **Helen REILLY** (1891-1962) was one of the most popular writers of police mysteries during the '30s, '40s and '50s. She wrote straightforward stories about the Manhattan Homicide Squad, including 31 books featuring the dour and dedicated detective Christopher McKee, known as the Scotchman among his colleagues. As head of the Manhattan Homicide Squad it was convenient that McKee had the "fatal gift of being too often in the right." This series, firmly rooted in correct police procedure, ran from 1930 until 1962. Reilly also wrote four nonseries mysteries under her own name and three more under the name Kiernan Abbey. She was born in New York City where her father, Dr. James Kiernan, was president of Columbia University. She and artist husband Paul Reilly were the parents of four daughters, two of whom grew up to write prize-winning mysteries—Ursula Curtiss and Mary McMullen, fashion designer and advertising executive.

Christopher McKee . . . Manhattan homicide squad detective
- ❑ ❑ 1 - The Diamond Feather (1930)
- ❑ ❑ 2 - Murder in the Mews (1931)
- ❑ ❑ 3 - McKee of Centre Street (1934)
- ❑ ❑ 4 - The Line-up (1934)
- ❑ ❑ 5 - Mr. Smith's Hat (1936)
- ❑ ❑ 6 - Dead Man's Control (1936)
- ❑ ❑ 7 - Dead for a Ducat (1939)
- ❑ ❑ 8 - All Concerned Notified (1939)
- ❑ ❑ 9 - Murder in Shinbone Alley (1940)
- ❑ ❑ 10 - Death Demands an Audience (1940)
- ❑ ❑ 11 - The Dead Can Tell (1940)
- ❑ ❑ 12 - Mourned on Sunday (1941)
- ❑ ❑ 13 - Three Women in Black (1941)
- ❑ ❑ 14 - Name Your Poison (1942)
- ❑ ❑ 15 - The Opening Door (1944)
- ❑ ❑ 16 - Murder on Angler's Island (1945)
- ❑ ❑ 17 - The Silver Leopard (1946)
- ❑ ❑ 18 - The Farmhouse (1947)
- ❑ ❑ 19 - Staircase 4 (1949)
- ❑ ❑ 20 - Murder at Arroways (1950)
- ❑ ❑ 21 - Lament for the Bride (1951)
- ❑ ❑ 22 - The Double Man (1952)
- ❑ ❑ 23 - The Velvet Hand (1953)
- ❑ ❑ 24 - Tell Her It's Murder (1954)
- ❑ ❑ 25 - Compartment K (1955) [Britain–Murder Rides the Express]
- ❑ ❑ 26 - The Canvas Dagger (1956)
- ❑ ❑ 27 - Ding Dong Bell (1958)
- ❑ ❑ 28 - Not Me, Inspector (1959)
- ❑ ❑ 29 - Follow Me (1960)

❏ ❏ 30 - Certain Sleep (1961)
❏ ❏ 31 - The Day She Died (1962)

■ **Ruth RENDELL** has been called the best mystery writer anywhere in the English-speaking world, the "Queen of Crime." With 48 books published in 22 languages, she has won three Edgars, three Gold Daggers, a Silver Dagger and a special National Book Award from the Arts Council of Great Britain. Since the beginning of her career she has alternated traditional detective stories featuring Chief Inspector Reginald Wexford with her more psychological crime novels, many of which appear under her own name, but several under the pseudonym Barbara Vine, including the critically acclaimed *Anna's Book* in 1994. Her first Barbara Vine title, *A Dark-Adapted Eye,* won the Edgar for best novel in 1986. Thirty years after his first case, *From Doon with Death* (1964), Inspector Wexford is back for this series' 16th installment, *Simisola* (1994). Although described as corpulent and heavy, with flint-colored eyes set in a snub-nosed ugly face, Wexford is a witty detective with a keen understanding of people. Born in London, Rendell worked for several years as a reporter and editor for newspapers in West Essex. On top of producing two books each year, she writes reviews and articles, assembles anthologies, actively supports the Labor Party, reads avidly and manages three homes—a Suffolk farmhouse, a London mews house near Regents Park and a seaside home in Aldeburgh.

Reginald Wexford . . . Sussex, England chief inspector
❏ ❏ 1 - From Doon with Death (1964)
❏ ❏ 2 - A Wolf to Slaughter (1967)
❏ ❏ 3 - A New Lease of Death (1967) [APA–Sins of the Fathers ('70)]
❏ ❏ 4 - The Best Man to Die (1969)
❏ ❏ 5 - A Guilty Thing Surprised (1970)
❏ ❏ 6 - No More Dying Then (1971)
❏ ❏ 7 - Murder Being Once Done (1972)
❏ ❏ 8 - Some Lie and Some Die (1973)
❏ ❏ 9 - Shake Hands Forever (1975)
❏ ❏ 10 - **A Sleeping Life** (1978) *Edgar nominee* ☆
❏ ❏ 11 - Put on by Cunning (1981) [U.S.–Death Notes]
❏ ❏ 12 - The Speaker of Mandarin (1983)
❏ ❏ 13 - **An Unkindness of Ravens** (1985) *Edgar nominee* ☆
❏ ❏ 14 - The Veiled One (1988)
❏ ❏ 15 - Kissing the Gunner's Daughter (1993)
❏ ❏ 16 - Simisola (1994)

■ **Craig RICE** is one of the pseudonyms of Georgiana Ann Randolph Craig (1908-1957) who also wrote as Ruth Malone, Daphne Sanders and Michael Venning. She served as a ghost writer for Gypsy Rose Lee and George Sanders while working as a publicity agent, radio writer and producer. Raised by an aunt and uncle named Rice, she was among the most successful practitioners of humor in detective fiction. Her series with John J. Malone and his friends the Justuses made her a celebrity. Even President Roosevelt wrote her a fan letter. She also created a gullible pair of city slickers named Bingo Riggs and Handsome Kusak, whose adventures are so packed with screwball characters that you may feel a bit wacky yourself after reading one (according to Bill Pronzini in *1001 Midnights*). Their third romp, three-quarters finished at the time of Rice's death, was completed by Ed McBain and published under their joint by-line. The first mystery writer ever to be featured on the cover of *Time* magazine (January 28, 1946), Rice died of an accidental combination of alcohol and barbiturates in 1957 at the age of 49. Her semiautobiographical mystery, *Home Sweet Homicide* (1944), where three children of a mystery writer solve a neighbor's murder while playing Cupid for their mother and the handsome police detective, was made into a 1946 film starring Lynn Bari and Randolph Scott.

Bingo Riggs & Handsome Kusak . . . gullible city slickers & reluctant detectives
- ❏ ❏ 1 - The Sunday Pigeon Murders (1942)
- ❏ ❏ 2 - The Thursday Turkey Murders (1943)
- ❏ ❏ 3 - The April Robin Murders (1958)

John J. Malone . . . hard-drinking, cigar-smoking lawyer in Chicago, Illinois
- ❏ ❏ 1 - 8 Faces at 3 (1939)
- ❏ ❏ 2 - The Corpse Steps Out (1940)
- ❏ ❏ 3 - The Wrong Murder (1940)
- ❏ ❏ 4 - The Right Murder (1941)
- ❏ ❏ 5 - Trial by Fury (1941)
- ❏ ❏ 6 - The Big Midget Murders (1942)
- ❏ ❏ 7 - Having a Wonderful Crime (1943)
- ❏ ❏ 8 - The Lucky Stiff (1945)
- ❏ ❏ 9 - The Fourth Postman (1948)
- ❏ ❏ 10 - My Kingdom for a Hearse (1957)
- ❏ ❏ 11 - Knocked for a Loop (1957) [Britain–The Double Frame]
- ❏ ❏ - The Name Is Malone [short stories] (1958)
- ❏ ❏ - People vs. Withers and Malone [short stories] (1963)
- ❏ ❏ 12 - But the Doctor Died (1967)

■ **Virginia RICH** is the creator of Eugenia Potter, congenial widow and good cook who divides her time between New England and Arizona, hosting lively dinner parties and delivering plenty of cooking wisdom. After Rich's death, Nancy Pickard was commissioned to complete the unfinished manuscript left by Rich. *The 27-Ingredient Chili Con Carne Murders* is the delightful result.

Eugenia Potter . . . widowed chef in Maine & Arizona
- ❏ ❏ 1 - The Cooking School Murders (1982)
- ❏ ❏ 2 - The Baked Bean Supper Murders (1983)
- ❏ ❏ 3 - The Nantucket Diet Murders (1985)
- ❏ ❏ 4 - The 27-Ingredient Chili Con Carne Murders (1993) [Nancy Pickard]

■ **Mary Roberts RINEHART** (1876-1958) was once the highest paid writer in America and the first mystery writer with a novel on the year's best seller list (1909). She covered criminal trials and the American war effort for magazines during World War I and began her mystery writing with serials that were later published in book length. Originally trained as a nurse, she used her medical experience to write her only mystery series—featuring nurse Hilda Adams, also known as Miss Pinkerton. She wrote more than 15 nonseries novels, in addition to several novelettes, numerous collections of short stories and her 1931 autobiography *My Story* which was revised in 1948. Early in her career she invested in the publishing company that was to become Farrar and Rinehart which published all her books after 1930. In 1953 she was awarded a special honor by the Mystery Writers of America.

Hilda Adams aka Miss Pinkerton . . . nurse & police agent in England
- ❏ ❏ 1 - Miss Pinkerton (1932)
- ❏ ❏ 2 - Haunted Lady (1942)
- ❏ ❏ 3 - The Wandering Knife (1952)

■ **Ann RIPLEY** is the creator of a new series featuring Louise Eldridge, organic gardener in suburban Washington DC. In the series opener, Louise finds a body amidst the grass clippings and leaves she has collected in the neighborhood. The sequel to *Mulch* is aptly titled *Death of a Garden Pest*. Ripley has worked as a stringer for the *New York Times*, writer and editor for a suburban daily and placement coordinator at Medill School of Journalism at Northwestern University. She is currently working on a new series set in a retirement home.

> **Louise Eldridge** . . . organic gardener in suburban Washington DC
> ❏ ❏ 1 - Mulch (1994)
> ❏ ❏ 2 - Death of a Garden Pest (1995)

■ **Candace M. ROBB** is the creator of a new medieval mystery series featuring Welsh marksman Owen Archer, blind in one eye after a longbow incident. First appearing in *The Apothecary Rose* (1993), the gentle Archer is, in fact, a spy for the Archbishop of York. His most recent case, *The Nun's Tale* (1995), involves disturbing stories about the resurrection of a young nun. A native of North Carolina, Robb has an MA in English literature from the University of Cincinnati and has completed her coursework for a PhD in medieval and Anglo-Saxon literature. A frequent visitor to England for her research, Robb lives in Seattle.

> **Owen Archer** . . . medieval Welsh spy for the Archbishop
> ❏ ❏ 1 - The Apothecary Rose (1993)
> ❏ ❏ 2 - The Lady Chapel (1994)
> ❏ ❏ 3 - The Nun's Tale (1995)

■ **J. D. ROBB** is the pseudonym of best-selling romance writer Nora Roberts for her futuristic police series set in 21st century New York, featuring homicide detective Eve Dallas and multi-billionaire Roarke, introduced in *Naked in Death* (1995). Roberts says she chose writing over a nervous breakdown one fierce winter while marooned with her two sons in western Maryland. The first to be inducted into the Romance Writers of America Hall of Fame, she has won virtually every award for excellence in her field, with more than 25 million books in print worldwide. Her 100th published novel, the hardcover epic romance *Montana Sky*, is scheduled for release in March 1996, not quite 15 years after publication of her first title, *Irish Thoroughbred* in May 1981.

> **Eve Dallas** . . . homicide lieutenant in 21st century New York City
> ❏ ❏ 1 - Naked in Death (1995)
> ❏ ❏ 2 - Glory in Death (1996)
> ❏ ❏ 3 - Immortal in Death (1996)

■ **Carey ROBERTS** is the creator of a police series featuring Washington DC homicide detective Anne Fitzhugh. Roberts, who has written about Washington in numerous national publications, is both a working writer and a practicing psychotherapist in suburban Maryland. She is currently working on the third installment of this series.

> **Anne Fitzhugh** . . . Washington DC police detective
> ❏ ❏ 1 - Touch a Cold Door (1989)
> ❏ ❏ 2 - Pray God to Die (1993)

■ **Gillian ROBERTS** is the pseudonym of Judith Greber for her award-winning series featuring Amanda Pepper, 30-something high school English teacher at a Philadelphia prep school introduced in the Anthony winner *Caught Dead in Philadelphia* (1987). Greber is a native Philadelphian, graduate of the University of Pennsylvania and a former high school English teacher. She presently lives in the San Francisco Bay area.

Amanda Pepper . . . Philadelphia, Pennsylvania high school teacher
- ❏ ❏ 1 - **Caught Dead in Philadelphia** (1987) *Anthony winner* ★
- ❏ ❏ 2 - **Philly Stakes** (1989) *Agatha nominee* ☆
- ❏ ❏ 3 - I'd Rather Be in Philadelphia (1991)
- ❏ ❏ 4 - With Friends Like These (1993)
- ❏ ❏ 5 - How I Spent My Summer Vacation (1994)
- ❏ ❏ 6 - In the Dead of Summer (1995)

■ **Lora ROBERTS**, born and raised in Missouri, has lived for 20 years in Palo Alto, California, the setting of her mystery series featuring vagabond writer Liz Sullivan. The first installment, *Revolting Development*, was published under the name Lora Roberts Smith. The sleuthing Liz, introduced in *Murder in a Nice Neighborhood,* returns in *Murder in the Marketplace* and will be back in *Murder Mile-High* in 1996.

Liz Sullivan . . . Palo Alto, California freelance writer
- ❏ ❏ 1 - Murder in a Nice Neighborhood (1994)
- ❏ ❏ 2 - Murder in the Marketplace (1995)
- ❏ ❏ 3 - Murder Mile-High (1996)

■ **Lynda S. ROBINSON's** first Lord Meren novel, *Murder in the Place of Anubis*, debuted with a starred review in *Publisher's Weekly*, as did the second and third installments of this critically-acclaimed series. Set in ancient Egypt, it features the chief investigator for the Pharaoh Tutankhamen. Robinson has a PhD in anthropology from the University of Texas at Austin and lives in San Antonio.

Lord Meren . . . chief investigator for Pharaoh Tutankhamen in Egypt
- ❏ ❏ 1 - Murder in the Place of Anubis (1994)
- ❏ ❏ 2 - Murder at the God's Gate (1995)
- ❏ ❏ 3 - Murder at the Feast of Rejoicing (1996)

■ **Julie ROBITAILLE** is the creator of a new mystery series featuring television sports reporter and part-time sportscaster Kit Powell of San Diego. Robitaille, who is a native of Los Angeles, has worked as a story analyst for several major motion picture studios in southern California where she currently lives.

Kit Powell . . . San Diego, California TV sports reporter
- ❏ ❏ 1 - Jinx (1992)
- ❏ ❏ 2 - Iced (1994)

■ **Nina ROMBERG**, of Richardson, Texas, is the creator of a new series featuring Texas Caddo-Commanche medicine woman Marian Winchester, introduced in *The Spirit Stalker*.

Marian Winchester . . . Texas Caddo-Commanche medicine woman
- ❏ ❏ 1 - The Spirit Stalker (1989)
- ❏ ❏ 2 - Shadow Walkers (1993)

■ **Annette ROOME**, of Guilford, England, won the Creasey award for best first crime novel with her 1989 series opener, *A Real Shot in the Arm,* featuring 40-something cub reporter Christine Martin.

Christine Martin . . . 40-something cub reporter in England
- ❏ ❏ 1 - **A Real Shot in the Arm** (1989) *Creasey winner* ★
- ❏ ❏ 2 - A Second Shot in the Dark (1990)

■ **Kate ROSS** is a trial attorney for a large Boston law firm. During her study of legal history at Yale Law School, she was fascinated by the lack of professional police in early 19th century England, a perfect setting for a clever amateur sleuth. Her series detective is the charming and elegant Julian Kestrel whose manservant Dipper is a former pickpocket. A Greek scholar as an undergraduate, Ross says she has virtually no life outside 19th century England because even though she walks fast and talks fast, she researches very slowly.

Julian Kestrel . . . 1820s dandy-about-town in London
❑ ❑   1 -   Cut to the Quick (1993)
❑ ❑   2 -   **A Broken Vessel** (1994) *Gargoyle winner* ★
❑ ❑   3 -   Whom the Gods Love (1995)

■ **Rebecca ROTHENBERG** of Los Angeles is the creator of a new series featuring MIT microbiologist Claire Sharples who leaves her Boston research post for a new job in the agricultural heartland of California. The first installment was nominated for an Anthony and an Agatha award and named one of the ten best mystery novels of 1992 by the *Los Angeles Times*. An amateur botanist, Rothenberg is a data analysis consultant in epidemiology and editor of her chapter's newsletter of the California Native Plant Society. Raised in northern New York state, Rothenberg attended Swarthmore College and after a stint in Nashville, spent five years trying to break into the world of country–western singing and song writing.

Claire Sharples . . . former MIT scholar/microbiologist in central California
❑ ❑   1 -   **The Bulrush Murders** (1991) *Agatha & Anthony nominee* ☆ ☆
❑ ❑   2 -   The Dandelion Murders (1994)
❑ ❑   3 -   The Shy Tulip Murders (1995)

■ **Jennifer ROWE** is an award-winning Australian writer and creator of a mystery series featuring Australian television researcher Birdie Birdwood. Rowe is also editor of *The Australian Women's Weekly*.

Verity "Birdie" Birdwood . . . Australian TV researcher
❑ ❑   1 -   Murder by the Book (1989)
❑ ❑   2 -   Grim Pickings (1991)
❑ ❑   -   Death in Store [short stories with Birdie] (1992)
❑ ❑   3 -   The Makeover Murders (1993)
❑ ❑   4 -   Stranglehold (1994)

■ **Betty ROWLANDS**, of Gloucestershire, England, is the creator of a mystery series featuring Melissa Craig, successful British crime novelist who leaves London to write from a quiet cottage in the Cotswolds. Rowlands has had a varied career as secretary, language teacher and writer of educational materials for students of English as a foreign language.

Melissa Craig . . . British mystery writer in Cotswolds, England
❑ ❑   1 -   Murder in the Cotswolds (1989)
❑ ❑   2 -   A Little Gentle Sleuthing (1990)
❑ ❑   3 -   Finishing Touch (1993)
❑ ❑   4 -   Over the Edge (1993)
❑ ❑   5 -   Exhaustive Inquiries (1994)
❑ ❑   6 -   Malice Poetic (1995)
❑ ❑   7 -   Smiling at Death (1996)

■ **S. J. ROZAN** is Shira J. Rozan (pronounced Rose-ANNE) whose first name is Hebrew for song. A graduate of Oberlin College and a practicing architect in New York City, Rozan has worked as a self-defense instructor, jewelry saleswoman, photographer and janitor. Her architectural specialties include police stations, firehouses and zoo buildings—especially aviaries. She is the creator of a new series featuring New York City private eyes Lydia Chin and Bill Smith. Chin, a 30-something Chinese American, and Smith, a 40-something Army brat and Chin's investigative partner, are also featured in Rozan's short stories. The series opener, *China Trade* (1994) is narrated by Lydia, and the second installment is told from Bill's point of view. Lydia will retake center stage in book #3 as part of Rozan's plan to let Lydia and Bill alternate as narrators.

Lydia Chin & Bill Smith . . . 30-something Chinese American & 40-something Army brat P. I.s in New York
- ❑ ❑ 1 - China Trade (1994)
- ❑ ❑ 2 - Concourse (1995)

■ **Jean RURYK** is the creator of a light-hearted new series featuring Catherine Wilde, a 60-something advertising executive turned antiques restorer. In the series opener, Cat robs a bank (to save the house she's about to lose) and ends up taking home her hostages who are fleeing an abusive husband and father. A former Young & Rubicam Creative Director and now a freelance writer, the author lives in Montreal where she is writing more Wilde tales.

Catherine Wilde . . . 60-something advertising exec turned antiques restorer
- ❑ ❑ 1 - Chicken Little Was Right (1994)

■ **Medora SALE** was born in Windsor, Ontario where her attorney father, a specialist in weaponry, was an official in the court system. With a BA in modern languages and a PhD in medieval studies from the University of Toronto, she has worked as a teacher, welfare case worker, advertising freelancer, translator and typist, while living in England, Switzerland, France and the United States. Her mystery series features Toronto homicide detective John Sanders, introduced in *Murder on the Run* (1986), which won the Arthur Ellis Award for best first novel from the Crime Writers of Canada. In book #2, Sanders is sent to Ottawa for a seminar on terrorism and he runs (quite literally) into architectural photographer Harriet Jeffries. Past president of Crime Writers of Canada, she currently serves on the board of Sisters in Crime International and lives in Toronto with her photographer husband, a professor of medieval studies, originally from Boston.

John Sanders & Harriet Jeffries . . . Toronto, Canada police detective & architectural photographer
- ❑ ❑ 1 - **Murder on the Run** (1986) *Ellis winner* ★
- ❑ ❑ 2 - Murder in Focus (1989)
- ❑ ❑ 3 - Murder in a Good Cause (1990)
- ❑ ❑ 4 - Sleep of the Innocent (1991)
- ❑ ❑ 5 - Pursued by Shadows (1992)
- ❑ ❑ 6 - Short Cut to Santa Fe (1994)

■ **Eve K. SANDSTROM** is a former award-winning reporter and columnist for the *Lawton Constitution* in Oklahoma, the home state for her series characters Sam and Nicky Titus after they are abruptly relocated from Germany soon after their marriage. Sam is an army criminal investigations officer and Nicky a working photojournalist and daughter of a general.

Sam & Nicky Titus . . . ex-Army CID sheriff/rancher & his photojournalist wife in Holton, Oklahoma
- ❏ ❏ 1 - Death Down Home (1990)
- ❏ ❏ 2 - The Devil down Home (1991)
- ❏ ❏ 3 - The Down Home Heifer Heist (1993)

■ **Karen SAUM** is the creator of a three-book series featuring Brigid Donovan, a 50-something ex-nun, whose first adventure, *Murder is Relative* (1990), takes place in Maine. In the third installment the action moves to Nova Scotia.

Brigid Donovan . . . 50-something ex-nun in Maine
- ❏ ❏ 1 - Murder Is Relative (1990)
- ❏ ❏ 2 - Murder Is Germane (1992)
- ❏ ❏ 3 - Murder Is Material (1994)

■ **Corinne Holt SAWYER**, former actor and TV writer, is a past director of academic special projects at Clemson University in South Carolina. She is also the creator of Angela Benbow and Caledonia Wingate, widows of Navy admirals and residents of a posh retirement community in southern California. They are physical and temperamental opposites—an engaging pair in the little old lady amateur tradition. Their first adventure was nominated for an Agatha.

Angela Benbow & Caledonia Wingate . . . 70-something admirals' widows in southern California
- ❏ ❏ 1 - **The J. Alfred Prufrock Murders** (1988) *Agatha nominee* ☆
- ❏ ❏ 2 - Murder in Gray & White (1989)
- ❏ ❏ 3 - Murder by Owl Light (1992)
- ❏ ❏ 4 - The Peanut Butter Murders (1993)
- ❏ ❏ 5 - Murder Has No Calories (1994)
- ❏ ❏ 6 - Ho-Ho Homicide (1995)

■ **Dorothy L. SAYERS** (1893-1957) was born in Oxford where her father was director of the Christchurch Cathedral Choir School. She learned Latin by the age of seven, picked up French from her governess, and later earned both BA and MA degrees from Oxford while teaching and working as a reader for a publishing company. During the 1920s she worked at a London advertising agency for seven years where she sold Coleman's mustard using the cartoon figures of a British colonel—which later inspired the creation of Colonel Mustard for the board game *Clue*. Sayers' renowned series detective is Lord Peter Wimsey, second son of the fifteenth Duke of Denver, pianist, bibliophile and criminologist. His love interest (apart from the author's infatuation) and future detecting partner Harriet Vane first appears in *Strong Poison*. Sayers was president of the Modern Language Association from 1939 to 1945 and also the Detection Club from 1949-1957. On a plaque near the door of the Witham house where she lived for more than 30 years are the words "Dorothy L. Sayers 1893-1957 novelist, theologian and Dante scholar." The "L," about which she was most particular, stood for Leigh.

Lord Peter Wimsey . . . London pianist, bibliophile & criminologist
- ❏ ❏ 1 - Whose Body? (1923)
- ❏ ❏ 2 - Clouds of Witness (1926)
- ❏ ❏ 3 - Unnatural Death (1927) [U.S.–The Dawson Pedigree]
- ❏ ❏ 4 - The Unpleasantness at the Bellona Club (1928)
- ❏ ❏ 5 - Lord Peter Views the Body (1929)
- ❏ ❏ 6 - Strong Poison (1930)

❏ ❏ 7 - Five Red Herrings (1931) [U.S.–Suspicious Characters]
❏ ❏ 8 - Have His Carcase (1932)
❏ ❏ 9 - Murder Must Advertise (1933)
❏ ❏ - Hangman's Holiday [short stories] (1933)
❏ ❏ 10 - The Nine Tailors (1934)
❏ ❏ 11 - Gaudy Night (1935)
❏ ❏ 12 - Busman's Honeymoon (1937)
❏ ❏ 13 - In the Teeth of the Evidence (1939)

■ **S. E. SCHENKEL** is Shirley Schenkel of Farmington, Michigan, creator of a new series featuring Ray Frederick, Tanglewood, Michigan chief of detectives and his wife of 30 years, Kate. Schenkel is a former nun who spent 19 years in the convent, including a total of 10 years in Africa where she taught in a school for girls in Ghana. In the series opener, a nun is struck by a hit-and-run driver, sending Kate and Ray on a search that goes back 40 years.

Ray & Kate Frederick . . . Michigan chief of detectives & his wife of 30 years
❏ ❏ 1 - In Blacker Moments (1994)
❏ ❏ 2 - Death Days (1995)

■ **Margaret SCHERF** (1908-1979) created several series detectives for mysteries she wrote starting in the 1940s, including New York City decorators, Henry and Emily Bryce, who first appear in 1949 in *The Gun in Daniel Webster's Bust*. Earlier she wrote a pair of novels featuring NYPD cop Lt. Ryan. A master at titles, she reserved some of her best for the series starring Rev. Martin Buell, who first appears in 1948 in *Always Murder a Friend*. Scherf also gets credit for what is probably the first woman pathologist in mysteries, Dr. Grace Sever-ance, who made her debut in 1968 in *The Banker's Bones*. During World War II Scherf was Secretary to the Naval Inspector at the Brooklyn Shipyard of Bethlehem Steel and later served one session in the House of the Montana Legislature in the mid-1960s.

Emily & Henry Bryce . . . Manhattan interior decorators
❏ ❏ 1 - The Gun in Daniel Webster's Bust (1949)
❏ ❏ 2 - The Green Plaid Pants (1951) [APA–The Corpse with One Shoe]
❏ ❏ 3 - Glass on the Stairs (1954)
❏ ❏ 4 - The Diplomat and the Gold Piano (1963)
         [Britain–Death and the Diplomat]

Dr. Grace Severance . . . Arizona retired pathologist
❏ ❏ 1 - The Banker's Bones (1968)
❏ ❏ 2 - The Beautiful Birthday Cake (1971)
❏ ❏ 3 - To Cache a Millionaire (1972)
❏ ❏ 4 - The Beaded Banana (1978)

Lt. Ryan . . . NYPD cop in New York
❏ ❏ 1 - The Owl in the Cellar (1945)
❏ ❏ 2 - Murder Makes Me Nervous (1948)

Reverend Martin Buell . . . Episcopal rector in Farrington, Montana
❏ ❏ 1 - Always Murder a Friend (1948)
❏ ❏ 2 - Gilbert's Last Toothache (1949) [APA–For the Love of Murder]
❏ ❏ 3 - The Curious Custard Pie (1950) [APA–Divine and Deadly]
❏ ❏ 4 - The Elk and the Evidence (1952)
❏ ❏ 5 - The Cautious Overshoes (1956)
❏ ❏ 6 - The Corpse in the Flannel Nightgown (1965)

■ **Norma SCHIER** is the author of a four-book series featuring Colorado district attorney Kay Barth, opening with *Death on the Slopes* (1978).

    Kay Barth . . . Colorado district attorney
- ❏ ❏ 1 - Death on the Slopes (1978)
- ❏ ❏ 2 - Murder by the Book (1979)
- ❏ ❏ 3 - Death Goes Skiing (1979)
- ❏ ❏ 4 - Demon at the Opera (1980)

■ **Carol SCHMIDT** is the author of a new lesbian series featuring amateur sleuth Laney Samms, a Los Angeles bar owner, introduced in *Silverlake Heat* (1993).

    Laney Samms . . . bar owner in Los Angeles
- ❏ ❏ 1 - Silverlake Heat (1993)
- ❏ ❏ 2 - Sweet Cherry Wine (1994)
- ❏ ❏ 3 - Cabin Fever (1994)

■ **Sandra SCOPPETTONE**, of Southold, New York, is the creator of lesbian private eye Lauren Laurano of Greenwich Village and her psychotherapist lover Kip who have now appeared in three titles. Scoppettone's first mysteries were published under the name Jack Early, including *A Creative Kind of Killer,* which won the Shamus for best first P. I. novel in 1984 and was also nominated for an Edgar. Scoppettone says she used a male pseudonym simply because the voice came to her as first person male. The three titles originally published under the Jack Early name are currently being re-released with the Scoppettone name on the cover. She is one of the founding members of Sisters in Crime.

    Lauren Laurano . . . Greenwich Village lesbian P. I.
- ❏ ❏ 1 - Everything You Have Is Mine (1991)
- ❏ ❏ 2 - I'll Be Leaving You Always (1993)
- ❏ ❏ 3 - My Sweet Untraceable You (1994)

■ **Rosie SCOTT** is the creator of amateur detective Glory Day, a New Zealand artist and singer.

    Glory Day . . . New Zealand artist & singer
- ❏ ❏ 1 - Glory Day (1989)

■ **Lisa SCOTTOLINE** is a Philadelphia lawyer, who like her first protagonist, is a good Italian girl who went to the University of Pennsylvania and started her legal career in a large corporate law firm. Scottoline previously worked part-time for the chief judge of a federal appeals court, a background she used for her second mystery. She now writes full-time and any one of her Philadelphia lawyers may yet become a series character. Scottoline says she's keeping her options open.

    Grace Rossi . . . Federal appeals attorney & law clerk in
- ❏ ❏ 1 - **Final Appeal** (1994) *Edgar winner* ★

    Mary DiNunzio . . . Philadelphia, Pennsylvania attorney
- ❏ ❏ 1 - **Everywhere That Mary Went** (1993) *Edgar nominee* ☆

    Rita Morrone Hamilton . . . attorney in Philadelphia
- ❏ ❏ 1 - Running from the Law (1995)

■ **Kate SEDLEY** is the pseudonym used by Brenda Margaret Lilian Honeyman Clarke for her history-mystery series featuring Roger the Chapman, a 15th century peddler in England. Although his mother originally sent him to a Benedictine monastery, Roger answers the call of the outside world where he makes the acquaintance of the Duke of Gloucester and future king Richard III.

Roger the Chapman . . . medieval chapman (peddler) in England
- ❑ ❑ 1 - Death and the Chapman (1991)
- ❑ ❑ 2 - The Plymouth Cloak (1992)
- ❑ ❑ 3 - The Weaver's Tale (1993)
- ❑ ❑ 4 - The Hanged Man (1993)
- ❑ ❑ 5 - The Holy Innocents (1994)
- ❑ ❑ 6 - Eve of St. Hyacinth (1996)

■ **Louise SHAFFER** is the creator of amateur sleuth Angie DaVito who is the producer of a television soap opera. Her debut in *All My Suspects* provides a laugh-a-minute look at daytime television from a woman who happens to be an Emmy-award winning soap opera star. Shaffer's credits include *All My Children*, *The Edge of Night* and *Ryan's Hope*. She divides her time between New York and a farm in Georgia.

Angie DaVito . . . TV soap opera producer in New York
- ❑ ❑ 1 - All My Suspects (1994)
- ❑ ❑ 2 - Talked to Death (1995)

■ **Diane K. SHAH** is an experienced journalist and mystery author who has recreated Hollywood in the late 1940s for her series with Paris Chandler, assistant to the gossip columnist on the *Los Angeles Examiner*. Shah is also co-author of LAPD chief Daryl Gates' autobiography, *Chief*.

Paris Chandler . . . 1940s Hollywood P. I.
- ❑ ❑ 1 - As Crime Goes By (1990)
- ❑ ❑ 2 - Dying Cheek to Cheek (1992)

■ **Sarah SHANKMAN** is the creator of Georgia journalist Samantha Adams, whose first two titles originally appeared under the name of Alice Storey. Shankman returned to the use of her own name for the third installment and continues perfecting her unique blend of wit and humor. In 1995 she introduced a new series set in Nashville with the opening title, *I Still Miss My Man But My Aim is Getting Better*.

Samantha Adams . . . Atlanta, Georgia investigative reporter
- ❑ ❑ 1 - First Kill All the Lawyers (1988)
- ❑ ❑ 2 - Then Hang All the Liars (1989)
- ❑ ❑ 3 - Now Let's Talk of Graves (1990)
- ❑ ❑ 4 - She Walks in Beauty (1991)
- ❑ ❑ 5 - The King Is Dead (1992)
- ❑ ❑ 6 - He Was Her Man (1993)

■ **Dell SHANNON** (1921-1988) is one of several pseudonyms used by Elizabeth Linington during a prolific writing career which produced mysteries, historical novels and romantic suspense. She also wrote as Anne Blaisdell, Lesley Egan and Egan O'Neill. For more than 20 years she completed an average of three books a year for a lifetime total of 88 novels. Writing in *Murderess Ink*, she described her writing style as total immersion. "It's all I do for 18 hours a day, for 10 or 12 days without a break, writing in longhand. I have a 22-foot flagpole outside my house and when I run up the *Don't Tread on Me* banner people know to leave me alone." Each February, March and June she produced a full-length novel in this fashion. Although she was single and lived alone most of her life, her series mysteries reverberate with family life. Shannon's first and perhaps favorite detective was Lieutenant Luis Rodolfo Vicente Mendoza, head of LAPD Homicide. Inheriting millions allowed him to drive fancy cars, dress like a prince and comfortably enjoy a wife, three kids, an adopted grandmother, cats, dogs and a flock of sheep on his refurbished country estate. An unusual detective indeed.

Luis Mendoza . . . Los Angeles, California dapper & wealthy homicide lieutenant

❑ ❑ 1 - **Case Pending** (1960) *Edgar nominee* ☆
❑ ❑ 2 - The Ace of Spades (1960)
❑ ❑ 3 - Extra Kill (1961)
❑ ❑ 4 - **Knave of Hearts** (1962) *Edgar nominee* ☆
❑ ❑ 5 - Death of a Busybody (1963)
❑ ❑ 6 - Double Bluff (1963)
❑ ❑ 7 - Mark of Murder (1964)
❑ ❑ 8 - Root of All Evil (1964)
❑ ❑ 9 - The Death-Bringers (1965)
❑ ❑ 10 - Death by Inches (1965)
❑ ❑ 11 - Coffin Corner (1966)
❑ ❑ 12 - With a Vengeance (1966)
❑ ❑ 13 - Chance to Kill (1966)
❑ ❑ 14 - Rain with Violence (1967)
❑ ❑ 15 - Kill with Kindness (1968)
❑ ❑ 16 - Schooled to Kill (1969)
❑ ❑ 17 - Crime on Their Hands (1969)
❑ ❑ 18 - Unexpected Death (1970)
❑ ❑ 19 - Whim to Kill (1971)
❑ ❑ 20 - The Ringer (1971)
❑ ❑ 21 - Murder with Love (1972)
❑ ❑ 22 - With Intent to Kill (1972)
❑ ❑ 23 - No Holiday for Crime (1973)
❑ ❑ 24 - Spring of Violence (1973)
❑ ❑ 25 - Crime File (1974)
❑ ❑ 26 - Deuces Wild (1975)
❑ ❑ 27 - Streets of Death (1976)
❑ ❑ 28 - Appearances of Death (1977)
❑ ❑ 29 - Cold Trail (1978)
❑ ❑ 30 - Felony at Random (1979)
❑ ❑ 31 - Felony File (1980)
❑ ❑ 32 - Murder Most Strange (1981)
❑ ❑ 33 - The Motive on Record (1982)
❑ ❑ 34 - Exploits of Death (1983)
❑ ❑ 35 - Destiny of Death (1984)
❑ ❑ 36 - Chaos of Crime (1985)
❑ ❑ 37 - Blood Count (1986)
❑ ❑   - Murder by Tale [short stories] (1987)

■ **Connie SHELTON** is both the author and publisher (for Intrigue Press) of a new series featuring investigator Charlie Parker, an Albuquerque CPA who's in partnership with her brother Ron. In book #2 of this series, Charlie meets a handsome helicopter pilot in Hawaii, not unlike the author herself who later married the helicopter pilot she met on her Hawaiian vacation. Shelton is a commercial hot air balloon pilot and currently holds the woman's world altitude record for a size AX-4 balloon. She and her helicopter pilot husband live in northern New Mexico.

> **Charlie Parker** . . . CPA turned reluctant investigator in New Mexico
> - ❏ ❏ 1 - Deadly Gamble (1995)
> - ❏ ❏ 2 - Vacations Can Be Murder (1995)
> - ❏ ❏ 3 - Relative Innocence (1996)

■ **Stella SHEPHERD**, who practiced medicine before she turned to writing, has special knowledge about the use of drugs and poisons to commit murder. Her Richard Montgomery titles are police procedurals with a diabolical medical twist.

> **Inspector Richard Montgomery** . . . Nottingham CID Inspector in England
> - ❏ ❏ 1 - Black Justice (1989)
> - ❏ ❏ 2 - Murderous Remedy (1990)
> - ❏ ❏ 3 - Thinner Than Blood (1992)
> - ❏ ❏ 4 - A Lethal Fixation (1993)
> - ❏ ❏ 5 - Nurse Dawes Is Dead (1994)
> - ❏ ❏ 6 - Something in the Cellar (1995)

■ **Juanita SHERIDAN** created the first Asian woman sleuth, Lily Wu, who along with her foster sister Janice, solves her first case in New York and later returns to her native Hawaii. In the series opener, Janice helps clear Lily of murder and is adopted by her grateful family. The four-book series featuring this indomitable pair ran from 1949 to 1953.

> **Lily Wu & Janice Cameron** . . . investigator & foster sister in Hawaii
> - ❏ ❏ 1 - The Chinese Chop (1949)
> - ❏ ❏ 2 - The Kahuna Killer (1951)
> - ❏ ❏ 3 - The Mamo Murders (1952) [Britain–While the Coffin Waited]
> - ❏ ❏ 4 - The Waikiki Widow (1953)

■ **Anna SHONE** is the creator of a new private eye series featuring Shakespeare-spouting Ulysses Finnegan Donaghue, who makes his first appearance in *Mr. Donaghue Investigates* (1995). Donaghue is vacationing in Provence when a notorious Hollywood film director is found dead during the opening weekend of a spiritual retreat at the abbey in St. Pierre la Croix. Although the death is made to look like suicide, the director's dying words—a quote from *Twelfth Night*—lead Ulysses to believe it was murder. Shone is a former English teacher who lives in the south of France. This series debut is her first mystery.

> **Ulysses Finnegan Donaghue** . . . Shakespeare-spouting P. I. in Provence France
> - ❏ ❏ 1 - Mr. Donaghue Investigates (1995)

■ **Sharon Gwyn SHORT** is an experienced technical and business writer in the computer industry, with her own computer whiz detective, P. I. Patricia Delaney. Short has a BA in English and an MA in Technical Communication from Bowling Green State University. She is an Ohio native.

> **Patricia Delaney** . . . Cincinnati, Ohio computer whiz P. I.
> - ❏ ❏ 1 - Angel's Bidding (1994)
> - ❏ ❏ 2 - Past Pretense (1994)
> - ❏ ❏ 3 - The Death We Share (1995)

■ **Celestine SIBLEY** first introduced her series detective Kathryn Kincaid in *The Malignant Heart* in 1958. The second installment was 33 years in the making and the once young Katy Kincaid is now a widow, but still a reporter. Like Kincaid, Sibley is also a veteran Atlanta newswriter.

Kate Kincaid Mulcay . . . veteran newspaperwoman in Atlanta, Georgia
- ❑ ❑ 1 - The Malignant Heart (1958)
- ❑ ❑ 2 - Ah, Sweet Mystery (1991)
- ❑ ❑ 3 - Straight as an Arrow (1992)
- ❑ ❑ 4 - Dire Happenings at Scratch Ankle (1993)
- ❑ ❑ 5 - A Plague of Kinfolks (1995)

■ **Linda Kay SILVA** is the creator of Delta Stevens, a gay woman police officer in California. Each of the four titles features strong weather, starting with the 1991 series opener *Taken by Storm*.

Delta Stevens . . . policewoman in California
- ❑ ❑ 1 - Taken by Storm (1991)
- ❑ ❑ 2 - Storm Shelter (1993)
- ❑ ❑ 3 - Weathering the Storm (1994)
- ❑ ❑ 4 - Storm Front (1995)

■ **Sheila SIMONSON** teaches history and English at Clark College in Vancouver, Washington and is the creator of the Lark Dodge series featuring a West coast book dealer and her homicide detective husband.

Lark Dailey Dodge . . . 6-ft. bookdealer in northern California
- ❑ ❑ 1 - Larkspur (1990)
- ❑ ❑ 2 - Skylark (1992)
- ❑ ❑ 3 - Mudlark (1993)
- ❑ ❑ 4 - Meadowlark (1996)

■ **Dorothy SIMPSON** began her Luke Thanet series about the family man police inspector in 1981. She was awarded the Silver Dagger by the British Crime Writers Association for the fifth book in the series and continues to charm her fans with contemporary tales of English urban family life.

Inspector Luke Thanet . . . British police inspector
- ❑ ❑ 1 - The Night She Died (1981)
- ❑ ❑ 2 - Six Feet Under (1982)
- ❑ ❑ 3 - Puppet for a Corpse (1983)
- ❑ ❑ 4 - Close Her Eyes (1984)
- ❑ ❑ 5 - **Last Seen Alive (1985)** *Silver Dagger* ★
- ❑ ❑ 6 - Dead on Arrival (1986)
- ❑ ❑ 7 - Element of Doubt (1987)
- ❑ ❑ 8 - Suspicious Death (1988)
- ❑ ❑ 9 - Dead by Morning (1989)
- ❑ ❑ 10 - Doomed To Die (1991)
- ❑ ❑ 11 - Wake Her Dead (1992)
- ❑ ❑ 12 - No Laughing Matter (1993)
- ❑ ❑ 13 - A Day for Dying (1995)

■ **L. V. SIMS** is the creator of the Dixie Struthers series featuring one of the first women to join the San Jose, California police department. As the daughter and granddaughter of Irish cops Dixie is prepared for the challenges of sexism and discrimination. High-tech crimes of the computer world provide an intriguing backdrop for these police procedurals penned by the wife of a San Jose police officer.

Dixie T. Struthers . . . San Jose, California police detective
- ❑ ❑ 1 - Murder Is Only Skin Deep (1987)
- ❑ ❑ 2 - Death Is a Family Affair (1987)
- ❑ ❑ 3 - To Sleep, Perchance to Kill (1988)

■ **Shelley SINGER** grew up in Minneapolis and began her career as a UPI reporter in Chicago. She currently lives in the San Francisco Bay area which is also the setting for her two series. Jake Samson is an ex-Chicago cop who lands in Oakland after leaving the Midwest. Using press credentials provided by his friend the magazine editor, Jake solves a series of crimes with the assistance of Rosie the carpenter who rents a small cottage on his property. Singer's newer series features Barrett Lake, the high school history teacher who'd rather be a P. I. Singer also teaches mystery writing and does book reviews for Pacifica Public Radio.

Barrett Lake . . . Berkeley, California high school history teacher
- ❑ ❑ 1 - Following Jane (1993)
- ❑ ❑ 2 - Picture of David (1993)
- ❑ ❑ 3 - Searching for Sara (1994)
- ❑ ❑ 4 - Interview with Mattie (1995)
- ❑ ❑ 5 - Anthony's Tattoo (1996)

Jake Samson & Rosie Vicente . . . Berkeley, California ex-cop & carpenter tenant
- ❑ ❑ 1 - Samson's Deal (1983)
- ❑ ❑ 2 - Free Draw (1984)
- ❑ ❑ 3 - Full House (1986)
- ❑ ❑ 4 - Spit in the Ocean (1987)
- ❑ ❑ 5 - Suicide King (1988)

■ **Maj SJÖWALL and Per WAHLÖÖ** (1926-1975), creators of chess-playing cop Martin Beck, are Sweden's premier mystery writers. This Communist wife and husband team wrote alternate chapters in their Stockholm police series which won an Edgar for best novel in 1970 with *The Laughing Policeman*. In 1973 the book made it to the big screen in America and although the movie retained the book's title, the action inexplicably moved to San Francisco, starring Walter Matthau and Bruce Dern. Subplots in the Beck series involve the lives of Stockholm's Homicide Squad—something like 87th Precinct without the levity. A search for the killer in the series opener is complicated by the victim's unknown identity. The case gets stranger when it is learned that the young woman is a librarian from Lincoln, Nebraska, found dead in a canal south of Stockholm.

Martin Beck . . . police officer in Stockholm Sweden
- ❑ ❑ 1 - Roseanna (1967)
- ❑ ❑ 2 - The Man on the Balcony (1968)
- ❑ ❑ 3 - The Man Who Went Up in Smoke (1969)
- ❑ ❑ 4 - **The Laughing Policeman** (1970) *Edgar winner* ★
- ❑ ❑ 5 - Murder at the Savoy (1971)
- ❑ ❑ 6 - The Fire Engine That Disappeared (1971)
- ❑ ❑ 7 - The Abominable Man (1972)
- ❑ ❑ 8 - The Locked Room (1973)
- ❑ ❑ 9 - Cop Killer (1975)
- ❑ ❑ 10 - The Terrorists (1976)

■ **Edith SKOM**, of Winnetka, Illinois, is the creator of college English professor Elizabeth Austin whose first adventure was nominated for three awards for best first mystery.

Elizabeth Austin . . . midwestern English professor
- ❏ ❏ 1 - **The Mark Twain Murders** (1989)
  Agatha, Anthony & Macavity nominee ☆ ☆ ☆
- ❏ ❏ 2 - The George Eliot Murders (1995)

■ **Gillian SLOVO** grew up in South Africa where her father is a senior official with the African National Congress and her mother was an anti-apartheid activist killed by a letter bomb. Slovo's character, Kate Baeier, is a left-wing Portuguese, saxophone-playing, freelance journalist-investigator whose milieu is a London of racial diversity, street politics and activist ferment.

Kate Baeier . . . London freelance journalist turned detective
- ❏ ❏ 1 - Morbid Symptoms (1984)
- ❏ ❏ 2 - Death Comes Staccato (1987)
- ❏ ❏ 3 - Death by Analysis (1988)
- ❏ ❏ 4 - Catnap (1994)
- ❏ ❏ 5 - Close Call (1995)

■ **April SMITH** is the creator of a new series featuring Los Angeles FBI agent Ana Grey, a seven-year veteran in line for promotion. James Ellroy called this debut novel a "righteously spirited cruise through present-day LA."

Ana Grey . . . FBI agent in Los Angeles
- ❏ ❏ 1 - North of Montana (1994)

■ **Barbara Burnett SMITH** is the creator of the Anthony-nominated series featuring Jolie Wyatt, aspiring novelist who debuts in *Writers of the Purple Sage* (1994). Smith, who writes and directs mystery dinner theatre and weekend plays, is also a training consultant in Austin, Texas.

Jolie Wyatt . . . aspiring novelist & writer's group member in Purple Sage, Texas
- ❏ ❏ 1 - **Writers of the Purple Sage** (1994) *Agatha nominee* ☆
- ❏ ❏ 2 - Dust Devils of the Purple Sage (1995)
- ❏ ❏ 3 - Celebration in Purple Sage (1996)

■ **Evelyn E. SMITH** is the creator of a zany series featuring art teacher and painter down-on-her-luck Susan Melville who inadvertently sets herself up as a freelance assassin when she shoots the speaker at a charity function. Miss Melville has high standards and will not take a contract unless the victim deserves to die. She is scrupulous about paying her income tax and always produces a painting to match a contract payment.

Susan Melville . . . New York City freelance assassin & painter
- ❏ ❏ 1 - Miss Melville Regrets (1986)
- ❏ ❏ 2 - Miss Melville Returns (1987)
- ❏ ❏ 3 - Miss Melville's Revenge (1989)
- ❏ ❏ 4 - Miss Melville Rides a Tiger (1991)
- ❏ ❏ 5 - Miss Melville Runs for Cover (1995)

■ **J. C. S. SMITH** is the name used by Jane S. Smith for her pair of detective novels featuring New York City private eye Quentin Jacoby, introduced in *Jacoby's First Case* (1980).

     Quentin Jacoby . . . New York city private eye
- ❏ ❏ 1 - Jacoby's First Case (1980)
- ❏ ❏ 2 - Nightcap (1984)

■ **Janet L. SMITH** is a Seattle attorney whose series character Annie MacPherson is similarly employed, starting with *Sea of Troubles* (1990), nominated for an Agatha as best first traditional mystery. If you enjoy law firm politics, this series delivers with latte. A fourth-generation Californian who has worked as a trial attorney in a large regional firm, Smith is now a part-time litigator for a much smaller law practice.

     Annie MacPherson . . . Seattle, Washington attorney
- ❏ ❏ 1 - **Sea of Troubles** (1990) *Agatha nominee* ☆
- ❏ ❏ 2 - Practice to Deceive (1992)
- ❏ ❏ 3 - A Vintage Murder (1994)

■ **Joan SMITH** was born in London where she was formerly a journalist and theatre critic on the London *Sunday Times*. Several of her series mysteries have been filmed for BBC television, featuring amateur detective Loretta Lawson, professor of English and active feminist scholar at the University of London. Smith, the author of several nonfiction books including *Misogynies: Reflections on Myths and Malice*, lives in Oxfordshire where she also writes articles and reviews for the *Guardian*, the *Observer*, the *Independent on Sunday* and *Harpers & Queen*.

     Loretta Lawson . . . British feminist professor
- ❏ ❏ 1 - A Masculine Ending (1987)
- ❏ ❏ 2 - Why Aren't They Screaming? (1988)
- ❏ ❏ 3 - Don't Leave Me This Way (1990)
- ❏ ❏ 4 - What Men Say (1993)
- ❏ ❏ 5 - Full Stop (1995)

■ **Joan G. SMITH**, is Joan Gerarda Smith, a Canadian novelist and author of more than 65 romance novels published between 1977 and 1993, who also wrote a pair of mystery novels featuring Cassie Newton, amateur sleuth and French major at McGill University in Montreal, Quebec. Smith, who holds a degree from Queen's University and a teaching diploma from Ontario College of Education, has taught high school English and French and English at St. Lawrence College in Cornwall, Ontario. Under the name Jennie Gallant she also wrote ten historical romance novels and a number of short stories for anthologies published by Regency. A third Cassie Newton installment (*Sipan Jaguar*) is in progress.

     Cassie Newton . . . French major at McGill University in Montreal Canada
- ❏ ❏ 1 - Capriccio (1989)
- ❏ ❏ 2 - A Brush with Death (1990)

■ **Julie SMITH**, born in Annapolis, raised in Savannah and educated at the University of Mississippi, is a former reporter for the *New Orleans Times-Picayune* and *San Francisco Chronicle*. She has three series detectives to her credit. Freelance writer Paul MacDonald solves real crimes so that he can afford to write the fictional ones. Attorney Rebecca Schwartz, a nice Jewish girl from Marin County, opens her first adventure playing the piano in a feminist bordello. Smith's newest series features Skip Langdon, a daughter of New Orleans high society who becomes a police officer.

Paul MacDonald . . . ex-reporter & mystery writer in San Francisco
- ❏ ❏ 1 - True-Life Adventure (1985)
- ❏ ❏ 2 - Huckleberry Fiend (1987)

Rebecca Schwartz . . . San Francisco defense attorney
- ❏ ❏ 1 - Death Turns a Trick (1982)
- ❏ ❏ 2 - The Sourdough Wars (1984)
- ❏ ❏ 3 - Tourist Trap (1986)
- ❏ ❏ 4 - Dead in the Water (1991)
- ❏ ❏ 5 - Other People's Skeletons (1993)

Skip Langdon . . . 6-ft. police detective in New Orleans, Louisiana
- ❏ ❏ 1 - **New Orleans Mourning** (1990) *Edgar winner* ★
- ❏ ❏ 2 - The Axeman's Jazz (1991)
- ❏ ❏ 3 - Jazz Funeral (1993)
- ❏ ❏ 4 - New Orleans Beat (1994)
- ❏ ❏ 5 - House of Blues (1995)

■ **Michelle SPRING**, of Cambridge, England, is the creator of Cambridge private investigator Laura Principal, introduced in *Every Breath You Take*, which was nominated for Anthony and Ellis awards as best first mystery of 1994. Laura came to Cambridge to read history at Newnham College. She stayed to do her graduate research, find a best friend, survive a failed marriage and forge a partnership (business and personal) with the oh-so-appealing Sonny Mendlowitz. Spring says that Cambridge is the outsider's dream of an English city, but she chose it as the venue for her mystery series because it represents the captivating conjuncture of real life in a fairy tale setting.

Laura Principal . . . British academic turned P. I.
- ❏ ❏ 1 - **Every Breath You Take** (1994) *Anthony & Ellis nominee* ☆ ☆
- ❏ ❏ 2 - Running for Shelter (1995)

■ **Patricia Houck SPRINKLE**, of Miami, Florida, is the creator of a series featuring widowed public relations executive Sheila Travis who spent a number of years in Japan with her husband, the abusive diplomat. But Sheila's foreign service experience lands her a job in Chicago training students for the diplomatic corps, and she soon returns to her native South where she joins a Japanese firm in Atlanta. Author of the nonfiction title *Women Who Do Too Much*, Sprinkle has also written *Women Home Alone: Learning To Thrive*, a 1996 title for Zondervan Press.

Sheila Travis . . . administrative assistant turned public relations executive in Atlanta, Georgia
- ❏ ❏ 1 - Murder at Markham (1988)
- ❏ ❏ 2 - Murder in the Charleston Manner (1990)
- ❏ ❏ 3 - Murder on Peachtree Street (1991)
- ❏ ❏ 4 - Somebody's Dead in Snellville (1992)
- ❏ ❏ 5 - Death of a Dunwoody Matron (1993)
- ❏ ❏ 6 - A Mystery Bred in Buckhead (1994)
- ❏ ❏ 7 - Deadly Secrets on the St. Johns (1995)

■ **Elizabeth Daniels SQUIRE** wrote two nonfiction books and another mystery (*Kill the Messenger*) before launching her series about the forgetful senior sleuth Peaches Dann. Squire was born into a newspaper publishing family where both her father and grandfather were controversial editors of *The News and Observer* in Raleigh, North Carolina. She has worked as a columnist in Beirut, a police reporter in Connecticut and once wrote a nation-ally-syndicated column called "How To Read Your Own Hand." She lives on an organic farm near Asheville and is a frequent speaker to library groups and writing workshops.

Peaches Dann . . . absent-minded 50-something North Carolina widow
- ❏ ❏ 1 - Who Killed What's-Her-Name? (1994)
- ❏ ❏ 2 - Remember the Alibi (1994)
- ❏ ❏ 3 - Memory Can Be Murder (1995)

■ **Dana STABENOW**, born in Alaska and raised on a fish tender, is the creator of Edgar award-winning series detective, Aleut Kate Shugak, a former investigator for the Anchorage district attorney's office, and her yellow-eyed half-dog, half-wolf Mutt. This series resonates with the exotic landscape of the Alaskan bush and the fiercely independent people who live there. Before introducing her Alaska mysteries, Stabenow launched a science fiction trilogy featuring Esther "Star" Svensdotter, project leader of the space colony Ellfive. Star's three adventures in Ace paperback original are *Second Star* (1991), *A Handful of Stars* (1991) and *Red Planet Run* (1995), where she accepts a commission to explore Mars.

Kate Shugak . . . native Alaskan ex-D.A. investigator
- ❏ ❏ 1 - **A Cold Day for Murder** (1992) *Edgar winner* ★
- ❏ ❏ 2 - A Fatal Thaw (1993)
- ❏ ❏ 3 - Dead in the Water (1993)
- ❏ ❏ 4 - A Cold-Blooded Business (1994)
- ❏ ❏ 5 - Play with Fire (1995)
- ❏ ❏ 6 - Blood Will Tell (1996)

■ **Susannah STACEY** is one of the pseudonyms used by Jill Staynes and Margaret Storey, former teachers and longtime friends who are writing partners for two mystery series. As Susannah Stacey, they are the creators of the Inspector Bone series featuring the wise and quiet Englishman who is raising his daughter alone after the death of his wife. In the U. K., the Inspector Bone series is published under their real names. As Elizabeth Eyre, Staynes and Storey write a historical series set in Renaissance Italy featuring Sigismondo, agent for the Duke of Rocca.

Inspector Robert Bone . . . widowed British police inspector
- ❏ ❏ 1 - **Goodbye Nanny Gray** (1987) *Agatha nominee* ☆
- ❏ ❏ 2 - A Knife at the Opera (1988)
- ❏ ❏ 3 - Body of Opinion (1988)
- ❏ ❏ 4 - Grave Responsibility (1990)
- ❏ ❏ 5 - The Late Lady (1992)
- ❏ ❏ 6 - Bone Idle (1993)
- ❏ ❏ 7 - Dead Serious (1995)

■ **Veronica STALLWOOD** is the creator of a new series featuring Oxford novelist Kate Ivory who makes her debut appearance in the 1993 title, *Death and the Oxford Box.*

Kate Ivory . . . Oxford novelist in England
- ❏ ❏ 1 - Death and the Oxford Box (1993)
- ❏ ❏ 2 - Oxford Exit (1995)
- ❏ ❏ 3 - Oxford Mourning (1996)

■ **Triss STEIN** is the creator of Kay Engles, a nationally-known reporter who finds murder at her class reunion in the opening installment.

Kay Engles . . . nationally-known reporter
    ❑ ❑   1 - Murder at the Class Reunion (1993)

■ **Janice STEINBERG** is the creator of a new mystery series featuring Margo Simon, a reporter for California Public Radio in San Diego.

    Margo Simon . . . California Public Radio reporter in San Diego, California
    ❑ ❑   1 - Death of a Postmodernist (1995)
    ❑ ❑   2 - Death Crosses the Border (1995)

■ **Susan STEINER**, of Forest Knolls, California, is the creator of Alex Winter, P. I. with the California firm of Abromowitz & Stewart and owner of a one-eyed black cat named Ms. Watson.

    Alex Winter . . . California P. I.
    ❑ ❑   1 - Murder on Her Mind (1991)
    ❑ ❑   2 - Library: No Murder Aloud (1993)

■ **Serita STEVENS** is a registered psychiatric nurse and graduate of the University of Illinois Medical Center in Chicago where she grew up. Her medical training was put to good use in her nonfiction work, *Deadly Doses: A Writer's Guide to Poisons*, which was nominated for an Anthony and a Macavity award. She is also the creator of the Fanny Zindel series featuring a Jewish grandmother sleuth introduced in *Red Sea, Dead Sea* (1991). Stevens has authored several video movies and radio plays and in 1985 produced a novelization of the Cagney and Lacey TV series (*Before the Fourteenth*). Other nonseries novels include *The Shrieking Shadow of Penporth Island* (1983) and *The Bloodstone Inheritance* (1985). A native of Chicago, she currently lives in north San Fernando Valley, California.

    Fanny Zindel . . . Jewish grandmother
    ❑ ❑   1 - Red Sea, Dead Sea (1991)
    ❑ ❑   2 - Bagels for Tea (1993)

■ **Dorothy SUCHER**, an experienced psychotherapist, mother and editor of a small-town weekly newspaper, is the creator of Sabina Swift, Washington DC, P. I. and her young side-kick Vic Newman. *Dead Men Don't Give Seminars* was nominated for an Agatha as best first traditional mystery.

    Sabina Swift . . . Georgetown detective agency owner
    ❑ ❑   1 - **Dead Men Don't Give Seminars** (1988) *Agatha nominee* ☆
    ❑ ❑   2 - Dead Men Don't Marry (1989)

■ **Winona SULLIVAN**'s first mystery was named best first P. I. novel of 1991 in a contest sponsored by St. Martin's Press, Macmillan London and the Private Eye Writers of America. Her unusual protagonist is Sister Cecile Buddenbrooks, an heiress and a nun whose father disapproved of her vocation. He left her his fortune on the condition that it not be spent for religious purposes, so she finances her P. I. work with her inheritance and later donates the fees to her Boston convent. A former teacher and CIA analyst, Sullivan is the mother of seven and lives with her husband and their four youngest in an ancient farmhouse in Carver, Massachusetts.

    Sister Cecile Buddenbrooks . . . nun & licensed P. I. in Boston, Massachusetts
    ❑ ❑   1 - **A Sudden Death at the Norfolk Cafe** (1993) *SMP/PWA winner* ★
    ❑ ❑   2 - Dead South (1996)

■ **Penny SUMNER** is the author of a new series starring Victoria Cross, British archivist turned private eye.

> **Victoria Cross** . . . archivist turned P. I. in England
> - ❏ ❏ 1 - The End of April (1992)
> - ❏ ❏ 2 - Crosswords (1995)

■ **Elizabeth Atwood TAYLOR**, of San Francisco, is a native of San Antonio, Texas, educated at Vassar (art history) and Bryn Mawr (social work). She worked as a film editor, TV news reporter, social worker and art therapist before starting her mystery series featuring Maggie Elliott, a former film maker turned P. I. in San Francisco. A young widow and recently reformed alcoholic, Maggie teams up with much older ex-cop, Richard Patrick O'Reagan, to solve the mystery of her half-sister's death in a cable car accident.

> **Maggie Elliott** . . . ex-film maker turned P. I. in San Francisco
> - ❏ ❏ 1 - The Cable Car Murder (1981)
> - ❏ ❏ 2 - Murder at Vassar (1987)
> - ❏ ❏ 3 - The Northwest Murders (1992)

■ **Jean TAYLOR** is a proofreader at a major San Francisco law firm and the creator of a new private eye series starring the red-haired Maggie Garrett, a young gay woman investigator in San Francisco. Taylor has worked as a kitchen helper, secretary, volunteer coordinator, seamstress and emergency room clerk. She lives in the Mission District with Tigey and Fearless, models for her overindulged series cats and sings soprano in the Metropolitan Community Church Choir. Fellow San Francisco crime writer and former P. I. Elizabeth Pincus called Maggie "a P. I.'s P. I.—witty and resourceful, reckless and wild. Just the woman to turn to in a pinch."

> **Maggie Garrett** . . . young lesbian P. I. in San Francisco, California
> - ❏ ❏ 1 - We Know Where You Live (1995)
> - ❏ ❏ 2 - The Last of Her Lies (1996)

■ **L. A. TAYLOR**, of Minneapolis, has been writing virtually all her life. Her published work includes a prize-winning volume of poetry titled *Changing the Past* and *Footnote to Murder*, a mystery featuring Minneapolis library researcher Marge Brock. Taylor is also the creator of the J. J. Jamison series featuring a Minneapolis computer engineer who is also an investigator for CATCH—the Committee for Analysis of Tropospheric and Celestial Happenings.

> **J. J. Jamison** . . . Minneapolis computer engineer & CATCH investigator
> - ❏ ❏ 1 - Only Half a Hoax (1984)
> - ❏ ❏ 2 - Deadly Objectives (1985)
> - ❏ ❏ 3 - Shed Light on Death (1985)
> - ❏ ❏ 4 - A Murder Waiting to Happen (1989)

■ **Phoebe Atwood TAYLOR** (1909-1976) was born in Boston, descended from Mayflower pilgrims and published her first novel (*The Cape Cod Mystery*) the year after she graduated from Barnard College. Her series detective is Asey Mayo, "The Codfish Sherlock," a man who never tells his age despite the number of characters who try to figure it out. Although Taylor published nothing in the mystery field after 1951, her Cape Cod mysteries remain popular and in print more than 40 years later. As Alice Tilton she also wrote a Boston series featuring Leonidas Witherall, retired professor, Shakespeare look-alike and secret author of pulp thrillers.

Asey Mayo . . . former sailor & auto racer in Cape Cod, Massachusetts
- ❑ ❑ 1 - The Cape Cod Mystery (1931)
- ❑ ❑ 2 - Death Lights a Candle (1932)
- ❑ ❑ 3 - The Mystery of the Cape Cod Players (1933)
- ❑ ❑ 4 - The Mystery of the Cape Cod Tavern (1934)
- ❑ ❑ 5 - Sandbar Sinister (1934)
- ❑ ❑ 6 - The Tinkling Symbol (1935)
- ❑ ❑ 7 - Deathblow Hill (1935)
- ❑ ❑ 8 - The Crimson Patch (1936)
- ❑ ❑ 9 - Out of Order (1936)
- ❑ ❑ 10 - Figure Away (1937)
- ❑ ❑ 11 - Octagon House (1937)
- ❑ ❑ 12 - The Annulet of Gilt (1938)
- ❑ ❑ 13 - Banbury Bog (1938)
- ❑ ❑ 14 - Spring Harrowing (1939)
- ❑ ❑ 15 - The Deadly Sunshade (1940)
- ❑ ❑ 16 - The Criminal C.O.D. (1940)
- ❑ ❑ 17 - The Perennial Border (1941)
- ❑ ❑ 18 - Three Plots for Asey Mayo (1942)
- ❑ ❑ 19 - The Six Iron Spiders (1942)
- ❑ ❑ 20 - Going, Going, Gone (1943)
- ❑ ❑ 21 - Proof of the Pudding (1945)
- ❑ ❑ 22 - Punch with Care (1946)
- ❑ ❑ 23 - The Asey Mayo Trio (1946)
- ❑ ❑ 24 - Diplomatic Corpse (1951)

■ **Dorothy TELL** is the creator of 60-something Texas amateur sleuth Poppy Dillworth who first appeared in *Murder at Red Rook Ranch* in 1990.

Poppy Dillworth . . . 60-something lesbian sleuth in Texas
- ❑ ❑ 1 - Murder at Red Rook Ranch (1990)
- ❑ ❑ 2 - Wilderness Trek (1990)
- ❑ ❑ 3 - The Hallelujah Murders (1991)

■ **Josephine TEY** (1896-1952) is the pseudonym used by playwright and mystery writer Elizabeth Mackintosh, often called "the mystery writer for people who hate mysteries," owing to her fondness for focusing on the characters rather than the hunt for the guilty. Her series detective, Alan Grant of Scotland Yard, is a gentleman of independent means who works because he enjoys it. The first Grant book was originally published under the pseudonym Gordon Daviot but later reissued under Josephine Tey. Before starting a writing career, Tey studied and taught physical education and at the age of 50 produced her only novel with a woman protagonist—Miss *Pym Disposes* (1946). Miss Lucy Pym, retired physical education teacher and writer of pop psychology, tries to use her knowledge to solve a murder at a girls physical education college.

Inspector Alan Grant . . . Scotland Yard inspector
- ❑ ❑ 1 - The Man in the Queue (1929) [APA–Killer in the Crowd ('54)]
- ❑ ❑ 2 - A Shilling for Candles (1936)
- ❑ ❑ 3 - The Franchise Affair (1949)
- ❑ ❑ 4 - To Love and Be Wise (1950)
- ❑ ❑ 5 - The Daughter of Time (1951)
- ❑ ❑ 6 - The Singing Sands (1952)

■ **Joyce THOMPSON** is the creator of Seattle forensic artist Freddy Bascomb, featured in the mystery thriller *Bones*. The author of four earlier novels and two collections of short fiction, Thompson has taught fiction workshops at universities and writing conferences throughout the West. She lives with her two children in a beachfront cabin on an island in Puget Sound.

> **Frederika Bascomb** . . . Seattle, Washington forensic artist
> ❏ ❏   1   -   Bones (1991)

■ **June THOMSON** earned her BA with honors from Bedford College, University of London and taught English for 20 years before turning to mystery writing. She is the creator of Inspector Finch, the simple Essex cop who lives with his unmarried sister. When this series was reprinted in the U.S., Inspector Finch mysteriously became Inspector Rudd. Thomson is also the author of two recent short story collections—*The Secret Files of Sherlock Holmes* (1990) and *The Secret Chronicles of Sherlock Holmes* (1992).

> **Inspector Finch (Inspector Rudd in the U.S.)** . . . Essex, England police inspector
> ❏ ❏   1   -   Not One of Us (1971)
> ❏ ❏   2   -   Death Cap [comes to the U.S. with Insp. renamed Rudd] (1973)
> ❏ ❏   3   -   The Long Revenge (1974)
> ❏ ❏   4   -   Case Closed (1977)
> ❏ ❏   5   -   A Question of Identity (1977)
> ❏ ❏   6   -   Deadly Relations (1979) [U.S.–The Habit of Loving]
> ❏ ❏   7   -   Alibi in Time (1980)
> ❏ ❏   8   -   Shadow of a Doubt (1981)
> ❏ ❏   9   -   To Make a Killing (1982) [U.S.–Portrait of Lilith]
> ❏ ❏ 10   -   Sound Evidence (1984)
> ❏ ❏ 11   -   A Dying Fall (1985)
> ❏ ❏ 12   -   The Dark Stream (1986)
> ❏ ❏ 13   -   No Flowers by Request (1987)
> ❏ ❏ 14   -   Rosemary for Remembrance (1988)
> ❏ ❏ 15   -   The Spoils of Time (1989)
> ❏ ❏ 16   -   Past Reckoning (1990)
> ❏ ❏ 17   -   Foul Play (1991)
> ❏ ❏ 18   -   Burden of Innocence (1996)

■ **Aimée and David THURLO** have been married over 20 years and writing together for nearly that long, beginning with articles for *Grit*, *Popular Mechanics* and *The National Examiner*. Their nearly 30 novels, written under Aimee's name as well as pseudonyms, have been published in more than 20 countries. Recent titles include *Timewalker*, *Black Mesa*, *Spirit Warrior* and *Strangers Who Linger*. They are creators of a new series featuring Navajo FBI agent Ella Clah who makes her debut in *Blackening Song* (1995). Ella returns to the Navajo Nation after the murder of her minister father to find that her brother the medicine man is the chief suspect. Aimee is a native of Cuba and David lived for 17 years in Shiprock on the Navajo Indian Nation. They currently live and write in New Mexico.

> **Ella Clah** . . . Navajo FBI agent in New Mexico
> ❏ ❏   1   -   Blackening Song (1995)
> ❏ ❏   2   -   Death Walker (1996)

■ **Alice TILTON** is the pseudonym used by Phoebe Atwood Taylor for her Boston series featuring Leonidas Witherall, retired professor, Shakespeare look-alike, hunter of rare books and secret author of pulp fiction. Witherall is financially well-to-do thanks to the commercial success of his fictional character, Lieutenant Haseltine, hero of thrillers and radio.

    Leonidas Witherall . . . retired Boston academic & secret pulp fiction author
- ❏ ❏ 1 - Beginning with a Bash (1937)
- ❏ ❏ 2 - The Cut Direct (1938)
- ❏ ❏ 3 - Cold Steal (1939)
- ❏ ❏ 4 - The Left Leg (1940)
- ❏ ❏ 5 - The Hollow Chest (1941)
- ❏ ❏ 6 - File for Record (1943)
- ❏ ❏ 7 - Dead Earnest (1944)
- ❏ ❏ 8 - The Iron Clew (1947) [Britain–The Iron Hand]

■ **Teona TONE** (pronounced Tee-AH-na TONE) is the creator of a pair of private eye novels set at the turn-of-the-century featuring Kyra Keaton, heir to one of America's great industrial fortunes. The aristocratic lady detective, who runs her own business in Washington DC, debuts in *Lady on the Line*, a tale of murder and intrigue in the telephone industry in 1899. The sequel involves a Virginia fox hunting club in 1906. A native of Abilene, Texas, Tone holds a PhD from UCLA and has worked as a private investigator in Los Angeles and an instructor in English at the University of California. She is a member of the Santa Ynez Valley Hunt Club and with Deanna Sclar is author of *Housemates: How to Live with Other People*.

    Kyra Keaton . . . P. I. at the turn-of-the-century in Washington DC
- ❏ ❏ 1 - Lady on the Line (1983)
- ❏ ❏ 2 - Full Cry (1985)

■ **Malcolm TORRIE** is the pseudonym used by Gladys Mitchell (1901-1983) for her series featuring British preservation society director Timothy Herring who appeared in six novels between 1966 and 1971. Mitchell had already begun her 40-year teaching career by the time she received her diploma in history from University College, London, in 1926. In addition to the 66 novels she wrote featuring Beatrice Lestrange Bradley, Mitchell also produced five nonmysteries under the name of Stephen Hockaby.

    Timothy Herring . . . preservation society director in England
- ❏ ❏ 1 - Heavy as Lead (1966)
- ❏ ❏ 2 - Late and Cold (1967)
- ❏ ❏ 3 - Your Secret Friend (1968)
- ❏ ❏ 4 - Churchyard Salad (1969)
- ❏ ❏ 5 - Shades of Darkness (1970)
- ❏ ❏ 6 - Bismarck Herrings (1971)

■ **Elizabeth TRAVIS** is the creator of a pair of novels featuring amateur sleuths and book publishers Ben and Carrie Porter in Riverdale, Connecticut. Ben and Carrie make their first appearance in the 1989 title *Under the Influence*.

    Ben & Carrie Porter . . . book publishers in Riverdale, Connecticut
- ❏ ❏ 1 - Under the Influence (1989)
- ❏ ❏ 2 - Finders Keepers (1990)

■ **Kathy Hogan TROCHECK** is a Florida native with a journalism degree from the University of Georgia who spent 14 years as a newspaper reporter, primarily with *The Atlanta Journal-Constitution*. Her first series detective, Julia Callahan Garrity, is a burned-out ex-cop and part-time P. I. who owns and operates the House Mouse cleaning service with her mother Edna Mae. Two of the funnier mice are Baby and Sister, two little-old-lady black women. One is almost blind and the other nearly deaf, but together they see and hear almost everything. Trocheck's new series features Truman Kicklighter, a retired wire service reporter in St. Petersburg, Florida, who makes his debut in 1996.

    Callahan Garrity . . . Atlanta, Georgia ex-cop cleaning service operator
- ❑ ❑ 1 - **Every Crooked Nanny** (1992) *Macavity nominee* ☆
- ❑ ❑ 2 - **To Live and Die in Dixie** (1993) *Agatha & Anthony nominee* ☆ ☆
- ❑ ❑ 3 - Homemade Sin (1994)
- ❑ ❑ 4 - Happy Never After (1995)

    Truman Kicklighter . . . retired wire service reporter in St. Petersburg, Florida
- ❑ ❑ 1 - Lickety Split (1996)

■ **Margaret TRUMAN** writes Washington DC mysteries with titles featuring national landmarks. Several of these classic puzzle cases (the ones listed below) involve the recurring characters of Mac Smith and Annabel Reed, law professor and his attorney wife turned gallery owner. As the daughter of a former president, the author is definitely in-the-know when it comes to power politics and political intrigue in our nation's capital.

    Mackenzie Smith & Annabel Reed . . . Washington DC law professor & attorney wife turned gallery owner
- ❑ ❑ 1 - Murder at the Kennedy Center (1989)
- ❑ ❑ 2 - Murder at the National Cathedral (1990)
- ❑ ❑ 3 - Murder at the Pentagon (1992)
- ❑ ❑ 4 - Murder on the Potomac (1994)
- ❑ ❑ 5 - Murder at the National Gallery (1995)

■ **Kerry TUCKER**, of Guilford, Connecticut, is the creator of Libby Kincaid, New York City photojournalist. Tucker is also the author of *Greetings from New York—A Visit to Manhattan in Postcards*.

    Libby Kincaid . . . New York City magazine photographer
- ❑ ❑ 1 - Still Waters (1991)
- ❑ ❑ 2 - Cold Feet (1992)
- ❑ ❑ 3 - Death Echo (1993)
- ❑ ❑ 4 - Drift Away (1994)

■ **Peg TYRE** is a Pulitzer Prize-winning crime reporter for *New York Newsday* and a former magazine writer for *New York* magazine. She is also the creator of a new series featuring a woman crime reporter in search of a front page story who meets a detective in search of love in the midst of murder in Brooklyn. Tyre is a graduate of Brown University and lives in New York with her husband, novelist Peter Blauner, and their son.

    Kate Murray . . . Brooklyn newspaper reporter for New York's *Daily Herald*
- ❑ ❑ 1 - Strangers in the Night (1994)
- ❑ ❑ 2 - In the Midnight Hour (1995)

■ **Dorothy UHNAK** was a New York transit cop for 14 years, 12 of them spent as a detective, before quitting the force to write *Policewoman: A Young Woman's Initiation into the Realities of Justice* in 1964. Her award-winning series with Christie Opara beginning in 1968 recounts much of the discrimination Uhnak herself experienced on the job. According to Marcia Muller in *1001 Midnights*, Uhnak's most compelling heroine is 38-year-old New York Assistant District Attorney Lynne Jacobi, bureau chief of the Violent Sex Crimes Division and star of *False Witness* (1981). Uhnak is perhaps best known for her big, best-selling police novels such as *Law and Order,* which became a three-hour TV-movie starring Darren McGavin and Suzanne Pleshette.

    Christine Opara . . . 20-something New York City police detective
- ❑ ❑ 1 – **The Bait** (1968) *Edgar winner* ★
- ❑ ❑ 2 – The Witness (1969)
- ❑ ❑ 3 – **The Ledger** (1970) *Grand Prix de Litteratue Policiere winner* ★

■ **Deborah VALENTINE** is the creator of ex-sheriff's detective Kevin Bryce and artist Katharine Craig who first meet when she is suspected of using a piece of sculpture as a murder weapon. The idyllic mystery setting is an upscale community near Lake Tahoe. The American-born Valentine, who previously pursued wine and gardening interests in a small port town between San Francisco and the Napa Valley, currently lives in London.

    Katharine Craig & Kevin Bryce . . . northern California sculptor & ex-sheriff's detective
- ❑ ❑ 1 – Unorthodox Methods (1989)
- ❑ ❑ 2 – **A Collector of Photographs** (1989) *Edgar & Shamus nominee* ☆ ☆
- ❑ ❑ 3 – **Fine Distinctions** (1991) *Edgar nominee* ☆

■ **Judith VAN GIESON**, a Northwestern University graduate, writes a hard-boiled attorney-investigator series featuring Neil Hamel of Albuquerque, New Mexico. Neil is passionate about the environment and tequila. Her accordion-playing auto mechanic (who is also her lover) calls her Chiquita. She calls him The Kid. Their fifth appearance (*The Lies That Bind*) was nominated for a Shamus award as Best Novel of 1993 according to the Private Eye Writers of America.

    Neil Hamel . . . Albuquerque, New Mexico attorney & investigator
- ❑ ❑ 1 – North of the Border (1988)
- ❑ ❑ 2 – Raptor (1990)
- ❑ ❑ 3 – The Other Side of Death (1991)
- ❑ ❑ 4 – The Wolf Path (1992)
- ❑ ❑ 5 – **The Lies That Bind** (1993) *Shamus nominee* ☆
- ❑ ❑ 6 – Parrot Blues (1995)

■ **Michael VENNING** is one of the pseudonyms of Georgiana Ann Randolph Craig (1908-1957), better known as Craig Rice, who also wrote as Ruth Malone and Daphne Sanders. She was born in Chicago, educated privately and worked as a journalist, radio writer and producer and free lance writer. As Venning, it has been said she produced stories more introspective and sensitive than much of her other lighthearted screwball comedy. Her Venning series character is that gentlemanly detective Melville Fairr, 1940s New York lawyer.

    Melville Fairr . . . lawyer in New York
- ❑ ❑ 1 – The Man Who Slept All Day (1942)
- ❑ ❑ 2 – Murder Through the Looking Glass (1943)
- ❑ ❑ 3 – Jethro Hammer (1944)

■ **Anca VLASOPOLOS**, of Grosse Pointe, Michigan, is a Rumanian-born poet and professor of English at Wayne State University. She is also the creator of crime fiction's only female Detroit detective—police lieutenant Sharon Dair of the sex crimes division. The series opener, featuring a Bobbitt crime before its time, was published by the author's husband as a Christmas surprise in 1990 after two literary agents were unsuccessful in finding a publisher. When Sharon returns in 1997 or 1998 she will be working as an art investigator in *A Little E.L.F. Can Hurt You.*

      Sharon Dair . . . sex crimes police detective in Detroit
        ❑ ❑ 1 – Missing Members (1990)

■ **Hannah WAKEFIELD** is the shared pseudonym for two American-born women, Sarah Burton and Judith Holland, who were raised in the U.S. but moved to London in the early 1970s. One is a former editor who divides her time between writing and teaching, while the other is a practicing lawyer who collaborates on the story and characters. Their novels feature Dee Street, an American attorney and partner in a women-owned London law firm.

      Dee Street . . . American attorney in London
        ❑ ❑ 1 – The Price You Pay (1987)
        ❑ ❑ 2 – A Woman's Own Mystery (1990) [Britain-A February Mourning]

■ **Mary Willis WALKER**, of Austin, Texas, is the creator of two new female detectives—Texas dog trainer Kate Driscoll, and Texas crime writer and reporter Mollie Cates. Her first series opener, *Zero at the Bone*, won both the Agatha and Macavity awards for best first novel and was nominated for an Edgar. When her second series debuted three years later, the opener won the Edgar for best novel and was nominated for a Macavity. Walker, who often rides patrol with the Austin police, shares her commitment to aerobic exercise classes with reporter Mollie Cates and her love of golden retrievers with Kate Driscoll. She is a graduate of Duke University.

      Kate Driscoll . . . Texas dog trainer
        ❑ ❑ 1 – **Zero at the Bone** (1991) *Agatha & Macavity winner* ★ ★
                  Edgar nominee ☆

      Mollie Cates . . . Texas true crime writer & reporter
        ❑ ❑ 1 – **The Red Scream** (1994) *Edgar winner* ★ *Macavity nominee* ☆
        ❑ ❑ 2 – **Under the Beetle's Cellar** (1995)

■ **Marilyn WALLACE** is the Brooklyn-born daughter of a New York City police officer. Her Macavity award winning mystery series featuring Oakland homicide detectives Jay Goldstein and Carlos Cruz has been twice nominated for an Anthony. She is the author of the Taconic Hills suspense series including *So Shall You Reap* and *The Seduction*, and *Speak of the Devil*, as well as editor of the five-volume *Sisters In Crime* short story anthologies and co-editor with Robert J. Randisi of *Deadly Allies.*

      Jay Goldstein & Carlos Cruz . . . Oakland, California homicide detectives
        ❑ ❑ 1 – **A Case of Loyalties** (1986) *Macavity winner* ★
        ❑ ❑ 2 – **Primary Target** (1988) *Anthony nominee* ☆
        ❑ ❑ 3 – **A Single Stone** (1991) *Anthony nominee* ☆

■ **Patricia WALLACE** is Patricia Wallace Estrada, author of 17 books, including the Sydney Bryant private eye series and eleven horror novels, in addition to her latest novel of suspense, *Dark Intent* (1995). San Diego P. I. Sidney Bryant is introduced in *Small Favors*

(1988), a baffling case of a missing spouse. In *Deadly Devotion* (1994), nominated for a Shamus award, Sydney finds a crucial piece of evidence overlooked by the police in their haste to arrest the philandering husband for his wife's murder. Some of Wallace's nonseries titles include *Night Whisper* (1987), *See No Evil* (1988), *Monday's Child* (1989), *Thrill* (1990). A resident of Nevada, she has degrees in both film and police science and has worked for NBC as a freelance story analyst.

Sydney Bryant . . . San Diego, California private investigator
❑ ❑ 1 – Small Favors (1988)
❑ ❑ 2 – Deadly Grounds (1989)
❑ ❑ 3 – Blood Lies (1991)
❑ ❑ 4 – **Deadly Devotion** (1994) *Shamus nominee* ☆

■ **Lee WALLINGFORD** is a former teacher and librarian who lives in Oregon where she writes a series featuring two officers of the U.S. Forest Service—Frank Carver and Ginny Trask. She has also written *Principal Suspect*, a novel based on her teaching experience.

Ginny Trask & Frank Carver . . . Oregon forest fire dispatcher & ex-cop
❑ ❑ 1 – Cold Tracks (1991)
❑ ❑ 2 – Clear Cut Murder (1993)

■ **Jill Paton WALSH** is the distinguished author of more than two dozen children's books including *The Emperor's Winding Sheet* (1974) for which she won the Whitbread Prize (shared with Russell Hoban) for a tale about loyalty in the midst of destruction in 15th century Byzantium. She is also the creator of a new mystery series featuring nurse Imogen Quy (rhymes with WHY) who makes her living tending to the ailments of the student population of the Cambridge University College of St. Agatha's. In the series opener, the body is found in the library, or more precisely, a locked library within a library—the Wyndham Case, a two-story oak bookcase with steps at one end and a gallery with access to the upper shelves. She earned an MA in English (with honors) at Oxford where she attended lectures on literature and philology by both C. S. Lewis and J. R. R. Tolkien. The example they set as serious scholars who were also writers of fantasy and children's books was not lost on her, Paton Walsh says. A native of London, she lives in Cambridge.

Imogen Quy . . . school nurse at St. Agatha's College in Cambridge England
❑ ❑ 1 – The Wyndham Case (1993)
❑ ❑ 2 – A Piece of Justice (1995)

■ **Lilla M. WALTCH** who lives in Cambridge, Massachusetts is the creator of a pair of mystery novels from the late 1980s featuring Lisa Davis, newspaper reporter in Braeton, Massachusetts. The author holds a BA from Radcliffe and a PhD from Brandeis University.

Lisa Davis . . . newspaper reporter in Braeton, Massachusetts
❑ ❑ 1 – The Third Victim (1987)
❑ ❑ 2 – Fearful Symmetry (1988)

■ **Jean WARMBOLD** is the author of a three-book San Francisco series featuring newspaper reporter Sarah Calloway. The third installment is set in Paris.

Sarah Calloway . . . San Francisco, California newspaper reporter
❑ ❑ 1 – June Mail (1986)
❑ ❑ 2 – The White Hand (1988)
❑ ❑ 3 – The Third Way (1989)

■ **Mignon WARNER** was born in Australia, but currently lives in England where she works with her husband in the design and manufacture of apparatus for magic. She spends much of her free time doing research on the occult and other psychic phenomena. Her series character is the clairvoyante Edwina Charles.

Edwina Charles . . . British clairvoyante in Little Gidding England
- ❏ ❏ 1 – A Medium for Murder (1976) [Britain-A Nice Way to Die]
- ❏ ❏ 2 – The Tarot Murders (1978)
- ❏ ❏ 3 – Death in Time (1980)
- ❏ ❏ 4 – The Girl Who Was Clairvoyant (1982)
- ❏ ❏ 5 – Devil's Knell (1983)
- ❏ ❏ 6 – Illusion (1984)
- ❏ ❏ 7 – Speak No Evil (1985)

■ **Clarissa WATSON** is co-owner and director of a New York art gallery which she helped to found. Her series detective is the delightful 30-something art curator and widow Persis Willum, whose adventures involve the art world and Long Island high society. For nonmystery fun, Watson served as editor of *The Sensuous Carrot*, a collection of gourmet recipes from artists around the world.

Persis Willum . . . New York City art curator in Long Island
- ❏ ❏ 1 – The Fourth Stage of Gainsborough Brown (1977)
- ❏ ❏ 2 – The Bishop in the Back Seat (1980)
- ❏ ❏ 3 – Runaway (1985)
- ❏ ❏ 4 – Last Plane from Nice (1988)
- ❏ ❏ 5 – Somebody Killed the Messenger (1988)

■ **Martha G. WEBB** is one of the pseudonyms used by Anne Wingate who also writes as Lee Martin. Under the Webb name she produced a pair of novels featuring Texas cop Tommy Inman. As Lee Martin she writes the longer running Ft. Worth series starring police officer Deb Ralston, now in her 11th adventure. Under her own name as Anne Wingate she has also written 5 novels in the series featuring Mark Shigata, Japanese-American former FBI-agent turned police chief in Bayport, Texas.

Tommy Inman . . . Texas cop
- ❏ ❏ 1 – A White Male Running (1985)
- ❏ ❏ 2 – Even Cops' Daughters (1986)

■ **Charlene WEIR** is a native of Kansas who studied and worked in the public health field in Oklahoma before moving to northern California. Her series detective moves from California to Kansas where she is unexpectedly widowed in the opening title which was nominated for an Anthony and won the Agatha for best first traditional mystery. Weir's short fiction has appeared in *Ellery Queen Mystery Magazine* and *Alfred Hitchcock Mystery Magazine* and one of her stories was transcribed into Braille for a magazine for blind readers.

Susan Wren . . . ex-San Francisco cop now Kansas police chief
- ❏ ❏ 1 – **The Winter Widow** (1992) *Agatha winner* ★ *Anthony nominee* ☆
- ❏ ❏ 2 – **Consider the Crows** (1993) *Anthony nominee* ☆
- ❏ ❏ 3 – Family Practice (1995)

■ **Pat WELCH** was born in an Air Force hospital in Japan where she lived for several years before moving to the rural South, later settling in Miami, then Los Angeles and San Francisco. She is the creator of Helen Black, lesbian private eye and ex-cop in Berkeley, California. The author, who has a degree in English, lives in Berkeley with an assortment of pets.

Helen Black . . . ex-cop lesbian P. I. in Berkeley CA

❏ ❏ 1 – Murder by the Book (1990)
❏ ❏ 2 - Still Waters (1992)
❏ ❏ 3 – A Proper Burial (1993)
❏ ❏ 4 – Open House (1995)

■ **Carolyn WELLS** (1869-1942), author of more than 80 mystery novels, first became known as a writer of books for girls and an editor of anthologies. But she is perhaps best known as the originator of master sleuth Fleming Stone who appeared in 61 titles between 1909 and 1942. Wells is also credited with another early contribution—the first how-to book about detective stories—*The Technique of the Mystery Story* (1913). Her non-Fleming mysteries include three novels with Kenneth Carlisle, movie actor turned detective in New York City, eight titles featuring psychic detective Pennington Wise and his unusual young female assistant Zizi. Wells also wrote several nonseries mysteries under the name Rowland Wright. For more than 25 years (1915-1942) she wrote three or four novels a year, in fact, it has been said that the woman never had an unpublished thought.

Fleming Stone . . . New York City intellectual private investigator

❏ ❏ 1 – The Clue (1909)
❏ ❏ 2 – The Gold Bag (1911)
❏ ❏ 3 – A Chain of Evidence (1912)
❏ ❏ 4 – The Maxwell Mystery (1913)
❏ ❏ 5 – Anybody but Anne (1914)
❏ ❏ 6 – The White Alley (1915)
❏ ❏ 7 – The Curved Blades (1916)
❏ ❏ 8 – The Mark of Cain (1917)
❏ ❏ 9 – Vicky Van (1918)
❏ ❏ 10 – The Diamond Pin (1919)
❏ ❏ 11 – Raspberry Jam (1920)
❏ ❏ 12 – The Mystery of the Sycamore (1921)
❏ ❏ 13 – The Mystery Girl (1922)
❏ ❏ 14 – Feathers Left Around (1923)
❏ ❏ 15 – Spooky Hollow (1923)
❏ ❏ 16 – The Furthest Fury (1924)
❏ ❏ 17 – Prilligirl (1924)
❏ ❏ 18 – Anything but the Truth (1925)
❏ ❏ 19 – The Daughter of the House (1925)
❏ ❏ 20 – The Bronze Hand (1926)
❏ ❏ 21 – The Red-Haired Girl (1926)
❏ ❏ 22 – All at Sea (1927)
❏ ❏ 23 – Where's Emily? (1927)
❏ ❏ 24 – The Crime in the Crypt (1928)
❏ ❏ 25 – The Tannahill Tangle (1928)
❏ ❏ 26 – The Tapestry Room Murder (1929)
❏ ❏ 27 – Triple Murder (1929)
❏ ❏ 28 – The Doomed Five (1930)
❏ ❏ 29 – The Ghosts' High Noon (1930)
❏ ❏ 30 – Horror House (1931)
❏ ❏ 31 – The Umbrella Murder (1931)
❏ ❏ 32 – Fuller's Earth (1932)
❏ ❏ 33 – The Roll-Top Desk Mystery (1932)
❏ ❏ 34 – The Broken O (1933)
❏ ❏ 35 – The Clue of the Eyelash (1933)
❏ ❏ 36 – The Master Murderer (1933)

❑ ❑ 37 – Eyes in the Wall (1934)
❑ ❑ 38 – The Visiting Villain (1934)
❑ ❑ 39 – For Goodness' Sake (1935)
❑ ❑ 40 – The Beautiful Derelict (1935)
❑ ❑ 41 – The Wooden Indian (1935)
❑ ❑ 42 – Money Musk (1936)
❑ ❑ 43 – The Huddle (1936)
❑ ❑ 44 – Murder in the Bookshop (1936)
❑ ❑ 45 – The Mystery of the Tarn (1937)
❑ ❑ 46 – In the Tiger's Cage (1936)
❑ ❑ 47 – The Radio Studio Murder (1937)
❑ ❑ 48 – Gilt-Edged Guilt (1938)
❑ ❑ 49 – The Killer (1938)
❑ ❑ 50 – The Missing Link (1938)
❑ ❑ 51 – Calling All Suspects (1939)
❑ ❑ 52 – Crime Tears On (1939)
❑ ❑ 53 – The Importance of Being Murdered (1939)
❑ ❑ 54 – Crime Incarnate (1940)
❑ ❑ 55 – Devil's Work (1940)
❑ ❑ 56 – Murder on Parade (1940)
❑ ❑ 57 – Murder Plus (1940)
❑ ❑ 58 – The Black Night Murders (1941)
❑ ❑ 59 – Murder at the Casino (1941)
❑ ❑ 60 – Murder Will In (1942)
❑ ❑ 61 – Who Killed Caldwell? (1942)

Kenneth Carlisle . . . movie actor turned detective in New York
❑ ❑ 1 – Sleeping Dogs (1929)
❑ ❑ 2 – The Doorstep Murders (1930)
❑ ❑ 3 – The Skeleton at the Feast (1931)

Pennington Wise . . . private detective in New York
❑ ❑ 1 – The Room with the Tassels (1918)
❑ ❑ 2 – The Man Who Fell Through the Earth (1919)
❑ ❑ 3 – In the Onyx Lobby (1920)
❑ ❑ 4 – The Come-Back (1921)
❑ ❑ 5 – The Luminous Face (1921)
❑ ❑ 6 – The Vanishing of Betty Varian (1922)
❑ ❑ 7 – The Affair at Flower Acres (1923)
❑ ❑ 8 – Wheels Within Wheels (1923)

■ **Tobias WELLS** is one of the pseudonyms of DeLoris Florine Stanton Forbes who also wrote as Stanton Forbes and Forbes Rydell (with Helen Rydell). Born in Kansas City, and educated at Oklahoma State University and the University of Chicago, she worked as editor, broadcaster and retail clothing shop owner. Her best known series detective, Massachusetts cop Knute Severson, stars in 16 cases between 1966 and 1988, including his 1975 trip to the Caribbean island of St. Martin in *Hark, Hark, The Watchdogs Bark*. As Stanton Forbes she authored two dozen nonseries novels including *If Laurel Shot Hardy the World Would End* (1970), described by Bill Pronzini (*1001 Midnights*) as poorly-executed and sophomoric but with one of the niftiest dust jackets of any modern crime novel—13 sad-faced Laurels on an orange background.

Knute Severson . . . police officer in Boston, Massachusetts
❑ ❑ 1 – A Matter of Love and Death (1966)
❑ ❑ 2 – Dead by the Light of the Moon (1967)

❑ ❑ 3 – What Should You Know of Dying? (1967)
❑ ❑ 4 – Murder Most Fouled Up (1968)
❑ ❑ 5 – The Young Can Die Protesting (1969)
❑ ❑ 6 – Die Quickly, Dear Mother (1969)
❑ ❑ 7 – Dinky Died (1970)
❑ ❑ 8 – The Foo Dog (1971) [Britain-The Lotus Affair]
❑ ❑ 9 – What To Do Until the Undertaker Comes (1971)
❑ ❑ 10 – A Die in the Country (1972)
❑ ❑ 11 – How to Kill a Man (1972)
❑ ❑ 12 – Brenda's Murder (1973)
❑ ❑ 13 – Have Mercy Upon Us (1974)
❑ ❑ 14 – Hark, Hark, the Watchdogs Bark (1975)
❑ ❑ 15 – A Creature Was Stirring (1977)
❑ ❑ 16 – Of Graves, Worms and Epitaphs (1988)

■ **Theodora WENDER**, a Latin professor who wrote "punny" stories while relearning to speak after a stroke, is the creator of a pair of late 1980s novels featuring Glad Gold and Alden Chase, English professor and chief of police in Massachusetts.

    Glad Gold & Alden Chase . . . English professor & chief of police in Massachusetts
❑ ❑ 1 - Knight Must Fall (1985)
❑ ❑ 2 – Murder Gets a Degree (1986)

■ **Patricia WENTWORTH** is the pseudonym of Dora Amy Elles (1878-1961) who wrote nine mysteries before introducing in 1928 the character who would make her famous—retired governess and professional private inquiry agent Miss Maud Silver. Although Miss Silver is the quintessential spinster sleuth, complete with funny hats (black felt in winter and black straw in summer) and the requisite bag of knitting, she is often quite well paid for her detecting. According to Marcia Muller in *1001 Midnights*, Miss Silver is at her charming best in the 1956 title *The Gazebo*, which unfortunately bore little resemblance to the 1959 movie of the same title, starring Glenn Ford and Debbie Reynolds. In the nine-year lapse between Miss Silver's first and second appearance, Wentworth wrote 16 nonseries titles and then wisely returned to her little old lady sleuth who would eventually star in 32 novels by 1961. Miss Silver became so popular in the U.S. during the 1940s that Lippincott of Philadelphia became her primary publisher and British editions were released after their American counterparts. Most of the Miss Silver titles are available today in trade paperback reprints. Wentworth also created the somewhat inept Inspector Lamb who appears in some of the Miss Silver books as well as center stage in two cases of his own—*The Blind Side* (1939) and *Pursuit of a Parcel* (1942). Born in Mussoorie, India, she was educated privately and at Blackheath High School in London. After her marriage to George Oliver Turnbull in 1920, she lived in Surrey until her death in 1961.

    Inspector Ernest Lamb . . . police inspector in London
❑ ❑ 1 – The Blind Side (1939)
❑ ❑ 2 – Pursuit of a Parcel (1942)

    Miss Maud Silver . . . London, England retired governess & spinster P. I.
❑ ❑ 1 – Grey Mask (1928)
❑ ❑ 2 – The Case Is Closed (1937)
❑ ❑ 3 – Lonesome Road (1939)
❑ ❑ 4 – In the Balance (1941) [Britain-Danger Point]
❑ ❑ 5 – The Chinese Shawl (1943)
❑ ❑ 6 – Miss Silver Deals in Death (1943) [Britain-Miss Silver Intervenes]
❑ ❑ 7 – The Clock Strikes Twelve (1944)

❑ ❑   8 – The Key (1944)
❑ ❑   9 – She Came Back (1945) [Britain-The Traveller Returns]
❑ ❑ 10 – Pilgrim's Rest (1946) [APA-Dark Threat]
❑ ❑ 11 – Latter End (1947)
❑ ❑ 12 – Wicked Uncle (1947) [Britain-The Spotlight]
❑ ❑ 13 – The Eternity Ring (1948)
❑ ❑ 14 – The Case of William Smith (1948)
❑ ❑ 15 – Miss Silver Comes to Stay (1949)
❑ ❑ 16 – The Catherine Wheel (1949)
❑ ❑ 17 – Through the Wall (1950)
❑ ❑ 18 – The Brading Collection (1950) [APA-Mr. Brading's Collection]
❑ ❑ 19 – The Ivory Dagger (1951)
❑ ❑ 20 – Anna, Where Are You? (1951) [APA-Death at Deep End]
❑ ❑ 21 – The Watersplash (1951)
❑ ❑ 22 – Ladies' Bane (1952)
❑ ❑ 23 – Out of the Past (1953)
❑ ❑ 24 – Vanishing Point (1953)
❑ ❑ 25 – The Silent Pool (1954)
❑ ❑ 26 – The Benevent Treasure (1954)
❑ ❑ 27 – The Listening Eye (1955)
❑ ❑ 28 – The Gazebo (1956) [APA-The Summerhouse]
❑ ❑ 29 – The Fingerprint (1956)
❑ ❑ 30 – Poison in the Pen (1957)
❑ ❑ 31 – The Alington Inheritance (1958)
❑ ❑ 32 – The Girl in the Cellar (1961)

■ **Valerie Wilson WESLEY** is a former executive editor of *Essence* magazine and creator of black P. I. Tamara Hayle, single parent and ex-cop from the mean streets of Newark, New Jersey, whose first adventure was Shamus-nominated. A graduate of Howard University and the Columbia Graduate School of Journalism, Wesley says she was inspired to write a black woman P. I. by Walter Mosley, Edgar-nominated creator of Los Angeles P. I. Easy Rawlins.

    Tamara Hayle . . . Newark, New Jersey black P. I. ex-cop
    ❑ ❑ 1 – **When Death Comes Stealing** (1994) *Shamus nominee* ☆
    ❑ ❑ 2 – Devil's Gonna Get Him (1995)

■ **Chassie WEST** is the creator of Leigh Ann Warren, a former street cop in Washington DC who returns home to the small town of Sunrise, North Carolina after a shooting incident involving her partner, Duck, who almost died because of her. A law school graduate, Leigh Ann introduces herself as free (well, unmarried anyway), black (on the toasted almond end of the spectrum) and solvent (one gas card and one credit card for emergencies). The first book in this new police series was nominated for an Edgar award. In addition to having written 19 books, West has acted in professional and community theaters, films and commercials. She lives in Columbia, Maryland.

    Leigh Ann Warren . . . former DC street cop in Sunrise, North Carolina
    ❑ ❑ 1 – **Sunrise** (1994) *Edgar nominee* ☆

■ **Carolyn WESTON** is the creator of a Santa Monica cop pair featuring a young college grad liberal and his partner, the hard-bitten, street-wise veteran who became the inspiration for a long-running TV series. Weston's cops were transplanted to northern California where they became the basis for the 1975 pilot that launched *The Streets of San Francisco*—

still running after 20 years—complete with credits for Weston as creator of the popular characters. According to *1001 Midnights*, the relationship between the characters is about all that the TV series accurately reflects, but the plot of the pilot is loosely based on Weston's series opener *Poor, Poor Ophelia*. She is also the author of *Danju Gig*, a 1969 nonseries novel set in West Africa.

> **Casey Kellog & Al Krug** . . . college grad liberal & hard-bitten veteran cop in Santa Monica, California
> ❏ ❏ 1 – Poor, Poor Ophelia (1972)
> ❏ ❏ 2 – Susannah Screaming (1975)
> ❏ ❏ 3 – Rouse the Demon (1976)

■ **Carolyn WHEAT** was once a Brooklyn defense attorney with the Legal Aid Society, much like her Cass Jameson character. After a nine-year hiatus, Wheat has revived her Edgar-nominated series with a third installment, *Fresh Kills* (1995), and the simultaneous re-release of the earlier two titles. Cass Jameson was a student at Kent State University the day four of her friends were gunned down by the National Guard and ten years later she's a disillusioned public defender in Brooklyn who wonders if she could support herself with her photography. In the series opener, *Dead Man's Thoughts* (1983), her lover Nathan is brutally murdered in what is made to look like the attack of a vicious homosexual lover. While exposing some of New York's finest in her investigation, Cass regains her commitment to public defense. After relocating from Brooklyn to southern California, Wheat is currently teaching writing in Oklahoma. She previously taught mystery writing at the New School in New York City and legal writing at Brooklyn Law School.

> **Cass Jameson** . . . Brooklyn, New York criminal lawyer
> ❏ ❏ 1 – **Dead Man's Thoughts** (1983) *Edgar nominee* ☆
> ❏ ❏ 2 – Where Nobody Dies (1986)
> ❏ ❏ 3 – Fresh Kills (1995)

■ **Gloria WHITE** is the creator of the Ronnie (Veronica) Ventana series featuring a San Francisco P. I. whose now-deceased parents were cat burglars. The first title in the series was nominated for an Edgar and named audio best of the year by *Publishers Weekly*. The entire series is available on audio book and has been translated to German, Japanese and Italian. White, who has a degree in economics, has worked at an equine veterinary clinic, investigated employment discrimination complaints and conducted computer background searches. Like her character, she lives in San Francisco.

> **Veronica "Ronnie" Ventana** . . . Anglo-Mexican P. I. daughter of cat burglars in San Francisco, California
> ❏ ❏ 1 – **Murder on the Run** (1991) *Anthony nominee* ☆
> ❏ ❏ 2 – Money to Burn (1993)
> ❏ ❏ 3 – Charged with Guilt (1995)

■ **Teri WHITE** won an Edgar in 1982 for best paperback original with her first novel about two Vietnam vets who hire out as hit men (*Triangle*). The killers, like their victims, are young male homosexuals, pursued by the unlikely cop pair of Spaceman Kolwalski and Blue Maguire. According to Julie Smith, writing in *1001 Midnights*, Spaceman is a reverse snob and Blue a rich kid who works as a cop because he likes it. Smith calls this a tale so brutal, bloody and compelling the book will stick to your fingers and hold you in a horrified trance until the story's done.

Spaceman Kowalski & Blue Maguire . . . Los Angeles cop pair with a prickly partnership
- ❑ ❑ 1 – Bleeding Hearts (1984)
- ❑ ❑ 2 – Tightrope (1986)

■ **Polly WHITNEY** commutes between her midtown Manhattan apartment, one block from Carneige Hall, and her rural writing roost in Missouri. Like her series characters, Ike and Abby, who've been called Nick and Nora Charles on rollerblades, Whitney has worked in network television. She also shares with Ike and Abby a love of rollerblading and ballroom dancing, but only Polly can claim to have danced with Arnold Schwarzenegger at his wedding to her friend Maria Shriver. Whitney holds an MA in English from Yale where she worked as a crime reporter and photographer for *The New Haven Register*.

Mary "Ike" Tygart & "Abby" Abagnarro . . . network producer & director of morning TV news show in New York
- ❑ ❑ 1 – **Until Death** (1994) *Agatha nominee* ☆
- ❑ ❑ 2 – Until the End of Time (1995)
- ❑ ❑ 3 – Until It Hurts (1996)

■ **Kate WILHELM** published her first short story in 1956 and her first novel in 1963. For more than 30 years she has been producing prize-winning science fiction, as well as horror, mystery, mainstream fiction, psychological novels, suspense and comic novels. She has won the two most prestigious prizes in science fiction—the Hugo and Nebula awards—for which she is best known. Wilhelm has also created several series detectives, including Charlie Meiklejohn and Constance Leidl. He is a former New York City arson investigator turned P. I., while she is a PhD practicing psychologist. Wilhelm's legal mystery protagonists are Oregon defense attorney Barbara Holloway and Oregon judge Sarah Drexler.

Barbara Holloway . . . Oregon defense attorney
- ❑ ❑ 1 – Death Qualified (1991)
- ❑ ❑ 2 – The Best Defense (1994)

Charlie Meiklejohn & Constance Leidl . . . ex-arson investigator P. I. & psychologist in New York
- ❑ ❑ 1 – The Hamlet Trap (1987)
- ❑ ❑ 2 – The Dark Door (1988)
- ❑ ❑ 3 – Smart House (1989)
- ❑ ❑ 4 – Sweet, Sweet Poison (1990)
- ❑ ❑ 5 – Seven Kinds of Death (1992)
- ❑ ❑ 6 – A Flush of Shadows [5 novellas] (1995)

Sarah Drexler . . . Oregon judge
- ❑ ❑ 1 – Justice for Some (1993)

■ **Barbara WILSON**, co-founder of Seattle's Seal Press, writes two lesbian feminist mystery series. Her first title featuring Cassandra Reilly, globe-trotting Spanish translator, won an award for best crime novel with a European setting from the British Crime Writers Association. The author herself is an award-winning translator. Her second series features Pam Nilsen and her twin sister Penny whose family business, Best Printing, is turned into a collective. Their 1984 series opener includes a lesson in U.S. involvement in the Philippines and American support of the Marcos regime, in addition to feminist politics, a lesbian love story, and a murder mystery.

Cassandra Reilly . . . London-based Spanish translator
    ❑ ❑   1 – **Gaudi Afternoon** (1990) *BCWA award winner* ★
    ❑ ❑   2 – Trouble in Transylvania (1993)

Pam Nilsen . . . Seattle, Washington lesbian printing company owner
    ❑ ❑   1 – Murder in the Collective (1984)
    ❑ ❑   2 – Sisters of the Road (1986)
    ❑ ❑   3 – The Dog Collar Murders (1989)

■ **Karen Ann WILSON** is the creator of a new animal series featuring Samantha Holt, veterinary assistant to Dr. Louis Augustin in Paradise Cay, Florida. In the series opener, the vet's estranged wife Rachel, who trains and races greyhounds, is accused of murder. The surly Dr. Augustin is no James Herriott, but there's plenty of canine lore for dog lovers. Sam's second adventure gives equal opportunity to cat lovers.

Samantha Holt . . . vet's assistant in Paradise Cay, Florida
    ❑ ❑   1 – Eight Dogs Flying (1994)
    ❑ ❑   2 – Copy Cat Crimes (1995)

■ **Chris WILTZ** is the creator of a three-book series starting in 1981 featuring Neal Rafferty, a third generation cop turned private eye in New Orleans.

Neal Rafferty . . . third generation cop turned P. I. in New Orleans, Louisiana
    ❑ ❑   1 – The Killing Circle (1981)
    ❑ ❑   2 – A Diamond Before You Die (1987)
    ❑ ❑   3 – The Emerald Lizard (1991)

■ **Anne WINGATE** is a former Texas police officer with a PhD in English who writes both fiction and nonfiction under three names. As Wingate she publishes the Mark Shigata series about a Japanese-American ex-FBI agent turned chief of police in Bayport, Texas and for Writer's Digest Books in 1992 she authored *Scene of the Crime: A Writer's Guide to Crime Scene Investigations*. Under the Lee Martin pseudonym she writes the Deb Ralston series and early in her writing career she produced several nonseries novels under the name of Martha G. Webb.

Mark Shigata . . . ex-FBI agent turned sheriff in Bayport, Texas
    ❑ ❑   1 – Death by Deception (1988)
    ❑ ❑   2 – The Eye of Anna (1989)
    ❑ ❑   3 – The Buzzards Must Also Be Fed (1991)
    ❑ ❑   4 – Exception to Murder (1992)
    ❑ ❑   5 – Yakuza, Go Home! (1993)

■ **Mary WINGS**, a Chicago native, lived in the Netherlands for eight years where she wrote the first two titles of her hard-boiled lesbian series featuring private investigator Emma Victor. While in Amsterdam she also did graphic design and book production work for a number of feminist research projects. She has also written three comic books, the gothic thriller *Divine Victim* (Lambda award winner for best lesbian mystery novel in 1993), and been nominated for the Raymond Chandler Fulbright award. She currently lives in San Francisco.

Emma Victor . . . lesbian activist & P. I. in San Francisco
    ❑ ❑   1 – She Came Too Late (1987)
    ❑ ❑   2 – She Came in a Flash (1990)
    ❑ ❑   3 – She Came by the Book (1996)

■ **Pauline Glen WINSLOW** is the creator of Scotland Yard detective Merle Capricorn, conventional offspring of a flamboyant show business family headed by Capricorn's father, the Great Capricornus, who taught his son all the tricks of the illusionist's trade. The detective's aunts, The Magic Merlinos are music hall veterans turned TV stars who provide their nephew with plenty of useful gossip. This American author, born and educated in England, later attended Hunter College, Columbia University and New School for Social Research in New York City where she later worked as a court reporter for city, state and federal governments. Her court reporting for the United Nations inspired her final Capricorn novel, *The Rockefeller Gift* (1992).

Merlin Capricorn . . . magician turned police superintendent in England
- ❏ ❏ 1 – Death of an Angel (1975)
- ❏ ❏ 2 – The Brandenburg Hotel (1976)
- ❏ ❏ 3 – The Witch Hill Murder (1977)
- ❏ ❏ 4 – Copper Gold (1978) [Britain-Coppergold]
- ❏ ❏ 5 – The Counsellor Heart (1980) [APA-Sister Death]
- ❏ ❏ 6 – The Rockefeller Gift (1982)

■ **Susan WOLFE** is a practicing attorney in Palo Alto, California who won an Edgar for best first novel of 1989. The Dean of Stanford Law School described her book as "a diverting tale of legal skullduggery" in the high-tech practice of law in Silicon Valley.

Sarah Nelson . . . Silicon Valley, California police inspector
- ❏ ❏ 1 – **The Last Billable Hour** (1989) *Edgar winner* ★

■ **Valerie WOLZIEN** is the creator of Susan Henshaw, a suburban Connecticut housewife whose neighborhood seems to have a crime for every holiday and social occasion. Susan's friend, police detective Kathleen Gordon, is also a private security consultant whose professional expertise helps solve local murders. In 1995 Wolzien launched a new series with Josie Pigeon, owner of the all-women construction crew introduced in *Remodeled to Death*. Wolzien, born in Ohio and raised in New Jersey, went to college in Colorado and Alaska. After living in Pennsylvania, Oklahoma, Wisconsin and Washington DC, she is now back in New Jersey.

Josie Pigeon . . . owner of an all-women construction firm in the Northeast U.S.
- ❏ ❏ 1 – Shore to Die (1996)

Susan Henshaw . . . Connecticut suburban housewife sleuth
- ❏ ❏ 1 – Murder at the PTA Luncheon (1987)
- ❏ ❏ 2 – The Fortieth Birthday Body (1989)
- ❏ ❏ 3 – We Wish You a Merry Murder (1991)
- ❏ ❏ 4 – All Hallow's Evil (1992)
- ❏ ❏ 5 – An Old Faithful Murder (1992)
- ❏ ❏ 6 – A Star-Spangled Murder (1993)
- ❏ ❏ 7 – A Good Year for a Corpse (1994)
- ❏ ❏ 8 – Tis the Season To Be Murdered (1994)
- ❏ ❏ 9 – Remodeled to Death (1995)
- ❏ ❏ 10 – Elected to Die (1996)

■ **Sara WOODS** is the pseudonym of Sara Hutton Bowen-Judd (1922-1985) who used her own experience working in a solicitor's office to produce 48 titles in the Antony Maitland series, where the title of each book is a quotation from Shakespeare. Although Maitland is often called the British Perry Mason, Woods was no Erle Stanley Gardner. She refrained entirely from courtroom tricks—no mystery witnesses or last-minute confessions. According to Marcia Muller in *1001 Midnights*, the Maitland novels are full of interesting characters, multiple secrets and firmly-grounded courtroom scenes which allow readers to detect right along with their lawyer hero. Maitland's wonderful family includes his wife Jenny and law partner and uncle, Sir Nicholas Harding, who owns the house where they all live. In later novels they are joined by fellow barrister Vera Langhorne who marries the confirmed bachelor uncle. Rounding out the family group are friends Meg and Roger Farrell and Chief Inspector Sykes who all play a part in these engaging legal puzzlers. Woods was born and educated in England, but didn't start writing seriously until she moved to Nova Scotia. Although her setting and character are distinctly British, she is considered Canada's most successful writer of mystery fiction. She also wrote as Anne Burton, Mary Challis and Margaret Leek.

Antony Maitland . . . English barrister drawn to murder cases

❑ ❑ 1 – Bloody Instructions (1962)
❑ ❑ 2 – Malice Domestic (1962)
❑ ❑ 3 – The Taste of Fears (1963) [APA-The Third Encounter]
❑ ❑ 4 – Error of the Moon (1963)
❑ ❑ 5 – Trusted Like the Fox (1964)
❑ ❑ 6 – This Little Measure (1964)
❑ ❑ 7 – The Windy Side of the Law (1965)
❑ ❑ 8 – Though I Know She Lies (1965)
❑ ❑ 9 – Enter Certain Murderers (1966)
❑ ❑ 10 – Let's Choose Executors (1966)
❑ ❑ 11 – The Case Is Altered (1967)
❑ ❑ 12 – And Shame the Devil (1967)
❑ ❑ 13 – Knives Have Edges (1968)
❑ ❑ 14 – Past Praying For (1968)
❑ ❑ 15 – Tarry and Be Hanged (1969)
❑ ❑ 16 – An Improbable Fiction (1970)
❑ ❑ 17 – Serpent's Tooth (1971)
❑ ❑ 18 – The Knavish Crows (1971)
❑ ❑ 19 – They Love Not Poison [prequel] (1972)
❑ ❑ 20 – Yet She Must Die (1973)
❑ ❑ 21 – Enter the Corpse (1973)
❑ ❑ 22 – Done to Death (1974)
❑ ❑ 23 – A Show of Violence (1975)
❑ ❑ 24 – My Life Is Done (1976)
❑ ❑ 25 – The Law's Delay (1977)
❑ ❑ 26 – A Thief or Two (1977)
❑ ❑ 27 – Exit Murderer (1978)
❑ ❑ 28 – This Fatal Writ (1979)
❑ ❑ 29 – Proceed to Judgement (1979)
❑ ❑ 30 – They Stay for Death (1980)
❑ ❑ 31 – Weep for Her (1980)
❑ ❑ 32 – Dearest Enemy (1981)
❑ ❑ 33 – Cry Guilty (1981)
❑ ❑ 34 – Villains by Necessity (1982)
❑ ❑ 35 – Enter a Gentlewoman (1982)
❑ ❑ 36 – Most Grievous Murder (1982)
❑ ❑ 37 – The Lie Direct (1983)
❑ ❑ 38 – Call Back Yesterday (1983)
❑ ❑ 39 – Where Should He Die? (1983)
❑ ❑ 40 – The Bloody Book of Law (1984)
❑ ❑ 41 – Defy the Devil (1984)
❑ ❑ 42 – Murder's Out of Tune (1984)

❏ ❏ 43 – An Obscure Grave (1985)
❏ ❏ 44 – Away with Them to Prison (1985)
❏ ❏ 45 – Put out the Light (1985)
❏ ❏ 46 – Nor Live so Long (1986)
❏ ❏ 47 – Most Deadly Hate (1986)
❏ ❏ 48 – Naked Villainy (1987)

■ **Sherryl WOODS** is the award-winning author of over 50 novels, many of which are best-selling romances translated into more than a dozen languages. She writes the Amanda Roberts series featuring a Georgia investigative reporter transplanted from New York and the Molly DeWitt series featuring a Miami film promoter and single mother. Woods divides her time between Key Biscayne and Los Angeles where several of her books have been optioned for television. She spent 14 years as a working journalist, including her stint as television critic for the *Miami News*.

Amanda Roberts . . . ex-New York investigative reporter in Atlanta, Georgia
❏ ❏ 1 – Reckless (1989)
❏ ❏ 2 – Body and Soul (1989)
❏ ❏ 3 – Stolen Moments (1990)
❏ ❏ 4 – Ties That Bind (1991)
❏ ❏ 5 – Bank on It (1993)
❏ ❏ 6 – Hide and Seek (1993)
❏ ❏ 7 – Wages of Sin (1994)
❏ ❏ 8 – Deadly Obsession (1995)
❏ ❏ 9 – White Lightning (1995)

Molly DeWitt . . . Miami, Florida film office public relations staffer
❏ ❏ 1 – Hot Property (1991)
❏ ❏ 2 – Hot Secret (1992)
❏ ❏ 3 – Hot Money (1993)
❏ ❏ 4 – Hot Schemes (1994)
❏ ❏ 5 – Hot Ticket (1995)

■ **M. K. WREN** is the pseudonym of Martha Kay Renfroe of Otis, Oregon, creator of Oregon bookshop owner Conan Flagg, former intelligence agent and reluctant P. I. He is also half Nez Perce Indian, art collector and Jaguar owner. Wren is the author of a 500,000-word science fiction trilogy titled *The Phoenix Legacy*, now out of print, and a 1990 mainstream novel set in the near future, *A Gift Upon the Shore*. She has a degree in fine arts from the University of Oklahoma and once tried to make her living as a painter.

Conan Flagg . . . Oregon bookstore owner & former intelligence agent
❏ ❏ 1 – Curiosity Didn't Kill the Cat (1973)
❏ ❏ 2 – A Multitude of Sins (1975)
❏ ❏ 3 – Oh Bury Me Not (1977)
❏ ❏ 4 – Nothing's Certain but Death (1978)
❏ ❏ 5 – Seasons of Death (1981)
❏ ❏ 6 – Wake Up, Darlin' Corey (1984)
❏ ❏ 7 – Dead Matter (1993)
❏ ❏ 8 – King of the Mountain (1995)

■ **L. R. WRIGHT** is Laurali Wright, a Canadian author who gave up journalism to write novels. She published three works of fiction before her first mystery—the opening title in the Karl Alberg series—which was awarded the Edgar for best novel of 1985. This series is set on the coast of British Columbia where Karl is a Royal Canadian Mounted Police (RCMP) officer in his late 40s, divorced, in a developing relationship with Cassandra Mitchell, the town librarian.

Martin Karl Alberg . . . RCMP staff sergeant on the coast of British Columbia
- ❏ ❏ 1 – **The Suspect** (1985) *Edgar winner* ★
- ❏ ❏ 2 – Sleep While I Sing (1986)
- ❏ ❏ 3 – **A Chill Rain in January** (1990) *Ellis winner* ☆
- ❏ ❏ 4 – Fall from Grace (1991)
- ❏ ❏ 5 – Prized Possessions (1993)
- ❏ ❏ 6 – **A Touch of Panic** (1994) *Ellis nominee* ☆
- ❏ ❏ 7 – Mother Love (1995)

■ **Chelsea Quinn YARBRO**, past president of Horror Writers of America, is best known for her historical horror novels, including the Olivia trilogy featuring a female vampire introduced in *A Flame in Byantium* (1987). Her much-acclaimed Saint Germain novels cast the Count as a surprisingly sympathetic character with each book in the series focusing on a particular period in history ranging from ancient Rome to the mid-20th century. Yarbro has written science fiction, fantasy, westerns, other historicals, books for children, nonfiction and a mystery series—more than 40 titles in all. Her mystery series protagonist is Charles Spotted Moon, a San Francisco attorney who is also an Ojibway tribal shaman. Two-time Edgar nominee and former vice president of Mystery Writers of America, Yarbro describes herself as a composer, fortune teller and lifetime student of history. She has written three nonfiction books about Ouija board messages received from an ancient entity named Michael. A native of Berkeley, California, Yarbro attended San Francisco State and once worked as a cartographer in the family map-making business. She is coauthor with Bill Fawcett of the new series written as Quinn Fawcett featuring Victoire Vernet, wife of a Napoleonic gendarme.

Charles Spotted Moon . . . San Francisco attorney & Ojibway tribal shaman
- ❏ ❏ 1 – Ogilvie, Tallant and Moon (1976) [APA-Bad Medicine ('90)]
- ❏ ❏ 2 – Music When Sweet Voices Die (1979) [APA-False Notes ('90)]
- ❏ ❏ 3 – Poison Fruit (1991)
- ❏ ❏ 4 – Cat's Claw (1992)

■ **Margaret (Evelyn) Tayler YATES** (1887-1952), born in California, was herself a newspaper correspondent. She was also the creator of a four-book series wartime series featuring newspaper correspondent Anne "Davvie" Davenport McLean. While the series opener was aboard ship, subsequent adventures took place in Cuba, Midway Island, and finally, Hawaii.

Anne "Davvie" Davenport McLean . . . newspaper correspondent aboard ship
- ❏ ❏ 1 – The Hush-Hush Murders (1937)
- ❏ ❏ 2 – Death Send a Cable (1939)
- ❏ ❏ 3 – Midway to Murder (1941)
- ❏ ❏ 4 – Murder by the Yard (1942)

■ **Dorian YEAGER** is a native of New Hampshire and a working actor, director and freelance magazine humor writer in New York City. Her newest series, introduced in 1994, features Elizabeth Will, a 30-something seasonal gallery owner who is forced to lobster fish commercially with her father off the coast of New Hampshire. Yeager's earlier series features Victoria Bowering, New York City actor, director and playwright who is a part-time psychic on the party circuit.

Elizabeth Will . . . art gallery owner & lobster fisherman in Dovekey, New Hampshire
- ❑ ❑ 1 – Murder Will Out (1994)
- ❑ ❑ 2 – Summer Will End (1995)

Victoria Bowering . . . New York City actor, writer, playwright
- ❑ ❑ 1 – Cancellation by Death (1992)
- ❑ ❑ 2 – Eviction by Death (1993)
- ❑ ❑ 3 – Ovation by Death (1995)

■ **Margaret YORKE** is the pseudonym of Margaret Beda Larminie Nicholson, Oxford college librarian, mystery author and wartime veteran of the Women's Royal Naval Service. She launched her mystery writing career with a five-book series featuring Oxford don Patrick Grant, after turning out eleven of what she called "family problem novels." She chaired the British Crime Writers Association in 1979 and received an award from the Swedish Academy of Detection in 1982. Her nonseries novels of psychological suspense, including *No Medals for the Major* (1974) and *The Hand of Death* (1981), are considered her best work.

Dr. Patrick Grant . . . Oxford don teaching English literature
- ❑ ❑ 1 – Dead in the Morning (1970)
- ❑ ❑ 2 – Silent Witness (1972)
- ❑ ❑ 3 – Grave Matters (1973)
- ❑ ❑ 4 – Mortal Remains (1974)
- ❑ ❑ 5 – Cast for Death (1976)

■ **Fay ZACHARY** is the creator of Dr. Liz Broward, family practice physician, and Zack James, single father and computer graphic artist and genealogist. Zack's wife Maryellen (a public health nurse) and Liz had known each other at Penn, but after her death from leukemia, Zack finds himself one of Liz's patients. The doctor's Main Line pedigree is strictly Mayflower, but she never appreciated genealogy until Zack helps her solve a medical mystery. Their professional and personal interests converge in a final plot twist that is downright spooky. The series opens with *Bloodwork* (1994) in Philadelphia where the author lived for eight years, but moves to Phoenix with the second installment. Zachary, who studied nursing at the University of Pittsburgh and the University of Pennsylvania, now lives in Scottsdale, Arizona.

Dr. Liz Broward & Zack James . . . family practice physician & computer graphic artist/genealogist in Phoenix, Arizona
- ❑ ❑ 1 – Blood Work (1994)
- ❑ ❑ 2 – A Poison in the Blood (1994)

■ **Sharon ZUKOWSKI** is a Manhattan executive by day and a mystery writer by night from her home in Hackensack, New Jersey. She is also the creator of P. I. Blaine Stewart who's in partnership with her attorney sister Eileen. Their clients are typically Fortune 500 and Wall Street firms with concerns too sensitive for in-house legal staffs. Before starting their very profitable investigations business, Blaine did a cop tour with the NYPD and Eileen worked for the Manhattan District Attorney. Zukowski is senior publications editor for a major New York financial services firm and has worked as a stockbroker, financial planner and housing coordinator.

Blaine Stewart . . . ex-NYPD cop turned P. I. in Manhattan
- ❑ ❑ 1 – The Hour of the Knife (1991)
- ❑ ❑ 2 – Dancing in the Dark (1992)
- ❑ ❑ 3 – Leap of Faith (1994)
- ❑ ❑ 4 – Prelude to Death (1996)

Two

Mystery Types

Police Procedurals

Author	❏ – #	Series Character	Occupation	Setting
Adamson, M. J.	'87 – 5	Balthazar Marten & Sixto Cardenas	NYPD homicide det. & Puerto Rican cop	Puerto Rico
Aird, Catherine	'66 – 13	Christopher Dennis "Seedy" Sloan	Berebury CID department head	West Calleshire, England
Allen, Kate	'93 – 2	Alison Kaine	lesbian cop	Denver, CO
Ayres, Noreen	'92 – 3	Samantha "Smokey" Brandon	sheriff's forensic expert	Orange Co., CA
Bannister, Jo	'93 – 4	F. Shapiro, C. Donovan & L. Graham	cops	Castlemere, England
Barber, Willetta Ann	'40 – 7	Christopher "Kit" Storm	police illustrator for the NYPD	New York, NY
Barr, Nevada	'93 – 4	Anna Pigeon	U. S. park ranger	National Parks, USA
Beaton, M. C.	'85 – 11	Hamish Macbeth	Scottish police constable	Scotland
Beecham, Rose	'92 – 3	Amanda Valentine	ex-NYPD cop turned detective inspector	New Zealand
Bell, Josephine	'38 – 1	Steven Mitchell	Scotland Yard Inspector	London, England
Bland, Eleanor T.	'92 – 4	Marti MacAlister	black police detective	Lincoln Prairie, IL
Brand, Christianna	'41 – 6	Cockrill, Insp.	police inspector	Kent County, England
Burden, Pat	'90 – 4	Henry Bassett	retired cop	Herefordshire, England
Butler, Gwendoline	'57 – 24	John Coffin, Insp.	police inspector	London, England
Carlson, P. M.	'92 – 2	Martine "Marty" LaForte Hopkins	deputy sheriff & mother	southern Indiana
Cleeves, Ann	'90 – 4	Stephen Ramsey	British inspector	England
Cooper, Susan R.	'88 – 6	Milton Kovak	chief deputy	Prophesy County, OK
Craig, Alisa	'80 – 5	Madoc & Janet Rhys	RCMP inspector & wife	Canada
Crombie, Deborah	'93 – 3	Duncan Kincaid & Gemma James	Scotland Yard superintendent & sergeant	London, England
Curzon, Clare	'83 – 10	Mike Yeadings	det. superintendent of Serious Crime Squad	Thames Valley, England
D'Amato, Barbara	'96 – 1	Suze Figueroa & Norm Bennis	pair of cops	Chicago, IL
Davis, Dorothy S.	'57 – 3	Jasper Tully & Norris, Mrs.	DA's investigator & Scottish housekeeper	New York, NY
Dengler, Sandy	'93 – 4	Jack Prester	U. S. park ranger	National Parks, USA
Dengler, Sandy	'93 – 4	Joe Rodriguez, Sgt.	police officer	Phoenix, AZ
Disney, Doris Miles	'43 – 5	Jim O'Neill	small town policeman	Connecticut
Drake, Alison	'88 – 4	Aline Scott	small resort town police detective	Tango key, FL
Dunlap, Susan	'81 – 9	Jill Smith	homicide detective	Berkeley, CA
Dymmoch, Michael	'93 – 2	John Thinnes & Jack Caleb, Dr.	cop & psychiatrist	Chicago, IL
Eberhart, Mignon G.	'29 – 7	Sarah Keate & Lance O'Leary	nurse & wealthy police detective	New York, NY
Eccles, Marjorie	'88 – 8	Gil Mayo	detective chief inspector	England

Police Procedurals . . . continued

Author	1 – #	Series Character	Occupation	Setting
Edwards, Ruth D.	'81 – 5	James Milton & Robert Amiss	police superintendent & ex-civil servant	England
Egan, Lesley	'62 – 13	Vic Varallo	small town cop moved to Glendale	Glendale, CA
Erskine, Margaret	'38 – 21	Septimus Finch	Scotland Yard Inspector	England
Fenisong, Ruth	'42 – 13	Gridley Nelson	wealthy young cop w/ Harlem housekeeper	New York, NY
Ferrars, E. X.	'71 – 2	Ditteridge, Supt.	police superintendent	England
Forrest, Katherine V.	'84 – 4	Kate Delafield	LAPD lesbian homicide detective	Los Angeles, CA
Fraser, Anthea	'86 – 13	David Webb	British police inspector	England
Gardiner, Dorothy	'56 – 3	Moss Magill	sheriff	Notlaw, CO
George, Elizabeth	'88 – 8	Thomas Lynley & Barbara Havers	Scotland Yard inspector & detective sergeant	London, England
Gill, B. M.	'80 – 3	Tom Maybridge	police inspector	England
Gilpatrick, Noreen	'93 – 2	Kate McLean	police detective	Seattle, WA
Glass, Leslie	'93 – 2	April Woo	police detective	New York, NY
Gosling, Paula	'94 – 2	Blackwater Bay Mystery	police series with a Great Lakes setting	Midwest, USA
Gosling, Paula	'85 – 3	Jack Stryker & Kate Trevorne	homicide cop & English professor	Grantham, OH
Gosling, Paula	'86 – 2	Luke Abbott	English cop	England
Graham, Caroline	'87 – 4	Tom Barnaby	chief inspector	England
Granger, Ann	'91 – 9	Alan Markby & Meredith Mitchell	detective inspector & Foreign Service officer	Cotswolds, England
Gray, Dulcie	'60 – 2	Cardiff, Insp. Supt.	police inspector	England
Green, Anna K.	1899 – 3	Caleb Sweetwater	policeman	New York, NY
Green, Anna K.	1878 – 12	Ebenezer Gryce	portly policeman	New York, NY
Green, Christine	'94 – 3	Connor O'Neill & Fran Wilson	village inspector & new policewoman	Fowchester, England
Green, Kate	'86 – 2	Theresa Fortunato & Oliver Jardino	professional psychic & LAPD detective	Los Angeles, CA
Grimes, Martha	'81 – 13	Richard Jury, Insp.	Scotland Yard investigator	London, England
Grindle, Lucretia	'93 – 2	H. W. Ross	detective superintendent	England
Gur, Batya	'88 – 3	Michael Ohayon	chief inspector	Jerusalem, Israel
Hager, Jean	'89 – 4	Mitch Bushyhead	police chief of Cherokee descent	Buckskin, OK
Hall, Patricia	'93 – 1	Alex Sinclair & Kate Weston	British inspector & social worker	England
Hall, Patricia	'94 – 3	Laura Ackroyd & Michael Thackeray	reporter & police inspector	Yorkshire, England
Harrison, Jamie	'95 – 1	Jules Clement	30-something archaeologist turned sheriff	Blue Deer, MT
Harrod-Eagles, C.	'91 – 5	Bill Slider	detective inspector	England
Hart, Jeanne	'87 – 3	Carl & Freda Pedersen	police lieutenant & wife	Bay Cove, CA
Haymon, S. T.	'80 – 7	Benjamin Jurnet, Insp.	detective inspector	Norwich, England
Herndon, Nancy	'95 – 2	Elena Jarvis	detective with Crimes Against Persons unit	Los Santos, TX
Hess, Joan	'87 – 9	Arly Hanks	small-town police chief	Maggody, AR
Heyer, Georgette	'35 – 4	Hannasyde, Supt.	police superintendent	England
Heyer, Georgette	'39 – 4	Hemingway, Insp.	one-time assistant to Supt. Hannasyde	England
Hightower, Lynn S.	'92 – 4	David Silver & String	homicide cop & alien partner	USA
Hightower, Lynn S.	'95 – 1	Sonora Blair	homicide detective	Cincinnati, OH
Horansky, Ruby	'90 – 2	Nikki Trakos	homicide detective	New York, NY
Hornsby, Wendy	'87 – 2	Kate Teague & Roger Tejeda	college professor & homicide detective	southern California
Huxley, Elspeth	'37 – 3	Vachell, Supt.	young Scotsman trained by the RCMP	Kenya
James, P. D.	'62 – 9	Adam Dalgleish	published poet of Scotland Yard	London, England
Jance, J. A.	'85 – 13	J. P. Beaumont	homicide detective	Seattle, WA
Jance, J. A.	'93 – 3	Joanna Brady	deputy sheriff's widow turned sheriff	Cochise County, AZ
Kellerman, Faye	'86 – 8	Peter Decker & Rina Lazarus	LAPD detective & wife	Los Angeles, CA
Kelly, Mary	'56 – 3	Brett Nightingale	Scottish Inspector	Edinburgh, Scotland
Knight, Alanna	'88 – 9	Jeremy Faro	Victorian detective inspector	Edinburgh, Scotland
Krich, Rochelle M.	'93 – 2	Jessie Drake	police detective	Los Angeles, CA
Langton, Jane	'64 – 11	Homer Kelly	Harvard professor & retired detective	Cambridge, MA
La Pierre, Janet	'87 – 5	Vince Gutierrez & Meg Halloran	police chief & school teacher	Port Silva, CA

Police Procedurals . . . *continued*

Author	❶ – #	Series Character	Occupation	Setting
La Plante, Lynda	'93 – 3	Jane Tennison	detective chief inspector	London, England
Lemarchand, E.	'67 – 17	Tom Pollard & Gregory Toye	Scotland Yard detectives	England
Leon, Donna	'92 – 5	Guido Brunetti	commissario of the Venice police	Venice, Italy
Linington, Elizabeth	'64 – 13	Ivor Maddox, Sgt.	book-collecting mystery-addict cop	Hollywood, CA
Lockridge, F. & R.	'47 – 24	Merton Heimrich, Insp.	State Police Bureau of Criminal Investigation	New York
Maron, Margaret	'81 – 8	Sigrid Harald	police lieutenant	New York, NY
Marsh, Ngaio	'34 – 32	Roderick Alleyn	inspector son of a baronet	London, England
Martin, Lee	'84 – 11	Deb Ralston	police detective & mother	Ft. Worth, TX
Mason, Sarah Jill	'93 – 4	D. S. Trewley & Stone, Sgt.	village detective partners	Allshire, England
Mathews, Francine	'94 – 2	Meredith "Merry" Folger	police detective	Nantucket, MA
McAllester, Melanie	'94 – 1	Elizabeth Mendoza & Ashley Johnson	lesbian homicide detectives	USA
McCrumb, Sharyn	'90 – 4	Spencer Arrowood	Appalachian sheriff	Tennessee
McGown, Jill	'83 – 7	Lloyd, Chief Inspector & Judy Hill	detective inspectors	East Anglia, England
McNab, Claire	'88 – 7	Carol Ashton	lesbian detective inspector & single mother	Sydney, Australia
Melville, Jennie	'62 – 17	Charmian Daniels	police detective	Deerham Hills, England
Meredith, D. R.	'84 – 5	Charles Matthews	sheriff	west Texas
Mickelbury, Penny	'94 – 2	Gianna Maglione & Mimi Patterson	lesbian police lieutenant & reporter	Washington, DC
Millar, Margaret	'43 – 2	Sands, Insp.	police inspector	Toronto, Canada
Mitchell, Kay	'90 – 5	John Morrissey	Chief Inspector	Malminster, England
Morell, Mary	'91 – 2	Lucia Ramos	lesbian police detective	San Antonio, TX
Moyes, Patricia	'59 – 19	Henry & Emmy Tibbett	Scotland Yard inspector & wife	London, England
Nabb, Magdalen	'81 – 10	Salvatore Guarnaccia	Italian police marshal	Florence, Italy
Neel, Janet	'88 – 4	John McLeish & Francesca Wilson	detective inspector & civil servant	England
O'Connell, Carol	'94 – 3	Kathleen Mallory	NYPD cop	New York, NY
O'Connell, Catherine	'93 – 1	Karen Levinson	NYPD homicide detective	New York, NY
O'Donnell, Lillian	'77 – 3	Mici Anhalt	criminal justice investigator	New York, NY
O'Donnell, Lillian	'72 – 15	Norah Mulcahaney	NYPD detective	New York, NY
Oleksiw, Susan	'93 – 3	Joe Silva	chief of police	Mellingham, MA
Olsen, D. B.	'40 – 2	Stephen Mayhew, Lt.	police detective	Los Angeles, CA
Page, Emma	'80 – 8	Kelsey, Insp.	police inspector	England
Paul, Barbara	'84 – 6	Marian Larch	NYPD officer	New York, NY
Perry, Anne	'79 – 16	Thomas & Charlotte Pitt	Victorian police inspector & wife	London, England
Perry, Anne	'90 – 6	William Monk	amnesiac Victorian police inspector	England
Peters, Ellis	'51 – 13	George, Bunty & Dominic Felse	family of detectives	Shropshire, England
Petrie, Rhona	'63 – 5	Marcus MacLurg	Inspector	England
Porter, Joyce	'64 – 21	Wilfred Dover	a fat lout of a Chief Inspector	England
Pulver, Mary Monica	'87 – 5	Peter & Kori Price Brichter	police detective & horse breeder	Illinois
Quest, Erica	'88 – 3	Kate Maddox	Det. Chief Inspector	Cotswolds, England
Radley, Sheila	'78 – 9	Douglas Quantrill & Hilary Lloyd	detective chief inspector & sergeant partner	Suffolk, England
Reilly, Helen	'30 – 31	Christopher McKee	Manhattan homicide squad detective	New York, NY
Rendell, Ruth	'64 – 16	Reginald Wexford	chief inspector	Sussex, England
Robb, J. D.	'95 – 3	Eve Dallas	NYPD lieutenant in the 21st century	New York, NY
Roberts, Carey	'89 – 2	Anne Fitzhugh	police detective	Washington, DC
Sale, Medora	'86 – 6	John Sanders & Harriet Jeffries	police detective & architectural photographer	Toronto, Canada
Sandstrom, Eve K.	'90 – 3	Sam & Nicky Titus	ex-army CID sheriff & photojournalist wife	Holton, OK
Schenkel, S. E.	'94 – 2	Ray & Kate Frederick	chief of detectives & wife of 30 yrs	Michigan
Scherf, Margaret	'45 – 2	Lt. Ryan	NYPD cop	New York, NY
Shannon, Dell	'60 – 37	Luis Mendoza	wealthy homicide lieutenant	Los Angeles, CA
Shepherd, Stella	'89 – 6	Richard Montgomery	CID Inspector	Nottingham, England
Silva, Linda Kay	'91 – 4	Delta Stevens	lesbian policewoman	California

Police Procedurals ... *continued*

Author	❶ – #	Series Character	Occupation	Setting
Simpson, Dorothy	'81 – 13	Luke Thanet	British police inspector	England
Sims, L. V.	'87 – 3	Dixie T. Struthers	police detective	San Jose, CA
Sjöwall, M. & P. W.	'67 – 10	Martin Beck	police officer	Stockholm, Sweden
Smith, April	'94 – 1	Ana Grey	FBI agent	Los Angeles, CA
Smith, Julie	'90 – 5	Skip Langdon	6-ft. police detective	New Orleans, LA
Stacey, Susannah	'87 – 7	Robert Bone	widowed British police inspector	England
Tey, Josephine	'29 – 6	Alan Grant	Scotland Yard inspector	London, England
Thomson, June	'71 – 18	Finch, Insp.	police inspector	Essex, England
Thurlo, A. & D.	'95 – 2	Ella Clah	Navajo FBI agent	New Mexico
Uhnak, Dorothy	'68 – 3	Christine Opara	20-something police detective	New York, NY
Vlasopolos, Anca	'90 – 1	Sharon Dair	sex crimes police detective	Detroit, MI
Wallace, Marilyn	'86 – 3	Jay Goldstein & Carlos Cruz	homicide detectives	Oakland, CA
Webb, Martha G.	'85 – 2	Tommy Inman	cop	Texas
Weir, Charlene	'92 – 3	Susan Wren	ex-cop turned police chief	Kansas
Wells, Tobias	'66 – 16	Knute Severson	police officer	Boston, MA
Wentworth, Patricia	'39 – 2	Ernest Lamb, Insp.	police inspector	London, England
West, Chassie	'94 – 1	Leigh Ann Warren	former DC street cop	Sunrise, NC
Weston, Carolyn	'72 – 3	Casey Kellog & Al Krug	college grad liberal & hard-bitten veteran cop	Santa Monica, CA
White, Teri	'84 – 2	Spaceman Kowalski & Blue Maguire	cop pair with prickly partnership	Los Angeles, CA
Wingate, Anne	'88 – 5	Mark Shigata	ex-FBI agent turned sheriff	Bayport, TX
Winslow, Pauline G.	'75 – 6	Merlin Capricorn	magician turned police superintendent	England
Wolfe, Susan	'89 – 1	Sarah Nelson	police inspector	Silicon Valley, CA
Wright, L. R.	'85 – 7	Martin Karl Alberg	RCMP staff sergeant	Vancouver, B.C., Canada

Private Investigators

Author	❶ – #	Series Character	Occupation	Setting
Barnes, Linda	'87 – 6	Carlotta Carlyle	6'1" cab-driving ex-cop P. I.	Boston, MA
Barnes, Linda	'82 – 4	Michael Spraggue III	wealthy actor & ex-P. I.	Boston, MA
Bedford, Jean	'90 – 3	Anna Southwood	P. I.	Sydney, Australia
Borton, D. B.	'93 – 5	Cat Caliban	60-something P. I.-in-training	Cincinnati, OH
Bowers, Elisabeth	'88 – 2	Meg Lacey	P. I.	Vancouver, B.C., Canada
Bradley, Lynn	'94 – 1	Coleman January	insurance investigator	Houston, TX
Brod, D. C.	'89 – 4	Quint McCauley	ex-cop turned P. I.	Chicago suburb, IL
Bushell, Agnes	'89 – 2	Wilson & Wilder	P. I.s	Maine
Chapman, Sally	'91 – 3	Juliet Blake	Silicon Valley fraud investigator	Silicon Valley, CA
Christie, Agatha	'20 – 35	Hercule Poirot	former Belgian cop turned private detective	London, England
Clark, Carol Higgins	'92 – 3	Regan Reilly	P. I.	Los Angeles, CA
Clark, Carolyn C.	'94 – 1	Theresa Franco	P. I.	Florida
Cody, Liza	'80 – 6	Anna Lee	P. I.	London, England
Dain, Catherine	'92 – 5	Freddie O'Neal	plane-flying P. I.	Reno, NV
Davis, Lindsey	'89 – 8	Marcus Didius Falco	P. I. in ancient Rome	Rome, Italy
Dawson, Janet	'90 – 5	Jeri Howard	P. I.	Oakland, CA
Day, Marele	'88 – 4	Claudia Valentine	Australian P. I.	Australia
Disney, Doris Miles	'46 – 8	Jeff Di Marco	insurance investigator	Boston, MA
Donald, Anabel	'91 – 4	Alex Tanner	part-time P. I. & TV researcher	London, England
Douglas, Lauren W.	'87 – 6	Caitlin Reece	lesbian detective	Victoria, Canada
Duffy, Margaret	'94 – 2	Joanna MacKenzie	former CID turned P. I.	Bath, England
Dunant, Sarah	'92 – 3	Hannah Wolfe	P. I.	London, England
Dunlap, Susan	'89 – 3	Kiernan O'Shaughnessy	San Francisco medical examiner turned P. I.	La Jolla, CA
Eichler, Selma	'94 – 4	Desiree Shapiro	5'2" queen-size Manhattan P. I.	New York, NY
Evanovich, Janet	'94 – 2	Stephanie Plum	neophyte bounty hunter	Trenton, NJ

Private Investigators ... *continued*

Author	🔢 – #	Series Character	Occupation	Setting
Farrell, Gillian B.	'92 – 2	Annie McGrogan	P. I. & actor just back from LA	New York, NY
Femling, Jean	'89 – 2	Martha "Moz" Brant	insurance claims investigator	southern, CA
Fennelly, Tony	'85 – 3	Matthew Arthur Sinclair	gay ex-D.A. turned P. I.	New Orleans, LA
Fickling, G. G.	'62 – 3	Erik March	P. I.	California
Fickling, G. G.	'57 – 11	Honey West	sexiest P. I. ever to pull a trigger	California
Frankel, Valerie	'91 – 4	Wanda Mallory	detective agency owner	New York, NY
Furie, Ruthe	'95 – 3	Fran Kirk	former battered wife & P. I. in training	Cheektowaga, NY
Gallison, Kate	'86 – 3	Nick Magaracz	P. I.	Trenton, NJ
Geason, Susan	'93 – 3	Syd Fish	P. I.	Sydney, Australia
Grafton, Sue	'82 – 12	Kinsey Millhone	ex-cop P. I.	Santa Teresa, CA
Grant, Linda	'88 – 5	Catherine Sayler	P. I.	San Francisco, CA
Grant-Adamson, L.	'91 – 2	Laura Flynn	P. I.	London, England
Haddam, Jane	'90 – 12	Gregor Demarkian	former FBI department head	Philadelphia, PA
Heberden, M. V.	'39 – 17	Desmond Shannon	high-priced Irish-American P. I.	New York, NY
Heberden, M. V.	'46 – 3	Rick Vanner	former Naval Intelligence officer	New York, NY
Hightower, Lynn S.	'93 – 1	Lena Padget	P. I.	Lexington, KY
Hitchens, Dolores	'57 – 2	Jim Sader	P. I.	Long Beach, CA
Hollingsworth, G.	'95 – 1	Frances Finn	P. I.	Kansas City, KS
Hooper, Kay	'91 – 2	Lane Montana & Trey Fortier	finder of lost things & homicide detective	Atlanta, GA
Howe, Melodie J.	'89 – 2	Claire Conrad & Maggie Hill	P. I. & secretary	southern California
Huff, Tanya	'92 – 4	Vicki Nelson	ex-cop turned P. I.	Toronto, Canada
Jackson, Marian J.A.	'90 – 5	Abigail Patience Danforth	turn-of-the-century consulting detective	USA
Jacobs, Nancy B.	'91 – 3	Devon MacDonald	ex-teacher P. I.	Minneapolis, MN
James, P. D.	'72 – 2	Cordelia Gray	fledgling P. I.	London, England
Kelly, Mary	'61 – 2	Hedley Nicholson	P. I.	England
Kelner, Toni L. P.	'93 – 3	Laura Fleming	small-town detective	Byerly, NC
Kijewski, Karen	'88 – 6	Kat Colorado	P. I.	Sacramento, CA
King, Laurie R.	'93 – 3	Kate Martinelli & Alonzo Hawkin	SFPD homicide detectives	San Francisco, CA
King, Laurie R.	'94 – 2	Mary Russell	teenage student of Sherlock Holmes	London, England
Knight, Phyllis	'92 – 3	Lil Ritchie	ex-rocker & gay woman P. I.	coastal Maine
Komo, Dolores	'88 – 1	Clio Browne	cop's widow & P. I. agency owner	St. Louis, MO
Kreuter, Katherine E.	'94 – 1	Paige Taylor	mystery writer & P. I.	USA
Lackey, Mercedes	'89 – 3	Diana Tregarde	romance author & practicing witch	Hartford, CT
Law, Janice	'76 – 8	Anna Peters	international oil company exec turned P. I.	Washington, DC
Lawrence, Hilda	'44 – 3	Mark East, B. Petty & B. Pond	NYC P. I. & New England little old ladies	northeast USA
Lawrence, Martha	'95 – 1	Elizabeth Chase, Dr.	Stanford-trained parapsychologist turned P. I.	San Diego, CA
Lee, W. W. (Wendi)	'94 – 2	Angela Matelli	ex-Marine turned P. I.	Boston, MA
Lee, W. W. (Wendi)	'89 – 6	Jefferson Birch	P. I. in the Old West	Western, USA
Leonard, Charles L.	'42 – 11	Paul Kilgerrin	P. I. spy	Washington, DC
Lorden, Randye	'93 – 2	Sydney Sloane	upper west side P. I.	New York, NY
Lucke, Margaret	'91 – 2	Jessica Randolph	artist working as a P. I.	San Francisco, CA
MacGregor, T. J.	'86 – 10	Quin St. James & Mike McCleary	wife & husband P. I. team	Florida
MacLeod, Charlotte	'79 – 11	Sarah Kelling & Max Bittersohn	investigative couple	Boston, MA
Maiman, Jaye	'91 – 4	Robin Miller	travel & romance writer turned P. I.	New York, NY
McCafferty, Taylor	'90 – 5	Haskell Blevins	small-town P. I.	Pigeon Fork, KY
McDermid, Val	'92 – 5	Kate Brannigan	P. I.	Manchester, England
McKenna, Bridget	'93 – 3	Caley Burke	30-something P. I.	northern California
McKevett, G. A.	'95 – 2	Savannah Reid	ex-cop & owner of a new detective agency	southern California
Muller, Marcia	'86 – 3	Joanna Stark	international art investigator	Napa Valley, CA
Muller, Marcia	'77 – 17	Sharon McCone	legal co-op investigator turned P. I.	San Francisco, CA

Private Investigators ... *continued*

Author	▯ – #	Series Character	Occupation	Setting
O'Callaghan, Maxine	'80 – 5	Delilah West	P. I.	Orange County, CA
O'Donnell, Lillian	'90 – 3	Gwenn Ramadge	P. I. for corporate investigations	New York, NY
Oliver, Maria Antonia	'87 – 2	Lonia Gulu	Catalan P. I.	Spain
Padgett, Abigail	'93 – 3	Barbara Joan "Bo" Bradley	child abuse investigator	San Diego, CA
Paretsky, Sara	'82 – 8	V. I. Warshawski	attorney turned P. I.	Chicago, IL
Pincus, Elizabeth	'92 – 3	Nell Fury	lesbian P. I.	San Francisco, CA
Popkin, Zelda	'38 – 5	Mary Carner	former department store detective	New York, NY
Prowell, Sandra W.	'93 – 3	Phoebe Siegel	ex-cop P. I.	Billings, MT
Redmann, J. M.	'90 – 3	Michelle "Micky" Knight	lesbian P. I.	New Orleans, LA
Robinson, Lynda S.	'94 – 3	Meren, Lord	chief investigator for Pharaoh Tutankhamen	Egypt
Rozan, S. J.	'94 – 2	Lydia Chin & Bill Smith	Chinese American & Army brat P. I.s	New York, NY
Scoppettone, Sandra	'91 – 3	Lauren Laurano	Greenwich Village lesbian P. I.	New York, NY
Shah, Diane K.	'90 – 2	Paris Chandler	1940s P. I.	Hollywood, CA
Sheridan, Juanita	'49 – 4	Lily Wu & Janice Cameron	investigator & adopted sister	Hawaii
Shone, Anna	'95 – 1	Ulysses Finnegan Donaghue	Shakespeare-spouting P. I.	Provence, France
Short, Sharon Gwyn	'94 – 3	Patricia Delaney	computer whiz P. I.	Cincinnati, OH
Singer, Shelley	'83 – 5	Jake Samson & Rosie Vicente	ex-cop & carpenter tenant	Berkeley, CA
Slovo, Gillian	'84 – 5	Kate Baeier	freelance journalist turned detective	London, England
Smith, J. C. S.	'80 – 2	Quentin Jacoby	P. I.	New York, NY
Spring, Michelle	'94 – 2	Laura Principal	British academic turned P. I.	England
Stabenow, Dana	'92 – 6	Kate Shugak	native Alaskan ex-D.A. investigator	Alaska
Steiner, Susan	'91 – 2	Alex Winter	P. I.	California
Sucher, Dorothy	'88 – 2	Sabina Swift	Georgetown detective agency owner	Washington, DC
Sullivan, Winona	'93 – 2	Cecile Buddenbrooks, Sister	licensed P. I. nun	Boston, MA
Sumner, Penny	'92 – 2	Victoria Cross	archivist turned P. I.	England
Taylor, Elizabeth A.	'81 – 3	Maggie Elliott	ex-film maker turned P. I.	San Francisco, CA
Taylor, Jean	'95 – 2	Maggie Garrett	young lesbian P. I.	San Francisco, CA
Tone, Teona	'83 – 2	Kyra Keaton	P. I. at the turn-of-the-century	Washington, DC
Wallace, Patricia	'88 – 4	Sydney Bryant	P. I.	San Diego, CA
Welch, Pat	'90 – 4	Helen Black	ex-cop lesbian P. I.	San Francisco, CA
Wells, Carolyn	'09 – 61	Fleming Stone	intellectual P. I.	New York, NY
Wells, Carolyn	'29 – 3	Kenneth Carlisle	actor turned detective	New York, NY
Wells, Carolyn	'18 – 8	Pennington Wise	private detective	New York, NY
Wentworth, Patricia	'28 – 32	Maud Silver, Miss	retired governess & spinster P. I.	London, England
Wesley, Valerie W.	'94 – 2	Tamara Hayle	black ex-cop P. I. & single mother	Newark, NJ
White, Gloria	'91 – 3	Veronica "Ronnie" Ventana	Anglo-Mexican P. I. daughter of cat burglars	San Francisco, CA
Wilhelm, Kate	'87 – 6	Charlie Meiklejohn & Constance Leidl	ex-arson investigator P. I. & psychologist	New York, NY
Wiltz, Chris	'81 – 3	Neal Rafferty	third generation cop turned P. I.	New Orleans, LA
Wings, Mary	'87 – 3	Emma Victor	lesbian activist & P. I.	San Francisco, CA
Zukowski, Sharon	'91 – 4	Blaine Stewart	ex-NYPD cop turned P. I. in Manhattan	New York, NY

Amateurs

Author	🔢 – #	Series Character	Occupation	Setting

Academic

Author	🔢 – #	Series Character	Occupation	Setting
Armstrong, Charlotte	'42 – 3	MacDougal Duff	retired history professor	New York, NY
Arnold, Margot	'79 – 12	Penny Spring & Toby Glendower, Sir	Amer anthropologist & Brit archlgst	World Travelers
Belfort, Sophie	'86 – 3	Molly Rafferty	college history professor	Boston, MA
Borthwick, J. S.	'82 – 7	Sarah Deane & Alex McKenzie, Dr.	English professor & internist	Boston, MA
Bowen, Gail	'90 – 4	Joanne Kilbourn	political science professor	Regina, Sask., Canada
Carlson, P. M.	'85 – 8	Maggie Ryan	college student turned statistician & mother	New York, NY
Caudwell, Sarah	'81 – 3	Hilary Tamar	Oxford professor of medieval law	Oxford, England
Clarke, Anna	'85 – 8	Paula Glenning	British professor & writer	London, England
Cleary, Melissa	'92 – 8	Jackie Walsh & Jake	college film instructor with her ex-police dog	Palmer, MA
Crane, Hamilton	'68 – 19	Emily D. Seeton	retired British art teacher	Kent, England
Cross, Amanda	'64 – 11	Kate Fansler	university English professor	New York, NY
Dunant, Sarah	'88 – 1	Marla Masterson	young British professor	USA
Ferrars, E. X.	'83 – 8	Andrew Basnett	retired botany professor	England
Flora, Kate Clark	'95 – 1	Ross McIntyre	small town high school biology teacher	Maine
Kelly, Nora	'84 – 3	Gillian Adams	Univ. of the Pacific Northwest history chair	Canada
Lee, Marie	'95 – 1	Marguerite Smith	retired science teacher	Cape Cod, MA
Lorens, M. K.	'90 – 5	William Marlowe Sherman	Shakespeare professor & mystery writer	New York, NY
Mackay, Amanda	'76 – 2	Hannah Land	divorced New York PhD at Duke University	Durham, NC
MacLeod, Charlotte	'78 – 9	Peter Shandy & Helen Marsh Shandy	botany professor & librarian wife	Balaclava Co., MA
Mann, Jessica	'82 – 6	Tamara Hoyland	British secret agent archaeologist	England
Mann, Jessica	'72 – 2	Thea Crawford	archaeology professor	England
Mariz, Linda French	'92 – 2	Laura Ireland	grad student volleyball player	Seattle, WA
McCrumb, Sharyn	'84 – 8	Elizabeth MacPherson	forensic anthropologist	Southern, USA
McCrumb, Sharyn	'88 – 2	James Owens Mega, Dr.	science fiction author & college professor	USA
McFall, Patricia	'92 – 1	Nora James	American linguistics graduate student	Japan
Olsen, D. B.	'45 – 6	A. Pennyfather, Prof.	professor at Clarendon College	Los Angeles, CA
Peterson, Audrey	'92 – 3	Claire Camden	California English professor in Britain	London, England
Roberts, Gillian	'87 – 6	Amanda Pepper	high school teacher	Philadelphia, PA
Singer, Shelley	'93 – 5	Barrett Lake	high school history teacher	Berkeley, CA
Skom, Edith	'89 – 2	Elizabeth Austin	English professor	Midwest, USA
Smith, Joan	'87 – 5	Loretta Lawson	British feminist professor	London, England
Smith, Joan G.	'89 – 2	Cassie Newton	French major at McGill University	Montreal, Canada
Walsh, Jill Paton	'93 – 2	Imogen Quy	school nurse at St. Agatha's College	Cambridge, England
Wender, Theodora	'85 – 2	Glad Gold & Alden Chase	English professor & chief of police	Massachusetts
Yorke, Margaret	'70 – 5	Patrick Grant, Dr.	Oxford don teaching English literature	Oxford, England

Animals, cat

Author	🔢 – #	Series Character	Occupation	Setting
Braun, Lilian Jackson	'66 – 18	Jim Qwilleran, Koko & Yum Yum	ex-police reporter & cats	Midwest USA
Brown, Rita Mae	'90 – 4	Mary Minor Haristeen	small-town postmistress & cat	Crozet, VA
Douglas, Carole N.	'92 – 5	Temple Barr & Midnight Louie	public relations freelancer & tomcat sleuth	Las Vegas, NV
Matthews, Alex	'96 – 2	Cassidy McCabe	psychotherapirst	Oak Park, IL
Olsen, D. B.	'39 – 13	Rachel & Jennifer Murdock	sister sleuths	Los Angeles, CA
Olsen, D. B.	'40 – 2	Stephen Mayhew, Lt.	police detective	Los Angeles, CA

Amateurs . . . *continued*

Author	**1** – #	Series Character	Occupation	Setting

Animals, dog

Author	1 – #	Series Character	Occupation	Setting
Berenson, Laurien	'95 – 3	Melanie Travis	special ed teacher posing as poodle breeder	Connecticut
Cleary, Melissa	'92 – 8	Jackie Walsh & Jake	college film instructor with her ex-police dog	Palmer, MA
Conant, Susan	'89 – 8	Holly Winter	dog trainer & magazine columnist	Cambridge, MA
Henry, Sue	'91 – 3	Jessie Arnold & Alex Jensen	sled dog racer & Alaska state trooper	Anchorage, AK
Lee, Barbara	'95 – 1	Eve Elliott	ex-New York advertising exec turned realtor	Anne Arundel Co., MD
Moore, Barbara	'83 – 2	Gordon Christy, Dr.	veterinarian	New Mexico
Walker, Mary Willis	'91 – 1	Kate Driscoll	dog trainer	Texas
Wilson, Karen Ann	'94 – 2	Samantha Holt	vet's assistant	Paradise Cay, FL

Animals, horse

Author	1 – #	Series Character	Occupation	Setting
Banks, Carolyn	'93 – 3	Robin Vaughn	equestrienne sleuth	Texas
Crum, Laura	'94 – 2	Gail McCarthy	horse veterinarian	Santa Cruz, CA
Jaffe, Jody	'95 – 2	Natalie Gold	newspaper reporter on horse show circuit	Charlotte, NC

Animals, other

Author	1 – #	Series Character	Occupation	Setting
Block, Barbara	'94 – 2	Robin Light	pet store owner	Syracuse, NY

Art & Antiques

Author	1 – #	Series Character	Occupation	Setting
Brown, Lizbie	'92 – 2	Elizabeth Blair	American widow from Virginia selling quilts	Bath, England
Coker, Carolyn	'84 – 4	Andrea Perkins	museum art historian & restorer of paintings	Boston, MA
Comfort, Barbara	'86 – 4	Tish McWhinney	70-something artist & painter	Vermont
Dunnett, Dorothy	'68 – 7	Johnson Johnson	portrait painter & British agent w/his yacht	International
Fowler, Earlene	'94 – 3	Albenia "Benni" Harper	ex-rancher & folk art museum curator	San Celina, CA
Frommer, Sara H.	'93 – 2	Joan Spencer	symphony orchestra manager	Oliver, IN
Hardwick, Mollie	'86 – 6	Doran Fairweather	British antiques dealer	Kent, England
Kenney, Susan	'83 – 3	Roz Howard & Alan Stewart	American professor & British painter	Maine
Logan, Margaret	'94 – 2	Olivia Chapman	interior decorator	Boston, MA
McClendon, Lise	'94 – 2	Alix Thorssen	gallery owner & art forgery expert	Jackson, WY
Muller, Marcia	'83 – 3	Elena Oliverez	Mexican arts museum curator	Santa Barbara, CA
Orde, A. J.	'89 – 5	Jason Lynx	antiques dealer & interior decorator	Denver, CO
Peters, Elizabeth	'73 – 5	Vicky Bliss	art historian	Germany
Ruryk, Jean	'94 – 1	Catherine Wilde	retired ad exec turned antiques restorer	USA
Scherf, Margaret	'49 – 4	Emily & Henry Bryce	Manhattan interior decorators	New York, NY
Smith, Evelyn E.	'86 – 5	Susan Melville	freelance assassin & painter	New York, NY
Torrie, Malcolm	'66 – 6	Timothy Herring	preservation society director	England
Valentine, Deborah	'89 – 3	Katharine Craig & Kevin Bryce	sculptor & ex-sheriff's detective	northern California
Watson, Clarissa	'77 – 5	Persis Willum	New York art curator	Long Island, NY
Yeager, Dorian	'94 – 2	Elizabeth Will	art gallery owner & lobster fisherman	Dovekey, NH

Authors & Writers

Author	1 – #	Series Character	Occupation	Setting
Bannister, Jo	'84 – 3	Clio Rees, Dr. & Harry Marsh	physician/mystery writer & chief inspector	England
Blackmur, L. L.	'89 – 2	Galen Shaw & Julian Baugh	writer & financier	New England
Brill, Toni	'91 – 2	Midge Cohen	children's author fluent in Russian	New York, NY
Cooper, Natasha	'90 – 5	Willow King & Cressida Woodruffe	civil servant & romance novelist	London, England
Cooper, Susan R.	'92 – 2	E. J. Pugh	housewife, mother & romance writer	Texas

Amateurs . . . *continued*

Author	❶ – #	Series Character	Occupation	Setting

Authors & Writers . . . *continued*

Author	❶ – #	Series Character	Occupation	Setting
Daly, Elizabeth	'40 – 16	Henry Gamadge	children's author & bibliophile	New York, NY
Dank, Gloria	'89 – 4	Bernard Woodrull & "Snooky" Randolph	children's author & visiting brother-in-law	CT
Duffy, Margaret	'87 – 6	Ingrid Langley & Patrick Gillard	novelist/British agent & British army major	England
Friedman, Mickey	'88 – 2	Georgia Lee Maxwell	freelance writer	Paris, France
Glen, Alison	'92 – 2	Charlotte Sams	freelance writer	Columbus, OH
Holbrook, Teri	'95 – 2	Gale Grayson	American expatriate historian	Fetherbridge, England
Jordan, Jennifer	'87 – 3	Barry & Dee Vaughan	spoofy crime writer & office temp wife	Woodfield, England
Kittredge, Mary	'87 – 3	Charlotte Kent	freelance writer	Connecticut
Kreuter, Katherine E.	'94 – 1	Paige Taylor	mystery writer & P. I.	USA
Maiman, Jaye	'91 – 4	Robin Miller	travel & romance writer turned P. I.	New York, NY
Malmont, Valerie S.	'94 – 1	Tori Miracle	ex-NYC crime writer turned novelist	Pennsylvania
Moffat, Gwen	'73 – 14	Melinda Pink	writer & mountain climber	Utah
Offord, Lenore Glen	'43 – 4	Todd McKinnon & Georgine Wyeth	pulp writer & single working mother	Berkeley, CA
Osborne, Denise	'94 – 2	Queenie Davilow	Hollywood screenwriter	Hollywood, CA
Paige, Robin	'94 – 2	Kathryn Ardleigh	25-yr-old American author	Dedham, England
Papazoglou, Orania	'84 – 5	Patience Campbell McKenna	6-ft romance novelist turned crime writer	New York, NY
Peters, Elizabeth	'72 – 4	Jacqueline Kirby	librarian turned romance novelist	New York, NY
Roberts, Lora	'94 – 3	Liz Sullivan	freelance writer	Palo Alto, CA
Rowlands, Betty	'89 – 7	Melissa Craig	British mystery writer	Cotswolds, England
Saum, Karen	'90 – 3	Brigid Donovan	50-something lesbian ex-nun	Maine
Smith, Barbara B.	'94 – 3	Jolie Wyatt	aspiring novelist & writer's group member	Purple Sage, TX
Smith, Julie	'85 – 2	Paul MacDonald	ex-reporter & mystery writer	San Francisco, CA
Stallwood, Veronica	'93 – 3	Kate Ivory	novelist	Oxford, England

Bed & Breakfast

Author	❶ – #	Series Character	Occupation	Setting
Bishop, Claudia	'94 – 4	Sarah & Meg Quilliam	inn owner & chef (sisters)	Hemlock Falls, NY
Daheim, Mary	'91 – 9	Judith McMonigle	bed & breakfast owner	Seattle, WA
Hager, Jean	'94 – 3	Tess Darcy	Ozarks bed & breakfast owner	Victoria Springs, MO
Kingsbury, Kate	'93 – 7	Cecily Sinclair	hotel owner in Edwardian England	Badger's End, England
Myers, Tamar	'94 – 3	Magdalena Yoder	Mennonite inn owner & operator	Hernia, PA

Black

Author	❶ – #	Series Character	Occupation	Setting
Bland, Eleanor T.	'92 – 4	Marti MacAlister	black police detective	Lincoln Prairie, IL
Johns, Veronica P.	'53 – 2	Webster Flagg	60-something Harlem actor/butler/houseman	New York, NY
Komo, Dolores	'88 – 1	Clio Browne	cop's widow & P. I. agency owner	St. Louis, MO
Moody, Susan	'84 – 7	Penny Wanawake	6-ft. photographer daughter of UN diplomat	England
Neely, Barbara	'92 – 2	Blanche White	middle-aged black domestic	North Carolina
Wesley, Valerie W.	'94 – 2	Tamara Hayle	black ex-cop P. I. & single mother	Newark, NJ
West, Chassie	'94 – 1	Leigh Ann Warren	former DC street cop	Sunrise, NC

Books & Libraries

Author	❶ – #	Series Character	Occupation	Setting
de la Torre, Lillian	'46 – 4	Samuel Johnson, Dr. & James Boswell	18th century lexicographer & biographer	London, England
Dereske, Jo	'94 – 4	Helma Zukas	state librarian	Washington
Harris, Charlaine	'90 – 5	Aurora Teagarden	librarian turned real estate agent	Georgia
Hart, Carolyn G.	'87 – 9	Annie Laurance & Max Darling	bookstore owner & investigator	South Carolina
Hess, Joan	'86 – 10	Claire Malloy	small-town bookstore owner	Farberville, AR

Amateurs . . . *continued*

Author	**1** – #	Series Character	Occupation	Setting

Books & Libraries . . . *continued*

Author	1 – #	Series Character	Occupation	Setting
Knight, Kathryn L.	'86 – 4	Calista Jacobs	award-winning illustrator of children's books	Cambridge, MA
Linington, Elizabeth	'64 – 13	Ivor Maddox, Sgt.	book-collecting mystery-addict cop	Hollywood, CA
Lockridge, F. & R.	'40 – 26	Pam & Jerry North	book publisher & wife	New York, NY
Morgan, Kate	'90 – 6	Dewey James	60-something small-town librarian	New York
Simonson, Sheila	'90 – 4	Lark Dailey	6-ft. bookdealer	northern California
Sumner, Penny	'92 – 2	Victoria Cross	archivist turned P. I.	England
Tilton, Alice	'37 – 8	Leonidas Witherall	retired academic & secret pulp fiction author	Boston, MA
Travis, Elizabeth	'89 – 2	Ben & Carrie Porter	book publishers	Riverdale, CT
Wren, M. K.	'73 – 8	Conan Flagg	bookstore owner & ex-intelligence agent	Oregon

Botanical

Author	1 – #	Series Character	Occupation	Setting
Albert, Susan Wittig	'92 – 4	China Bayles	herb shop owner & former attorney	Pecan Springs, TX
Craig, Alisa	'81 – 5	Dittany Henbit Monk & Osbert Monk	garden club member & author of westerns	Lobelia Falls, Ont, Canada
Ripley, Ann	'94 – 2	Louise Eldridge	organic gardener	Washington DC
Rothenberg, Rebecca	'91 – 3	Claire Sharples	former MIT scholar/microbiologist	central California

Business & Finance

Author	1 – #	Series Character	Occupation	Setting
Amey, Linda	'92 – 2	Blair Emerson	funeral director	Austin, TX
Babson, Marian	'71 – 4	Douglas Perkins	London-based public relations agent	London, England
Baker, Nikki	'91 – 3	Virginia Kelly	black lesbian stockbroker	Chicago, IL
Beaton, M. C.	'92 – 4	Agatha Raisin	London advertising retiree	Cotswolds, England
Bennett, Liza	'89 – 2	Peg Goodenough	ad agency creative director	New York, NY
Berry, Carole	'87 – 6	Bonnie Indermill	tap-dancing Manhattan office temp	New York, NY
Brennan, Carol	'91 – 2	Liz Wareham	Manhattan public relations consultant	New York, NY
Burton, Anne	'80 – 3	Richard Trenton	banker	England
Christmas, Joyce	'93 – 2	Betty Trenka	retired office manager	Connecticut
Collins, Anna A.	'94 – 2	Abigail Doyle	efficiency expert	New York
Day, Dianne	'95 – 3	Fremont Jones	owner of a typewriting service circa 1900	San Francisco, CA
Feddersen, Connie	'93 – 4	Amanda Hazard	small-town Certified Public Accountant	Vamoose, OK
Flora, Kate Clark	'94 – 2	Thea Kozak	educational consultant	Massachusetts
Froetschel, Susan	'94 – 1	Jane McBride	finance director	Sitka, AK
Girdner, Jaqueline	'91 – 7	Kate Jasper	gag gift wholesaler	Marin County, CA
Gray, Gallagher	'91 – 3	Theodore S. Hubbert & Auntie Lil	retired personnel mgr & dress designer	New York, NY
Gunning, Sally	'90 – 6	Peter Bartholomew	small business owner	Cape Cod, MA
Harris, Charlaine	'90 – 5	Aurora Teagarden	librarian turned real estate agent	Georgia
Knight, Kathleen M.	'35 – 16	Elisha Macomber	selectman & owner of a fish market	Cape Cod, MA
Knight, Kathleen M.	'40 – 4	Margot Blair	partner in a PR agency	New York, NY
Kraft, Gabrielle	'87 – 4	Jerry Zalman	Beverly Hills deal maker	Los Angeles, CA
Kunz, Kathleen	'93 – 2	Terry Girard	genealogist for hire	St. Louis, MO
Lacey, Sarah	'92 – 4	Leah Hunter	tax inspector	Yorkshire, England
Lamb, J. Dayne	'93 – 3	Teal Stewart	Certified Public Accountant	Boston, MA
Lathen, Emma	'61 – 22	John Putnam Thatcher	Wall Street financial whiz	New York, NY
Lee, Barbara	'95 – 1	Eve Elliott	ex-New York advertising exec turned realtor	Anne Arundel Cty, MD
Maxwell, A. E.	'85 – 8	Fiddler & Fiora Flynn	ex-husband & investment banker	southern California
McClellan, Tierney	'95 – 3	Schuyler Ridgway	40-something real estate agent	Louisville, KY
Meyers, Annette	'89 – 7	Xenia Smith & Leslie Wetzon	Wall Street headhunters	New York, NY
Montgomery, Y. E.	'87 – 2	Finny Aletter	stockbroker turned carpenter	Denver, CO

Amateurs . . . *continued*

Author	▣ – #	Series Character	Occupation	Setting

Business & Finance . . . *continued*

Author	▣ – #	Series Character	Occupation	Setting
Pickard, Nancy	'84 – 10	Jenny Cain	New England foundation director	Port Frederick, MA
Pugh, Dianne G.	'93 – 2	Iris Thorne	investment counselor	Los Angeles, CA
Shelton, Connie	'95 – 3	Charlie Parker	CPA turned reluctant investigator	New Mexico
Sprinkle, Patricia H.	'88 – 7	Sheila Travis	admin asst turned PR executive	Atlanta, GA
Wilson, Barbara	'90 – 2	Cassandra Reilly	Spanish translator	London, England
Wolzien, Valerie	'96 – 1	Josie Pigeon	owner of an all-women construction firm	northeast USA
Yeager, Dorian	'94 – 2	Elizabeth Will	art gallery owner & lobster fisherman	Dovekey, NH

Computers & Technology

Author	▣ – #	Series Character	Occupation	Setting
Chapman, Sally	'91 – 3	Juliet Blake	Silicon Valley fraud investigator	Silicon Valley, CA
D'Amato, Barbara	'96 – 1	Suze Figueroa & Norm Bennis	pair of cops	Chicago, IL
Danks, Denise	'89 – 3	Georgina Powers	British computer journalist	London, England
Haddad, Carolyn A.	'92 – 1	Becky Belski	computer investigator	Chicago, IL
Holtzer, Susan	'94 – 2	Anneke Haagen	computer consultant	Ann Arbor, MI
Kelly, Susan B.	'90 – 5	Alison Hope & Nick Trevellyan	software designer & detective inspector	Hop Valley, England
Taylor, L. A.	'84 – 4	J. J. Jamison	computer engineer & CATCH investigator	Minneapolis, MN
Zachary, Fay	'94 – 2	Liz Broward, Dr. & Zack James	family physician & computer artist/genealogist	Phoenix, AZ

Criminal

Author	▣ – #	Series Character	Occupation	Setting
Highsmith, Patricia	'55 – 5	Tom Ripley	charming forger & psychopath	England

Cross genre

Author	▣ – #	Series Character	Occupation	Setting
Douglas, Carole N.	'85 – 2	Kevin Blake, Dr.	psychiatrist	Minnesota
Elrod, P. N.	'90 – 6	Jack Fleming	reporter, ladies' man & vampire	Chicago, IL
Hambly, Barbara	'88 – 2	James Asher	professor & one-time spy	London, England
Hamilton, Laurell K.	'93 – 4	Anita Blake	reanimator & vampire hunter	St. Louis, MO
Hightower, Lynn S.	'92 – 4	David Silver & String	homicide cop & alien partner	USA
Huff, Tanya	'92 – 4	Vicki Nelson	ex-cop turned P. I. w/vampire lover	Toronto, Canada
Lackey, Mercedes	'89 – 3	Diana Tregarde	romance author & practicing witch	Hartford, CT

Domestic

Author	▣ – #	Series Character	Occupation	Setting
Neely, Barbara	'92 – 2	Blanche White	middle-aged black domestic	North Carolina
Trocheck, Kathy H.	'92 – 4	Callahan Garrity	ex-cop cleaning service operator	Atlanta, GA

Ecclesiastical & Religious

Author	▣ – #	Series Character	Occupation	Setting
Black, Veronica	'90 – 8	Joan, Sister	British investigative nun	Cornwall, England
Charles, Kate	'91 – 5	Lucy Kingsley & D. Middleton-Brown	artist & solicitor	London, England
Frazer, Margaret	'92 – 6	Frevisse, Sister	Medieval nun	Oxfordshire, England
Gallison, Kate	'95 – 2	Lavinia Grey, Mother	Episcopal vicar & practicing therapist	Fishersville, NJ
Greenwood, Diane M.	'91 – 6	Theodora Braithwaite, Rev.	British deaconess	England
Harris, Lee	'92 – 7	Christine Bennett	ex-nun	New York, NY
Highsmith, Domini	'95 – 1	Simeon, Father & Elvira	medieval priest & nurse	East Yorkshire, England
Holland, Isabelle	'83 – 6	Claire Aldington, Rev.	Episcopal priest	New York, NY
Newman, Sharan	'93 – 3	Catherine LeVendeur	novice & scholar in 12th century	France
O'Marie, Sister C. A.	'84 – 6	Mary Helen, Sister	70-something nun	San Francisco, CA

Amateurs . . . continued

Author	🔲 – #	Series Character	Occupation	Setting

Ecclesiastical & Religious . . . continued

Author	🔲 – #	Series Character	Occupation	Setting
Peters, Ellis	'77 – 20	Brother Cadfael	medieval monk & herbalist	Shrewsbury, England
Robb, Candace M.	'93 – 3	Owen Archer	medieval Welsh spy for the archbishop	England
Scherf, Margaret	'48 – 6	Martin Buell, Rev.	Episcopal rector	Farrington, MT

Environment & Wilderness

Author	🔲 – #	Series Character	Occupation	Setting
Andrews, Sarah	'94 – 2	Em Hansen	oil worker	Wyoming
Barr, Nevada	'93 – 4	Anna Pigeon	U. S. park ranger	National Parks, USA
Cleeves, Ann	'86 – 8	George & Molly Palmer-Jones	ex-Home Office & bird-watcher & wife	Surrey, England
Dengler, Sandy	'93 – 4	Jack Prester	U. S. park ranger	National Parks, USA
Dunlap, Susan	'83 – 3	Vejay Haskell	utility meter reader for Pacific Gas & Electric	northern California
Henry, Sue	'91 – 3	Jessie Arnold & Alex Jensen	sled dog racer & Alaska state trooper	Anchorage, AK
Huxley, Elspeth	'37 – 3	Vachell, Supt.	young Scotsman trained by the RCMP	Kenya
McQuillan, Karin	'90 – 3	Jazz Jasper	American safari guide	Kenya
Oliphant, B. J.	'90 – 6	Shirley McClintock	50-something rancher	Colorado
Quinn, Elizabeth	'93 – 3	Lauren Maxwell	wildlife investigator PhD	Alaska
Stabenow, Dana	'92 – 6	Kate Shugak	native Alaskan ex-D.A. investigator	Alaska
Wallingford, Lee	'91 – 2	Ginny Trask & Frank Carver	forest fire dispatcher & ex-cop	Oregon

Ethnic & Native American

Author	🔲 – #	Series Character	Occupation	Setting
Coel, Margaret	'95 – 2	John A. O'Malley & Vicky Holden	Jesuit missionary & Arapaho attorney	Wind River Reserv., WY
Hager, Jean	'92 – 3	Molly Bearpaw	Cherokee civil rights investigator	Tahlequah, OK
Romberg, Nina	'89 – 2	Marian Winchester	Caddo-Commanche medicine woman	Texas
Thurlo, A. & D.	'95 – 2	Ella Clah	Navajo FBI agent	New Mexico

Gay & Lesbian

Author	🔲 – #	Series Character	Occupation	Setting
Allen, Kate	'93 – 2	Alison Kaine	lesbian cop	Denver, CO
Baker, Nikki	'91 – 3	Virginia Kelly	black lesbian stockbroker	Chicago, IL
Beecham, Rose	'92 – 3	Amanda Valentine	ex-NYPD cop turned detective inspector	New Zealand
Douglas, Lauren W.	'87 – 6	Caitlin Reece	lesbian detective	Victoria, Canada
Dreher, Sarah	'85 – 6	Stoner McTavish	lesbian travel agent	Boston, MA
Ennis, Catherine	'91 – 2	Bernadette Hebert, Dr.	lesbian crime lab expert	Louisiana
Fennelly, Tony	'85 – 3	Matthew Arthur Sinclair	gay ex-D.A. turned P. I.	New Orleans, LA
Forrest, Katherine V.	'84 – 4	Kate Delafield	LAPD lesbian homicide detective	Los Angeles, CA
Haddock, Lisa	'94 – 2	Carmen Ramirez	lesbian newspaper copy editor	Frontier City, OK
Hart, Ellen	'89 – 7	Jane Lawless	lesbian restaurateur	Minneapolis, MN
Knight, Phyllis	'92 – 3	Lil Ritchie	ex-rocker & gay woman P. I.	coastal Maine
Maiman, Jaye	'91 – 4	Robin Miller	lesbian travel & romance writer turned P. I.	New York, NY
Maney, Mabel	'93 – 3	Nancy Clue	gay-lesbian parody of Nancy Drew	River Depths, IL
Manthorne, Jackie	'94 – 3	Harriett Hubley	intrepid lesbian sleuth	Montreal, Canada
McConnell, Vickie P.	'82 – 3	Nyla Wade	lesbian journalist	Denver, CO
McDermid, Val	'87 – 4	Lindsay Gordon	lesbian journalist & socialist	Glasgow, Scotland
McNab, Claire	'88 – 7	Carol Ashton	lesbian detective inspector & single mother	Sydney, Australia
Mickelbury, Penny	'94 – 2	Gianna Maglione & Mimi Patterson	lesbian police lieutenant & reporter	Washington, DC
Morell, Mary	'91 – 2	Lucia Ramos	lesbian police detective	San Antonio, TX
Pincus, Elizabeth	'92 – 3	Nell Fury	lesbian P. I.	San Francisco, CA

Amateurs ... *continued*

Author	🔲 – #	Series Character	Occupation	Setting

Gay & Lesbian ... *continued*

Author	🔲 – #	Series Character	Occupation	Setting
Powell, Deborah	'91 – 2	Hollis Carpenter	gay woman crime reporter	Houston, TX
Redmann, J. M.	'90 – 3	Michelle "Micky" Knight	lesbian P. I.	New Orleans, LA
Saum, Karen	'90 – 3	Brigid Donovan	50-something lesbian ex-nun	Maine
Schmidt, Carol	'93 – 3	Laney Samms	lesbian bar owner	Los Angeles, CA
Scoppettone, Sandra	'91 – 3	Lauren Laurano	Greenwich Village lesbian P. I.	New York, NY
Silva, Linda Kay	'91 – 4	Delta Stevens	lesbian policewoman	California
Taylor, Jean	'95 – 2	Maggie Garrett	young lesbian P. I.	San Francisco, CA
Tell, Dorothy	'90 – 3	Poppy Dillworth	60-something lesbian sleuth	Texas
Welch, Pat	'90 – 4	Helen Black	ex-cop lesbian P. I.	San Francisco, CA
Wilson, Barbara	'84 – 3	Pam Nilsen	lesbian printing company owner	Seattle, WA
Wings, Mary	'87 – 3	Emma Victor	lesbian activist & P. I.	San Francisco, CA

Gourmet & Food

Author	🔲 – #	Series Character	Occupation	Setting
Crespi, Camilla	'91 – 6	Simona Griffo	advertising executive & gourmet cook	New York, NY
Davidson, Diane M.	'90 – 6	Goldy Bear	caterer & single mother	Aspen Meadow, CO
Dietz, Denise	'93 – 2	Ellie Bernstein	diet group leader	USA
Hart, Ellen	'89 – 7	Jane Lawless	lesbian restaurateur	Minneapolis, MN
Hart, Ellen	'94 – 3	Sophie Greenway	magazine editor & food critic for newspaper	Minneapolis, MN
Laurence, Janet	'89 – 8	Darina Lisle	British caterer, chef & food writer	England
Lyons, Nan & Ivan	'76 – 2	Natasha O'Brien & Millie Ogden	pair of culinary artists	USA
Myers, Amy	'82 – 8	Auguste Didier	British-French Victorian master chef	England
Page, Katherine H.	'90 – 7	Faith Sibley Fairchild	minister's wife & culinary artist	Massachusetts
Pence, Joanne	'93 – 4	Angelina Amalfi	food columnist & restaurant reviewer	San Francisco, CA
Rich, Virginia	'82 – 4	Eugenia Potter	widowed chef	Maine

Government

Author	🔲 – #	Series Character	Occupation	Setting
Cooper, Natasha	'90 – 5	Willow King & Cressida Woodruffe	civil servant & romance novelist	London, England
Dominic, R. B.	'68 – 7	Ben Safford	Democratic congressman	Ohio
Edwards, Ruth D.	'81 – 5	James Milton & Robert Amiss	police superintendent & ex-civil servant	England
Gilbert, Anthony	'27 – 9	Scott Egerton	Liberal M.P. & man about town	England
Neel, Janet	'88 – 4	John McLeish & Francesca Wilson	detective inspector & civil servant	England

Historical, Ancient

Author	🔲 – #	Series Character	Occupation	Setting
Davis, Lindsey	'89 – 8	Marcus Didius Falco	P. I. in ancient Rome	Rome, Italy
Robinson, Lynda S.	'94 – 3	Meren, Lord	chief investigator for Pharaoh Tutankhamen	Egypt

Historical, Medieval

Author	🔲 – #	Series Character	Occupation	Setting
Highsmith, Domini	'95 – 1	Simeon, Father & Elvira	medieval priest & nurse	East Yorkshire, England
Newman, Sharan	'93 – 3	Catherine LeVendeur	novice & scholar in 12th century	France
Sedley, Kate	'91 – 6	Roger the Chapman	medieval chapman (peddler)	England

Historical, Renaissance

Author	🔲 – #	Series Character	Occupation	Setting
Eyre, Elizabeth	'92 – 5	Sigismondo	agent of a Renaissance duke	Italy

Amateurs . . . *continued*

Author	🔲 – #	Series Character	Occupation	Setting
Historical, 18th century				
de la Torre, Lillian	'46 – 4	Sam Johnson, Dr. & James Boswell	lexicographer & biographer	London, England
Historical, 19th century				
Brightwell, Emily	'93 – 7	Witherspoon, Insp. & Jeffries, Mrs.	Victorian police inspector & housekeeper	London, England
Crowleigh, Ann	'93 – 2	Mirinda & Clare Clively	Victorian London twin sisters	London, England
Day, Dianne	'95 – 3	Fremont Jones	owner of a typewriting service circa 1900	San Francisco, CA
Douglas, Carole N.	'90 – 4	Irene Adler	19th century French sleuth	Paris, France
Fawcett, Quinn	'93 – 2	Victoire Vernet	wife of Napoleonic gendarme	France
Hambly, Barbara	'88 – 2	James Asher	professor & one-time spy	London, England
Jackson, Marian J. A.	'90 – 5	Abigail Patience Danforth	turn-of-the-century consulting detective	USA
Kingsbury, Kate	'93 – 7	Cecily Sinclair	hotel owner in Edwardian England	Badger's End, England
Knight, Alanna	'88 – 9	Jeremy Faro	Victorian detective inspector	Edinburgh, Scotland
Kruger, Mary	'94 – 2	Brooke Cassidy & Matt Devlin	mystery writer & P. I.	Newport, RI
Lee, W. W. (Wendi)	'89 – 6	Jefferson Birch	P. I. in the Old West	Western USA
Linscott, Gillian	'91 – 5	Nell Bray	British suffragette	England
Monfredo, Miriam G.	'92 – 4	Glynis Tryon	librarian & suffragette in mid-19th century	Seneca Falls, NY
Myers, Amy	'82 – 8	Auguste Didier	British-French Victorian master chef	England
Paige, Robin	'94 – 2	Kathryn Ardleigh	25-yr-old American author	Dedham, England
Perry, Anne	'79 – 16	Thomas & Charlotte Pitt	Victorian police inspector & wife	England
Perry, Anne	'90 – 6	William Monk	amnesiac Victorian police inspector	England
Peters, Elizabeth	'75 – 7	Amelia Peabody	Victorian feminist archaeologist	Kent, England
Ross, Kate	'93 – 3	Julian Kestrel	1820s dandy-about-town	London, England
Tone, Teona	'83 – 2	Kyra Keaton	P. I. at the turn-of-the-century	Washington, DC
Historical, 1920s				
Beck, K. K.	'84 – 3	Iris Cooper	Roaring 20s co-ed at Stanford University	Palo Alto, CA
Dunn, Carola	'94 – 4	Daisy Dalrymple	young aristocratic woman writer	Hampshire, England
Greenwood, Kerry	'89 – 8	Phryne Fisher	1920s sleuth	Melbourne, Australia
King, Laurie R.	'94 – 2	Mary Russell	teenage student of Sherlock Holmes	London, England
Historical, other				
Chisholm, P. F.	'95 – 3	Robert Carey, Sir	Elizabethan nobleman (1592)	England
Meyers, Maan	'92 – 4	The Tonnemans	New Amsterdam historical series (1664-1808)	New York, NY
Journalism, magazine				
Buckstaff, Kathryn	'94 – 1	Morgana Dalton	Florida-based travel writer	Florida
D'Amato, Barbara	'90 – 6	Cat Marsala	freelance investigative journalist	Chicago, IL
Dunn, Carola	'94 – 4	Daisy Dalrymple	young aristocratic woman writer	Hampshire, England
Hart, Ellen	'94 – 3	Sophie Greenway	magazine editor & food critic for newspaper	Minneapolis, MN
Holt, Hazel	'89 – 7	Sheila Malory	British literary magazine writer	Devon, England
Hyde, Eleanor	'95 – 2	Lydia Miller	30-something fashion editor	New York, NY
Kelly, Susan	'85 – 6	Liz Connors	freelance crime writer	Cambridge, MA
Woods, Sherryl	'89 – 9	Amanda Roberts	ex-New York investigative reporter	Atlanta, GA

Amateurs . . . continued

Author	❶ – #	Series Character	Occupation	Setting

Journalism, newspaper

Author	❶ – #	Series Character	Occupation	Setting
Braun, Lilian J.	'66 – 18	Jim Qwilleran, Koko & Yum Yum	ex-police reporter & cats	Midwest USA
Bridge, Ann	'56 – 7	Julia Probyn Jamieson	freelance journalist & part-time agent	England
Buchanan, Edna	'92 – 4	Britt Montero	newspaper crime reporter	Miami, FL
Burke, Jan	'93 – 4	Irene Kelly	newspaper reporter	southern California
Cail, Carol	'93 – 2	Maxey Burnell	investigative reporter	Colorado
Chase, Elaine Raco	'87 – 2	Nikki Holden & Roman Cantrell	reporter & P. I.	Florida
Daheim, Mary	'92 – 7	Emma Lord	small-town newspaper owner & editor	Alpine, WA
Danks, Denise	'89 – 3	Georgina Powers	British computer journalist	London, England
Elrod, P. N.	'90 – 6	Jack Fleming	reporter, ladies' man & vampire	Chicago, IL
Fennelly, Tony	'94 – 2	Margo Fortier	ex-stripper turned columnist	New Orleans, LA
Gordon, Alison	'89 – 4	Kate Henry	baseball newswriter	Toronto, Canada
Grant-Adamson, L.	'85 – 5	Rain Morgan	newspaper reporter	London, England
Haddock, Lisa	'94 – 2	Carmen Ramirez	lesbian newspaper copy editor	Frontier City, OK
Hall, Patricia	'94 – 3	Laura Ackroyd & Michael Thackeray	reporter	Yorkshire, England
Hart, Carolyn G.	'93 – 3	Henrietta O'Dwyer Collins	70-something reporter	South Carolina
Jaffe, Jody	'95 – 2	Natalie Gold	reporter on the horse show circuit	Charlotte, NC
Jorgensen, C. T.	'94 – 3	Stella the Stargazer	astrologer & lovelorn columnist	Denver, CO
Kallen, Lucille	'79 – 5	Maggie Rome & C. B. Greenfield	reporter & editor/publisher	Connecticut
Karr, Leona	'93 – 1	Addie Devore	small-town newspaper owner	Colorado
Logue, Mary	'93 – 1	Laura Malloy	journalist	Minneapolis, MN
McConnell, Vickie P.	'82 – 3	Nyla Wade	lesbian journalist	Denver, CO
McDermid, Val	'87 – 4	Lindsay Gordon	lesbian journalist & socialist	Glasgow, Scotland
Mickelbury, Penny	'94 – 2	Gianna Maglione & Mimi Patterson	lesbian police lieutenant & reporter	Washington, DC
O'Brien, Meg	'90 – 4	Jessica James	newspaper reporter	Rochester, NY
Peterson, Audrey	'88 – 6	Jane Winfield	British journalist & music writer	London, England
Porter, Anna	'85 – 2	Judith Hayes	journalist	Toronto, Ontario, Canada
Powell, Deborah	'91 – 2	Hollis Carpenter	gay woman crime reporter	Houston, TX
Roome, Annette	'89 – 2	Christine Martin	40-something cub reporter	England
Shankman, Sarah	'88 – 6	Samantha Adams	investigative reporter	Atlanta, GA
Sibley, Celestine	'58 – 5	Kate Kincaid Mulcay	veteran newspaperwoman	Atlanta, GA
Stein, Triss	'93 – 1	Kay Engles	nationally-known reporter	USA
Trocheck, Kathy H.	'96 – 1	Truman Kicklighter	retired wire service reporter	St. Petersburg, FL
Tyre, Peg	'94 – 2	Kate Murray	newspaper reporter for Daily Herald	Brooklyn, NY
Walker, Mary Willis	'94 – 2	Mollie Cates	true crime writer & reporter	Texas
Waltch, Lilla M.	'87 – 2	Lisa Davis	newspaper reporter	Braeton, MA
Warmbold, Jean	'86 – 3	Sarah Calloway	newspaper reporter	San Francisco, CA
Yates, Margaret E.T.	'37 – 4	Anne "Davvie" Davenport McLean	newspaper correspondent	World Traveler

Journalism, photography

Author	❶ – #	Series Character	Occupation	Setting
Hornsby, Wendy	'92 – 4	Maggie MacGowen	investigative filmmaker	California
Jones, Hazel Wynn	'88 – 2	Emma Shaw	documentary film director	Italy
Kelly, Mary Ann	'90 – 3	Claire Breslinsky	freelance photographer	New York, NY
Moody, Susan	'84 – 7	Penny Wanawake	photographer daughter of black diplomat	England
North, Suzanne	'94 – 1	Phoebe Fairfax	TV video photographer	Calgary, Canada
OCork, Shannon	'80 – 3	Theresa Tracy Baldwin	sports photographer for New York daily	New York, NY
Sale, Medora	'86 – 6	John Sanders & Harriet Jeffries	police detective & architectural photographer	Toronto, Canada
Tucker, Kerry	'91 – 4	Libby Kincaid	magazine photographer	New York, NY

Amateurs . . . *continued*

Author	🔲 – #	Series Character	Occupation	Setting

Journalism, radio & television

Author	🔲 – #	Series Character	Occupation	Setting
Babbin, Jacqueline	'72 – 2	Clovis Kelly	ex-NYPD homicide det. & crime consultant	New York , NY
Donald, Anabel	'91 – 4	Alex Tanner	part-time P. I. & TV researcher	London, England
Fraser, Antonia	'77 – 8	Jemima Shore	British TV interviewer	London, England
Hayter, Sparkle	'94 – 2	Robin Hudson	cable news reporter	New York, NY
Robitaille, Julie	'92 – 2	Kit Powell	TV sports reporter	San Diego, CA
Rowe, Jennifer	'89 – 4	Verity "Birdie" Birdwood	TV researcher	Australia
Shaffer, Louise	'94 – 2	Angie DaVito	TV soap opera producer	New York, NY
Steinberg, Janice	'95 – 2	Margo Simon	California Public Radio reporter	San Diego, CA
Whitney, Polly	'94 – 3	Ike Tygart & Abby Abagnarro	network producer & TV news director	New York, NY

Legal, attorney

Author	🔲 – #	Series Character	Occupation	Setting
Bell, Josephine	'59 – 3	Claude Warrington-Reeve	barrister	London, England
Cannon, Taffy	'93 – 3	Nan Robinson	investigator for the California State Bar	Los Angeles, CA
Challis, Mary	'80 – 4	Jeremy Locke	attorney	England
Dominic, R. B.	'68 – 7	Ben Safford	Democratic congressman from Ohio	Washington, DC
Egan, Lesley	'61 – 13	Jesse Falkenstein	lawyer	Los Angeles, CA
Fallon, Ann C.	'90 – 5	James Fleming	solicitor	Dublin, Ireland
Fyfield, Frances	'88 – 5	Helen West	London Crown prosecutor	London, England
Fyfield, Frances	'89 – 2	Sarah Fortune	lawyer in prestigious British firm	England
Gilbert, Anthony	'36 – 50	Arthur G. Crook	Cockney lawyer-detective	England
Giroux, E. X.	'84 – 10	Robert Forsythe & Abigail Sanderson	barrister & secretary	London, England
Hartzmark, Gini	'92 – 3	Katherine Prescott Milholland	corporate attorney	Chicago, IL
Jacobs, Jonnie	'96 – 1	Kali O'Brien	attorney	Gold Country, CA
Lachnit, Carroll	'95 – 2	Hannah Barlow	ex-cop turned law student	Orange County, CA
Lambert, Mercedes	'91 – 1	Whitney Logan	20-something attorney	Los Angeles, CA
Leek, Margaret	'80 – 3	Stephen Marryat	attorney	England
Matera, Lia	'88 – 5	Laura Di Palma	attorney	San Francisco, CA
Matera, Lia	'86 – 5	Willa Jansson	law student turned attorney	San Francisco, CA
McGuire, Christine	'93 – 2	Kathryn Mackay	prosecuting attorney	northern California
Meek, M. R. D.	'83 – 10	Lennox Kemp	solicitor detective	London, England
Meredith, D. R.	'88 – 5	John Lloyd Branson & Lydia Fairchild	defense attorney & legal assistant	Canadian, TX
Millar, Margaret	'76 – 3	Tom Aragon	attorney	California
Nielsen, Helen	'51 – 6	Simon Drake	attorney transplanted from Chicago	southern California
Parker, Barbara	'94 – 2	Gail Connor	corporate attorney	Miami, FL
Piesman, Marissa	'89 – 5	Nina Fischman	legal services attorney	New York, NY
Rice, Craig	'39 – 12	John J. Malone	hard-drinking, cigar-smoking lawyer	Chicago, IL
Schier, Norma	'78 – 4	Kay Barth	district attorney	Colorado
Scottoline, Lisa	'94 – 1	Grace Rossi	Federal appeals attorney & law clerk	Philadelphia, PA
Scottoline, Lisa	'93 – 1	Mary DiNunzio	attorney	Philadelphia, PA
Scottoline, Lisa	'95 – 1	Rita Morrone Hamilton	attorney	Philadelphia, PA
Smith, Janet L.	'90 – 3	Annie MacPherson	attorney	Seattle, WA
Smith, Julie	'82 – 5	Rebecca Schwartz	defense attorney	San Francisco, CA
Truman, Margaret	'89 – 5	Mackenzie Smith & Annabel Reed	law professor & gallery owner	Washington, DC
Van Gieson, Judith	'88 – 6	Neil Hamel	attorney & investigator	Albuquerque, NM
Venning, Michael	'42 – 3	Melville Fairr	lawyer	New York, NY
Wakefield, Hannah	'87 – 2	Dee Street	American attorney	London, England

Amateurs . . . *continued*

Author	❶ – #	Series Character	Occupation	Setting

Legal, attorney . . . *continued*

Author	❶ – #	Series Character	Occupation	Setting
Wheat, Carolyn	'83 – 3	Cass Jameson	Brooklyn criminal lawyer	New York, NY
Wilhelm, Kate	'91 – 2	Barbara Holloway	defense attorney	Oregon
Woods, Sara	'62 – 48	Antony Maitland	barrister drawn to murder cases	England
Yarbro, Chelsea Q.	'76 – 4	Charles Spotted Moon	attorney & Ojibway tribal shaman	San Francisco, CA

Legal, judge

Author	❶ – #	Series Character	Occupation	Setting
Maron, Margaret	'92 – 4	Deborah Knott	district judge	North Carolina
Wilhelm, Kate	'93 – 1	Sarah Drexler	judge	Oregon

Medical

Author	❶ – #	Series Character	Occupation	Setting
Bannister, Jo	'84 – 3	Clio Rees, Dr. & Harry Marsh	physician/mystery writer & chief inspector	England
Bell, Josephine	'37 – 14	David Wintringham, Dr.	British physician	London, England
Bell, Josephine	'64 – 2	Henry Frost, Dr.	British physician	London, England
Clark, Carolyn C.	'93 – 1	Megan Baldwin	registered nurse	St. Petersburg, FL
Cohen, Anthea	'82 – 13	Agnes Carmichael	hospital staff nurse	England
Cornwell, Patricia	'90 – 6	Kay Scarpetta, Dr.	chief medical examiner	Richmond, VA
D'Amato, Barbara	'80 – 2	Gerritt DeGraaf, Dr.	forensic pathologist	Chicago, IL
Douglas, Carole N.	'85 – 2	Kevin Blake, Dr.	psychiatrist	Minnesota
Dymmoch, Michael	'93 – 2	John Thinnes & Jack Caleb, Dr.	cop & psychiatrist	Chicago, IL
Ennis, Catherine	'91 – 2	Bernadette Hebert, Dr.	lesbian crime lab expert	Louisiana
Ferrars, E. X.	'78 – 9	Virginia & Felix Freer	physiotherapist & businessman	England
Fromer, Margot J.	'91 – 2	Amanda Knight	hospital director of nursing	Washington, DC
Green, Christine	'91 – 3	Kate Kinsella	British nurse & medical investigator	England
Hendricksen, Louise	'93 – 3	Amy Prescott, Dr.	crime lab physician	Seattle, WA
Kittredge, Mary	'90 – 6	Edwina Crusoe	RN & medical consultant	New Haven, CT
Landreth, Marsha	'92 – 3	Samantha Turner, Dr.	medical examiner	Sheridan, WY
Lovett, Sarah	'95 – 2	Sylvia Strange, Dr.	forensic psychologist	Sante Fe, NM
Matthews, Alex	'96 – 2	Cassidy McCabe	psychotherapirst	Oak Park, IL
McCloy, Helen	'38 – 13	Basil Willing, Dr.	psychiatrist & FBI consultant	New York, NY
McGiffin, Janet	'92 – 3	Maxene St. Clair, Dr.	emergency room physician	Milwaukee, WI
Millar, Margaret	'41 – 3	Paul Prye, Dr.	psychiatrist	Toronto, Canada
O'Callaghan, Maxine	'96 – 2	Anne Menlo, Dr.	child psychologist	Phoenix, AZ
Rinehart, Mary R.	'32 – 3	Hilda Adams aka Miss Pinkerton	nurse & police agent	England
Scherf, Margaret	'68 – 4	Grace Severance, Dr.	retired pathologist	Arizona
Thompson, Joyce	'91 – 1	Frederika Bascomb	forensic artist	Seattle, WA
Walsh, Jill Paton	'93 – 2	Imogen Quy	school nurse at St. Agatha's College	Cambridge, England
Zachary, Fay	'94 – 2	Liz Broward, Dr. & Zack James	family physician & computer artist/genealogist	Phoenix, AZ

Military

Author	❶ – #	Series Character	Occupation	Setting
Ford, Leslie	'34 – 16	John Primrose, Col. & Grace Latham	career soldier & attractive widow	Washington DC

Amateurs . . . *continued*

Author	❶ – #	Series Character	Occupation	Setting
Miscellaneous				
Allingham, Margery	'29 – 22	Albert Campion	suave sleuth with noble blood	London, England
Andreae, Christine	'92 – 2	Lee Squires	English professor & poet	Montana
Ballard, Mignon	'93 – 1	Eliza Figg	former Peace Corps volunteer	USA
Bell, Josephine	'79 – 2	Amy Tupper	amateur sleuth	London, England
Christmas, Joyce	'88 – 7	Margaret Priam, Lady	English noblewoman	New York, NY
Dunbar, Sophie	'93 – 3	Claire & Dan Claiborne	sleuthing pair	New Orleans, LA
Ferrars, E. X.	'40 – 5	Toby Dyke	amateur sleuth	England
Foley, Rae	'55 – 11	Hiram Potter	mild-mannered Old Money sleuth	New York
Frome, David	'30 – 11	Evan Pinkerton	Welshman	England
Gardiner, Dorothy	'33 – 2	Watson, Mr.	amateur sleuth	California
Grant-Adamson, L.	'92 – 2	Jim Rush	American on the run from British police	England
Greth, Roma	'88 – 2	Hana Shaner	carpet company heiress in Dutch country	Conover, PA
Jackson, Muriel R.	'92 – 1	Merrie Lee Spencer	Manhattan transplant	North Carolina
Johns, Veronica P.	'40 – 2	Agatha Welch	middle-aged woman sleuth	Connecticut
Jordan, Jennifer	'92 – 2	Kristin Ashe	amateur sleuth	Woodfield, England
Michaels, Barbara	'68 – 3	Georgetown house	historic home	Washington, DC
Moody, Susan	'93 – 4	Cassandra Swann	British biology teacher turned bridge pro	Cotswolds, England
Morison, B. J.	'82 – 5	Elizabeth Lamb Worthington	pre-teenager in the 1970s	coastal Maine
Murray, Donna H.	'95 – 2	Ginger Struve Barnes	amateur sleuth	Philadelphia, PA
Offord, Lenore Glen	'38 – 2	Bill & Coco Hastings	sleuthing pair	San Francisco, CA
Porath, Sharon	'95 – 1	Kendra MacFarlane	amateur sleuth	
Rice, Craig	'42 – 3	Bingo Riggs & Handsome Kusak	gullible city slickers & reluctant detectives	USA
Sayers, Dorothy L.	'23 – 13	Peter Wimsey, Lord	pianist, bibliophile & criminologist	London, England
Taylor, Phoebe A.	'31 – 24	Asey Mayo	former sailor & auto racer	Cape Cod, MA
Occult				
Edghill, Rosemary	'94 – 2	Karen Hightower	Manhattan graphic designer & white witch	New York, NY
Green, Kate	'86 – 2	Theresa Fortunato & Oliver Jardino	professional psychic & LAPD detective	Los Angeles, CA
Jorgensen, C. T.	'94 – 3	Stella the Stargazer	astrologer & lovelorn columnist	Denver, CO
Lawrence, Martha	'95 – 1	Elizabeth Chase, Dr.	Stanford-trained parapsychologist turned P. I.	San Diego, CA
Mather, Linda	'94 – 3	Jo Hughes	professional astrologer	USA
Warner, Mignon	'76 – 7	Edwina Charles	British clairvoyant	Little Gidding, England
Romantic				
Atherton, Nancy	'92 – 3	Aunt Dimity	romantic ghost	England
Cannell, Dorothy	'84 – 7	Ellie & Ben Haskell	interior decorator & writer/chef	Chitterton Falls, England
Feddersen, Connie	'93 – 4	Amanda Hazard	small-town Certified Public Accountant	Vamoose, OK
Florian, S. L.	'92 – 1	Delia Ross-Merlani, Viscountess	English-Italian noblewoman	New York, NY
Fulton, Eileen	'88 – 6	Nina McFall & Dino Rossi, Lt.	glamorous TV soap star & NYPD cop	New York, NY
Robb, J. D.	'95 – 3	Eve Dallas	NYPD lieutenant in the 21st century	New York, NY
Shaffer, Louise	'94 – 2	Angie DaVito	TV soap opera producer	New York, NY

Amateurs . . . *continued*

Author	❶ – #	Series Character	Occupation	Setting
Secret Agents				
Bridge, Ann	'56 – 7	Julia Probyn Jamieson	freelance journalist & part-time agent	England
Christie, Agatha	'22 – 4	Tuppence & Tommy Beresford	adventurers for hire & intelligence agents	London, England
Hooper, Kay	'87 – 11	Hagen	government agent	USA
McGerr, Patricia	'64 – 2	Selena Mead	British government agent	England
Mitchell, Gladys	'29 – 66	Beatrice Lestrange Bradley	psychiatrist & consultant to Home Office	London, England
Porter, Joyce	'66 – 4	Eddie Brown	comic spy	England
Senior Sleuths				
Allen, Irene	'92 – 2	Elizabeth Elliot	widowed Quaker meeting clerk	Pennsylvania
Beaton, M. C.	'92 – 4	Agatha Raisin	London advertising retiree	Cotswolds, England
Borton, D. B.	'93 – 5	Cat Caliban	60-something P. I.-in-training	Cincinnati, OH
Boylan, Eleanor	'89 – 4	Clara Gamadge	widow of Henry the forgery expert	New York, NY
Brightwell, Emily	'93 – 7	Witherspoon, Insp. & Jeffries, Mrs.	Victorian police inspector & housekeeper	London, England
Christie, Agatha	'30 – 12	Jane Marple, Miss	elderly spinster	St. Mary's Mead, Eng.
Christmas, Joyce	'93 – 2	Betty Trenka	retired office manager	Connecticut
Cleeves, Ann	'86 – 8	George & Molly Palmer-Jones	ex-Home Office/bird-watcher & wife	Surrey, England
Comfort, Barbara	'86 – 4	Tish McWhinney	70-something artist & painter	Vermont
Crane, Hamilton	'68 – 19	Emily D. Seeton	retired British art teacher	Kent, England
Dolson, Hildegarde	'71 – 4	Lucy Ramsdale & James McDougal	illustrator & homicide inspector	Wingate, CT
Gilman, Dorothy	'66 – 12	Emily Pollifax	grandmother CIA agent	New Jersey
Gray, Gallagher	'91 – 3	Theodore S. Hubbert & Auntie Lil	retired personnel manager & dress designer	New York, NY
Green, Edith Pinero	'77 – 3	Dearborn V. Pinch	70-something ladies man	New York, NY
Haddam, Jane	'90 – 12	Gregor Demarkian	former FBI department head	Philadelphia, PA
Hall, Mary Bowen	'89 – 4	Emma Chizzit	salvage dealer	Sacramento, CA
Hart, Carolyn G.	'93 – 3	Henrietta O'Dwyer Collins	70-something reporter	South Carolina
Johns, Veronica P.	'53 – 2	Webster Flagg	60-something Harlem actor/butler/houseman	New York, NY
Knight, Kathleen M.	'35 – 16	Elisha Macomber	selectman & owner of a fish market	Cape Cod, MA
Lawrence, Hilda	'44 – 3	Mark East, Bessie Petty & Beulah Pond	NYC P. I. & New England little old ladies	USA
Lewis, Sherry	'95 – 2	Fred Vickery	70-something retiree	Cutler, CO
Livingston, Nancy	'85 – 8	G. D. H. Pringle	retired tax inspector	England
Matteson, Stefanie	'90 – 7	Charlotte Graham	Oscar-winning actress	New York, NY
McShea, Susanna	'90 – 3	Mildred Bennett & friends	a quartet of senior sleuths	Raven's Wing, CT
Mitchell, Gladys	'29 – 66	Beatrice Lestrange Bradley	psychiatrist & consultant to Home Office	London, England
Morgan, Kate	'90 – 6	Dewey James	60-something small-town librarian	New York
Olsen, D. B.	'39 – 13	Rachel & Jennifer Murdock	sister sleuths	Los Angeles, CA
Porter, Joyce	'70 – 5	Constance E. M. Burke, Hon.	comic senior sleuth	England
Rich, Virginia	'82 – 4	Eugenia Potter	widowed chef	Maine
Ruryk, Jean	'94 – 1	Catherine Wilde	retired ad exec turned antiques restorer	USA
Sawyer, Corinne H.	'88 – 6	Angela Benbow & Caledonia Wingate	70-something admirals' widows	southern California
Squire, Elizabeth D.	'94 – 3	Peaches Dann	absent-minded 50-something widow	North Carolina
Stevens, Serita	'91 – 2	Fanny Zindel	Jewish grandmother	USA
Tell, Dorothy	'90 – 3	Poppy Dillworth	60-something lesbian sleuth	Texas
Trocheck, Kathy H.	'96 – 1	Truman Kicklighter	retired wire service reporter	St. Petersburg, FL
Warner, Mignon	'76 – 7	Edwina Charles	British clairvoyant	Little Gidding, England
Wentworth, Patricia	'28 – 32	Maud Silver, Miss	retired governess & spinster P. I.	London, England

Amateurs . . . *continued*

Author	❶ – #	Series Character	Occupation	Setting

Small Town

Author	❶ – #	Series Character	Occupation	Setting
Adams, Deborah	'92 – 5	Jesus Creek TN	eccentric small town	Jesus Creek, TN
Hess, Joan	'87 – 9	Arly Hanks	small-town police chief	Maggody, AR
West, Chassie	'94 – 1	Leigh Ann Warren	former DC street cop	Sunrise, NC

Sports

Author	❶ – #	Series Character	Occupation	Setting
Cody, Liza	'93 – 2	Eva Wylie	wrestler & security guard	London, England
Dunnett, Dorothy	'68 – 7	Johnson Johnson	portrait painter & British agent w/his yacht	International
Elkins, C. & A.	'89 – 2	Lee Ofsted & Graham Sheldon	golf pro & homicide detective	Washington
McKernan, Victoria	'90 – 3	Chicago Nordejoong	professional scuba diver	Florida
Robitaille, Julie	'92 – 2	Kit Powell	TV sports reporter	San Diego, CA

Suburban

Author	❶ – #	Series Character	Occupation	Setting
Berenson, Laurien	'94 – 1	Gwen Harding	NYC journalist turned suburban wife & mother	New York
Berenson, Laurien	'95 – 3	Melanie Travis	special ed teacher posing as poodle breeder	Connecticut
Churchill, Jill	'89 – 7	Jane Jeffry	suburban single mother	Chicago, IL
Jacobs, Jonnie	'94 – 2	Kate Austen	Bay area single mother	Walnut Hills, CA
Meier, Leslie	'93 – 2	Lucy Stone	small-town sleuth	Maine
Wolzien, Valerie	'96 – 1	Josie Pigeon	owner of an all-women construction firm	Northeast USA
Wolzien, Valerie	'87 – 10	Susan Henshaw	suburban housewife	Connecticut

Theatre & Performing Arts

Author	❶ – #	Series Character	Occupation	Setting
Babson, Marian	'86 – 5	Eve Sinclair & Trixie Dolan	aging British ex-movie queens	London, England
Beck, K. K.	'92 – 4	Jane da Silva	former lounge singer	Seattle, WA
Brennan, Carol	'94 – 2	Emily Silver	New York actress	New York, NY
Cooper, Susan R.	'93 – 2	Kimmey Kruse	stand-up comic	Austin, TX
Davis, Dorothy S.	'76 – 4	Julie Hayes	former actress & columnist	New York, NY
Dentinger, Jane	'83 – 6	Jocelyn O'Roarke	Broadway actress & director	New York, NY
Frommer, Sara H.	'93 – 2	Joan Spencer	symphony orchestra manager	Oliver, IN
Fulton, Eileen	'88 – 6	Nina McFall & Dino Rossi, Lt.	glamorous TV soap star & NYPD cop	New York, NY
Johns, Veronica P.	'53 – 2	Webster Flagg	60-something Harlem actor/butler/houseman	New York, NY
Knight, Phyllis	'92 – 3	Lil Ritchie	ex-rocker & gay woman P. I.	coastal Maine
Matteson, Stefanie	'90 – 7	Charlotte Graham	Oscar-winning actress	New York, NY
Meyers, Annette	'89 – 7	Xenia Smith & Leslie Wetzon	Wall Street headhunters	New York, NY
Millhiser, Marlys	'92 – 3	Charlie Greene	literary agent	Hollywood, CA
Morice, Anne	'70 – 23	Tessa Crichton	English actress sleuth	England
Paul, Barbara	'84 – 3	Enrico Caruso	Italian tenor	New York, NY
Scott, Rosie	'89 – 1	Glory Day	artist & singer	New Zealand
Woods, Sherryl	'91 – 5	Molly DeWitt	film office public relations staffer	Miami, FL
Yeager, Dorian	'92 – 3	Victoria Bowering	NYC actor, writer & playwright	New York, NY

Travel

Author	❶ – #	Series Character	Occupation	Setting
Crane, Frances	'41 – 26	Pat & Jean Abbot	husband & wife detection team	World Travelers
Dreher, Sarah	'85 – 6	Stoner McTavish	lesbian travel agent	Boston, MA
Gilman, Dorothy	'66 – 12	Emily Pollifax	grandmother CIA agent	New Jersey
Linscott, Gillian	'84 – 3	Birdie Linnet	ex-cop fitness trainer	England
Peters, Elizabeth	'75 – 7	Amelia Peabody	Victorian feminist archaeologist	Kent, England
Yates, Margaret E.T.	'37 – 4	Anne "Davvie" Davenport McLean	newspaper correspondent	World Traveler

Three

Series Characters

Series Character	Author	1 – #	Occupation	Setting
A				
A. Pennyfather, Prof.	Olsen, D. B.	'45 – 6	professor at Clarendon College	Los Angeles, CA
Abby Abagnarro & Ike Tygart	Whitney, Polly	'94 – 3	TV news director & network producer	New York, NY
Abigail Doyle	Collins, Anna A.	'94 – 2	efficiency expert	New York
Abigail Patience Danforth	Jackson, Marian J. A.	'90 – 5	turn-of-the-century consulting detective	USA
Abigail Sanderson & Robert Forsythe	Giroux, E. X.	'84 – 10	secretary & barrister	London, England
Adam Dalgleish	James, P. D.	'62 – 9	published poet of Scotland Yard	London, England
Addie Devore	Karr, Leona	'93 – 1	small-town newspaper owner	Colorado
Agatha Raisin	Beaton, M. C.	'92 – 4	London advertising retiree	Cotswolds, England
Agatha Welch	Johns, Veronica P.	'40 – 2	middle-aged woman sleuth	Connecticut
Agnes Carmichael	Cohen, Anthea	'82 – 13	hospital staff nurse	England
Al Krug & Casey Kellog	Weston, Carolyn	'72 – 3	hard-bitten veteran cop & college grad liberal	Santa Monica, CA
Alan Grant	Tey, Josephine	'29 – 6	Scotland Yard inspector	London, England
Alan Markby, Insp. & Meredith Mitchell	Granger, Ann	'91 – 9	detective inspector & Foreign Service officer	Cotswolds, England
Alan Stewart & Roz Howard	Kenney, Susan	'83 – 3	British painter & American professor	Maine
Albenia "Benni" Harper	Fowler, Earlene	'94 – 3	ex-rancher & folk art museum curator	San Celina, CA
Albert Campion	Allingham, Margery	'29 – 22	suave sleuth with noble blood	London, England
Alden Chase & Glad Gold	Wender, Theodora	'85 – 2	chief of police & English professor	Massachusetts
Alex Jensen & Jessie Arnold	Henry, Sue	'91 – 3	Alaska state trooper & sled dog racer	Anchorage, AK
Alex McKenzie, Dr. & Sarah Deane	Borthwick, J. S.	'82 – 7	internist & English professor	Boston, MA
Alex Sinclair & Kate Weston	Hall, Patricia	'93 – 1	British inspector & social worker	England
Alex Tanner	Donald, Anabel	'91 – 4	part-time P. I. & TV researcher	London, England
Alex Winter	Steiner, Susan	'91 – 2	P. I.	California
Aline Scott	Drake, Alison	'88 – 4	small resort town police detective	Tango Key, FL
Alison Hope & Nick Trevellyan	Kelly, Susan B.	'90 – 5	software designer & detective inspector	Hop Valley, England
Alison Kaine	Allen, Kate	'93 – 2	lesbian cop	Denver, CO

A . . . B

Series Character	Author	❶ – #	Occupation	Setting

A . . . continued

Series Character	Author	❶ – #	Occupation	Setting
Alix Thorssen	McClendon, Lise	'94 – 2	gallery owner & art forgery expert	Jackson, WY
Alonzo Hawkin & Kate Martinelli	King, Laurie R.	'93 – 3	SFPD homicide detectives	San Francisco, CA
Amanda Hazard	Feddersen, Connie	'93 – 4	small-town Certified Public Accountant	Vamoose, OK
Amanda Knight	Fromer, Margot J.	'91 – 2	hospital director of nursing	Washington, DC
Amanda Pepper	Roberts, Gillian	'87 – 6	high school teacher	Philadelphia, PA
Amanda Roberts	Woods, Sherryl	'89 – 9	ex-New York investigative reporter	Atlanta, GA
Amanda Valentine	Beecham, Rose	'92 – 3	ex-NYPD cop turned detective inspector	New Zealand
Amelia Peabody	Peters, Elizabeth	'75 – 7	Victorian feminist archaeologist	Kent, England
Amy Prescott, Dr.	Hendricksen, Louise	'93 – 3	crime lab physician	Seattle, WA
Amy Tupper	Bell, Josephine	'79 – 2	amateur sleuth	London, England
Ana Grey	Smith, April	'94 – 1	FBI agent	Los Angeles, CA
Andrea Perkins	Coker, Carolyn	'84 – 4	museum art historian & restorer of paintings	Boston, MA
Andrew Basnett	Ferrars, E. X.	'83 – 8	retired botany professor	England
Angela Benbow & Caledonia Wingate	Sawyer, Corinne Holt	'88 – 6	70-something admirals' widows	southern California
Angela Matelli	Lee, W. W. (Wendi)	'94 – 2	ex-Marine turned P. I.	Boston, MA
Angelina Amalfi	Pence, Joanne	'93 – 4	food columnist & restaurant reviewer	San Francisco, CA
Angie DaVito	Shaffer, Louise	'94 – 2	TV soap opera producer	New York, NY
Anita Blake	Hamilton, Laurell K.	'93 – 4	reanimator & vampire hunter	St. Louis, MO
Anna Lee	Cody, Liza	'80 – 6	P. I.	London, England
Anna Peters	Law, Janice	'76 – 8	international oil company exec turned P. I.	Washington, DC
Anna Pigeon	Barr, Nevada	'93 – 4	U. S. park ranger	National Parks, USA
Anna Southwood	Bedford, Jean	'90 – 3	P. I.	Sydney, Australia
Annabel Reed & Mackenzie Smith	Truman, Margaret	'89 – 5	gallery owner & law professor	Washington, DC
Anne "Davvie" Davenport McLean	Yates, Margaret E. T.	'37 – 4	newspaper correspondent	World Traveler
Anne Fitzhugh	Roberts, Carey	'89 – 2	police detective	Washington, DC
Anne Menlo, Dr.	O'Callaghan, Maxine	'96 – 2	child psychologist	Phoenix, AZ
Anneke Haagen	Holtzer, Susan	'94 – 2	computer consultant	Ann Arbor, MI
Annie Laurance & Max Darling	Hart, Carolyn G.	'87 – 9	bookstore owner & investigator	South Carolina
Annie MacPherson	Smith, Janet L.	'90 – 3	attorney	Seattle, WA
Annie McGrogan	Farrell, Gillian B.	'92 – 2	P. I. & actor just back from LA	New York, NY
Antony Maitland	Woods, Sara	'62 – 48	barrister drawn to murder cases	England
April Woo	Glass, Leslie	'93 – 2	police detective	New York, NY
Arly Hanks	Hess, Joan	'87 – 9	small-town police chief	Maggody, AR
Arthur "Snooky" Randolph & B. Woodrull	Dank, Gloria	'89 – 4	children's author & visiting brother-in-law	Connecticut
Arthur G. Crook	Gilbert, Anthony	'36 – 50	Cockney lawyer-detective	England
Asey Mayo	Taylor, Phoebe A.	'31 – 24	former sailor & auto racer	Cape Cod, MA
Ashley Johnson & Elizabeth Mendoza	McAllester, Melanie	'94 – 1	lesbian homicide detectives	USA
Auguste Didier	Myers, Amy	'82 – 8	British-French Victorian master chef	England
Aunt Dimity	Atherton, Nancy	'92 – 3	romantic ghost	England
Auntie Lil & Theodore S. Hubbert	Gray, Gallagher	'91 – 3	dress designer & retired personnel manager	New York, NY
Aurora Teagarden	Harris, Charlaine	'90 – 5	librarian turned real estate agent	GA

B

Series Character	Author	❶ – #	Occupation	Setting
Balthazar Marten & Sixto Cardenas	Adamson, M. J.	'87 – 5	NYPD homicide det. & Puerto Rican cop	Puerto Rico
Barbara Havers & Thomas Lynley	George, Elizabeth	'88 – 8	detective sergeant & Scotland Yard inspector	London, England
Barbara Holloway	Wilhelm, Kate	'91 – 2	defense attorney	OR
Barbara Joan "Bo" Bradley	Padgett, Abigail	'93 – 3	child abuse investigator	San Diego, CA
Barrett Lake	Singer, Shelley	'93 – 5	high school history teacher	Berkeley, CA

B . . . C

Series Character	Author	1 – #	Occupation	Setting

B . . . *continued*

Series Character	Author	1 – #	Occupation	Setting
Barry & Dee Vaughan	Jordan, Jennifer	'87 – 3	spoofy crime writer & office temp wife	Woodfield, England
Basil Willing, Dr.	McCloy, Helen	'38 – 13	psychiatrist & FBI consultant	New York, NY
Beatrice Lestrange Bradley	Mitchell, Gladys	'29 – 66	psychiatrist & consultant to Home Office	London, England
Becky Belski	Haddad, Carolyn A.	'92 – 1	computer investigator	Chicago, IL
Ben & Carrie Porter	Travis, Elizabeth	'89 – 2	book publishers	Riverdale, CT
Ben & Ellie Haskell	Cannell, Dorothy	'84 – 7	writer/chef & interior decorator	Chitterton Falls, England
Ben Safford	Dominic, R. B.	'68 – 7	Democratic congressman from Ohio	Washington, DC
Benjamin Jurnet, Insp.	Haymon, S. T.	'80 – 7	detective inspector	Norwich, England
Bernadette Hebert, Dr.	Ennis, Catherine	'91 – 2	lesbian crime lab expert	Louisiana
Bernard Woodrull & A. "Snooky" Randolph	Dank, Gloria	'89 – 4	children's author & visiting brother-in-law	Connecticut
Bessie Petty, B. Pond & M. East	Lawrence, Hilda	'44 – 3	New England little old ladies & New York city P. I.	Northeast USA
Betty Trenka	Christmas, Joyce	'93 – 2	retired office manager	Connecticut
Beulah Pond, Mark East & Bessie Petty	Lawrence, Hilda	'44 – 3	New York city P. I. & New England little old ladies	Northeast USA
Bill & Coco Hastings	Offord, Lenore Glen	'38 – 2	sleuthing pair	San Francisco, CA
Bill Slider	Harrod-Eagles, C.	'91 – 5	detective inspector	England
Bill Smith & Lydia Chin	Rozan, S. J.	'94 – 2	Army brat & Chinese American P. I.s	New York, NY
Bingo Riggs & Handsome Kusak	Rice, Craig	'42 – 3	gullible city slickers & reluctant detectives	USA
Birdie Linnet	Linscott, Gillian	'84 – 3	ex-cop fitness trainer	England
Blackwater Bay Mystery	Gosling, Paula	'94 – 2	police series with a Great Lakes setting	Midwest USA
Blaine Stewart	Zukowski, Sharon	'91 – 4	ex-NYPD cop turned P. I. in Manhattan	New York, NY
Blair Emerson	Amey, Linda	'92 – 2	funeral director	Austin, TX
Blanche White	Neely, Barbara	'92 – 2	middle-aged black domestic	North Carolina
Blue Maguire & Spaceman Kowalski	White, Teri	'84 – 2	cop pair with prickly partnership	Los Angeles, CA
Bonnie Indermill	Berry, Carole	'87 – 6	tap-dancing Manhattan office temp	New York, NY
Brett Nightingale	Kelly, Mary	'56 – 3	Scottish Inspector	Edinburgh, Scotland
Brigid Donovan	Saum, Karen	'90 – 3	50-something lesbian ex-nun	Maine
Britt Montero	Buchanan, Edna	'92 – 4	newspaper crime reporter	Miami, FL
Brooke Cassidy & Matt Devlin	Kruger, Mary	'94 – 2	mystery writer & P. I.	Newport, RI
Brother Cadfael	Peters, Ellis	'77 – 20	medieval monk & herbalist	Shrewsbury, England
Bunty, Dominic & George Felse	Peters, Ellis	'51 – 13	family of detectives	Shropshire, England

C

Series Character	Author	1 – #	Occupation	Setting
C. B. Greenfield & Maggie Rome	Kallen, Lucille	'79 – 5	editor/publisher & reporter	Connecticut
Caitlin Reece	Douglas, Lauren W.	'87 – 6	lesbian detective	Victoria, Canada
Cal Donovan, L. Graham & F. Shapiro	Bannister, Jo	'93 – 4	cops	Castlemere, England
Caleb Sweetwater	Green, Anna K.	1899 – 3	policeman	New York, NY
Caledonia Wingate & Angela Benbow	Sawyer, Corinne Holt	'88 – 6	70-something admirals' widows	southern California
Caley Burke	McKenna, Bridget	'93 – 3	30-something P. I.	northern, CA
Calista Jacobs	Knight, Kathryn L.	'86 – 4	award-winning illustrator of children's books	Cambridge, MA
Callahan Garrity	Trocheck, Kathy H.	'92 – 4	ex-cop cleaning service operator	Atlanta, GA
Cardiff, Insp. Supt.	Gray, Dulcie	'60 – 2	police inspector	England
Carl & Freda Pedersen	Hart, Jeanne	'87 – 3	police lieutenant & wife	Bay Cove, CA
Carlos Cruz & Jay Goldstein	Wallace, Marilyn	'86 – 3	homicide detectives	Oakland, CA
Carlotta Carlyle	Barnes, Linda	'87 – 6	6'1" cab-driving ex-cop P. I.	Boston, MA
Carmen Ramirez	Haddock, Lisa	'94 – 2	lesbian newspaper copy editor	Frontier City, OK
Carol Ashton	McNab, Claire	'88 – 7	lesbian detective inspector & single mother	Sydney, Australia
Carrie & Ben Porter	Travis, Elizabeth	'89 – 2	book publishers	Riverdale, CT

C

Series Character	Author	1 – #	Occupation	Setting

C . . . continued

Series Character	Author	1 – #	Occupation	Setting
Casey Kellog & Al Krug	Weston, Carolyn	'72 – 3	college grad liberal & hard-bitten veteran cop	Santa Monica, CA
Cass Jameson	Wheat, Carolyn	'83 – 3	Brooklyn criminal lawyer	New York, NY
Cassandra Reilly	Wilson, Barbara	'90 – 2	Spanish translator	London, England
Cassandra Swann	Moody, Susan	'93 – 4	British biology teacher turned bridge pro	Cotswolds, England
Cassidy McCabe	Matthews, Alex	'96 – 2	psychotherapirst	Oak Park, IL
Cassie Newton	Smith, Joan G.	'89 – 2	French major at McGill University	Montreal, Canada
Cat Caliban	Borton, D. B.	'93 – 5	60-something P. I.-in-training	Cincinnati, OH
Cat Marsala	D'Amato, Barbara	'90 – 6	freelance investigative journalist	Chicago, IL
Catherine LeVendeur	Newman, Sharan	'93 – 3	novice & scholar in 12th century	France
Catherine Sayler	Grant, Linda	'88 – 5	P. I.	San Francisco, CA
Catherine Wilde	Ruryk, Jean	'94 – 1	retired ad exec turned antiques restorer	USA
Cecile Buddenbrooks, Sister	Sullivan, Winona	'93 – 2	licensed P. I. nun	Boston, MA
Cecily Sinclair	Kingsbury, Kate	'93 – 7	hotel owner in Edwardian England	Badger's End, England
Charles Matthews	Meredith, D. R.	'84 – 5	sheriff	west Texas
Charles Spotted Moon	Yarbro, Chelsea Q.	'76 – 4	attorney & Ojibway tribal shaman	San Francisco, CA
Charlie Greene	Millhiser, Marlys	'92 – 3	literary agent	Hollywood, CA
Charlie Meiklejohn & Constance Leidl	Wilhelm, Kate	'87 – 6	ex-arson investigator P. I. & psychologist	New York, NY
Charlie Parker	Shelton, Connie	'95 – 3	CPA turned reluctant investigator	New Mexico
Charlotte & Thomas Pitt	Perry, Anne	'79 – 16	wife & Victorian police inspector	London, England
Charlotte Graham	Matteson, Stefanie	'90 – 7	Oscar-winning actress	New York, NY
Charlotte Kent	Kittredge, Mary	'87 – 3	freelance writer	Connecticut
Charlotte Sams	Glen, Alison	'92 – 2	freelance writer	Columbus, OH
Charmian Daniels	Melville, Jennie	'62 – 17	police detective	Deerham Hills, England
Chicago Nordejoong	McKernan, Victoria	'90 – 3	professional scuba diver	Florida
China Bayles	Albert, Susan Wittig	'92 – 4	herb shop owner & former attorney	Pecan Springs, TX
Christine Bennett	Harris, Lee	'92 – 7	ex-nun	New York, NY
Christine Martin	Roome, Annette	'89 – 2	40-something cub reporter	England
Christine Opara	Uhnak, Dorothy	'68 – 3	20-something police detective	New York, NY
Christopher Dennis "Seedy" Sloan, Insp.	Aird, Catherine	'66 – 13	Berebury CID department head	W. Calleshire, England
Christopher "Kit" Storm	Barber, Willetta Ann	'40 – 7	police illustrator for the NYPD	New York, NY
Christopher McKee	Reilly, Helen	'30 – 31	Manhattan homicide squad detective	New York, NY
Claire & Dan Claiborne	Dunbar, Sophie	'93 – 3	sleuthing pair	New Orleans, LA
Claire Aldington, Rev.	Holland, Isabelle	'83 – 6	Episcopal priest	New York, NY
Claire Breslinsky	Kelly, Mary Ann	'90 – 3	freelance photographer	New York, NY
Claire Camden	Peterson, Audrey	'92 – 3	California English professor in Britain	London, England
Claire Conrad & Maggie Hill	Howe, Melodie J.	'89 – 2	P. I. & secretary	southern California
Claire Malloy	Hess, Joan	'86 – 10	small-town bookstore owner	Farberville, AR
Claire Sharples	Rothenberg, Rebecca	'91 – 3	former MIT scholar/microbiologist	central, CA
Clara Gamadge	Boylan, Eleanor	'89 – 4	widow of Henry the forgery expert	New York, NY
Clare & Mirinda Clively	Crowleigh, Ann	'93 – 2	Victorian London twin sisters	London, England
Claude Warrington-Reeve	Bell, Josephine	'59 – 3	barrister	London, England
Claudia Valentine	Day, Marele	'88 – 4	Australian P. I.	Australia
Clio Browne	Komo, Dolores	'88 – 1	cop's widow & P. I. agency owner	St. Louis, MO
Clio Rees, Dr. & Harry Marsh	Bannister, Jo	'84 – 3	physician/mystery writer & chief inspector	England
Clovis Kelly	Babbin, Jacqueline	'72 – 2	ex-NYPD homicide det. & crime consultant	New York , NY

C . . . D

Series Character	Author	▯ – #	Occupation	Setting

C . . . continued

Series Character	Author	▯ – #	Occupation	Setting
Cockrill, Insp.	Brand, Christianna	'41 – 6	police inspector	Kent County, England
Coco & Bill Hastings	Offord, Lenore Glen	'38 – 2	sleuthing pair	San Francisco, CA
Coleman January	Bradley, Lynn	'94 – 1	insurance investigator	Houston, TX
Conan Flagg	Wren, M. K.	'73 – 8	bookstore owner & ex-intelligence agent	Oregon
Connor O'Neill & Fran Wilson	Green, Christine	'94 – 3	village inspector & new policewoman	Fowchester, England
Constance Ethel Morrison Burke, Hon.	Porter, Joyce	'70 – 5	comic senior sleuth	England
Constance Leidl & Charlie Meiklejohn	Wilhelm, Kate	'87 – 6	psychologist & ex-arson investigator P. I.	New York, NY
Cordelia Gray	James, P. D.	'72 – 2	fledgling P. I.	London, England
Cressida Woodruffe & Willow King	Cooper, Natasha	'90 – 5	civil servant & romance novelist	London, England

D

Series Character	Author	▯ – #	Occupation	Setting
D. S. Trewley & Sgt. Stone	Mason, Sarah Jill	'93 – 4	village detective partners	Allshire, England
Daisy Dalrymple	Dunn, Carola	'94 – 4	young aristocratic woman writer	Hampshire, England
Dan & Claire Claiborne	Dunbar, Sophie	'93 – 3	sleuthing pair	New Orleans, LA
Darina Lisle	Laurence, Janet	'89 – 8	British caterer, chef & food writer	England
David Middleton-Brown & Lucy Kingsley	Charles, Kate	'91 – 5	solicitor & artist	London, England
David Silver & String	Hightower, Lynn S.	'92 – 4	homicide cop & alien partner	USA
David Webb	Fraser, Anthea	'86 – 13	British police inspector	England
David Wintringham, Dr.	Bell, Josephine	'37 – 14	British physician	London, England
Dearborn V. Pinch	Green, Edith Pinero	'77 – 3	70-something ladies man	New York, NY
Deb Ralston	Martin, Lee	'84 – 11	police detective & mother	Ft. Worth, TX
Deborah Knott	Maron, Margaret	'92 – 4	district judge	North Carolina
Dee & Barry Vaughan	Jordan, Jennifer	'87 – 3	office temp wife & spoofy crime writer	Woodfield, England
Dee Street	Wakefield, Hannah	'87 – 2	American attorney	London, England
Delia Ross-Merlani, Viscountess	Florian, S. L.	'92 – 1	English-Italian noblewoman	New York, NY
Delilah West	O'Callaghan, Maxine	'80 – 5	P. I.	Orange County, CA
Delta Stevens	Silva, Linda Kay	'91 – 4	lesbian policewoman	California
Desiree Shapiro	Eichler, Selma	'94 – 2	5'2" queen-size Manhattan P. I.	New York, NY
Desmond Shannon	Heberden, M. V.	'39 – 17	high-priced Irish-American P. I.	New York, NY
Devon MacDonald	Jacobs, Nancy Baker	'91 – 3	ex-teacher P. I.	Minneapolis, MN
Dewey James	Morgan, Kate	'90 – 6	60-something small-town librarian	New York
Diana Tregarde	Lackey, Mercedes	'89 – 3	romance author & practicing witch	Hartford, CT
Dino Rossi, Lt. & Nina McFall	Fulton, Eileen	'88 – 6	NYPD cop & glamorous TV soap star	New York, NY
Dittany Henbit Monk & Osbert Monk	Craig, Alisa	'81 – 5	garden club member & author of westerns	Lobelia Falls, Ont., Canada
Ditteridge, Supt.	Ferrars, E. X.	'71 – 2	police superintendent	England
Dixie T. Struthers	Sims, L. V.	'87 – 3	police detective	San Jose, CA
Dolly Rawlins	La Plante, Lynda	'83 – 2	young English widow	England
Dominic, George & Bunty Felse	Peters, Ellis	'51 – 13	family of detectives	Shropshire, England
Doran Fairweather	Hardwick, Mollie	'86 – 6	British antiques dealer	Kent, England
Douglas Perkins	Babson, Marian	'71 – 4	London-based public relations agent	London, England
Douglas Quantrill & Hilary Lloyd	Radley, Sheila	'78 – 9	detective chief inspector & sergeant partner	Suffolk, England
Duncan Kincaid & Gemma James	Crombie, Deborah	'93 – 3	Scotland Yard superintendent & sergeant	London, England

E...F

Series Character	Author	❶ – #	Occupation	Setting
E				
E. J. Pugh	Cooper, Susan R.	'92 – 2	housewife, mother & romance writer	Texas
Ebenezer Gryce	Green, Anna K.	1878 – 12	portly policeman	New York, NY
Eddie Brown	Porter, Joyce	'66 – 4	comic spy	England
Edwina Charles	Warner, Mignon	'76 – 7	British clairvoyant	Little Gidding, England
Edwina Crusoe	Kittredge, Mary	'90 – 6	RN & medical consultant	New Haven, CT
Elena Jarvis	Herndon, Nancy	'95 – 2	detective with Crimes Against Persons unit	Los Santos, TX
Elena Oliverez	Muller, Marcia	'83 – 3	Mexican arts museum curator	Santa Barbara, CA
Elisha Macomber	Knight, Kathleen M.	'35 – 16	selectman & owner of a fish market	Cape Cod, MA
Eliza Figg	Ballard, Mignon	'93 – 1	former Peace Corps volunteer	USA
Elizabeth Austin	Skom, Edith	'89 – 2	English professor	Midwest USA
Elizabeth Blair	Brown, Lizbie	'92 – 2	American widow from Virginia selling quilts	Bath, England
Elizabeth Chase, Dr.	Lawrence, Martha	'95 – 1	Stanford-trained parapsychologist turned P. I.	San Diego, CA
Elizabeth Elliot	Allen, Irene	'92 – 2	widowed Quaker meeting clerk	Pennsylvania
Elizabeth Lamb Worthington	Morison, B. J.	'82 – 5	pre-teenager in the 1970s	coastal, ME
Elizabeth MacPherson	McCrumb, Sharyn	'84 – 8	forensic anthropologist	Southern USA
Elizabeth Mendoza & Ashley Johnson	McAllester, Melanie	'94 – 1	lesbian homicide detectives	USA
Elizabeth Will	Yeager, Dorian	'94 – 2	art gallery owner & lobster fisherman	Dovekey, NH
Ella Clah	Thurlo, Aimée & David	'95 – 2	Navajo FBI agent	NM
Ellie & Ben Haskell	Cannell, Dorothy	'84 – 7	interior decorator & writer/chef	Chitterton Falls, England
Ellie Bernstein	Dietz, Denise	'93 – 2	diet group leader	USA
Elvira & Father Simeon	Highsmith, Domini	'95 – 1	nurse & medieval priest	E. Yorkshire, England
Em Hansen	Andrews, Sarah	'94 – 2	oil worker	Wyoming
Emily & Henry Bryce	Scherf, Margaret	'49 – 4	Manhattan interior decorators	New York, NY
Emily D. Seeton	Crane, Hamilton	'68 – 19	retired British art teacher	Kent, England
Emily Pollifax	Gilman, Dorothy	'66 – 12	grandmother CIA agent	New Jersey
Emily Silver	Brennan, Carol	'94 – 2	New York actress	New York, NY
Emma Chizzit	Hall, Mary Bowen	'89 – 4	salvage dealer	Sacramento, CA
Emma Lord	Daheim, Mary	'92 – 7	small-town newspaper owner & editor	Alpine, WA
Emma Shaw	Jones, Hazel Wynn	'88 – 2	documentary film director	Italy
Emma Victor	Wings, Mary	'87 – 3	lesbian activist & P. I.	San Francisco, CA
Emmy & Henry Tibbett	Moyes, Patricia	'59 – 19	Scotland Yard inspector & wife	London, England
Enrico Caruso	Paul, Barbara	'84 – 3	Italian tenor	New York, NY
Erik March	Fickling, G. G.	'62 – 3	P. I.	California
Ernest Lamb, Insp.	Wentworth, Patricia	'39 – 2	police inspector	London, England
Eugenia Potter	Rich, Virginia	'82 – 4	widowed chef	Maine
Eva Wylie	Cody, Liza	'93 – 2	wrestler & security guard	London, England
Evan Pinkerton	Frome, David	'30 – 11	Welshman	England
Eve Dallas	Robb, J. D.	'95 – 3	NYPD lieutenant in the 21st century	New York, NY
Eve Elliott	Lee, Barbara	'95 – 1	ex-New York advertising exec turned realtor	Anne Arundel Co., MD
Eve Sinclair & Trixie Dolan	Babson, Marian	'86 – 5	aging British ex-movie queens	London, England
F				
Faith Sibley Fairchild	Page, Katherine Hall	'90 – 7	minister's wife & culinary artist	Massachusetts
Fanny Zindel	Stevens, Serita	'91 – 2	Jewish grandmother	USA
Felix & Virginia Freer	Ferrars, E. X.	'78 – 9	businessman & physiotherapist	England
Fiddler & Fiora Flynn	Maxwell, A. E.	'85 – 8	ex-husband & investment banker	California
Finch, Insp.	Thomson, June	'71 – 18	police inspector	Essex, England

F . . . G

Series Character	Author	■ – #	Occupation	Setting

F . . . *continued*

Series Character	Author	■ – #	Occupation	Setting
Finny Aletter	Montgomery, Yvonne	'87 – 2	stockbroker turned carpenter	Denver, CO
Fiora & Fiddler Flynn	Maxwell, A. E.	'85 – 8	investment banker & ex-husband	California
Fleming Stone	Wells, Carolyn	'09 – 61	intellectual P. I.	New York, NY
Fran Kirk	Furie, Ruthe	'95 – 3	former battered wife & P. I. in training	Cheektowaga, NY
Fran Wilson & Connor O'Neill	Green, Christine	'94 – 3	new policewoman & village inspector	Fowchester, England
Frances Finn	Hollingsworth, Gerelyn	'95 – 1	P. I.	Kansas City, KS
Francesca Wilson & John McLeish	Neel, Janet	'88 – 4	civil servant & detective inspector	England
Frank Carver & Ginny Trask	Wallingford, Lee	'91 – 2	ex-cop & forest fire dispatcher	Oregon
Frank Shapiro, C. Donovan & L. Graham	Bannister, Jo	'93 – 4	cops	Castlemere, England
Fred Vickery	Lewis, Sherry	'95 – 2	70-something retiree	Cutler, CO
Freda & Carl Pedersen	Hart, Jeanne	'87 – 3	wife & police lieutenant	Bay Cove, CA
Freddie O'Neal	Dain, Catherine	'92 – 5	plane-flying P. I.	Reno, NV
Frederika Bascomb	Thompson, Joyce	'91 – 1	forensic artist	Seattle, WA
Fremont Jones	Day, Dianne	'95 – 3	owner of a typewriting service circa 1900	San Francisco, CA
Frevisse, Sister	Frazer, Margaret	'92 – 6	Medieval nun	Oxfordshire, England

G

Series Character	Author	■ – #	Occupation	Setting
G. D. H. Pringle	Livingston, Nancy	'85 – 8	retired tax inspector	England
Gail Connor	Parker, Barbara	'94 – 2	corporate attorney	Miami, FL
Gail McCarthy	Crum, Laura	'94 – 1	horse veterinarian	Santa Cruz, CA
Gale Grayson	Holbrook, Teri	'95 – 2	American expatriate historian	Fetherbridge, England
Galen Shaw & Julian Baugh	Blackmur, L. L.	'89 – 2	writer & financier	New England
Gemma James & Duncan Kincaid	Crombie, Deborah	'93 – 3	Scotland Yard sergeant & superintendent	London, England
George & Molly Palmer-Jones	Cleeves, Ann	'86 – 8	ex-Home Office bird-watcher & wife	Surrey, England
George, Bunty & Dominic Felse	Peters, Ellis	'51 – 13	family of detectives	Shropshire, England
Georgetown house	Michaels, Barbara	'68 – 3	historic home	Washington, DC
Georgia Lee Maxwell	Friedman, Mickey	'88 – 2	freelance writer	Paris, France
Georgina Powers	Danks, Denise	'89 – 3	British computer journalist	London, England
Georgine Wyeth & Todd McKinnon	Offord, Lenore Glen	'43 – 4	single working mother & pulp writer	Berkeley, CA
Gerritt DeGraaf, Dr.	D'Amato, Barbara	'80 – 2	forensic pathologist	Chicago, IL
Gianna Maglione & Mimi Patterson	Mickelbury, Penny	'94 – 2	lesbian police lieutenant & reporter	Washington, DC
Gil Mayo	Eccles, Marjorie	'88 – 8	detective chief inspector	England
Gillian Adams	Kelly, Nora	'84 – 3	Univ. of the Pacific Northwest history chair	Canada
Ginger Struve Barnes	Murray, Donna H.	'95 – 2	amateur sleuth	Philadelphia, PA
Ginny Trask & Frank Carver	Wallingford, Lee	'91 – 2	forest fire dispatcher & ex-cop	Oregon
Glad Gold & Alden Chase	Wender, Theodora	'85 – 2	English professor & chief of police	Massachusetts
Glory Day	Scott, Rosie	'89 – 1	artist & singer	New Zealand
Glynis Tryon	Monfredo, Miriam G.	'92 – 4	librarian & suffragette in mid-19th century	Seneca Falls, NY
Goldy Bear	Davidson, Diane M.	'90 – 6	caterer & single mother	Aspen Meadow, CO
Gordon Christy, Dr.	Moore, Barbara	'83 – 2	veterinarian	New Mexico
Grace Latham & John Primrose, Col.	Ford, Leslie	'34 – 16	attractive widow & career soldier	Washington DC
Grace Rossi	Scottoline, Lisa	'94 – 1	Federal appeals attorney & law clerk	Philadelphia, PA
Grace Severance, Dr.	Scherf, Margaret	'68 – 4	retired pathologist	Arizona
Graham Sheldon & Lee Ofsted	Elkins, Charlotte & Aaron	'89 – 2	homicide detective & golf pro	Washington
Gregor Demarkian	Haddam, Jane	'90 – 12	former FBI department head	Philadelphia, PA
Gregory Toye & Tom Pollard	Lemarchand, Elizabeth	'67 – 17	Scotland Yard detectives	England
Gridley Nelson	Fenisong, Ruth	'42 – 13	wealthy young cop with Harlem housekeeper	New York, NY

G...H...I

Series Character	Author	❶ – #	Occupation	Setting

G ... continued

Series Character	Author	❶ – #	Occupation	Setting
Guido Brunetti	Leon, Donna	'92 – 5	commissario of the Venice police	Venice, Italy
Gwen Harding	Berenson, Laurien	'94 – 1	NYC journalist turned suburban wife & mother	New York
Gwenn Ramadge	O'Donnell, Lillian	'90 – 3	P. I. for corporate investigations	New York, NY

H

Series Character	Author	❶ – #	Occupation	Setting
H. W. Ross	Grindle, Lucretia	'93 – 2	detective superintendent	England
Hagen	Hooper, Kay	'87 – 11	government agent	USA
Hamish Macbeth	Beaton, M. C.	'85 – 11	Scottish police constable	Scotland
Hana Shaner	Greth, Roma	'88 – 2	carpet company heiress in Dutch country	Conover, PA
Handsome Kusak & Bingo Riggs	Rice, Craig	'42 – 3	gullible city slickers & reluctant detectives	USA
Hannah Barlow	Lachnit, Carroll	'95 – 2	ex-cop turned law student	Orange County, CA
Hannah Land	Mackay, Amanda	'76 – 2	divorced New York PhD at Duke University	Durham, NC
Hannah Wolfe	Dunant, Sarah	'92 – 3	P. I.	London, England
Hannasyde, Supt.	Heyer, Georgette	'35 – 4	police superintendent	England
Harriet Jeffries & John Sanders	Sale, Medora	'86 – 6	police detective & architectural photographer	Toronto, Canada
Harriett Hubley	Manthorne, Jackie	'94 – 3	intrepid lesbian sleuth	Montreal, Canada
Harry Marsh & Clio Rees, Dr.	Bannister, Jo	'84 – 3	chief inspector & physician/mystery writer	England
Haskell Blevins	McCafferty, Taylor	'90 – 5	small-town P. I.	Pigeon Fork, KY
Hedley Nicholson	Kelly, Mary	'61 – 2	P. I.	England
Helen Black	Welch, Pat	'90 – 4	ex-cop lesbian P. I.	San Francisco, CA
Helen Marsh Shandy & Peter Shandy	MacLeod, Charlotte	'78 – 9	botany professor & librarian wife	Balaclava Co., MA
Helen West	Fyfield, Frances	'88 – 5	London Crown prosecutor	London, England
Helma Zukas	Dereske, Jo	'94 – 4	state librarian	Washington
Hemingway, Insp.	Heyer, Georgette	'39 – 4	one-time assistant to Supt. Hannasyde	England
Henrietta O'Dwyer Collins	Hart, Carolyn G.	'93 – 3	70-something reporter	South Carolina
Henry & Emily Bryce	Scherf, Margaret	'49 – 4	Manhattan interior decorators	New York, NY
Henry & Emmy Tibbett	Moyes, Patricia	'59 – 19	Scotland Yard inspector & wife	London, England
Henry Bassett	Burden, Pat	'90 – 4	retired cop	Herefordshire, England
Henry Frost, Dr.	Bell, Josephine	'64 – 2	British physician	London, England
Henry Gamadge	Daly, Elizabeth	'40 – 16	author & bibliophile	New York, NY
Hercule Poirot	Christie, Agatha	'20 – 35	former Belgian cop turned private detective	London, England
Hilary Lloyd & Douglas Quantrill	Radley, Sheila	'78 – 9	sergeant partner & detective chief inspector	Suffolk, England
Hilary Tamar	Caudwell, Sarah	'81 – 3	Oxford professor of medieval law	Oxford, England
Hilda Adams aka Miss Pinkerton	Rinehart, Mary R.	'32 – 3	nurse & police agent	England
Hiram Potter	Foley, Rae	'55 – 11	mild-mannered Old Money sleuth	New York
Hollis Carpenter	Powell, Deborah	'91 – 2	gay woman crime reporter	Houston, TX
Holly Winter	Conant, Susan	'89 – 8	dog trainer & magazine columnist	Cambridge, MA
Homer Kelly	Langton, Jane	'64 – 11	Harvard professor & retired detective	Cambridge, MA
Honey West	Fickling, G. G.	'57 – 11	sexiest P. I. ever to pull a trigger	California

I

Series Character	Author	❶ – #	Occupation	Setting
Ike Tygart & Abby Abagnarro	Whitney, Polly	'94 – 3	network producer & TV news director	New York, NY
Imogen Quy	Walsh, Jill Paton	'93 – 2	school nurse at St. Agatha's College	Cambridge, England
Ingrid Langley & Patrick Gillard	Duffy, Margaret	'87 – 6	novelist/British agent & British army major	England
Irene Adler	Douglas, Carole N.	'90 – 4	19th century French sleuth	Paris, France
Irene Kelly	Burke, Jan	'93 – 4	newspaper reporter	southern California

I . . . J

Series Character	Author	❶ – #	Occupation	Setting

I . . . continued

Series Character	Author	❶ – #	Occupation	Setting
Iris Cooper	Beck, K. K.	'84 – 3	Roaring 20s co-ed at Stanford University	Palo Alto, CA
Iris Thorne	Pugh, Dianne G.	'93 – 2	investment counselor	Los Angeles, CA
Ivor Maddox, Sgt.	Linington, Elizabeth	'64 – 13	book-collecting mystery-addict cop	Hollywood, CA

J

Series Character	Author	❶ – #	Occupation	Setting
J. J. Jamison	Taylor, L. A.	'84 – 4	computer engineer & CATCH investigator	Minneapolis, MN
J. P. Beaumont	Jance, J. A.	'85 – 13	homicide detective	Seattle, WA
Jack Caleb, Dr. & John Thinnes	Dymmoch, Michael A.	'93 – 2	cop & psychiatrist	Chicago, IL
Jack Fleming	Elrod, P. N.	'90 – 6	reporter, ladies' man & vampire	Chicago, IL
Jack Prester	Dengler, Sandy	'93 – 4	U. S. park ranger	National Parks, USA
Jack Stryker & Kate Trevorne	Gosling, Paula	'85 – 3	homicide cop & English professor	Grantham, OH
Jackie Walsh & Jake	Cleary, Melissa	'92 – 8	college film instructor with her ex-police dog	Palmer, MA
Jacqueline Kirby	Peters, Elizabeth	'72 – 4	librarian turned romance novelist	New York, NY
Jake & Jackie Walsh	Cleary, Melissa	'92 – 8	college film instructor with her ex-police dog	Palmer, OH
Jake Samson & Rosie Vicente	Singer, Shelley	'83 – 5	ex-cop & carpenter tenant	Berkeley, CA
James Asher	Hambly, Barbara	'88 – 2	professor & one-time spy	London, England
James Boswell & Samuel Johnson, Dr.	de la Torre, Lillian	'46 – 4	biographer & 18th century lexicographer	London, England
James Fleming	Fallon, Ann C.	'90 – 5	solicitor	Dublin, Ireland
James McDougal & Lucy Ramsdale	Dolson, Hildegarde	'71 – 4	illustrator & homicide inspector	Wingate, CT
James Milton & Robert Amiss	Edwards, Ruth D.	'81 – 5	police superintendent & ex-civil servant	England
James Owens Mega, Dr.	McCrumb, Sharyn	'88 – 2	college professor & science fiction author	USA
Jane da Silva	Beck, K. K.	'92 – 4	former lounge singer	Seattle, WA
Jane Jeffry	Churchill, Jill	'89 – 7	suburban single mother	Chicago, IL
Jane Lawless	Hart, Ellen	'89 – 7	lesbian restaurateur	Minneapolis, MN
Jane Marple, Miss	Christie, Agatha	'30 – 12	elderly spinster	St. Mary's Mead, England
Jane McBride	Froetschel, Susan	'94 – 1	finance director	Sitka, AK
Jane Tennison	La Plante, Lynda	'93 – 3	detective chief inspector	London, England
Jane Winfield	Peterson, Audrey	'88 – 6	British journalist & music writer	London, England
Janet & Madoc Rhys	Craig, Alisa	'80 – 5	RCMP inspector & wife	Canada
Janice Cameron & Lily Wu	Sheridan, Juanita	'49 – 4	investigator & adopted sister	Hawaii
Jason Lynx	Orde, A. J.	'89 – 5	antiques dealer & interior decorator	Denver, CO
Jasper Tully & Mrs. Norris	Davis, Dorothy S.	'57 – 3	DA's investigator & Scottish housekeeper	New York, NY
Jay Goldstein & Carlos Cruz	Wallace, Marilyn	'86 – 3	homicide detectives	Oakland, CA
Jazz Jasper	McQuillan, Karin	'90 – 3	American safari guide	Kenya
Jean & Pat Abbot	Crane, Frances	'41 – 26	wife & husband detection team	World Travelers
Jeff Di Marco	Disney, Doris Miles	'46 – 8	insurance investigator	Boston, MA
Jefferson Birch	Lee, W. W. (Wendi)	'89 – 6	P. I. in the Old West	Western USA
Jeffries, Mrs. & Witherspoon, Insp.	Brightwell, Emily	'93 – 7	housekeeper & Victorian police inspector	London, England
Jemima Shore	Fraser, Antonia	'77 – 8	British TV interviewer	London, England
Jennifer & Rachel Murdock	Olsen, D. B.	'39 – 13	sister sleuths	Los Angeles, CA
Jenny Cain	Pickard, Nancy	'84 – 10	New England foundation director	Port Frederick, MA
Jeremy Faro	Knight, Alanna	'88 – 9	Victorian detective inspector	Edinburgh, Scotland
Jeremy Locke	Challis, Mary	'80 – 4	attorney	England
Jeri Howard	Dawson, Janet	'90 – 5	P. I.	Oakland, CA
Jerry & Pam North	Lockridge, F. & R.	'40 – 26	book publisher & wife	New York, NY
Jerry Zalman	Kraft, Gabrielle	'87 – 4	Beverly Hills deal maker	Los Angeles, CA

J

Series Character	Author	☐ – #	Occupation	Setting

J . . . continued

Series Character	Author	☐ – #	Occupation	Setting
Jesse Falkenstein	Egan, Lesley	'61 – 13	lawyer	Los Angeles, CA
Jessica James	O'Brien, Meg	'90 – 4	newspaper reporter	Rochester, NY
Jessica Randolph	Lucke, Margaret	'91 – 2	artist working as a P. I.	San Francisco, CA
Jessie Arnold & Alex Jensen	Henry, Sue	'91 – 3	sled dog racer & Alaska state trooper	Anchorage, AK
Jessie Drake	Krich, Rochelle Majer	'93 – 2	police detective	Los Angeles, CA
Jesus Creek, TN	Adams, Deborah	'92 – 5	eccentric small town	Jesus Creek, TN
Jill Smith	Dunlap, Susan	'81 – 9	homicide detective	Berkeley, CA
Jim O'Neill	Disney, Doris Miles	'43 – 5	small town policeman	Connecticut
Jim Qwilleran, Koko & Yum Yum	Braun, Lilian Jackson	'66 – 18	ex-police reporter & cats	Midwest USA
Jim Rush	Grant-Adamson, Lesley	'92 – 2	American on the run from British police	England
Jim Sader	Hitchens, Dolores	'57 – 2	P. I.	Long Beach, CA
Jo Hughes	Mather, Linda	'94 – 3	professional astrologer	USA
Joan, Sister	Black, Veronica	'90 – 8	British investigative nun	Cornwall, England
Joan Spencer	Frommer, Sara H.	'93 – 2	symphony orchestra manager	Oliver, IN
Joanna Brady	Jance, J. A.	'93 – 3	deputy sheriff's widow turned sheriff	Cochise County, AZ
Joanna MacKenzie	Duffy, Margaret	'94 – 2	former CID turned P. I.	Bath, England
Joanna Stark	Muller, Marcia	'86 – 3	international art investigator	Napa Valley, CA
Joanne Kilbourn	Bowen, Gail	'90 – 4	political science professor	Regina, Sask., Canada
Jocelyn O'Roarke	Dentinger, Jane	'83 – 6	Broadway actress & director	New York, NY
Joe Rodriguez, Sgt.	Dengler, Sandy	'93 – 4	police officer	Phoenix, AZ
Joe Silva	Oleksiw, Susan	'93 – 3	chief of police	Mellingham, MA
John Aloysius O'Malley & Vicky Holden	Coel, Margaret	'95 – 2	Jesuit missionary & Arapaho attorney	Wind River Reserv., WY
John Coffin, Insp.	Butler, Gwendoline	'57 – 24	police inspector	London, England
John J. Malone	Rice, Craig	'39 – 12	hard-drinking, cigar-smoking lawyer	Chicago, IL
John Lloyd Branson & Lydia Fairchild	Meredith, D. R.	'88 – 5	defense attorney & legal assistant	Canadian, TX
John McLeish & Francesca Wilson	Neel, Janet	'88 – 4	detective inspector & civil servant	England
John Morrissey	Mitchell, Kay	'90 – 5	Chief Inspector	Malminster, England
John Primrose, Col. & Grace Latham	Ford, Leslie	'34 – 16	career soldier & attractive widow	Washington DC
John Putnam Thatcher	Lathen, Emma	'61 – 22	Wall Street financial whiz	New York, NY
John Sanders & Harriet Jeffries	Sale, Medora	'86 – 6	police detective & architectural photographer	Toronto, Canada
John Thinnes & Jack Caleb, Dr.	Dymmoch, Michael A.	'93 – 2	cop & psychiatrist	Chicago, IL
Johnson Johnson	Dunnett, Dorothy	'68 – 7	portrait painter & British agent w/his yacht	International
Jolie Wyatt	Smith, Barbara B.	'94 – 3	aspiring novelist & writer's group member	Purple Sage, TX
Josie Pigeon	Wolzien, Valerie	'96 – 1	owner of an all-women construction firm	Northeast USA
Judith Hayes	Porter, Anna	'85 – 2	journalist	Toronto, Ont., Canada
Judith McMonigle	Daheim, Mary	'91 – 9	bed & breakfast owner	Seattle, WA
Judy Hill & Chief Inspector Lloyd	McGown, Jill	'83 – 7	detective inspectors	East Anglia, England
Jules Clement	Harrison, Jamie	'95 – 1	30-something archaeologist turned sheriff	Blue Deer, MT
Julia Probyn Jamieson	Bridge, Ann	'56 – 7	freelance journalist & part-time agent	England
Julian Baugh & Galen Shaw	Blackmur, L. L.	'89 – 2	writer & financier	New England
Julian Kestrel	Ross, Kate	'93 – 3	1820s dandy-about-town	London, England
Julie Hayes	Davis, Dorothy S.	'76 – 4	former actress & columnist	New York, NY
Juliet Blake	Chapman, Sally	'91 – 3	Silicon Valley fraud investigator	Silicon Valley, CA

K

Series Character	Author	'❚ – #	Occupation	Setting

K

Series Character	Author	'❚ – #	Occupation	Setting
Kali O'Brien	Jacobs, Jonnie	'96 – 1	attorney	Gold Country, CA
Karen Hightower	Edghill, Rosemary	'94 – 2	Manhattan graphic designer & white witch	New York, NY
Karen Levinson	O'Connell, Catherine	'93 – 1	NYPD homicide detective	New York, NY
Kat Colorado	Kijewski, Karen	'88 – 6	P. I.	Sacramento, CA
Kate & Ray Frederick	Schenkel, S. E.	'94 – 2	chief of detectives & wife of 30 yrs	Michigan
Kate Austen	Jacobs, Jonnie	'94 – 2	Bay area single mother	Walnut Hills, CA
Kate Baeier	Slovo, Gillian	'84 – 5	freelance journalist turned detective	London, England
Kate Brannigan	McDermid, Val	'92 – 5	P. I.	Manchester, England
Kate Delafield	Forrest, Katherine V.	'84 – 4	LAPD lesbian homicide detective	Los Angeles, CA
Kate Driscoll	Walker, Mary Willis	'91 – 1	dog trainer	Texas
Kate Fansler	Cross, Amanda	'64 – 11	university English professor	New York, NY
Kate Henry	Gordon, Alison	'89 – 4	baseball newswriter	Toronto, Canada
Kate Ivory	Stallwood, Veronica	'93 – 3	novelist	Oxford, England
Kate Jasper	Girdner, Jaqueline	'91 – 7	gag gift wholesaler	Marin County, CA
Kate Kincaid Mulcay	Sibley, Celestine	'58 – 5	veteran newspaperwoman	Atlanta, GA
Kate Kinsella	Green, Christine	'91 – 3	British nurse & medical investigator	England
Kate Maddox	Quest, Erica	'88 – 3	Det. Chief Inspector	Cotswolds, England
Kate Martinelli & Alonzo Hawkin	King, Laurie R.	'93 – 3	SFPD homicide detectives	San Francisco, CA
Kate McLean	Gilpatrick, Noreen	'93 – 2	police detective	Seattle, WA
Kate Murray	Tyre, Peg	'94 – 2	newspaper reporter for Daily Herald	Brooklyn, NY
Kate Shugak	Stabenow, Dana	'92 – 6	native Alaskan ex-D.A. investigator	Alaska
Kate Teague & Roger Tejeda	Hornsby, Wendy	'87 – 2	college professor & homicide detective	southern, CA
Kate Trevorne & Jack Stryker	Gosling, Paula	'85 – 3	homicide cop & English professor	Grantham, OH
Kate Weston & Alex Sinclair	Hall, Patricia	'93 – 1	social worker & British inspector	England
Katharine Craig & Kevin Bryce	Valentine, Deborah	'89 – 3	sculptor & ex-sheriff's detective	northern California
Katherine Prescott Milholland	Hartzmark, Gini	'92 – 3	corporate attorney	Chicago, IL
Kathleen Mallory	O'Connell, Carol	'94 – 3	NYPD cop	New York, NY
Kathryn Ardleigh	Paige, Robin	'94 – 2	25-yr-old American author	Dedham, England
Kathryn Mackay	McGuire, Christine	'93 – 2	prosecuting attorney	northern, CA
Kay Barth	Schier, Norma	'78 – 4	district attorney	Colorado
Kay Engles	Stein, Triss	'93 – 1	nationally-known reporter	USA
Kay Scarpetta, Dr.	Cornwell, Patricia	'90 – 6	chief medical examiner	Richmond, VA
Kelsey, Insp.	Page, Emma	'80 – 8	police inspector	England
Kendra MacFarlane	Porath, Sharon	'95 – 1	amateur sleuth	USA
Kenneth Carlisle	Wells, Carolyn	'29 – 3	actor turned detective	New York, NY
Kevin Blake, Dr.	Douglas, Carole N.	'85 – 2	psychiatrist	Minnesota
Kevin Bryce & Katharine Craig	Valentine, Deborah	'89 – 3	sculptor & ex-sheriff's detective	northern California
Kiernan O'Shaughnessy	Dunlap, Susan	'89 – 3	former San Francisco medical examiner turned P. I.	La Jolla, CA
Kimmey Kruse	Cooper, Susan R.	'93 – 2	stand-up comic	Austin, TX
Kinsey Millhone	Grafton, Sue	'82 – 12	ex-cop P. I.	Santa Teresa, CA
Kit Powell	Robitaille, Julie	'92 – 2	TV sports reporter	San Diego, CA
Knute Severson	Wells, Tobias	'66 – 16	police officer	Boston, MA
Koko, Yum Yum & Jim Qwilleran	Braun, Lilian Jackson	'66 – 18	ex-police reporter & cats	Midwest USA
Kori Price Brichter & Peter Brichter	Pulver, Mary Monica	'87 – 5	police detective & horse breeder	Illinois
Kristin Ashe	Jordan, Jennifer	'92 – 2	amateur sleuth	Woodfield, England
Kyra Keaton	Tone, Teona	'83 – 2	P. I. at the turn-of-the-century	Washington, DC

L

Series Character	Author	❶ – #	Occupation	Setting
Lance O'Leary & Sarah Keate	Eberhart, Mignon G.	'29 – 7	nurse & wealthy police detective	New York, NY
Lane Montana & Trey Fortier	Hooper, Kay	'91 – 2	finder of lost things & homicide detective	Atlanta, GA
Laney Samms	Schmidt, Carol	'93 – 3	lesbian bar owner	Los Angeles, CA
Lark Dailey	Simonson, Sheila	'90 – 4	6-ft. bookdealer	northern, CA
Laura Ackroyd & Michael Thackeray	Hall, Patricia	'94 – 3	reporter & police inspector	Yorkshire, England
Laura Di Palma	Matera, Lia	'88 – 5	attorney	San Francisco, CA
Laura Fleming	Kelner, Toni L. P.	'93 – 3	small-town detective	Byerly, NC
Laura Flynn	Grant-Adamson, Lesley	'91 – 2	P. I.	London, England
Laura Ireland	Mariz, Linda French	'92 – 2	grad student volleyball player	Seattle, WA
Laura Malloy	Logue, Mary	'93 – 1	journalist	Minneapolis, MN
Laura Principal	Spring, Michelle	'94 – 2	British academic turned P. I.	England
Lauren Laurano	Scoppettone, Sandra	'91 – 3	Greenwich Village lesbian P. I.	New York, NY
Lauren Maxwell	Quinn, Elizabeth	'93 – 3	wildlife investigator PhD	Alaska
Lavinia Grey, Mother	Gallison, Kate	'95 – 2	Episcopal vicar & practicing therapist	Fishersville, NJ
Leah Hunter	Lacey, Sarah	'92 – 4	tax inspector	Yorkshire, England
Lee Ofsted & Graham Sheldon	Elkins, Charlotte & Aaron	'89 – 2	golf pro & homicide detective	Washington
Lee Squires	Andreae, Christine	'92 – 2	English professor & poet	Montana
Leigh Ann Warren	West, Chassie	'94 – 1	former DC street cop	Sunrise, NC
Lena Padget	Hightower, Lynn S.	'93 – 1	P. I.	Lexington, KY
Lennox Kemp	Meek, M. R. D.	'83 – 10	solicitor detective	London, England
Leonidas Witherall	Tilton, Alice	'37 – 8	retired academic & secret pulp fiction author	Boston, MA
Leslie Wetzon & Xenia Smith	Meyers, Annette	'89 – 7	Wall Street headhunters	New York, NY
Libby Kincaid	Tucker, Kerry	'91 – 4	magazine photographer	New York, NY
Lil Ritchie	Knight, Phyllis	'92 – 3	ex-rocker & gay woman P. I.	coastal Maine
Lily Wu & Janice Cameron	Sheridan, Juanita	'49 – 4	investigator & adopted sister	Hawaii
Lindsay Gordon	McDermid, Val	'87 – 4	lesbian journalist & socialist	Glasgow, Scotland
Lisa Davis	Waltch, Lilla M.	'87 – 2	newspaper reporter	Braeton, MA
Liz Broward, Dr. & Zack James	Zachary, Fay	'94 – 2	family physician & computer artist/genealogist	Phoenix, AZ
Liz Connors	Kelly, Susan	'85 – 6	freelance crime writer	Cambridge, MA
Liz Graham, F. Shapiro & C. Donovan	Bannister, Jo	'93 – 4	cops	Castlemere, England
Liz Sullivan	Roberts, Lora	'94 – 3	freelance writer	Palo Alto, CA
Liz Wareham	Brennan, Carol	'91 – 2	Manhattan public relations consultant	New York, NY
Lloyd, Chief Inspector & Judy Hill	McGown, Jill	'83 – 7	detective inspectors	East Anglia, England
Lonia Gulu	Oliver, Maria Antonia	'87 – 2	Catalan P. I.	Spain
Loretta Lawson	Smith, Joan	'87 – 5	British feminist professor	London, England
Louise Eldridge	Ripley, Ann	'94 – 2	organic gardener	Washington DC
Lucia Ramos	Morell, Mary	'91 – 2	lesbian police detective	San Antonio, TX
Lucy Kingsley & David Middleton-Brown	Charles, Kate	'91 – 5	artist & solicitor	London, England
Lucy Ramsdale & James McDougal	Dolson, Hildegarde	'71 – 4	illustrator & homicide inspector	Wingate, CT
Lucy Stone	Meier, Leslie	'93 – 2	small-town sleuth	Maine
Luis Mendoza	Shannon, Dell	'60 – 37	wealthy homicide lieutenant	Los Angeles, CA
Luke Abbott	Gosling, Paula	'86 – 2	English cop	England
Luke Thanet	Simpson, Dorothy	'81 – 13	British police inspector	England
Lydia Chin & Bill Smith	Rozan, S. J.	'94 – 2	Chinese American & Army brat P. I.s	New York, NY
Lydia Fairchild & John Lloyd Branson	Meredith, D. R.	'88 – 5	legal assistant & defense attorney	Canadian, TX
Lydia Miller	Hyde, Eleanor	'95 – 2	30-something fashion editor	New York, NY

M

Series Character	Author	❶ – #	Occupation	Setting
M				
MacDougal Duff	Armstrong, Charlotte	'42 – 3	retired history professor	New York, NY
Mackenzie Smith & Annabel Reed	Truman, Margaret	'89 – 5	law professor & gallery owner	Washington, DC
Madoc & Janet Rhys	Craig, Alisa	'80 – 5	RCMP inspector & wife	Canada
Magdalena Yoder	Myers, Tamar	'94 – 3	Mennonite inn owner & operator	Hernia, PA
Maggie Elliott	Taylor, Elizabeth A.	'81 – 3	ex-film maker turned P. I.	San Francisco, CA
Maggie Garrett	Taylor, Jean	'95 – 2	young lesbian P. I.	San Francisco, CA
Maggie Hill & Claire Conrad	Howe, Melodie J.	'89 – 2	secretary & P. I.	southern California
Maggie MacGowen	Hornsby, Wendy	'92 – 4	investigative filmmaker	California
Maggie Rome & C. B. Greenfield	Kallen, Lucille	'79 – 5	reporter & editor/publisher	Connecticut
Maggie Ryan	Carlson, P. M.	'85 – 8	college student turned statistician & mother	New York, NY
Marcus Didius Falco	Davis, Lindsey	'89 – 8	P. I. in ancient Rome	Rome, Italy
Marcus MacLurg	Petrie, Rhona	'63 – 5	Inspector	England
Margaret Priam, Lady	Christmas, Joyce	'88 – 7	English noblewoman	New York, NY
Margo Fortier	Fennelly, Tony	'94 – 2	ex-stripper turned columnist	New Orleans, LA
Margo Simon	Steinberg, Janice	'95 – 2	California Public Radio reporter	San Diego, CA
Margot Blair	Knight, Kathleen M.	'40 – 4	partner in a PR agency	New York, NY
Marguerite Smith	Lee, Marie	'95 – 1	retired science teacher	Cape Cod, MA
Marian Larch	Paul, Barbara	'84 – 6	NYPD officer	New York, NY
Marian Winchester	Romberg, Nina	'89 – 2	Caddo-Commanche medicine woman	Texas
Mark East, Bessie Petty & Beulah Pond	Lawrence, Hilda	'44 – 3	New York city P. I. & New England little old ladies	Northeast USA
Mark Shigata	Wingate, Anne	'88 – 5	ex-FBI agent turned sheriff	Bayport, TX
Marla Masterson	Dunant, Sarah	'88 – 1	young British professor of literature	USA
Martha "Moz" Brant	Femling, Jean	'89 – 2	insurance claims investigator	southern, CA
Marti MacAlister	Bland, Eleanor Taylor	'92 – 4	black police detective	Lincoln Prairie, IL
Martin Beck	Sjöwall, M. & P. Wahlöö	'67 – 10	police officer	Stockholm, Sweden
Martin Buell, Rev.	Scherf, Margaret	'48 – 6	Episcopal rector	Farrington, MT
Martin Karl Alberg	Wright, L. R.	'85 – 7	RCMP staff sergeant	Vancouver, BC, Canada
Martine "Marty" LaForte Hopkins	Carlson, P. M.	'92 – 2	deputy sheriff & mother	southern Indiana
Mary Carner	Popkin, Zelda	'38 – 5	former department store detective	New York, NY
Mary DiNunzio	Scottoline, Lisa	'93 – 1	attorney	Philadelphia, PA
Mary Helen, Sister	O'Marie, Carol A., Sister	'84 – 6	70-something nun	San Francisco, CA
Mary Minor Haristeen	Brown, Rita Mae	'90 – 4	small-town postmistress & cat	Crozet, VA
Mary Russell	King, Laurie R.	'94 – 2	teenage student of Sherlock Holmes	London, England
Matt Devlin & Brooke Cassidy	Kruger, Mary	'94 – 2	P. I. & mystery writer	Newport, RI
Matthew Arthur Sinclair	Fennelly, Tony	'85 – 3	gay ex-D.A. turned P. I.	New Orleans, LA
Maud Silver, Miss	Wentworth, Patricia	'28 – 32	retired governess & spinster P. I.	London, England
Max Bittersohn & Sarah Kelling	MacLeod, Charlotte	'79 – 11	investigative couple	Boston, MA
Max Darling & Annie Laurance	Hart, Carolyn G.	'87 – 9	investigator & bookstore owner	South Carolina
Maxene St. Clair, Dr.	McGiffin, Janet	'92 – 3	emergency room physician	Milwaukee, WI
Maxey Burnell	Cail, Carol	'93 – 2	investigative reporter	Colorado
Meg & Sarah Quilliam	Bishop, Claudia	'94 – 4	chef & inn owner (sisters)	Hemlock Falls, NY
Meg Halloran & Vince Gutierrez	La Pierre, Janet	'87 – 5	police chief & school teacher	Port Silva, CA
Meg Lacey	Bowers, Elisabeth	'88 – 2	P. I.	Vancouver, B.C., Canada
Megan Baldwin	Clark, Carolyn C.	'93 – 1	registered nurse	St. Petersburg, FL
Melanie Travis	Berenson, Laurien	'95 – 3	special ed teacher posing as poodle breeder	Connecticut

M . . . N

Series Character	Author	❶ – #	Occupation	Setting

M . . . *continued*

Series Character	Author	❶ – #	Occupation	Setting
Melinda Pink	Moffat, Gwen	'73 – 14	writer & mountain climber	Utah
Melissa Craig	Rowlands, Betty	'89 – 7	British mystery writer	Cotswolds, England
Melville Fairr	Venning, Michael	'42 – 3	lawyer	New York, NY
Meredith "Merry" Folger	Mathews, Francine	'94 – 2	police detective	Nantucket, MA
Meredith Mitchell & Alan Markby, Insp.	Granger, Ann	'91 – 9	Foreign Service officer & detective inspector	Cotswolds, England
Merlin Capricorn	Winslow, Pauline G.	'75 – 6	magician turned police superintendent	England
Merrie Lee Spencer	Jackson, Muriel R.	'92 – 1	Manhattan transplant	North Carolina
Meren, Lord	Robinson, Lynda S.	'94 – 3	chief investigator for Pharaoh Tutankhamen	Egypt
Merton Heimrich, Insp.	Lockridge, F. & R.	'47 – 24	State Police Bureau of Criminal Investigation	New York
Michael Ohayon	Gur, Batya	'88 – 3	chief inspector	Jerusalem, Israel
Michael Spraggue III	Barnes, Linda	'82 – 4	wealthy actor & ex-P. I.	Boston, MA
Michael Thackeray & Laura Ackroyd	Hall, Patricia	'94 – 3	police inspector & reporter	Yorkshire, England
Michelle "Micky" Knight	Redmann, J. M.	'90 – 3	lesbian P. I.	New Orleans, LA
Mici Anhalt	O'Donnell, Lillian	'77 – 3	criminal justice investigator	New York, NY
Midge Cohen	Brill, Toni	'91 – 2	children's author fluent in Russian	New York, NY
Midnight Louie & Temple Barr	Douglas, Carole N.	'92 – 5	tomcat sleuth & public relations freelancer	Las Vegas, NV
Mike McCleary & Quin St. James	MacGregor, T. J.	'86 – 10	husband & wife P. I. team	Florida
Mike Yeadings	Curzon, Clare	'83 – 10	det. superintendent of Serious Crime Squad	Thames Valley, England
Mildred Bennett & friends	McShea, Susanna H.	'90 – 3	a quartet of senior sleuths	Raven's Wing, CT
Millie Ogden & Natasha O'Brien	Lyons, Nan & Ivan	'76 – 2	pair of culinary artists	USA
Milton Kovak	Cooper, Susan R.	'88 – 6	chief deputy	Prophesy County, OK
Mimi Patterson & Gianna Maglione	Mickelbury, Penny	'94 – 2	lesbian police lieutenant & reporter	Washington, DC
Mirinda & Clare Clively	Crowleigh, Ann	'93 – 2	Victorian London twin sisters	London, England
Mitch Bushyhead	Hager, Jean	'89 – 4	police chief of Cherokee descent	Buckskin, OK
Mollie Cates	Walker, Mary Willis	'94 – 2	true crime writer & reporter	Texas
Molly & George Palmer-Jones	Cleeves, Ann	'86 – 8	wife & ex-Home Office bird-watcher	Surrey, England
Molly Bearpaw	Hager, Jean	'92 – 3	Cherokee civil rights investigator	Tahlequah, OK
Molly DeWitt	Woods, Sherryl	'91 – 5	film office public relations staffer	Miami, FL
Molly Rafferty	Belfort, Sophie	'86 – 3	college history professor	Boston, MA
Morgana Dalton	Buckstaff, Kathryn	'94 – 1	Florida-based travel writer	Florida
Moss Magill	Gardiner, Dorothy	'56 – 3	sheriff	Notlaw, CO

N

Series Character	Author	❶ – #	Occupation	Setting
Nan Robinson	Cannon, Taffy	'93 – 3	investigator for the California State Bar	Los Angeles, CA
Nancy Clue	Maney, Mabel	'93 – 3	gay-lesbian parody of Nancy Drew	River Depths, IL
Natalie Gold	Jaffe, Jody	'95 – 2	newspaper reporter on horse show circuit	Charlotte, NC
Natasha O'Brien & Millie Ogden	Lyons, Nan & Ivan	'76 – 2	pair of culinary artists	USA
Neal Rafferty	Wiltz, Chris	'81 – 3	third generation cop turned P. I.	New Orleans, LA
Neil Hamel	Van Gieson, Judith	'88 – 6	attorney & investigator	Albuquerque, NM
Nell Bray	Linscott, Gillian	'91 – 5	British suffragette	England
Nell Fury	Pincus, Elizabeth	'92 – 3	lesbian P. I.	San Francisco, CA
Nick Magaracz	Gallison, Kate	'86 – 3	P. I.	Trenton, NJ
Nick Trevellyan & Alison Hope	Kelly, Susan B.	'90 – 5	detective inspector & software designer	Hop Valley, England
Nicky & Sam Titus	Sandstrom, Eve K.	'90 – 3	photojournalist wife & ex-army CID sheriff	Holton, OK
Nikki Holden & Roman Cantrell	Chase, Elaine Raco	'87 – 2	reporter & P. I.	Florida
Nikki Trakos	Horansky, Ruby	'90 – 2	homicide detective	New York, NY
Nina Fischman	Piesman, Marissa	'89 – 5	legal services attorney	New York, NY

N...O...P

Series Character	Author	🏁 – #	Occupation	Setting
N ... *continued*				
Nina McFall & Dino Rossi, Lt.	Fulton, Eileen	'88 – 6	glamorous TV soap star & NYPD cop	New York, NY
Nora James	McFall, Patricia	'92 – 1	American linguistics graduate student	Japan
Norah Mulcahaney	O'Donnell, Lillian	'72 – 15	NYPD detective	New York, NY
Norm Bennis & Suze Figueroa	D'Amato, Barbara	'96 – 1	pair of cops	Chicago, IL
Norris, Mrs. & Jasper Tully	Davis, Dorothy S.	'57 – 3	Scottish housekeeper & DA's investigator	New York, NY
Nyla Wade	McConnell, Vickie P.	'82 – 3	lesbian journalist	Denver, CO
O				
Oliver Jardino & Theresa Fortunato	Green, Kate	'86 – 2	LAPD detective & professional psychic	Los Angeles, CA
Olivia Chapman	Logan, Margaret	'94 – 2	interior decorator	Boston, MA
Osbert Monk & Dittany Henbit Monk	Craig, Alisa	'81 – 5	author of westerns & garden club member	Lobelia Falls, Ont., Canada
Owen Archer	Robb, Candace M.	'93 – 3	medieval Welsh spy for the archbishop	England
P				
Paige Taylor	Kreuter, Katherine E.	'94 – 1	mystery writer & P. I.	USA
Pam & Jerry North	Lockridge, F. & R.	'40 – 26	wife & book publisher husband	New York, NY
Pam Nilsen	Wilson, Barbara	'84 – 3	lesbian printing company owner	Seattle, WA
Paris Chandler	Shah, Diane K.	'90 – 2	'40s P. I.	Hollywood, CA
Pat & Jean Abbot	Crane, Frances	'41 – 26	husband & wife detection team	World Travelers
Patience Campbell McKenna	Papazoglou, Orania	'84 – 5	6-ft romance novelist turned crime writer	New York, NY
Patricia Delaney	Short, Sharon Gwyn	'94 – 3	computer whiz P. I.	Cincinnati, OH
Patrick Gillard & Ingrid Langley	Duffy, Margaret	'87 – 6	British army major & novelist/British agent	England
Patrick Grant, Dr.	Yorke, Margaret	'70 – 5	Oxford don teaching English literature	Oxford, England
Paul Kilgerrin	Leonard, Charles L.	'42 – 11	P. I. spy	Washington, DC
Paul MacDonald	Smith, Julie	'85 – 2	ex-reporter & mystery writer	San Francisco, CA
Paul Prye, Dr.	Millar, Margaret	'41 – 3	psychiatrist	Toronto, Canada
Paula Glenning	Clarke, Anna	'85 – 8	British professor & writer	London, England
Peaches Dann	Squire, Elizabeth D.	'94 – 3	absent-minded 50-something widow	North Carolina
Peg Goodenough	Bennett, Liza	'89 – 2	ad agency creative director	New York, NY
Pennington Wise	Wells, Carolyn	'18 – 8	private detective	New York, NY
Penny Spring & Toby Glendower, Sir	Arnold, Margot	'79 – 12	Amer anthropologist & Brit archlgst	World Travelers
Penny Wanawake	Moody, Susan	'84 – 7	photographer daughter of black diplomat	England
Persis Willum	Watson, Clarissa	'77 – 5	New York art curator	Long Island, NY
Peter & Kori Price Brichter	Pulver, Mary Monica	'87 – 5	police detective & horse breeder	Illinois
Peter Bartholomew	Gunning, Sally	'90 – 6	small business owner	Cape Cod, MA
Peter Decker & Rina Lazarus	Kellerman, Faye	'86 – 8	LAPD detective & wife	Los Angeles, CA
Peter Shandy & Helen Marsh Shandy	MacLeod, Charlotte	'78 – 9	botany professor & librarian wife	Balaclava Co., MA
Peter Wimsey, Lord	Sayers, Dorothy L.	'23 – 13	pianist, bibliophile & criminologist	London, England
Phoebe Fairfax	North, Suzanne	'94 – 1	TV video photographer	Calgary, Canada
Phoebe Siegel	Prowell, Sandra West	'93 – 3	ex-cop P. I.	Billings, MT
Phryne Fisher	Greenwood, Kerry	'89 – 8	'20s sleuth	Melbourne, Australia
Poppy Dillworth	Tell, Dorothy	'90 – 3	60-something lesbian sleuth	Texas

Q . . . R . . . S

Series Character	Author	🄳 – #	Occupation	Setting
Q				
Queenie Davilow	Osborne, Denise	'94 – 2	Hollywood screenwriter	Hollywood, CA
Quentin Jacoby	Smith, J. C. S.	'80 – 2	P. I.	New York, NY
Quin St. James & Mike McCleary	MacGregor, T. J.	'86 – 10	wife & husband P. I. team	Florida
Quint McCauley	Brod, D. C.	'89 – 4	ex-cop turned P. I.	Chicago suburb, IL
R				
Rachel & Jennifer Murdock	Olsen, D. B.	'39 – 13	sister sleuths	Los Angeles, CA
Rain Morgan	Grant-Adamson, Lesley	'85 – 5	newspaper reporter	London, England
Ray & Kate Frederick	Schenkel, S. E.	'94 – 2	chief of detectives & wife of 30 yrs	Michigan
Rebecca Schwartz	Smith, Julie	'82 – 5	defense attorney	San Francisco, CA
Regan Reilly	Clark, Carol Higgins	'92 – 3	P. I.	Los Angeles, CA
Reginald Wexford	Rendell, Ruth	'64 – 16	chief inspector	Sussex, England
Richard Jury, Insp.	Grimes, Martha	'81 – 13	Scotland Yard investigator	London, England
Richard Montgomery	Shepherd, Stella	'89 – 6	CID Inspector	Nottingham, England
Richard Trenton	Burton, Anne	'80 – 3	banker	England
Rick Vanner	Heberden, M. V.	'46 – 3	former Naval Intelligence officer	New York, NY
Rina Lazarus & Peter Decker	Kellerman, Faye	'86 – 8	wife & LAPD detective	Los Angeles, CA
Rita Morrone Hamilton	Scottoline, Lisa	'95 – 1	attorney	Philadelphia, PA
Robert Amiss & James Milton	Edwards, Ruth D.	'81 – 5	ex-civil servant & police superintendent	England
Robert Bone	Stacey, Susannah	'87 – 7	widowed British police inspector	England
Robert Carey, Sir	Chisholm, P. F.	'95 – 3	Elizabethan nobleman (1592)	England
Robert Forsythe & Abigail Sanderson	Giroux, E. X.	'84 – 10	barrister & secretary	London, England
Robin Hudson	Hayter, Sparkle	'94 – 2	cable news reporter	New York, NY
Robin Light	Block, Barbara	'94 – 2	pet store owner	Syracuse, NY
Robin Miller	Maiman, Jaye	'91 – 4	lesbian travel & romance writer turned P. I.	New York, NY
Robin Vaughn	Banks, Carolyn	'93 – 3	equestrienne sleuth	Texas
Roderick Alleyn	Marsh, Ngaio	'34 – 32	inspector son of a baronet	London, England
Roger Tejeda & Kate Teague	Hornsby, Wendy	'87 – 2	homicide detective & college professor	southern California
Roger the Chapman	Sedley, Kate	'91 – 6	medieval chapman (peddler)	England
Roman Cantrell & Nikki Holden	Chase, Elaine Raco	'87 – 2	P. I. & reporter	Florida
Rosie Vicente & Jake Samson	Singer, Shelley	'83 – 5	carpenter tenant & ex-cop	Berkeley, CA
Ross McIntyre	Flora, Kate Clark	'95 – 1	small town high school biology teacher	Maine
Roz Howard & Alan Stewart	Kenney, Susan	'83 – 3	American professor & British painter	Maine
Ryan, Lt.	Scherf, Margaret	'45 – 2	NYPD cop	New York, NY
S				
Sabina Swift	Sucher, Dorothy	'88 – 2	Georgetown detective agency owner	Washington, DC
Salvatore Guarnaccia	Nabb, Magdalen	'81 – 10	Italian police marshal	Florence, Italy
Sam & Nicky Titus	Sandstrom, Eve K.	'90 – 3	ex-army CID sheriff & photojournalist wife	Holton, OK
Samantha Adams	Shankman, Sarah	'88 – 6	investigative reporter	Atlanta, GA
Samantha Holt	Wilson, Karen Ann	'94 – 2	vet's assistant	Paradise Cay, FL
Samantha "Smokey" Brandon	Ayres, Noreen	'92 – 3	sheriff's forensic expert	Orange County, CA
Samantha Turner, Dr.	Landreth, Marsha	'92 – 3	medical examiner	Sheridan, WY
Samuel Johnson, Dr. & James Boswell	de la Torre, Lillian	'46 – 4	18th century lexicographer & biographer	London, England
Sands, Insp.	Millar, Margaret	'43 – 2	police inspector	Toronto, Canada
Sarah & Meg Quilliam	Bishop, Claudia	'94 – 4	inn owner & chef (sisters)	Hemlock Falls, NY

S

Series Character	Author	❶ – #	Occupation	Setting

S . . . continued

Series Character	Author	❶ – #	Occupation	Setting
Sarah Calloway	Warmbold, Jean	'86 – 3	newspaper reporter	San Francisco, CA
Sarah Deane & Alex McKenzie, Dr.	Borthwick, J. S.	'82 – 7	English professor & internist	Boston, MA
Sarah Drexler	Wilhelm, Kate	'93 – 1	judge	Oregon
Sarah Fortune	Fyfield, Frances	'89 – 2	lawyer in prestigious British firm	England
Sarah Keate & Lance O'Leary	Eberhart, Mignon G.	'29 – 7	nurse & wealthy police detective	New York, NY
Sarah Kelling & Max Bittersohn	MacLeod, Charlotte	'79 – 11	investigative couple	Boston, MA
Sarah Nelson	Wolfe, Susan	'89 – 1	police inspector	Silicon Valley, CA
Savannah Reid	McKevett, G. A.	'95 – 2	ex-cop & owner of a new detective agency	southern California
Schuyler Ridgway	McClellan, Tierney	'95 – 3	40-something real estate agent	Louisville, KY
Scott Egerton	Gilbert, Anthony	'27 – 9	Liberal M.P. & man about town	England
Selena Mead	McGerr, Patricia	'64 – 2	British government agent	England
Septimus Finch	Erskine, Margaret	'38 – 21	Scotland Yard Inspector	England
Sharon Dair	Vlasopolos, Anca	'90 – 1	sex crimes police detective	Detroit, MI
Sharon McCone	Muller, Marcia	'77 – 17	legal co-op investigator turned P. I.	San Francisco, CA
Sheila Malory	Holt, Hazel	'89 – 7	British literary magazine writer	Devon, England
Sheila Travis	Sprinkle, Patricia H.	'88 – 7	admin asst turned PR executive	Atlanta, GA
Shirley McClintock	Oliphant, B. J.	'90 – 6	50-something rancher	Colorado
Simeon, Father & Elvira	Highsmith, Domini	'95 – 1	medieval priest & nurse	E. Yorkshire, England
Sigismondo	Eyre, Elizabeth	'92 – 5	agent of a Renaissance duke	Italy
Sigrid Harald	Maron, Margaret	'81 – 8	police lieutenant	New York, NY
Simon Drake	Nielsen, Helen	'51 – 6	attorney transplanted from Chicago	southern, CA
Simona Griffo	Crespi, Camilla	'91 – 6	advertising executive & gourmet cook	New York, NY
Sixto Cardenas & Balthazar Marten	Adamson, M. J.	'87 – 5	Puerto Rican cop & NYPD homicide det.	Puerto Rico
Skip Langdon	Smith, Julie	'90 – 5	6-ft. police detective	New Orleans, LA
Sonora Blair	Hightower, Lynn S.	'95 – 1	homicide detective	Cincinnati, OH
Sophie Greenway	Hart, Ellen	'94 – 3	magazine editor & food critic for newspaper	Minneapolis, MN
Spaceman Kowalski & Blue Maguire	White, Teri	'84 – 2	cop pair with prickly partnership	Los Angeles, CA
Spencer Arrowood	McCrumb, Sharyn	'90 – 4	Appalachian sheriff	Tennessee
Stella the Stargazer	Jorgensen, Christine	'94 – 3	astrologer & lovelorn columnist	Denver, CO
Stephanie Plum	Evanovich, Janet	'94 – 2	neophyte bounty hunter	Trenton, NJ
Stephen Marryat	Leek, Margaret	'80 – 3	attorney	England
Stephen Mayhew, Lt.	Olsen, D. B.	'40 – 2	police detective	Los Angeles, CA
Stephen Ramsey	Cleeves, Ann	'90 – 4	British inspector	England
Steven Mitchell	Bell, Josephine	'38 – 1	Scotland Yard Inspector	London, England
Stone, Sgt. & D. S. Trewley	Mason, Sarah Jill	'93 – 4	village detective partners	Allshire, England
Stoner McTavish	Dreher, Sarah	'85 – 6	lesbian travel agent	Boston, MA
String & David Silver	Hightower, Lynn S.	'92 – 4	alien partner & homicide cop	USA
Susan Henshaw	Wolzien, Valerie	'87 – 10	suburban housewife	Connecticut
Susan Melville	Smith, Evelyn E.	'86 – 5	freelance assassin & painter	New York, NY
Susan Wren	Weir, Charlene	'92 – 3	ex-cop turned police chief	Kansas
Suze Figueroa & Norm Bennis	D'Amato, Barbara	'96 – 1	pair of cops	Chicago, IL
Syd Fish	Geason, Susan	'93 – 3	P. I.	Sydney, Australia
Sydney Bryant	Wallace, Patricia	'88 – 4	P. I.	San Diego, CA
Sydney Sloane	Lorden, Randye	'93 – 2	upper west side P. I.	New York, NY
Sylvia Strange, Dr.	Lovett, Sarah	'95 – 2	forensic psychologist	Sante Fe, NM

T . . . U . . . V

Series Character	Author	❶ – #	Occupation	Setting
T				
Tamara Hayle	Wesley, Valerie W.	'94 – 2	black ex-cop P. I. & single mother	Newark, NJ
Tamara Hoyland	Mann, Jessica	'82 – 6	British secret agent archaeologist	England
Teal Stewart	Lamb, J. Dayne	'93 – 3	Certified Public Accountant	Boston, MA
Temple Barr & Midnight Louie	Douglas, Carole N.	'92 – 5	public relations freelancer & tomcat sleuth	Las Vegas, NV
Terry Girard	Kunz, Kathleen	'93 – 2	genealogist for hire	St. Louis, MO
Tess Darcy	Hager, Jean	'94 – 3	Ozarks bed & breakfast owner	Victoria Springs, MO
Tessa Crichton	Morice, Anne	'70 – 23	English actress sleuth	England
Thea Crawford	Mann, Jessica	'72 – 2	archaeology professor	England
Thea Kozak	Flora, Kate Clark	'94 – 2	educational consultant	Massachusetts
Theodora Braithwaite, Rev.	Greenwood, Diane M.	'91 – 6	British deaconess	England
Theodore S. Hubbert & Auntie Lil	Gray, Gallagher	'91 – 3	retired personnel manager & dress designer	New York, NY
Theresa Fortunato & Oliver Jardino	Green, Kate	'86 – 2	professional psychic & LAPD detective	Los Angeles, CA
Theresa Franco	Clark, Carolyn C.	'94 – 1	P. I.	Florida
Theresa Tracy Baldwin	OCork, Shannon	'80 – 3	sports photographer for New York daily	New York, NY
Thomas & Charlotte Pitt	Perry, Anne	'79 – 16	Victorian police inspector & wife	London, England
Thomas Lynley & Barbara Havers	George, Elizabeth	'88 – 8	Scotland Yard inspector & detective sergeant	London, England
Timothy Herring	Torrie, Malcolm	'66 – 6	preservation society director	England
Tish McWhinney	Comfort, Barbara	'86 – 4	70-something artist & painter	Vermont
Toby Dyke	Ferrars, E. X.	'40 – 5	amateur sleuth	England
Toby Glendower, Sir & Penny Spring	Arnold, Margot	'79 – 12	Brit archeologist & Amer anthropologist	World Travelers
Todd McKinnon & Georgine Wyeth	Offord, Lenore Glen	'43 – 4	pulp writer & single working mother	Berkeley, CA
Tom Aragon	Millar, Margaret	'76 – 3	attorney	California
Tom Barnaby	Graham, Caroline	'87 – 4	chief inspector	England
Tom Maybridge	Gill, B. M.	'80 – 3	police inspector	England
Tom Pollard & Gregory Toye	Lemarchand, Elizabeth	'67 – 17	Scotland Yard detectives	England
Tom Ripley	Highsmith, Patricia	'55 – 5	charming forger & psychopath	England
Tommy & Tuppence Beresford	Christie, Agatha	'22 – 4	adventurers for hire & intelligence agents	London, England
Tommy Inman	Webb, Martha G.	'85 – 2	cop	Texas
Tonnemans	Meyers, Maan	'92 – 4	New Amsterdam historical series (l664-l808)	New York, NY
Tori Miracle	Malmont, Valerie S.	'94 – 1	ex-NYC crime writer turned novelist	Pennsylvania
Trey Fortier & Lane Montana	Hooper, Kay	'91 – 2	homicide detective & finder of lost things	Atlanta, GA
Trixie Dolan & Eve Sinclair	Babson, Marian	'86 – 5	aging British ex-movie queens	London, England
Truman Kicklighter	Trocheck, Kathy H.	'96 – 1	retired wire service reporter	St. Petersburg, FL
Tuppence & Tommy Beresford	Christie, Agatha	'22 – 4	adventurers for hire & intelligence agents	London, England
U				
Ulysses Finnegan Donaghue	Shone, Anna	'95 – 1	Shakespeare-spouting P. I.	Provence, France
V				
V. I. Warshawski	Paretsky, Sara	'82 – 8	attorney turned P. I.	Chicago, IL
Vachell, Supt.	Huxley, Elspeth	'37 – 3	young Scotsman trained by the RCMP	Kenya
Vejay Haskell	Dunlap, Susan	'83 – 3	utility meter reader for Pacific Gas & Electric	northern, CA
Verity "Birdie" Birdwood	Rowe, Jennifer	'89 – 4	TV researcher	Australia
Veronica "Ronnie" Ventana	White, Gloria	'91 – 3	Anglo-Mexican P. I. daughter of cat burglars	San Francisco, CA

V . . . W . . . X . . . Y . . . Z

Series Character	Author	1 – #	Occupation	Setting
V . . . continued				
Vic Varallo	Egan, Lesley	'62 – 13	small town cop moved to Glendale	Glendale, CA
Vicki Nelson	Huff, Tanya	'92 – 4	ex-cop turned P. I. with vampire lover	Toronto, Canada
Vicky Bliss	Peters, Elizabeth	'73 – 5	art historian	Germany
Vicky Holden & John Aloysius O'Malley	Coel, Margaret	'95 – 2	Arapaho attorney & Jesuit missionary	Wind River Reserv., WY
Victoire Vernet	Fawcett, Quinn	'93 – 2	wife of Napoleonic gendarme	France
Victoria Bowering	Yeager, Dorian	'92 – 3	NYC actor, writer & playwright	New York, NY
Victoria Cross	Sumner, Penny	'92 – 2	archivist turned P. I.	England
Vince Gutierrez & Meg Halloran	La Pierre, Janet	'87 – 5	police chief & school teacher	Port Silva, CA
Virginia & Felix Freer	Ferrars, E. X.	'78 – 9	physiotherapist & businessman	England
Virginia Kelly	Baker, Nikki	'91 – 3	black lesbian stockbroker	Chicago, IL
W				
Wanda Mallory	Frankel, Valerie	'91 – 4	detective agency owner	New York, NY
Watson, Mr.	Gardiner, Dorothy	'33 – 2	amateur sleuth	California
Webster Flagg	Johns, Veronica P.	'53 – 2	60-something Harlem actor/butler/houseman	New York, NY
Whitney Logan	Lambert, Mercedes	'91 – 1	20-something attorney	Los Angeles, CA
Wilder & Wilson	Bushell, Agnes	'89 – 2	P. I.s	Maine
Wilfred Dover	Porter, Joyce	'64 – 21	a fat lout of a Chief Inspector	England
Willa Jansson	Matera, Lia	'86 – 5	law student turned attorney	San Francisco, CA
William Marlowe Sherman	Lorens, M. K.	'90 – 5	Shakespeare professor & mystery writer	New York, NY
William Monk	Perry, Anne	'90 – 6	amnesiac Victorian police inspector	England
Willow King & Cressida Woodruffe	Cooper, Natasha	'90 – 5	civil servant & romance novelist	London, England
Wilson & Wilder	Bushell, Agnes	'89 – 2	P. I.s	Maine
Witherspoon, Insp. & Mrs. Jeffries	Brightwell, Emily	'93 – 7	Victorian police inspector & housekeeper	London, England
X				
Xenia Smith & Leslie Wetzon	Meyers, Annette	'89 – 7	Wall Street headhunters	New York, NY
Y				
Yum Yum, Koko & Jim Qwilleran	Braun, Lilian Jackson	'66 – 18	cats & ex-police reporter	Midwest USA
Z				
Zack James & Liz Broward, Dr.	Zachary, Fay	'94 – 2	computer artist/genealogist & family physician	Phoenix, AZ

Series Character	Author	1 – #	Occupation	Setting

Settings

4

United States

Setting	Author	1 – #	Series Character	Occupation

Alaska

Setting	Author	1 – #	Series Character	Occupation
	Quinn, Elizabeth	'93 – 3	Lauren Maxwell	wildlife investigator PhD
	Stabenow, Dana	'92 – 6	Kate Shugak	native Alaskan ex-D.A. investigator
Anchorage	Henry, Sue	'91 – 3	Jessie Arnold & Alex Jensen	sled dog racer & Alaska state trooper
Sitka	Froetschel, Susan	'94 – 1	Jane McBride	finance director

Arizona

Setting	Author	1 – #	Series Character	Occupation
	Scherf, Margaret	'68 – 4	Grace Severance, Dr.	retired pathologist
Cochise County	Jance, J. A.	'93 – 3	Joanna Brady	deputy sheriff's widow turned sheriff
Phoenix	Dengler, Sandy	'93 – 4	Joe Rodriguez, Sgt.	police officer
Phoenix	O'Callaghan, Maxine	'96 – 2	Anne Menlo, Dr.	child psychologist
Phoenix	Zachary, Fay	'94 – 2	Liz Broward, Dr. & Zack James	family physician & computer artist/genealogist

Arkansas

Setting	Author	1 – #	Series Character	Occupation
Farberville	Hess, Joan	'86 – 10	Claire Malloy	small-town bookstore owner
Maggody	Hess, Joan	'87 – 9	Arly Hanks	small-town police chief

California

Setting	Author	1 – #	Series Character	Occupation
	Fickling, G. G.	'62 – 3	Erik March	P. I.
	Fickling, G. G.	'57 – 11	Honey West	sexiest P. I. ever to pull a trigger
	Gardiner, Dorothy	'33 – 2	Watson, Mr.	amateur sleuth
	Hornsby, Wendy	'92 – 4	Maggie MacGowen	investigative filmmaker
	Millar, Margaret	'76 – 3	Tom Aragon	attorney
	Silva, Linda Kay	'91 – 4	Delta Stevens	lesbian policewoman
	Steiner, Susan	'91 – 2	Alex Winter	P. I.
Bay Cove	Hart, Jeanne	'87 – 3	Carl & Freda Pedersen	police lieutenant & wife
Berkeley	Dunlap, Susan	'81 – 9	Jill Smith	homicide detective
Berkeley	Offord, Lenore Glen	'43 – 4	Todd McKinnon & Georgine Wyeth	pulp writer & single working mother

United States . . . continued

Setting	Author	⊞ – #	Series Character	Occupation

California . . . continued

Setting	Author	⊞ – #	Series Character	Occupation
Berkeley	Singer, Shelley	'93 – 5	Barrett Lake	high school history teacher
Berkeley	Singer, Shelley	'83 – 5	Jake Samson & Rosie Vicente	ex-cop & carpenter tenant
central	Rothenberg, Rebecca	'91 – 3	Claire Sharples	former MIT scholar/microbiologist
Glendale	Egan, Lesley	'62 – 13	Vic Varallo	small town cop moved to Glendale
Gold Country	Jacobs, Jonnie	'96 – 1	Kali O'Brien	attorney
Hollywood	Linington, Elizabeth	'64 – 13	Ivor Maddox, Sgt.	book-collecting mystery-addict cop
Hollywood	Millhiser, Marlys	'92 – 3	Charlie Greene	literary agent
Hollywood	Osborne, Denise	'94 – 2	Queenie Davilow	Hollywood screenwriter
Hollywood	Shah, Diane K.	'90 – 2	Paris Chandler	'40s P. I.
La Jolla	Dunlap, Susan	'89 – 3	Kiernan O'Shaughnessy	former San Fran. medical examiner turned P. I.
Long Beach	Hitchens, Dolores	'57 – 2	Jim Sader	P. I.
Los Angeles	Cannon, Taffy	'93 – 3	Nan Robinson	investigator for the California State Bar
Los Angeles	Clark, Carol Higgins	'92 – 3	Regan Reilly	P. I.
Los Angeles	Egan, Lesley	'61 – 13	Jesse Falkenstein	lawyer
Los Angeles	Forrest, Katherine V.	'84 – 4	Kate Delafield	LAPD lesbian homicide detective
Los Angeles	Green, Kate	'86 – 2	Theresa Fortunato & Oliver Jardino	professional psychic & LAPD detective
Los Angeles	Kellerman, Faye	'86 – 8	Peter Decker & Rina Lazarus	LAPD detective & wife
Los Angeles	Kraft, Gabrielle	'87 – 4	Jerry Zalman	Beverly Hills deal maker
Los Angeles	Krich, Rochelle Majer	'93 – 2	Jessie Drake	police detective
Los Angeles	Lambert, Mercedes	'91 – 1	Whitney Logan	20-something attorney
Los Angeles	Olsen, D. B.	'45 – 6	A. Pennyfather, Prof.	professor at Clarendon College
Los Angeles	Olsen, D. B.	'39 – 13	Rachel & Jennifer Murdock	sister sleuths
Los Angeles	Olsen, D. B.	'40 – 2	Stephen Mayhew, Lt.	police detective
Los Angeles	Pugh, Dianne G.	'93 – 2	Iris Thorne	investment counselor
Los Angeles	Schmidt, Carol	'93 – 3	Laney Samms	lesbian bar owner
Los Angeles	Shannon, Dell	'60 – 37	Luis Mendoza	wealthy homicide lieutenant
Los Angeles	Smith, April	'94 – 1	Ana Grey	FBI agent
Los Angeles	White, Teri	'84 – 2	Spaceman Kowalski & Blue Maguire	cop pair with prickly partnership
Marin County	Girdner, Jaqueline	'91 – 7	Kate Jasper	gag gift wholesaler
Napa Valley	Muller, Marcia	'86 – 3	Joanna Stark	international art investigator
northern	Dunlap, Susan	'83 – 3	Vejay Haskell	utility meter reader for Pacific Gas & Electric
northern	McGuire, Christine	'93 – 2	Kathryn Mackay	prosecuting attorney
northern	McKenna, Bridget	'93 – 3	Caley Burke	30-something P. I.
northern	Simonson, Sheila	'90 – 4	Lark Dailey	6-ft. bookdealer
northern	Valentine, Deborah	'89 – 3	Katharine Craig & Kevin Bryce	sculptor & ex-sheriff's detective
Oakland	Dawson, Janet	'90 – 5	Jeri Howard	P. I.
Oakland	Wallace, Marilyn	'86 – 3	Jay Goldstein & Carlos Cruz	homicide detectives
Orange County	Ayres, Noreen	'92 – 3	Samantha "Smokey" Brandon	sheriff's forensic expert
Orange County	Lachnit, Carroll	'95 – 2	Hannah Barlow	ex-cop turned law student
Orange County	O'Callaghan, Maxine	'80 – 5	Delilah West	P. I.
Palo Alto	Beck, K. K.	'84 – 3	Iris Cooper	Roaring 20s co-ed at Stanford University
Palo Alto	Roberts, Lora	'94 – 3	Liz Sullivan	freelance writer
Port Silva	La Pierre, Janet	'87 – 5	Vince Gutierrez & Meg Halloran	police chief & school teacher
Sacramento	Hall, Mary Bowen	'89 – 4	Emma Chizzit	salvage dealer
Sacramento	Kijewski, Karen	'88 – 6	Kat Colorado	P. I.
San Celina	Fowler, Earlene	'94 – 3	Albenia "Benni" Harper	ex-rancher & folk art museum curator
San Diego	Lawrence, Martha	'95 – 1	Elizabeth Chase, Dr.	Stanford-trained parapsychologist turned P. I.
San Diego	Padgett, Abigail	'93 – 3	Barbara Joan "Bo" Bradley	child abuse investigator

United States . . . *continued*

Setting	Author	🔢 – #	Series Character	Occupation

California . . . *continued*

Setting	Author	# – #	Series Character	Occupation
San Diego	Robitaille, Julie	'92 – 2	Kit Powell	TV sports reporter
San Diego	Steinberg, Janice	'95 – 2	Margo Simon	California Public Radio reporter
San Diego	Wallace, Patricia	'88 – 4	Sydney Bryant	P. I.
San Francisco	Day, Dianne	'95 – 3	Fremont Jones	owner of a typewriting service circa 1900
San Francisco	Grant, Linda	'88 – 5	Catherine Sayler	P. I.
San Francisco	King, Laurie R.	'93 – 3	Kate Martinelli & Alonzo Hawkin	SFPD homicide detectives
San Francisco	Lucke, Margaret	'91 – 2	Jessica Randolph	artist working as a P. I.
San Francisco	Matera, Lia	'88 – 5	Laura Di Palma	attorney
San Francisco	Matera, Lia	'86 – 5	Willa Jansson	law student turned attorney
San Francisco	Muller, Marcia	'77 – 17	Sharon McCone	legal co-op investigator turned P. I.
San Francisco	O'Marie, Carol, Sister	'84 – 6	Mary Helen, Sister	70-something nun
San Francisco	Offord, Lenore Glen	'38 – 2	Bill & Coco Hastings	sleuthing pair
San Francisco	Pence, Joanne	'93 – 4	Angelina Amalfi	food columnist & restaurant reviewer
San Francisco	Pincus, Elizabeth	'92 – 3	Nell Fury	lesbian P. I.
San Francisco	Smith, Julie	'85 – 2	Paul MacDonald	ex-reporter & mystery writer
San Francisco	Smith, Julie	'82 – 5	Rebecca Schwartz	defense attorney
San Francisco	Taylor, Elizabeth A.	'81 – 3	Maggie Elliott	ex-film maker turned P. I.
San Francisco	Taylor, Jean	'95 – 2	Maggie Garrett	young lesbian P. I.
San Francisco	Warmbold, Jean	'86 – 3	Sarah Calloway	newspaper reporter
San Francisco	Welch, Pat	'90 – 4	Helen Black	ex-cop lesbian P. I.
San Francisco	White, Gloria	'91 – 3	Veronica "Ronnie" Ventana	Anglo-Mexican P. I. daughter of cat burglars
San Francisco	Wings, Mary	'87 – 3	Emma Victor	lesbian activist & P. I.
San Francisco	Yarbro, Chelsea Quinn	'76 – 4	Charles Spotted Moon	attorney & Ojibway tribal shaman
San Jose	Sims, L. V.	'87 – 3	Dixie T. Struthers	police detective
Santa Barbara	Muller, Marcia	'83 – 3	Elena Oliverez	Mexican arts museum curator
Santa Cruz	Crum, Laura	'94 – 2	Gail McCarthy	horse veterinarian
Santa Monica	Weston, Carolyn	'72 – 3	Casey Kellog & Al Krug	college grad liberal & hard-bitten veteran cop
Santa Teresa	Grafton, Sue	'82 – 12	Kinsey Millhone	ex-cop P. I.
Silicon Valley	Chapman, Sally	'91 – 3	Juliet Blake	Silicon Valley fraud investigator
Silicon Valley	Wolfe, Susan	'89 – 1	Sarah Nelson	police inspector
southern	Burke, Jan	'93 – 4	Irene Kelly	newspaper reporter
southern	Femling, Jean	'89 – 2	Martha "Moz" Brant	insurance claims investigator
southern	Hornsby, Wendy	'87 – 2	Kate Teague & Roger Tejeda	college professor & homicide detective
southern	Howe, Melodie J.	'89 – 2	Claire Conrad & Maggie Hill	P. I. & secretary
southern	Maxwell, A. E.	'85 – 8	Fiddler & Fiora Flynn	ex-husband & investment banker
southern	McKevett, G. A.	'95 – 2	Savannah Reid	ex-cop & owner of a new detective agency
southern	Nielsen, Helen	'51 – 6	Simon Drake	attorney transplanted from Chicago
southern	Sawyer, Corinne Holt	'88 – 6	Angela Benbow & Caledonia Wingate	70-something admirals' widows
Walnut Hills	Jacobs, Jonnie	'94 – 2	Kate Austen	Bay area single mother

Colorado

Setting	Author	# – #	Series Character	Occupation
	Cail, Carol	'93 – 2	Maxey Burnell	investigative reporter
	Karr, Leona	'93 – 1	Addie Devore	small-town newspaper owner
	Oliphant, B. J.	'90 – 6	Shirley McClintock	50-something rancher
	Schier, Norma	'78 – 4	Kay Barth	district attorney
Aspen Meadow	Davidson, Diane Mott	'90 – 6	Goldy Bear	caterer & single mother
Cutler	Lewis, Sherry	'95 – 2	Fred Vickery	70-something retiree
Denver	Allen, Kate	'93 – 2	Alison Kaine	lesbian cop

United States . . . *continued*

Setting	Author	❶ – #	Series Character	Occupation

Colorado . . . *continued*

Setting	Author	❶ – #	Series Character	Occupation
Denver	Jorgensen, Christine	'94 – 3	Stella the Stargazer	astrologer & lovelorn columnist
Denver	McConnell, Vickie P.	'82 – 3	Nyla Wade	lesbian journalist
Denver	Montgomery, Yvonne	'87 – 2	Finny Aletter	stockbroker turned carpenter
Denver	Orde, A. J.	'89 – 5	Jason Lynx	antiques dealer & interior decorator
Notlaw	Gardiner, Dorothy	'56 – 3	Moss Magill	sheriff

Connecticut

Setting	Author	❶ – #	Series Character	Occupation
	Berenson, Laurien	'95 – 3	Melanie Travis	special ed teacher posing as poodle breeder
	Christmas, Joyce	'93 – 2	Betty Trenka	retired office manager
	Dank, Gloria	'89 – 4	B. Woodrull & A.Randolph	children's author & visiting brother-in-law
	Disney, Doris Miles	'43 – 5	Jim O'Neill	small town policeman
	Johns, Veronica P.	'40 – 2	Agatha Welch	middle-aged woman sleuth
	Kallen, Lucille	'79 – 5	Maggie Rome & C. B. Greenfield	reporter & editor/publisher
	Kittredge, Mary	'87 – 3	Charlotte Kent	freelance writer
	Wolzien, Valerie	'87 – 10	Susan Henshaw	suburban housewife
Hartford	Lackey, Mercedes	'89 – 3	Diana Tregarde	romance author & practicing witch
New Haven	Kittredge, Mary	'90 – 6	Edwina Crusoe	RN & medical consultant
Raven's Wing	McShea, Susanna H.	'90 – 3	Mildred Bennett & friends	a quartet of senior sleuths
Riverdale	Travis, Elizabeth	'89 – 2	Ben & Carrie Porter	book publishers
Wingate	Dolson, Hildegarde	'71 – 4	Lucy Ramsdale & J. McDougal	illustrator & homicide inspector

District of Columbia

Setting	Author	❶ – #	Series Character	Occupation
Washington	Dominic, R. B.	'68 – 7	Ben Safford	Democratic congressman from Ohio
Washington	Ford, Leslie	'34 – 16	John Primrose & Grace Latham	career soldier & attractive widow
Washington	Fromer, Margot J.	'91 – 2	Amanda Knight	hospital director of nursing
Washington	Law, Janice	'76 – 8	Anna Peters	international oil company exec turned P. I.
Washington	Leonard, Charles L.	'42 – 11	Paul Kilgerrin	P. I. spy
Washington	Michaels, Barbara	'68 – 3	Georgetown house	historic home
Washington	Mickelbury, Penny	'94 – 2	Gianna Maglione & Mimi Patterson	lesbian police lieutenant & reporter
Washington	Ripley, Ann	'94 – 2	Louise Eldridge	organic gardener
Washington	Roberts, Carey	'89 – 2	Anne Fitzhugh	police detective
Washington	Sucher, Dorothy	'88 – 2	Sabina Swift	Georgetown detective agency owner
Washington	Tone, Teona	'83 – 2	Kyra Keaton	P. I. at the turn-of-the-century
Washington	Truman, Margaret	'89 – 5	Mackenzie Smith & Annabel Reed	law professor & gallery owner

Florida

Setting	Author	❶ – #	Series Character	Occupation
	Buckstaff, Kathryn	'94 – 1	Morgana Dalton	Florida-based travel writer
	Chase, Elaine Raco	'87 – 2	Nikki Holden & Roman Cantrell	reporter & P. I.
	Clark, Carolyn C.	'94 – 1	Theresa Franco	P. I.
	MacGregor, T. J.	'86 – 10	Quin St. James & Mike McCleary	wife & husband P. I. team
	McKernan, Victoria	'90 – 3	Chicago Nordejoong	professional scuba diver
Miami	Buchanan, Edna	'92 – 4	Britt Montero	newspaper crime reporter
Miami	Parker, Barbara	'94 – 2	Gail Connor	corporate attorney
Miami	Woods, Sherryl	'91 – 5	Molly DeWitt	film office public relations staffer
Paradise Cay	Wilson, Karen Ann	'94 – 2	Samantha Holt	vet's assistant
St. Petersburg	Clark, Carolyn C.	'93 – 1	Megan Baldwin	registered nurse
St. Petersburg	Trocheck, Kathy H.	'96 – 1	Truman Kicklighter	retired wire service reporter
Tango Key	Drake, Alison	'88 – 4	Aline Scott	small resort town police detective

United States . . . *continued*

Setting	Author	🔲 – #	Series Character	Occupation

Georgia

Setting	Author	🔲 – #	Series Character	Occupation
	Harris, Charlaine	'90 – 5	Aurora Teagarden	librarian turned real estate agent
Atlanta	Hooper, Kay	'91 – 2	Lane Montana & Trey Fortier	finder of lost things & homicide detective
Atlanta	Shankman, Sarah	'88 – 6	Samantha Adams	investigative reporter
Atlanta	Sibley, Celestine	'58 – 5	Kate Kincaid Mulcay	veteran newspaperwoman
Atlanta	Sprinkle, Patricia H.	'88 – 7	Sheila Travis	admin asst turned PR executive
Atlanta	Trocheck, Kathy H.	'92 – 4	Callahan Garrity	ex-cop cleaning service operator
Atlanta	Woods, Sherryl	'89 – 9	Amanda Roberts	ex-New York investigative reporter

Hawaii

Setting	Author	🔲 – #	Series Character	Occupation
	Sheridan, Juanita	'49 – 4	Lily Wu & Janice Cameron	investigator & adopted sister

Illinois

Setting	Author	🔲 – #	Series Character	Occupation
	Pulver, Mary Monica	'87 – 5	Peter & Kori Price Brichter	police detective & horse breeder
Chicago	Baker, Nikki	'91 – 3	Virginia Kelly	black lesbian stockbroker
Chicago	Churchill, Jill	'89 – 7	Jane Jeffry	suburban single mother
Chicago	D'Amato, Barbara	'90 – 6	Cat Marsala	freelance investigative journalist
Chicago	D'Amato, Barbara	'80 – 2	Gerritt DeGraaf, Dr.	forensic pathologist
Chicago	D'Amato, Barbara	'96 – 1	Suze Figueroa & Norm Bennis	pair of cops
Chicago	Dymmoch, Michael A.	'93 – 2	John Thinnes & Jack Caleb, Dr.	cop & psychiatrist
Chicago	Elrod, P. N.	'90 – 6	Jack Fleming	reporter, ladies' man & vampire
Chicago	Haddad, Carolyn A.	'92 – 1	Becky Belski	computer investigator
Chicago	Hartzmark, Gini	'92 – 3	Katherine Prescott Milholland	corporate attorney
Chicago	Paretsky, Sara	'82 – 8	V. I. Warshawski	attorney turned P. I.
Chicago	Rice, Craig	'39 – 12	John J. Malone	hard-drinking, cigar-smoking lawyer
Chicago suburb	Brod, D. C.	'89 – 4	Quint McCauley	ex-cop turned P. I.
Lincoln Prairie	Bland, Eleanor Taylor	'92 – 4	Marti MacAlister	black police detective
Oak Park	Matthews, Alex	'96 – 2	Cassidy McCabe	psychotherapirst
River Depths	Maney, Mabel	'93 – 3	Nancy Clue	gay-lesbian parody of Nancy Drew

Indiana

Setting	Author	🔲 – #	Series Character	Occupation
Oliver	Frommer, Sara H.	'93 – 2	Joan Spencer	symphony orchestra manager
southern	Carlson, P. M.	'92 – 2	Martine "Marty" LaForte Hopkins	deputy sheriff & mother

Kansas

Setting	Author	🔲 – #	Series Character	Occupation
	Weir, Charlene	'92 – 3	Susan Wren	ex-cop turned police chief
Kansas City	Hollingsworth, Gerelyn	'95 – 1	Frances Finn	P. I.

Kentucky

Setting	Author	🔲 – #	Series Character	Occupation
Lexington	Hightower, Lynn S.	'93 – 1	Lena Padget	P. I.
Louisville	McClellan, Tierney	'95 – 3	Schuyler Ridgway	40-something real estate agent
Pigeon Fork	McCafferty, Taylor	'90 – 5	Haskell Blevins	small-town P. I.

United States . . . continued

Setting	Author	🗓 – #	Series Character	Occupation
Louisiana				
	Ennis, Catherine	'91 – 2	Bernadette Hebert, Dr.	lesbian crime lab expert
New Orleans	Dunbar, Sophie	'93 – 3	Claire & Dan Claiborne	sleuthing pair
New Orleans	Fennelly, Tony	'94 – 2	Margo Fortier	ex-stripper turned columnist
New Orleans	Fennelly, Tony	'85 – 3	Matthew Arthur Sinclair	gay ex-D.A. turned P. I.
New Orleans	Redmann, J. M.	'90 – 3	Michelle "Micky" Knight	lesbian P. I.
New Orleans	Smith, Julie	'90 – 5	Skip Langdon	6-ft. police detective
New Orleans	Wiltz, Chris	'81 – 3	Neal Rafferty	third generation cop turned P. I.
Maine				
	Bushell, Agnes	'89 – 2	Wilson & Wilder	P. I.s
	Flora, Kate Clark	'95 – 1	Ross McIntyre	small town high school biology teacher
	Kenney, Susan	'83 – 3	Roz Howard & Alan Stewart	American professor & British painter
	Meier, Leslie	'93 – 2	Lucy Stone	small-town sleuth
	Rich, Virginia	'82 – 4	Eugenia Potter	widowed chef
	Saum, Karen	'90 – 3	Brigid Donovan	50-something lesbian ex-nun
coastal	Knight, Phyllis	'92 – 3	Lil Ritchie	ex-rocker & gay woman P. I.
coastal	Morison, B. J.	'82 – 5	Elizabeth Lamb Worthington	pre-teenager in the 1970s
Maryland				
Anne Arundel Co.	Lee, Barbara	'95 – 1	Eve Elliott	ex-New York advertising exec turned realtor
Massachusetts				
	Flora, Kate Clark	'94 – 2	Thea Kozak	educational consultant
	Page, Katherine Hall	'90 – 7	Faith Sibley Fairchild	minister's wife & culinary artist
	Wender, Theodora	'85 – 2	Glad Gold & Alden Chase	English professor & chief of police
Balaclava Co.	MacLeod, Charlotte	'78 – 9	Peter Shandy & Helen M. Shandy	botany professor & librarian wife
Boston	Barnes, Linda	'87 – 6	Carlotta Carlyle	6'1" cab-driving ex-cop P. I.
Boston	Barnes, Linda	'82 – 4	Michael Spraggue III	wealthy actor & ex-P. I.
Boston	Belfort, Sophie	'86 – 3	Molly Rafferty	college history professor
Boston	Borthwick, J. S.	'82 – 7	Sarah Deane & Alex McKenzie, Dr.	English professor & internist
Boston	Coker, Carolyn	'84 – 4	Andrea Perkins	museum art historian & restorer of paintings
Boston	Disney, Doris Miles	'46 – 8	Jeff Di Marco	insurance investigator
Boston	Dreher, Sarah	'85 – 6	Stoner McTavish	lesbian travel agent
Boston	Lamb, J. Dayne	'93 – 3	Teal Stewart	Certified Public Accountant
Boston	Lee, W. W. (Wendi)	'94 – 2	Angela Matelli	ex-Marine turned P. I.
Boston	Logan, Margaret	'94 – 2	Olivia Chapman	interior decorator
Boston	MacLeod, Charlotte	'79 – 11	Sarah Kelling & Max Bittersohn	investigative couple
Boston	Sullivan, Winona	'93 – 2	Cecile Buddenbrooks, Sister	licensed P. I. nun
Boston	Tilton, Alice	'37 – 8	Leonidas Witherall	retired academic & secret pulp fiction author
Boston	Wells, Tobias	'66 – 16	Knute Severson	police officer
Braeton	Waltch, Lilla M.	'87 – 2	Lisa Davis	newspaper reporter
Cambridge	Conant, Susan	'89 – 8	Holly Winter	dog trainer & magazine columnist
Cambridge	Kelly, Susan	'85 – 6	Liz Connors	freelance crime writer
Cambridge	Knight, Kathryn Lasky	'86 – 4	Calista Jacobs	award-winning illustrator of children's books
Cambridge	Langton, Jane	'64 – 11	Homer Kelly	Harvard professor & retired detective
Cape Cod	Gunning, Sally	'90 – 6	Peter Bartholomew	small business owner
Cape Cod	Knight, Kathleen M.	'35 – 16	Elisha Macomber	selectman & owner of a fish market

United States . . . *continued*

Setting	Author	❶ – #	Series Character	Occupation
Massachusetts . . . *continued*				
Cape Cod	Lee, Marie	'95 – 1	Marguerite Smith	retired science teacher
Cape Cod	Taylor, Phoebe A.	'31 – 24	Asey Mayo	former sailor & auto racer
Mellingham	Oleksiw, Susan	'93 – 3	Joe Silva	chief of police
Nantucket	Mathews, Francine	'94 – 2	Meredith "Merry" Folger	police detective
Palmer	Cleary, Melissa	'92 – 8	Jackie Walsh & Jake	college film instructor with her ex-police dog
Port Frederick	Pickard, Nancy	'84 – 10	Jenny Cain	New England foundation director
Michigan				
	Schenkel, S. E.	'94 – 2	Ray & Kate Frederick	chief of detectives & wife of 30 yrs
Ann Arbor	Holtzer, Susan	'94 – 2	Anneke Haagen	computer consultant
Detroit	Vlasopolos, Anca	'90 – 1	Sharon Dair	sex crimes police detective
Minnesota				
	Douglas, Carole N.	'85 – 2	Kevin Blake, Dr.	psychiatrist
Minneapolis	Hart, Ellen	'89 – 7	Jane Lawless	lesbian restaurateur
Minneapolis	Hart, Ellen	'94 – 3	Sophie Greenway	magazine editor & food critic for newspaper
Minneapolis	Jacobs, Nancy Baker	'91 – 3	Devon MacDonald	ex-teacher P. I.
Minneapolis	Logue, Mary	'93 – 1	Laura Malloy	journalist
Minneapolis	Taylor, L. A.	'84 – 4	J. J. Jamison	computer engineer & CATCH investigator
Missouri				
St. Louis	Hamilton, Laurell K.	'93 – 4	Anita Blake	reanimator & vampire hunter
St. Louis	Komo, Dolores	'88 – 1	Clio Browne	cop's widow & P. I. agency owner
St. Louis	Kunz, Kathleen	'93 – 2	Terry Girard	genealogist for hire
Victoria Springs	Hager, Jean	'94 – 3	Tess Darcy	Ozarks bed & breakfast owner
Montana				
	Andreae, Christine	'92 – 2	Lee Squires	English professor & poet
Billings	Prowell, Sandra West	'93 – 3	Phoebe Siegel	ex-cop P. I.
Blue Deer	Harrison, Jamie	'95 – 1	Jules Clement	30-something archaeologist turned sheriff
Farrington	Scherf, Margaret	'48 – 6	Martin Buell, Rev.	Episcopal rector
Nevada				
Las Vegas	Douglas, Carole N.	'92 – 5	Temple Barr & Midnight Louie	public relations freelancer & tomcat sleuth
Reno	Dain, Catherine	'92 – 5	Freddie O'Neal	plane-flying P. I.
New Hampshire				
Dovekey	Yeager, Dorian	'94 – 2	Elizabeth Will	art gallery owner & lobster fisherman
New Jersey				
	Gilman, Dorothy	'66 – 12	Emily Pollifax	grandmother CIA agent
Fishersville	Gallison, Kate	'95 – 2	Lavinia Grey, Mother	Episcopal vicar & practicing therapist
Newark	Wesley, Valerie Wilson	'94 – 2	Tamara Hayle	black ex-cop P. I. & single mother
Trenton	Evanovich, Janet	'94 – 2	Stephanie Plum	neophyte bounty hunter
Trenton	Gallison, Kate	'86 – 3	Nick Magaracz	P. I.

United States . . . continued

Setting	Author	❶ – #	Series Character	Occupation
New Mexico				
	Moore, Barbara	'83 – 2	Gordon Christy, Dr.	veterinarian
	Shelton, Connie	'95 – 3	Charlie Parker	CPA turned reluctant investigator
	Thurlo, Aimée & David	'95 – 2	Ella Clah	Navajo FBI agent
Albuquerque	Van Gieson, Judith	'88 – 6	Neil Hamel	attorney & investigator
Sante Fe	Lovett, Sarah	'95 – 2	Sylvia Strange, Dr.	forensic psychologist
New York				
	Berenson, Laurien	'94 – 1	Gwen Harding	NYC journalist turned suburban wife & mother
	Collins, Anna Ashwood	'94 – 2	Abigail Doyle	efficiency expert
	Foley, Rae	'55 – 11	Hiram Potter	mild-mannered Old Money sleuth
	Lockridge, F. & R.	'47 – 24	Merton Heimrich, Insp.	State Police Bureau of Criminal Investigation
	Morgan, Kate	'90 – 6	Dewey James	60-something small-town librarian
Brooklyn	Tyre, Peg	'94 – 2	Kate Murray	newspaper reporter for Daily Herald
Cheektowaga	Furie, Ruthe	'95 – 3	Fran Kirk	former battered wife & P. I. in training
Hemlock Falls	Bishop, Claudia	'94 – 4	Sarah & Meg Quilliam	inn owner & chef (sisters)
Long Island	Watson, Clarissa	'77 – 5	Persis Willum	New York art curator
New York	Armstrong, Charlotte	'42 – 3	MacDougal Duff	retired history professor
New York	Babbin, Jacqueline	'72 – 2	Clovis Kelly	ex-NYPD homicide detective & crime consultant
New York	Barber, Willetta Ann	'40 – 7	Christopher "Kit" Storm	police illustrator for the NYPD
New York	Bennett, Liza	'89 – 2	Peg Goodenough	ad agency creative director
New York	Berry, Carole	'87 – 6	Bonnie Indermill	tap-dancing Manhattan office temp
New York	Boylan, Eleanor	'89 – 4	Clara Gamadge	widow of Henry the forgery expert
New York	Brennan, Carol	'94 – 2	Emily Silver	New York actress
New York	Brennan, Carol	'91 – 2	Liz Wareham	Manhattan public relations consultant
New York	Brill, Toni	'91 – 2	Midge Cohen	children's author fluent in Russian
New York	Carlson, P. M.	'85 – 8	Maggie Ryan	college student turned statistician & mother
New York	Christmas, Joyce	'88 – 7	Margaret Priam, Lady	English noblewoman
New York	Crespi, Camilla	'91 – 6	Simona Griffo	advertising executive & gourmet cook
New York	Cross, Amanda	'64 – 11	Kate Fansler	university English professor
New York	Daly, Elizabeth	'40 – 16	Henry Gamadge	author & bibliophile
New York	Davis, Dorothy S.	'57 – 3	Jasper Tully & Norris, Mrs.	DA's investigator & Scottish housekeeper
New York	Davis, Dorothy S.	'76 – 4	Julie Hayes	former actress & columnist
New York	Dentinger, Jane	'83 – 6	Jocelyn O'Roarke	Broadway actress & director
New York	Eberhart, Mignon G.	'29 – 7	Sarah Keate & Lance O'Leary	nurse & wealthy police detective
New York	Edghill, Rosemary	'94 – 2	Karen Hightower	Manhattan graphic designer & white witch
New York	Eichler, Selma	'94 – 4	Desiree Shapiro	5'2" queen-size Manhattan P. I.
New York	Farrell, Gillian B.	'92 – 2	Annie McGrogan	P. I. & actor just back from LA
New York	Fenisong, Ruth	'42 – 13	Gridley Nelson	wealthy young cop with Harlem housekeeper
New York	Florian, S. L.	'92 – 1	Delia Ross-Merlani, Viscountess	English-Italian noblewoman
New York	Frankel, Valerie	'91 – 4	Wanda Mallory	detective agency owner
New York	Fulton, Eileen	'88 – 6	Nina McFall & Dino Rossi, Lt.	glamorous TV soap star & NYPD cop
New York	Glass, Leslie	'93 – 2	April Woo	police detective
New York	Gray, Gallagher	'91 – 3	Theodore S. Hubbert & Auntie Lil	retired personnel manager & dress designer
New York	Green, Anna K.	1899 – 3	Caleb Sweetwater	policeman
New York	Green, Anna K.	1878 – 12	Ebenezer Gryce	portly policeman
New York	Green, Edith Pinero	'77 – 3	Dearborn V. Pinch	70-something ladies man
New York	Harris, Lee	'92 – 7	Christine Bennett	ex-nun

United States . . . *continued*

Setting	Author	❶ – #	Series Character	Occupation

New York . . . *continued*

Setting	Author	❶ – #	Series Character	Occupation
New York	Hayter, Sparkle	'94 – 2	Robin Hudson	cable news reporter
New York	Heberden, M. V.	'39 – 17	Desmond Shannon	high-priced Irish-American P. I.
New York	Heberden, M. V.	'46 – 3	Rick Vanner	former Naval Intelligence officer
New York	Holland, Isabelle	'83 – 6	Claire Aldington, Rev.	Episcopal priest
New York	Horansky, Ruby	'90 – 2	Nikki Trakos	homicide detective
New York	Hyde, Eleanor	'95 – 2	Lydia Miller	30-something fashion editor
New York	Johns, Veronica P.	'53 – 2	Webster Flagg	60-something Harlem actor/butler/houseman
New York	Kelly, Mary Ann	'90 – 3	Claire Breslinsky	freelance photographer
New York	Knight, Kathleen M.	'40 – 4	Margot Blair	partner in a PR agency
New York	Lathen, Emma	'61 – 22	John Putnam Thatcher	Wall Street financial whiz
New York	Lockridge, F. & R.	'40 – 26	Pam & Jerry North	book publisher & wife
New York	Lorden, Randye	'93 – 2	Sydney Sloane	upper west side P. I.
New York	Lorens, M. K.	'90 – 5	William Marlowe Sherman	Shakespeare professor & mystery writer
New York	Maiman, Jaye	'91 – 4	Robin Miller	lesbian travel & romance writer turned P. I.
New York	Maron, Margaret	'81 – 8	Sigrid Harald	police lieutenant
New York	Matteson, Stefanie	'90 – 7	Charlotte Graham	Oscar-winning actress
New York	McCloy, Helen	'38 – 13	Basil Willing, Dr.	psychiatrist & FBI consultant
New York	Meyers, Annette	'89 – 7	Xenia Smith & Leslie Wetzon	Wall Street headhunters
New York	Meyers, Maan	'92 – 4	The Tonnemans	New Amsterdam historical series (1664-1808)
New York	O'Connell, Carol	'94 – 3	Kathleen Mallory	NYPD cop
New York	O'Connell, Catherine	'93 – 1	Karen Levinson	NYPD homicide detective
New York	O'Donnell, Lillian	'90 – 3	Gwenn Ramadge	P. I. for corporate investigations
New York	O'Donnell, Lillian	'77 – 3	Mici Anhalt	criminal justice investigator
New York	O'Donnell, Lillian	'72 – 15	Norah Mulcahaney	NYPD detective
New York	OCork, Shannon	'80 – 3	Theresa Tracy Baldwin	sports photographer for New York daily
New York	Papazoglou, Orania	'84 – 5	Patience Campbell McKenna	6-ft romance novelist turned crime writer
New York	Paul, Barbara	'84 – 3	Enrico Caruso	Italian tenor
New York	Paul, Barbara	'84 – 6	Marian Larch	NYPD officer
New York	Peters, Elizabeth	'72 – 4	Jacqueline Kirby	librarian turned romance novelist
New York	Piesman, Marissa	'89 – 5	Nina Fischman	legal services attorney
New York	Popkin, Zelda	'38 – 5	Mary Carner	former department store detective
New York	Reilly, Helen	'30 – 31	Christopher McKee	Manhattan homicide squad detective
New York	Robb, J. D.	'95 – 3	Eve Dallas	NYPD lieutenant in the 21st century
New York	Rozan, S. J.	'94 – 2	Lydia Chin & Bill Smith	Chinese American & Army brat P. I.s
New York	Scherf, Margaret	'49 – 4	Emily & Henry Bryce	Manhattan interior decorators
New York	Scherf, Margaret	'45 – 2	Ryan, Lt.	NYPD cop
New York	Scoppettone, Sandra	'91 – 3	Lauren Laurano	Greenwich Village lesbian P. I.
New York	Shaffer, Louise	'94 – 2	Angie DaVito	TV soap opera producer
New York	Smith, Evelyn E.	'86 – 5	Susan Melville	freelance assassin & painter
New York	Smith, J. C. S.	'80 – 2	Quentin Jacoby	P. I.
New York	Tucker, Kerry	'91 – 4	Libby Kincaid	magazine photographer
New York	Uhnak, Dorothy	'68 – 3	Christine Opara	20-something police detective
New York	Venning, Michael	'42 – 3	Melville Fairr	lawyer
New York	Wells, Carolyn	'09 – 61	Fleming Stone	intellectual P. I.
New York	Wells, Carolyn	'29 – 3	Kenneth Carlisle	actor turned detective
New York	Wells, Carolyn	'18 – 8	Pennington Wise	private detective
New York	Wheat, Carolyn	'83 – 3	Cass Jameson	Brooklyn criminal lawyer
New York	Whitney, Polly	'94 – 3	Ike Tygart & Abby Abagnarro	network producer & TV news director

United States . . . *continued*

Setting	Author	1 – #	Series Character	Occupation
New York . . . *continued*				
New York	Wilhelm, Kate	'87 – 6	Charlie Meiklejohn & Constance Leidl	ex-arson investigator P. I. & psychologist
New York	Yeager, Dorian	'92 – 3	Victoria Bowering	NYC actor, writer & playwright
New York	Zukowski, Sharon	'91 – 4	Blaine Stewart	ex-NYPD cop turned P. I. in Manhattan
Rochester	O'Brien, Meg	'90 – 5	Jessica James	newspaper reporter
Seneca Falls	Monfredo, Miriam G.	'92 – 4	Glynis Tryon	librarian & suffragette in mid-19th century
Syracuse	Block, Barbara	'94 – 2	Robin Light	pet store owner
North Carolina				
	Jackson, Muriel R.	'92 – 1	Merrie Lee Spencer	Manhattan transplant
	Maron, Margaret	'92 – 4	Deborah Knott	district judge
	Neely, Barbara	'92 – 2	Blanche White	middle-aged black domestic
	Squire, Elizabeth D.	'94 – 3	Peaches Dann	absent-minded 50-something widow
Byerly	Kelner, Toni L. P.	'93 – 3	Laura Fleming	small-town detective
Charlotte	Jaffe, Jody	'95 – 2	Natalie Gold	reporter on horse show circuit
Durham	Mackay, Amanda	'76 – 2	Hannah Land	divorced New York PhD at Duke University
Sunrise	West, Chassie	'94 – 1	Leigh Ann Warren	former DC street cop
Ohio				
Cincinnati	Borton, D. B.	'93 – 5	Cat Caliban	60-something P. I.-in-training
Cincinnati	Hightower, Lynn S.	'95 – 1	Sonora Blair	homicide detective
Cincinnati	Short, Sharon Gwyn	'94 – 3	Patricia Delaney	computer whiz P. I.
Columbus	Glen, Alison	'92 – 2	Charlotte Sams	freelance writer
Grantham	Gosling, Paula	'85 – 3	Jack Stryker & Kate Trevorne	homicide cop & English professor
Oklahoma				
Buckskin	Hager, Jean	'89 – 4	Mitch Bushyhead	police chief of Cherokee descent
Frontier City	Haddock, Lisa	'94 – 2	Carmen Ramirez	lesbian newspaper copy editor
Holton	Sandstrom, Eve K.	'90 – 3	Sam & Nicky Titus	ex-army CID sheriff & photojournalist wife
Prophesy County	Cooper, Susan Rogers	'88 – 6	Milton Kovak	chief deputy
Tahlequah	Hager, Jean	'92 – 3	Molly Bearpaw	Cherokee civil rights investigator
Vamoose	Feddersen, Connie	'93 – 4	Amanda Hazard	small-town Certified Public Accountant
Oregon				
	Wallingford, Lee	'91 – 2	Ginny Trask & Frank Carver	forest fire dispatcher & ex-cop
	Wilhelm, Kate	'91 – 2	Barbara Holloway	defense attorney
	Wilhelm, Kate	'93 – 1	Sarah Drexler	judge
	Wren, M. K.	'73 – 8	Conan Flagg	bookstore owner & ex-intelligence agent
Pennsylvania				
	Allen, Irene	'92 – 2	Elizabeth Elliot	widowed Quaker meeting clerk
	Malmont, Valerie S.	'94 – 1	Tori Miracle	ex-NYC crime writer turned novelist
Conover	Greth, Roma	'88 – 2	Hana Shaner	carpet company heiress in Dutch country
Hernia	Myers, Tamar	'94 – 3	Magdalena Yoder	Mennonite inn owner & operator
Philadelphia	Haddam, Jane	'90 – 12	Gregor Demarkian	former FBI department head

United States . . . continued

Setting	Author	1 – #	Series Character	Occupation

Pennsylvania . . . continued

Setting	Author	1 – #	Series Character	Occupation
Philadelphia	Murray, Donna Huston	'95 – 2	Ginger Struve Barnes	amateur sleuth
Philadelphia	Roberts, Gillian	'87 – 6	Amanda Pepper	high school teacher
Philadelphia	Scottoline, Lisa	'94 – 1	Grace Rossi	Federal appeals attorney & law clerk
Philadelphia	Scottoline, Lisa	'93 – 1	Mary DiNunzio	attorney
Philadelphia	Scottoline, Lisa	'95 – 1	Rita Morrone Hamilton	attorney

Rhode Island

Setting	Author	1 – #	Series Character	Occupation
Newport	Kruger, Mary	'94 – 2	Brooke Cassidy & Matt Devlin	mystery writer & P. I.

South Carolina

Setting	Author	1 – #	Series Character	Occupation
	Hart, Carolyn G.	'87 – 9	Annie Laurance & Max Darling	bookstore owner & investigator
	Hart, Carolyn G.	'93 – 3	Henrietta O'Dwyer Collins	70-something reporter

Tennessee

Setting	Author	1 – #	Series Character	Occupation
	McCrumb, Sharyn	'90 – 4	Spencer Arrowood	Appalachian sheriff
Jesus Creek	Adams, Deborah	'92 – 5	Jesus Creek TN	eccentric small town

Texas

Setting	Author	1 – #	Series Character	Occupation
	Banks, Carolyn	'93 – 3	Robin Vaughn	equestrienne sleuth
	Cooper, Susan Rogers	'92 – 2	E. J. Pugh	housewife, mother & romance writer
	Romberg, Nina	'89 – 2	Marian Winchester	Caddo-Commanche medicine woman
	Tell, Dorothy	'90 – 3	Poppy Dillworth	60-something lesbian sleuth
	Walker, Mary Willis	'91 – 1	Kate Driscoll	dog trainer
	Walker, Mary Willis	'94 – 2	Mollie Cates	true crime writer & reporter
	Webb, Martha G.	'85 – 2	Tommy Inman	cop
Austin	Amey, Linda	'92 – 2	Blair Emerson	funeral director
Austin	Cooper, Susan Rogers	'93 – 2	Kimmey Kruse	stand-up comic
Bayport	Wingate, Anne	'88 – 5	Mark Shigata	ex-FBI agent turned sheriff
Canadian	Meredith, D. R.	'88 – 5	John L. Branson & Lydia Fairchild	defense attorney & legal assistant
Ft. Worth	Martin, Lee	'84 – 11	Deb Ralston	police detective & mother
Houston	Bradley, Lynn	'94 – 1	Coleman January	insurance investigator
Houston	Powell, Deborah	'91 – 2	Hollis Carpenter	gay woman crime reporter
Los Santos	Herndon, Nancy	'95 – 2	Elena Jarvis	detective with the Crimes Against Persons unit
Pecan Springs	Albert, Susan Wittig	'92 – 4	China Bayles	herb shop owner & former attorney
Purple Sage	Smith, Barbara B.	'94 – 3	Jolie Wyatt	aspiring novelist & writer's group member
San Antonio	Morell, Mary	'91 – 2	Lucia Ramos	lesbian police detective
west	Meredith, D. R.	'84 – 5	Charles Matthews	sheriff

Utah

Setting	Author	1 – #	Series Character	Occupation
	Moffat, Gwen	'73 – 14	Melinda Pink	writer & mountain climber

Vermont

Setting	Author	1 – #	Series Character	Occupation
	Comfort, Barbara	'86 – 4	Tish McWhinney	70-something artist & painter

United States . . . *continued*

Setting	Author	❶ – #	Series Character	Occupation

Virginia

Setting	Author	❶ – #	Series Character	Occupation
Crozet	Brown, Rita Mae	'90 – 4	Mary Minor Haristeen	small-town postmistress & cat
Richmond	Cornwell, Patricia	'90 – 6	Kay Scarpetta, Dr.	chief medical examiner

Washington

Setting	Author	❶ – #	Series Character	Occupation
	Dereske, Jo	'94 – 4	Helma Zukas	state librarian
	Elkins, Charlotte & Aaron	'89 – 2	Lee Ofsted & Graham Sheldon	golf pro & homicide detective
Alpine	Daheim, Mary	'92 – 7	Emma Lord	small-town newspaper owner & editor
Seattle	Beck, K. K.	'92 – 4	Jane da Silva	former lounge singer
Seattle	Daheim, Mary	'91 – 9	Judith McMonigle	bed & breakfast owner

Washington . . . continued

Setting	Author	❶ – #	Series Character	Occupation
Seattle	Gilpatrick, Noreen	'93 – 2	Kate McLean	police detective
Seattle	Hendricksen, Louise	'93 – 3	Amy Prescott, Dr.	crime lab physician
Seattle	Jance, J. A.	'85 – 13	J. P. Beaumont	homicide detective
Seattle	Mariz, Linda French	'92 – 2	Laura Ireland	grad student volleyball player
Seattle	Smith, Janet L.	'90 – 3	Annie MacPherson	attorney
Seattle	Thompson, Joyce	'91 – 1	Frederika Bascomb	forensic artist
Seattle	Wilson, Barbara	'84 – 3	Pam Nilsen	lesbian printing company owner

Wisconsin

Setting	Author	❶ – #	Series Character	Occupation
Milwaukee	McGiffin, Janet	'92 – 3	Maxene St. Clair, Dr.	emergency room physician

Wyoming

Setting	Author	❶ – #	Series Character	Occupation
	Andrews, Sarah	'94 – 2	Em Hansen	oil worker
Jackson	McClendon, Lise	'94 – 2	Alix Thorssen	gallery owner & art forgery expert
Sheridan	Landreth, Marsha	'92 – 3	Samantha Turner, Dr.	medical examiner
Wind River Reserv.	Coel, Margaret	'95 – 2	John A. O'Malley & Vicky Holden	Jesuit missionary & Arapaho attorney

Miscellaneous U.S.

Setting	Author	❶ – #	Series Character	Occupation
	Ballard, Mignon	'93 – 1	Eliza Figg	former Peace Corps volunteer
	Dietz, Denise	'93 – 2	Ellie Bernstein	diet group leader
	Dunant, Sarah	'88 – 1	Marla Masterson	young British professor of literature
	Hightower, Lynn S.	'92 – 4	David Silver & String	homicide cop & alien partner
	Hooper, Kay	'87 – 11	Hagen	government agent
	Jackson, Marian J. A.	'90 – 5	Abigail Patience Danforth	turn-of-the-century consulting detective
	Kreuter, Katherine E.	'94 – 1	Paige Taylor	mystery writer & P. I.
	Lyons, Nan & Ivan	'76 – 2	Natasha O'Brien & Millie Ogden	pair of culinary artists
	Mather, Linda	'94 – 3	Jo Hughes	professional astrologer
	McAllester, Melanie	'94 – 1	Elizabeth Mendoza & Ashley Johnson	lesbian homicide detectives
	McCrumb, Sharyn	'88 – 2	James Owens Mega, Dr.	college professor & science fiction author
	Porath, Sharon	'95 – 1	Kendra MacFarlane	amateur sleuth
	Rice, Craig	'42 – 3	Bingo Riggs & Handsome Kusak	gullible city slickers & reluctant detectives
	Ruryk, Jean	'94 – 1	Catherine Wilde	retired ad exec turned antiques restorer
	Stein, Triss	'93 – 1	Kay Engles	nationally-known reporter

United States . . . continued

Setting	Author	◨ – #	Series Character	Occupation

Miscellaneous U.S. . . . continued

Setting	Author	◨ – #	Series Character	Occupation
	Stevens, Serita	'91 – 2	Fanny Zindel	Jewish grandmother
Midwest	Braun, Lilian Jackson	'66 – 18	Jim Qwilleran, Koko & Yum Yum	ex-police reporter & cats
Midwest	Gosling, Paula	'94 – 2	Blackwater Bay Mystery	police series with a Great Lakes setting
Midwest	Skom, Edith	'89 – 2	Elizabeth Austin	English professor
National Parks	Barr, Nevada	'93 – 4	Anna Pigeon	U. S. park ranger
National Parks	Dengler, Sandy	'93 – 4	Jack Prester	U. S. park ranger
New England	Blackmur, L. L.	'89 – 2	Galen Shaw & Julian Baugh	writer & financier
Northeast	Lawrence, Hilda	'44 – 3	Mark East, Bessie Petty & Beulah Pond	New York city P. I. & New England little old ladies
Northeast	Wolzien, Valerie	'96 – 1	Josie Pigeon	owner of an all-women construction firm
Puerto Rico	Adamson, M. J.	'87 – 5	Balthazar Marten & Sixto Cardenas	NYPD homicide det. & Puerto Rican cop
Southern	McCrumb, Sharyn	'84 – 8	Elizabeth MacPherson	forensic anthropologist
Western	Lee, W. W. (Wendi)	'89 – 6	Jefferson Birch	P. I. in the Old West

United Kingdom

England

Setting	Author	◨ – #	Series Character	Occupation
	Atherton, Nancy	'92 – 3	Aunt Dimity	romantic ghost
	Bannister, Jo	'84 – 3	Clio Rees, Dr. & Harry Marsh	physician/mystery writer & chief inspector
	Bridge, Ann	'56 – 7	Julia Probyn Jamieson	freelance journalist & part-time agent
	Burton, Anne	'80 – 3	Richard Trenton	banker
	Challis, Mary	'80 – 4	Jeremy Locke	attorney
	Chisholm, P. F.	'95 – 3	Robert Carey, Sir	Elizabethan nobleman (1592)
	Cleeves, Ann	'90 – 4	Stephen Ramsey	British inspector
	Cohen, Anthea	'82 – 13	Agnes Carmichael	hospital staff nurse
	Duffy, Margaret	'87 – 6	Ingrid Langley & Patrick Gillard	novelist/British agent & British army major
	Eccles, Marjorie	'88 – 8	Gil Mayo	detective chief inspector
	Edwards, Ruth D.	'81 – 5	James Milton & Robert Amiss	police supt & ex-civil servant
	Erskine, Margaret	'38 – 21	Septimus Finch	Scotland Yard Inspector
	Ferrars, E. X.	'83 – 8	Andrew Basnett	retired botany professor
	Ferrars, E. X.	'71 – 2	Ditteridge, Supt.	police superintendent
	Ferrars, E. X.	'40 – 5	Toby Dyke	amateur sleuth
	Ferrars, E. X.	'78 – 9	Virginia & Felix Freer	physiotherapist & businessman
	Fraser, Anthea	'86 – 13	David Webb	British police inspector
	Frome, David	'30 – 11	Evan Pinkerton	Welshman
	Fyfield, Frances	'89 – 2	Sarah Fortune	lawyer in prestigious British firm
	Gilbert, Anthony	'36 – 50	Arthur G. Crook	Cockney lawyer-detective
	Gilbert, Anthony	'27 – 9	Scott Egerton	Liberal M.P. & man about town
	Gill, B. M.	'80 – 3	Tom Maybridge	police inspector
	Gosling, Paula	'86 – 2	Luke Abbott	English cop
	Graham, Caroline	'87 – 4	Tom Barnaby	chief inspector
	Grant-Adamson, L.	'92 – 2	Jim Rush	American on the run from British police
	Gray, Dulcie	'60 – 2	Cardiff, Insp. Supt.	police inspector
	Green, Christine	'91 – 3	Kate Kinsella	British nurse & medical investigator
	Greenwood, Diane M.	'91 – 6	Theodora Braithwaite, Rev.	British deaconess
	Grindle, Lucretia	'93 – 2	H. W. Ross	detective superintendent
	Hall, Patricia	'93 – 1	Alex Sinclair & Kate Weston	British inspector & social worker

United Kingdom . . . *continued*

Setting	Author	❶ – #	Series Character	Occupation
England . . . *continued*				
	Harrod-Eagles, C.	'91 – 5	Bill Slider	detective inspector
	Heyer, Georgette	'35 – 4	Hannasyde, Supt.	police superintendent
	Heyer, Georgette	'39 – 4	Hemingway, Insp.	one-time assistant to Supt. Hannasyde
	Highsmith, Patricia	'55 – 5	Tom Ripley	charming forger & psychopath
	Kelly, Mary	'61 – 2	Hedley Nicholson	P. I.
	La Plante, Lynda	'83 – 2	Dolly Rawlins	young English widow
	Laurence, Janet	'89 – 8	Darina Lisle	British caterer, chef & food writer
	Leek, Margaret	'80 – 3	Stephen Marryat	attorney
	Lemarchand, Elizabeth	'67 – 17	Tom Pollard & Gregory Toye	Scotland Yard detectives
	Linscott, Gillian	'84 – 3	Birdie Linnet	ex-cop fitness trainer
	Linscott, Gillian	'91 – 5	Nell Bray	British suffragette
	Livingston, Nancy	'85 – 8	G. D. H. Pringle	retired tax inspector
	Mann, Jessica	'82 – 6	Tamara Hoyland	British secret agent archaeologist
	Mann, Jessica	'72 – 2	Thea Crawford	archaeology professor
	McGerr, Patricia	'64 – 2	Selena Mead	British government agent
	Moody, Susan	'84 – 7	Penny Wanawake	photographer daughter of black diplomat
	Morice, Anne	'70 – 23	Tessa Crichton	English actress sleuth
	Myers, Amy	'82 – 8	Auguste Didier	British-French Victorian master chef
	Neel, Janet	'88 – 4	John McLeish & Francesca Wilson	detective inspector & civil servant
	Page, Emma	'80 – 8	Kelsey, Insp.	police inspector
	Perry, Anne	'90 – 6	William Monk	amnesiac Victorian police inspector
	Petrie, Rhona	'63 – 5	Marcus MacLurg	Inspector
	Porter, Joyce	'70 – 5	Constance Ethel Morrison Burke	comic senior sleuth
	Porter, Joyce	'66 – 4	Eddie Brown	comic spy
	Porter, Joyce	'64 – 21	Wilfred Dover	a fat lout of a Chief Inspector
	Rinehart, Mary Roberts	'32 – 3	Hilda Adams aka Miss Pinkerton	nurse & police agent
	Robb, Candace M.	'93 – 3	Owen Archer	medieval Welsh spy for the archbishop
	Roome, Annette	'89 – 2	Christine Martin	40-something cub reporter
	Sedley, Kate	'91 – 6	Roger the Chapman	medieval chapman (peddler)
	Simpson, Dorothy	'81 – 13	Luke Thanet	British police inspector
	Spring, Michelle	'94 – 2	Laura Principal	British academic turned P. I.
	Stacey, Susannah	'87 – 7	Robert Bone	widowed British police inspector
	Sumner, Penny	'92 – 2	Victoria Cross	archivist turned P. I.
	Torrie, Malcolm	'66 – 6	Timothy Herring	preservation society director
	Winslow, Pauline Glen	'75 – 6	Merlin Capricorn	magician turned police superintendent
	Woods, Sara	'62 – 48	Antony Maitland	barrister drawn to murder cases
Allshire	Mason, Sarah Jill	'93 – 4	D. S. Trewley & Stone, Sgt.	village detective partners
Badger's End	Kingsbury, Kate	'93 – 7	Cecily Sinclair	hotel owner in Edwardian England
Bath	Brown, Lizbie	'92 – 2	Elizabeth Blair	widow from Turkey Creek, VA selling quilts
Bath	Duffy, Margaret	'94 – 2	Joanna MacKenzie	former CID turned P. I.
Cambridge	Walsh, Jill Paton	'93 – 2	Imogen Quy	school nurse at St. Agatha's College
Castlemere	Bannister, Jo	'93 – 4	F. Shapiro, C. Donovan & L. Graham	cops
Chitterton Falls	Cannell, Dorothy	'84 – 7	Ellie & Ben Haskell	interior decorator & writer/chef
Cornwall	Black, Veronica	'90 – 8	Joan, Sister	British investigative nun
Cotswolds	Beaton, M. C.	'92 – 4	Agatha Raisin	London advertising retiree
Cotswolds	Granger, Ann	'91 – 9	Alan Markby & Meredith Mitchell	detective inspector & Foreign Service officer
Cotswolds	Moody, Susan	'93 – 4	Cassandra Swann	British biology teacher turned bridge pro
Cotswolds	Quest, Erica	'88 – 3	Kate Maddox	Det. Chief Inspector

United Kingdom . . . continued

Setting	Author	▣ – #	Series Character	Occupation

England . . . continued

Setting	Author	▣ – #	Series Character	Occupation
Cotswolds	Rowlands, Betty	'89 – 7	Melissa Craig	British mystery writer
Dedham	Paige, Robin	'94 – 2	Kathryn Ardleigh	25-yr-old American author
Deerham Hills	Melville, Jennie	'62 – 17	Charmian Daniels	police detective
Devon	Holt, Hazel	'89 – 7	Sheila Malory	British literary magazine writer
East Anglia	McGown, Jill	'83 – 7	Lloyd, Chief Inspector & Judy Hill	detective inspectors
East Yorkshire	Highsmith, Domini	'95 – 1	Simeon, Father & Elvira	medieval priest & nurse
Essex	Thomson, June	'71 – 18	Finch, Insp.	police inspector
Fetherbridge	Holbrook, Teri	'95 – 2	Gale Grayson	American expatriate historian
Fowchester	Green, Christine	'94 – 3	Connor O'Neill & Fran Wilson	village inspector & new policewoman
Hampshire	Dunn, Carola	'94 – 4	Daisy Dalrymple	young aristocratic woman writer
Herefordshire	Burden, Pat	'90 – 4	Henry Bassett	retired cop
Hop Valley	Kelly, Susan B.	'90 – 5	Alison Hope & Nick Trevellyan	software designer & detective inspector
Kent	Crane, Hamilton	'68 – 19	Emily D. Seeton	retired British art teacher
Kent	Hardwick, Mollie	'86 – 6	Doran Fairweather	British antiques dealer
Kent	Peters, Elizabeth	'75 – 7	Amelia Peabody	Victorian feminist archaeologist
Kent County	Brand, Christianna	'41 – 6	Cockrill, Insp.	police inspector
Little Gidding	Warner, Mignon	'76 – 7	Edwina Charles	British clairvoyant
London	Allingham, Margery	'29 – 22	Albert Campion	suave sleuth with noble blood
London	Babson, Marian	'71 – 4	Douglas Perkins	London-based public relations agent
London	Babson, Marian	'86 – 5	Eve Sinclair & Trixie Dolan	aging British ex-movie queens
London	Bell, Josephine	'79 – 2	Amy Tupper	amateur sleuth
London	Bell, Josephine	'59 – 3	Claude Warrington-Reeve	barrister
London	Bell, Josephine	'37 – 14	David Wintringham, Dr.	British physician
London	Bell, Josephine	'64 – 2	Henry Frost, Dr.	British physician
London	Bell, Josephine	'38 – 1	Steven Mitchell	Scotland Yard Inspector
London	Brightwell, Emily	'93 – 7	Witherspoon, Insp. & Jeffries, Mrs.	Victorian police inspector & housekeeper
London	Butler, Gwendoline	'57 – 24	John Coffin, Insp.	police inspector
London	Charles, Kate	'91 – 5	Lucy Kingsley & D. Middleton-Brown	artist & solicitor
London	Christie, Agatha	'20 – 35	Hercule Poirot	former Belgian cop turned private detective
London	Christie, Agatha	'22 – 4	Tuppence & Tommy Beresford	adventurers for hire & intelligence agents
London	Clarke, Anna	'85 – 8	Paula Glenning	British professor & writer
London	Cody, Liza	'80 – 6	Anna Lee	P. I.
London	Cody, Liza	'93 – 2	Eva Wylie	wrestler & security guard
London	Cooper, Natasha	'90 – 5	Willow King & Cressida Woodruffe	civil servant & romance novelist
London	Crombie, Deborah	'93 – 3	Duncan Kincaid & Gemma James	Scotland Yard superintendent & sergeant
London	Crowleigh, Ann	'93 – 2	Mirinda & Clare Clively	Victorian London twin sisters
London	Danks, Denise	'89 – 3	Georgina Powers	British computer journalist
London	de la Torre, Lillian	'46 – 4	Samuel Johnson, Dr. & J. Boswell	18th century lexicographer & biographer
London	Donald, Anabel	'91 – 4	Alex Tanner	part-time P. I. & TV researcher
London	Dunant, Sarah	'92 – 3	Hannah Wolfe	P. I.
London	Fraser, Antonia	'77 – 8	Jemima Shore	British TV interviewer
London	Fyfield, Frances	'88 – 5	Helen West	London Crown prosecutor
London	George, Elizabeth	'88 – 8	Thomas Lynley & Barbara Havers	Scotland Yard inspector & detective sergeant
London	Giroux, E. X.	'84 – 10	Robert Forsythe & Abigail Sanderson	barrister & secretary
London	Grant-Adamson, L.	'91 – 2	Laura Flynn	P. I.
London	Grant-Adamson, L.	'85 – 5	Rain Morgan	newspaper reporter England
London	Grimes, Martha	'81 – 13	Richard Jury, Insp.	Scotland Yard investigator
London	Hambly, Barbara	'88 – 2	James Asher	professor & one-time spy

United Kingdom . . . *continued*

Setting	Author	❶ – #	Series Character	Occupation

England . . . *continued*

Setting	Author	❶ – #	Series Character	Occupation
London	James, P. D.	'62 – 9	Adam Dalgleish	published poet of Scotland Yard
London	James, P. D.	'72 – 2	Cordelia Gray	fledgling P. I.
London	King, Laurie R.	'94 – 2	Mary Russell	teenage student of Sherlock Holmes
London	La Plante, Lynda	'93 – 3	Jane Tennison	detective chief inspector
London	Marsh, Ngaio	'34 – 32	Roderick Alleyn	inspector son of a baronet
London	Meek, M. R. D.	'83 – 10	Lennox Kemp	solicitor detective
London	Mitchell, Gladys	'29 – 66	Beatrice Lestrange Bradley	psychiatrist & consultant to Home Office
London	Moyes, Patricia	'59 – 19	Henry & Emmy Tibbett	Scotland Yard inspector & wife
London	Perry, Anne	'79 – 16	Thomas & Charlotte Pitt	Victorian police inspector & wife
London	Peterson, Audrey	'92 – 3	Claire Camden	California English professor in Britain
London	Peterson, Audrey	'88 – 6	Jane Winfield	British journalist & music writer
London	Ross, Kate	'93 – 3	Julian Kestrel	1820s dandy-about-town
London	Sayers, Dorothy L.	'23 – 13	Peter Wimsey, Lord	pianist, bibliophile & criminologist
London	Slovo, Gillian	'84 – 5	Kate Baeier	freelance journalist turned detective
London	Smith, Joan	'87 – 5	Loretta Lawson	British feminist professor
London	Tey, Josephine	'29 – 6	Alan Grant	Scotland Yard inspector
London	Wakefield, Hannah	'87 – 2	Dee Street	American attorney
London	Wentworth, Patricia	'39 – 2	Ernest Lamb, Insp.	police inspector
London	Wentworth, Patricia	'28 – 32	Maud Silver, Miss	retired governess & spinster P. I.
London	Wilson, Barbara	'90 – 2	Cassandra Reilly	Spanish translator
Malminster	Mitchell, Kay	'90 – 5	John Morrissey	Chief Inspector
Manchester	McDermid, Val	'92 – 5	Kate Brannigan	P. I.
Norwich	Haymon, S. T.	'80 – 7	Benjamin Jurnet, Insp.	detective inspector
Nottingham	Shepherd, Stella	'89 – 6	Richard Montgomery	CID Inspector
Oxford	Caudwell, Sarah	'81 – 3	Hilary Tamar	Oxford professor of medieval law
Oxford	Stallwood, Veronica	'93 – 3	Kate Ivory	novelist
Oxford	Yorke, Margaret	'70 – 5	Patrick Grant, Dr.	Oxford don teaching English literature
Oxfordshire	Frazer, Margaret	'92 – 6	Frevisse, Sister	Medieval nun
Shrewsbury	Peters, Ellis	'77 – 20	Brother Cadfael	medieval monk & herbalist
Shropshire	Peters, Ellis	'51 – 13	George, Bunty & Dominic Felse	family of detectives
St. Mary's Mead	Christie, Agatha	'30 – 12	Jane Marple, Miss	elderly spinster
Suffolk	Radley, Sheila	'78 – 9	Douglas Quantrill & Hilary Lloyd	detective chief inspector & sergeant partner
Surrey	Cleeves, Ann	'86 – 8	George & Molly Palmer-Jones	ex-Home Office bird-watcher & wife
Sussex	Rendell, Ruth	'64 – 16	Reginald Wexford	chief inspector
Thames Valley	Curzon, Clare	'83 – 10	Mike Yeadings	detective superintendent of Serious Crime Squad
West Calleshire	Aird, Catherine	'66 – 13	Christopher Dennis "Seedy" Sloan	Berebury CID department head
Woodfield	Jordan, Jennifer	'87 – 3	Barry & Dee Vaughan	spoofy crime writer & office temp wife
Woodfield	Jordan, Jennifer	'92 – 2	Kristin Ashe	amateur sleuth
Yorkshire	Hall, Patricia	'94 – 3	Laura Ackroyd & Michael Thackeray	reporter & police inspector
Yorkshire	Lacey, Sarah	'92 – 4	Leah Hunter	tax inspector

Ireland

Setting	Author	❶ – #	Series Character	Occupation
Dublin	Fallon, Ann C.	'90 – 5	James Fleming	solicitor

United Kingdom . . . *continued*

Setting	Author	❶ – #	Series Character	Occupation

Scotland

Setting	Author	❶ – #	Series Character	Occupation
	Beaton, M. C.	'85 – 11	Hamish Macbeth	Scottish police constable
Edinburgh	Kelly, Mary	'56 – 3	Brett Nightingale	Scottish Inspector
Edinburgh	Knight, Alanna	'88 – 9	Jeremy Faro	Victorian detective inspector
Glasgow	McDermid, Val	'87 – 4	Lindsay Gordon	lesbian journalist & socialist

Other Nations

Australia

Setting	Author	❶ – #	Series Character	Occupation
	Day, Marele	'88 – 4	Claudia Valentine	Australian P. I.
	Rowe, Jennifer	'89 – 4	Verity "Birdie" Birdwood	TV researcher
Melbourne	Greenwood, Kerry	'89 – 8	Phryne Fisher	'20s sleuth
Sydney	Bedford, Jean	'90 – 3	Anna Southwood	P. I.
Sydney	Geason, Susan	'93 – 3	Syd Fish	P. I.
Sydney	McNab, Claire	'88 – 7	Carol Ashton	lesbian detective inspector & single mother

Canada

Setting	Author	❶ – #	Series Character	Occupation
	Craig, Alisa	'80 – 5	Madoc & Janet Rhys	RCMP inspector & wife
	Kelly, Nora	'84 – 3	Gillian Adams	Univ. of the Pacific Northwest history chair
Calgary	North, Suzanne	'94 – 1	Phoebe Fairfax	TV video photographer
Lobelia Falls, Ont.	Craig, Alisa	'81 – 5	Dittany Henbit Monk & Osbert Monk	garden club member & author of westerns
Montreal	Manthorne, Jackie	'94 – 3	Harriett Hubley	intrepid lesbian sleuth
Montreal	Smith, Joan G.	'89 – 2	Cassie Newton	French major at McGill University
Regina, Sask.	Bowen, Gail	'90 – 4	Joanne Kilbourn	political science professor
Toronto, Ontario	Gordon, Alison	'89 – 4	Kate Henry	baseball newswriter
Toronto, Ontario	Huff, Tanya	'92 – 4	Vicki Nelson	ex-cop turned P. I. with vampire lover
Toronto, Ontario	Millar, Margaret	'41 – 3	Paul Prye, Dr.	psychiatrist
Toronto, Ontario	Millar, Margaret	'43 – 2	Sands, Insp.	police inspector
Toronto, Ontario	Sale, Medora	'86 – 6	John Sanders & Harriet Jeffries	police detective & architectural photographer
Toronto, Ontario	Porter, Anna	'85 – 2	Judith Hayes	journalist
Vancouver, B.C.	Wright, L. R.	'85 – 7	Martin Karl Alberg	RCMP staff sergeant
Vancouver, B.C.	Bowers, Elisabeth	'88 – 2	Meg Lacey	P. I.
Victoria	Douglas, Lauren W.	'87 – 6	Caitlin Reece	lesbian detective

Egypt

Setting	Author	❶ – #	Series Character	Occupation
	Robinson, Lynda S.	'94 – 3	Meren, Lord	chief investigator for Pharaoh Tutankhamen

France

Setting	Author	❶ – #	Series Character	Occupation
	Fawcett, Quinn	'93 – 2	Victoire Vernet	wife of Napoleonic gendarme
	Newman, Sharan	'93 – 3	Catherine LeVendeur	novice & scholar in 12th century
Paris	Douglas, Carole N.	'90 – 4	Irene Adler	19th century French sleuth
Paris	Friedman, Mickey	'88 – 2	Georgia Lee Maxwell	freelance writer
Provence	Shone, Anna	'95 – 1	Ulysses Finnegan Donaghue	Shakespeare-spouting P. I.

Other Nations . . . *continued*

Setting	Author	❶ – #	Series Character	Occupation
Germany				
	Peters, Elizabeth	'73 – 5	Vicky Bliss	art historian
Israel				
Jerusalem	Gur, Batya	'88 – 3	Michael Ohayon	chief inspector
Italy				
	Eyre, Elizabeth	'92 – 5	Sigismondo	agent of a Renaissance duke
	Jones, Hazel Wynn	'88 – 2	Emma Shaw	documentary film director
Florence	Nabb, Magdalen	'81 – 10	Salvatore Guarnaccia	Italian police marshal
Rome	Davis, Lindsey	'89 – 8	Marcus Didius Falco	P. I. in ancient Rome
Venice	Leon, Donna	'92 – 5	Guido Brunetti	commissario of the Venice police
Japan				
	McFall, Patricia	'92 – 1	Nora James	American linguistics graduate student
Kenya				
	Huxley, Elspeth	'37 – 3	Vachell, Supt.	young Scotsman trained by the RCMP
	McQuillan, Karin	'90 – 3	Jazz Jasper	American safari guide
New Zealand				
	Beecham, Rose	'92 – 3	Amanda Valentine	ex-NYPD cop turned detective inspector
	Scott, Rosie	'89 – 1	Glory Day	artist & singer
Spain				
	Oliver, Maria Antonia	'87 – 2	Lonia Gulu	Catalan P. I.
Sweden				
Stockholm	Sjöwall & Wahlöö	'67 – 10	Martin Beck	police officer
World Travelers				
	Arnold, Margot	'79 – 12	Penny Spring & Toby Glendower	Amer anthropologist & Brit archlgst
	Crane, Frances	'41 – 26	Pat & Jean Abbot	husband & wife detection team
	Dunnett, Dorothy	'68 – 7	Johnson Johnson	portrait painter & British agent w/his yacht
	Gilman, Dorothy	'66 – 12	Emily Pollifax	grandmother CIA agent
	Yates, Margaret E. T.	'37 – 4	Anne "Davvie" Davenport McLean	newspaper correspondent

Five

Mystery chronology

The explosion of series mystery titles written by women, published in the 15 years since 1980, is a stunning phenomenon. As shown in Figure A, *110 Years of Series Mysteries Written by Women, 1890 to 1999*, the number of new mystery titles introduced by women writers grew at a steady pace in each decade from 1900 to 1980, notwithstanding the brief wartime surge of titles in the 1940s.

But starting in 1980, the mystery floodgates began releasing a virtual torrent of new titles and new series detectives created by women writers. During the 1980s, the number of new series mystery titles jumped 504 over the previous decade (793 vs. 289), while the number of new series increased more than fivefold (207 new series vs. a mere 40 new series introduced during the 1970s).

The average number of new series introduced each year during the 1980s increased by a factor of 5 over the prior decade (21 vs. 4). In fact, the 1980s was the first decade in which the number of new series introduced every year was in double digits. Not once during the previous 90 years had more than nine new series detectives appeared from women authors in a single year.

On the next page, Figure B, *New Mystery Titles and Series from Women Writers, 1960 to 1995*, shows the number of new titles and new series introduced each year beginning in 1960.

Decade	New Titles	New Series	Avg Titles per Year	Avg Series per Year
1890–1899	5	1	–	–
1900–1909	4	1	–	–
1910–1919	14	1	1	–
1920–1929	46	10	5	1
1930–1939	168	25	17	2
1940–1949	271	28	27	3
1950–1959	202	15	20	1
1960–1969	240	32	24	3
1970–1979	289	40	29	4
1980–1989	793	207	79	21
100 years	**2032**	**360**	**20**	**4**
1990–1994	1130	282	226	56
5 years actual	1130	282	226	56
1995–99 (est)	1250	225	250	45
1990–99 (est)	2380	507	238	51
10 years (est)	**2380**	**507**	**238**	**51**

Figure A

110 Years of Series Mysteries Written by Women, 1890 to 1999

Year	New Titles	New Series
1960	17	2
1961	16	3
1962	22	4
1963	24	2
1964	27	7
1965	21	0
1966	26	6
1967	27	2
1968	33	6
1969	27	–
1970	31	3
1971	36	4
1972	29	6
1973	30	3
1974	20	–
1975	27	2
1976	28	7
1977	31	6
1978	30	4
1979	27	5
1980	48	12
1981	44	10
1982	50	11
1983	49	14
1984	73	21
1985	81	17
1986	82	19
1987	98	29
1988	120	33
1989	148	41
1990	168	48
1991	175	40
1992	216	57
1993	279	68
1994	292	69
1995	288*	32*

undercount due to incomplete reporting

Figure B

New Mystery Titles and Series from Women Writers, 1960 to 1995

The upsurge which starts building in 1980 (48 new titles vs. 27 in 1979) shifts into overdrive in 1988 (121 titles vs. 95 in the prior year) and just keeps climbing.

Likewise the number of new series introduced each year by women mystery writers just keeps growing. In 1994 almost 6 new series each month (69 for the year) appeared on the scene, with close to 300 new series titles overall. When the official tally for 1994 is complete, the number will probably exceed 300.

The numbers shown thus far for 1995 also represent an undercount and may again hit the 300-title mark. It is doubtful, however, that the number of new series introduced in 1995 will reach the 1994 peak of 69. And this may be the first sign that the slowdown and perhaps even the retreat has begun.

The bar graphs on the opposite page (see Figure C, *36 Years of Series Mysteries Written by Women, 1960 to 1995*) paint a powerful picture of the 15-year run-up in mystery series titles from women. Another look at Figure A shows how this activity compares with what came before 1960.

Assuming the last four years of the '90s (1996 to 1999) will yield a mystery output in the 250-titles-per-year range, the decade's total will top out just under 2400 titles, approximately 15% more series mysteries from women than in the preceding 100 years (1890 to 1989).

An obvious question at this point is how does this activity compare with what's been happening with series titles written by men? The answer is that we do not know, yet. Perhaps the forthcoming **Detecting Men** will answer some of these questions, but until the new data is collected and analyzed, we can only guess. We do have our suspicions though. We're betting the surge in mystery titles written by women indicates that women who write mysteries are finally approaching parity with men (at least in numbers of titles), rather than taking over the field.

In the meantime, we continue to marvel at the increasing height of our to-be-read stacks of books and give thanks for new fictional friends and the pleasures of return visits with our favorites. Stay tuned.

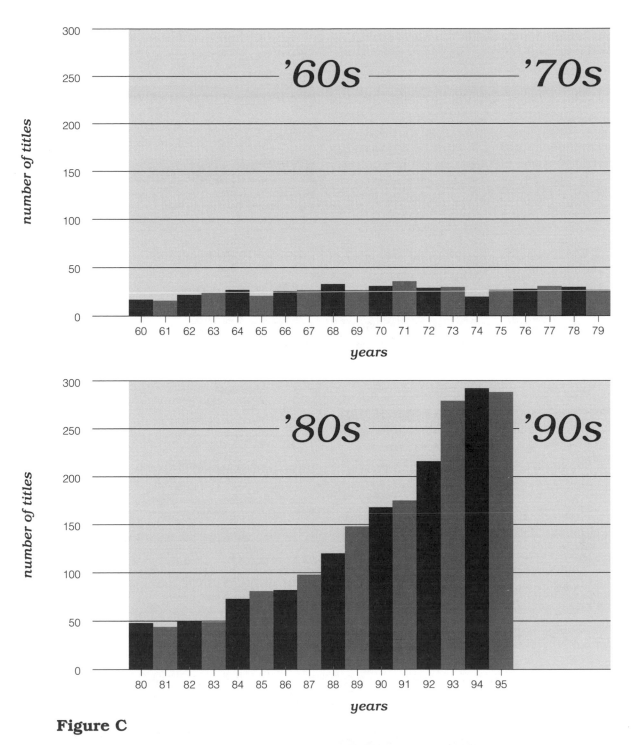

Figure C

36 Years of Series Mysteries Written by Women, 1960 to 1995

On the following pages, presented in chronological order, are more than 3,600 series mystery titles written by women, beginning with nine titles from Anna Katherine Green published before 1900. Titles from the same year are listed alphabetically by author, which means that in 1982 *'A' is for Alibi* (Grafton) is listed ahead of *Indemnity Only* (Paretsky). Both titles are marked with a small black square containing the number '1.' Whenever you see this symbol, it indicates first-in-a-series.

Prior to 1990, titles are grouped by decade with a black bar used as a divider every ten years. The total number of series mystery titles and the number of new series for the decade are printed on each bar. Starting with 1990, titles are summarized by year, owing to their large number.

Each title is listed according to its earliest known date of publication. This means that British, Canadian and Australian titles are likely to appear earlier than their U.S. editions. If the title has not changed, the book is not re-listed for U.S. publication. In cases where the title does change and there is a long period between first and second publication, both titles are listed, with cross references.

For example, when Chelsea Quinn Yarbro's first Charles Spotted Moon title appeared in 1976, it was published as *Ogilvie, Tallant and Moon*, but when it was re-issued in 1990 it was titled *Bad Medicine*. You'll find the *Ogilvie* entry in 1976 with a cross-reference to *Bad Medicine* (1990) and the *Bad Medicine* title in 1990 with a cross-reference to 1976.

pre-1900	9 titles	2 ∎

1878 ∎	The Leavenworth Case (Green, Anna Katherine)
1880	A Strange Disappearance (Green, Anna Katherine)
1883	Hand and Ring (Green, Anna Katherine)
1888	Behind Closed Doors (Green, Anna Katherine)
1890	A Matter of Millions (Green, Anna Katherine)
1895	The Doctor, His Wife, and the Clock (Green, A. K.)
1897	That Affair Next Door (Green, Anna Katherine)
1898	Lost Man's Lane (Green, Anna Katherine)
1899 ∎	Agatha Webb (Green, Anna Katherine)

1900s	4 titles	1 ∎

1900	The Circular Study (Green, Anna Katherine)
1901	One of My Sons (Green, Anna Katherine)
1906	The Woman in the Alcove (Green, Anna Katherine)
1909 ∎	The Clue (Wells, Carolyn)

1910s	14 titles	1 ∎

1910	The House of the Whispering Pines (Green, Anna Katherine)
1911	Initials Only (Green, Anna Katherine)
1911	The Mystery of the Hasty Arrow (Green, Anna K.)
1911	The Gold Bag (Wells, Carolyn)
1912	A Chain of Evidence (Wells, Carolyn)
1913	The Maxwell Mystery (Wells, Carolyn)
1914	Anybody but Anne (Wells, Carolyn)

1915	The White Alley (Wells, Carolyn)
1916	The Curved Blades (Wells, Carolyn)
1917	The Mark of Cain (Wells, Carolyn)
1918 ∎	The Room with the Tassels (Wells, Carolyn)
1918	Vicky Van (Wells, Carolyn)
1919	The Man Who Fell Through the Earth (Wells, C.)
1919	The Diamond Pin (Wells, Carolyn)

1920s	46 titles	10 ∎

1920 ∎	The Mysterious Affair at Styles (Christie, Agatha)
1920	In the Onyx Lobby (Wells, Carolyn)
1920	Raspberry Jam (Wells, Carolyn)
1921	The Come-Back (Wells, Carolyn)
1921	The Luminous Face (Wells, Carolyn)
1921	The Mystery of the Sycamore (Wells, Carolyn)
1922 ∎	The Secret Adversary (Christie, Agatha)
1922	The Vanishing of Betty Varian (Wells, Carolyn)
1922	The Mystery Girl (Wells, Carolyn)
1923	Murder on the Links (Christie, Agatha)
1923 ∎	Whose Body? (Sayers, Dorothy L.)
1923	The Affair at Flower Acres (Wells, Carolyn)
1923	Wheels Within Wheels (Wells, Carolyn)
1923	Feathers Left Around (Wells, Carolyn)
1923	Spooky Hollow (Wells, Carolyn)
1924	Poirot Investigates [14 stories] (Christie, Agatha)
1924	The Furthest Fury (Wells, Carolyn)
1924	Prilligirl (Wells, Carolyn)
1925	Anything but the Truth (Wells, Carolyn)
1925	The Daughter of the House (Wells, Carolyn)
1926	The Murder of Roger Ackroyd (Christie, Agatha)
1926	Clouds of Witness (Sayers, Dorothy L.)
1926	The Bronze Hand (Wells, Carolyn)
1926	The Red-Haired Girl (Wells, Carolyn)
1927	The Big Four (Christie, Agatha)
1927 ∎	The Tragedy at Freyne (Gilbert, Anthony)
1927	Unnatural Death [U.S.–The Dawson Pedigree] (Sayers, Dorothy L.)
1927	All at Sea (Wells, Carolyn)
1927	Where's Emily? (Wells, Carolyn)
1928	The Mystery of the Blue Train (Christie, Agatha)
1928	The Murder of Mrs. Davenport (Gilbert, Anthony)
1928	The Unpleasantness at the Bellona Club (Sayers, D. L.)
1928	The Crime in the Crypt (Wells, Carolyn)
1928	The Tannahill Tangle (Wells, Carolyn)
1928 ∎	Grey Mask (Wentworth, Patricia)
1929 ∎	The Crime at Black Dudley [U.S.–The Black Dudley Murder] (Allingham, Margery)
1929	Partners in Crime [short stories] (Christie, Agatha)
1929 ∎	The Patient in Room 18 (Eberhart, Mignon G.)
1929	Death at Four Corners (Gilbert, Anthony)
1929	The Mystery of the Open Window (Gilbert, Anthony)
1929 ∎	Speedy Death (Mitchell, Gladys)
1929	The Mystery of a Butcher's Shop (Mitchell, Gladys)
1929	Lord Peter Views the Body (Sayers, Dorothy L.)
1929 ∎	The Man in the Queue [APA–Killer in the Crowd ('54)] (Tey, Josephine)
1929 ∎	Sleeping Dogs (Wells, Carolyn)
1929	The Tapestry Room Murder (Wells, Carolyn)
1929	Triple Murder (Wells, Carolyn)

1930s   168 titles   25 ☐

1930	Mystery Mile (Allingham, Margery)
1930 ☐	The Murder at the Vicarage (Christie, Agatha)
1930	While the Patient Slept (Eberhart, Mignon G.)
1930	The Mystery of Hunting's End (Eberhart, Mignon G.)
1930 ☐	The Hammersmith Murders (Frome, David)
1930	The Night of the Fog (Gilbert, Anthony)
1930	The Longer Bodies (Mitchell, Gladys)
1930 ☐	The Diamond Feather (Reilly, Helen)
1930	Strong Poison (Sayers, Dorothy L.)
1930	The Doorstep Murders (Wells, Carolyn)
1930	The Doomed Five (Wells, Carolyn)
1930	The Ghosts' High Noon (Wells, Carolyn)

1931	Look to the Lady [U.S.–The Gryth Chalice Mystery] (Allingham, Margery)
1931	Police at the Funeral (Allingham, Margery)
1931	From This Dark Stairway (Eberhart, Mignon G.)
1931	Two Against Scotland Yard [Britain–The By-Pass Murder] (Frome, David)
1931	Murder in the Mews (Reilly, Helen)
1931	Five Red Herrings [U.S.–Suspicious Characters] (Sayers, Dorothy L.)
1931 ☐	The Cape Cod Mystery (Taylor, Phoebe Atwood)
1931	The Skeleton at the Feast (Wells, Carolyn)
1931	Horror House (Wells, Carolyn)
1931	The Umbrella Murder (Wells, Carolyn)

1932	Peril at End House (Christie, Agatha)
1932	Murder by an Aristocrat (Eberhart, Mignon G.)
1932	The Man from Scotland Yard [Britain–Mr. Simpson Finds a Body] (Frome, David)
1932	The Body on the Beam (Gilbert, Anthony)
1932	The Long Shadow (Gilbert, Anthony)
1932	The Saltmarsh Murders (Mitchell, Gladys)
1932 ☐	Miss Pinkerton (Rinehart, Mary Roberts)
1932	Have His Carcase (Sayers, Dorothy L.)
1932	Death Lights a Candle (Taylor, Phoebe Atwood)
1932	Fuller's Earth (Wells, Carolyn)
1932	The Roll-Top Desk Mystery (Wells, Carolyn)

1933	Sweet Danger [U.S.–Kingdom of Death] [APA–The Fear Sign] (Allingham, Margery)
1933	Lord Edgware Dies [U.S.–Thirteen at Dinner] (Christie, Agatha)
1933	The Eel Pie Murders [Britain–The Eel Pie Mystery] (Frome, David)
1933 ☐	The Transatlantic Ghost (Gardiner, Dorothy)
1933	Murder Must Advertise (Sayers, Dorothy L.)
1933	Hangman's Holiday [short stories] (Sayers, D. L.)
1933	The Mystery of the Cape Cod Players (Taylor, P. A.)
1933	The Broken O (Wells, Carolyn)
1933	The Clue of the Eyelash (Wells, Carolyn)
1933	The Master Murderer (Wells, Carolyn)

1934	Death of a Ghost (Allingham, Margery)
1934	Three-Act Tragedy [U.S.–Murder in Three Acts] (Christie, Agatha)
1934	Murder on the Orient Express [U.S.–Murder in the Calais Coach] (Christie, Agatha)
1934 ☐	The Strangled Witness (Ford, Leslie)
1934	Mr. Pinkerton Goes to Scotland Yard [Britain–Arsenic in Richmond] (Frome, David)
1934	Mr. Pinkerton Finds a Body [Britain–The Body in the Turl] (Frome, David)
1934	A Drink for Mr. Cherry [Britain–Mr. Watson Intervenes] (Gardiner, Dorothy)
1934	An Old Lady Dies (Gilbert, Anthony)

1934 ☐	A Man Lay Dead (Marsh, Ngaio)
1934	Death at the Opera [Britain–Death in the Wet] (Mitchell, Gladys)
1934	McKee of Centre Street (Reilly, Helen)
1934	The Line-up (Reilly, Helen)
1934	The Nine Tailors (Sayers, Dorothy L.)
1934	The Mystery of the Cape Cod Tavern (Taylor, P. A.)
1934	Sandbar Sinister (Taylor, Phoebe Atwood)
1934	Eyes in the Wall (Wells, Carolyn)
1934	The Visiting Villain (Wells, Carolyn)

1935	Death in the Clouds [U.S.–Death in the Air] (Christie, Agatha)
1935	The ABC Murders [APA–The Alphabet Murders] (Christie, Agatha)
1935	Mr. Pinkerton Grows a Beard [Britain–The Body in Bedford Square] (Frome, David)
1935	The Man Who Was Too Clever (Gilbert, Anthony)
1935 ☐	Death in the Stocks [U.S.–Merely Murder] (Heyer, G.)
1935 ☐	Death Blew Out the Match (Knight, Kathleen Moore)
1935	Enter a Murderer (Marsh, Ngaio)
1935	The Nursing-Home Murder (Marsh, Ngaio)
1935	The Devil at Saxon Wall (Mitchell, Gladys)
1935	Gaudy Night (Sayers, Dorothy L.)
1935	The Tinkling Symbol (Taylor, Phoebe Atwood)
1935	Deathblow Hill (Taylor, Phoebe Atwood)
1935	For Goodness' Sake (Wells, Carolyn)
1935	The Beautiful Derelict (Wells, Carolyn)
1935	The Wooden Indian (Wells, Carolyn)

1936	Flowers for the Judge [APA–Legacy in Blood] (Allingham, Margery)
1936	Murder in Mesopotamia (Christie, Agatha)
1936	Cards on the Table (Christie, Agatha)
1936	Mr. Pinkerton Has the Clue (Frome, David)
1936 ☐	Murder by Experts (Gilbert, Anthony)
1936	Behold, Here's Poison (Heyer, Georgette)
1936	The Clue of the Poor Man's Shilling [Britain–The Poor Man's Shilling] (Knight, Kathleen Moore)
1936	The Wheel That Turned [APA–Murder Greets Jean Holton] (Knight, Kathleen Moore)
1936	Death in Ecstasy (Marsh, Ngaio)
1936	Dead Men's Morris (Mitchell, Gladys)
1936	Mr. Smith's Hat (Reilly, Helen)
1936	Dead Man's Control (Reilly, Helen)
1936	The Crimson Patch (Taylor, Phoebe Atwood)
1936	Out of Order (Taylor, Phoebe Atwood)
1936	A Shilling for Candles (Tey, Josephine)
1936	Money Musk (Wells, Carolyn)
1936	The Huddle (Wells, Carolyn)
1936	Murder in the Bookshop (Wells, Carolyn)
1936	In the Tiger's Cage (Wells, Carolyn)

1937	Dancers in Mourning [APA–Who Killed Chloe?] (Allingham, Margery)
1937	The Case of the Late Pig (Allingham, Margery)
1937 ☐	Murder in Hospital (Bell, Josephine)
1937	Death on the Borough Council (Bell, Josephine)
1937	Dumb Witness [U.S.–Poirot Loses a Client] (Christie, Agatha)
1937	Death on the Nile (Christie, Agatha)
1937	Murder in the Mews [U.S.–Dead Man's Mirror] (Christie, Agatha)
1937	Ill-Met by Moonlight (Ford, Leslie)
1937	The Simple Way of Poison (Ford, Leslie)
1937	The Black Envelope [Britain–The Guilt is Plain] (Frome, David)
1937	The Man Who Wasn't There (Gilbert, Anthony)

1930s . . . continued   168 titles   25 **1**

1937	Murder Has No Tongue (Gilbert, Anthony)
1937	They Found Him Dead (Heyer, Georgette)
1937 **1**	Murder at Government House (Huxley, Elspeth)
1937	Seven Were Veiled [Britain–Seven Were Suspect] [APA–Death Wears a (Bridal) Veil] (Knight, K. M.)
1937	Vintage Murder (Marsh, Ngaio)
1937	Come Away, Death (Mitchell, Gladys)
1937	Busman's Honeymoon (Sayers, Dorothy L.)
1937	Figure Away (Taylor, Phoebe Atwood)
1937	Octagon House (Taylor, Phoebe Atwood)
1937 **1**	Beginning with a Bash (Tilton, Alice)
1937	The Mystery of the Tarn (Wells, Carolyn)
1937	The Radio Studio Murder (Wells, Carolyn)
1937	The Case Is Closed (Wentworth, Patricia)
1937 **1**	The Hush-Hush Murders (Yates, Margaret Evelyn T.)

1938	The Fashion in Shrouds (Allingham, Margery)
1938 **1**	The Port of London (Bell, Josephine)
1938	Fall Over Cliff (Bell, Josephine)
1938	A Holiday for Murder (Christie, Agatha)
1938	Appointment with Death (Christie, Agatha)
1938	Hercule Poirot's Christmas [U.S.–Murder for Christmas] (Christie, Agatha)
1938 **1**	And Being Dead [U.S.–The Limping Man] [APA–The Painted Mask] (Erskine, Margaret)
1938	Three Bright Pebbles (Ford, Leslie)
1938	Treason in My Breast (Gilbert, Anthony)
1938	A Blunt Instrument (Heyer, Georgette)
1938	Murder on Safari (Huxley, Elspeth)
1938	The Tainted Token [APA–The Case of the Tainted Token] (Knight, Kathleen Moore)
1938	Acts of Black Night (Knight, Kathleen Moore)
1938	Artists in Crime (Marsh, Ngaio)
1938	Death in a White Tie (Marsh, Ngaio)
1938 **1**	Dance of Death [APA–Design for Dying] (McCloy, H.)
1938	St. Peter's Finger (Mitchell, Gladys)
1938 **1**	Murder on Russian Hill [Britain–Murder Before Breakfast] (Offord, Lenore Glen)
1938 **1**	Death Wears a White Gardenia (Popkin, Zelda)
1938	The Annulet of Gilt (Taylor, Phoebe Atwood)
1938	Banbury Bog (Taylor, Phoebe Atwood)
1938	The Cut Direct (Tilton, Alice)
1938	Gilt-Edged Guilt (Wells, Carolyn)
1938	The Killer (Wells, Carolyn)
1938	The Missing Link (Wells, Carolyn)

1939	Death at Half-Term [APA–Curtain Call for a Corpse] (Bell, Josephine)
1939	From Natural Causes (Bell, Josephine)
1939	Sad Cypress (Christie, Agatha)
1939	Reno Rendezvous [Britain–Mr. Cromwell is Dead] (Ford, Leslie)
1939	False to Any Man [Britain–Snow-White Murder] (Ford, Leslie)
1939	Mr. Pinkerton at the Old Angel [Britain–Mr. Pinkerton and the Old Angel] (Frome, David)
1939	The Bell of Death (Gilbert, Anthony)
1939	The Clock in the Hatbox (Gilbert, Anthony)
1939 **1**	Death on the Door Mat (Heberden, M. V.)
1939 **1**	No Wind of Blame (Heyer, Georgette)
1939	The African Poison Murders [Britain–Death of an Aryan] (Huxley, Elspeth)
1939	Overture to Death (Marsh, Ngaio)
1939	Printer's Error (Mitchell, Gladys)
1939 **1**	The Cat Saw Murder (Olsen, D. B.)

1939	Dead for a Ducat (Reilly, Helen)
1939	All Concerned Notified (Reilly, Helen)
1939 **1**	8 Faces at 3 (Rice, Craig)
1939	In the Teeth of the Evidence (Sayers, Dorothy L.)
1939	Spring Harrowing (Taylor, Phoebe Atwood)
1939	Cold Steal (Tilton, Alice)
1939	Calling All Suspects (Wells, Carolyn)
1939	Crime Tears On (Wells, Carolyn)
1939	The Importance of Being Murdered (Wells, Carolyn)
1939 **1**	The Blind Side (Wentworth, Patricia)
1939	Lonesome Road (Wentworth, Patricia)
1939	Death Send a Cable (Yates, Margaret Evelyn Tayler)

1940s   271 titles   28 **1**

1940 **1**	Murder Draws a Line (Barber, Willetta Ann)
1940	All Is Vanity (Bell, Josephine)
1940	One, Two, Buckle My Shoe [U.S.–The Patriotic Murders] (Christie, Agatha)
1940 **1**	Unexpected Night (Daly, Elizabeth)
1940	Deadly Nightshade (Daly, Elizabeth)
1940 **1**	Give a Corpse a Bad Name (Ferrars, E. X.)
1940	Remove the Bodies [U.S.–Rehearsals for Murder] (Ferrars, E. X.)
1940	Old Lover's Ghost (Ford, Leslie)
1940	Dear Dead Woman [U.S.–Death Takes a Redhead] (Gilbert, Anthony)
1940	Fugitive from Murder (Heberden, M. V.)
1940	Subscription to Murder (Heberden, M. V.)
1940	Aces, Eights and Murder (Heberden, M. V.)
1940	The Lobster Pick Murder (Heberden, M. V.)
1940 **1**	Hush, Gabriel! (Johns, Veronica Parker)
1940 **1**	Rendezvous with the Past (Knight, Kathleen Moore)
1940	Death Came Dancing (Knight, Kathleen Moore)
1940 **1**	The Norths Meet Murder (Lockridge, F. & R.)
1940	Death at the Bar (Marsh, Ngaio)
1940	Death of a Peer [Britain–Surfeit of Lampreys] (Marsh, Ngaio)
1940	The Man in the Moonlight (McCloy, Helen)
1940	Brazen Tongue (Mitchell, Gladys)
1940 **1**	The Ticking Heart (Olsen, D. B.)
1940	Murder in the Mist (Popkin, Zelda)
1940	Time Off for Murder (Popkin, Zelda)
1940	Murder in Shinbone Alley (Reilly, Helen)
1940	Death Demands an Audience (Reilly, Helen)
1940	The Dead Can Tell (Reilly, Helen)
1940	The Corpse Steps Out (Rice, Craig)
1940	The Wrong Murder (Rice, Craig)
1940	The Deadly Sunshade (Taylor, Phoebe Atwood)
1940	The Criminal C.O.D. (Taylor, Phoebe Atwood)
1940	The Left Leg (Tilton, Alice)
1940	Crime Incarnate (Wells, Carolyn)
1940	Devil's Work (Wells, Carolyn)
1940	Murder on Parade (Wells, Carolyn)
1940	Murder Plus (Wells, Carolyn)

1941	Traitor's Purse [APA–The Sabotage Murder Mystery] (Allingham, Margery)
1941	Pencil Points to Murder (Barber, Willetta Ann)
1941 **1**	Heads You Lose (Brand, Christianna)
1941	N or M? (Christie, Agatha)
1941	Evil Under the Sun (Christie, Agatha)
1941	Five Little Pigs [U.S.–Murder in Retrospect] (Christie, Agatha)
1941 **1**	The Turquoise Shop (Crane, Frances)
1941	Murder in Volume 2 (Daly, Elizabeth)
1941	Death in Botanist's Bay [U.S.–Murder of a Suicide] (Ferrars, E. X.)

1940s . . . continued   271 titles   28 ▮

1941 The Murder of a Fifth Columnist [Britain–A Capital Crime] (Ford, Leslie)
1941 The Vanishing Corpse [U.S.–She Vanished in the Dawn] (Gilbert, Anthony)
1941 The Woman in Red [APA–The Mystery of the Woman in Red] (Gilbert, Anthony)
1941 Envious Casca (Heyer, Georgette)
1941 Shady Doings (Johns, Veronica Parker)
1941 Exit a Star (Knight, Kathleen Moore)
1941 Murder Out of Turn (Lockridge, Frances & Richard)
1941 A Pinch of Poison (Lockridge, Frances & Richard)
1941 Death and the Dancing Footman (Marsh, Ngaio)
1941 The Deadly Truth (McCloy, Helen)
1941 ▮ The Invisible Worm (Millar, Margaret)
1941 When Last I Died (Mitchell, Gladys)
1941 Hangman's Curfew (Mitchell, Gladys)
1941 Dead Man's Gift (Popkin, Zelda)
1941 Mourned on Sunday (Reilly, Helen)
1941 Three Women in Black (Reilly, Helen)
1941 The Right Murder (Rice, Craig)
1941 Trial by Fury (Rice, Craig)
1941 The Perennial Border (Taylor, Phoebe Atwood)
1941 The Hollow Chest (Tilton, Alice)
1941 The Black Night Murders (Wells, Carolyn)
1941 Murder at the Casino (Wells, Carolyn)
1941 In the Balance [Britain–Danger Point] (Wentworth, P.)
1941 Midway to Murder (Yates, Margaret Evelyn Tayler)

1942 ▮ Lay on, Mac Duff! (Armstrong, Charlotte)
1942 Drawn Conclusion (Barber, Willetta Ann)
1942 Murder Enters the Picture (Barber, Willetta Ann)
1942 The Moving Finger (Christie, Agatha)
1942 The Body in the Library (Christie, Agatha)
1942 The Golden Box (Crane, Frances)
1942 The House Without the Door (Daly, Elizabeth)
1942 Wolf in Man's Clothing (Eberhart, Mignon G.)
1942 ▮ Murder Needs a Face (Fenisong, Ruth)
1942 Murder Needs a Name (Fenisong, Ruth)
1942 Don't Monkey with Murder [U.S.–The Shape of a Stain] (Ferrars, E. X.)
1942 Your Neck in a Noose [U.S.–Neck in a Noose] (Ferrars, E. X.)
1942 Murder in the O.P.M. [Britain–The Priority Murder] (Ford, Leslie)
1942 Something Nasty in the Woodshed [U.S.–Mystery in the Woodshed] (Gilbert, Anthony)
1942 The Case of the Tea-Cosy's Aunt [U.S.–Death in the Blackout] (Gilbert, Anthony)
1942 Murder Follows Desmond Shannon (Heberden, M. V.)
1942 Murder Makes a Racket (Heberden, M. V.)
1942 Terror by Twilight (Knight, Kathleen Moore)
1942 ▮ The Stolen Squadron (Leonard, Charles L.)
1942 Deadline for Destruction (Leonard, Charles L.)
1942 Death on the Aisle (Lockridge, Frances & Richard)
1942 Hanged for a Sheep (Lockridge, Frances & Richard)
1942 Who's Calling? (McCloy, Helen)
1942 Cue for Murder (McCloy, Helen)
1942 The Weak-Eyed Bat (Millar, Margaret)
1942 The Devil Loves Me (Millar, Margaret)
1942 Laurels are Poison (Mitchell, Gladys)
1942 Clues to Burn (Offord, Lenore Glen)
1942 The Alarm of the Black Cat (Olsen, D. B.)
1942 No Crime for a Lady (Popkin, Zelda)
1942 Name Your Poison (Reilly, Helen)
1942 ▮ The Sunday Pigeon Murders (Rice, Craig)

1942 The Big Midget Murders (Rice, Craig)
1942 Haunted Lady (Rinehart, Mary Roberts)
1942 Three Plots for Asey Mayo (Taylor, Phoebe Atwood)
1942 The Six Iron Spiders (Taylor, Phoebe Atwood)
1942 ▮ The Man Who Slept All Day (Venning, Michael)
1942 Murder Will In (Wells, Carolyn)
1942 Who Killed Caldwell? (Wells, Carolyn)
1942 Pursuit of a Parcel (Wentworth, Patricia)
1942 Murder by the Yard (Yates, Margaret Evelyn Tayler)

1943 The Case of the Weird Sisters (Armstrong, Charlotte)
1943 The Yellow Violet (Crane, Frances)
1943 The Pink Umbrella (Crane, Frances)
1943 The Applegreen Cat (Crane, Frances)
1943 Nothing Can Rescue Me (Daly, Elizabeth)
1943 Evidence of Things Seen (Daly, Elizabeth)
1943 ▮ Compound for Death (Disney, Doris Miles)
1943 The Butler Died in Brooklyn (Fenisong, Ruth)
1943 Murder Runs a Fever (Fenisong, Ruth)
1943 Siren in the Night (Ford, Leslie)
1943 The Mouse Who Wouldn't Play Ball [U.S.–30 Days to Live] (Gilbert, Anthony)
1943 Murder Goes Astray (Heberden, M. V.)
1943 The Fanatic of Fez [APA–Assignment to Death] (Leonard, Charles L.)
1943 Death Takes a Bow (Lockridge, Frances & Richard)
1943 Colour Scheme (Marsh, Ngaio)
1943 The Goblin Market (McCloy, Helen)
1943 ▮ Wall of Eyes (Millar, Margaret)
1943 The Worsted Viper (Mitchell, Gladys)
1943 Sunset Over Soho (Mitchell, Gladys)
1943 ▮ Skeleton Key (Offord, Lenore Glen)
1943 Cat's Claw (Olsen, D. B.)
1943 Catspaw for Murder (Olsen, D. B.)
1943 The Thursday Turkey Murders (Rice, Craig)
1943 Having a Wonderful Crime (Rice, Craig)
1943 Going, Going, Gone (Taylor, Phoebe Atwood)
1943 File for Record (Tilton, Alice)
1943 Murder Through the Looking Glass (Venning, Michael)
1943 The Chinese Shawl (Wentworth, Patricia)
1943 Miss Silver Deals in Death [Britain–Miss Silver Intervenes] (Wentworth, Patricia)

1944 Death at the Medical Board (Bell, Josephine)
1944 Green for Danger (Brand, Christianna)
1944 The Amethyst Spectacles (Crane, Frances)
1944 Arrow Pointing Nowhere [APA–Murder Listens In ('49)] (Daly, Elizabeth)
1944 The Book of the Dead (Daly, Elizabeth)
1944 All for the Love of a Lady [Britain–Crack of Dawn] (Ford, Leslie)
1944 He Came by Night [U.S.–Death at the Door] (Gilbert, Anthony)
1944 The Scarlet Button [APA–Murder is Cheap] (Gilbert, Anthony)
1944 Murder of a Stuffed Shirt (Heberden, M. V.)
1944 Design in Diamonds (Knight, Kathleen Moore)
1944 ▮ Blood Upon the Snow (Lawrence, Hilda)
1944 A Time to Die (Lawrence, Hilda)
1944 The Secret of the Spa (Leonard, Charles L.)
1944 Killing the Goose (Lockridge, Frances & Richard)
1944 The Glass Mask (Offord, Lenore Glen)
1944 The Cat Wears a Noose (Olsen, D. B.)
1944 The Opening Door (Reilly, Helen)
1944 Dead Earnest (Tilton, Alice)
1944 Jethro Hammer (Venning, Michael)
1944 The Clock Strikes Twelve (Wentworth, Patricia)

1940s... *continued*   271 titles   28 **1**

1944	The Key (Wentworth, Patricia)

1945 Coroner's Pidgin [U.S.–Pearls Before Swine] (Allingham, Margery)
1945 The Innocent Flower (Armstrong, Charlotte)
1945 The Noose Is Drawn (Barber, Willetta Ann)
1945 The Indigo Necklace (Crane, Frances)
1945 Any Shape or Form (Daly, Elizabeth)
1945 Murder on a Tangent (Disney, Doris Miles)
1945 The Philadelphia Murder Story (Ford, Leslie)
1945 Don't Open the Door! [U.S.–Death Lifts the Latch] (Gilbert, Anthony)
1945 Lift up the Lid [U.S.–The Innocent Bottle] (Gilbert, Anthony)
1945 The Black Stage [U.S.–Murder Cheats the Bride] (Gilbert, Anthony)
1945 Vicious Pattern (Heberden, M. V.)
1945 Expert in Murder (Leonard, Charles L.)
1945 Payoff for the Banker (Lockridge, Frances & Richard)
1945 Died in the Wool (Marsh, Ngaio)
1945 The One That Got Away (McCloy, Helen)
1945 The Iron Gates (Millar, Margaret)
1945 The Rising of the Moon (Mitchell, Gladys)
1945 **1** Bring the Bride a Shroud [APA–A Shroud for the Bride] (Olsen, D. B.)
1945 Cats Don't Smile (Olsen, D. B.)
1945 Murder on Angler's Island (Reilly, Helen)
1945 The Lucky Stiff (Rice, Craig)
1945 **1** The Owl in the Cellar (Scherf, Margaret)
1945 Proof of the Pudding (Taylor, Phoebe Atwood)
1945 She Came Back [Britain–The Traveller Returns] (Wentworth, Patricia)

1946 Suddenly at His Residence [U.S.–The Crooked Wreath] (Brand, Christianna)
1946 The Hollow [U.S.–Murder After Hours] (Christie, A.)
1946 The Cinnamon Murder (Crane, Frances)
1946 The Shocking Pink Hat (Crane, Frances)
1946 Somewhere in the House (Daly, Elizabeth)
1946 The Wrong Way Down [APA–Shroud for a Lady ('56)] (Daly, Elizabeth)
1946 **1** Dr. Sam: Johnson, Detector (de la Torre, Lillian)
1946 **1** Dark Road (Disney, Doris Miles)
1946 Honolulu Story [Britain–Honolulu Murder Story] (Ford, Leslie)
1946 The Spinster's Secret [U.S.–By Hook or By Crook] (Gilbert, Anthony)
1946 **1** Murder Cancels All Debts (Heberden, M. V.)
1946 The Trouble at Turkey Hill (Knight, Kathleen Moore)
1946 Pursuit in Peru (Leonard, Charles L.)
1946 Death of a Tall Man (Lockridge, Frances & Richard)
1946 Murder Within Murder (Lockridge, F. & R.)
1946 Here Comes a Chopper (Mitchell, Gladys)
1946 Cats Don't Need Coffins (Olsen, D. B.)
1946 The Silver Leopard (Reilly, Helen)
1946 Punch with Care (Taylor, Phoebe Atwood)
1946 The Asey Mayo Trio (Taylor, Phoebe Atwood)
1946 Pilgrim's Rest [APA–Dark Threat] (Wentworth, P.)

1947 Drawback to Murder (Barber, Willetta Ann)
1947 Murder on the Purple Water (Crane, Frances)
1947 Night Walk (Daly, Elizabeth)
1947 Appointment at Nine (Disney, Doris Miles)
1947 The Whispering House [U.S.–The Voice of the House] (Erskine, Margaret)
1947 The Woman in Black (Ford, Leslie)

1947 Death in the Wrong Room (Gilbert, Anthony)
1947 Die in the Dark [U.S.–The Missing Widow] (Gilbert, A.)
1947 Drinks on the Victim (Heberden, M. V.)
1947 They Can't All Be Guilty (Heberden, M. V.)
1947 The Case of the Eight Brothers (Heberden, M. V.)
1947 Footbridge to Death (Knight, Kathleen Moore)
1947 Death of a Doll (Lawrence, Hilda)
1947 **1** Think of Death (Lockridge, Frances & Richard)
1947 Untidy Murder (Lockridge, Frances & Richard)
1947 Final Curtain (Marsh, Ngaio)
1947 Death and the Maiden (Mitchell, Gladys)
1947 Gallows for the Groom (Olsen, D. B.)
1947 The Farmhouse (Reilly, Helen)
1947 The Iron Clew [Britain–The Iron Hand] (Tilton, Alice)
1947 Latter End (Wentworth, Patricia)
1947 Wicked Uncle [Britain–The Spotlight] (Wentworth, P.)

1948 Death of a Jezebel (Brand, Christianna)
1948 Taken at the Flood [U.S.–There is a Tide] (Christie, A.)
1948 Black Cypress (Crane, Frances)
1948 The Book of the Lion (Daly, Elizabeth)
1948 I Knew MacBean [APA–Caravan of Night] (Erskine, M.)
1948 The Devil's Stronghold (Ford, Leslie)
1948 Bait for Murder (Knight, Kathleen Moore)
1948 Search for a Scientist (Leonard, Charles L.)
1948 The Fourth Funeral (Leonard, Charles L.)
1948 I Want to Go Home (Lockridge, Frances & Richard)
1948 Murder Is Served (Lockridge, Frances & Richard)
1948 The Dancing Druids (Mitchell, Gladys)
1948 The Clue in the Clay (Olsen, D. B.)
1948 Devious Design (Olsen, D. B.)
1948 Cats Have Tall Shadows (Olsen, D. B.)
1948 The Fourth Postman (Rice, Craig)
1948 **1** Always Murder a Friend (Scherf, Margaret)
1948 Murder Makes Me Nervous (Scherf, Margaret)
1948 The Eternity Ring (Wentworth, Patricia)
1948 The Case of William Smith (Wentworth, Patricia)

1949 More Work for the Undertaker (Allingham, Margery)
1949 The Deed Is Drawn (Barber, Willetta Ann)
1949 Death in Clairvoyance (Bell, Josephine)
1949 The Flying Red Horse (Crane, Frances)
1949 Murder Listens In [APA–Arrow Pointing Nowhere ('44)] (Daly, Elizabeth)
1949 And Dangerous to Know (Daly, Elizabeth)
1949 Family Skeleton (Disney, Doris Miles)
1949 Give up the Ghost (Erskine, Margaret)
1949 Death Knocks Three Times (Gilbert, Anthony)
1949 Engaged to Murder (Heberden, M. V.)
1949 The Bass Derby Murder (Knight, Kathleen Moore)
1949 Sinister Shelter (Leonard, Charles L.)
1949 Spin Your Web, Lady! (Lockridge, F. & R.)
1949 The Dishonest Murder (Lockridge, F. & R.)
1949 Swing, Brother, Swing [U.S.–A Wreath for Rivera] (Marsh, Ngaio)
1949 Tom Brown's Body (Mitchell, Gladys)
1949 The Smiling Tiger (Offord, Lenore Glen)
1949 The Cat Wears a Mask (Olsen, D. B.)
1949 Staircase 4 (Reilly, Helen)
1949 **1** The Gun in Daniel Webster's Bust (Scherf, Margaret)
1949 Gilbert's Last Toothache [APA–For the Love of Murder] (Scherf, Margaret)
1949 **1** The Chinese Chop (Sheridan, Juanita)
1949 The Franchise Affair (Tey, Josephine)
1949 Miss Silver Comes to Stay (Wentworth, Patricia)
1949 The Catherine Wheel (Wentworth, Patricia)

1950s 202 titles 15 ▪

1950 The Summer School Mystery (Bell, Josephine)
1950 A Murder is Announced (Christie, Agatha)
1950 The Daffodil Blonde (Crane, Frances)
1950 Death and Letters (Daly, Elizabeth)
1950 Fire at Will (Disney, Doris Miles)
1950 The Disappearing Bridegroom [U.S.–The Silver Ladies] (Erskine, Margaret)
1950 Grim Rehearsal (Fenisong, Ruth)
1950 Homicide House [Britain–Murder on the Square] (Frome, David)
1950 A Nice Cup of Tea [U.S.–The Wrong Body] (Gilbert, A.)
1950 Murder Comes Home (Gilbert, Anthony)
1950 Exit This Way [APA–You'll Fry Tomorrow] (Heberden, M. V.)
1950 That's the Spirit [Britain–Ghosts Can't Kill] (Heberden, M. V.)
1950 Secrets for Sale (Leonard, Charles L.)
1950 Foggy, Foggy Death (Lockridge, Frances & Richard)
1950 Murder in a Hurry (Lockridge, Frances & Richard)
1950 Through a Glass Darkly (McCloy, Helen)
1950 Groaning Spinney (Mitchell, Gladys)
1950 Something About Midnight (Olsen, D. B.)
1950 Death Wears Cat's Eyes (Olsen, D. B.)
1950 Murder at Arroways (Reilly, Helen)
1950 The Curious Custard Pie [APA–Divine and Deadly] (Scherf, Margaret)
1950 To Love and Be Wise (Tey, Josephine)
1950 Through the Wall (Wentworth, Patricia)
1950 The Brading Collection [APA–Mr. Brading's Collection] (Wentworth, Patricia)

1951 Murder in Blue Street [Britain-Murder in Blue Hour] (Crane, Frances)
1951 The Polkadot Murder (Crane, Frances)
1951 The Book of the Crime (Daly, Elizabeth)
1951 Straw Man [Britain–The Case of the Straw Man] (Disney, Doris Miles)
1951 Dead Yesterday (Fenisong, Ruth)
1951 Lady Killer (Gilbert, Anthony)
1951 The Sleeping Witness (Heberden, M. V.)
1951 Duplicate Death (Heyer, Georgette)
1951 Treachery in Trieste (Leonard, Charles L.)
1951 A Client Is Cancelled (Lockridge, Frances & Richard)
1951 Murder Comes First (Lockridge, Frances & Richard)
1951 Opening Night [U.S.–Night at the Vulcan] (Marsh, N.)
1951 Alias Basil Willing (McCloy, Helen)
1951 The Devil's Elbow (Mitchell, Gladys)
1951 ▪ Gold Coast Nocturne [Britain–Murder by Proxy] (Nielsen, Helen)
1951 Love Me in Death (Olsen, D. B.)
1951 The Cat and Capricorn (Olsen, D. B.)
1951 ▪ Fallen into the Pit (Peters, Ellis)
1951 Lament for the Bride (Reilly, Helen)
1951 The Green Plaid Pants [APA–The Corpse with One Shoe] (Scherf, Margaret)
1951 The Kahuna Killer (Sheridan, Juanita)
1951 Diplomatic Corpse (Taylor, Phoebe Atwood)
1951 The Daughter of Time (Tey, Josephine)
1951 The Ivory Dagger (Wentworth, Patricia)
1951 Anna, Where Are You? [APA–Death at Deep End] (Wentworth, Patricia)
1951 The Watersplash (Wentworth, Patricia)

1952 The Tiger in the Smoke (Allingham, Margery)
1952 They Do It with Mirrors [U.S.–Murder with Mirrors] (Christie, Agatha)

1952 Mrs. McGinty's Dead [U.S.–Blood Will Tell] (Christie, A.)
1952 Death of Our Dear One [U.S.–Look Behind You Lady] [APA–Don't Look Behind You] (Erskine, Margaret)
1952 Deadlock (Fenisong, Ruth)
1952 And Death Came Too (Gilbert, Anthony)
1952 Miss Pinnegar Disappears [U.S.–A Case For Mr. Crook] (Gilbert, Anthony)
1952 Tragic Target (Heberden, M. V.)
1952 Death Goes to a Reunion (Knight, Kathleen Moore)
1952 Valse Macabre (Knight, Kathleen Moore)
1952 Death by Association (Lockridge, Frances & Richard)
1952 Stand up and Die (Lockridge, Frances & Richard)
1952 Dead as a Dinosaur (Lockridge, Frances & Richard)
1952 The Echoing Strangers (Mitchell, Gladys)
1952 Enrollment Cancelled [APA–Dead Babes in the Wood] (Olsen, D. B.)
1952 The Double Man (Reilly, Helen)
1952 The Wandering Knife (Rinehart, Mary Roberts)
1952 The Elk and the Evidence (Scherf, Margaret)
1952 The Mamo Murders [Britain–While the Coffin Waited] (Sheridan, Juanita)
1952 The Singing Sands (Tey, Josephine)
1952 Ladies' Bane (Wentworth, Patricia)

1953 Bones in the Barrow (Bell, Josephine)
1953 London Particular [U.S.–Fog of Doubt] (Brand, C.)
1953 A Pocket Full of Rye (Christie, Agatha)
1953 After the Funeral [U.S.–Funerals are Fatal] (Christie, A.)
1953 Thirteen White Tulips (Crane, Frances)
1953 Murder in Bright Red (Crane, Frances)
1953 Dead by Now (Erskine, Margaret)
1953 The Wench Is Dead (Fenisong, Ruth)
1953 Washington Whispers Murder [Britain–The Lying Jade] (Ford, Leslie)
1953 Footsteps Behind Me [U.S.–Black Death] [APA–Dark Death] (Gilbert, Anthony)
1953 Murder Unlimited (Heberden, M. V.)
1953 Detection Unlimited (Heyer, Georgette)
1953 ▪ Murder by the Day (Johns, Veronica Parker)
1953 Three of Diamonds (Knight, Kathleen Moore)
1953 Akin to Murder (Knight, Kathleen Moore)
1953 Death Has a Small Voice (Lockridge, F. & R.)
1953 Curtain for a Jester (Lockridge, Frances & Richard)
1953 Spinsters in Jeopardy [APA–The Bride of Death] (Marsh, Ngaio)
1953 Merlin's Furlong (Mitchell, Gladys)
1953 The Cat Walk (Olsen, D. B.)
1953 The Velvet Hand (Reilly, Helen)
1953 The Waikiki Widow (Sheridan, Juanita)
1953 Out of the Past (Wentworth, Patricia)
1953 Vanishing Point (Wentworth, Patricia)

1954 No Love Lost (Allingham, Margery)
1954 Fires at Fairlawn (Bell, Josephine)
1954 The Coral Princess Murders (Crane, Frances)
1954 The Last Straw [Britain–Driven to Kill] (Disney, D. M.)
1954 Man Missing (Eberhart, Mignon G.)
1954 Miscast for Murder [APA–Too Lovely to Live] (Fenisong, Ruth)
1954 Snake in the Grass [U.S.–Death Won't Wait] (Gilbert, Anthony)
1954 Death and the Gentle Bull (Lockridge, F. & R.)
1954 A Key to Death (Lockridge, Frances & Richard)
1954 Faintly Speaking (Mitchell, Gladys)
1954 Tell Her It's Murder (Reilly, Helen)
1954 Glass on the Stairs (Scherf, Margaret)
1954 Killer in the Crowd [APA–The Man in the Queue ('29)] (Tey, Josephine)

1950s ... *continued*　　202 titles　　15 **1**

1954	The Silent Pool (Wentworth, Patricia)
1954	The Benevent Treasure (Wentworth, Patricia)

1955	The Beckoning Lady [U.S.–The Estate of the Beckoning Lady] (Allingham, Margery)
1955	Tour de Force (Brand, Christianna)
1955	Hickory, Dickory, Dock [U.S.–Hickory, Dickory, Death] (Christie, Agatha)
1955	Death in Lilac Time (Crane, Frances)
1955	Trick or Treat [Britain-The Halloween Murder (Disney, Doris Miles)
1955	Fatal Relations [U.S.–Old Mrs. Ommanney Is Dead] [APA–The Dead Don't Speak] (Erskine, Margaret)
1955 **1**	Death and Mr. Potter [APA–The Peacock Is a Bird of Prey] (Foley, Rae)
1955	Is She Dead Too? [U.S.–A Question of Murder] (Gilbert, Anthony)
1955 **1**	The Talented Mr. Ripley (Highsmith, Patricia) ☆
1955	Burnt Offering (Lockridge, Frances & Richard)
1955	Death of an Angel (Lockridge, Frances & Richard)
1955	Scales of Justice (Marsh, Ngaio) ★
1955	The Long Body (McCloy, Helen)
1955	Watson's Choice (Mitchell, Gladys)
1955	Compartment K [Britain–Murder Rides the Express] (Reilly, Helen)
1955	The Listening Eye (Wentworth, Patricia)

1956	Death in Retirement (Bell, Josephine)
1956	The China Roundabout [U.S.–Murder on the Merry-Go-Round] (Bell, Josephine)
1956 **1**	The Lighthearted Quest (Bridge, Ann)
1956	Dead Man's Folly (Christie, Agatha)
1956	Horror on the Ruby X (Crane, Frances)
1956	The Ultraviolet Widow (Crane, Frances)
1956	Bite the Hand [Britain–The Blackmailer] (Fenisong, R.)
1956	The Last Gamble (Foley, Rae)
1956	Run for Your Life (Foley, Rae)
1956 **1**	What Crime Is It? [Britain–The Case of the Hula Clock] (Gardiner, Dorothy)
1956	Riddle of a Lady (Gilbert, Anthony)
1956 **1**	A Cold Coming (Kelly, Mary)
1956	Let Dead Enough Alone (Lockridge, F. & R.)
1956	Voyage into Violence (Lockridge, Frances & Richard)
1956	Death of a Fool [Britain–Off with His Head] (Marsh, N.)
1956	Two-thirds of a Ghost (McCloy, Helen)
1956	Twelve Horses and the Hangman's Noose (Mitchell, G.)
1956	Death Walks on Cat Feet (Olsen, D. B.)
1956	The Canvas Dagger (Reilly, Helen)
1956	The Cautious Overshoes (Scherf, Margaret)
1956	The Gazebo [APA–The Summerhouse] (Wentworth, P.)
1956	The Fingerprint (Wentworth, Patricia)

1957 **1**	Dead in a Row (Butler, Gwendoline)
1957	4:50 from Paddington [U.S.–What Mrs. McGillicuddy Saw!] (Christie, Agatha)
1957 **1**	Death of an Old Sinner (Davis, Dorothy Salisbury)
1957	Method in Madness [Britain-Quiet Violence] (Disney, Doris Miles)
1957 **1**	This Girl for Hire (Fickling, G. G.)
1957	Give Death a Name (Gilbert, Anthony)
1957 **1**	Sleep with Strangers (Hitchens, Dolores)
1957	Dead Man's Riddle (Kelly, Mary)
1957	Practice to Deceive (Lockridge, Frances & Richard)
1957	The Twenty-Third Man (Mitchell, Gladys)
1957	My Kingdom for a Hearse (Rice, Craig)

1957	Knocked for a Loop [Britain–The Double Frame] (Rice, Craig)
1957	Poison in the Pen (Wentworth, Patricia)

1958	Hide My Eyes [U.S.–Tether's End] [APA–Ten Were Missing] (Allingham, Margery) ★
1958	The Seeing Eye (Bell, Josephine)
1958	The Portuguese Escape (Bridge, Ann)
1958	The Dull Dead (Butler, Gwendoline)
1958	The Murdering Kind (Butler, Gwendoline)
1958	The Man in Gray [Britain-The Gray Stranger] (Crane, Frances)
1958	The Buttercup Case (Crane, Frances)
1958	A Gentleman Called (Davis, Dorothy Salisbury)
1958	Sleep No More (Erskine, Margaret)
1958	Death of the Party (Fenisong, Ruth)
1958	Girl on the Loose (Fickling, G. G.)
1958	A Gun for Honey (Fickling, G. G.)
1958	Where Is Mary Bostwick? [APA–Escape to Fear] (Foley, Rae)
1958	The Seventh Mourner (Gardiner, Dorothy)
1958	Death Against the Clock (Gilbert, Anthony)
1958	Servant's Problem (Johns, Veronica Parker)
1958	The Christmas Egg (Kelly, Mary)
1958	Accent on Murder (Lockridge, Frances & Richard)
1958	The Long Skeleton (Lockridge, Frances & Richard)
1958	Singing in the Shrouds (Marsh, Ngaio)
1958	Spotted Hemlock (Mitchell, Gladys)
1958	Ding Dong Bell (Reilly, Helen)
1958	The April Robin Murders (Rice, Craig)
1958	The Name Is Malone [short stories] (Rice, Craig)
1958 **1**	The Malignant Heart (Sibley, Celestine)
1958	The Alington Inheritance (Wentworth, Patricia)

1959 **1**	Easy Prey (Bell, Josephine)
1959	Cat Among the Pigeons (Christie, Agatha)
1959	Old Sinners Never Die (Davis, Dorothy Salisbury)
1959	Did She Fall or Was She Pushed? (Disney, D. M.)
1959	The House of the Enchantress [U.S.–A Graveyard Plot] (Erskine, Margaret)
1959	Girl on the Prowl (Fickling, G. G.)
1959	Honey in the Flesh (Fickling, G. G.)
1959	Dangerous to Me (Foley, Rae)
1959	Death Takes a Wife [U.S.–Death Casts a Long Shadow] (Gilbert, Anthony)
1959	Third Crime Lucky [U.S.–Prelude to Murder] (Gilbert, Anthony)
1959	Beauty Is a Beast (Knight, Kathleen Moore)
1959	Murder Is Suggested (Lockridge, Frances & Richard)
1959	False Scent (Marsh, Ngaio)
1959	The Man Who Grew Tomatoes (Mitchell, Gladys)
1959 **1**	Dead Men Don't Ski (Moyes, Patricia)
1959	Walking Shadow (Offord, Lenore Glen)
1959	Not Me, Inspector (Reilly, Helen)

1960s　　　　240 titles　　32 **1**

1960	A Well-Known Face (Bell, Josephine)
1960	The Numbered Account (Bridge, Ann)
1960	Death Lives Next Door (Butler, Gwendoline)
1960	Death Wish Green (Crane, Frances)
1960	The Detections of Dr. Sam: Johnson (de la Torre, L.)
1960	But Not Forgotten [Britain–Sinister Assignment] (Fenisong, Ruth)
1960	Dig a Dead Doll (Fickling, G. G.)
1960	Kiss for a Killer (Fickling, G. G.)
1960	Out for the Kill (Gilbert, Anthony)
1960 **1**	Epitaph for a Dead Actor (Gray, Dulcie)

1960s . . . continued   240 titles   32 **1**

1960	Sleep with Slander (Hitchens, Dolores)
1960	Show Red for Danger (Lockridge, F. & R.)
1960	The Judge Is Reversed (Lockridge, F. & R.)
1960	Say It with Flowers (Mitchell, Gladys)
1960	Follow Me (Reilly, Helen)
1960 **1**	Case Pending (Shannon, Dell) ☆
1960	The Ace of Spades (Shannon, Dell)

1961	Make Me a Murderer (Butler, Gwendoline)
1961 **1**	A Case for Appeal (Egan, Lesley)
1961	The Woman at Belguardo (Erskine, Margaret)
1961	Blood and Honey (Fickling, G. G.)
1961	It's Murder Mr. Potter [APA–Curtain Call] (Foley, Rae)
1961	She Shall Die [U.S.–After the Verdict] (Gilbert, A.)
1961	Uncertain Death (Gilbert, Anthony)
1961 **1**	The Spoilt Kill (Kelly, Mary) ★
1961 **1**	Banking on Death (Lathen, Emma)
1961	With One Stone (Lockridge, Frances & Richard)
1961	Murder Has Its Points (Lockridge, Frances & R.)
1961	Nodding Canaries (Mitchell, Gladys)
1961	Down Among the Dead Men (Moyes, Patricia)
1961	Certain Sleep (Reilly, Helen)
1961	Extra Kill (Shannon, Dell)
1961	The Girl in the Cellar (Wentworth, Patricia)

1962	The China Governess (Allingham, Margery)
1962	Coffin in Oxford (Butler, Gwendoline)
1962	The Mirror Crack'd from Side to Side [U.S.–The Mirror Crack'd] (Christie, Agatha)
1962	The Amber Eyes (Crane, Frances)
1962	Find the Woman (Disney, Doris Miles)
1962 **1**	The Borrowed Alibi (Egan, Lesley)
1962	Against the Evidence (Egan, Lesley)
1962	Dead Weight (Fenisong, Ruth)
1962	Repent at Leisure [Britain–The Deadly Noose] (Foley, Rae)
1962	No Dust in the Attic (Gilbert, Anthony)
1962 **1**	Cover Her Face (James, P. D.)
1962	Due to a Death [U.S.–The Dead of Summer] (Kelly, M.)
1962	First Come, First Kill (Lockridge, Frances & Richard)
1962	Hand in Glove (Marsh, Ngaio)
1962 **1**	Come Home and Be Killed (Melville, Jennie)
1962	My Bones Will Keep (Mitchell, Gladys)
1962	Death on the Agenda (Moyes, Patricia)
1962	Death and the Joyful Woman (Peters, Ellis) ★
1962	The Day She Died (Reilly, Helen)
1962	Knave of Hearts (Shannon, Dell) ☆
1962 **1**	Bloody Instructions (Woods, Sara)
1962	Malice Domestic (Woods, Sara)

1963	A Flat Tire in Fulham [U.S.–Fiasco in Fulham] [APA–Room for a Body] (Bell, Josephine)
1963	The Dangerous Islands (Bridge, Ann)
1963	A Coffin for Baby (Butler, Gwendoline)
1963	The Clocks (Christie, Agatha)
1963	Run to Evil (Egan, Lesley)
1963	The Case in Belmont Square [U.S.–No. 9 Belmont Square] (Erskine, Margaret)
1963 **1**	The Case of the Radioactive Redhead (Fickling, G. G.)
1963	Back Door to Death [APA–Nightmare Honeymoon] (Foley, Rae)
1963	Lion in Wait [Britain–Lion? or Murderer?] (Gardiner, D.)
1963	Ring for a Noose (Gilbert, Anthony)
1963	A Mind to Murder (James, P. D.)
1963	A Place for Murder (Lathen, Emma)
1963	The Distant Clue (Lockridge, Frances & Richard)

1963	Murder by the Book (Lockridge, Frances & Richard)
1963	Dead Water (Marsh, Ngaio)
1963	Burning Is a Substitute for Loving (Melville, Jennie)
1963	Adders on the Heath (Mitchell, Gladys)
1963	Murder a la Mode (Moyes, Patricia)
1963 **1**	Death in Deakins Wood (Petrie, Rhona)
1963	People vs. Withers and Malone (Rice, Craig)
1963	The Diplomat and the Gold Piano [Britain–Death and the Diplomat] (Scherf, Margaret)
1963	Death of a Busybody (Shannon, Dell)
1963	Double Bluff (Shannon, Dell)
1963	The Taste of Fears [APA–The Third Encounter] (Woods, Sara)
1963	Error of the Moon (Woods, Sara)

1964 **1**	The Upfold Witch (Bell, Josephine)
1964	Coffin Waiting (Butler, Gwendoline)
1964	A Caribbean Mystery (Christie, Agatha)
1964 **1**	In the Last Analysis (Cross, Amanda) ☆
1964	My Name Is Death (Egan, Lesley)
1964	The Crazy Mixed-Up Nude (Fickling, G. G.)
1964	Bombshell (Fickling, G. G.)
1964	Fatal Lady (Foley, Rae)
1964	Knock, Knock, Who's There? [U.S.–The Voice] (Gilbert, Anthony)
1964	The Fingerprint (Gilbert, Anthony)
1964 **1**	The Transcendental Murder [APA–The Minuteman Murder ('76)] (Langton, Jane)
1964	Accounting for Murder (Lathen, Emma) ★
1964 **1**	Greenmask! (Linington, Elizabeth)
1964	No Evil Angel (Linington, Elizabeth)
1964	Murder Can't Wait (Lockridge, Frances & Richard)
1964 **1**	Is There a Traitor in the House (McGerr, Patricia)
1964	Murderer's Houses (Melville, Jennie)
1964	Death of a Delft Blue (Mitchell, Gladys)
1964	Falling Star (Moyes, Patricia)
1964	Flight of a Witch (Peters, Ellis)
1964	Murder by Precedent (Petrie, Rhona)
1964 **1**	Dover One (Porter, Joyce)
1964 **1**	From Doon with Death (Rendell, Ruth)
1964	Mark of Murder (Shannon, Dell)
1964	Root of All Evil (Shannon, Dell)
1964	Trusted Like the Fox (Woods, Sara)
1964	This Little Measure (Woods, Sara)

1965	The Mind Readers (Allingham, Margery)
1965	Emergency in the Pyrenees (Bridge, Ann)
1965	At Bertram's Hotel (Christie, Agatha)
1965	The Body Beneath a Mandarin Tree (Crane, F.)
1965	Detective's Due (Egan, Lesley)
1965	Take a Dark Journey [U.S.–The Family at Tammerron] (Erskine, Margaret)
1965	The Voice of Murder (Erskine, Margaret)
1965	Call It Accident (Foley, Rae)
1965	Passenger to Nowhere (Gilbert, Anthony)
1965	There Lies Your Love (Melville, Jennie)
1965	Pageant of Murder (Mitchell, Gladys)
1965	Johnny Underground (Moyes, Patricia)
1965	A Nice Derangement of Epitaphs [U.S.-Who Lies Here?] (Peters, Ellis)
1965	Running Deep (Petrie, Rhona)
1965	Dover Two (Porter, Joyce)
1965	Dover Three (Porter, Joyce)
1965	The Corpse in the Flannel Nightgown (Scherf, M.)
1965	The Death-Bringers (Shannon, Dell)
1965	Death by Inches (Shannon, Dell)
1965	The Windy Side of the Law (Woods, Sara)

1960s . . . *continued*   240 titles   32 ∎

1965   Though I Know She Lies (Woods, Sara)

1966 ∎ The Religious Body (Aird, Catherine)
1966   Death on the Reserve (Bell, Josephine)
1966 ∎ The Cat Who Could Read Backwards (Braun, L. J.)
1966   The Episode at Toledo (Bridge, Ann)
1966   A Nameless Coffin (Butler, Gwendoline)
1966   Third Girl (Christie, Agatha)
1966   Some Avenger, Rise (Egan, Lesley)
1966   The Looking Glass Murder (Gilbert, Anthony)
1966 ∎ The Unexpected Mrs. Pollifax (Gilman, Dorothy)
1966   Murder Makes the Wheels Go 'Round (Lathen, E.)
1966   Death Shall Overcome (Lathen, Emma)
1966   Date with Death (Linington, Elizabeth)
1966   Murder Roundabout (Lockridge, Frances & Richard)
1966   Killer Dolphin [Britain–Death at the Dolphin]
           (Marsh, Ngaio) ☆
1966   Nell Alone (Melville, Jennie)
1966   After Midnight (Nielsen, Helen)
1966   The Piper on the Mountain (Peters, Ellis)
1966   Dead Loss (Petrie, Rhona)
1966 ∎ Sour Cream with Everything (Porter, Joyce)
1966   Coffin Corner (Shannon, Dell)
1966   With a Vengeance (Shannon, Dell)
1966   Chance to Kill (Shannon, Dell)
1966 ∎ Heavy as Lead (Torrie, Malcolm)
1966 ∎ A Matter of Love and Death (Wells, Tobias)
1966   Enter Certain Murderers (Woods, Sara)
1966   Let's Choose Executors (Woods, Sara)

1967   The Cat Who Ate Danish Modern (Braun, Lilian J.)
1967   The James Joyce Murder (Cross, Amanda)
1967   The Nameless Ones (Egan, Lesley)
1967   Case with Three Husbands (Erskine, Margaret)
1967   The Visitor (Gilbert, Anthony)
1967   Unnatural Causes (James, P. D.)
1967   Murder Against the Grain (Lathen, Emma) ★
1967 ∎ Death of an Old Girl (Lemarchand, Elizabeth)
1967   Something Wrong (Linington, Elizabeth)
1967   With Option to Die (Lockridge, Frances & Richard)
1967   A Different Kind of Summer (Melville, Jennie)
1967   Skeleton Island (Mitchell, Gladys)
1967   Murder Fantastical (Moyes, Patricia)
1967   A Killer in the Street (Nielsen, Helen)
1967   Black Is the Colour of My True Love's Heart (Peters, E.)
1967   The Chinks in the Curtain (Porter, Joyce)
1967   Dover and the Unkindest Cut of All (Porter, Joyce)
1967   A Wolf to Slaughter (Rendell, Ruth)
1967   A New Lease of Death [APA–Sins of the Fathers ('70)]
           (Rendell, Ruth)
1967   But the Doctor Died (Rice, Craig)
1967   Rain with Violence (Shannon, Dell)
1967 ∎ Roseanna (Sjöwall, Maj & Per Wahlöö)
1967   Late and Cold (Torrie, Malcolm)
1967   Dead by the Light of the Moon (Wells, Tobias)
1967   What Should You Know of Dying? (Wells, Tobias)
1967   The Case Is Altered (Woods, Sara)
1967   And Shame the Devil (Woods, Sara)

1968   Henrietta Who? (Aird, Catherine)
1968   Cargo of Eagles (Allingham, Margery)
1968   The Cat Who Turned On and Off (Braun, Lilian J.)
1968   Coffin Following (Butler, Gwendoline)
1968   By the Pricking of My Thumbs (Christie, Agatha)
1968 ∎ Picture Miss Seeton (Crane, Hamilton) ☆
1968 ∎ Murder Sunny Side Up (Dominic, R. B.)

1968 ∎ The Photogenic Soprano [Britain–Dolly and the
           Singing Bird] (Dunnett, Dorothy)
1968   A Serious Investigation (Egan, Lesley)
1968   The Ewe Lamb (Erskine, Margaret)
1968   Night Encounter [U.S.–Murder Anonymous] (Gilbert, A.)
1968   Died in the Red (Gray, Dulcie)
1968   A Stitch in Time (Lathen, Emma)
1968   Come to Dust (Lathen, Emma)
1968   The Affacombe Affair (Lemarchand, Elizabeth)
1968   Policeman's Lot (Linington, Elizabeth)
1968   Clutch of Constables (Marsh, Ngaio)
1968   Mr. Splitfoot (McCloy, Helen)
1968 ∎ Ammie, Come Home (Michaels, Barbara)
1968   Three Quick and Five Dead (Mitchell, Gladys)
1968   Death and the Dutch Uncle (Moyes, Patricia)
1968   The Grass-Widow's Tale (Peters, Ellis)
1968   MacLurg Goes West (Petrie, Rhona)
1968   Dover and the Sense of Justice (Porter, Joyce)
1968   Dover Goes to Pott (Porter, Joyce)
1968 ∎ The Banker's Bones (Scherf, Margaret)
1968   Kill with Kindness (Shannon, Dell)
1968   The Man on the Balcony (Sjöwall, Maj & Per Wahlöö)
1968   Your Secret Friend (Torrie, Malcolm)
1968 ∎ The Bait (Uhnak, Dorothy) ★
1968   Murder Most Fouled Up (Wells, Tobias)
1968   Knives Have Edges (Woods, Sara)
1968   Past Praying For (Woods, Sara)

1969   The Complete Steel [U.S.–The Stately Home Murder]
           (Aird, Catherine)
1969   Mr. Campion's Farthing (Allingham, Margery)
1969   The Malady in Madeira (Bridge, Ann)
1969   Coffin's Dark Number (Butler, Gwendoline)
1969   Hallowe'en Party (Christie, Agatha)
1969   Miss Seeton Draws the Line (Crane, Hamilton)
1969   The Wine of Violence (Egan, Lesley)
1969   Missing from Her Home (Gilbert, Anthony)
1969   When in Greece (Lathen, Emma) ☆
1969   Murder To Go (Lathen, Emma)
1969   Alibi for a Corpse (Lemarchand, Elizabeth)
1969   A Risky Way to Kill (Lockridge, Frances & Richard)
1969   Dance to Your Daddy (Mitchell, Gladys)
1969   Darkest Hour (Nielsen, Helen)
1969   The House of Green Turf (Peters, Ellis)
1969   Morning Raga (Peters, Ellis)
1969   Neither a Candle nor a Pitchfork (Porter, Joyce)
1969   Dover Pulls a Rabbit (Porter, Joyce)
1969   The Best Man to Die (Rendell, Ruth)
1969   Schooled to Kill (Shannon, Dell)
1969   Crime on Their Hands (Shannon, Dell)
1969   The Man Who Went Up in Smoke (Sjöwall, M. & P. W.)
1969   Churchyard Salad (Torrie, Malcolm)
1969   The Witness (Uhnak, Dorothy)
1969   The Young Can Die Protesting (Wells, Tobias)
1969   Die Quickly, Dear Mother (Wells, Tobias)
1969   Tarry and Be Hanged (Woods, Sara)

1970s   289 titles   40 ∎

1970   A Late Phoenix (Aird, Catherine)
1970   Mr. Campion's Falcon [U.S.–Mr. Campion's Quarry]
           (Allingham, Margery)
1970   A Coffin from the Past (Butler, Gwendoline)
1970   Poetic Justice (Cross, Amanda)
1970   Murder in High Place (Dominic, R. B.)
1970   Murder in the Round [Britain–Dolly and the Cookie
           Bird] (Dunnett, Dorothy)
1970   In the Death of a Man (Egan, Lesley)

1970s . . . *continued*   289 titles   40 ∎

1970 The Case of Mary Fielding (Erskine, Margaret)
1970 A Calculated Risk (Foley, Rae)
1970 Death Wears a Mask [U.S.–Mr. Crook Lifts the Mask] (Gilbert, Anthony)
1970 The Amazing Mrs. Pollifax (Gilman, Dorothy)
1970 Ripley Underground (Highsmith, Patricia)
1970 Pick up Sticks (Lathen, Emma)
1970 When in Rome (Marsh, Ngaio)
1970 Legacy of Danger (McGerr, Patricia)
1970 A New Kind of Killer (Melville, Jennie)
1970 Gory Dew (Mitchell, Gladys)
1970 ∎ Death in the Grand Manor (Morice, Anne)
1970 Many Deadly Returns [Britain–Who Saw Her Die?] (Moyes, Patricia) ☆
1970 The Knocker on Death's Door (Peters, Ellis)
1970 ∎ Rather a Common Sort of Crime (Porter, Joyce)
1970 Dover Fails to Make His Mark (Porter, Joyce)
1970 Dover Strikes Again (Porter, Joyce)
1970 Sins of the Fathers [APA–A New Lease of Death ('67)] (Rendell, Ruth)
1970 A Guilty Thing Surprised (Rendell, Ruth)
1970 Unexpected Death (Shannon, Dell)
1970 The Laughing Policeman (Sjöwall, Maj & Per W.) ★
1970 Shades of Darkness (Torrie, Malcolm)
1970 The Ledger (Uhnak, Dorothy) ★
1970 Dinky Died (Wells, Tobias)
1970 An Improbable Fiction (Woods, Sara)
1970 ∎ Dead in the Morning (Yorke, Margaret)

1971 ∎ Cover-up Story (Babson, Marian)
1971 Nemesis (Christie, Agatha)
1971 Witch Miss Seeton [Britain–Miss Seeton, Bewitched] (Crane, Hamilton)
1971 The Chandler Policy (Disney, Doris Miles)
1971 ∎ To Spite Her Face (Dolson, Hildegarde) ☆
1971 There is No Justice (Dominic, R. B.)
1971 Match for a Murderer [Britain–Dolly and the Doctor Bird] (Dunnett, Dorothy)
1971 Malicious Mischief (Egan, Lesley)
1971 The Brood of Folly (Erskine, Margaret)
1971 ∎ A Stranger and Afraid (Ferrars, E. X.)
1971 Honey on Her Tail (Fickling, G. G.)
1971 Tenant for the Tomb (Gilbert, Anthony)
1971 The Elusive Mrs. Pollifax (Gilman, Dorothy)
1971 Shroud for a Nightingale (James, P. D.) ★ ☆
1971 Ashes to Ashes (Lathen, Emma)
1971 The Longer the Thread (Lathen, Emma)
1971 Death on Doomsday (Lemarchand, Elizabeth)
1971 Practice to Deceive (Linington, Elizabeth)
1971 Inspector's Holiday (Lockridge, Frances & Richard)
1971 Lament for Leto (Mitchell, Gladys)
1971 Murder in Married Life (Morice, Anne)
1971 Season of Snows and Sins (Moyes, Patricia) ★
1971 Only with a Bargepole (Porter, Joyce)
1971 A Terrible Drag for Dover (Porter, Joyce)
1971 No More Dying Then (Rendell, Ruth)
1971 The Beautiful Birthday Cake (Scherf, Margaret)
1971 Whim to Kill (Shannon, Dell)
1971 The Ringer (Shannon, Dell)
1971 Murder at the Savoy (Sjöwall, Maj & Per Wahlöö)
1971 The Fire Engine That Disappeared (Sjöwall, M. & P. W.)
1971 ∎ Not One of Us (Thomson, June)
1971 Bismarck Herrings (Torrie, Malcolm)
1971 The Foo Dog [Britain–The Lotus Affair] (Wells, T.)
1971 What To Do Until the Undertaker Comes (Wells, T)

1971 Serpent's Tooth (Woods, Sara)
1971 The Knavish Crows (Woods, Sara)

1972 ∎ Prime Time Corpse [APA–Bloody Special ('89)] (Babbin, Jacqueline)
1972 Murder on Show [U.S.–Murder at the Cat Show] (Babson, Marian)
1972 Elephants Can Remember (Christie, Agatha)
1972 The Theban Mysteries (Cross, Amanda)
1972 Murder in Focus [Britain–Dolly and the Starry Bird] (Dunnett, Dorothy)
1972 Paper Chase (Egan, Lesley)
1972 Stiff as a Broad (Fickling, G. G.)
1972 Murder's a Waiting Game (Gilbert, Anthony)
1972 ∎ An Unsuitable Job for a Woman (James, P. D.) ☆
1972 Murder Without Icing (Lathen, Emma)
1972 Cyanide with Compliments (Lemarchand, Elizabeth)
1972 ∎ The Only Security [U.S.–Troublecross] (Mann, J.)
1972 Tied up in Tinsel (Marsh, Ngaio) ☆
1972 A Hearse in May-Day (Mitchell, Gladys)
1972 ∎ The Phone Calls (O'Donnell, Lillian)
1972 ∎ The Seventh Sinner (Peters, Elizabeth)
1972 Death To the Landlords! (Peters, Ellis)
1972 A Meddler and Her Murder (Porter, Joyce)
1972 Dover and the Dark Lady (Porter, Joyce)
1972 Murder Being Once Done (Rendell, Ruth)
1972 To Cache a Millionaire (Scherf, Margaret)
1972 Murder with Love (Shannon, Dell)
1972 With Intent to Kill (Shannon, Dell)
1972 The Abominable Man (Sjöwall, Maj & Per Wahlöö)
1972 A Die in the Country (Wells, Tobias)
1972 How to Kill a Man (Wells, Tobias)
1972 ∎ Poor, Poor Ophelia (Weston, Carolyn)
1972 They Love Not Poison [prequel] (Woods, Sara)
1972 Silent Witness (Yorke, Margaret)

1973 His Burial Too (Aird, Catherine)
1973 Postern of Fate (Christie, Agatha)
1973 Miss Seeton Sings (Crane, Hamilton)
1973 A Dying Fall (Dolson, Hildegarde)
1973 Besides the Wench Is Dead (Erskine, Margaret)
1973 Foot in the Grave (Ferrars, E. X.)
1973 A Palm for Mrs. Pollifax (Gilman, Dorothy)
1973 Let or Hindrance [U.S.–No Vacation from Murder] (Lemarchand, Elizabeth)
1973 Crime by Chance (Linington, Elizabeth)
1973 Not I, Said the Sparrow (Lockridge, F. & R.)
1973 The Murder of Busy Lizzie (Mitchell, Gladys)
1973 ∎ Lady with a Cool Eye (Moffat, Gwen)
1973 Death of a Gay Dog (Morice, Anne)
1973 Murder on French Leave (Morice, Anne)
1973 The Curious Affair of the Third Dog (Moyes, Patricia)
1973 The Severed Key (Nielsen, Helen)
1973 Don't Wear Your Wedding Ring (O'Donnell, Lillian)
1973 ∎ Borrower of the Night (Peters, Elizabeth)
1973 City of Gold and Shadows (Peters, Ellis)
1973 It's Murder with Dover (Porter, Joyce)
1973 Some Lie and Some Die (Rendell, Ruth)
1973 No Holiday for Crime (Shannon, Dell)
1973 Spring of Violence (Shannon, Dell)
1973 The Locked Room (Sjöwall, Maj & Per Wahlöö)
1973 Death Cap (Thomson, June)
1973 Brenda's Murder (Wells, Tobias)
1973 Yet She Must Die (Woods, Sara)
1973 Enter the Corpse (Woods, Sara)
1973 ∎ Curiosity Didn't Kill the Cat (Wren, M. K.)
1973 Grave Matters (Yorke, Margaret)

1970s . . . continued   289 titles   40 ▮

1974	A Coffin for the Canary [U.S.–Sarsen Place] (Butler, G.)
1974	Epitaph for a Lobbyist (Dominic, R. B.)
1974	A Nice Little Killing (Gilbert, Anthony)
1974	Ripley's Game (Highsmith, Patricia)
1974	Sweet and Low (Lathen, Emma)
1974	Buried in the Past (Lemarchand, Elizabeth)
1974	Black as He's Painted (Marsh, Ngaio)
1974	Winking at the Brim (Mitchell, Gladys)
1974	A Javelin for Jonah (Mitchell, Gladys)
1974	My Father Sleeps (Mitchell, Gladys)
1974	Mingled with Venom (Mitchell, Gladys)
1974	Death and the Dutiful Daughter (Morice, Anne)
1974	Death of a Heavenly Twin (Morice, Anne)
1974	Dial 557 R-A-P-E (O'Donnell, Lillian)
1974	The Murders of Richard III (Peters, Elizabeth)
1974	Crime File (Shannon, Dell)
1974	The Long Revenge (Thomson, June)
1974	Have Mercy Upon Us (Wells, Tobias)
1974	Done to Death (Woods, Sara)
1974	Mortal Remains (Yorke, Margaret)

1975	Slight Mourning (Aird, Catherine)
1975	Curtain (Christie, Agatha)
1975	Odds on Miss Seeton (Crane, Hamilton)
1975	Please Omit Funeral (Dolson, Hildegarde)
1975	Harriet Farewell (Erskine, Margaret)
1975	The Black Tower (James, P. D.) ★
1975	Dark Nantucket Noon (Langton, Jane)
1975	By Hook or by Crook (Lathen, Emma)
1975	Captive Audience (Mann, Jessica)
1975	Convent on Styx (Mitchell, Gladys)
1975	The Croaking Raven (Mitchell, Gladys)
1975	Miss Pink at the Edge of the World (Moffat, Gwen)
1975	Killing with Kindness (Morice, Anne)
1975	Nursery Tea and Poison (Morice, Anne)
1975	Black Widower (Moyes, Patricia)
1975	The Baby Merchants (O'Donnell, Lillian)
1975 ▮	Crocodile on the Sandbank (Peters, Elizabeth)
1975	The Package Included Murder (Porter, Joyce)
1975	Dover Tangles with High Finance (Porter, Joyce)
1975	Shake Hands Forever (Rendell, Ruth)
1975	Deuces Wild (Shannon, Dell)
1975	Cop Killer (Sjöwall, Maj & Per Wahlöö)
1975	Hark, Hark, the Watchdogs Bark (Wells, Tobias)
1975	Susannah Screaming (Weston, Carolyn)
1975 ▮	Death of an Angel (Winslow, Pauline Glen)
1975	A Show of Violence (Woods, Sara)
1975	A Multitude of Sins (Wren, M. K.)

1976	Sleeping Murder (Christie, Agatha)
1976	The Question of Max (Cross, Amanda)
1976 ▮	A Death in the Life (Davis, Dorothy Salisbury)
1976	Murder Out of Commission (Dominic, R. B.)
1976	Split Code [Britain–Dolly and the Nanny Bird] (Dunnett, Dorothy)
1976	Scenes of Crime (Egan, Lesley)
1976	Mrs. Pollifax on Safari (Gilman, Dorothy)
1976 ▮	The Minuteman Murder [APA–The Transcendental Murder ('64)] (Langton, Jane)
1976 ▮	The Big Pay-off (Law, Janice) ☆
1976	Step in the Dark (Lemarchand, Elizabeth)
1976	Dead Run (Lockridge, Frances & Richard)
1976 ▮	Someone Is Killing the Great Chefs of Europe (Lyons, Nan & Ivan)
1976 ▮	Murder Is Academic (Mackay, Amanda)

1976 ▮	Ask Me for Tomorrow (Millar, Margaret)
1976	Late, Late in the Evening (Mitchell, Gladys)
1976	Over the Sea to Death (Moffat, Gwen)
1976	A Short Time to Live (Moffat, Gwen)
1976	Death of a Wedding Guest (Morice, Anne)
1976	The Brink of Murder (Nielsen, Helen)
1976	Leisure Dying (O'Donnell, Lillian)
1976	Dover and the Claret Tappers (Porter, Joyce)
1976	Streets of Death (Shannon, Dell)
1976	The Terrorists (Sjöwall, Maj & Per Wahlöö)
1976 ▮	A Medium for Murder [Britain–A Nice Way to Die] (Warner, Mignon)
1976	Rouse the Demon (Weston, Carolyn)
1976	The Brandenburg Hotel (Winslow, Pauline Glen)
1976	My Life Is Done (Woods, Sara)
1976 ▮	Ogilvie, Tallant and Moon [APA–Bad Medicine ('90)] (Yarbro, Chelsea Quinn)
1976	Cast for Death (Yorke, Margaret)

1977	Parting Breath (Aird, Catherine)
1977	Beauty Sleep (Dolson, Hildegarde)
1977	The Blind Search (Egan, Lesley)
1977 ▮	Quiet as a Nun (Fraser, Antonia)
1977 ▮	Rotten Apples (Green, Edith Pinero)
1977	Death of an Expert Witness (James, P. D.)
1977	Gemini Trip (Law, Janice)
1977	Unhappy Returns (Lemarchand, Elizabeth)
1977	Perchance of Death (Linington, Elizabeth)
1977	The Tenth Life (Lockridge, Frances & Richard)
1977	Last Ditch (Marsh, Ngaio)
1977	Fault in the Structure (Mitchell, Gladys)
1977	Noonday and Night (Mitchell, Gladys)
1977	Murder in Mimicry (Morice, Anne)
1977	Scared to Death (Morice, Anne)
1977	The Coconut Killings (Moyes, Patricia)
1977 ▮	Edwin of the Iron Shoes (Muller, Marcia)
1977 ▮	Aftershock (O'Donnell, Lillian)
1977 ▮	A Morbid Taste for Bones (Peters, Ellis)
1977	Who the Heck Is Sylvia? (Porter, Joyce)
1977	Dover Does Some Spadework (Porter, Joyce)
1977	When Dover Gets Knotted (Porter, Joyce)
1977	Appearances of Death (Shannon, Dell)
1977	Case Closed (Thomson, June)
1977	A Question of Identity (Thomson, June)
1977 ▮	The Fourth Stage of Gainsborough Brown (Watson, C.)
1977	A Creature Was Stirring (Wells, Tobias)
1977	The Witch Hill Murder (Winslow, Pauline Glen)
1977	The Law's Delay (Woods, Sara)
1977	A Thief or Two (Woods, Sara)
1977	Oh Bury Me Not (Wren, M. K.)

1978	A Dream Apart (Egan, Lesley)
1978	Back on Death (Egan, Lesley)
1978	The House in Hook Street (Erskine, Margaret)
1978 ▮	Last Will and Testament (Ferrars, E. X.)
1978	In at the Kill (Ferrars, E. X.)
1978	The Wild Island (Fraser, Antonia)
1978	The Memorial Hall Murder (Langton, Jane)
1978	Double, Double, Oil and Trouble (Lathen, Emma)
1978	Under Orion (Law, Janice)
1978	Suddenly While Gardening (Lemarchand, Elizabeth)
1978 ▮	Rest You Merry (MacLeod, Charlotte)
1978	Grave Mistake (Marsh, Ngaio)
1978	Wraiths and Changelings (Mitchell, Gladys)
1978	Persons Unknown (Moffat, Gwen)
1978	Murder by Proxy (Morice, Anne)
1978	Street of the Five Moons (Peters, Elizabeth)

1970s . . . *continued*   289 titles   40 🔢

1978	Rainbow's End (Peters, Ellis)
1978	Dover Without Perks (Porter, Joyce)
1978	Dover Doesn't Dilly-Dally (Porter, Joyce)
1978	Dead Easy for Dover (Porter, Joyce)
1978	Dover Goes to School (Porter, Joyce)
1978 🔢	Death and the Maiden [U.S.-Death in the Morning] (Radley, Sheila)
1978	A Sleeping Life (Rendell, Ruth) ☆
1978	The Beaded Banana (Scherf, Margaret)
1978 🔢	Death on the Slopes (Schier, Norma)
1978	Cold Trail (Shannon, Dell)
1978	The Tarot Murders (Warner, Mignon)
1978	Copper Gold [Britain–Coppergold] (Winslow, P. G.)
1978	Exit Murderer (Woods, Sara)
1978	Nothing's Certain but Death (Wren, M. K.)

1979	Some Die Eloquent (Aird, Catherine)
1979 🔢	Exit Actors, Dying (Arnold, Margot)
1979	Zadock's Treasure (Arnold, Margot)
1979 🔢	Wolf! Wolf! (Bell, Josephine)
1979	The Hunter and the Hunted (Egan, Lesley)
1979	Sneaks (Green, Edith Pinero)
1979 🔢	Introducing C. B. Greenfield (Kallen, Lucille)
1979	No Villian Need Be (Linington, Elizabeth)
1979 🔢	The Family Vault (MacLeod, Charlotte)
1979	The Luck Runs Out (MacLeod, Charlotte)
1979	The Murder of Miranda (Millar, Margaret)
1979	Nest of Vipers (Mitchell, Gladys)
1979	The Mudflats of the Dead (Mitchell, Gladys)
1979	Murder in Outline (Morice, Anne)
1979	Who Is Simon Warwick? (Moyes, Patricia)
1979	Falling Star (O'Donnell, Lillian)
1979	No Business Being a Cop (O'Donnell, Lillian)
1979 🔢	The Cater Street Hangman (Perry, Anne)
1979	One Corpse Too Many (Peters, Ellis)
1979	The Cart Before the Crime (Porter, Joyce)
1979	Murder by the Book (Schier, Norma)
1979	Death Goes Skiing (Schier, Norma)
1979	Felony at Random (Shannon, Dell)
1979	Deadly Relations [U.S.–The Habit of Loving] (Thomson, June)
1979	This Fatal Writ (Woods, Sara)
1979	Proceed to Judgement (Woods, Sara)
1979	Music When Sweet Voices Die [APA–False Notes ('90)] (Yarbro, Chelsea Quinn)

1980s   793 titles   207 🔢

1980	Passing Strange (Aird, Catherine)
1980	The Cape Cod Caper (Arnold, Margot)
1980	A Question of Inheritance (Bell, Josephine)
1980 🔢	The Dear Departed (Burton, Anne)
1980	Where There's a Will (Burton, Anne)
1980 🔢	Burden of Proof (Challis, Mary)
1980	Crimes Past (Challis, Mary)
1980 🔢	Dupe (Cody, Liza) ★ ☆
1980 🔢	A Pint of Murder (Craig, Alisa)
1980 🔢	The Hands of Healing Murder (D'Amato, Barbara)
1980	Scarlet Night (Davis, Dorothy Salisbury)
1980	The Attending Physician (Dominic, R. B.)
1980	A Choice of Crimes (Egan, Lesley)
1980	Motive in Shadow (Egan, Lesley)
1980	Frog in the Throat (Ferrars, E. X.)
1980 🔢	Victims [U.S.–Suspect] (Gill, B. M.)
1980 🔢	Death and the Pregnant Virgin (Haymon, S. T.)

1980	The Boy Who Followed Ripley (Highsmith, Patricia)
1980	The Tanglewood Murder (Kallen, Lucille)
1980	The Shadow of the Palms (Law, Janice)
1980 🔢	We Must Have a Trial (Leek, Margaret)
1980	The Healthy Grave (Leek, Margaret)
1980	Change for the Worse (Lemarchand, Elizabeth)
1980	Consequence of Crime (Linington, Elizabeth)
1980	The Withdrawing Room (MacLeod, Charlotte)
1980	Photo-Finish (Marsh, Ngaio)
1980	Burn This (McCloy, Helen)
1980	The Whispering Knights (Mitchell, Gladys)
1980	Uncoffin'd Clay (Mitchell, Gladys)
1980	Death in the Round (Morice, Anne)
1980	Angel Death (Moyes, Patricia)
1980 🔢	Death Is Forever (O'Callaghan, Maxine)
1980	Wicked Designs (O'Donnell, Lillian)
1980 🔢	Sports Freak (OCork, Shannon)
1980 🔢	Missing Woman (Page, Emma)
1980	Callander Square (Perry, Anne)
1980	Monk's Hood (Peters, Ellis) ★
1980	Dover Beats the Band (Porter, Joyce)
1980	The Chief Inspector's Daughter (Radley, Sheila)
1980	Demon at the Opera (Schier, Norma)
1980	Felony File (Shannon, Dell)
1980 🔢	Jacoby's First Case (Smith, J. C. S.)
1980	Alibi in Time (Thomson, June)
1980	Death in Time (Warner, Mignon)
1980	The Bishop in the Back Seat (Watson, Clarissa)
1980	The Counsellor Heart [APA–Sister Death] (Winslow, Pauline Glen)
1980	They Stay for Death (Woods, Sara)
1980	Weep for Her (Woods, Sara)

1981	Worse Than a Crime (Burton, Anne)
1981 🔢	Thus Was Adonis Murdered (Caudwell, Sarah)
1981	The Ghost of an Idea (Challis, Mary)
1981	A Very Good Hater (Challis, Mary)
1981 🔢	The Grub-and-Stakers Move a Mountain (Craig, A.)
1981	Murder Goes Mumming (Craig, Alisa)
1981	Death in a Tenured Position [Britain–A Death in the Faculty] (Cross, Amanda)
1981	The Eyes on Utopia Murders (D'Amato, Barbara)
1981 🔢	Karma (Dunlap, Susan)
1981 🔢	Corridors of Death (Edwards, Ruth Dudley)
1981	The Miser (Egan, Lesley)
1981	Thinner Than Water (Ferrars, E. X.)
1981	A Splash of Red (Fraser, Antonia)
1981 🔢	The Man with a Load of Mischief (Grimes, Martha)
1981	Going for the Gold (Lathen, Emma)
1981	Death Under Par (Law, Janice)
1981	Voice of the Past (Leek, Margaret)
1981	Nothing To Do with the Case (Lemarchand, E.)
1981	Death on the Eno (Mackay, Amanda)
1981	The Palace Guard (MacLeod, Charlotte)
1981 🔢	One Coffee With (Maron, Margaret)
1981	Murder Has a Pretty Face (Melville, Jennie)
1981	The Death-Cap Dancers (Mitchell, Gladys)
1981	Lovers, Make Moan (Mitchell, Gladys)
1981	The Men in Her Death (Morice, Anne)
1981 🔢	Death of an Englishman (Nabb, Magdalen)
1981	Run from Nightmare (O'Callaghan, Maxine)
1981	The Children's Zoo (O'Donnell, Lillian)
1981	End of the Line (OCork, Shannon)
1981	Every Second Thursday (Page, Emma)
1981	Paragon Walk (Perry, Anne)
1981	Resurrection Row (Perry, Anne)
1981	The Curse of the Pharaohs (Peters, Elizabeth)

1980s ... *continued*   793 titles   207 🔳

1981	St. Peter's Fair (Peters, Ellis)
1981	The Leper of St. Giles (Peters, Ellis)
1981	Put on by Cunning [U.S.–Death Notes] (Rendell, R.)
1981	Murder Most Strange (Shannon, Dell)
1981 🔳	The Night She Died (Simpson, Dorothy)
1981 🔳	The Cable Car Murder (Taylor, Elizabeth Atwood)
1981	Shadow of a Doubt (Thomson, June)
1981 🔳	The Killing Circle (Wiltz, Chris)
1981	Dearest Enemy (Woods, Sara)
1981	Cry Guilty (Woods, Sara)
1981	Seasons of Death (Wren, M. K.)

1982	Last Respects (Aird, Catherine)
1982	Death of a Voodoo Doll (Arnold, Margot)
1982	Lament for a Lady Laird (Arnold, Margot)
1982	Death on a Dragon's Tongue (Arnold, Margot)
1982 🔳	Blood Will Have Blood (Barnes, Linda)
1982 🔳	The Case of the Hook-Billed Kites (Borthwick, J. S.)
1982	Bad Company (Cody, Liza)
1982 🔳	Angel Without Mercy (Cohen, Anthea)
1982	Angel of Vengeance (Cohen, Anthea)
1982	Random Death (Egan, Lesley)
1982	Cool Repentance (Fraser, Antonia)
1982 🔳	"A" is for Alibi (Grafton, Sue) ★ ☆
1982	Perfect Fools (Green, Edith Pinero)
1982	The Old Fox Deceived (Grimes, Martha)
1982	Ritual Murder (Haymon, S. T.) ★
1982	The Skull Beneath the Skin (James, P. D.)
1982	No Lady in the House (Kallen, Lucille)
1982	Natural Enemy (Langton, Jane)
1982	Green Grow the Dollars (Lathen, Emma) ★
1982	Troubled Waters (Lemarchand, Elizabeth)
1982	Skeletons in the Closet (Linington, Elizabeth)
1982	Wrack and Rune (MacLeod, Charlotte)
1982 🔳	Funeral Sites (Mann, Jessica)
1982	Light Thickens (Marsh, Ngaio)
1982 🔳	Mrs. Porter's Letter (McConnell, Vickie P.)
1982	Mermaid (Millar, Margaret)
1982	Death of a Burrowing Mole (Mitchell, Gladys)
1982	Here Lies Gloria Mundy (Mitchell, Gladys)
1982	The Buckskin Girl (Moffat, Gwen)
1982	Miss Pink's Mistake (Moffat, Gwen)
1982	Die Like a Dog (Moffat, Gwen)
1982	Sleep of Death (Morice, Anne)
1982	Hollow Vengeance (Morice, Anne)
1982 🔳	Champagne and a Gardener (Morison, B. J.)
1982	Ask the Cards a Question (Muller, Marcia)
1982	Death of a Dutchman (Nabb, Magdalen)
1982	Last Walk Home (Page, Emma)
1982 🔳	Indemnity Only (Paretsky, Sara)
1982	The Virgin in the Ice (Peters, Ellis)
1982	A Talent for Destruction (Radley, Sheila)
1982 🔳	The Cooking School Murders (Rich, Virginia)
1982	The Motive on Record (Shannon, Dell)
1982	Six Feet Under (Simpson, Dorothy)
1982 🔳	Death Turns a Trick (Smith, Julie)
1982	To Make a Killing [U.S.–Portrait of Lilith] (Thomson, J.)
1982	The Girl Who Was Clairvoyant (Warner, Mignon)
1982	The Rockefeller Gift (Winslow, Pauline Glen)
1982	Villains by Necessity (Woods, Sara)
1982	Enter a Gentlewoman (Woods, Sara)
1982	Most Grievous Murder (Woods, Sara)

1983	Bitter Finish (Barnes, Linda)
1983	Angel of Death (Cohen, Anthea)

1983 🔳	I Give You Five Days (Curzon, Clare)
1983 🔳	Murder on Cue (Dentinger, Jane)
1983 🔳	An Equal Opportunity Death (Dunlap, Susan)
1983	Tropical Issue [Britain–Dolly and the Bird of Paradise] (Dunnett, Dorothy)
1983	Crime for Christmas (Egan, Lesley)
1983	Little Boy Lost (Egan, Lesley)
1983 🔳	Something Wicked (Ferrars, E. X.)
1983	Death of a Minor Character (Ferrars, E. X.)
1983	Mrs. Pollifax on the China Station (Gilman, Dorothy)
1983	The Anodyne Necklace (Grimes, Martha)
1983 🔳	The Lost Madonna (Holland, Isabelle)
1983 🔳	Garden of Malice (Kenney, Susan)
1983 🔳	The Widows (La Plante, Lynda)
1983	The Wheel Turns (Lemarchand, Elizabeth)
1983	Something the Cat Dragged In (MacLeod, Charlotte)
1983	The Bilbao Looking Glass (MacLeod, Charlotte)
1983	No Man's Island (Mann, Jessica)
1983 🔳	A Perfect Match (McGown, Jill)
1983 🔳	With Flowers That Fell (Meek, M. R. D.)
1983	Cold, Lone and Still (Mitchell, Gladys)
1983	The Greenstone Griffins (Mitchell, Gladys)
1983	Last Chance Country (Moffat, Gwen)
1983 🔳	The Doberman Wore Black (Moore, Barbara)
1983	Murder Post-Dated (Morice, Anne)
1983	A Six-Letter Word for Death (Moyes, Patricia)
1983 🔳	The Tree of Death (Muller, Marcia)
1983	The Cheshire Cat's Eye (Muller, Marcia)
1983	Death in Springtime (Nabb, Magdalen)
1983	Cop Without a Shield (O'Donnell, Lillian)
1983	Hell Bent for Heaven (OCork, Shannon)
1983	Cold Light of Day (Page, Emma)
1983	Rutland Place (Perry, Anne)
1983	Silhouette in Scarlet (Peters, Elizabeth)
1983	The Sanctuary Sparrow (Peters, Ellis)
1983	The Devil's Novice (Peters, Ellis)
1983	Blood on the Happy Highway [U.S.-The Quiet Road to Death] (Radley, Sheila)
1983	The Speaker of Mandarin (Rendell, Ruth)
1983	The Baked Bean Supper Murders (Rich, Virginia)
1983	Exploits of Death (Shannon, Dell)
1983	Puppet for a Corpse (Simpson, Dorothy)
1983 🔳	Samson's Deal (Singer, Shelley)
1983 🔳	Lady on the Line (Tone, Teona)
1983	Devil's Knell (Warner, Mignon)
1983 🔳	Dead Man's Thoughts (Wheat, Carolyn) ☆
1983	The Lie Direct (Woods, Sara)
1983	Call Back Yesterday (Woods, Sara)
1983	Where Should He Die? (Woods, Sara)

1984 🔳	Striving with Gods (Bannister, Jo)
1984	Dead Heat (Barnes, Linda)
1984 🔳	Death in a Deck Chair (Beck, K. K.)
1984 🔳	The Thin Woman (Cannell, Dorothy)
1984	Stalker (Cody, Liza)
1984	Fallen Angel (Cohen, Anthea)
1984 🔳	The Other David (Coker, Carolyn)
1984	Sweet Death, Kind Death (Cross, Amanda)
1984	Masks and Faces (Curzon, Clare)
1984	Lullaby of Murder (Davis, Dorothy Salisbury)
1984	The Return of Dr. Sam: Johnson, Detector (de la Torre, Lillian)
1984	First Hit of the Season (Dentinger, Jane)
1984	Unexpected Developments (Dominic, R. B.)
1984	As a Favor (Dunlap, Susan)
1984	Root of All Evil (Ferrars, E. X.)
1984 🔳	Amateur City (Forrest, Katherine V.)

1980s . . . continued   793 titles   207 ∎

1984   A Shroud for Delilah (Fraser, Anthea)
1984 ∎ A Death for Adonis (Giroux, E. X.)
1984   The Dirty Duck (Grimes, Martha)
1984   Jerusalem Inn (Grimes, Martha)
1984   Stately Homicide (Haymon, S. T.)
1984   A Death at St. Anselm's (Holland, Isabelle)
1984   The Piano Bird (Kallen, Lucille)
1984 ∎ In the Shadow of King's (Kelly, Nora)
1984   Emily Dickinson Is Dead (Langton, Jane) ☆
1984   Light through the Glass (Lemarchand, Elizabeth)
1984   Felony Report (Linington, Elizabeth)
1984 ∎ A Healthy Body (Linscott, Gillian)
1984   The Convivial Codfish (MacLeod, Charlotte)
1984   Grave Goods (Mann, Jessica)
1984   Death of a Butterfly (Maron, Margaret)
1984 ∎ Too Sane a Murder (Martin, Lee)
1984   The Burnton Widows (McConnell, Vickie P.)
1984 ∎ Sick of Shadows (McCrumb, Sharyn)
1984   Hang the Consequences (Meek, M. R. D.)
1984 ∎ The Sheriff & the Panhandle Murders (Meredith, D. R.)
1984   The Crozier Pharaohs (Mitchell, Gladys)
1984   No Winding-Sheet (Mitchell, Gladys)
1984   Grizzly Trail (Moffat, Gwen)
1984 ∎ Penny Black (Moody, Susan)
1984   Penny Dreadful (Moody, Susan)
1984   Getting Away with Murder (Morice, Anne)
1984   Port and a Star Border (Morison, B. J.)
1984   Games to Keep the Dark Away (Muller, Marcia)
1984   Leave a Message for Willie (Muller, Marcia)
1984   Double (Muller, Marcia)
1984   Death in Autumn (Nabb, Magdalen)
1984   Ladykiller (O'Donnell, Lillian)
1984 ∎ A Novena for Murder (O'Marie, Carol Anne, Sister)
1984 ∎ Sweet, Savage Death (Papazoglou, Orania) ☆
1984   Deadlock (Paretsky, Sara)
1984 ∎ A Cadenza for Caruso (Paul, Barbara)
1984 ∎ The Renewable Virgin (Paul, Barbara)
1984   Bluegate Fields (Perry, Anne)
1984   Die for Love (Peters, Elizabeth)
1984   The Dead Man's Ransom (Peters, Ellis)
1984   The Pilgrim of Hate (Peters, Ellis)
1984 ∎ Generous Death (Pickard, Nancy)
1984   Destiny of Death (Shannon, Dell)
1984   Close Her Eyes (Simpson, Dorothy)
1984   Free Draw (Singer, Shelley)
1984 ∎ Morbid Symptoms (Slovo, Gillian)
1984   Nightcap (Smith, J. C. S.)
1984   The Sourdough Wars (Smith, Julie)
1984 ∎ Only Half a Hoax (Taylor, L. A.)
1984   Sound Evidence (Thomson, June)
1984   Illusion (Warner, Mignon)
1984 ∎ Bleeding Hearts (White, Teri)
1984 ∎ Murder in the Collective (Wilson, Barbara)
1984   The Bloody Book of Law (Woods, Sara)
1984   Defy the Devil (Woods, Sara)
1984   Murder's Out of Tune (Woods, Sara)
1984   Wake Up, Darlin' Corey (Wren, M. K.)

1985 ∎ Death of a Gossip (Beaton, M. C.)
1985   Murder in a Mummy Case (Beck, K. K.)
1985   The Down East Murders (Borthwick, J. S.)
1985   Down the Garden Path: A Pastoral Mystery (Cannell, Dorothy)
1985 ∎ Audition for Murder (Carlson, P. M.)
1985   Murder Is Academic (Carlson, P. M.) ☆

1985   The Shortest Way to Hades (Caudwell, Sarah)
1985 ∎ Last Judgment (Clarke, Anna)
1985   Head Case (Cody, Liza)
1985   Guardian Angel (Cohen, Anthea)
1985   The Grub-and-Stakers Quilt a Bee (Craig, Alisa)
1985   The Trojan Hearse (Curzon, Clare)
1985 ∎ Probe (Douglas, Carole Nelson)
1985 ∎ Stoner McTavish (Dreher, Sarah)
1985   The Bohemian Connection (Dunlap, Susan)
1985   Not Exactly a Brahmin (Dunlap, Susan)
1985   St. Valentine's Day Murders (Edwards, Ruth Dudley)
1985   Chain of Violence (Egan, Lesley)
1985   The Wine of Life (Egan, Lesley)
1985 ∎ The Glory Hole Murders (Fennelly, Tony) ☆
1985   The Crime and the Crystal (Ferrars, E. X.)
1985   I Met Murder (Ferrars, E. X.)
1985 ∎ A Necessary End (Fraser, Anthea)
1985   Oxford Blood (Fraser, Antonia)
1985   Seminar for Murder (Gill, B. M.)
1985   Mrs. Pollifax and the Hong Kong Buddha (Gilman, D.)
1985   A Death for a Darling (Giroux, E. X.)
1985 ∎ Monkey Puzzle (Gosling, Paula) ★
1985   "B" is for Burglar (Grafton, Sue) ★ ★
1985 ∎ Death on Widow's Walk [Britain–Patterns in the Dust] (Grant-Adamson, Lesley)
1985   The Face of Death (Grant-Adamson, Lesley)
1985   Help the Poor Struggler (Grimes, Martha)
1985   The Deer Leap (Grimes, Martha)
1985   Flight of the Archangel (Holland, Isabelle)
1985 ∎ Until Proven Guilty (Jance, J. A.)
1985 ∎ The Gemini Man (Kelly, Susan) ☆
1985   Graves of Academe (Kenney, Susan)
1985   The Widows II (La Plante, Lynda)
1985   Murder Makes Tracks (Linscott, Gillian)
1985 ∎ The Trouble at Aquitaine (Livingston, Nancy)
1985   The Curse of the Giant Hogweed (MacLeod, C.)
1985   The Plain Old Man (MacLeod, Charlotte)
1985   Death in Blue Folders (Maron, Margaret)
1985 ∎ Just Another Day in Paradise (Maxwell, A. E.)
1985   Lovely in Her Bones (McCrumb, Sharyn)
1985   The Split Second (Meek, M. R. D.)
1985   The Sheriff & the Branding Iron Murders (Meredith, D. R.)
1985   Penny Post (Moody, Susan)
1985   Dead on Cue (Morice, Anne)
1985   Beer and Skittles (Morison, B. J.)
1985   Night Ferry to Death (Moyes, Patricia)
1985   The Legend of the Slain Soldiers (Muller, Marcia)
1985   There's Nothing To Be Afraid Of (Muller, Marcia)
1985   Casual Affairs (O'Donnell, Lillian)
1985   Scent of Death (Page, Emma)
1985   Wicked, Loving Murder (Papazoglou, Orania)
1985   Killing Orders (Paretsky, Sara)
1985   Prima Donna at Large (Paul, Barbara)
1985   Death in Devil's Acre (Perry, Anne)
1985   The Mummy Case (Peters, Elizabeth)
1985   An Excellent Mystery (Peters, Ellis)
1985   Say No to Murder (Pickard, Nancy) ★
1985 ∎ Hidden Agenda (Porter, Anna)
1985   Fate Worse Than Death (Radley, Sheila)
1985   An Unkindness of Ravens (Rendell, Ruth) ☆
1985   The Nantucket Diet Murders (Rich, Virginia)
1985   Chaos of Crime (Shannon, Dell)
1985   Last Seen Alive (Simpson, Dorothy) ★
1985 ∎ True-Life Adventure (Smith, Julie)
1985   Deadly Objectives (Taylor, L. A.)
1985   Shed Light on Death (Taylor, L. A.)

1980s ... continued　793 titles　207 ▮

1985	A Dying Fall (Thomson, June)
1985	Full Cry (Tone, Teona)
1985	Speak No Evil (Warner, Mignon)
1985	Runaway (Watson, Clarissa)
1985 ▮	A White Male Running (Webb, Martha G.)
1985 ▮	Knight Must Fall (Wender, Theodora)
1985	An Obscure Grave (Woods, Sara)
1985	Away with Them to Prison (Woods, Sara)
1985	Put out the Light (Woods, Sara)
1985 ▮	The Suspect (Wright, L. R.) ★

1986 ▮	Reel Murder (Babson, Marian)
1986	Cities of the Dead (Barnes, Linda)
1986 ▮	The Lace Curtain Murders (Belfort, Sophie)
1986	The Student Body (Borthwick, J. S.)
1986	The Cat Who Saw Red (Braun, Lilian Jackson) ☆
1986	Coffin on the Water (Butler, Gwendoline)
1986	Murder is Pathological (Carlson, P. M.)
1986	Cabin 3033 (Clarke, Anna)
1986	The Mystery Lady (Clarke, Anna)
1986 ▮	A Bird in the Hand (Cleeves, Ann)
1986	Under Contract (Cody, Liza)
1986	Hell's Angel (Cohen, Anthea)
1986	Ministering Angel (Cohen, Anthea)
1986 ▮	Phoebe's Knee (Comfort, Barbara)
1986	A Dismal Thing To Do (Craig, Alisa)
1986	No Word from Winifred (Cross, Amanda)
1986	The Quest for K (Curzon, Clare)
1986	Something Shady (Dreher, Sarah)
1986	The Last Annual Slugfest (Dunlap, Susan)
1986	The Other Devil's Name (Ferrars, E. X.)
1986	Murder at the Nightwood Bar (Forrest, Katherine V.)
1986	Pretty Maids All in a Row (Fraser, Anthea)
1986	Jemima Shore's First Case & Other Stories (Fraser, A.)
1986 ▮	Unblanced Accounts (Gallison, Kate)
1986	A Death for a Dancer (Giroux, E. X.)
1986	A Death for a Doctor (Giroux, E. X.)
1986 ▮	The Wychford Murders (Gosling, Paula)
1986	"C" is for Corpse (Grafton, Sue) ★ ☆
1986	Guilty Knowledge (Grant-Adamson, Lesley)
1986 ▮	Shattered Moon (Green, Kate) ☆
1986	I Am the Only Running Footman (Grimes, Martha)
1986 ▮	Malice Domestic (Hardwick, Mollie)
1986 ▮	Strangled Prose (Hess, Joan) ☆
1986	The Murder at the Murder at the Mimosa Inn (Hess, J.)
1986	A Lover Scorned (Holland, Isabelle)
1986	A Taste for Death (James, P. D.) ★ ★
1986	Injustice for All (Jance, J. A.)
1986	Trial by Fury (Jance, J. A.)
1986	A Little Madness (Kallen, Lucille)
1986 ▮	The Ritual Bath (Kellerman, Faye) ★
1986	The Summertime Soldiers (Kelly, Susan)
1986 ▮	Trace Elements (Knight, Kathryn Lasky)
1986	Good and Dead (Langton, Jane)
1986	Who Goes Home? (Lemarchand, Elizabeth)
1986	Strange Felony (Linington, Elizabeth)
1986	Fatality at Bath & Wells (Livingston, Nancy)
1986 ▮	Dark Fields (MacGregor, T. J.) ☆
1986	The Corpse in Oozak's Pond (MacLeod, Charlotte) ☆
1986	A Kind of Healthy Grave (Mann, Jessica)
1986	A Conspiracy of Strangers (Martin, Lee)
1986 ▮	Where Lawyers Fear to Tread (Matera, Lia) ☆
1986	The Frog and the Scorpion (Maxwell, A. E.)
1986	Highland Laddie Gone (McCrumb, Sharyn)
1986	In Remembrance of Rose (Meek, M. R. D.)

1986	Shattered Silk (Michaels, Barbara)
1986	Penny Royal (Moody, Susan)
1986	The Wolf Whispered Death (Moore, Barbara)
1986	Publish and Be Killed (Morice, Anne)
1986 ▮	The Cavalier in White (Muller, Marcia)
1986	Beyond the Grave (Muller, Marcia)
1986	Advent of Dying (O'Marie, Carol Anne, Sister)
1986	Death's Savage Passion (Papazoglou, Orania)
1986	Lion in the Valley (Peters, Elizabeth)
1986	The Raven in the Foregate (Peters, Ellis)
1986	The Rose Rent (Peters, Ellis)
1986	No Body (Pickard, Nancy) ☆
1986 ▮	Murder on the Run (Sale, Medora) ★
1986	Blood Count (Shannon, Dell)
1986	Dead on Arrival (Simpson, Dorothy)
1986	Full House (Singer, Shelley)
1986 ▮	Miss Melville Regrets (Smith, Evelyn E.)
1986	Tourist Trap (Smith, Julie)
1986	The Dark Stream (Thomson, June)
1986 ▮	A Case of Loyalties (Wallace, Marilyn) ★
1986 ▮	June Mail (Warmbold, Jean)
1986	Even Cops' Daughters (Webb, Martha G.)
1986	Murder Gets a Degree (Wender, Theodora)
1986	Where Nobody Dies (Wheat, Carolyn)
1986	Tightrope (White, Teri)
1986	Sisters of the Road (Wilson, Barbara)
1986	Nor Live so Long (Woods, Sara)
1986	Most Deadly Hate (Woods, Sara)
1986	Sleep While I Sing (Wright, L. R.)

1987 ▮	Not Till a Hot January (Adamson, M. J.)
1987	A February Face (Adamson, M. J.)
1987	A Dead Liberty (Aird, Catherine)
1987 ▮	A Trouble of Fools (Barnes, Linda) ★ ☆ ☆
1987	Death of a Cad (Beaton, M. C.)
1987 ▮	The Letter of the Law (Berry, Carole)
1987	The Cat Who Played Brahms (Braun, Lilian J.) ☆
1987	The Cat Who Played Post Office (Braun, Lilian J.)
1987	Coffin in Fashion (Butler, Gwendoline)
1987	Murder Unrenovated (Carlson, P. M.) ☆ ☆
1987 ▮	Dangerous Places (Chase, Elaine Raco)
1987	Last Seen in London (Clarke, Anna)
1987	Come Death and High Water (Cleeves, Ann)
1987	The Hand of the Lion (Coker, Carolyn)
1987	The Habit of Fear (Davis, Dorothy Salisbury)
1987	The Exploits of Dr. Sam: Johnson (de la Torre, Lillian)
1987 ▮	The Always Anonymous Beast (Douglas, Lauren W.)
1987	Gray Magic (Dreher, Sarah)
1987 ▮	A Murder of Crows (Duffy, Margaret)
1987	Too Close to the Edge (Dunlap, Susan)
1987	A Dinner to Die For (Dunlap, Susan)
1987	The Closet Hanging (Fennelly, Tony)
1987	Death Speaks Softly (Fraser, Anthea)
1987	The Nine Bright Shiners (Fraser, Anthea)
1987	Your Royal Hostage (Fraser, Antonia)
1987	The Death Tape (Gallison, Kate)
1987	A Death for a Dilletante (Giroux, E. X.)
1987	"D" is for Deadbeat (Grafton, Sue)
1987 ▮	The Killings at Badger's Drift (Graham, Caroline) ★ ☆
1987	Wild Justice (Grant-Adamson, Lesley)
1987	The Five Bells and Bladebone (Grimes, Martha)
1987	Parson's Pleasure (Hardwick, Mollie)
1987 ▮	Death on Demand (Hart, Carolyn G.) ☆ ☆
1987	Design for Murder (Hart, Carolyn G.)
1987 ▮	Fetish [Britain–A Personal Possession] (Hart, J.) ☆
1987	Death of a God (Haymon, S. T.)
1987 ▮	Malice in Maggody (Hess, Joan)

1980s . . . continued   793 titles   207 ■

1987   Dear Miss Demeanor (Hess, Joan)
1987 ■ Zach's Law (Hooper, Kay)
1987   Rafferty's Wife (Hooper, Kay)
1987   Raven on the Wing (Hooper, Kay)
1987   In Serena's Web (Hooper, Kay)
1987 ■ No Harm (Hornsby, Wendy)
1987   Taking the Fifth (Jance, J. A.)
1987 ■ A Good Weekend for Murder (Jordan, Jennifer)
1987   Sacred and Profane (Kellerman, Faye)
1987 ■ Murder in Mendocino (Kittredge, Mary)
1987 ■ Bullshot (Kraft, Gabrielle) ☆
1987 ■ Unquiet Grave (La Pierre, Janet) ☆
1987   A Whiff of Sulphur (Linscott, Gillian)
1987   Incident at Parga (Livingston, Nancy)
1987   Kill Flash (MacGregor, T. J.)
1987   The Silver Ghost (MacLeod, Charlotte)
1987   The Recycled Citizen (MacLeod, Charlotte)
1987   The Right Jack (Maron, Margaret)
1987   A Radical Departure (Matera, Lia) ☆
1987   Gatsby's Vineyard (Maxwell, A. E.)
1987 ■ Report for Murder (McDermid, Val)
1987   A Worm of Doubt (Meek, M. R. D.)
1987   The Sheriff & the Folsom Man Murders (Meredith, D. R.)
1987   Snare (Moffat, Gwen)
1987 ■ Scavengers (Montgomery, Yvonne E.)
1987   Treble Exposure (Morice, Anne)
1987   The Voyage of the Chianti (Morison, B. J.)
1987 ■ Murder in Pug's Parlour (Myers, Amy)
1987   Murder in the Limelight (Myers, Amy)
1987   The Marshal and the Murderer (Nabb, Magdalen)
1987   The Other Side of the Door (O'Donnell, Lillian)
1987 ■ A Study in Lilac (Oliver, Maria Antonia)
1987   Final Moments (Page, Emma)
1987   Bitter Medicine (Paretsky, Sara)
1987   A Chorus of Detectives (Paul, Barbara)
1987   Cardington Crescent (Perry, Anne)
1987   Trojan Gold (Peters, Elizabeth)
1987   The Hermit of Eyton Forest (Peters, Ellis)
1987   Marriage Is Murder (Pickard, Nancy) ★ ☆
1987   Mortal Sins (Porter, Anna)
1987 ■ Murder at the War [APA–Knight Fall] (Pulver, Mary M.)
1987   Who Saw Him Die? (Radley, Sheila)
1987 ■ Caught Dead in Philadelphia (Roberts, Gillian) ★
1987   Murder by Tale [short stories] (Shannon, Dell)
1987   Element of Doubt (Simpson, Dorothy)
1987 ■ Murder Is Only Skin Deep (Sims, L. V.)
1987   Death Is a Family Affair (Sims, L. V.)
1987   Spit in the Ocean (Singer, Shelley)
1987   Death Comes Staccato (Slovo, Gillian)
1987   Miss Melville Returns (Smith, Evelyn E.)
1987 ■ A Masculine Ending (Smith, Joan)
1987   Huckleberry Fiend (Smith, Julie)
1987 ■ Goodbye Nanny Gray (Stacey, Susannah) ☆
1987   Murder at Vassar (Taylor, Elizabeth Atwood)
1987   No Flowers by Request (Thomson, June)
1987 ■ The Price You Pay (Wakefield, Hannah)
1987 ■ The Third Victim (Waltch, Lilla M.)
1987 ■ The Hamlet Trap (Wilhelm, Kate)
1987   A Diamond Before You Die (Wiltz, Chris)
1987 ■ She Came Too Late (Wings, Mary)
1987 ■ Murder at the PTA Luncheon (Wolzien, Valerie)
1987   Naked Villainy (Woods, Sara)

1988   Remember March (Adamson, M. J.)
1988   April When They Woo (Adamson, M. J.)

1988   Death of an Outsider (Beaton, M. C.)
1988   The Year of the Monkey (Berry, Carole)
1988 ■ Ladies' Night (Bowers, Elisabeth)
1988   The Cat Who Knew Shakespeare (Braun, Lilian J.)
1988   The Cat Who Sniffed Glue (Braun, Lilian Jackson)
1988   Coffin Underground (Butler, Gwendoline)
1988   The Widow's Club (Cannell, Dorothy) ☆ ☆
1988   Rehearsal for Murder (Carlson, P. M.)
1988   Dark Corners (Chase, Elaine Raco)
1988 ■ Suddenly in Her Sorbet (Christmas, Joyce)
1988   Murder in Writing (Clarke, Anna)
1988   Destroying Angel (Cohen, Anthea)
1988 ■ The Man in the Green Chevy (Cooper, Susan R.)
1988   The Grub-and-Stakers Pinch a Poke (Craig, Alisa)
1988   Three-Core Lead (Curzon, Clare)
1988 ■ The Life and Crimes of Harry Lavender (Day, Marele)
1988   Death Mask (Dentinger, Jane)
1988 ■ Tango Key (Drake, Alison)
1988   Fevered (Drake, Alison)
1988   Death of a Raven (Duffy, Margaret)
1988 ■ Snowstorms in a Hot Climate (Dunant, Sarah)
1988 ■ Cast a Cold Eye (Eccles, Marjorie)
1988   A Murder Too Many (Ferrars, E. X.)
1988   Six Proud Walkers (Fraser, Anthea)
1988 ■ Magic Mirror [Britain–Deadly Reflections] (Friedman, Mickey)
1988 ■ Take One for Murder (Fulton, Eileen)
1988   Death of a Golden Girl (Fulton, Eileen)
1988   Dying for Stardom (Fulton, Eileen)
1988   Lights, Camera, Death (Fulton, Eileen)
1988   A Setting for Murder (Fulton, Eileen)
1988 ■ A Question of Guilt (Fyfield, Frances) ☆ ☆ ☆
1988 ■ A Great Deliverance (George, Elizabeth) ★ ★ ☆ ☆
1988   Mrs. Pollifax and the Golden Triangle (Gilman, D.)
1988   A Death for a Dietician (Giroux, E. X.)
1988   "E" is for Evidence (Grafton, Sue)
1988 ■ Random Access Murder (Grant, Linda) ☆
1988 ■ Now You Don't (Greth, Roma)
1988 ■ Saturday Morning Murder (Gur, Batya)
1988 ■ Those Who Hunt the Night (Hambly, Barbara)
1988   Uneaseful Death (Hardwick, Mollie)
1988   Something Wicked (Hart, Carolyn G.) ★ ★
1988   Honeymoon with Murder (Hart, Carolyn G.) ★
1988   Mischief in Maggody (Hess, Joan) ☆
1988   A Really Cute Corpse (Hess, Joan)
1988   Captain's Paradise (Hooper, Kay)
1988   Outlaw Derek (Hooper, Kay)
1988   Shades of Gray (Hooper, Kay)
1988   The Fall of Lucas Kendrick (Hooper, Kay)
1988   Unmasking Kelsey (Hooper, Kay)
1988   Improbable Cause (Jance, J. A.)
1988   A More Perfect Union (Jance, J. A.)
1988 ■ Death and the Trumpets of Tuscany (Jones, Hazel W.)
1988   Murder Under the Mistletoe (Jordan, Jennifer)
1988   Trail of the Dragon (Kelly, Susan)
1988 ■ Katwalk (Kijewski, Karen) ★ ★ ★
1988 ■ Enter Second Murderer (Knight, Alanna)
1988 ■ Clio Browne: Private Investigator (Komo, Dolores)
1988   Screwdriver (Kraft, Gabrielle)
1988   Murder at the Gardner (Langton, Jane)
1988   Something in the Air (Lathen, Emma)
1988   The Glade Manor Murder (Lemarchand, Elizabeth)
1988   Death in a Distant Land (Livingston, Nancy)
1988   Death Sweet (MacGregor, T. J.)
1988   Death Beyond the Nile (Mann, Jessica)
1988   Baby Doll Games (Maron, Margaret)
1988   Death Warmed Over (Martin, Lee)

1980s . . . *continued*   793 titles   207 ⓵

1988   Murder at the Blue Owl (Martin, Lee)
1988 ⓵ The Smart Money (Matera, Lia)
1988   Just Enough Light to Kill (Maxwell, A. E.)
1988   Double Daughter (McConnell, Vickie P.)
1988 ⓵ Bimbos of the Death Sun (McCrumb, Sharyn) ★ ☆
1988   Paying the Piper (McCrumb, Sharyn) ☆ ☆
1988   Redemption [U.S.–Murder at the Old Vicarage ('89)] (McGown, Jill)
1988 ⓵ Lessons in Murder [APA–Silver Moon ('90)] (McNab, C.)
1988   A Mouthful of Sand (Meek, M. R. D.)
1988   Windsor Red (Melville, Jennie)
1988 ⓵ Murder by Impulse (Meredith, D. R.) ☆
1988   Penny Wise (Moody, Susan)
1988   Fatal Charm (Morice, Anne)
1988   There Hangs the Knife (Muller, Marcia)
1988   Eye of the Storm (Muller, Marcia)
1988   The Marshal and the Madwoman (Nabb, Magdalen)
1988 ⓵ Death's Bright Angel (Neel, Janet) ★
1988   The Missing Madonna (O'Marie, Carol Anne, Sister)
1988   A Violent End (Page, Emma)
1988   Rich, Radiant Slaughter (Papazoglou, Orania)
1988   Blood Shot [Britain–Toxic Shock] (Paretsky, S.) ★ ☆ ☆
1988   Silence in Hanover Close (Perry, Anne)
1988   The Deeds of the Disturber (Peters, Elizabeth)
1988   The Confession of Brother Haluin (Peters, Ellis)
1988 ⓵ The Nocturne Murder (Peterson, Audrey)
1988   Dead Crazy (Pickard, Nancy) ☆ ☆
1988   The Unforgiving Minutes [prequel] (Pulver, Mary M.)
1988   Ashes to Ashes (Pulver, Mary Monica)
1988 ⓵ Death Walk (Quest, Erica)
1988   The Veiled One (Rendell, Ruth)
1988 ⓵ The J. Alfred Prufrock Murders (Sawyer, Corinne H.) ☆
1988 ⓵ First Kill All the Lawyers (Shankman, Sarah)
1988   Suspicious Death (Simpson, Dorothy)
1988   To Sleep, Perchance to Kill (Sims, L. V.)
1988   Suicide King (Singer, Shelley)
1988   Death by Analysis (Slovo, Gillian)
1988   Why Aren't They Screaming? (Smith, Joan)
1988 ⓵ Murder at Markham (Sprinkle, Patricia H.)
1988   A Knife at the Opera (Stacey, Susannah)
1988   Body of Opinion (Stacey, Susannah)
1988 ⓵ Dead Men Don't Give Seminars (Sucher, Dorothy) ☆
1988   Rosemary for Remembrance (Thomson, June)
1988 ⓵ North of the Border (Van Gieson, Judith)
1988   Primary Target (Wallace, Marilyn) ☆
1988 ⓵ Small Favors (Wallace, Patricia)
1988   Fearful Symmetry (Waltch, Lilla M.)
1988   The White Hand (Warmbold, Jean)
1988   Last Plane from Nice (Watson, Clarissa)
1988   Somebody Killed the Messenger (Watson, Clarissa)
1988   Of Graves, Worms and Epitaphs (Wells, Tobias)
1988   The Dark Door (Wilhelm, Kate)
1988 ⓵ Death by Deception (Wingate, Anne)

1989   May's Newfangled Mirth (Adamson, M. J.)
1989   The Menehune Murders (Arnold, Margot)
1989 ⓵ Bloody Special [APA–Prime Time Corpse ('72)] (Babbin, Jacqueline)
1989   Bloody Soaps (Babbin, Jacqueline)
1989   Encore Murder (Babson, Marian)
1989   Tourists are for Trapping (Babson, Marian)
1989   Gilgamesh (Bannister, Jo)
1989   The Snake Tattoo (Barnes, Linda)
1989   Death of a Perfect Wife (Beaton, M. C.)
1989   Peril Under the Palms (Beck, K. K.)

1989 ⓵ Madison Avenue Murder (Bennett, Liza)
1989 ⓵ Love Lies Slain (Blackmur, L. L.)
1989   Love Lies Bleeding (Blackmur, L. L.)
1989 ⓵ Working Murder (Boylan, Eleanor) ☆
1989   The Cat Who Went Underground (Braun, Lilian J.)
1989 ⓵ Murder in Store (Brod, D. C.)
1989 ⓵ Shadowdance (Bushell, Agnes)
1989   Coffin in the Black Museum (Butler, Gwendoline)
1989   Coffin in the Museum of Crime (Butler, Gwendoline)
1989   The Sirens Sang of Murder (Caudwell, Sarah) ★ ☆
1989   Simply to Die For (Christmas, Joyce)
1989 ⓵ Grime & Punishment (Churchill, Jill) ★ ★ ☆
1989   The Whitelands Affair (Clarke, Anna)
1989   Murder in Paradise (Cleeves, Ann)
1989   A Prey to Murder (Cleeves, Ann)
1989   Angel Dust (Cohen, Anthea)
1989   Grave Consequences (Comfort, Barbara)
1989 ⓵ A New Leash on Death (Conant, Susan)
1989   Trouble in the Brasses (Craig, Alisa)
1989   A Trap for Fools (Cross, Amanda)
1989 ⓵ Friends Till the End (Dank, Gloria)
1989 ⓵ User Deadly [Britain–The Pizza House Crash] (Danks, Denise)
1989 ⓵ Silver Pigs (Davis, Lindsey)
1989   Ninth Life (Douglas, Lauren Wright)
1989   Black Moon (Drake, Alison)
1989   Brass Eagle (Duffy, Margaret)
1989 ⓵ Pious Deception (Dunlap, Susan)
1989   Death of a Good Woman (Eccles, Marjorie)
1989 ⓵ A Wicked Slice (Elkins, Charlotte & Aaron)
1989 ⓵ Hush, Money (Femling, Jean)
1989   Kiss Yourself Goodbye (Fennelly, Tony)
1989   Woman Slaughter (Ferrars, E. X.)
1989   The Beverly Malibu (Forrest, Katherine V.) ★
1989   The April Rainers (Fraser, Anthea)
1989   A Temporary Ghost (Friedman, Mickey)
1989   Fatal Flashback (Fulton, Eileen)
1989 ⓵ Shadows on the Mirror (Fyfield, Frances)
1989   Payment in Blood (George, Elizabeth)
1989   A Death for a Dreamer (Giroux, E. X.)
1989 ⓵ The Dead Pull Hitter (Gordon, Alison)
1989   Backlash (Gosling, Paula)
1989   "F" is for Fugitive (Grafton, Sue)
1989   Death of a Hollow Man (Graham, Caroline)
1989 ⓵ Cocaine Blues [U.S.–Death by Misadventure] (Greenwood, Kerry)
1989   Plain Murder (Greth, Roma)
1989   The Old Silent (Grimes, Martha)
1989 ⓵ The Grandfather Medicine (Hager, Jean)
1989 ⓵ Emma Chizzit and the Queen Anne Killer (Hall, M. B.)
1989   The Bandersnatch (Hardwick, Mollie)
1989   Perish in July (Hardwick, Mollie)
1989   A Little Class on Murder (Hart, Carolyn G.) ★ ☆ ☆
1989 ⓵ Hallowed Murder (Hart, Ellen) ☆
1989   A Very Particular Murder (Haymon, S. T.)
1989   Much Ado in Maggody (Hess, Joan)
1989   A Diet to Die For (Hess, Joan) ★
1989   A Fatal Advent (Holland, Isabelle)
1989 ⓵ Mrs. Malory Investigates [Britain–Gone Away] (Holt, H.)
1989   Aces High (Hooper, Kay)
1989   It Takes a Thief (Hooper, Kay)
1989 ⓵ The Mother Shadow (Howe, Melodie Johnson) ☆ ☆ ☆
1989   Devices and Desires (James, P. D.)
1989   Dismissed with Prejudice (Jance, J. A.)
1989   Dead and Gone (Kittredge, Mary)
1989   Bloodline (Knight, Alanna)
1989   Deadly Beloved (Knight, Alanna)

1980s . . . continued   793 titles   207 ▣

1989		Let's Rob Roy (Kraft, Gabrielle)
1989		Children's Games (La Pierre, Janet)
1989	▣	Burning Water (Lackey, Mercedes)
1989	▣	A Deepe Coffyn (Laurence, Janet)
1989	▣	Rogue's Gold (Lee, W. W.)
1989		Death in Close-Up (Livingston, Nancy)
1989		On Ice (MacGregor, T. J.)
1989		Vane Pursuit (MacLeod, Charlotte)
1989		The Gladstone Bag (MacLeod, Charlotte)
1989		Corpus Christmas (Maron, Margaret) ☆ ☆
1989		Hal's Own Murder Case (Martin, Lee)
1989		Hidden Agenda (Matera, Lia)
1989		The Art of Survival (Maxwell, A. E.)
1989		Common Murder (McDermid, Val)
1989		Murder at the Old Vicarage [Britain–Redemption ('88)] (McGown, Jill)
1989		Death of a Dancer [U.S.–Gone to Her Death ('90)] (McGown, Jill)
1989		Fatal Reunion (McNab, Claire)
1989		A Loose Connection (Meek, M. R. D.)
1989		Murder in the Garden (Melville, Jennie)
1989		Making Good Blood (Melville, Jennie)
1989		Murder by Deception (Meredith, D. R.) ☆
1989	▣	The Big Killing (Meyers, Annette)
1989		The Stone Hawk (Moffat, Gwen)
1989		Penny Pinching (Moody, Susan)
1989		Black Girl, White Girl (Moyes, Patricia)
1989		Dark Star (Muller, Marcia)
1989		There's Something in a Sunday (Muller, Marcia)
1989		The Shape of Dread (Muller, Marcia) ★ ☆
1989		Murder at Plum's (Myers, Amy)
1989		Death on Site (Neel, Janet)
1989		Hit and Run (O'Callaghan, Maxine)
1989		A Good Night to Kill (O'Donnell, Lillian) ★
1989		Antipodes (Oliver, Maria Antonia)
1989	▣	A Little Neighborhood Murder (Orde, A. J.)
1989		He Huffed and He Puffed (Paul, Barbara)
1989		Good King Sauerkraut (Paul, Barbara)
1989		Naked Once More (Peters, Elizabeth) ★ ★
1989		The Heretic's Apprentice (Peters, Ellis)
1989		The Potter's Field (Peters, Ellis) ☆
1989		Death in Wessex (Peterson, Audrey)
1989		Murder in Burgundy (Peterson, Audrey)
1989		Bum Steer (Pickard, Nancy) ★
1989	▣	Unorthodox Practices (Piesman, Marissa)
1989		This Way Out (Radley, Sheila)
1989	▣	Touch a Cold Door (Roberts, Carey)
1989		Philly Stakes (Roberts, Gillian) ☆
1989	▣	The Spirit Stalker (Romberg, Nina)
1989	▣	A Real Shot in the Arm (Roome, Annette) ★
1989	▣	Murder by the Book (Rowe, Jennifer)
1989	▣	Murder in the Cotswolds (Rowlands, Betty)
1989		Murder in Focus (Sale, Medora)
1989		Murder in Gray & White (Sawyer, Corinne Holt)
1989	▣	Glory Day (Scott, Rosie)
1989		Then Hang All the Liars (Shankman, Sarah)
1989	▣	Black Justice (Shepherd, Stella)
1989		Dead by Morning (Simpson, Dorothy)
1989	▣	The Mark Twain Murders (Skom, Edith) ☆ ☆ ☆
1989		Miss Melville's Revenge (Smith, Evelyn E.)
1989	▣	Capriccio (Smith, Joan G.)
1989		Dead Men Don't Marry (Sucher, Dorothy)
1989		A Murder Waiting to Happen (Taylor, L. A.)
1989		The Spoils of Time (Thomson, June)

1989	▣	Under the Influence (Travis, Elizabeth)
1989	▣	Murder at the Kennedy Center (Truman, Margaret)
1989	▣	Unorthodox Methods (Valentine, Deborah) ☆ ☆
1989		A Collector of Photographs (Valentine, Deborah)
1989		Deadly Grounds (Wallace, Patricia)
1989		The Third Way (Warmbold, Jean)
1989		Smart House (Wilhelm, Kate)
1989		The Dog Collar Murders (Wilson, Barbara)
1989		The Eye of Anna (Wingate, Anne)
1989	▣	The Last Billable Hour (Wolfe, Susan) ★
1989		The Fortieth Birthday Body (Wolzien, Valerie)
1989	▣	Reckless (Woods, Sherryl)
1989		Body and Soul (Woods, Sherryl)

Series Mystery Titles Written by Women, 1878–1995
3,434 titles

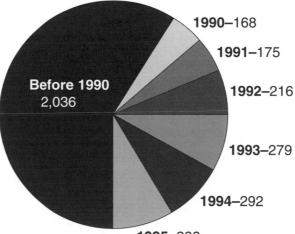

Before 1990 2,036
1990–168
1991–175
1992–216
1993–279
1994–292
1995–288

Owing to the huge number of titles in the current decade, the format of the chronology changes slightly at this point. Starting with 1990, a horizontal rule separates titles alphabetically by author's last name.

1990   168 titles   48 **1**

1990   Toby's Folly (Arnold, Margot)

1990   In the Teeth of Adversity (Babson, Marian)
1990   The Going Down of the Sun (Bannister, Jo)
1990   Coyote (Barnes, Linda)
1990   Death of a Hussy (Beaton, M. C.)
1990 **1** To Make a Killing (Bedford, Jean)
1990   Seventh Avenue Murder (Bennett, Liza)
1990   Good Night, Sweet Prince (Berry, Carole)
1990 **1** A Vow of Silence (Black, Veronica)
1990   Bodies of Water (Borthwick, J. S.)
1990 **1** Deadly Appearances (Bowen, Gail)
1990   Murder Observed (Boylan, Eleanor)
1990   The Cat Who Talked to Ghosts (Braun, Lilian J.)
1990   The Cat Who Lived High (Braun, Lilian Jackson)
1990   Error In Judgment (Brod, D. C.)
1990 **1** Wish You Were Here (Brown, Rita Mae)
1990 **1** Screaming Bones (Burden, Pat) ☆
1990   Wreath of Honesty (Burden, Pat)

1990   Mum's the Word (Cannell, Dorothy)
1990   Murder in the Dog Days (Carlson, P. M.) ☆
1990   Murder Misread (Carlson, P. M.)
1990   A Fete Worse than Death (Christmas, Joyce)
1990 **1** A Lesson in Dying (Cleeves, Ann)
1990   The Balmoral Nude (Coker, Carolyn)
1990   Dead and Doggone (Conant, Susan)
1990 **1** Festering Lilies [U.S.–A Common Death] (Cooper, N.)
1990   Houston in the Rear View Mirror (Cooper, Susan R.)
1990   Other People's Houses (Cooper, Susan Rogers)
1990 **1** Postmortem (Cornwell, Patricia) ★ ★ ★ ★
1990   The Grub-and-Stakers Spin a Yarn (Craig, Alisa)
1990   Advantage Miss Seeton (Crane, Hamilton)
1990   Miss Seeton at the Helm (Crane, Hamilton)
1990   Miss Seeton, by Appointment (Crane, Hamilton)
1990   The Players Come Again (Cross, Amanda)
1990   The Blue-Eyed Boy (Curzon, Clare)

1990 **1** Hardball (D'Amato, Barbara)
1990   Going Out in Style (Dank, Gloria)
1990 **1** Catering to Nobody (Davidson, Diane Mott) ☆ ☆ ☆
1990   Shadows in Bronze (Davis, Lindsey)
1990 **1** Kindred Crimes (Dawson, Janet) ★ ☆ ☆ ☆
1990   The Case of the Chinese Boxes (Day, Marele)
1990   Good Morning, Irene (Douglas, Carole Nelson)
1990   Counterprobe (Douglas, Carole Nelson)
1990   A Captive in Time (Dreher, Sarah)
1990   Who Killed Cock Robin? (Duffy, Margaret)
1990   Diamond in the Buff (Dunlap, Susan)

1990   Requiem for a Dove (Eccles, Marjorie)
1990   More Deaths Than One (Eccles, Marjorie)
1990   The English School of Murder [APA–The School of
          English Murder] (Edwards, Ruth Dudley)
1990 **1** Bloodlust (Elrod, P. N.)
1990   Lifeblood (Elrod, P. N.)
1990   Bloodcircle (Elrod, P. N.)

1990 **1** Blood Is Thicker (Fallon, Ann C.)
1990   Smoke Without Fire (Ferrars, E. X.)
1990   Sleep of the Unjust (Ferrars, E. X.)
1990   Symbols at Your Door (Fraser, Anthea)
1990   Not That Kind of Place [Britain–Trial by Fire] (Fyfield, F.)

1990   Well-Schooled in Murder (George, Elizabeth)
1990   The Fifth Rapunzel (Gill, B. M.)
1990   Mrs. Pollifax and the Whirling Dervish (Gilman, D.)
1990   A Death for a Double (Giroux, E. X.)
1990   "G" is for Gumshoe (Grafton, Sue) ★ ★
1990   Blind Trust (Grant, Linda)
1990   Curse the Darkness (Grant-Adamson, Lesley)
1990   Flying Too High (Greenwood, Kerry)
1990   The Old Contemptibles (Grimes, Martha)
1990 **1** Hot Water (Gunning, Sally)

1990 **1** Not a Creature Was Stirring (Haddam, Jane) ☆ ☆
1990   Night Walker (Hager, Jean)
1990   Emma Chizzit and the Sacramento Stalker (Hall, M. B.)
1990   The Dreaming Damozel (Hardwick, Mollie)
1990 **1** Real Murders (Harris, Charlaine) ☆
1990   Deadly Valentine (Hart, Carolyn G.) ☆ ☆
1990   Some Die Young (Hart, Jeanne)
1990   The Long Search (Holland, Isabelle)
1990 **1** Dead Ahead (Horansky, Ruby)
1990   Half a Mind (Hornsby, Wendy)

1990 **1** The Punjat's Ruby (Jackson, Marian J. A.)
1990   The Arabian Pearl (Jackson, Marian J. A.)
1990   Minor in Possession (Jance, J. A.)
1990   Shot on Location (Jones, Hazel Wynn)
1990   Book Early for Murder (Jordan, Jennifer)

1990   Milk and Honey (Kellerman, Faye)
1990 **1** Parklane South, Queens (Kelly, Mary Ann)
1990   Until Proven Innocent (Kelly, Susan)
1990 **1** Hope Against Hope (Kelly, Susan B.)
1990   Time of Hope (Kelly, Susan B.)
1990   One Fell Sloop (Kenney, Susan)
1990   Katapult (Kijewski, Karen)
1990 **1** Fatal Diagnosis (Kittredge, Mary)
1990   Poison Pen (Kittredge, Mary)
1990   Killing Cousins (Knight, Alanna)
1990   Mortal Words (Knight, Kathryn Lasky)
1990   Bloody Mary (Kraft, Gabrielle)

1990   Cruel Mother (La Pierre, Janet)
1990   Children of the Night (Lackey, Mercedes)
1990   A Tasty Way to Die (Laurence, Janet)
1990   Rustler's Venom (Lee, W. W.)
1990   Mayhem in Parva (Livingston, Nancy)
1990 **1** Sweet Narcissus (Lorens, M. K.)
1990   Ropedancer's Fall (Lorens, M. K.)

1990   Kin Dread (MacGregor, T. J.)
1990   Deficit Ending (Martin, Lee)
1990   The Mensa Murders (Martin, Lee)
1990   The Good Fight (Matera, Lia)
1990 **1** Murder at the Spa (Matteson, Stefanie)
1990 **1** Pet Peeves (McCafferty, Taylor)
1990 **1** If Ever I Return, Pretty Peggy-O (McCrumb, S.) ★ ☆
1990   The Windsor Knot (McCrumb, Sharyn)
1990   Gone to Her Death [Britain–Death of a Dancer ('89)]
          (McGown, Jill)
1990 **1** Osprey Reef (McKernan, Victoria)
1990   Death Down Under (McNab, Claire)
1990 **1** Deadly Safari (McQuillan, Karin)
1990 **1** Hometown Heroes (McShea, Susanna Hofmann)
1990   This Blessed Plot (Meek, M. R. D.)

1990 ... *continued*   168 titles   48 🔳

1990   Witching Murder (Melville, Jennie)
1990   Murder by Masquerade (Meredith, D. R.)
1990   Tender Death (Meyers, Annette)
1990 🔳 A Lively Form of Death (Mitchell, Kay)
1990   Rage (Moffat, Gwen)
1990   Obstacle Course (Montgomery, Yvonne E.)
1990 🔳 A Slay at the Races (Morgan, Kate)
1990   Trophies and Dead Things (Muller, Marcia)

1990   The Marshal's Own Case (Nabb, Magdalen)

1990 🔳 The Daphne Decisions (O'Brien, Meg)
1990   Salmon in the Soup (O'Brien, Meg)
1990 🔳 A Wreath for the Bride (O'Donnell, Lillian)
1990 🔳 Dead in the Scrub (Oliphant, B. J.) ☆
1990   The Unexpected Corpse (Oliphant, B. J.)
1990   Death and the Dogwalker (Orde, A. J.)

1990 🔳 The Body in the Belfry (Page, Katherine Hall) ★
1990   Once and Always Murder (Papazoglou, Orania)
1990   Burn Marks (Paretsky, Sara)
1990 🔳 The Face of a Stranger (Perry, Anne) ☆
1990   Bethlehem Road (Perry, Anne)
1990   Deadly Rehearsal (Peterson, Audrey)
1990   Elegy in a Country Graveyard (Peterson, Audrey)

1990   Cold Coffin (Quest, Erica)

1990 🔳 Death by the Riverside (Redmann, J. M.)
1990   A Second Shot in the Dark (Roome, Annette)
1990   A Little Gentle Sleuthing (Rowlands, Betty)
1990   Murder in a Good Cause (Sale, Medora)
1990 🔳 Death Down Home (Sandstrom, Eve K.)
1990 🔳 Murder Is Relative (Saum, Karen)
1990 🔳 As Crime Goes By (Shah, Diane K.)
1990   Now Let's Talk of Graves (Shankman, Sarah)
1990   Murderous Remedy (Shepherd, Stella)
1990 🔳 Larkspur (Simonson, Sheila)
1990 🔳 Sea of Troubles (Smith, Janet L.) ☆
1990   A Brush with Death (Smith, Joan G.)
1990   Don't Leave Me This Way (Smith, Joan)
1990 🔳 New Orleans Mourning (Smith, Julie) ★
1990   Murder in the Charleston Manner (Sprinkle, P. H.)
1990   Grave Responsibility (Stacey, Susannah)

1990 🔳 Murder at Red Rook Ranch (Tell, Dorothy)
1990   Wilderness Trek (Tell, Dorothy)
1990   Past Reckoning (Thomson, June)
1990   Finders Keepers (Travis, Elizabeth)
1990   Murder at the National Cathedral (Truman, Margaret)

1990   Raptor (Van Gieson, Judith)
1990 🔳 Missing Members (Vlasopolos, Anca)

1990   A Woman's Own Mystery [Britain–A February
          Mourning] (Wakefield, Hannah)
1990 🔳 Murder by the Book (Welch, Pat)
1990   Sweet, Sweet Poison (Wilhelm, Kate)
1990 🔳 Gaudi Afternoon (Wilson, Barbara) ★
1990   She Came in a Flash (Wings, Mary)
1990   Stolen Moments (Woods, Sherryl)
1990   A Chill Rain in January (Wright, L. R.) ☆
1990 🔳 Bad Medicine [APA–Ogilvie, Tallant and Moon ('76)]
          (Yarbro, Chelsea Quinn)
1990   False Notes [APA–Music When Sweet Voices Die
          ('79)] (Yarbro, Chelsea Quinn)

1991   175 titles   40 🔳

1991   The Catacomb Conspiracy (Arnold, Margot)

1991 🔳 In the Game (Baker, Nikki)
1991   Steel Guitar (Barnes, Linda)
1991   Death of a Snob (Beaton, M. C.)
1991   The Marvell College Murders (Belfort, Sophie)
1991   Island Girl (Berry, Carole)
1991   Love and Murder [APA–Murder at the Mendel]
          (Bowen, Gail)
1991   No Forwarding Address (Bowers, Elisabeth)
1991   The Cat Who Knew a Cardinal (Braun, Lilian J.)
1991 🔳 Headhunt (Brennan, Carol)
1991 🔳 Date with a Dead Doctor (Brill, Toni)
1991   Masquerade in Blue [APA–Framed in Blue] (Brod, D. C.)
1991   Coffin and the Paper Man (Butler, Gwendoline)

1991   Bad Blood (Carlson, P. M.)
1991 🔳 Raw Data (Chapman, Sally)
1991 🔳 A Drink of Deadly Wine (Charles, Kate)
1991   A Stunning Way to Die (Christmas, Joyce)
1991   Friend or Faux (Christmas, Joyce)
1991   A Farewell to Yarns (Churchill, Jill)
1991   The Case of the Paranoid Patient (Clarke, Anna)
1991   Murder in My Backyard (Cleeves, Ann)
1991   Sea Fever (Cleeves, Ann)
1991   Backhand (Cody, Liza) ☆
1991   Recording Angel (Cohen, Anthea)
1991   A Bite of Death (Conant, Susan)
1991   Poison Flowers (Cooper, Natasha)
1991   Chasing Away the Devil (Cooper, Susan Rogers)
1991   Body of Evidence (Cornwell, Patricia)
1991   Miss Seeton Cracks the Case (Crane, Hamilton)
1991   Miss Seeton Paints the Town (Crane, Hamilton)
1991 🔳 The Trouble with a Small Raise (Crespi, Camilla)
1991   The Trouble with Moonlighting (Crespi, Camilla)

1991   Hard Tack (D'Amato, Barbara)
1991 🔳 Just Desserts (Daheim, Mary) ☆
1991   Fowl Prey (Daheim, Mary)
1991   Venus in Copper (Davis, Lindsey)
1991 🔳 Smile, Honey (Donald, Anabel)
1991   The Daughters of Artemis (Douglas, Lauren Wright)
1991   Rook-Shoot (Duffy, Margaret)
1991   Rogue Wave (Dunlap, Susan)

1991   Art in the Blood (Elrod, P. N.)
1991   Fire in the Blood (Elrod, P. N.)
1991 🔳 Clearwater (Ennis, Catherine)

1991   Where Death Lies (Fallon, Ann C.)
1991   Getting Mine (Femling, Jean)
1991   Murder by Tradition (Forrest, Katherine V.) ★
1991 🔳 A Deadline for Murder (Frankel, Valerie)
1991   The Lily-White Boys (Fraser, Anthea)
1991   The Cavalier Case (Fraser, Antonia)
1991 🔳 Scalpel's Edge (Fromer, Margot J.)
1991   Deep Sleep (Fyfield, Frances)

1991   A Suitable Vengeance (George, Elizabeth)
1991 🔳 Adjusted to Death (Girdner, Jaqueline)
1991   The Last Resort (Girdner, Jaqueline)
1991   A Death for a Dancing Doll (Giroux, E. X.)
1991   Safe at Home (Gordon, Alison)
1991   Death Penalties (Gosling, Paula)
1991   "H" is for Homicide (Grafton, Sue)
1991 🔳 Say It with Poison (Granger, Ann)
1991   Love nor Money (Grant, Linda) ☆

1991 . . . continued   175 titles   40 ∎

1991 ∎ Too Many Questions [Britain–Flynn] (Grant-
        Adamson, Lesley)
1991 ∎ Partners in Crime (Gray, Gallagher)
1991 ∎ Deadly Errand (Green, Christine)
1991 ∎ Clerical Errors (Greenwood, Diane M.)
1991   Murder on the Ballarat Train (Greenwood, Kerry)

1991   Precious Blood (Haddam, Jane)
1991   Act of Darkness (Haddam, Jane)
1991   Quoth the Raven (Haddam, Jane)
1991 ∎ Orchestrated Death (Harrod-Eagles, Cynthia)
1991   The Christie Caper (Hart, Carolyn G.) ☆ ☆ ☆
1991   Vital Lies (Hart, Ellen)
1991   Threnody for Two [Britain–Lament for Two Ladies]
        (Hart, Jeanne)
1991   Death of a Warrior Queen (Haymon, S. T.)
1991 ∎ Murder on the Iditarod Trail (Henry, Sue) ★ ★
1991   Mortal Remains in Maggody (Hess, Joan)
1991   Madness in Maggody (Hess, Joan)
1991   Roll Over and Play Dead (Hess, Joan)
1991   The Cruellest Month (Holt, Hazel)
1991 ∎ Crime of Passion (Hooper, Kay)
1991   House of Cards (Hooper, Kay) ☆

1991   Cat's Eye (Jackson, Marian J. A.)
1991 ∎ The Turquoise Tattoo (Jacobs, Nancy Baker)
1991   Payment in Kind (Jance, J. A.)

1991   And Soon I'll Come to Kill You (Kelly, Susan)
1991   Kat's Cradle (Kijewski, Karen)
1991   Rigor Mortis (Kittredge, Mary)
1991   A Quiet Death (Knight, Alanna)
1991   Mumbo Jumbo (Knight, Kathryn Lasky)

1991   Grandmother's House (La Pierre, Janet)
1991   Jinx High (Lackey, Mercedes)
1991 ∎ Dogtown (Lambert, Mercedes)
1991   The Dante Game (Langton, Jane)
1991   East Is East (Lathen, Emma)
1991   Hotel Morgue (Laurence, Janet)
1991   Rancher's Blood (Lee, W. W.)
1991 ∎ Sister Beneath the Sheet (Linscott, Gillian)
1991   Unwilling to Vegas (Livingston, Nancy)
1991   Deception Island (Lorens, M. K.)
1991 ∎ A Relative Stranger (Lucke, Margaret) ☆

1991   Death Flats (MacGregor, T. J.)
1991   An Owl Too Many (MacLeod, Charlotte) ☆
1991 ∎ I Left My Heart (Maiman, Jaye)
1991   Faith, Hope and Homicide (Mann, Jessica)
1991   Past Imperfect (Maron, Margaret)
1991   Prior Convictions (Matera, Lia) ☆
1991   Murder on the Cliff (Matteson, Stefanie)
1991   Murder at Teatime (Matteson, Stefanie)
1991   Money Burns (Maxwell, A. E.)
1991   Missing Susan (McCrumb, Sharyn)
1991   Final Edition [U.S.–Open and Shut] (McDermid, Val)
1991   The Murders of Mrs. Austin & Mrs. Beale (McGown, J.)
1991   Cop Out (McNab, Claire)
1991   Murder by Reference (Meredith, D. R.)
1991   The Deadliest Option (Meyers, Annette)
1991   In Stony Places (Mitchell, Kay)
1991   Murder Most Fowl (Morgan, Kate)
1991 ∎ Final Session (Morell, Mary)
1991   Where Echoes Live (Muller, Marcia) ☆
1991   Murder at the Masque (Myers, Amy)

1991   The Marshal Makes His Report (Nabb, Magdalen)
1991   Death of a Partner (Neel, Janet)

1991   Hare Today, Gone Tomorrow (O'Brien, Meg)
1991   Set-Up (O'Callaghan, Maxine)
1991   A Private Crime (O'Donnell, Lillian)
1991   Murder in Ordinary Time (O'Marie, Carol Anne, Sister)

1991   The Body in the Kelp (Page, Katherine Hall)
1991   The Body in the Bouillon (Page, Katherine Hall)
1991   Guardian Angel (Paretsky, Sara)
1991   A Dangerous Mourning (Perry, Anne)
1991   Highgate Rise (Perry, Anne)
1991   The Last Camel Died at Noon (Peters, Elizabeth) ☆
1991   Summer of the Danes (Peters, Ellis)
1991   Lament for Christabel (Peterson, Audrey)
1991   I. O. U. (Pickard, Nancy) ★ ★ ☆
1991   Personal Effects (Piesman, Marissa)
1991 ∎ Bayou City Streets (Powell, Deborah)
1991   Original Sin (Pulver, Mary Monica)

1991   Model Murder (Quest, Erica)

1991   I'd Rather Be in Philadelphia (Roberts, Gillian)
1991 ∎ The Bulrush Murders (Rothenberg, Rebecca) ☆ ☆
1991   Grim Pickings (Rowe, Jennifer)

1991   Sleep of the Innocent (Sale, Medora)
1991   The Devil down Home (Sandstrom, Eve K.)
1991 ∎ Everything You Have Is Mine (Scoppettone, Sandra)
1991 ∎ Death and the Chapman (Sedley, Kate)
1991   She Walks in Beauty (Shankman, Sarah)
1991   Ah, Sweet Mystery (Sibley, Celestine)
1991 ∎ Taken by Storm (Silva, Linda Kay)
1991   Doomed To Die (Simpson, Dorothy)
1991   Miss Melville Rides a Tiger (Smith, Evelyn E.)
1991   The Axeman's Jazz (Smith, Julie)
1991   Dead in the Water (Smith, Julie)
1991   Murder on Peachtree Street (Sprinkle, Patricia H.)
1991 ∎ Murder on Her Mind (Steiner, Susan)
1991 ∎ Red Sea, Dead Sea (Stevens, Serita)

1991   The Hallelujah Murders (Tell, Dorothy)
1991 ∎ Bones (Thompson, Joyce)
1991   Foul Play (Thomson, June)
1991 ∎ Still Waters (Tucker, Kerry)

1991   Fine Distinctions (Valentine, Deborah) ☆
1991   The Other Side of Death (Van Gieson, Judith)

1991 ∎ Zero at the Bone (Walker, Mary Willis) ★ ★ ☆
1991   A Single Stone (Wallace, Marilyn) ☆
1991   Blood Lies (Wallace, Patricia)
1991 ∎ Cold Tracks (Wallingford, Lee)
1991 ∎ Murder on the Run (White, Gloria) ☆
1991 ∎ Death Qualified (Wilhelm, Kate)
1991   The Emerald Lizard (Wiltz, Chris)
1991   The Buzzards Must Also Be Fed (Wingate, Anne)
1991   We Wish You a Merry Murder (Wolzien, Valerie)
1991 ∎ Hot Property (Woods, Sherryl)
1991   Ties That Bind (Woods, Sherryl)
1991   Fall from Grace (Wright, L. R.)

1991   Poison Fruit (Yarbro, Chelsea Quinn)

1991 ∎ The Hour of the Knife (Zukowski, Sharon)

1992   216 titles   57 **1**

1992 **1** All the Great Pretenders (Adams, Deborah) ☆
1992   All the Crazy Winters (Adams, Deborah)
1992 **1** Thyme of Death (Albert, Susan Wittig) ☆
1992 **1** Quaker Silence (Allen, Irene)
1992 **1** Bury Her Sweetly (Amey, Linda)
1992 **1** Trail of Murder (Andreae, Christine) ☆
1992   Cape Cod Conundrum (Arnold, Margot)
1992 **1** Aunt Dimity's Death (Atherton, Nancy)
1992 **1** A World the Color of Salt (Ayres, Noreen)

1992   The Lavender House Murder (Baker, Nikki)
1992 **1** Agatha Raisin and the Quiche of Death (Beaton, M. C.)
1992   Death of a Prankster (Beaton, M. C.)
1992 **1** A Hopeless Case (Beck, K. K.)
1992   Worse Than Death (Bedford, Jean)
1992 **1** Introducing Amanda Valentine (Beecham, Rose)
1992   Eyewitness to Murder (Belfort, Sophie)
1992   A Vow of Chastity (Black, Veronica)
1992 **1** Dead Time (Bland, Eleanor Taylor)
1992   Dude on Arrival (Borthwick, J. S.)
1992   Murder Machree (Boylan, Eleanor)
1992   The Cat Who Moved a Mountain (Braun, Lilian J.)
1992   Full Commission (Brennan, Carol)
1992 **1** Broken Star (Brown, Lizbie)
1992   Rest in Pieces (Brown, Rita Mae)
1992 **1** Contents Under Pressure (Buchanan, Edna)
1992   Bury Him Kindly (Burden, Pat)
1992   Coffin on Murder Street (Butler, Gwendoline)

1992   Femmes Fatal (Cannell, Dorothy)
1992 **1** Gravestone (Carlson, P. M.)
1992   It's Her Funeral (Christmas, Joyce)
1992 **1** Decked (Clark, Carol Higgins) ☆
1992 **1** A Tail of Two Murders (Cleary, Melissa)
1992   A Day in the Death of Dorothea Cassidy (Cleeves, A.)
1992   Angel in Action (Cohen, Anthea)
1992   Paws Before Dying (Conant, Susan)
1992   Gone to the Dogs (Conant, Susan)
1992   Bloodlines (Conant, Susan)
1992   Bloody Roses (Cooper, Natasha)
1992 **1** One, Two, What Did Daddy Do? (Cooper, Susan R.)
1992   All That Remains (Cornwell, Patricia)
1992   The Wrong Rite (Craig, Alisa)
1992   Miss Seeton Rocks the Cradle (Crane, Hamilton)
1992   Hands up, Miss Seeton (Crane, Hamilton)
1992   Miss Seeton by Moonlight (Crane, Hamilton)
1992   The Trouble with Too Much Sun (Crespi, Camilla)
1992   Cat's Cradle (Curzon, Clare)

1992   Hard Luck (D'Amato, Barbara)
1992 **1** The Alpine Advocate (Daheim, Mary) ☆
1992   Holy Terrors (Daheim, Mary)
1992 **1** Lay It on the Line (Dain, Catherine) ☆
1992   As the Sparks Fly Upward (Dank, Gloria)
1992   Frame Grabber (Danks, Denise)
1992   Dying for Chocolate (Davidson, Diane Mott)
1992   Iron Hand of Mars (Davis, Lindsey)
1992   The Last Tango of Delores Delgado (Day, Marele) ★
1992   Dead Pan (Dentinger, Jane)
1992 **1** Catnap (Douglas, Carole Nelson)
1992   Irene at Large (Douglas, Carole Nelson)
1992   A Tiger's Heart (Douglas, Lauren Wright)
1992   High Strangeness (Drake, Alison)
1992 **1** Birth Marks (Dunant, Sarah)
1992   Death and Taxes (Dunlap, Susan)

1992   Moroccan Traffic [Britain–Send a Fax to the Kasbah] (Dunnett, Dorothy)

1992   Late of This Parish (Eccles, Marjorie)
1992   Clubbed to Death (Edwards, Ruth Dudley)
1992   Blood on the Water (Elrod, P. N.)
1992 **1** Death of a Duchess (Eyre, Elizabeth)

1992   Dead Ends (Fallon, Ann C.)
1992 **1** Alibi for an Actress (Farrell, Gillian B.)
1992   Beware of the Dog (Ferrars, E. X.)
1992 **1** Born to the Purple (Florian, S. L.)
1992   Murder on Wheels (Frankel, Valerie)
1992   Three, Three the Rivals (Fraser, Anthea)
1992 **1** The Novice's Tale (Frazer, Margaret)

1992   The Jersey Monkey (Gallison, Kate)
1992   For the Sake of Elena (George, Elizabeth)
1992   Murder Most Mellow (Girdner, Jaqueline)
1992 **1** Showcase (Glen, Alison)
1992   The Body in Blackwater Bay (Gosling, Paula)
1992   "I" is for Innocent (Grafton, Sue) ★
1992   A Season for Murder (Granger, Ann)
1992 **1** A Life of Adventure (Grant-Adamson, Lesley)
1992   A Cast of Killers (Gray, Gallagher)
1992   Deadly Admirer (Green, Christine)
1992   Unholy Ghosts (Greenwood, Diane M.)
1992   Death at Victoria Dock (Greenwood, Kerry)
1992   Under Water (Gunning, Sally)

1992 **1** Caught in the Shadows (Haddad, Carolyn A.)
1992   A Great Day for the Deadly (Haddam, Jane)
1992   Feast of Murder (Haddam, Jane)
1992   A Stillness in Bethlehem (Haddam, Jane)
1992 **1** Ravenmocker (Hager, Jean)
1992   Ghostland (Hager, Jean)
1992   Emma Chizzit and the Napa Nemesis (Hall, Mary B.)
1992   A Bone to Pick (Harris, Charlaine)
1992 **1** The Good Friday Murder (Harris, Lee) ☆
1992   The Yom Kippur Murder (Harris, Lee)
1992   Death Watch (Harrod-Eagles, Cynthia)
1992   Southern Ghost (Hart, Carolyn G.) ☆ ☆
1992   Stage Fright (Hart, Ellen)
1992 **1** Principal Defense (Hartzmark, Gini) ☆
1992   Maggody in Manhattan (Hess, Joan)
1992   Death by the Light of the Moon (Hess, Joan)
1992   Ripley Under Water (Highsmith, Patricia)
1992 **1** Alien Blues (Hightower, Lynn S.)
1992   The Shortest Journey (Holt, Hazel)
1992 **1** Telling Lies (Hornsby, Wendy)
1992 **1** Blood Price (Huff, Tanya)
1992   Blood Trail (Huff, Tanya)

1992   Diamond Head (Jackson, Marian J. A.)
1992 **1** The Garden Club (Jackson, Muriel Resnick)
1992   A Slash of Scarlet (Jacobs, Nancy Baker)
1992   Without Due Process (Jance, J. A.) ★
1992 **1** A Safe Place to Sleep (Jordan, Jennifer)

1992   Day of Atonement (Kellerman, Faye)
1992   False Prophet (Kellerman, Faye)
1992   Foxglove (Kelly, Mary Ann)
1992   My Sister's Keeper (Kelly, Nora)
1992   Out of the Darkness (Kelly, Susan)
1992   Copy Kat (Kijewski, Karen)
1992   Cadaver (Kittredge, Mary)
1992   Walking Dead Man (Kittredge, Mary)
1992   To Kill a Queen (Knight, Alanna)
1992 **1** Switching the Odds (Knight, Phyllis) ☆

1992 . . . *continued*   216 titles   57 **1**

1992 **1** File Under: Deceased (Lacey, Sarah)
1992 **1** The Holiday Murders (Landreth, Marsha)
1992 God in Concord (Langton, Jane)
1992 Recipe for Death (Laurence, Janet)
1992 Time Lapse (Law, Janice)
1992 Robber's Trail (Lee, W. W.)
1992 **1** Death at la Fenice (Leon, Donna)
1992 Hanging on the Wire (Linscott, Gillian)
1992 Quiet Murder (Livingston, Nancy)
1992 Dreamland (Lorens, M. K.)

1992 Spree (MacGregor, T. J.)
1992 The Resurrection Man (MacLeod, Charlotte)
1992 Crazy for Loving (Maiman, Jaye) ★
1992 **1** Body English (Mariz, Linda French)
1992 Snake Dance (Mariz, Linda French)
1992 **1** Bootlegger's Daughter (Maron, Margaret) ★ ★ ★
1992 Hacker (Martin, Lee)
1992 A Hard Bargain (Matera, Lia)
1992 Murder on the Silk Road (Matteson, Stefanie)
1992 The King of Nothing (Maxwell, A. E.)
1992 Ruffled Feathers (McCafferty, Taylor)
1992 Bed Bugs (McCafferty, Taylor)
1992 Zombies of the Gene Pool (McCrumb, Sharyn)
1992 The Hangman's Beautiful Daughter
       (McCrumb, Sharyn) ☆ ☆
1992 MacPherson's Lament (McCrumb, Sharyn)
1992 **1** Dead Beat (McDermid, Val)
1992 **1** Night Butterfly (McFall, Patricia)
1992 **1** Emergency Murder (McGiffin, Janet)
1992 The Other Woman (McGown, Jill)
1992 Point Deception (McKernan, Victoria)
1992 Dead Certain [APA–Off Key] (McNab, Claire)
1992 The Pumpkin Shell Wife (McShea, Susannah H.)
1992 Blood on the Street (Meyers, Annette)
1992 **1** The Dutchman (Meyers, Maan)
1992 **1** Murder at Moot Point (Millhiser, Marlys)
1992 Veronica's Sisters (Moffat, Gwen)
1992 **1** Seneca Falls Inheritance (Monfredo, Miriam G.) ☆ ☆
1992 Home Sweet Homicide (Morgan, Kate)
1992 Mystery Loves Company (Morgan, Kate)
1992 Days of Crime and Roses (Morgan, Kate)
1992 The Martini Effect (Morison, B. J.)
1992 Pennies on a Dead Woman's Eyes (Muller, Marcia)
1992 Murder Makes an Entree (Myers, Amy)
1992 Murder Under the Kissing Bough (Myers, Amy)

1992 **1** Blanche on the Lam (Neely, Barbara) ★ ★

1992 Eagles Die Too (O'Brien, Meg)
1992 Pushover (O'Donnell, Lillian)
1992 Deservedly Dead (Oliphant, B. J.)
1992 Death and the Delinquent (Oliphant, B. J.)
1992 Death for Old Times' Sake (Orde, A. J.)

1992 The Body in the Vestibule (Page, Katherine Hall)
1992 You Have the Right to Remain Silent (Paul, Barbara)
1992 Defend and Betray (Perry, Anne) ★ ☆
1992 Belgrave Square (Perry, Anne)
1992 The Snake, the Crocodile and the Dog (Peters, E.) ☆
1992 The Holy Thief (Peters, Ellis)
1992 **1** Dartmoor Burial (Peterson, Audrey)
1992 **1** The Two-Bit Tango (Pincus, Elizabeth)
1992 Houston Town (Powell, Deborah)
1992 Show Stopper (Pulver, Mary Monica)

1992 Cross My Heart and Hope to Die (Radley, Sheila)

1992 **1** Jinx (Robitaille, Julie)
1992 Death in Store [short stories with Birdie] (Rowe, J.)

1992 Pursued by Shadows (Sale, Medora)
1992 Murder Is Germane (Saum, Karen)
1992 Murder by Owl Light (Sawyer, Corinne Holt)
1992 The Plymouth Cloak (Sedley, Kate)
1992 Dying Cheek to Cheek (Shah, Diane K.)
1992 The King Is Dead (Shankman, Sarah)
1992 Thinner Than Blood (Shepherd, Stella)
1992 Straight as an Arrow (Sibley, Celestine)
1992 Skylark (Simonson, Sheila)
1992 Wake Her Dead (Simpson, Dorothy)
1992 Practice to Deceive (Smith, Janet L.)
1992 Somebody's Dead in Snellville (Sprinkle, Patricia H.)
1992 **1** A Cold Day for Murder (Stabenow, Dana) ★
1992 The Late Lady (Stacey, Susannah)
1992 **1** The End of April (Sumner, Penny)

1992 The Northwest Murders (Taylor, Elizabeth Atwood)
1992 **1** Every Crooked Nanny (Trocheck, Kathy Hogan) ☆
1992 **1** Murder at the Pentagon (Truman, Margaret)
1992 Cold Feet (Tucker, Kerry)

1992 The Wolf Path (Van Gieson, Judith)

1992 **1** The Winter Widow (Weir, Charlene) ★ ☆
1992 Still Waters (Welch, Pat)
1992 Seven Kinds of Death (Wilhelm, Kate)
1992 Exception to Murder (Wingate, Anne)
1992 All Hallow's Evil (Wolzien, Valerie)
1992 An Old Faithful Murder (Wolzien, Valerie)
1992 Hot Secret (Woods, Sherryl)

1992 Cat's Claw (Yarbro, Chelsea Quinn)
1992 **1** Cancellation by Death (Yeager, Dorian)

1992 Dancing in the Dark (Zukowski, Sharon)

1993   279 titles   68 **1**

1993 All the Dark Disguises (Adams, Deborah)
1993 All the Hungry Mothers (Adams, Deborah)
1993 A Going Concern (Aird, Catherine)
1993 Witches' Bane (Albert, Susan Wittig)
1993 Quaker Witness (Allen, Irene)
1993 **1** Tell Me What You Like (Allen, Kate)

1993 Shadows in Their Blood (Babson, Marian)
1993 Even Yuppies Die (Babson, Marian)
1993 Long Goodbyes (Baker, Nikki)
1993 **1** Minerva Cries Murder (Ballard, Mignon)
1993 **1** Death by Dressage (Banks, Carolyn)
1993 **1** A Bleeding of Innocents (Bannister, Jo)
1993 Snapshot (Barnes, Linda)
1993 **1** Track of the Cat (Barr, Nevada) ★ ★
1993 Agatha Raisin and the Vicious Vet (Beaton, M. C.)
1993 Death of a Glutton (Beaton, M. C.)
1993 Death of a Travelling Man (Beaton, M. C.)
1993 Amateur Night (Beck, K. K.)
1993 Signs of Murder (Bedford, Jean)
1993 A Vow of Sanctity (Black, Veronica)
1993 A Vow of Obedience (Black, Veronica)
1993 Slow Burn (Bland, Eleanor Taylor)
1993 **1** One for the Money (Borton, D. B.)
1993 Two Points for Murder (Borton, D. B.)
1993 The Wandering Soul Murders (Bowen, Gail)
1993 Pushing Murder (Boylan, Eleanor)
1993 The Cat Who Wasn't There (Braun, Lilian Jackson)
1993 **1** The Inspector and Mrs. Jeffries (Brightwell, Emily)

1993 . . . continued   279 titles   68 ∎

1993   Mrs. Jeffries Dusts for Clues (Brightwell, Emily)
1993   The Ghost and Mrs. Jeffries (Brightwell, Emily)
1993   Date with a Plummeting Publisher (Brill, Toni)
1993   Brothers in Blood (Brod, D. C.)
1993   Father, Forgive Me (Burden, Pat)
1993 ∎ Goodnight, Irene (Burke, Jan) ☆ ☆
1993   Death by Chrystal (Bushell, Agnes)
1993   Cracking Open a Coffin (Butler, Gwendoline)

1993 ∎ Private Lies (Cail, Carol)
1993 ∎ A Pocketful of Karma (Cannon, Taffy)
1993   The Snares of Death (Charles, Kate)
1993 ∎ This Business Is Murder (Christmas, Joyce)
1993   A Quiche Before Dying (Churchill, Jill)
1993   The Class Menagerie (Churchill, Jill)
1993   Snagged (Clark, Carol Higgins)
1993 ∎ Deadlier Than Death (Clark, Carolyn Chambers)
1993   Dog Collar Crime (Cleary, Melissa)
1993   Hounded to Death (Cleary, Melissa)
1993   Another Man's Poison (Cleeves, Ann)
1993 ∎ Bucket Nut (Cody, Liza) ★
1993   Angel in Love (Cohen, Anthea)
1993   Appearance of Evil (Coker, Carolyn)
1993   The Cashmere Kid (Comfort, Barbara)
1993   Ruffly Speaking (Conant, Susan)
1993   Bitter Herbs (Cooper, Natasha)
1993 ∎ Funny as a Dead Comic (Cooper, Susan Rogers)
1993   Cruel and Unusual (Cornwell, Patricia) ★
1993   The Grub-and-Stakers House a Haunt (Craig, Alisa)
1993   Miss Seeton Plants Suspicion (Crane, Hamilton)
1993   Miss Seeton Goes to Bat (Crane, Hamilton)
1993   The Trouble with Thin Ice (Crespi, Camilla)
1993 ∎ A Share in Death (Crombie, Deborah) ☆ ☆
1993 ∎ Dead as Dead Can Be (Crowleigh, Ann)
1993   Wait for the Dark (Crowleigh, Ann)
1993   First Wife, Twice Removed (Curzon, Clare)

1993   Hard Women (D'Amato, Barbara)
1993   The Alpine Betrayal (Daheim, Mary)
1993   The Alpine Christmas (Daheim, Mary)
1993   Dune to Death (Daheim, Mary)
1993   Bantam of the Opera (Daheim, Mary)
1993   Sing a Song of Death (Dain, Catherine)
1993   The Misfortune of Others (Dank, Gloria)
1993   Cereal Murders (Davidson, Diane Mott)
1993   Poseidon's Gold (Davis, Lindsey)
1993   Till the Old Men Die (Dawson, Janet)
1993   Take a Number (Dawson, Janet)
1993 ∎ Death Valley (Dengler, Sandy)
1993 ∎ Cat Killer (Dengler, Sandy)
1993   A Model Murder (Dengler, Sandy)
1993   Mouse Trapped (Dengler, Sandy)
1993 ∎ Throw Darts at a Cheesecake (Dietz, Denise)
1993   An Uncommon Murder (Donald, Anabel)
1993   Pussyfoot (Douglas, Carole Nelson)
1993   Goblin Market (Douglas, Lauren Wright)
1993   Otherworld (Dreher, Sarah)
1993   Gallows Bird (Duffy, Margaret)
1993   Fat Lands (Dunant, Sarah) ★
1993 ∎ Behind Eclaire's Doors (Dunbar, Sophie)
1993   Time Expired (Dunlap, Susan)
1993 ∎ The Man Who Understood Cats (Dymmoch, M. A.) ★

1993   The Company She Kept (Eccles, Marjorie)
1993   Chatauqua (Ennis, Catherine)
1993   Curtains for the Cardinal (Eyre, Elizabeth)

1993   Potter's Field (Fallon, Ann C.)
1993 ∎ Napoleon Must Die (Fawcett, Quinn)
1993   Death Wears a Crown (Fawcett, Quinn)
1993 ∎ Dead in the Water (Feddersen, Connie)
1993   Jemima Shore at the Sunny Grave [9 stories] (Fraser, Antonia)
1993   The Servant's Tale (Frazer, Margaret) ☆
1993   Night Shift (Fromer, Margot J.)
1993 ∎ Murder in C Major (Frommer, Sara Hoskinson)
1993   Shadow Play (Fyfield, Frances)

1993 ∎ Shaved Fish (Geason, Susan)
1993   Dogfish (Geason, Susan)
1993   Sharkbait (Geason, Susan)
1993   Missing Joseph (George, Elizabeth)
1993   Mrs. Pollifax and the Second Thief (Gilman, Dorothy)
1993 ∎ Final Design (Gilpatrick, Noreen)
1993   Fat-Free and Fatal (Girdner, Jaqueline)
1993   A Death for a Dodo (Giroux, E. X.)
1993 ∎ Burning Time (Glass, Leslie)
1993   Night Game (Gordon, Alison)
1993   "J" is for Judgment (Grafton, Sue)
1993   Death in Disguise (Graham, Caroline)
1993   Cold in the Earth (Granger, Ann)
1993   Murder Among Us (Granger, Ann)
1993 ∎ Where Old Bones Lie (Granger, Ann)
1993   The Dangerous Edge (Grant-Adamson, Lesley)
1993   Black Dreams (Green, Kate)
1993   Idol Bones (Greenwood, Diane M.)
1993   The Green Mill Murder (Greenwood, Kerry)
1993   The Horse You Came in On (Grimes, Martha)
1993 ∎ The Killing of Ellis Martin (Grindle, Lucretia)
1993   Ice Water (Gunning, Sally)
1993   Troubled Water (Gunning, Sally)
1993   Literary Murder (Gur, Batya)

1993   Murder Superior (Haddam, Jane)
1993   Festival of Deaths (Haddam, Jane)
1993   Emma Chizzit and the Mother Lode Marauder (Hall, Mary Bowen)
1993 ∎ The Poison Pool (Hall, Patricia)
1993 ∎ Guilty Pleasures (Hamilton, Laurell K.)
1993   The Christening Day Murder (Harris, Lee)
1993   Death To Go [APA—Necrochip] (Harrod-Eagles, C.)
1993 ∎ Dead Man's Island (Hart, Carolyn G.) ★
1993   A Killing Cure (Hart, Ellen)
1993 ∎ With Deadly Intent (Hendricksen, Louise)
1993   O Little Town of Maggody (Hess, Joan) ☆ ☆
1993   Poisoned Pins (Hess, Joan)
1993 ∎ Satan's Lambs (Hightower, Lynn S.) ★
1993   Alien Eyes (Hightower, Lynn S.)
1993   Mrs. Malory and the Festival Murders [Britain—Uncertain Death] (Holt, Hazel)
1993   Midnight Baby (Hornsby, Wendy)
1993   Blood Lines (Huff, Tanya)
1993   Blood Pact (Huff, Tanya)

1993   The Silver Scalpel (Jacobs, Nancy Baker)
1993 ∎ Desert Heat (Jance, J. A.)
1993   Failure to Appear (Jance, J. A.) ★
1993   Existing Solutions (Jordan, Jennifer)

1993 ∎ Murder in Bandora (Karr, Leona)
1993   Grievous Sin (Kellerman, Faye)
1993   Bad Chemistry (Kelly, Nora)
1993   Hope Will Answer (Kelly, Susan B.)
1993 ∎ Down Home Murder (Kelner, Toni L. P.)
1993 ∎ A Grave Talent (King, Laurie R.) ★ ☆

1993 . . . continued   279 titles   68 🔳

1993 🔳 Room with a Clue (Kingsbury, Kate)
1993   Desperate Remedy (Kittredge, Mary)
1993   The Evil That Men Do (Knight, Alanna)
1993 🔳 Fair Game (Krich, Rochelle Majer) ☆
1993 🔳 Murder Once Removed (Kunz, Kathleen)

1993   Old Enemies (La Pierre, Janet) ☆
1993 🔳 Prime Suspect (La Plante, Lynda)
1993   Prime Suspect 2 (La Plante, Lynda)
1993   File Under: Missing (Lacey, Sarah)
1993 🔳 Questionable Behavior (Lamb, J. Dayne)
1993   A Clinic for Murder (Landreth, Marsha)
1993   Divine Inspiration (Langton, Jane)
1993   Right on the Money (Lathen, Emma)
1993   Death and the Epicure (Laurence, Janet)
1993   A Safe Place to Die (Law, Janice)
1993   Outlaw's Fortune (Lee, W. W.)
1993   Death in a Strange Country (Leon, Donna)
1993   Stage Fright (Linscott, Gillian)
1993 🔳 Still Explosion (Logue, Mary)
1993 🔳 Brotherly Love (Lorden, Randye) ☆
1993   Sorrowheart (Lorens, M. K.)
1993   Someone Is Killing the Great Chefs of America
           (Lyons, Nan & Ivan)

1993   Storm Surge (MacGregor, T. J.)
1993   Under My Skin (Maiman, Jaye)
1993 🔳 The Case of the Not-So-Nice Nurse (Maney, Mabel)
1993   Southern Discomfort (Maron, Margaret) ☆ ☆
1993   The Day That Dusty Died (Martin, Lee)
1993 🔳 Murder in the Maze (Mason, Sarah Jill)
1993   Frozen Stiff (Mason, Sarah Jill)
1993   Murder at the Falls (Matteson, Stefanie)
1993   Murder Hurts (Maxwell, A. E.)
1993   Kick Back (McDermid, Val)
1993   Union Jack (McDermid, Val)
1993   Prescription for Death (McGiffin, Janet)
1993   Murder Now and Then (McGown, Jill)
1993 🔳 Until Proven Guilty (McGuire, Christine)
1993 🔳 Murder Beach (McKenna, Bridget)
1993   Elephants' Graveyard (McQuillan, Karin)
1993   Touch & Go (Meek, M. R. D.)
1993 🔳 Mail-Order Murder (Meier, Leslie)
1993   Dead Set (Melville, Jennie)
1993   Footsteps in the Blood (Melville, Jennie)
1993   The Sheriff & the Pheasant Hunt Murders
           (Meredith, D. R.)
1993   Murder by Sacrilege (Meredith, D. R.)
1993   Murder: The Musical (Meyers, Annette)
1993   The Kingsbridge Plot (Meyers, Maan)
1993   Death of the Office Witch (Millhiser, Marlys)
1993   North Star Conspiracy (Monfredo, Miriam Grace)
1993 🔳 Death Takes a Hand [Britain–Takeout Double]
           (Moody, Susan)
1993   Penny Saving (Moody, Susan)
1993   Final Rest (Morell, Mary)
1993   Twice in a Blue Moon (Moyes, Patricia)
1993   Wolf in the Shadows (Muller, Marcia) ★ ☆ ☆

1993   Death Among the Dons (Neel, Janet)
1993 🔳 Death Comes as Epiphany (Newman, Sharan) ★ ☆ ☆

1993 🔳 Skins (O'Connell, Catherine)
1993   Used to Kill (O'Donnell, Lillian)
1993   Murder Makes a Pilgrimmage (O'Marie, C. A., Sister)
1993 🔳 Murder in Mellingham (Oleksiw, Susan)

1993   Looking for the Aardvark [APA–Dead on Sunday]
           (Orde, A. J.)

1993 🔳 Child of Silence (Padgett, Abigail) ☆ ☆
1993   The Body in the Cast (Page, Katherine Hall)
1993   The Apostrophe Thief (Paul, Barbara)
1993 🔳 Something's Cooking (Pence, Joanne)
1993   A Sudden, Fearful Death (Perry, Anne)
1993   Farrier's Lane (Perry, Anne)
1993   But I Wouldn't Want to Die There (Pickard, Nancy)
1993   Heading Uptown (Piesman, Marissa)
1993   The Solitary Twist (Pincus, Elizabeth)
1993 🔳 By Evil Means (Prowell, Sandra West) ☆
1993 🔳 Cold Call (Pugh, Dianne G.)

1993 🔳 Murder Most Grizzly (Quinn, Elizabeth)
1993   Deaths of Jocasta (Redmann, J. M.) ☆
1993   Kissing the Gunner's Daughter (Rendell, Ruth)
1993   The 27-Ingredient Chili Con Carne Murders
           (Rich, Virginia)
1993 🔳 The Apothecary Rose (Robb, Candace M.)
1993 🔳 Pray God to Die (Roberts, Carey)
1993   With Friends Like These (Roberts, Gillian)
1993   Shadow Walkers (Romberg, Nina)
1993 🔳 Cut to the Quick (Ross, Kate)
1993   The Makeover Murders (Rowe, Jennifer)
1993   Finishing Touch (Rowlands, Betty)
1993   Over the Edge (Rowlands, Betty)

1993   The Down Home Heifer Heist (Sandstrom, Eve K.)
1993   The Peanut Butter Murders (Sawyer, Corinne Holt)
1993 🔳 Silverlake Heat (Schmidt, Carol)
1993   I'll Be Leaving You Always (Scoppettone, Sandra)
1993 🔳 Everywhere That Mary Went (Scottoline, Lisa) ☆
1993   The Weaver's Tale (Sedley, Kate)
1993   The Hanged Man (Sedley, Kate)
1993   He Was Her Man (Shankman, Sarah)
1993   A Lethal Fixation (Shepherd, Stella)
1993   Dire Happenings at Scratch Ankle (Sibley, Celestine)
1993   Storm Shelter (Silva, Linda Kay)
1993   Mudlark (Simonson, Sheila)
1993   No Laughing Matter (Simpson, Dorothy)
1993 🔳 Following Jane (Singer, Shelley)
1993   Picture of David (Singer, Shelley)
1993   What Men Say (Smith, Joan)
1993   Jazz Funeral (Smith, Julie)
1993   Other People's Skeletons (Smith, Julie)
1993   Death of a Dunwoody Matron (Sprinkle, Patricia H.)
1993   A Fatal Thaw (Stabenow, Dana)
1993   Dead in the Water (Stabenow, Dana)
1993   Bone Idle (Stacey, Susannah)
1993 🔳 Death and the Oxford Box (Stallwood, Veronica)
1993 🔳 Murder at the Class Reunion (Stein, Triss)
1993   Library: No Murder Aloud (Steiner, Susan)
1993   Bagels for Tea (Stevens, Serita)
1993 🔳 A Sudden Death at the Norfolk Cafe (Sullivan, W.) ★

1993   To Live and Die in Dixie (Trocheck, Kathy Hogan) ☆ ☆
1993   Death Echo (Tucker, Kerry)

1993   The Lies That Bind (Van Gieson, Judith) ☆

1993   Clear Cut Murder (Wallingford, Lee)
1993 🔳 The Wyndham Case (Walsh, Jill Paton)
1993   Consider the Crows (Weir, Charlene) ☆
1993   A Proper Burial (Welch, Pat)
1993   Money to Burn (White, Gloria)
1993 🔳 Justice for Some (Wilhelm, Kate)
1993   Trouble in Transylvania (Wilson, Barbara)
1993   Yakuza, Go Home! (Wingate, Anne)

1993 . . . *continued* ◦ 279 titles 68 **1**

1993	A Star-Spangled Murder (Wolzien, Valerie)
1993	Hot Money (Woods, Sherryl)
1993	Bank on It (Woods, Sherryl)
1993	Hide and Seek (Woods, Sherryl)
1993	Dead Matter (Wren, M. K.)
1993	Prized Possessions (Wright, L. R.)

1993	Eviction by Death (Yeager, Dorian)

1994 292 titles 69 **1**

1994	Hangman's Root (Albert, Susan Wittig)
1994	Grizzly, A Murder (Andreae, Christine)
1994 **1**	Tensleep (Andrews, Sarah)
1994	Dirge for a Dorset Druid (Arnold, Margot)
1994	Aunt Dimity and the Duke (Atherton, Nancy)
1994	Carcass Trade (Ayres, Noreen)

1994	Groomed for Death (Banks, Carolyn)
1994	Charisma [Britain–Sins of the Heart] (Bannister, Jo)
1994	A Superior Death (Barr, Nevada)
1994	Agatha Raisin and the Potted Gardener (Beaton, M. C.)
1994	Death of a Charming Man (Beaton, M. C.)
1994	Electric City (Beck, K. K.)
1994	Second Guess (Beecham, Rose)
1994 **1**	Deep Cover (Berenson, Laurien)
1994	The Death of a Difficult Woman (Berry, Carole)
1994 **1**	A Taste for Murder (Bishop, Claudia)
1994	A Vow of Penance (Black, Veronica)
1994	A Vow of Devotion (Black, Veronica)
1994	Gone Quiet (Bland, Eleanor Taylor)
1994 **1**	Chutes and Adders (Block, Barbara)
1994	Twister (Block, Barbara)
1994	The Bridled Groom (Borthwick, J. S.)
1994	Three Is a Crowd (Borton, D. B.)
1994	A Colder Kind of Death (Bowen, Gail) ★
1994 **1**	Stand-in for Murder (Bradley, Lynn)
1994	The Cat Who Came to Breakfast (Braun, Lilian J.)
1994	The Cat Who Went into the Closet (Braun, Lilian J.)
1994 **1**	In the Dark (Brennan, Carol)
1994	Mrs. Jeffries Takes Stock (Brightwell, Emily)
1994	Mrs. Jeffries on the Ball (Brightwell, Emily)
1994	Turkey Tracks (Brown, Lizbie)
1994	Murder at Monticello (Brown, Rita Mae)
1994	Miami, It's Murder (Buchanan, Edna) ☆
1994 **1**	No One Dies in Branson (Buckstaff, Kathryn)
1994	Sweet Dreams, Irene (Burke, Jan)
1994	A Coffin for Charley (Butler, Gwendoline)
1994	The Coffin Tree (Butler, Gwendoline)

1994	How to Murder Your Mother-in-law (Cannell, Dorothy)
1994	Love Bytes (Chapman, Sally)
1994	Appointed to Die (Charles, Kate)
1994	A Perfect Day for Dying (Christmas, Joyce)
1994	A Knife to Remember (Churchill, Jill)
1994 **1**	Dangerous Alibis (Clark, Carolyn Chambers)
1994	The Case of the Ludicrous Letters (Clarke, Anna)
1994	Skull and Dog Bones (Cleary, Melissa)
1994	First Pedigree Murder (Cleary, Melissa)
1994	Dead and Buried (Cleary, Melissa)
1994	The Mill on the Shore (Cleeves, Ann)
1994	Monkey Wrench (Cody, Liza)
1994 **1**	Deadly Resolutions (Collins, Anna Ashwood)
1994	Funny as a Dead Relative (Cooper, Susan Rogers)
1994	Dead Moon on the Rise (Cooper, Susan Rogers)

1994	The Body Farm (Cornwell, Patricia)
1994	Starring Miss Seeton (Crane, Hamilton)
1994	Miss Seeton Undercover (Crane, Hamilton)
1994	Miss Seeton Rules (Crane, Hamilton)
1994	All Shall Be Well (Crombie, Deborah)
1994 **1**	Cutter (Crum, Laura)
1994	Death Prone (Curzon, Clare)

1994	Hard Case (D'Amato, Barbara)
1994	The Alpine Decoy (Daheim, Mary)
1994	Fit of Tempera (Daheim, Mary)
1994	Walk a Crooked Mile (Dain, Catherine)
1994	Lament for a Dead Cowboy (Dain, Catherine) ☆
1994	Wink a Hopeful Eye (Danks, Denise)
1994	The Last Suppers (Davidson, Diane Mott)
1994	Last Act in Palmyra (Davis, Lindsey)
1994	Don't Turn Your Back on the Ocean (Dawson, Janet)
1994	The Disappearance of Madalena Grimaldi (Day, M.)
1994	Murder on the Mount (Dengler, Sandy)
1994	The Last Dinosaur (Dengler, Sandy)
1994	Gila Monster (Dengler, Sandy)
1994	The Queen Is Dead (Dentinger, Jane)
1994 **1**	Miss Zukas and the Library Murders (Dereske, Jo)
1994	Beat up a Cookie (Dietz, Denise)
1994	In at the Deep End (Donald, Anabel)
1994	Cat on a Blue Monday (Douglas, Carole Nelson)
1994	Irene's Last Waltz (Douglas, Carole Nelson)
1994	A Rage of Maidens (Douglas, Lauren Wright)
1994 **1**	Dressed to Kill (Duffy, Margaret)
1994	High Fall (Dunlap, Susan)
1994 **1**	Death at Wentwater Court (Dunn, Carola)

1994	An Accidental Shroud (Eccles, Marjorie)
1994 **1**	Speak Daggers to Her (Edghill, Rosemary)
1994	Matricide at St. Martha's (Edwards, Ruth Dudley)
1994 **1**	Murder Can Kill Your Social Life (Eichler, Selma)
1994 **1**	One for the Money (Evanovich, Janet) ☆ ☆ ☆ ☆
1994	Poison for the Prince (Eyre, Elizabeth)
1994	Bravo for the Bride (Eyre, Elizabeth)

1994	Murder and a Muse (Farrell, Gillian B.)
1994	Dead in the Cellar (Feddersen, Connie)
1994 **1**	The Hippie in the Wall (Fennelly, Tony)
1994	A Hobby of Murder (Ferrars, E. X.)
1994 **1**	Chosen for Death (Flora, Kate Clark)
1994 **1**	Fool's Puzzle (Fowler, Earlene) ☆
1994	Prime Time for Murder (Frankel, Valerie)
1994	The Gospel Makers (Fraser, Anthea)
1994	Political Death (Fraser, Antonia)
1994	The Outlaw's Tale (Frazer, Margaret)
1994	The Bishop's Tale (Frazer, Margaret)
1994 **1**	Alaska Gray (Froetschel, Susan)
1994	Buried in Quilts (Frommer, Sara Hoskinson)
1994	Perfectly Pure and Good (Fyfield, Frances)
1994	A Clear Conscience (Fyfield, Frances)

1994	Playing for the Ashes (George, Elizabeth)
1994	Tea-Totally Dead (Girdner, Jaqueline)
1994 **1**	A Few Dying Words (Gosling, Paula)
1994	"K" is for Killer (Grafton, Sue) ★ ☆
1994	Flowers for His Funeral (Granger, Ann)
1994	A Woman's Place (Grant, Linda)
1994	Dangerous Games (Grant-Adamson, Lesley)
1994 **1**	Death in the Country (Green, Christine)
1994	Deadly Practice (Green, Christine)
1994	Holy Terrors (Greenwood, Diane M.)
1994	Blood and Circuses (Greenwood, Kerry)
1994	So Little to Die For (Grindle, Lucretia)

1994 ... *continued*   **292 titles**   **69** 🆔

1994 Rough Water (Gunning, Sally)
1994 Murder on the Kibbutz: A Communal Case (Gur, B.) ☆

1994 Bleeding Hearts (Haddam, Jane)
1994 Dear Old Dead (Haddam, Jane)
1994 ▌ Edited Out (Haddock, Lisa)
1994 ▌ Blooming Murder (Hager, Jean)
1994 The Redbird's Cry (Hager, Jean)
1994 ▌ Death by Election (Hall, Patricia)
1994 The Laughing Corpse (Hamilton, Laurell K.)
1994 Three Bedrooms, One Corpse (Harris, Charlaine)
1994 The St. Patrick's Day Murder (Harris, Lee)
1994 The Christmas Night Murder (Harris, Lee)
1994 Grave Music [Britain–Dead End] (Harrod-Eagles, C.)
1994 Scandal in Fair Haven (Hart, Carolyn G.) ☆
1994 ▌ This Little Piggy Went to Murder (Hart, Ellen)
1994 A Small Sacrifice (Hart, Ellen) ★
1994 Final Option (Hartzmark, Gini)
1994 A Beautiful Death (Haymon, S. T.)
1994 ▌ What's a Girl Gotta Do? (Hayter, Sparkle) ★
1994 Grave Secrets (Hendricksen, Louise)
1994 Martians in Maggody (Hess, Joan)
1994 Tickled to Death (Hess, Joan)
1994 Alien Heat (Hightower, Lynn S.)
1994 Mrs. Malory: Detective in Residence [Britain–Murder on Campus] (Holt, Hazel)
1994 ▌ Something To Kill For (Holtzer, Susan) ★
1994 Dead Center (Horansky, Ruby)
1994 Bad Intent (Hornsby, Wendy)
1994 Beauty Dies (Howe, Melodie Johnson)

1994 The Sunken Treasure (Jackson, Marian J. A.)
1994 ▌ Murder Among Neighbors (Jacobs, Jonnie)
1994 Original Sin (James, P. D.)
1994 Tombstone Courage (Jance, J. A.)
1994 Lying in Wait (Jance, J. A.)
1994 ▌ A Love to Die For (Jorgensen, Christine T.)

1994 Sanctuary (Kellerman, Faye)
1994 Kid's Stuff (Kelly, Susan B.)
1994 Dead Ringer (Kelner, Toni L. P.)
1994 Wild Kat (Kijewski, Karen)
1994 ▌ The Beekeeper's Apprentice (King, Laurie R.) ☆
1994 Do Not Disturb (Kingsbury, Kate)
1994 Service for Two (Kingsbury, Kate)
1994 Eat, Drink, and Be Buried (Kingsbury, Kate)
1994 The Missing Duchess (Knight, Alanna)
1994 Dark Swain (Knight, Kathryn Lasky)
1994 Shattered Rhythms (Knight, Phyllis)
1994 ▌ Fool Me Once (Kreuter, Katherine E.)
1994 Angel of Death (Krich, Rochelle Majer) ☆
1994 ▌ Death on the Cliff Walk (Kruger, Mary)

1994 Prime Suspect 3 (La Plante, Lynda)
1994 File Under: Arson (Lacey, Sarah)
1994 A Question of Preference (Lamb, J. Dayne)
1994 Death at the Table (Laurence, Janet)
1994 Backfire (Law, Janice)
1994 ▌ The Good Daughter (Lee, W. W.)
1994 Dressed for Death [Britain–The Anonymous Venetian] (Leon, Donna)
1994 An Easy Day for a Lady [Britain–Widow's Peak] (Linscott, Gillian)
1994 ▌ The End of an Altruist (Logan, Margaret)
1994 Sister's Keeper (Lorden, Randye)

1994 Blue Pearl (MacGregor, T. J.)

1994 Something in the Water (MacLeod, Charlotte)
1994 ▌ Death Pays the Rose Rent (Malmont, Valerie S.)
1994 The Case of the Good-for-Nothing Girlfriend (Maney, Mabel)
1994 ▌ Ghost Motel (Manthorne, Jackie)
1994 Shooting at Loons (Maron, Margaret)
1994 Inherited Murder (Martin, Lee)
1994 Corpse in the Kitchen (Mason, Sarah Jill)
1994 Dying Breath (Mason, Sarah Jill)
1994 Face Value (Matera, Lia)
1994 ▌ Blood of an Aries (Mather, Linda)
1994 Beware Taurus (Mather, Linda)
1994 ▌ Death in the Off-Season (Mathews, Francine)
1994 Murder on High (Matteson, Stefanie)
1994 ▌ The Lessons (McAllester, Melanie)
1994 Thin Skins (McCafferty, Taylor)
1994 ▌ The Bluejay Shaman (McClendon, Lise)
1994 She Walks These Hills (McCrumb, Sharyn) ★ ★ ★
1994 Crack Down (McDermid, Val) ☆
1994 Until Justice is Done (McGuire, Christine)
1994 Dead Ahead (McKenna, Bridget) ☆
1994 Crooked Island (McKernan, Victoria)
1994 Body Guard (McNab, Claire)
1994 The Cheetah Chase (McQuillan, Karin)
1994 Ladybug, Ladybug (McShea, Susanna Hofmann)
1994 Tippy-Toe Murder (Meier, Leslie)
1994 Death in the Family [Britain–Baby Drop] (Melville, J.)
1994 The High Constable (Meyers, Maan)
1994 ▌ Keeping Secrets (Mickelbury, Penny)
1994 A Strange Desire [U.S.–Roots of Evil] (Mitchell, Kay)
1994 Grand Slam (Moody, Susan)
1994 Wanted Dude or Alive (Morgan, Kate)
1994 Till the Butchers Cut Him Down (Muller, Marcia)
1994 Murder in the Smokehouse (Myers, Amy)
1994 ▌ Too Many Crooks Spoil the Broth (Myers, Tamar)
1994 The Marshal at the Villa Torrini (Nabb, Magdalen)

1994 Blanche Among the Talented Tenth (Neely, Barbara)
1994 The Devil's Door (Newman, Sharan)
1994 ▌ Healthy, Wealthy & Dead (North, Suzanne) ☆

1994 Trade-Off (O'Callaghan, Maxine)
1994 ▌ Mallory's Oracle (O'Connell, Carol) ☆
1994 Lockout (O'Donnell, Lillian)
1994 Double Take (Oleksiw, Susan)
1994 Death Served up Cold (Oliphant, B. J.)
1994 ▌ Murder Offscreen (Osborne, Denise)

1994 Strawgirl (Padgett, Abigail)
1994 The Body in the Basement (Page, Katherine Hall)
1994 ▌ Death at Bishop's Keep (Paige, Robin)
1994 Tunnel Vision (Paretsky, Sara)
1994 ▌ Suspicion of Innocence (Parker, Barbara) ☆
1994 Too Many Cooks (Pence, Joanne)
1994 Sins of the Wolf (Perry, Anne)
1994 The Hyde Park Headsman (Perry, Anne)
1994 Night Train to Memphis (Peters, Elizabeth) ☆
1994 Brother Cadfael's Penance (Peters, Ellis)
1994 Death Too Soon (Peterson, Audrey)
1994 Confession (Pickard, Nancy)
1994 Close Quarters (Piesman, Marissa)
1994 The Killing of Monday Brown (Prowell, Sandra West) ☆
1994 Slow Squeeze (Pugh, Dianne G.)

1994 Fair Game (Radley, Sheila)
1994 Simisola (Rendell, Ruth)
1994 ▌ Mulch (Ripley, Ann)
1994 The Lady Chapel (Robb, Candace M.)
1994 How I Spent My Summer Vacation (Roberts, Gillian)

1994 . . . *continued* 292 titles 69 ∎

1994 ∎ Murder in a Nice Neighborhood (Roberts, Lora)
1994 ∎ Murder in the Place of Anubis (Robinson, Lynda S.)
1994 Iced (Robitaille, Julie)
1994 A Broken Vessel (Ross, Kate) ★
1994 The Dandelion Murders (Rothenberg, Rebecca)
1994 Stranglehold (Rowe, Jennifer)
1994 Exhaustive Inquiries (Rowlands, Betty)
1994 ∎ China Trade (Rozan, S. J.)
1994 ∎ Chicken Little Was Right (Ruryk, Jean)

1994 Short Cut to Santa Fe (Sale, Medora)
1994 Murder Is Material (Saum, Karen)
1994 Murder Has No Calories (Sawyer, Corinne Holt)
1994 ∎ In Blacker Moments (Schenkel, S. E.)
1994 Sweet Cherry Wine (Schmidt, Carol)
1994 Cabin Fever (Schmidt, Carol)
1994 My Sweet Untraceable You (Scoppettone, Sandra)
1994 ∎ Final Appeal (Scottoline, Lisa) ★
1994 The Holy Innocents (Sedley, Kate)
1994 ∎ All My Suspects (Shaffer, Louise)
1994 Nurse Dawes Is Dead (Shepherd, Stella)
1994 ∎ Angel's Bidding (Short, Sharon Gwyn)
1994 Past Pretense (Short, Sharon Gwyn)
1994 Weathering the Storm (Silva, Linda Kay)
1994 Searching for Sara (Singer, Shelley)
1994 Catnap (Slovo, Gillian)
1994 ∎ North of Montana (Smith, April)
1994 ∎ Writers of the Purple Sage (Smith, Barbara Burnett) ☆
1994 A Vintage Murder (Smith, Janet L.)
1994 New Orleans Beat (Smith, Julie)
1994 ∎ Every Breath You Take (Spring, Michelle) ☆ ☆
1994 A Mystery Bred in Buckhead (Sprinkle, Patricia H.)
1994 ∎ Who Killed What's-Her-Name? (Squire, Elizabeth D.)
1994 Remember the Alibi (Squire , Elizabeth Daniels)
1994 A Cold-Blooded Business (Stabenow, Dana)

1994 Homemade Sin (Trocheck, Kathy Hogan)
1994 Murder on the Potomac (Truman, Margaret)
1994 Drift Away (Tucker, Kerry)
1994 ∎ Strangers in the Night (Tyre, Peg)

1994 ∎ The Red Scream (Walker, Mary Willis) ★ ☆
1994 Deadly Devotion (Wallace, Patricia) ☆
1994 ∎ When Death Comes Stealing (Wesley, Valerie W.) ☆
1994 ∎ Sunrise (West, Chassie) ☆
1994 ∎ Until Death (Whitney, Polly) ☆
1994 The Best Defense (Wilhelm, Kate)
1994 ∎ Eight Dogs Flying (Wilson, Karen Ann)
1994 A Good Year for a Corpse (Wolzien, Valerie)
1994 Tis the Season To Be Murdered (Wolzien, Valerie)
1994 Hot Schemes (Woods, Sherryl)
1994 Wages of Sin (Woods, Sherryl)
1994 A Touch of Panic (Wright, L. R.) ☆

1994 ∎ Murder Will Out (Yeager, Dorian)

1994 ∎ Blood Work (Zachary, Fay)
1994 A Poison in the Blood (Zachary, Fay)
1994 Leap of Faith (Zukowski, Sharon)

1995 288 titles 32 ∎

1995 All the Deadly Beloved (Adams, Deborah)
1995 Rosemary Remembered (Albert, Susan Wittig)
1995 Give My Secrets Back (Allen, Kate)
1995 At Dead of Night (Amey, Linda)
1995 A Fall in Denver (Andrews, Sarah)

1995 The Midas Murders (Arnold, Margot)
1995 Break a Leg Darlings (Babson, Marian)
1995 Murder Well-Bred (Banks, Carolyn)
1995 A Taste for Burning [Britain–Burning Desires] (Bannister, Jo)
1995 Hardware (Barnes, Linda)
1995 Ill Wind (Barr, Nevada)
1995 Agatha Raisin and the Walkers of Dembley (Beaton, M. C.)
1995 Death of a Nag (Beaton, M. C.)
1995 Cold Smoked (Beck, K. K.)
1995 Fair Play (Beecham, Rose)
1995 ∎ A Pedigree to Die For (Berenson, Laurien)
1995 A Dash of Death (Bishop, Claudia)
1995 A Pinch of Poison (Bishop, Claudia)
1995 Vow of Poverty (Black, Veronica)
1995 Done Wrong (Bland, Eleanor Taylor)
1995 Dolly Is Dead (Borthwick, J. S.)
1995 Four Elements of Murder (Borton, D. B.)
1995 The Cat Who Blew the Whistle (Braun, Lilian J.)
1995 Chill of Summer (Brennan, Carol)
1995 Mrs. Jeffries on the Trail (Brightwell, Emily)
1995 Mrs. Jeffries Plays the Cook (Brightwell, Emily)
1995 Pay Dirt (Brown, Rita Mae)
1995 Suitable for Framing (Buchanan, Edna)
1995 Dear Irene, (Burke, Jan)

1995 A Dark Coffin (Butler, Gwendoline)
1995 Unsafe Keeping (Cail, Carol)
1995 How to Murder the Man of Your Dreams (Cannell, D.)
1995 Tangled Roots (Cannon, Taffy)
1995 Bloodstream (Carlson, P. M.)
1995 A Dead Man Out of Mind (Charles, Kate)
1995 Evil Angels Among Them (Charles, Kate)
1995 ∎ A Famine of Horses (Chisholm, P. F.)
1995 Death at Face Value (Christmas, Joyce)
1995 From Here to Paternity (Churchill, Jill)
1995 Iced (Clark, Carol Higgins)
1995 The Maltese Puppy (Cleary, Melissa)
1995 Killjoy (Cleeves, Ann)
1995 ∎ The Eagle Catcher (Coel, Margaret)
1995 Angel in Autumn (Cohen, Anthea)
1995 Elusive Quarry (Comfort, Barbara)
1995 Black Ribbon (Conant, Susan)
1995 Rotten Apples (Cooper, Natasha)
1995 Doctors and Lawyers and Such (Cooper, Susan R.)
1995 From Potter's Field (Cornwell, Patricia)
1995 Sold to Miss Seeton (Crane, Hamilton)
1995 The Trouble with Going Home (Crespi, Camilla)
1995 Leave the Grave Green (Crombie, Deborah)
1995 An Imperfect Spy (Cross, Amanda)
1995 Nice People (Curzon, Clare)

1995 Hard Christmas (D'Amato, Barbara)
1995 The Alpine Escape (Daheim, Mary)
1995 The Alpine Fury (Daheim, Mary)
1995 Major Vices (Daheim, Mary)
1995 Murder My Suite (Daheim, Mary)
1995 Bet Against the House (Dain, Catherine)
1995 Killer Pancake (Davidson, Diane Mott)
1995 Time to Depart (Davis, Lindsey)
1995 Nobody's Child (Dawson, Janet)
1995 ∎ The Strange Files of Fremont Jones (Day, Dianne)
1995 The Quick and the Dead (Dengler, Sandy)
1995 Who Dropped Peter Pan? (Dentinger, Jane)
1995 Miss Zukas and the Island Murders (Dereske, Jo)
1995 The Glass Ceiling (Donald, Anabel)

1995 . . . *continued*   288 titles   32 🆔

1995   Cat in a Crimson Haze (Douglas, Carole Nelson)
1995   Bad Company (Dreher, Sarah)
1995   Prospect of Death (Duffy, Margaret)
1995   Under My Skin (Dunant, Sarah)
1995   Redneck Riviera (Dunbar, Sophie)
1995   The Winter Garden Mystery (Dunn, Carola)
1995   The Death of Blue Mountain Cat (Dymmoch, M. A.)

1995   A Death of Distinction (Eccles, Marjorie)
1995   Book of Moons (Edghill, Rosemary)
1995   Murder Can Ruin Your Looks (Eichler, Selma)
1995   Rotten Lies (Elkins, Charlotte & Aaron)

1995   Hour of Our Death (Fallon, Ann C.)
1995   Dead in the Melon Patch (Feddersen, Connie)
1995   A Choice of Evils (Ferrars, E. X.)
1995 🆔 Silent Buddy (Flora, Kate Clark)
1995   Death in a Funhouse Mirror (Flora, Kate Clark)
1995   Irish Chain (Fowler, Earlene)
1995   A Body to Die For (Frankel, Valerie)
1995   Seven Stars (Fraser, Anthea)
1995   The Boy's Tale (Frazer, Margaret)
1995 🆔 If Looks Could Kill (Furie, Ruthe)

1995 🆔 Bury the Bishop (Gallison, Kate)
1995   Mrs. Pollifax Pursued (Gilman, Dorothy)
1995   Shadow of Death (Gilpatrick, Noreen)
1995   A Stiff Critique (Girdner, Jaqueline)
1995   Hanging Time (Glass, Leslie)
1995   Trunk Show (Glen, Alison)
1995   Striking Out (Gordon, Alison)
1995   The Dead of Winter (Gosling, Paula)
1995   "L" is for Lawless (Grafton, Sue)
1995   Written in Blood (Graham, Caroline)
1995   A Fine Place for Death (Granger, Ann)
1995   Candle for a Corpse (Granger, Ann)
1995   Death of a Dream Maker (Gray, Gallagher)
1995   Die in My Dreams (Green, Christine)
1995   Every Deadly Sin (Greenwood, Diane M.)
1995   Ruddy Gore (Greenwood, Kerry)
1995   Rainbow's End (Grimes, Martha)

1995   Fountain of Death (Haddam, Jane)
1995   Final Cut (Haddock, Lisa)
1995   Dead and Buried (Hager, Jean)
1995   Seven Black Stones (Hager, Jean)
1995   Dying Fall (Hall, Patricia)
1995   Traveling with the Dead (Hambly, Barbara)
1995   Circus of the Damned (Hamilton, Laurell K.)
1995   The Julius House (Harris, Charlaine)
1995   The Thanksgiving Day Murder (Harris, Lee)
1995 🆔 The Edge of the Crazies (Harrison, Jamie)
1995   The Mint Julep Murder (Hart, Carolyn G.)
1995   For Every Evil (Hart, Ellen)
1995   Faint Praise (Hart, Ellen)
1995   Bitter Business (Hartzmark, Gini)
1995   Lethal Legacy (Hendricksen, Louise)
1995   Termination Dust (Henry, Sue)
1995 🆔 Acid Bath (Herndon, Nancy)
1995   Widows' Watch (Herndon, Nancy)
1995   Miracles in Maggody (Hess, Joan)
1995   Busy Bodies (Hess, Joan)
1995 🆔 Keeper at the Shrine (Highsmith, Domini)
1995 🆔 Flashpoint (Hightower, Lynn S.)
1995   Alien Rites (Hightower, Lynn S.)
1995 🆔 A Far and Deadly Cry (Holbrook, Teri)

1995 🆔 Murder at St. Adelaide's (Hollingsworth, Gerelyn)
1995   Mrs. Malory Wonders Why [Britain–Superfluous Death] (Holt, Hazel)
1995   Curly Smoke (Holtzer, Susan)
1995   77th Street Requiem (Hornsby, Wendy)
1995 🆔 In Murder We Trust (Hyde, Eleanor)

1995   Murder Among Friends (Jacobs, Jonnie)
1995 🆔 Horse of a Different Killer (Jaffe, Jody)
1995   Shoot, Don't Shoot (Jance, J. A.)
1995   Name Withheld (Jance, J. A.)
1995   You Bet Your Life (Jorgensen, Christine T.)

1995   Justice (Kellerman, Faye)
1995   Keeper of the Mill (Kelly, Mary Ann)
1995   Trouble Looking for a Place to Happen (Kelner, T. L. P.)
1995   Alley Cat Blues (Kijewski, Karen)
1995   A Monstrous Regiment of Women (King, Laurie R.)
1995   To Play the Fool (King, Laurie R.)
1995   Check-out Time (Kingsbury, Kate)
1995   Grounds for Murder (Kingsbury, Kate)
1995   Kill or Cure (Kittredge, Mary)

1995   The Bull Slayers (Knight, Alanna)
1995   No Honeymoon for Death (Kruger, Mary)
1995   File Under: Jeopardy (Lacey, Sarah)
1995 🆔 Murder in Brief (Lachnit, Carroll)
1995   Unquestioned Loyalty (Lamb, J. Dayne)
1995   Vial Murders (Landreth, Marsha)
1995   The Shortest Day (Langton, Jane)
1995   Death a la Provencale (Laurence, Janet)
1995 🆔 Murder in Scorpio (Lawrence, Martha)
1995 🆔 Death in Still Waters (Lee, Barbara) ★
1995 🆔 The Curious Cape Cod Skull (Lee, Marie)
1995   Cannon's Revenge (Lee, W. W.)
1995   Death and Judgment [APA–A Venetian Reckoning] (Leon, Donna)
1995 🆔 No Place for Secrets (Lewis, Sherry)
1995   Crown Witness (Linscott, Gillian)
1995   Never Let a Stranger in Your House (Logan, M.)
1995 🆔 Dangerous Attachments (Lovett, Sarah)

1995   Mistress of the Bones (MacGregor, T. J.)
1995   The Odd Job (MacLeod, Charlotte)
1995   Someone to Watch (Maiman, Jaye)
1995   The Ghost in the Closet (Maney, Mabel)
1995   Deadly Reunion (Manthorne, Jackie)
1995   Last Resort (Manthorne, Jackie)
1995   Fugitive Colors (Maron, Margaret)
1995   Bird in a Cage (Martin, Lee)
1995   Designer Crimes (Matera, Lia)
1995   Gemini Doublecross (Mather, Linda)
1995   Death in Rough Water (Mathews, Francine)
1995   Hanky Panky (McCafferty, Taylor)
1995 🆔 Heir Condition (McClellan, Tierney)
1995   Closing Statement (McClellan, Tierney)
1995   Painted Truth (McClendon, Lise)
1995   If I'd Killed Him When I Met Him (McCrumb, Sharyn)
1995   Clean Break (McDermid, Val)
1995   Elective Murder (McGiffin, Janet)
1995   A Shred of Evidence (McGown, Jill)
1995   Caught Dead (McKenna, Bridget)
1995 🆔 Just Desserts (McKevett, G. A.)
1995   Double Bluff [apa–Silver Moon '90] (McNab, Claire)
1995   The Morbid Kitchen (Melville, Jennie)
1995   The Homefront Murders (Meredith, D. R.)
1995   These Bones Were Made for Dancin' (Meyers, A.)
1995   The Dutchman's Dilemma (Meyers, Maan)

1995 . . . continued   288 titles   32 [1]

1995	Stitches in Time (Michaels, Barbara)
1995	Night Songs (Mickelbury, Penny)
1995	Murder in a Hot Flash (Millhiser, Marlys)
1995	A Portion for Foxes (Mitchell, Kay)
1995	Blackwater Spirits (Monfredo, Miriam Grace)
1995	King of Hearts (Moody, Susan)
1995	The McCone Files [15 short stories] (Muller, Marcia)
1995	A Wild and Lonely Place (Muller, Marcia)
1995 [1]	The Main Line Is Murder (Murray, Donna Huston)
1995	Murder at the Music Hall (Myers, Amy)
1995	Parsley, Sage, Rosemary and Crime (Myers, Tamar)
1995	The Marshal and the Forgery (Nabb, Magdalen)
1995	The Wandering Arm (Newman, Sharan)

1995	The Man Who Cast Two Shadows (O'Connell, Carol)
1995	Raggedy Man (O'Donnell, Lillian)
1995	Death Goes on Retreat (O'Marie, Carol Anne, Sister)
1995	Family Album (Oleksiw, Susan)
1995	A Long Time Dead (Orde, A. J.)
1995	Cut to: Murder (Osborne, Denise)

1995	Turtle Baby (Padgett, Abigail)
1995	Death at Gallows Green (Paige, Robin)
1995	Murder Comes Caller (Page, Emma)
1995	Windy City Blues [short stories] (Paretsky, Sara)
1995	Suspicion of Guilt (Parker, Barbara)
1995	Fare Play (Paul, Barbara)
1995	Cooking up Trouble (Pence, Joanne)
1995	Cain His Brother (Perry, Anne)
1995	Traitor's Gate (Perry, Anne)
1995	Shroud for a Scholar (Peterson, Audrey)
1995	Twilight (Pickard, Nancy)
1995	Alternate Sides (Piesman, Marissa)
1995	The Hangdog Hustle (Pincus, Elizabeth)
1995 [1]	Dead File (Porath, Sharon)
1995	Death of a Wallflower (Prowell, Sandra West)

1995	A Wolf in Death's Clothing (Quinn, Elizabeth)

1995	The Intersection of Law and Desire (Redmann, J. M.)
1995	Death of a Garden Pest (Ripley, Ann)
1995	The Nun's Tale (Robb, Candace M.)
1995 [1]	Naked in Death (Robb, J. D.)
1995	In the Dead of Summer (Roberts, Gillian)
1995	Murder in the Marketplace (Roberts, Lora)
1995	Murder at the God's Gate (Robinson, Lynda S.)
1995	Whom the Gods Love (Ross, Kate)
1995	The Shy Tulip Murders (Rothenberg, Rebecca)
1995	Malice Poetic (Rowlands, Betty)
1995	Concourse (Rozan, S. J.)

1995	Ho-Ho Homicide (Sawyer, Corinne Holt)
1995	Death Days (Schenkel, S. E.)
1995 [1]	Running from the Law (Scottoline, Lisa)
1995	Talked to Death (Shaffer, Louise)
1995 [1]	Deadly Gamble (Shelton, Connie)
1995	Vacations Can Be Murder (Shelton, Connie)
1995	Something in the Cellar (Shepherd, Stella)
1995 [1]	Mr. Donaghue Investigates (Shone, Anna)
1995	The Death We Share (Short, Sharon Gwyn)
1995	A Plague of Kinfolks (Sibley, Celestine)
1995	Storm Front (Silva, Linda Kay)
1995	A Day for Dying (Simpson, Dorothy)
1995	Interview with Mattie (Singer, Shelley)
1995	The George Eliot Murders (Skom, Edith)
1995	Close Call (Slovo, Gillian)

1995	Dust Devils of the Purple Sage (Smith, Barbara B.)
1995	Miss Melville Runs for Cover (Smith, Evelyn E.)
1995	Full Stop (Smith, Joan)
1995	House of Blues (Smith, Julie)
1995	Running for Shelter (Spring, Michelle)
1995	Deadly Secrets on the St. Johns (Sprinkle, Patricia H.)
1995	Memory Can Be Murder (Squire, Elizabeth Daniels)
1995	Play with Fire (Stabenow, Dana)
1995	Dead Serious (Stacey, Susannah)
1995	Oxford Exit (Stallwood, Veronica)
1995 [1]	Death of a Postmodernist (Steinberg, Janice)
1995	Death Crosses the Border (Steinberg, Janice)
1995	Crosswords (Sumner, Penny)

1995 [1]	We Know Where You Live (Taylor, Jean)
1995 [1]	Blackening Song (Thurlo, Aimée & David)
1995	Happy Never After (Trocheck, Kathy Hogan)
1995	Murder at the National Gallery (Truman, Margaret)
1995	In the Midnight Hour (Tyre, Peg)

1995	Parrot Blues (Van Gieson, Judith)

1995	Under the Beetle's Cellar (Walker, Mary Willis)
1995	A Piece of Justice (Walsh, Jill Paton)
1995	Family Practice (Weir, Charlene)
1995	Open House (Welch, Pat)
1995	Devil's Gonna Get Him (Wesley, Valerie Wilson)
1995	Fresh Kills (Wheat, Carolyn)
1995	Charged with Guilt (White, Gloria)
1995	Until the End of Time (Whitney, Polly)
1995	A Flush of Shadows [5 novellas] (Wilhelm, Kate)
1995	Copy Cat Crimes (Wilson, Karen Ann)
1995	Remodeled to Death (Wolzien, Valerie)
1995	Hot Ticket (Woods, Sherryl)
1995	Deadly Obsession (Woods, Sherryl)
1995	White Lightning (Woods, Sherryl)
1995	King of the Mountain (Wren, M. K.)
1995	Mother Love (Wright, L. R.)

1995	Summer Will End (Yeager, Dorian)
1995	Ovation by Death (Yeager, Dorian)

1996   132 titles   6 [1]

1996	After Effects (Aird, Catherine)
1996	Aunt Dimity's Good Deed (Atherton, Nancy)
1996	The Long Slow Whistle of the Moon (Ayres, Noreen)

1996	No Birds Sing (Bannister, Jo)
1996	Firestorm (Barr, Nevada)
1996	Underdog (Berenson, Laurien)
1996	Dog Eat Dog (Berenson, Laurien)
1996	The Death of a Dancing Fool (Berry, Carole)
1996	Murder Well-Done (Bishop, Claudia)
1996	Vow of Felicity (Black, Veronica)
1996	Five Alarm Fire (Borton, D. B.)
1996	The Cat Who Said Cheese (Braun, Lilian Jackson)
1996	Act of Betrayal (Buchanan, Edna)
1996	Remember Me, Irene (Burke, Jan)

1996	Class Reunions are Murder (Cannon, Taffy)
1996	Cyber Kiss (Chapman, Sally)
1996	A Season of Knives (Chisholm, P. F.)
1996	Silence of the Hams (Churchill, Jill)
1996	Murder Most Beastly (Cleary, Melissa)
1996	High Island Blues (Cleeves, Ann)
1996	The Ghost Walker (Coel, Margaret)

1996	Red Roses for a Dead Trucker (Collins, Anna A.)
1996	Hickory, Dickory Stock (Cooper, Susan Rogers)

1996 . . . continued   132 titles   6 ■

1996	The Trouble with a Bad Fit (Crespi, Camilla)
1996	Hoofprints (Crum, Laura)
1996 ■	KILLER.app (D'Amato, Barbara)
1996	The Alpine Gamble (Daheim, Mary)
1996	Auntie Mayhem (Daheim, Mary)
1996	The Main Course (Davidson, Diane Mott)
1996	A Dying Light in Corduba (Davis, Lindsey)
1996	Fire and Fog (Day, Dianne)
1996	Miss Zukas and the Stroke of Death (Dereske, Jo)
1996	Miss Zukas and the Raven's Dance (Dereske , Jo)
1996	Cat in a Diamond Dazzle (Douglas, Carole Nelson)
1996	A Bad Hair Day (Dunbar, Sophie)
1996	Sudden Exposure (Dunlap, Susan)

1996	Requiem for a Mezzo (Dunn, Carola)
1996	Murder Can Stunt Your Growth (Eichler, Selma)
1996	Murder Can Wreck Your Reunion (Eichler, Selma)
1996	Two for the Dough (Evanovich, Janet)

1996	Axe for an Abbot (Eyre, Elizabeth)
1996	Dead in the Dirt (Feddersen, Connie)
1996	1(900)D-E-A-D (Fennelly, Tony)
1996	Kansas Troubles (Fowler, Earlene)
1996	One is One and All Alone (Fraser, Anthea)
1996	The Murderer's Tale (Frazer, Margaret)
1996	Natural Death (Furie, Ruthe)

1996	The Devil's Workshop (Gallison, Kate)
1996	In the Presence of the Enemy (George, Elizabeth)
1996	Mrs. Pollifax and the Lion Killer (Gilman, Dorothy)
1996	Most Likely to Die (Girdner, Jaqueline)
1996	A Touch of Mortality (Granger, Ann)
1996	Lethal Genes (Grant, Linda)
1996	Fatal Cut (Green, Christine)
1996	Mortal Spoils (Greenwood, Diane M.)
1996	Urn Burial (Greenwood, Kerry)
1996	Still Water (Gunning, Sally)

1996	Death on the Drunkard's Path (Hager, Jean)
1996	The Fire Carrier (Hager, Jean)
1996	In the Bleak Midwinter (Hall, Patricia)
1996	The Lunatic Cafe (Hamilton, Laurell K.)
1996	Dead Over Heels (Harris, Charlaine)
1996	The Passover Murder (Harris, Lee)
1996	Blood Lines (Harrod-Eagles, Cynthia)
1996	Death in Lovers' Lane (Hart, Carolyn G.)
1996	Robber's Wine (Hart, Ellen)
1996	Nice Girls Finish Last (Hayter, Sparkle)
1996	Sleeping Lady (Henry, Sue)
1996	The Grass Widow (Holbrook, Teri)

1996	Death of a Dean (Holt, Hazel)
1996	Animal Instincts (Hyde, Eleanor)
1996 ■	Shadow of Doubt (Jacobs, Jonnie)
1996	Chestnut Mare, Beware (Jaffe, Jody)

1996	Curl Up and Die (Jorgensen, Christine T.)
1996	Death is Sweet (Kelly, Susan B.)
1996	With Child (King, Laurie R.)
1996	Pay the Piper (Kingsbury, Kate)
1996	Lost to Sight (Knight, Phyllis)
1996	Death in a Private Place (Kunz, Kathleen)

1996	A Blessed Death (Lachnit, Carroll)
1996	Diet for Death (Laurence, Janet)
1996	Missing Eden (Lee, Wendi)
1996	Acqua Alta (Leon, Donna)
1996	No Place Like Home (Lewis, Sherry)

1996	Acquired Motive (Lovett, Sarah)
1996	Bridge to Nowhere (Lucke, Margaret)

1996	Up Jumps the Devil (Maron, Margaret)
1996	Last Chants (Matera, Lia)
1996	Murder Among the Angels (Matteson, Stefanie)
1996 ■	Secret's Shadow (Matthews, Alex)
1996	A Killing in Real Estate (McClellan, Tierney)
1996	The Rosewood Casket (McCrumb, Sharyn)
1996	Blue Genes (McDermid, Val)
1996	Bitter Sweets (McKevett, G. A.)
1996	Postscript to Murder (Meek, M. R. D.)
1996	The Woman Who Was Not There (Melville, Jennie)
1996	A Rage of Innocence (Mitchell, Kay)
1996	Through a Gold Eagle (Monfredo, Miriam Grace)
1996	Doubled in Spades (Moody, Susan)
1996	The Broken Promise Land (Muller, Marcia)
1996	Final Arrangements (Murray, Donna Huston)

1996	No Use Dying Over Spilled Milk (Myers, Tamar)
1996 ■	Shadow of a Child (O'Callaghan, Maxine)

1996	Killing Critics (O'Connell, Carol)
1996	A Ceremonial Death (Oliphant, B. J.)
1996	The Body in the Bog (Page, Katherine Hall)

1996	Cooking Most Deadly (Pence, Joanne)
1996	Pentecost Alley (Perry, Anne)
1996	Lamb to the Slaughter (Quinn, Elizabeth)
1996	Glory in Death (Robb, J. D.)
1996	Immortal in Death (Robb, J. D.)
1996	Murder Mile-High (Roberts, Lora)
1996	Murder at the Feast of Rejoicing (Robinson, Lynda S.)

1996	Smiling at Death (Rowlands, Betty)
1996	Eve of St. Hyacinth (Sedley, Kate)
1996	Relative Innocence (Shelton, Connie)
1996	Meadowlark (Simonson, Sheila)
1996	Anthony's Tattoo (Singer, Shelley)
1996	Celebration in Purple Sage (Smith, Barbara Burnett)
1996	Blood Will Tell (Stabenow, Dana)
1996	Oxford Mourning (Stallwood, Veronica)

1996	Dead South (Sullivan, Winona)
1996	The Last of Her Lies (Taylor, Jean)
1996	Burden of Innocence (Thomson, June)
1996	Death Walker (Thurlo, Aimée & David)
1996 ■	Lickety Split (Trocheck, Kathy Hogan)

1996	Until It Hurts (Whitney, Polly)
1996	She Came by the Book (Wings, Mary)
1996 ■	Shore to Die (Wolzien, Valerie)
1996	Elected to Die (Wolzien, Valerie)

1996	Prelude to Death (Zukowski, Sharon)

1997   8 titles

1997	A Surfeit of Guns (Chisholm, P. F.)

1997	The Bohemian Murders (Day, Dianne)
1997	Murder on the Flying Scotsman (Dunn, Carola)

1997	A Deadly Paté (Furie, Ruthe)

1997	The Oldest Sin (Hart, Ellen)

1997	Satan's Silence (Matthews, Alex)
1997	The Groaning Board (Meyers, Annette)

1997	Ashes to Ashes (O'Callaghan, Maxine)

Six

✎ Alphabetical list of titles

6

1(900)D-E-A-D [1996] (Fennelly, Tony)
27-Ingredient Chili Con Carne Murders [1993] (Rich, V.)
30 Days to Live [1943] (Gilbert, Anthony)
4:50 from Paddington [1957] (Christie, Agatha)
77th Street Requiem [1995] (Hornsby, Wendy)
∎ 8 Faces at 3 [1939] (Rice, Craig)

A

∎ "A" is for Alibi [1982] (Grafton, Sue) ★ ☆
ABC Murders [1935] (Christie, Agatha)
Abominable Man [1972] (Sjöwall, Maj & Per Wahlöö)
Accent on Murder [1958] (Lockridge, Frances & Richard)
Accidental Shroud [1994] (Eccles, Marjorie)
Accounting for Murder [1964] (Lathen, Emma) ★
Ace of Spades [1960] (Shannon, Dell)
Aces, Eights and Murder [1940] (Heberden, M. V.)
Aces High [1989] (Hooper, Kay)
∎ Acid Bath [1995] (Herndon, Nancy)
Acqua Alta [1996] (Leon, Donna)
Acquired Motive [1996] (Lovett, Sarah)
Act of Betrayal [1996] (Buchanan, Edna)
Act of Darkness [1991] (Haddam, Jane)
Acts of Black Night [1938] (Knight, Kathleen Moore)
Adders on the Heath [1963] (Mitchell, Gladys)
∎ Adjusted to Death [1991] (Girdner, Jaqueline)
Advantage Miss Seeton [1990] (Crane, Hamilton)
Advent of Dying [1986] (O'Marie, Sister Carol Anne)
Affacombe Affair [1968] (Lemarchand, Elizabeth)
Affair at Flower Acres [1923] (Wells, Carolyn)
African Poison Murders [1939] (Huxley, Elspeth)
After Effects [1996] (Aird, Catherine)
After Midnight [1966] (Nielsen, Helen)
After the Funeral [1953] (Christie, Agatha)
After the Verdict [1961] (Gilbert, Anthony)
∎ Aftershock [1977] (O'Donnell, Lillian)
Against the Evidence [1962] (Egan, Lesley)
Agatha Raisin and the Potted Gardener ['94] (Beaton, M. C.)
∎ Agatha Raisin and the Quiche of Death [1992] (Beaton, M. C.)
Agatha Raisin and the Vicious Vet [1993] (Beaton, M. C.)
Agatha Raisin and the Walkers of Dembley ['95] (Beaton, M. C.)
∎ Agatha Webb [1899] (Green, Anna Katherine)
Ah, Sweet Mystery [1991] (Sibley, Celestine)

Akin to Murder [1953] (Knight, Kathleen Moore)
Alarm of the Black Cat [1942] (Olsen, D. B.)
∎ Alaska Gray [1994] (Froetschel, Susan)
Alias Basil Willing [1951] (McCloy, Helen)
Alibi for a Corpse [1969] (Lemarchand, Elizabeth)
∎ Alibi for an Actress [1992] (Farrell, Gillian B.)
Alibi in Time [1980] (Thomson, June)
∎ Alien Blues [1992] (Hightower, Lynn S.)
Alien Eyes [1993] (Hightower, Lynn S.)
Alien Heat [1994] (Hightower, Lynn S.)
Alien Rites [1995] (Hightower, Lynn S.)
Alington Inheritance [1958] (Wentworth, Patricia)
All at Sea [1927] (Wells, Carolyn)
All Concerned Notified [1939] (Reilly, Helen)
All for the Love of a Lady [1944] (Ford, Leslie)
All Hallow's Evil [1992] (Wolzien, Valerie)
All Is Vanity [1940] (Bell, Josephine)
∎ All My Suspects [1994] (Shaffer, Louise)
All Shall Be Well [1994] (Crombie, Deborah)
All That Remains [1992] (Cornwell, Patricia)
All the Crazy Winters [1992] (Adams, Deborah)
All the Dark Disguises [1993] (Adams, Deborah)
All the Deadly Beloved [1995] (Adams, Deborah)
∎ All the Great Pretenders [1992] (Adams, Deborah) ☆
All the Hungry Mothers [1993] (Adams, Deborah)
Alley Cat Blues [1995] (Kijewski, Karen)
Alphabet Murders [1936] (Christie, Agatha)
∎ Alpine Advocate [1992] (Daheim, Mary) ☆
Alpine Betrayal [1993] (Daheim, Mary)
Alpine Christmas [1993] (Daheim, Mary)
Alpine Decoy [1994] (Daheim, Mary)
Alpine Escape [1995] (Daheim, Mary)
Alpine Fury [1995] (Daheim, Mary)
Alpine Gamble [1996] (Daheim, Mary)
Alternate Sides [1995] (Piesman, Marissa)
∎ Always Anonymous Beast [1987] (Douglas, Lauren W.)
∎ Always Murder a Friend [1948] (Scherf, Margaret)
∎ Amateur City [1984] (Forrest, Katherine V.)
Amateur Night [1993] (Beck, K. K.)
Amazing Mrs. Pollifax [1970] (Gilman, Dorothy)
Amber Eyes [1962] (Crane, Frances)
Amethyst Spectacles [1944] (Crane, Frances)
∎ Ammie, Come Home [1968] (Michaels, Barbara)

A . . . continued

🔳 And Being Dead [1938] (Erskine, Margaret)
And Dangerous to Know [1949] (Daly, Elizabeth)
And Death Came Too [1952] (Gilbert, Anthony)
And Shame the Devil [1967] (Woods, Sara)
And Soon I'll Come to Kill You [1991] (Kelly, Susan)
Angel Death [1980] (Moyes, Patricia)
Angel Dust [1989] (Cohen, Anthea)
Angel in Action [1992] (Cohen, Anthea)
Angel in Autumn [1995] (Cohen, Anthea)
Angel in Love [1993] (Cohen, Anthea)
Angel of Death [1983] (Cohen, Anthea)
Angel of Death [1994] (Krich, Rochelle Majer) ☆
Angel of Vengeance [1982] (Cohen, Anthea)
🔳 Angel Without Mercy [1982] (Cohen, Anthea)
🔳 Angel's Bidding [1994] (Short, Sharon Gwyn)
Animal Instincts [1996] (Hyde, Eleanor)
Anna, Where Are You? [1951] (Wentworth, Patricia)
Annulet of Gilt [1938] (Taylor, Phoebe Atwood)
Anodyne Necklace [1983] (Grimes, Martha)
Anonymous Venetian [1994] (Leon, Donna)
Another Man's Poison [1993] (Cleeves, Ann)
Anthony's Tattoo [1996] (Singer, Shelley)
Antipodes [1989] (Oliver, Maria Antonia)
Any Shape or Form [1945] (Daly, Elizabeth)
Anybody but Anne [1914] (Wells, Carolyn)
Anything but the Truth [1925] (Wells, Carolyn)
Apostrophe Thief [1993] (Paul, Barbara)
🔳 Apothecary Rose [1993] (Robb, Candace M.)
Appearance of Evil [1993] (Coker, Carolyn)
Appearances of Death [1977] (Shannon, Dell)
Applegreen Cat [1943] (Crane, Frances)
Appointed to Die [1994] (Charles, Kate)
Appointment at Nine [1947] (Disney, Doris Miles)
Appointment with Death [1938] (Christie, Agatha)
April Rainers [1989] (Fraser, Anthea)
April Robin Murders [1958] (Rice, Craig)
April When They Woo [1988] (Adamson, M. J.)
Arabian Pearl [1990] (Jackson, Marian J. A.)
Arrow Pointing Nowhere [1944] (Daly, Elizabeth)
Arsenic in Richmond [1934] (Frome, David)
Art in the Blood [1991] (Elrod, P. N.)
Art of Survival [1989] (Maxwell, A. E.)
Artists in Crime [1938] (Marsh, Ngaio)
As a Favor [1984] (Dunlap, Susan)
🔳 As Crime Goes By [1990] (Shah, Diane K.)
As the Sparks Fly Upward [1992] (Dank, Gloria)
Asey Mayo Trio [1946] (Taylor, Phoebe Atwood)
Ashes to Ashes [1971] (Lathen, Emma)
Ashes to Ashes [1997] (O'Callaghan, Maxine)
Ashes to Ashes [1988] (Pulver, Mary Monica)
🔳 Ask Me for Tomorrow [1976] (Millar, Margaret)
Ask the Cards a Question [1982] (Muller, Marcia)
Assignment to Death [1943] (Leonard, Charles L.)
At Bertram's Hotel [1965] (Christie, Agatha)
At Dead of Night [1995] (Amey, Linda)
Attending Physician [1980] (Dominic, R. B.)
🔳 Audition for Murder [1985] (Carlson, P. M.)
Aunt Dimity and the Duke [1994] (Atherton, Nancy)
🔳 Aunt Dimity's Death [1992] (Atherton, Nancy)
Aunt Dimity's Good Deed [1996] (Atherton, Nancy)
Auntie Mayhem [1996] (Daheim, Mary)
Away with Them to Prison [1985] (Woods, Sara)
Axe for an Abbot [1996] (Eyre, Elizabeth)
Axeman's Jazz [1991] (Smith, Julie)

B

"B" is for Burglar [1985] (Grafton, Sue) ★ ★
Baby Doll Games [1988] (Maron, Margaret)
Baby Drop [1994] (Melville, Jennie)
Baby Merchants [1975] (O'Donnell, Lillian)
Back Door to Death [1963] (Foley, Rae)
Back on Death [1978] (Egan, Lesley)
Backfire [1994] (Law, Janice)
Backhand [1991] (Cody, Liza) ☆
Backlash [1989] (Gosling, Paula)
Bad Blood [1991] (Carlson, P. M.)
Bad Chemistry [1993] (Kelly, Nora)
Bad Company [1982] (Cody, Liza)
Bad Company [1995] (Dreher, Sarah)
Bad Hair Day [1996] (Dunbar, Sophie)
Bad Intent [1994] (Hornsby, Wendy)
🔳 Bad Medicine [1990] (Yarbro, Chelsea Quinn)
Bagels for Tea [1993] (Stevens, Serita)
🔳 Bait [1968] (Uhnak, Dorothy) ★
Bait for Murder [1948] (Knight, Kathleen Moore)
Baked Bean Supper Murders [1983] (Rich, Virginia)
Balmoral Nude [1990] (Coker, Carolyn)
Banbury Bog [1938] (Taylor, Phoebe Atwood)
Bandersnatch [1989] (Hardwick, Mollie)
Bank on It [1993] (Woods, Sherryl)
🔳 Banker's Bones [1968] (Scherf, Margaret)
🔳 Banking on Death [1961] (Lathen, Emma)
Bantam of the Opera [1993] (Daheim, Mary)
Bass Derby Murder [1949] (Knight, Kathleen Moore)
🔳 Bayou City Streets [1991] (Powell, Deborah)
Beaded Banana [1978] (Scherf, Margaret)
Beat up a Cookie [1994] (Dietz, Denise)
Beautiful Birthday Cake [1971] (Scherf, Margaret)
Beautiful Death [1994] (Haymon, S. T.)
Beautiful Derelict [1935] (Wells, Carolyn)
Beauty Dies [1994] (Howe, Melodie Johnson)
Beauty Is a Beast [1959] (Knight, Kathleen Moore)
Beauty Sleep [1977] (Dolson, Hildegarde)
Beckoning Lady [1955] (Allingham, Margery)
Bed Bugs [1992] (McCafferty, Taylor)
🔳 Beekeeper's Apprentice [1994] (King, Laurie R.) ☆
Beer and Skittles [1985] (Morison, B. J.)
🔳 Beginning with a Bash [1937] (Tilton, Alice)
Behind Closed Doors [1888] (Green, Anna Katherine)
🔳 Behind Eclaire's Doors [1993] (Dunbar, Sophie)
Behold, Here's Poison [1936] (Heyer, Georgette)
Belgrave Square [1992] (Perry, Anne)
Bell of Death [1939] (Gilbert, Anthony)
Benevent Treasure [1954] (Wentworth, Patricia)
Besides the Wench Is Dead [1973] (Erskine, Margaret)
Best Defense [1994] (Wilhelm, Kate)
Best Man to Die [1969] (Rendell, Ruth)
Bet Against the House [1995] (Dain, Catherine)
Bethlehem Road [1990] (Perry, Anne)
Beverly Malibu [1989] (Forrest, Katherine V.) ★
Beware of the Dog [1992] (Ferrars, E. X.)
Beware Taurus [1994] (Mather, Linda)
Beyond the Grave [1986] (Muller, Marcia)
Big Four [1927] (Christie, Agatha)
🔳 Big Killing [1989] (Meyers, Annette)
Big Midget Murders [1942] (Rice, Craig)
🔳 Big Pay-off [1976] (Law, Janice) ☆
Bilbao Looking Glass [1983] (MacLeod, Charlotte)
🔳 Bimbos of the Death Sun [1988] (McCrumb, Sharyn) ★ ☆
Bird in a Cage [1995] (Martin, Lee)

B . . . continued

1 Bird in the Hand [1986] (Cleeves, Ann)
1 Birth Marks [1992] (Dunant, Sarah)
Bishop in the Back Seat [1980] (Watson, Clarissa)
Bishop's Tale [1994] (Frazer, Margaret)
Bismarck Herrings [1971] (Torrie, Malcolm)
Bite of Death [1991] (Conant, Susan)
Bite the Hand [1956] (Fenisong, Ruth)
Bitter Business [1995] (Hartzmark, Gini)
Bitter Finish [1983] (Barnes, Linda)
Bitter Herbs [1993] (Cooper, Natasha)
Bitter Medicine [1987] (Paretsky, Sara)
Bitter Sweets [1996] (McKevett, G. A.)
Black as He's Painted [1974] (Marsh, Ngaio)
Black Cypress [1948] (Crane, Frances)
Black Death [1953] (Gilbert, Anthony)
Black Dreams [1993] (Green, Kate)
1 Black Dudley Murder [1929] (Allingham, Margery)
Black Envelope [1937] (Frome, David)
Black Girl, White Girl [1989] (Moyes, Patricia)
Black Is the Colour of My True Love's Heart [1967]
     (Peters, Ellis)
1 Black Justice [1989] (Shepherd, Stella)
Black Moon [1989] (Drake, Alison)
Black Night Murders [1941] (Wells, Carolyn)
Black Ribbon [1995] (Conant, Susan)
Black Stage [1945] (Gilbert, Anthony)
Black Tower [1975] (James, P. D.) ★
Black Widower [1975] (Moyes, Patricia)
1 Blackening Song [1995] (Thurlo, Aimée & David)
Blackmailer [1956] (Fenisong, Ruth)
Blackwater Spirits [1995] (Monfredo, Miriam Grace)
Blanche Among the Talented Tenth [1994] (Neely, B.)
1 Blanche on the Lam [1992] (Neely, Barbara) ★ ★ ★
Bleeding Hearts [1994] (Haddam, Jane)
1 Bleeding Hearts [1984] (White, Teri)
1 Bleeding of Innocents [1993] (Bannister, Jo)
Blessed Death [1996] (Lachnit, Carroll)
Blind Search [1977] (Egan, Lesley)
1 Blind Side [1939] (Wentworth, Patricia)
Blind Trust [1990] (Grant, Linda)
Blood and Circuses [1994] (Greenwood, Kerry)
Blood and Honey [1961] (Fickling, G. G.)
Blood Count [1986] (Shannon, Dell)
1 Blood Is Thicker [1990] (Fallon, Ann C.)
Blood Lies [1991] (Wallace, Patricia)
Blood Lines [1996] (Harrod-Eagles, Cynthia)
Blood Lines [1993] (Huff, Tanya)
1 Blood of an Aries [1994] (Mather, Linda)
Blood on the Happy Highway [1983] (Radley, Sheila)
Blood on the Street [1992] (Meyers, Annette)
Blood on the Water [1992] (Elrod, P. N.)
Blood Pact [1993] (Huff, Tanya)
1 Blood Price [1992] (Huff, Tanya)
Blood Shot [1988] (Paretsky, Sara) ★ ☆ ☆
Blood Trail [1992] (Huff, Tanya)
1 Blood Upon the Snow [1944] (Lawrence, Hilda)
1 Blood Will Have Blood [1982] (Barnes, Linda)
Blood Will Tell [1952] (Christie, Agatha)
Blood Will Tell [1996] (Stabenow, Dana)
1 Blood Work [1994] (Zachary, Fay)
Bloodcircle [1990] (Elrod, P. N.)
Bloodline [1989] (Knight, Alanna)
Bloodlines [1992] (Conant, Susan)
1 Bloodlust [1990] (Elrod, P. N.)

Bloodstream [1995] (Carlson, P. M.)
Bloody Book of Law [1984] (Woods, Sara)
1 Bloody Instructions [1962] (Woods, Sara)
Bloody Mary [1990] (Kraft, Gabrielle)
Bloody Roses [1992] (Cooper, Natasha)
Bloody Soaps [1989] (Babbin, Jacqueline)
1 Bloody Special [1989] (Babbin, Jacqueline)
1 Blooming Murder [1994] (Hager, Jean)
Blue Pearl [1994] (MacGregor, T. J.)
Blue-Eyed Boy [1990] (Curzon, Clare)
Blue Genes [1996] (McDermid, Val)
Bluegate Fields [1984] (Perry, Anne)
1 Bluejay Shaman [1994] (McClendon, Lise)
Blunt Instrument [1938] (Heyer, Georgette)
Bodies of Water [1990] (Borthwick, J. S.)
Body and Soul [1989] (Woods, Sherryl)
Body Beneath a Mandarin Tree [1965] (Crane, Frances)
1 Body English [1992] (Mariz, Linda French)
Body Farm [1994] (Cornwell, Patricia)
Body Guard [1994] (McNab, Claire)
Body in Bedford Square [1935] (Frome, David)
Body in Blackwater Bay [1992] (Gosling, Paula)
Body in the Basement [1994] (Page, Katherine Hall)
1 Body in the Belfry [1990] (Page, Katherine Hall) ★
Body in the Bog [1996] (Page, Katherine Hall)
Body in the Bouillon [1991] (Page, Katherine Hall)
Body in the Cast [1993] (Page, Katherine Hall)
Body in the Kelp [1991] (Page, Katherine Hall)
Body in the Library [1942] (Christie, Agatha)
Body in the Turl [1934] (Frome, David)
Body in the Vestibule [1992] (Page, Katherine Hall)
Body of Evidence [1991] (Cornwell, Patricia)
Body of Opinion [1988] (Stacey, Susannah)
Body on the Beam [1932] (Gilbert, Anthony)
Body to Die For [1995] (Frankel, Valerie)
Bohemian Connection [1985] (Dunlap, Susan)
Bohemian Murders [1997] (Day, Dianne)
Bombshell [1964] (Fickling, G. G.)
Bone Idle [1993] (Stacey, Susannah)
Bone to Pick [1992] (Harris, Charlaine)
1 Bones [1991] (Thompson, Joyce)
Bones in the Barrow [1953] (Bell, Josephine)
Book Early for Murder [1990] (Jordan, Jennifer)
Book of Moons [1995] (Edghill, Rosemary)
Book of the Crime [1951] (Daly, Elizabeth)
Book of the Dead [1944] (Daly, Elizabeth)
Book of the Lion [1948] (Daly, Elizabeth)
1 Bootlegger's Daughter [1992] (Maron, Margaret) ★ ★ ★ ★
1 Born to the Purple [1992] (Florian, S. L.)
1 Borrowed Alibi [1962] (Egan, Lesley)
1 Borrower of the Night [1973] (Peters, Elizabeth)
Boy Who Followed Ripley [1980] (Highsmith, Patricia)
Boy's Tale [1995] (Frazer, Margaret)
Brading Collection [1950] (Wentworth, Patricia)
Brandenburg Hotel [1976] (Winslow, Pauline Glen)
Brass Eagle [1989] (Duffy, Margaret)
Bravo for the Bride [1994] (Eyre, Elizabeth)
Brazen Tongue [1940] (Mitchell, Gladys)
Break a Leg Darlings [1995] (Babson, Marian)
Brenda's Murder [1973] (Wells, Tobias)
Bride of Death [1953] (Marsh, Ngaio)
Bridge to Nowhere [1996] (Lucke, Margaret)
Bridled Groom [1994] (Borthwick, J. S.)
1 Bring the Bride a Shroud [1945] (Olsen, D. B.)
Brink of Murder [1976] (Nielsen, Helen)
Broken O [1933] (Wells, Carolyn)

B . . . continued

Broken Promise Land [1996] (Muller, Marcia)
■ Broken Star [1992] (Brown, Lizbie)
Broken Vessel [1994] (Ross, Kate) ★
Bronze Hand [1926] (Wells, Carolyn)
Brood of Folly [1971] (Erskine, Margaret)
Brother Cadfael's Penance [1994] (Peters, Ellis)
■ Brotherly Love [1993] (Lorden, Randye) ☆
Brothers in Blood [1993] (Brod, D. C.)
Brush with Death [1990] (Smith, Joan G.)
■ Bucket Nut [1993] (Cody, Liza) ★
Buckskin Girl [1982] (Moffat, Gwen)
Bull Slayers [1995] (Knight, Alanna)
■ Bullshot [1987] (Kraft, Gabrielle) ☆
■ Bulrush Murders [1991] (Rothenberg, Rebecca) ☆ ☆
Bum Steer [1989] (Pickard, Nancy) ★
Burden of Innocence [1996] (Thomson, June)
■ Burden of Proof [1980] (Challis, Mary)
Buried in Quilts [1994] (Frommer, Sara Hoskinson)
Buried in the Past [1974] (Lemarchand, Elizabeth)
Burn Marks [1990] (Paretsky, Sara)
Burn This [1980] (McCloy, Helen)
Burning Is a Substitute for Loving [1963] (Melville, Jennie)
Burning Desires [1995] (Bannister, Jo)
■ Burning Time [1993] (Glass, Leslie)
■ Burning Water [1989] (Lackey, Mercedes)
Burnt Offering [1955] (Lockridge, Frances & Richard)
Burnton Widows [1984] (McConnell, Vickie P.)
■ Bury Her Sweetly [1992] (Amey, Linda)
Bury Him Kindly [1992] (Burden, Pat)
■ Bury the Bishop [1995] (Gallison, Kate)
Busman's Honeymoon [1937] (Sayers, Dorothy L.)
Busy Bodies [1995] (Hess, Joan)
But I Wouldn't Want to Die There [1993] (Pickard, Nancy)
But Not Forgotten [1960] (Fenisong, Ruth)
But the Doctor Died [1967] (Rice, Craig)
Butler Died in Brooklyn [1943] (Fenisong, Ruth)
Buttercup Case [1958] (Crane, Frances)
Buzzards Must Also Be Fed [1991] (Wingate, Anne)
■ By Evil Means [1993] (Prowell, Sandra West) ☆
By Hook or by Crook [1975] (Lathen, Emma)
By Hook or By Crook [1946] (Gilbert, Anthony)
By the Pricking of My Thumbs [1968] (Christie, Agatha)
By-Pass Murder [1931] (Frome, David)

C

"C" is for Corpse [1986] (Grafton, Sue) ★ ☆
Cabin 3033 [1986] (Clarke, Anna)
Cabin Fever [1994] (Schmidt, Carol)
■ Cable Car Murder [1981] (Taylor, Elizabeth Atwood)
Cadaver [1992] (Kittredge, Mary)
■ Cadenza for Caruso [1984] (Paul, Barbara)
Cain His Brother [1995] (Perry, Anne)
Calculated Risk [1970] (Foley, Rae)
Call Back Yesterday [1983] (Woods, Sara)
Call It Accident [1965] (Foley, Rae)
Callander Square [1980] (Perry, Anne)
Calling All Suspects [1939] (Wells, Carolyn)
■ Cancellation by Death [1992] (Yeager, Dorian)
Candle for a Corpse [1995] (Granger, Ann)
Cannon's Revenge [1995] (Lee W. W.)
Canvas Dagger [1956] (Reilly, Helen)
Cape Cod Caper [1980] (Arnold, Margot)
Cape Cod Conundrum [1992] (Arnold, Margot)

■ Cape Cod Mystery [1931] (Taylor, Phoebe Atwood)
Capital Crime [1941] (Ford, Leslie)
■ Capriccio [1989] (Smith, Joan G.)
Captain's Paradise [1988] (Hooper, Kay)
Captive Audience [1975] (Mann, Jessica)
Captive in Time [1990] (Dreher, Sarah)
Caravan of Night [1948] (Erskine, Margaret)
Carcass Trade [1994] (Ayres, Noreen)
Cardington Crescent [1987] (Perry, Anne)
Cards on the Table [1936] (Christie, Agatha)
Cargo of Eagles [1968] (Allingham, Margery)
Caribbean Mystery [1964] (Christie, Agatha)
Cart Before the Crime [1979] (Porter, Joyce)
Case Closed [1977] (Thomson, June)
■ Case for Appeal [1961] (Egan, Lesley)
Case For Mr. Crook [1952] (Gilbert, Anthony)
Case in Belmont Square [1963] (Erskine, Margaret)
Case Is Altered [1967] (Woods, Sara)
Case Is Closed [1937] (Wentworth, Patricia)
■ Case of Loyalties [1986] (Wallace, Marilyn) ★
Case of Mary Fielding [1970] (Erskine, Margaret)
Case of the Chinese Boxes [1990] (Day, Marele)
Case of the Eight Brothers [1947] (Heberden, M. V.)
Case of the Good-for-Nothing Girlfriend [1994] (Maney, M.)
■ Case of the Hook-Billed Kites [1982] (Borthwick, J. S.)
■ Case of the Hula Clock [1956] (Gardiner, Dorothy)
Case of the Late Pig [1937] (Allingham, Margery)
Case of the Ludicrous Letters [1994] (Clarke, Anna)
■ Case of the Not-So-Nice Nurse [1993] (Maney, Mabel)
Case of the Paranoid Patient [1991] (Clarke, Anna)
■ Case of the Radioactive Redhead [1963] (Fickling, G. G.)
Case of the Straw Man [1951] (Disney, Doris Miles)
Case of the Tainted Token [1938] (Knight, Kathleen M.)
Case of the Tea-Cosy's Aunt [1942] (Gilbert, Anthony)
Case of the Weird Sisters [1943] (Armstrong, Charlotte)
Case of William Smith [1948] (Wentworth, Patricia)
■ Case Pending [1960] (Shannon, Dell) ☆
Case with Three Husbands [1967] (Erskine, Margaret)
Cashmere Kid [1993] (Comfort, Barbara)
■ Cast a Cold Eye [1988] (Eccles, Marjorie)
Cast for Death [1976] (Yorke, Margaret)
Cast of Killers [1992] (Gray, Gallagher)
Casual Affairs [1985] (O'Donnell, Lillian)
Cat Among the Pigeons [1959] (Christie, Agatha)
Cat and Capricorn [1951] (Olsen, D. B.)
Cat in a Crimson Haze [1995] (Douglas, Carole Nelson)
Cat in a Diamond Dazzle [1996] (Douglas, Carole Nelson)
■ Cat Killer [1993] (Dengler, Sandy)
Cat on a Blue Monday [1994] (Douglas, Carole Nelson)
■ Cat Saw Murder [1939] (Olsen, D. B.)
Cat Walk [1953] (Olsen, D. B.)
Cat Wears a Mask [1949] (Olsen, D. B.)
Cat Wears a Noose [1944] (Olsen, D. B.)
Cat Who Ate Danish Modern [1967] (Braun, Lilian J.)
Cat Who Blew the Whistle [1995] (Braun, Lilian J.)
Cat Who Came to Breakfast [1994] (Braun, Lilian J.)
■ Cat Who Could Read Backwards [1966] (Braun, Lilian J.)
Cat Who Knew a Cardinal [1991] (Braun, Lilian J.)
Cat Who Knew Shakespeare [1988] (Braun, Lilian J.)
Cat Who Lived High [1990] (Braun, Lilian J.)
Cat Who Moved a Mountain [1992] (Braun, Lilian J.)
Cat Who Played Brahms [1987] (Braun, Lilian J.) ☆
Cat Who Played Post Office [1987] (Braun, Lilian J.)
Cat Who Said Cheese [1996] (Braun, Lilian J.)
Cat Who Saw Red [1986] (Braun, Lilian J.) ☆
Cat Who Sniffed Glue [1988] (Braun, Lilian J.)

C . . . continued

Cat Who Talked to Ghosts [1990] (Braun, Lilian J.)
Cat Who Turned On and Off [1968] (Braun, Lilian J.)
Cat Who Wasn't There [1993] (Braun, Lilian J.)
Cat Who Went into the Closet [1994] (Braun, Lilian J.)
Cat Who Went Underground [1989] (Braun, Lilian J.)
Cat's Claw [1943] (Olsen, D. B.)
Cat's Claw [1992] (Yarbro, Chelsea Quinn)
Cat's Cradle [1992] (Curzon, Clare)
Cat's Eye [1991] (Jackson, Marian J. A.)
Catacomb Conspiracy [1991] (Arnold, Margot)
🔳 Cater Street Hangman [1979] (Perry, Anne)
🔳 Catering to Nobody [1990] (Davidson, Diane Mott) ☆ ☆ ☆
Catherine Wheel [1949] (Wentworth, Patricia)
🔳 Catnap [1992] (Douglas, Carole Nelson)
Catnap [1994] (Slovo, Gillian)
Cats Don't Need Coffins [1946] (Olsen, D. B.)
Cats Don't Smile [1945] (Olsen, D. B.)
Cats Have Tall Shadows [1948] (Olsen, D. B.)
Catspaw for Murder [1943] (Olsen, D. B.)
Caught Dead [1995] (McKenna, Bridget)
🔳 Caught Dead in Philadelphia [1987] (Roberts, Gillian) ★
🔳 Caught in the Shadows [1992] (Haddad, Carolyn A.)
Cautious Overshoes [1956] (Scherf, Margaret)
Cavalier Case [1991] (Fraser, Antonia)
🔳 Cavalier in White [1986] (Muller, Marcia)
Celebration in Purple Sage [1996] (Smith, Barbara B.)
Cereal Murders [1993] (Davidson, Diane Mott)
Ceremonial Death [1996] (Oliphant, B. J.)
Certain Sleep [1961] (Reilly, Helen)
Chain of Evidence [1912] (Wells, Carolyn)
Chain of Violence [1985] (Egan, Lesley)
🔳 Champagne and a Gardener [1982] (Morison, B. J.)
Chance to Kill [1966] (Shannon, Dell)
Chandler Policy [1971] (Disney, Doris Miles)
Change for the Worse [1980] (Lemarchand, Elizabeth)
Chaos of Crime [1985] (Shannon, Dell)
Charged with Guilt [1995] (White, Gloria)
Charisma [1994] (Bannister, Jo)
Chasing Away the Devil [1991] (Cooper, Susan Rogers)
Chatauqua [1993] (Ennis, Catherine)
Check-out Time [1995] (Kingsbury, Kate)
Cheetah Chase [1994] (McQuillan, Karin)
Cheshire Cat's Eye [1983] (Muller, Marcia)
Chestnut Mare, Beware [1996] (Jaffe, Jody)
🔳 Chicken Little Was Right [1994] (Ruryk, Jean)
Chief Inspector's Daughter [1980] (Radley, Sheila)
🔳 Child of Silence [1993] (Padgett, Abigail) ☆ ☆
Children of the Night [1990] (Lackey, Mercedes)
Children's Games [1989] (La Pierre, Janet)
Children's Zoo [1981] (O'Donnell, Lillian)
Chill of Summer [1995] (Brennan, Carol)
Chill Rain in January [1990] (Wright, L. R.) ☆
China Governess [1962] (Allingham, Margery)
China Roundabout [1956] (Bell, Josephine)
🔳 China Trade [1994] (Rozan, S. J.)
🔳 Chinese Chop [1949] (Sheridan, Juanita)
Chinese Shawl [1943] (Wentworth, Patricia)
Chinks in the Curtain [1967] (Porter, Joyce)
Choice of Crimes [1980] (Egan, Lesley)
Choice of Evils [1995] (Ferrars, E. X.)
Chorus of Detectives [1987] (Paul, Barbara)
🔳 Chosen for Death [1994] (Flora, Kate Clark)
Christening Day Murder [1993] (Harris, Lee)
Christie Caper [1991] (Hart, Carolyn G.) ☆ ☆ ☆

Christmas Egg [1958] (Kelly, Mary)
Christmas Night Murder [1994] (Harris, Lee)
Churchyard Salad [1969] (Torrie, Malcolm)
🔳 Chutes and Adders [1994] (Block, Barbara)
Cinnamon Murder [1946] (Crane, Frances)
Circular Study [1900] (Green, Anna Katherine)
Circus of the Damned [1995] (Hamilton, Laurell K.)
Cities of the Dead [1986] (Barnes, Linda)
City of Gold and Shadows [1973] (Peters, Ellis)
Class Menagerie [1993] (Churchill, Jill)
Class Reunions are Murder [1996] (Cannon, Taffy)
Clean Break [1995] (McDermid, Val)
Clear Conscience [1994] (Fyfield, Frances)
Clear Cut Murder [1993] (Wallingford, Lee)
🔳 Clearwater [1991] (Ennis, Catherine)
🔳 Clerical Errors [1991] (Greenwood, Diane M.)
Client Is Cancelled [1951] (Lockridge, Frances & Richard)
Clinic for Murder [1993] (Landreth, Marsha)
🔳 Clio Browne: Private Investigator [1988] (Komo, Dolores)
Clock in the Hatbox [1939] (Gilbert, Anthony)
Clock Strikes Twelve [1944] (Wentworth, Patricia)
Clocks [1963] (Christie, Agatha)
Close Call [1995] (Slovo, Gillian)
Close Her Eyes [1984] (Simpson, Dorothy)
Close Quarters [1994] (Piesman, Marissa)
Closet Hanging [1987] (Fennelly, Tony)
Closing Statement [1995] (McClellan, Tierney)
Clouds of Witness [1926] (Sayers, Dorothy L.)
Clubbed to Death [1992] (Edwards, Ruth Dudley)
🔳 Clue [1909] (Wells, Carolyn)
Clue in the Clay [1948] (Olsen, D. B.)
Clue of the Eyelash [1933] (Wells, Carolyn)
Clue of the Poor Man's Shilling [1936] (Knight, Kathleen M.)
Clues to Burn [1942] (Offord, Lenore Glen)
Clutch of Constables [1968] (Marsh, Ngaio)
🔳 Cocaine Blues [1989] (Greenwood, Kerry)
Coconut Killings [1977] (Moyes, Patricia)
Coffin and the Paper Man [1991] (Butler, Gwendoline)
Coffin Corner [1966] (Shannon, Dell)
Coffin Following [1968] (Butler, Gwendoline)
Coffin for Baby [1963] (Butler, Gwendoline)
Coffin for Charley [1994] (Butler, Gwendoline)
Coffin for the Canary [1974] (Butler, Gwendoline)
Coffin from the Past [1970] (Butler, Gwendoline)
Coffin in Fashion [1987] (Butler, Gwendoline)
Coffin in Oxford [1962] (Butler, Gwendoline)
Coffin in the Black Museum [1989] (Butler, Gwendoline)
Coffin in the Museum of Crime [1989] (Butler, G.)
Coffin on Murder Street [1992] (Butler, Gwendoline)
Coffin on the Water [1986] (Butler, Gwendoline)
Coffin Tree [1994] (Butler, Gwendoline)
Coffin Underground [1988] (Butler, Gwendoline)
Coffin Waiting [1964] (Butler, Gwendoline)
Coffin's Dark Number [1969] (Butler, Gwendoline)
🔳 Cold Call [1993] (Pugh, Dianne G.)
Cold Coffin [1990] (Quest, Erica)
🔳 Cold Coming [1956] (Kelly, Mary)
🔳 Cold Day for Murder [1992] (Stabenow, Dana) ★
Cold Feet [1992] (Tucker, Kerry)
Cold in the Earth [1993] (Granger, Ann)
Cold Light of Day [1983] (Page, Emma)
Cold, Lone and Still [1983] (Mitchell, Gladys)
Cold Smoked [1995] (Beck, K. K.)
Cold Steal [1939] (Tilton, Alice)
🔳 Cold Tracks [1991] (Wallingford, Lee)
Cold Trail [1978] (Shannon, Dell)

C . . . continued

Cold-Blooded Business [1994] (Stabenow, Dana)
Colder Kind of Death [1994] (Bowen, Gail) ★
Collector of Photographs [1989] (Valentine, Deborah) ☆ ☆
Colour Scheme [1943] (Marsh, Ngaio)
Come Away, Death [1937] (Mitchell, Gladys)
Come Death and High Water [1987] (Cleeves, Ann)
◧ Come Home and Be Killed [1962] (Melville, Jennie)
Come to Dust [1968] (Lathen, Emma)
Come-Back [1921] (Wells, Carolyn)
◧ Common Death [1990] (Cooper, Natasha)
Common Murder [1989] (McDermid, Val)
Company She Kept [1993] (Eccles, Marjorie)
Compartment K [1955] (Reilly, Helen)
Complete Steel [1969] (Aird, Catherine)
◧ Compound for Death [1943] (Disney, Doris Miles)
Concourse [1995] (Rozan, S. J.)
Confession [1994] (Pickard, Nancy)
Confession of Brother Haluin [1988] (Peters, Ellis)
Consequence of Crime [1980] (Linington, Elizabeth)
Consider the Crows [1993] (Weir, Charlene) ☆
Conspiracy of Strangers [1986] (Martin, Lee)
◧ Contents Under Pressure [1992] (Buchanan, Edna)
Convent on Styx [1975] (Mitchell, Gladys)
Convivial Codfish [1984] (MacLeod, Charlotte)
Cooking Most Deadly [1996] (Pence, Joanne)
◧ Cooking School Murders [1982] (Rich, Virginia)
Cooking up Trouble [1995] (Pence, Joanne)
Cool Repentance [1982] (Fraser, Antonia)
Cop Killer [1975] (Sjöwall, Maj & Per Wahlöö)
Cop Out [1991] (McNab, Claire)
Cop Without a Shield [1983] (O'Donnell, Lillian)
Copper Gold [1978] (Winslow, Pauline Glen)
Coppergold [1978] (Winslow, Pauline Glen)
Copy Cat Crimes [1995] (Wilson, Karen Ann)
Copy Kat [1992] (Kijewski, Karen)
Coral Princess Murders [1954] (Crane, Frances)
Coroner's Pidgin [1945] (Allingham, Margery)
Corpse in Oozak's Pond [1986] (MacLeod, Charlotte) ☆
Corpse in the Flannel Nightgown [1965] (Scherf, M.)
Corpse in the Kitchen [1994] (Mason, Sarah Jill)
Corpse Steps Out [1940] (Rice, Craig)
Corpse with One Shoe [1951] (Scherf, Margaret)
Corpus Christmas [1989] (Maron, Margaret) ☆ ☆
◧ Corridors of Death [1981] (Edwards, Ruth Dudley)
Counsellor Heart [1980] (Winslow, Pauline Glen)
Counterprobe [1990] (Douglas, Carole Nelson)
◧ Cover Her Face [1962] (James, P. D.)
◧ Cover-up Story [1971] (Babson, Marian)
Coyote [1990] (Barnes, Linda)
Crack Down [1994] (McDermid, Val) ☆
Crack of Dawn [1944] (Ford, Leslie)
Cracking Open a Coffin [1993] (Butler, Gwendoline)
Crazy for Loving [1992] (Maiman, Jaye) ★
Crazy Mixed-Up Nude [1964] (Fickling, G. G.)
Creature Was Stirring [1977] (Wells, Tobias)
Crime and the Crystal [1985] (Ferrars, E. X.)
◧ Crime at Black Dudley [1929] (Allingham, Margery)
Crime by Chance [1973] (Linington, Elizabeth)
Crime File [1974] (Shannon, Dell)
Crime for Christmas [1983] (Egan, Lesley)
Crime in the Crypt [1928] (Wells, Carolyn)
Crime Incarnate [1940] (Wells, Carolyn)
◧ Crime of Passion [1991] (Hooper, Kay)
Crime on Their Hands [1969] (Shannon, Dell)

Crime Tears On [1939] (Wells, Carolyn)
Crimes Past [1980] (Challis, Mary)
Criminal C.O.D. [1940] (Taylor, Phoebe Atwood)
Crimson Patch [1936] (Taylor, Phoebe Atwood)
Croaking Raven [1975] (Mitchell, Gladys)
◧ Crocodile on the Sandbank [1975] (Peters, Elizabeth)
Crooked Island [1994] (McKernan, Victoria)
Crooked Wreath [1946] (Brand, Christianna)
Cross My Heart and Hope to Die [1992] (Radley, Sheila)
Crosswords [1995] (Sumner, Penny)
Crown Witness [1995] (Linscott, Gillian)
Crozier Pharaohs [1984] (Mitchell, Gladys)
Cruel and Unusual [1993] (Cornwell, Patricia) ★
Cruel Mother [1990] (La Pierre, Janet)
Cruellest Month [1991] (Holt, Hazel)
Cry Guilty [1981] (Woods, Sara)
Cue for Murder [1942] (McCloy, Helen)
◧ Curiosity Didn't Kill the Cat [1973] (Wren, M. K.)
Curious Affair of the Third Dog [1973] (Moyes, Patricia)
◧ Curious Cape Cod Skull [1995] (Lee, Marie)
Curious Custard Pie [1950] (Scherf, Margaret)
Curl Up and Die [1996] (Jorgensen, Christine T.)
Curly Smoke [1995] (Holtzer, Susan)
Curse of the Giant Hogweed [1985] (MacLeod, Charlotte)
Curse of the Pharaohs [1981] (Peters, Elizabeth)
Curse the Darkness [1990] (Grant-Adamson, Lesley)
Curtain [1975] (Christie, Agatha)
Curtain Call [1961] (Foley, Rae)
Curtain Call for a Corpse [1939] (Bell, Josephine)
Curtain for a Jester [1953] (Lockridge, Frances & Richard)
Curtains for the Cardinal [1993] (Eyre, Elizabeth)
Curved Blades [1916] (Wells, Carolyn)
Cut Direct [1938] (Tilton, Alice)
Cut to: Murder [1995] (Osborne, Denise)
◧ Cut to the Quick [1993] (Ross, Kate)
◧ Cutter [1994] (Crum, Laura)
Cyanide with Compliments [1972] (Lemarchand, E.)
Cyber Kiss [1996] (Chapman, Sally)

D

"D" is for Deadbeat [1987] (Grafton, Sue)
Daffodil Blonde [1950] (Crane, Frances)
◧ Dance of Death [1938] (McCloy, Helen)
Dance to Your Daddy [1969] (Mitchell, Gladys)
Dancers in Mourning [1937] (Allingham, Margery)
Dancing Druids [1948] (Mitchell, Gladys)
Dancing in the Dark [1992] (Zukowski, Sharon)
Dandelion Murders [1994] (Rothenberg, Rebecca)
Danger Point [1941] (Wentworth, Patricia)
◧ Dangerous Alibis [1994] (Clark, Carolyn Chambers)
◧ Dangerous Attachments [1995] (Lovett, Sarah)
Dangerous Edge [1994] (Grant-Adamson, Lesley)
Dangerous Games [1994] (Grant-Adamson, Lesley)
Dangerous Islands [1963] (Bridge, Ann)
Dangerous Mourning [1991] (Perry, Anne)
◧ Dangerous Places [1987] (Chase, Elaine Raco)
Dangerous to Me [1959] (Foley, Rae)
Dante Game [1991] (Langton, Jane)
◧ Daphne Decisions [1990] (O'Brien, Meg)
Dark Coffin [1995] (Butler, Gwendoline)
Dark Corners [1988] (Chase, Elaine Raco)
Dark Death [1953] (Gilbert, Anthony)
Dark Door [1988] (Wilhelm, Kate)
◧ Dark Fields [1986] (MacGregor, T. J.) ☆
Dark Nantucket Noon [1975] (Langton, Jane)
◧ Dark Road [1946] (Disney, Doris Miles)

D . . . continued

Dark Star [1989] (Muller, Marcia)
Dark Stream [1986] (Thomson, June)
Dark Swain [1994] (Knight, Kathryn Lasky)
Dark Threat [1946] (Wentworth, Patricia)
Darkest Hour [1969] (Nielsen, Helen)
🔲 Dartmoor Burial [1992] (Peterson, Audrey)
Dash of Death [1995] (Bishop, Claudia)
🔲 Date with a Dead Doctor [1991] (Brill, Toni)
Date with a Plummeting Publisher [1993] (Brill, Toni)
Date with Death [1966] (Linington, Elizabeth)
Daughter of the House [1925] (Wells, Carolyn)
Daughter of Time [1951] (Tey, Josephine)
Daughters of Artemis [1991] (Douglas, Lauren Wright)
Dawson Pedigree [1927] (Sayers, Dorothy L.)
Day for Dying [1995] (Simpson, Dorothy)
Day in the Death of Dorothea Cassidy [1992] (Cleeves, A.)
Day of Atonement [1992] (Kellerman, Faye)
Day She Died [1962] (Reilly, Helen)
Day That Dusty Died [1993] (Martin, Lee)
Days of Crime and Roses [1992] (Morgan, Kate)
🔲 Dead Ahead [1990] (Horansky, Ruby)
Dead Ahead [1994] (McKenna, Bridget) ☆
Dead and Buried [1994] (Cleary, Melissa)
Dead and Buried [1995] (Hager, Jean)
Dead and Doggone [1990] (Conant, Susan)
Dead and Gone [1989] (Kittredge, Mary)
Dead as a Dinosaur [1952] (Lockridge, Frances & R.)
🔲 Dead as Dead Can Be [1993] (Crowleigh, Ann)
Dead Babes in the Wood [1952] (Olsen, D. B.)
🔲 Dead Beat [1992] (McDermid, Val)
Dead by Morning [1989] (Simpson, Dorothy)
Dead by Now [1953] (Erskine, Margaret)
Dead by the Light of the Moon [1967] (Wells, Tobias)
Dead Can Tell [1940] (Reilly, Helen)
Dead Center [1994] (Horansky, Ruby)
Dead Certain [1992] (McNab, Claire)
Dead Crazy [1988] (Pickard, Nancy) ☆ ☆
Dead Don't Speak [1955] (Erskine, Margaret)
Dead Earnest [1944] (Tilton, Alice)
Dead Easy for Dover [1978] (Porter, Joyce)
Dead End [1994] (Harrod-Eagles, Cynthia)
Dead Ends [1992] (Fallon, Ann C.)
🔲 Dead File [1995] (Porath, Sharon)
Dead for a Ducat [1939] (Reilly, Helen)
Dead Heat [1984] (Barnes, Linda)
🔲 Dead in a Row [1957] (Butler, Gwendoline)
Dead in the Cellar [1994] (Feddersen, Connie)
Dead in the Dirt [1996] (Feddersen, Connie)
Dead in the Melon Patch [1995] (Feddersen, Connie)
🔲 Dead in the Morning [1970] (Yorke, Margaret)
🔲 Dead in the Scrub [1990] (Oliphant, B. J.) ☆
🔲 Dead in the Water [1993] (Feddersen, Connie)
Dead in the Water [1991] (Smith, Julie)
Dead in the Water [1993] (Stabenow, Dana)
Dead Liberty [1987] (Aird, Catherine)
Dead Loss [1966] (Petrie, Rhona)
Dead Man Out of Mind [1995] (Charles, Kate)
Dead Man's Control [1936] (Reilly, Helen)
Dead Man's Folly [1956] (Christie, Agatha)
Dead Man's Gift [1941] (Popkin, Zelda)
🔲 Dead Man's Island [1993] (Hart, Carolyn G.) ★
Dead Man's Mirror [1937] (Christie, Agatha)
Dead Man's Ransom [1984] (Peters, Ellis)
Dead Man's Riddle [1957] (Kelly, Mary)

🔲 Dead Man's Thoughts [1983] (Wheat, Carolyn) ☆
Dead Matter [1993] (Wren, M. K.)
🔲 Dead Men Don't Give Seminars [1988] (Sucher, Dorothy) ☆
Dead Men Don't Marry [1989] (Sucher, Dorothy)
🔲 Dead Men Don't Ski [1959] (Moyes, Patricia)
Dead Men's Morris [1936] (Mitchell, Gladys)
Dead Moon on the Rise [1994] (Cooper, Susan Rogers)
Dead of Summer [1962] (Kelly, Mary)
Dead of Winter [1995] (Gosling, Paula)
Dead on Arrival [1986] (Simpson, Dorothy)
Dead on Cue [1985] (Morice, Anne)
Dead on Sunday [1993] (Orde, A. J.)
Dead Over Heels [1996] (Harris, Charlaine)
Dead Pan [1992] (Dentinger, Jane)
🔲 Dead Pull Hitter [1989] (Gordon, Alison)
Dead Ringer [1994] (Kelner, Toni L. P.)
Dead Run [1976] (Lockridge, Frances & Richard)
Dead Serious [1995] (Stacey, Susannah)
Dead Set [1993] (Melville, Jennie)
Dead South [1996] (Sullivan, Winona)
🔲 Dead Time [1992] (Bland, Eleanor Taylor)
Dead Water [1963] (Marsh, Ngaio)
Dead Weight [1962] (Fenisong, Ruth)
Dead Yesterday [1951] (Fenisong, Ruth)
🔲 Deadlier Than Death [1993] (Clark, Carolyn Chambers)
Deadliest Option [1991] (Meyers, Annette)
Deadline for Destruction [1942] (Leonard, Charles L.)
🔲 Deadline for Murder [1991] (Frankel, Valerie)
Deadlock [1952] (Fenisong, Ruth)
Deadlock [1984] (Paretsky, Sara)
Deadly Admirer [1992] (Green, Christine)
🔲 Deadly Appearances [1990] (Bowen, Gail)
Deadly Beloved [1989] (Knight, Alanna)
Deadly Devotion [1994] (Wallace, Patricia) ☆
🔲 Deadly Errand [1991] (Green, Christine)
🔲 Deadly Gamble [1995] (Shelton, Connie)
Deadly Grounds [1989] (Wallace, Patricia)
Deadly Nightshade [1940] (Daly, Elizabeth)
Deadly Noose [1962] (Foley, Rae)
Deadly Objectives [1985] (Taylor, L. A.)
Deadly Obsession [1995] (Woods, Sherryl)
Deadly Paté [1997] (Furie, Ruthe)
Deadly Practice [1994] (Green, Christine)
🔲 Deadly Reflections [1988] (Friedman, Mickey)
Deadly Rehearsal [1990] (Peterson, Audrey)
Deadly Relations [1979] (Thomson, June)
🔲 Deadly Resolutions [1994] (Collins, Anna Ashwood)
Deadly Reunion [1995] (Manthorne, Jackie)
🔲 Deadly Safari [1990] (McQuillan, Karin)
Deadly Secrets on the St. Johns [1995] (Sprinkle, P. H.)
Deadly Sunshade [1940] (Taylor, Phoebe Atwood)
Deadly Truth [1941] (McCloy, Helen)
Deadly Valentine [1990] (Hart, Carolyn G.) ☆ ☆
Dear Dead Woman [1940] (Gilbert, Anthony)
🔲 Dear Departed [1980] (Burton, Anne)
Dear Irene, [1995] (Burke, Jan)
Dear Miss Demeanor [1987] (Hess, Joan)
Dear Old Dead [1994] (Haddam, Jane)
Dearest Enemy [1981] (Woods, Sara)
Death a la Provencale [1995] (Laurence, Janet)
Death Against the Clock [1958] (Gilbert, Anthony)
Death Among the Dons [1993] (Neel, Janet)
Death and Judgment [1995] (Leon, Donna)
Death and Letters [1950] (Daly, Elizabeth)
🔲 Death and Mr. Potter [1955] (Foley, Rae)
Death and Taxes [1992] (Dunlap, Susan)

D . . . continued

1 Death and the Chapman [1991] (Sedley, Kate)
Death and the Dancing Footman [1941] (Marsh, Ngaio)
Death and the Delinquent [1992] (Oliphant, B. J.)
Death and the Diplomat [1963] (Scherf, Margaret)
Death and the Dogwalker [1990] (Orde, A. J.)
Death and the Dutch Uncle [1968] (Moyes, Patricia)
Death and the Dutiful Daughter [1974] (Morice, Anne)
Death and the Epicure [1993] (Laurence, Janet)
Death and the Gentle Bull [1954] (Lockridge, F. & R.)
Death and the Joyful Woman [1962] (Peters, Ellis) ★
Death and the Maiden [1947] (Mitchell, Gladys)
1 Death and the Maiden [1978] (Radley, Sheila)
1 Death and the Oxford Box [1993] (Stallwood, Veronica)
1 Death and the Pregnant Virgin [1980] (Haymon, S. T.)
1 Death and the Trumpets of Tuscany [1988] (Jones, H. W.)
1 Death at Bishop's Keep [1994] (Paige, Robin)
Death at Deep End [1951] (Wentworth, Patricia)
Death at Face Value [1995] (Christmas, Joyce)
Death at Four Corners [1929] (Gilbert, Anthony)
Death at Gallows Green [1995] (Paige, Robin)
Death at Half-Term [1939] (Bell, Josephine)
1 Death at la Fenice [1992] (Leon, Donna)
Death at St. Anselm's [1984] (Holland, Isabelle)
Death at the Bar [1940] (Marsh, Ngaio)
Death at the Dolphin [1966] (Marsh, Ngaio) ☆
Death at the Door [1944] (Gilbert, Anthony)
Death at the Medical Board [1944] (Bell, Josephine)
Death at the Opera [1934] (Mitchell, Gladys)
Death at the Table [1994] (Laurence, Janet)
Death at Victoria Dock [1992] (Greenwood, Kerry)
1 Death at Wentwater Court [1994] (Dunn, Carola)
Death Beyond the Nile [1988] (Mann, Jessica)
1 Death Blew Out the Match [1935] (Knight, Kathleen M.)
Death by Analysis [1988] (Slovo, Gillian)
Death by Association [1952] (Lockridge, Frances & R.)
Death by Chrystal [1993] (Bushell, Agnes)
1 Death by Deception [1988] (Wingate, Anne)
1 Death by Dressage [1993] (Banks, Carolyn)
1 Death by Election [1994] (Hall, Patricia)
Death by Inches [1965] (Shannon, Dell)
1 Death by Misadventure [1989] (Greenwood, Kerry)
Death by the Light of the Moon [1992] (Hess, Joan)
1 Death by the Riverside [1990] (Redmann, J. M.)
Death Came Dancing [1940] (Knight, Kathleen Moore)
Death Cap [1973] (Thomson, June)
Death Casts a Long Shadow [1959] (Gilbert, Anthony)
1 Death Comes as Epiphany [1993] (Newman, Sharan) ★ ☆ ☆
Death Comes Staccato [1987] (Slovo, Gillian)
Death Crosses the Border [1995] (Steinberg, Janice)
Death Days [1995] (Schenkel, S. E.)
Death Demands an Audience [1940] (Reilly, Helen)
1 Death Down Home [1990] (Sandstrom, Eve K.)
Death Down Under [1990] (McNab, Claire)
Death Echo [1993] (Tucker, Kerry)
Death Flats [1991] (MacGregor, T. J.)
Death for a Dancer [1986] (Giroux, E. X.)
Death for a Dancing Doll [1991] (Giroux, E. X.)
Death for a Darling [1985] (Giroux, E. X.)
Death for a Dietician [1988] (Giroux, E. X.)
Death for a Dilletante [1987] (Giroux, E. X.)
Death for a Doctor [1986] (Giroux, E. X.)
Death for a Dodo [1993] (Giroux, E. X.)
Death for a Double [1990] (Giroux, E. X.)
Death for a Dreamer [1989] (Giroux, E. X.)

1 Death for Adonis [1984] (Giroux, E. X.)
Death for Old Times' Sake [1992] (Orde, A. J.)
Death Goes on Retreat [1995] (O'Marie, Sister Carol A.)
Death Goes Skiing [1979] (Schier, Norma)
Death Goes to a Reunion [1952] (Knight, Kathleen Moore)
Death Has a Small Voice [1953] (Lockridge, Frances & R.)
1 Death in a Deck Chair [1984] (Beck, K. K.)
Death in a Distant Land [1988] (Livingston, Nancy)
Death in a Funhouse Mirror [1995] (Flora, Kate Clark)
Death in a Private Place [1996] (Kunz, Kathleen)
Death in a Strange Country [1993] (Leon, Donna)
Death in a Tenured Position [1981] (Cross, Amanda)
Death in a White Tie [1938] (Marsh, Ngaio)
Death in Autumn [1984] (Nabb, Magdalen)
Death in Blue Folders [1985] (Maron, Margaret)
Death in Botanist's Bay [1941] (Ferrars, E. X.)
Death in Clairvoyance [1949] (Bell, Josephine)
Death in Close-Up [1989] (Livingston, Nancy)
1 Death in Deakins Wood [1963] (Petrie, Rhona)
Death in Devil's Acre [1985] (Perry, Anne)
Death in Disguise [1993] (Graham, Caroline)
Death in Ecstasy [1936] (Marsh, Ngaio)
Death in Lilac Time [1955] (Crane, Frances)
Death in Lovers' Lane [1996] (Hart, Carolyn G.)
Death in Retirement [1956] (Bell, Josephine)
Death in Rough Water [1995] (Mathews, Francine)
Death in Springtime [1983] (Nabb, Magdalen)
1 Death in Still Waters [1995] (Lee, Barbara) ★
Death in Store [1992] (Rowe, J.)
Death in the Air [1935] (Christie, Agatha)
Death in the Blackout [1942] (Gilbert, Anthony)
Death in the Clouds [1935] (Christie, Agatha)
1 Death in the Country [1994] (Green, Christine)
Death in the Faculty [1981] (Cross, Amanda)
Death in the Family [1994] (Melville, Jennie)
1 Death in the Grand Manor [1970] (Morice, Anne)
1 Death in the Life [1976] (Davis, Dorothy Salisbury)
1 Death in the Morning [1978] (Radley, Sheila)
1 Death in the Off-Season [1994] (Mathews, Francine)
Death in the Round [1980] (Morice, Anne)
1 Death in the Stocks [1935] (Heyer, Georgette)
Death in the Wet [1934] (Mitchell, Gladys)
Death in the Wrong Room [1947] (Gilbert, Anthony)
Death in Time [1980] (Warner, Mignon)
Death in Wessex [1989] (Peterson, Audrey)
Death Is a Family Affair [1987] (Sims, L. V.)
1 Death Is Forever [1980] (O'Callaghan, Maxine)
Death Is Sweet [1996] (Kelly, Susan B.)
Death Knocks Three Times [1949] (Gilbert, Anthony)
Death Lifts the Latch [1945] (Gilbert, Anthony)
Death Lights a Candle [1932] (Taylor, Phoebe Atwood)
Death Lives Next Door [1960] (Butler, Gwendoline)
Death Mask [1988] (Dentinger, Jane)
Death Notes [1981] (Rendell, Ruth)
Death of a Burrowing Mole [1982] (Mitchell, Gladys)
Death of a Busybody [1963] (Shannon, Dell)
Death of a Butterfly [1984] (Maron, Margaret)
Death of a Cad [1987] (Beaton, M. C.)
Death of a Charming Man [1994] (Beaton, M. C.)
Death of a Dancing Fool [1996] (Berry, Carole)
Death of a Dean [1996] (Holt, Hazel)
Death of a Delft Blue [1964] (Mitchell, Gladys)
Death of a Difficult Woman [1994] (Berry, Carole)
Death of a Doll [1947] (Lawrence, Hilda)
Death of a Dream Maker [1995] (Gray, Gallagher)
Death of a Dunwoody Matron [1993] (Sprinkle, Patricia H.)

D ... continued

Death of a Dutchman [1982] (Nabb, Magdalen)
Death of a Fool [1956] (Marsh, Ngaio)
Death of a Garden Pest [1995] (Ripley, Ann)
Death of a Gay Dog [1973] (Morice, Anne)
Death of a Ghost [1934] (Allingham, Margery)
Death of a Glutton [1993] (Beaton, M. C.)
Death of a God [1987] (Haymon, S. T.)
Death of a Golden Girl [1988] (Fulton, Eileen)
Death of a Good Woman [1989] (Eccles, Marjorie)
❶ Death of a Gossip [1985] (Beaton, M. C.)
Death of a Heavenly Twin [1974] (Morice, Anne)
Death of a Hollow Man [1989] (Graham, Caroline)
Death of a Hussy [1990] (Beaton, M. C.)
Death of a Jezebel [1948] (Brand, Christianna)
Death of a Minor Character [1983] (Ferrars, E. X.)
Death of a Nag [1995] (Beaton, M. C.)
Death of a Partner [1991] (Neel, Janet)
Death of a Peer [1940] (Marsh, Ngaio)
Death of a Perfect Wife [1989] (Beaton, M. C.)
❶ Death of a Postmodernist [1995] (Steinberg, Janice)
Death of a Prankster [1992] (Beaton, M. C.)
Death of a Raven [1988] (Duffy, Margaret)
Death of a Snob [1991] (Beaton, M. C.)
Death of a Tall Man [1946] (Lockridge, Frances & Richard)
Death of a Travelling Man [1993] (Beaton, M. C.)
Death of a Voodoo Doll [1982] (Arnold, Margot)
Death of a Wallflower [1995] (Prowell, Sandra West)
Death of a Warrior Queen [1991] (Haymon, S. T.)
Death of a Wedding Guest [1976] (Morice, Anne)
Death of an Angel [1955] (Lockridge, Frances & Richard)
❶ Death of an Angel [1975] (Winslow, Pauline Glen)
Death of an Aryan [1939] (Huxley, Elspeth)
❶ Death of an Englishman [1981] (Nabb, Magdalen)
Death of an Expert Witness [1977] (James, P. D.)
❶ Death of an Old Girl [1967] (Lemarchand, Elizabeth)
❶ Death of an Old Sinner [1957] (Davis, Dorothy Salisbury)
Death of an Outsider [1988] (Beaton, M. C.)
Death of Blue Mountain Cat [1995] (Dymmoch, M. A.)
Death of Our Dear One [1952] (Erskine, Margaret)
Death of a Dancer [1989] (McGown, Jill)
❶ Death of a Duchess [1992] (Eyre, Elizabeth)
Death of the Office Witch [1993] (Millhiser, Marlys)
Death of the Party [1958] (Fenisong, Ruth)
Death on a Dragon's Tongue [1982] (Arnold, Margot)
❶ Death on Demand [1987] (Hart, Carolyn G.) ☆ ☆
Death of Distinction [1995] (Eccles, Marjorie)
Death on Doomsday [1971] (Lemarchand, Elizabeth)
Death on Site [1989] (Neel, Janet)
Death on the Agenda [1962] (Moyes, Patricia)
Death on the Aisle [1942] (Lockridge, Frances & Richard)
Death on the Borough Council [1937] (Bell, Josephine)
❶ Death on the Cliff Walk [1994] (Kruger, Mary)
❶ Death on the Door Mat [1939] (Heberden, M. V.)
Death on the Drunkard's Path [1996] (Hager, Jean)
Death on the Eno [1981] (Mackay, Amanda)
Death on the Nile [1937] (Christie, Agatha)
Death on the Reserve [1966] (Bell, Josephine)
❶ Death on the Slopes [1978] (Schier, Norma)
❶ Death on Widow's Walk [1985] (Grant-Adamson, Lesley)
❶ Death Pays the Rose Rent [1994] (Malmont, Valerie S.)
Death Penalties [1991] (Gosling, Paula)
Death Prone [1994] (Curzon, Clare)
❶ Death Qualified [1991] (Wilhelm, Kate)
Death Send a Cable [1939] (Yates, Margaret Evelyn T.)

Death Served up Cold [1994] (Oliphant, B. J.)
Death Shall Overcome [1966] (Lathen, Emma)
Death Speaks Softly [1987] (Fraser, Anthea)
Death Sweet [1988] (MacGregor, T. J.)
Death Takes a Bow [1943] (Lockridge, Frances & Richard)
❶ Death Takes a Hand [1993] (Moody, Susan)
Death Takes a Redhead [1940] (Gilbert, Anthony)
Death Takes a Wife [1959] (Gilbert, Anthony)
Death Tape [1987] (Gallison, Kate)
Death To Go [1993] (Harrod-Eagles, Cynthia)
Death To the Landlords! [1972] (Peters, Ellis)
Death Too Soon [1994] (Peterson, Audrey)
❶ Death Turns a Trick [1982] (Smith, Julie)
Death Under Par [1981] (Law, Janice)
❶ Death Valley [1993] (Dengler, Sandy)
❶ Death Walk [1988] (Quest, Erica)
Death Walker [1996] (Thurlo, Aimée & David)
Death Walks on Cat Feet [1956] (Olsen, D. B.)
Death Warmed Over [1988] (Martin, Lee)
Death Watch [1992] (Harrod-Eagles, Cynthia)
Death We Share [1995] (Short, Sharon Gwyn)
Death Wears a (Bridal) Veil [1937] (Knight, Kathleen M.)
Death Wears a Crown [1993] (Fawcett, Quinn)
Death Wears a Mask [1970] (Gilbert, Anthony)
❶ Death Wears a White Gardenia [1938] (Popkin, Zelda)
Death Wears Cat's Eyes [1950] (Olsen, D. B.)
Death Wish Green [1960] (Crane, Frances)
Death Won't Wait [1954] (Gilbert, Anthony)
❶ Death's Bright Angel [1988] (Neel, Janet) ★
Death's Savage Passion [1986] (Papazoglou, Orania)
Death-Bringers [1965] (Shannon, Dell)
Death-Cap Dancers [1981] (Mitchell, Gladys)
Deathblow Hill [1935] (Taylor, Phoebe Atwood)
Deaths of Jocasta [1993] (Redmann, J. M.) ☆
Deception Island [1991] (Lorens, M. K.)
❶ Decked [1992] (Clark, Carol Higgins) ☆
Deed Is Drawn [1949] (Barber, Willetta Ann)
Deeds of the Disturber [1988] (Peters, Elizabeth)
❶ Deep Cover [1994] (Berenson, Laurien)
Deep Sleep [1991] (Fyfield, Frances)
❶ Deepe Coffyn [1989] (Laurence, Janet)
Deer Leap [1985] (Grimes, Martha)
Defend and Betray [1992] (Perry, Anne) ★ ☆
Deficit Ending [1990] (Martin, Lee)
Defy the Devil [1984] (Woods, Sara)
Demon at the Opera [1980] (Schier, Norma)
❶ Desert Heat [1993] (Jance, J. A.)
Deservedly Dead [1992] (Oliphant, B. J.)
❶ Design for Dying [1938] (McCloy, Helen) ★
Design for Murder [1987] (Hart, Carolyn G.)
Design in Diamonds [1944] (Knight, Kathleen Moore)
Designer Crimes [1995] (Matera, Lia)
Desperate Remedy [1993] (Kittredge, Mary)
Destiny of Death [1984] (Shannon, Dell)
Destroying Angel [1988] (Cohen, Anthea)
Detection Unlimited [1953] (Heyer, Georgette)
Detections of Dr. Sam: Johnson [1960] (de la Torre, L.)
Detective's Due [1965] (Egan, Lesley)
Deuces Wild [1975] (Shannon, Dell)
Devices and Desires [1989] (James, P. D.)
Devil at Saxon Wall [1935] (Mitchell, Gladys)
Devil down Home [1991] (Sandstrom, Eve K.)
Devil Loves Me [1942] (Millar, Margaret)
Devil's Door [1994] (Newman, Sharan)
Devil's Elbow [1951] (Mitchell, Gladys)
Devil's Gonna Get Him [1995] (Wesley, Valerie Wilson)

D . . . continued

Devil's Knell [1983] (Warner, Mignon)
Devil's Novice [1983] (Peters, Ellis)
Devil's Stronghold [1948] (Ford, Leslie)
Devil's Work [1940] (Wells, Carolyn)
Devil's Workshop [1996] (Gallison, Kate)
Devious Design [1948] (Olsen, D. B.)
Dial 557 R-A-P-E [1974] (O'Donnell, Lillian)
Diamond Before You Die [1987] (Wiltz, Chris)
1 Diamond Feather [1930] (Reilly, Helen)
Diamond Head [1992] (Jackson, Marian J. A.)
Diamond in the Buff [1990] (Dunlap, Susan)
Diamond Pin [1919] (Wells, Carolyn)
Did She Fall or Was She Pushed? [1959] (Disney, Doris M.)
Die for Love [1984] (Peters, Elizabeth)
Die in My Dreams [1995] (Green, Christine)
Die in the Country [1972] (Wells, Tobias)
Die in the Dark [1947] (Gilbert, Anthony)
Die Like a Dog [1982] (Moffat, Gwen)
Die Quickly, Dear Mother [1969] (Wells, Tobias)
Died in the Red [1968] (Gray, Dulcie)
Died in the Wool [1945] (Marsh, Ngaio)
Diet for Death [1996] (Laurence, Janet)
Diet to Die For [1989] (Hess, Joan) ★
Different Kind of Summer [1967] (Melville, Jennie)
Dig a Dead Doll [1960] (Fickling, G. G.)
Ding Dong Bell [1958] (Reilly, Helen)
Dinky Died [1970] (Wells, Tobias)
Dinner to Die For [1987] (Dunlap, Susan)
Diplomat and the Gold Piano [1963] (Scherf, Margaret)
Diplomatic Corpse [1951] (Taylor, Phoebe Atwood)
Dire Happenings at Scratch Ankle [1993] (Sibley, C.)
Dirge for a Dorset Druid [1994] (Arnold, Margot)
Dirty Duck [1984] (Grimes, Martha)
Disappearance of Madalena Grimaldi [1994] (Day, Marele)
Disappearing Bridegroom [1950] (Erskine, Margaret)
Dishonest Murder [1949] (Lockridge, Frances & Richard)
Dismal Thing To Do [1986] (Craig, Alisa)
Dismissed with Prejudice [1989] (Jance, J. A.)
Distant Clue [1963] (Lockridge, Frances & Richard)
Divine and Deadly [1950] (Scherf, Margaret)
Divine Inspiration [1993] (Langton, Jane)
Do Not Disturb [1994] (Kingsbury, Kate)
1 Doberman Wore Black [1983] (Moore, Barbara)
Doctor, His Wife, and the Clock [1895] (Green, Anna K.)
Doctors and Lawyers and Such [1995] (Cooper, Susan R.)
Dog Collar Crime [1993] (Cleary, Melissa)
Dog Collar Murders [1989] (Wilson, Barbara)
Dog Eat Dog [1996] (Berenson, Laurien)
Dogfish [1993] (Geason, Susan)
1 Dogtown [1991] (Lambert, Mercedes)
Dolly and the Bird of Paradise [1983] (Dunnett, Dorothy)
Dolly and the Cookie Bird [1970] (Dunnett, Dorothy)
Dolly and the Doctor Bird [1971] (Dunnett, Dorothy)
Dolly and the Nanny Bird [1976] (Dunnett, Dorothy)
1 Dolly and the Singing Bird [1968] (Dunnett, Dorothy)
Dolly and the Starry Bird [1972] (Dunnett, Dorothy)
Dolly Is Dead [1995] (Borthwick, J. S.)
Don't Leave Me This Way [1990] (Smith, Joan)
Don't Look Behind You [1952] (Erskine, Margaret)
Don't Monkey with Murder [1942] (Ferrars, E. X.)
Don't Open the Door! [1945] (Gilbert, Anthony)
Don't Turn Your Back on the Ocean [1994] (Dawson, J.)
Don't Wear Your Wedding Ring [1973] (O'Donnell, Lillian)
Done to Death [1974] (Woods, Sara)

Done Wrong [1995] (Bland, Eleanor Taylor)
Doomed Five [1930] (Wells, Carolyn)
Doomed To Die [1991] (Simpson, Dorothy)
Doorstep Murders [1930] (Wells, Carolyn)
Double Bluff [1963] (Shannon, Dell)
Double Bluff [1995] (McNab, Claire)
Double Daughter [1988] (McConnell, Vickie P.)
Double, Double, Oil and Trouble [1978] (Lathen, Emma)
Double Frame [1957] (Rice, Craig)
Double Man [1952] (Reilly, Helen)
Double Take [1994] (Oleksiw, Susan)
Double [1984] (Muller, Marcia)
Doubled in Spades [1996] (Moody, Susan)
Dying Light in Corduba [1996] (Davis, Lindsey)
Dover and the Claret Tappers [1976] (Porter, Joyce)
Dover and the Dark Lady [1972] (Porter, Joyce)
Dover and the Sense of Justice [1968] (Porter, Joyce)
Dover and the Unkindest Cut of All [1967] (Porter, Joyce)
Dover Beats the Band [1980] (Porter, Joyce)
Dover Does Some Spadework [1977] (Porter, Joyce)
Dover Doesn't Dilly-Dally [1978] (Porter, Joyce)
Dover Fails to Make His Mark [1970] (Porter, Joyce)
Dover Goes to Pott [1968] (Porter, Joyce)
Dover Goes to School [1978] (Porter, Joyce)
1 Dover One [1964] (Porter, Joyce)
Dover Pulls a Rabbit [1969] (Porter, Joyce)
Dover Strikes Again [1970] (Porter, Joyce)
Dover Tangles with High Finance [1975] (Porter, Joyce)
Dover Three [1965] (Porter, Joyce)
Dover Two [1965] (Porter, Joyce)
Dover Without Perks [1978] (Porter, Joyce)
Down Among the Dead Men [1961] (Moyes, Patricia)
Down East Murders [1985] (Borthwick, J. S.)
Down Home Heifer Heist [1993] (Sandstrom, Eve K.)
1 Down Home Murder [1993] (Kelner, Toni L. P.)
Down the Garden Path [1985] (Cannell, Dorothy)
1 Dr. Sam: Johnson, Detector [1946] (de la Torre, Lillian)
Drawback to Murder [1947] (Barber, Willetta Ann)
Drawn Conclusion [1942] (Barber, Willetta Ann)
Dream Apart [1978] (Egan, Lesley)
Dreaming Damozel [1990] (Hardwick, Mollie)
Dreamland [1992] (Lorens, M. K.)
Dressed for Death [1994] (Leon, Donna)
1 Dressed to Kill [1994] (Duffy, Margaret)
Drift Away [1994] (Tucker, Kerry)
Drink for Mr. Cherry [1934] (Gardiner, Dorothy)
1 Drink of Deadly Wine [1991] (Charles, Kate)
Drinks on the Victim [1947] (Heberden, M. V.)
Driven to Kill [1954] (Disney, Doris Miles)
Dude on Arrival [1992] (Borthwick, J. S.)
Due to a Death [1962] (Kelly, Mary)
Dull Dead [1958] (Butler, Gwendoline)
Dumb Witness [1937] (Christie, Agatha)
Dune to Death [1993] (Daheim, Mary)
1 Dupe [1980] (Cody, Liza) ★ ☆
Duplicate Death [1951] (Heyer, Georgette)
Dust Devils of the Purple Sage [1995] (Smith, Barbara B.)
1 Dutchman [1992] (Meyers, Maan)
Dutchman's Dilemma [1995] (Meyers, Maan)
Dying Breath [1994] (Mason, Sarah Jill)
Dying Cheek to Cheek [1992] (Shah, Diane K.)
Dying Fall [1973] (Dolson, Hildegarde)
Dying Fall [1995] (Hall, Patricia)
Dying Fall [1985] (Thomson, June)
Dying for Chocolate [1992] (Davidson, Diane Mott)
Dying for Stardom [1988] (Fulton, Eileen)
Dying Light in Corduba [1996] (Davis, Lindsey)

E

"E" is for Evidence [1988] (Grafton, Sue)
◻ Eagle Catcher [1995] (Coel, Margaret)
Eagles Die Too [1992] (O'Brien, Meg)
East Is East [1991] (Lathen, Emma)
Easy Day for a Lady [1994] (Linscott, Gillian)
◻ Easy Prey [1959] (Bell, Josephine)
Eat, Drink, and Be Buried [1994] (Kingsbury, Kate)
Echoing Strangers [1952] (Mitchell, Gladys)
◻ Edge of the Crazies [1995] (Harrison, Jamie)
◻ Edited Out [1994] (Haddock, Lisa)
◻ Edwin of the Iron Shoes [1977] (Muller, Marcia)
Eel Pie Murders [1933] (Frome, David)
Eel Pie Mystery [1933] (Frome, David)
◻ Eight Dogs Flying [1994] (Wilson, Karen Ann)
◻ 8 Faces at 3 [1939] (Rice, Craig)
Elected to Die [1996] (Wolzien, Valerie)
Elective Murder [1995] (McGiffin, Janet)
Electric City [1994] (Beck, K. K.)
Elegy in a Country Graveyard [1990] (Peterson, Audrey)
Element of Doubt [1987] (Simpson, Dorothy)
Elephants Can Remember [1972] (Christie, Agatha)
Elephants' Graveyard [1993] (McQuillan, Karin)
Elk and the Evidence [1952] (Scherf, Margaret)
Elusive Mrs. Pollifax [1971] (Gilman, Dorothy)
Elusive Quarry [1995] (Comfort, Barbara)
Emerald Lizard [1991] (Wiltz, Chris)
Emergency in the Pyrenees [1965] (Bridge, Ann)
◻ Emergency Murder [1992] (McGiffin, Janet)
Emily Dickinson Is Dead [1984] (Langton, Jane) ☆
Emma Chizzit and the Mother Lode Marauder ['93] (Hall, M.B.)
Emma Chizzit and the Napa Nemesis [1992] (Hall, M. B.)
◻ Emma Chizzit and the Queen Anne Killer [1989] (Hall, M. B.)
Emma Chizzit and the Sacramento Stalker [1990] (Hall, M. B.)
Encore Murder [1989] (Babson, Marian)
◻ End of an Altruist [1994] (Logan, Margaret)
◻ End of April [1992] (Sumner, Penny)
End of the Line [1981] (OCork, Shannon)
Engaged to Murder [1949] (Heberden, M. V.)
English School of Murder [1990] (Edwards, Ruth Dudley)
Enrollment Cancelled [1952] (Olsen, D. B.)
Enter a Gentlewoman [1982] (Woods, Sara)
Enter a Murderer [1935] (Marsh, Ngaio)
Enter Certain Murderers [1966] (Woods, Sara)
◻ Enter Second Murderer [1988] (Knight, Alanna)
Enter the Corpse [1973] (Woods, Sara)
Envious Casca [1941] (Heyer, Georgette)
Episode at Toledo [1966] (Bridge, Ann)
◻ Epitaph for a Dead Actor [1960] (Gray, Dulcie)
Epitaph for a Lobbyist [1974] (Dominic, R. B.)
◻ Equal Opportunity Death [1983] (Dunlap, Susan)
Error In Judgment [1990] (Brod, D. C.)
Error of the Moon [1963] (Woods, Sara)
Escape to Fear [1958] (Foley, Rae)
Estate of the Beckoning Lady [1955] (Allingham, Margery)
Eternity Ring [1948] (Wentworth, Patricia)
Eve of St. Hyacinth [1996] (Sedley, Kate)
Even Cops' Daughters [1986] (Webb, Martha G.)
Even Yuppies Die [1993] (Babson, Marian)
◻ Every Breath You Take [1994] (Spring, Michelle) ☆ ☆
◻ Every Crooked Nanny [1992] (Trocheck, Kathy Hogan) ☆
Every Deadly Sin [1995] (Greenwood, Diane M.)
Every Second Thursday [1981] (Page, Emma)
◻ Everything You Have Is Mine [1991] (Scoppettone, S.)
◻ Everywhere That Mary Went [1993] (Scottoline, Lisa) ☆

Eviction by Death [1993] (Yeager, Dorian)
Evidence of Things Seen [1943] (Daly, Elizabeth)
Evil Angels Among Them [1995] (Charles, Kate)
Evil That Men Do [1993] (Knight, Alanna)
Evil Under the Sun [1941] (Christie, Agatha)
Ewe Lamb [1968] (Erskine, Margaret)
Excellent Mystery [1985] (Peters, Ellis)
Exception to Murder [1992] (Wingate, Anne)
Exhaustive Inquiries [1994] (Rowlands, Betty)
Existing Solutions [1993] (Jordan, Jennifer)
Exit a Star [1941] (Knight, Kathleen Moore)
◻ Exit Actors, Dying [1979] (Arnold, Margot)
Exit Murderer [1978] (Woods, Sara)
Exit This Way [1950] (Heberden, M. V.)
Expert in Murder [1945] (Leonard, Charles L.)
Exploits of Death [1983] (Shannon, Dell)
Exploits of Dr. Sam: Johnson [1987] (de la Torre, Lillian)
Extra Kill [1961] (Shannon, Dell)
Eye of Anna [1989] (Wingate, Anne)
Eye of the Storm [1988] (Muller, Marcia)
Eyes in the Wall [1934] (Wells, Carolyn)
Eyes on Utopia Murders [1981] (D'Amato, Barbara)
Eyewitness to Murder [1992] (Belfort, Sophie)

F

"F" is for Fugitive [1989] (Grafton, Sue)
◻ Face of a Stranger [1990] (Perry, Anne) ☆
Face of Death [1985] (Grant-Adamson, Lesley)
Face Value [1994] (Matera, Lia)
Failure to Appear [1993] (Jance, J. A.) ★
Faint Praise [1995] (Hart, Ellen)
Faintly Speaking [1954] (Mitchell, Gladys)
◻ Fair Game [1993] (Krich, Rochelle Majer) ☆
Fair Game [1994] (Radley, Sheila)
Fair Play [1995] (Beecham, Rose)
Faith, Hope and Homicide [1991] (Mann, Jessica)
Fall from Grace [1991] (Wright, L. R.)
Fall in Denver [1995] (Andrews, Sarah)
Fall of Lucas Kendrick [1988] (Hooper, Kay)
Fall Over Cliff [1938] (Bell, Josephine)
Fallen Angel [1984] (Cohen, Anthea)
◻ Fallen into the Pit [1951] (Peters, Ellis)
Falling Star [1964] (Moyes, Patricia)
Falling Star [1979] (O'Donnell, Lillian)
False Notes [1990] (Yarbro, Chelsea Quinn)
False Prophet [1992] (Kellerman, Faye)
False Scent [1959] (Marsh, Ngaio)
False to Any Man [1939] (Ford, Leslie)
Family Album [1995] (Oleksiw, Susan)
Family at Tammerron [1965] (Erskine, Margaret)
Family Practice [1995] (Weir, Charlene)
Family Skeleton [1949] (Disney, Doris Miles)
◻ Family Vault [1979] (MacLeod, Charlotte)
◻ Famine of Horses [1995] (Chisholm, P. F.)
Fanatic of Fez [1943] (Leonard, Charles L.)
◻ Far and Deadly Cry [1995] (Holbrook, Teri)
Fare Play [1995] (Paul, Barbara)
Farewell to Yarns [1991] (Churchill, Jill)
Farmhouse [1947] (Reilly, Helen)
Farrier's Lane [1993] (Perry, Anne)
Fashion in Shrouds [1938] (Allingham, Margery)
Fat Lands [1993] (Dunant, Sarah) ★
Fat-Free and Fatal [1993] (Girdner, Jaqueline)
Fatal Advent [1989] (Holland, Isabelle)
Fatal Charm [1988] (Morice, Anne)

F . . . continued

Fatal Cut [1996] (Green, Christine)
■ Fatal Diagnosis [1990] (Kittredge, Mary)
Fatal Flashback [1989] (Fulton, Eileen)
Fatal Lady [1964] (Foley, Rae)
Fatal Relations [1955] (Erskine, Margaret)
Fatal Reunion [1989] (McNab, Claire)
Fatal Thaw [1993] (Stabenow, Dana)
Fatality at Bath & Wells [1986] (Livingston, Nancy)
Fate Worse Than Death [1985] (Radley, Sheila)
Father, Forgive Me [1993] (Burden, Pat)
Fault in the Structure [1977] (Mitchell, Gladys)
Fear Sign [1933] (Allingham, Margery)
Fearful Symmetry [1988] (Waltch, Lilla M.)
Feast of Murder [1992] (Haddam, Jane)
Feathers Left Around [1923] (Wells, Carolyn)
February Face [1987] (Adamson, M. J.)
February Mourning [1990] (Wakefield, Hannah)
Felony at Random [1979] (Shannon, Dell)
Felony File [1980] (Shannon, Dell)
Felony Report [1984] (Linington, Elizabeth)
Femmes Fatal [1992] (Cannell, Dorothy)
■ Festering Lilies [1990] (Cooper, Natasha)
Festival of Deaths [1993] (Haddam, Jane)
Fete Worse than Death [1990] (Christmas, Joyce)
■ Fetish [1987] (Hart, Jeanne) ☆
Fevered [1988] (Drake, Alison)
■ Few Dying Words [1994] (Gosling, Paula)
Fiasco in Fulham [1963] (Bell, Josephine)
Fifth Rapunzel [1990] (Gill, B. M.)
Figure Away [1937] (Taylor, Phoebe Atwood)
File for Record [1943] (Tilton, Alice)
File Under: Arson [1994] (Lacey, Sarah)
■ File Under: Deceased [1992] (Lacey, Sarah)
File Under: Jeopardy [1995] (Lacey, Sarah)
File Under: Missing [1993] (Lacey, Sarah)
■ Final Appeal [1994] (Scottoline, Lisa) ★
Final Arrangements [1996] (Murray, Donna Huston)
Final Curtain [1947] (Marsh, Ngaio)
Final Cut [1995] (Haddock, Lisa)
■ Final Design [1993] (Gilpatrick, Noreen)
Final Moments [1987] (Page, Emma)
Final Option [1994] (Hartzmark, Gini)
Final Edition [1991] (McDermid, Val)
Final Rest [1993] (Morell, Mary)
■ Final Session [1991] (Morell, Mary)
Find the Woman [1962] (Disney, Doris Miles)
Finders Keepers [1990] (Travis, Elizabeth)
Fine Distinctions [1991] (Valentine, Deborah) ☆
Fine Place for Death [1995] (Granger, Ann)
Fingerprint [1964] (Gilbert, Anthony)
Fingerprint [1956] (Wentworth, Patricia)
Finishing Touch [1993] (Rowlands, Betty)
Fire and Fog [1996] (Day, Dianne)
Fire at Will [1950] (Disney, Doris Miles)
Fire Carrier [1996] (Hager, Jean)
Fire Engine That Disappeared [1971] (Sjöwall, Maj & Per W.)
Fire in the Blood [1991] (Elrod, P. N.)
Firestorm [1996] (Barr, Nevada)
Fires at Fairlawn [1954] (Bell, Josephine)
First Come, First Kill [1962] (Lockridge, Frances & R.)
First Hit of the Season [1984] (Dentinger, Jane)
■ First Kill All the Lawyers [1988] (Shankman, Sarah)
First Pedigree Murder [1994] (Cleary, Melissa)
First Wife, Twice Removed [1993] (Curzon, Clare)

Fit of Tempera [1994] (Daheim, Mary)
Five Alarm Fire [1996] (Borton, D. B.)
Five Bells and Bladebone [1987] (Grimes, Martha)
Five Little Pigs [1941] (Christie, Agatha)
Five Red Herrings [1931] (Sayers, Dorothy L.)
■ Flashpoint [1995] (Hightower, Lynn S.)
Flat Tire in Fulham [1963] (Bell, Josephine)
Flight of a Witch [1964] (Peters, Ellis)
Flight of the Archangel [1985] (Holland, Isabelle)
Flowers for His Funeral [1994] (Granger, Ann)
Flowers for the Judge [1936] (Allingham, Margery)
Flush of Shadows [1995] (Wilhelm, Kate)
Flying Red Horse [1949] (Crane, Frances)
Flying Too High [1990] (Greenwood, Kerry)
Flynn [1991] (Grant-Adamson, Lesley)
Fog of Doubt [1953] (Brand, Christianna)
Foggy, Foggy Death [1950] (Lockridge, Frances & R.)
Follow Me [1960] (Reilly, Helen)
■ Following Jane [1993] (Singer, Shelley)
Foo Dog [1971] (Wells, Tobias)
■ Fool Me Once [1994] (Kreuter, Katherine E.)
■ Fool's Puzzle [1994] (Fowler, Earlene) ☆
Foot in the Grave [1973] (Ferrars, E. X.)
Footbridge to Death [1947] (Knight, Kathleen Moore)
Footsteps Behind Me [1953] (Gilbert, Anthony)
Footsteps in the Blood [1993] (Melville, Jennie)
For Every Evil [1995] (Hart, Ellen)
For Goodness' Sake [1935] (Wells, Carolyn)
For the Love of Murder [1949] (Scherf, Margaret)
For the Sake of Elena [1992] (George, Elizabeth)
Fortieth Birthday Body [1989] (Wolzien, Valerie)
Foul Play [1991] (Thomson, June)
Fountain of Death [1995] (Haddam, Jane)
Four Elements of Murder [1995] (Borton, D. B.)
4:50 from Paddington [1957] (Christie, Agatha)
Fourth Funeral [1948] (Leonard, Charles L.)
Fourth Postman [1948] (Rice, Craig)
■ Fourth Stage of Gainsborough Brown [1977] (Watson, C.)
Fowl Prey [1991] (Daheim, Mary)
Foxglove [1992] (Kelly, Mary Ann)
Frame Grabber [1992] (Danks, Denise)
Framed in Blue [1991] (Brod, D. C.)
Franchise Affair [1949] (Tey, Josephine)
Free Draw [1984] (Singer, Shelley)
Fresh Kills [1995] (Wheat, Carolyn)
Friend or Faux [1991] (Christmas, Joyce)
■ Friends Till the End [1989] (Dank, Gloria)
Frog and the Scorpion [1986] (Maxwell, A. E.)
Frog in the Throat [1980] (Ferrars, E. X.)
■ From Doon with Death [1964] (Rendell, Ruth)
From Here to Paternity [1995] (Churchill, Jill)
From Natural Causes [1939] (Bell, Josephine)
From Potter's Field [1995] (Cornwell, Patricia)
From This Dark Stairway [1931] (Eberhart, Mignon G.)
Frozen Stiff [1993] (Mason, Sarah Jill)
Fugitive Colors [1995] (Maron, Margaret)
Fugitive from Murder [1940] (Heberden, M. V.)
Full Commission [1992] (Brennan, Carol)
Full Cry [1985] (Tone, Teona)
Full House [1986] (Singer, Shelley)
Full Stop [1995] (Smith, Joan)
Fuller's Earth [1932] (Wells, Carolyn)
■ Funeral Sites [1982] (Mann, Jessica)
Funerals are Fatal [1953] (Christie, Agatha)
■ Funny as a Dead Comic [1993] (Cooper, Susan Rogers)
Funny as a Dead Relative [1994] (Cooper, Susan Rogers)
Furthest Fury [1924] (Wells, Carolyn)

G

"G" is for Gumshoe [1990] (Grafton, Sue) ★ ★
Gallows Bird [1993] (Duffy, Margaret)
Gallows for the Groom [1947] (Olsen, D. B.)
Games to Keep the Dark Away [1984] (Muller, Marcia)
🔟 Garden Club [1992] (Jackson, Muriel Resnick)
🔟 Garden of Malice [1983] (Kenney, Susan)
Gatsby's Vineyard [1987] (Maxwell, A. E.)
🔟 Gaudi Afternoon [1990] (Wilson, Barbara) ★
Gaudy Night [1935] (Sayers, Dorothy L.)
Gazebo [1956] (Wentworth, Patricia)
Gemini Doublecross [1995] (Mather, Linda)
🔟 Gemini Man [1985] (Kelly, Susan) ☆
Gemini Trip [1977] (Law, Janice)
🔟 Generous Death [1984] (Pickard, Nancy)
Gentleman Called [1958] (Davis, Dorothy Salisbury)
George Eliot Murders [1995] (Skom, Edith)
Getting Away with Murder [1984] (Morice, Anne)
Getting Mine [1991] (Femling, Jean)
Ghost and Mrs. Jeffries [1993] (Brightwell, Emily)
Ghost in the Closet [1995] (Maney, Mabel)
🔟 Ghost Motel [1994] (Manthorne, Jackie)
Ghost of an Idea [1981] (Challis, Mary)
Ghost Walker [1996] (Coel, Margaret)
Ghostland [1992] (Hager, Jean)
Ghosts Can't Kill [1950] (Heberden, M. V.)
Ghosts' High Noon [1930] (Wells, Carolyn)
Gila Monster [1994] (Dengler, Sandy)
Gilbert's Last Toothache [1949] (Scherf, Margaret)
Gilgamesh [1989] (Bannister, Jo)
Gilt-Edged Guilt [1938] (Wells, Carolyn)
Girl in the Cellar [1961] (Wentworth, Patricia)
Girl on the Loose [1958] (Fickling, G. G.)
Girl on the Prowl [1959] (Fickling, G. G.)
Girl Who Was Clairvoyant [1982] (Warner, Mignon)
🔟 Give a Corpse a Bad Name [1940] (Ferrars, E. X.)
Give Death a Name [1957] (Gilbert, Anthony)
Give My Secrets Back [1995] (Allen, Kate)
Give up the Ghost [1949] (Erskine, Margaret)
Glade Manor Murder [1988] (Lemarchand, Elizabeth)
Gladstone Bag [1989] (MacLeod, Charlotte)
Glass Ceiling [1995] (Donald, Anabel)
Glass Mask [1944] (Offord, Lenore Glen)
Glass on the Stairs [1954] (Scherf, Margaret)
🔟 Glory Day [1989] (Scott, Rosie)
🔟 Glory Hole Murders [1985] (Fennelly, Tony) ☆
Glory in Death [1996] (Robb, J. D.)
Goblin Market [1993] (Douglas, Lauren Wright)
Goblin Market [1943] (McCloy, Helen)
God in Concord [1992] (Langton, Jane)
Going Concern [1993] (Aird, Catherine)
Going Down of the Sun [1990] (Bannister, Jo)
Going for the Gold [1981] (Lathen, Emma)
Going, Going, Gone [1943] (Taylor, Phoebe Atwood)
Going Out in Style [1990] (Dank, Gloria)
Gold Bag [1911] (Wells, Carolyn)
🔟 Gold Coast Nocturne [1951] (Nielsen, Helen)
Golden Box [1942] (Crane, Frances)
🔟 Gone Away [1989] (Holt, Hazel)
Gone Quiet [1994] (Bland, Eleanor Taylor)
Gone to Her Death [1990] (McGown, Jill)
Gone to the Dogs [1992] (Conant, Susan)
Good and Dead [1986] (Langton, Jane)
🔟 Good Daughter [1994] (Lee W. W.)

Good Fight [1990] (Matera, Lia)
🔟 Good Friday Murder [1992] (Harris, Lee) ☆
Good King Sauerkraut [1989] (Paul, Barbara)
Good Morning, Irene [1990] (Douglas, Carole Nelson)
🔟 Good Night, Mr. Holmes [1990] (Douglas, Carole N.) ★
Good Night, Sweet Prince [1990] (Berry, Carole)
Good Night to Kill [1989] (O'Donnell, Lillian) ★
🔟 Good Weekend for Murder [1987] (Jordan, Jennifer)
Good Year for a Corpse [1994] (Wolzien, Valerie)
🔟 Goodbye Nanny Gray [1987] (Stacey, Susannah) ☆
🔟 Goodnight, Irene [1993] (Burke, Jan) ☆ ☆
Gory Dew [1970] (Mitchell, Gladys)
Gospel Makers [1994] (Fraser, Anthea)
Grand Slam [1994] (Moody, Susan)
🔟 Grandfather Medicine [1989] (Hager, Jean)
Grandmother's House [1991] (La Pierre, Janet)
Grass Widow [1996] (Holbrook, Teri)
Grass-Widow's Tale [1968] (Peters, Ellis)
Grave Consequences [1989] (Comfort, Barbara)
Grave Goods [1984] (Mann, Jessica)
Grave Matters [1973] (Yorke, Margaret)
Grave Mistake [1978] (Marsh, Ngaio)
Grave Music [1994] (Harrod-Eagles, Cynthia)
Grave Responsibility [1990] (Stacey, Susannah)
Grave Secrets [1994] (Hendricksen, Louise)
🔟 Grave Talent [1993] (King, Laurie R.) ★ ☆
Graves of Academe [1985] (Kenney, Susan)
🔟 Gravestone [1992] (Carlson, P. M.)
Graveyard Plot [1959] (Erskine, Margaret)
Gray Magic [1987] (Dreher, Sarah)
Gray Stranger [1958] (Crane, Frances)
Great Day for the Deadly [1992] (Haddam, Jane)
🔟 Great Deliverance [1988] (George, Elizabeth) ★ ★ ☆ ☆
Green for Danger [1944] (Brand, Christianna)
Green Grow the Dollars [1982] (Lathen, Emma) ★
Green Mill Murder [1993] (Greenwood, Kerry)
Green Plaid Pants [1951] (Scherf, Margaret)
🔟 Greenmask! [1964] (Linington, Elizabeth)
Greenstone Griffins [1983] (Mitchell, Gladys)
🔟 Grey Mask [1928] (Wentworth, Patricia)
Grievous Sin [1993] (Kellerman, Faye)
Grim Pickings [1991] (Rowe, Jennifer)
Grim Rehearsal [1950] (Fenisong, Ruth)
🔟 Grime & Punishment [1989] (Churchill, Jill) ★ ★ ☆
Grizzly, A Murder [1994] (Andreae, Christine)
Grizzly Trail [1984] (Moffat, Gwen)
Gryth Chalice Mystery [1931] (Allingham, Margery)
Groaning Board [1997] (Meyers, Annette)
Groaning Spinney [1950] (Mitchell, Gladys)
Groomed for Death [1994] (Banks, Carolyn)
Grounds for Murder [1995] (Kingsbury, Kate)
Grub-and-Stakers House a Haunt [1993] (Craig, Alisa)
🔟 Grub-and-Stakers Move a Mountain [1981] (Craig, Alisa)
Grub-and-Stakers Pinch a Poke [1988] (Craig, Alisa)
Grub-and-Stakers Quilt a Bee [1985] (Craig, Alisa)
Grub-and-Stakers Spin a Yarn [1990] (Craig, Alisa)
Guardian Angel [1985] (Cohen, Anthea)
Guardian Angel [1991] (Paretsky, Sara)
Guilt is Plain [1937] (Frome, David)
Guilty Knowledge [1986] (Grant-Adamson, Lesley)
🔟 Guilty Pleasures [1993] (Hamilton, Laurell K.)
Guilty Thing Surprised [1970] (Rendell, Ruth)
Gun for Honey [1958] (Fickling, G. G.)
🔟 Gun in Daniel Webster's Bust [1949] (Scherf, Margaret)

H

"H" is for Homicide [1991] (Grafton, Sue)
Habit of Fear [1987] (Davis, Dorothy Salisbury)
Habit of Loving [1979] (Thomson, June)
Hacker [1992] (Martin, Lee)
Hal's Own Murder Case [1989] (Martin, Lee)
Half a Mind [1990] (Hornsby, Wendy)
Hallelujah Murders [1991] (Tell, Dorothy)
Hallowe'en Party [1969] (Christie, Agatha)
∎ Hallowed Murder [1989] (Hart, Ellen) ☆
He Huffed and He Puffed [1989] (Paul, Barbara)
Hickory, Dickory Stock [1996] (Cooper, Susan Rogers)
High Island Blues [1996] (Cleeves, Ann)
Hoofprints [1996] (Crum, Laura)
Halloween Murder [1955] (Disney, Doris Miles)
∎ Hamlet Trap [1987] (Wilhelm, Kate)
∎ Hammersmith Murders [1930] (Frome, David)
Hand and Ring [1883] (Green, Anna Katherine)
Hand in Glove [1962] (Marsh, Ngaio)
Hand of the Lion [1987] (Coker, Carolyn)
∎ Hands of Healing Murder [1980] (D'Amato, Barbara)
Hands up, Miss Seeton [1992] (Crane, Hamilton)
Hang the Consequences [1984] (Meek, M. R. D.)
Hangdog Hustle [1995] (Pincus, Elizabeth)
Hanged for a Sheep [1942] (Lockridge, Frances & R.)
Hanged Man [1993] (Sedley, Kate)
Hanging on the Wire [1992] (Linscott, Gillian)
Hanging Time [1995] (Glass, Leslie)
Hangman's Beautiful Daughter [1992] (McCrumb, S.) ☆ ☆
Hangman's Curfew [1941] (Mitchell, Gladys)
Hangman's Holiday [1933] (Sayers, D. L.)
Hangman's Root [1994] (Albert, Susan Wittig)
Hanky Panky [1995] (McCafferty, Taylor)
Happy Never After [1995] (Trocheck, Kathy Hogan)
Hard Bargain [1992] (Matera, Lia)
Hard Case [1994] (D'Amato, Barbara)
Hard Christmas [1995] (D'Amato, Barbara)
Hard Luck [1992] (D'Amato, Barbara)
Hard Tack [1991] (D'Amato, Barbara)
Hard Women [1993] (D'Amato, Barbara)
∎ Hardball [1990] (D'Amato, Barbara)
Hardware [1995] (Barnes, Linda)
Hare Today, Gone Tomorrow [1991] (O'Brien, Meg)
Hark, Hark, the Watchdogs Bark [1975] (Wells, Tobias)
Harriet Farewell [1975] (Erskine, Margaret)
Haunted Lady [1942] (Rinehart, Mary Roberts)
Have His Carcase [1932] (Sayers, Dorothy L.)
Have Mercy Upon Us [1974] (Wells, Tobias)
Having a Wonderful Crime [1943] (Rice, Craig)
He Came by Night [1944] (Gilbert, Anthony)
He Huffed and He Puffed [1989] (Paul, Barbara)
He Was Her Man [1993] (Shankman, Sarah)
Head Case [1985] (Cody, Liza)
∎ Headhunt [1991] (Brennan, Carol)
Heading Uptown [1993] (Piesman, Marissa)
∎ Heads You Lose [1941] (Brand, Christianna)
∎ Healthy Body [1984] (Linscott, Gillian)
Healthy Grave [1980] (Leek, Margaret)
∎ Healthy, Wealthy & Dead [1994] (North, Suzanne) ☆
Hearse in May-Day [1972] (Mitchell, Gladys)
∎ Heavy as Lead [1966] (Torrie, Malcolm)
∎ Heir Condition [1995] (McClellan, Tierney)
Hell Bent for Heaven [1983] (OCork, Shannon)
Hell's Angel [1986] (Cohen, Anthea)
Help the Poor Struggler [1985] (Grimes, Martha)

Henrietta Who? [1968] (Aird, Catherine)
Hercule Poirot's Christmas [1938] (Christie, Agatha)
Here Comes a Chopper [1946] (Mitchell, Gladys)
Here Lies Gloria Mundy [1982] (Mitchell, Gladys)
Heretic's Apprentice [1989] (Peters, Ellis)
Hermit of Eyton Forest [1987] (Peters, Ellis)
Hickory, Dickory, Death [1955] (Christie, Agatha)
Hickory, Dickory, Dock [1955] (Christie, Agatha)
Hickory, Dickory, Stock [1996] (Cooper, Susan Rogers)
Hidden Agenda [1989] (Matera, Lia)
∎ Hidden Agenda [1985] (Porter, Anna)
Hide and Seek [1993] (Woods, Sherryl)
Hide My Eyes [1958] (Allingham, Margery) ★
High Constable [1994] (Meyers, Maan)
High Fall [1994] (Dunlap, Susan)
High Island Blues [1996] (Cleeves, Ann)
High Strangeness [1992] (Drake, Alison)
Highgate Rise [1991] (Perry, Anne)
Highland Laddie Gone [1986] (McCrumb, Sharyn)
∎ Hippie in the Wall [1994] (Fennelly, Tony)
His Burial Too [1973] (Aird, Catherine)
Hit and Run [1989] (O'Callaghan, Maxine)
Ho-Ho Homicide [1995] (Sawyer, Corinne Holt)
Hobby of Murder [1994] (Ferrars, E. X.)
Holiday for Murder [1938] (Christie, Agatha)
∎ Holiday Murders [1992] (Landreth, Marsha)
Hollow [1946] (Christie, Agatha)
Hollow Chest [1941] (Tilton, Alice)
Hollow Vengeance [1982] (Morice, Anne)
Holy Innocents [1994] (Sedley, Kate)
Holy Terrors [1992] (Daheim, Mary)
Holy Terrors [1994] (Greenwood, Diane M.)
Holy Thief [1992] (Peters, Ellis)
Home Sweet Homicide [1992] (Morgan, Kate)
Homefront Murders [1995] (Meredith, D. R.)
Homemade Sin [1994] (Trocheck, Kathy Hogan)
∎ Hometown Heroes [1990] (McShea, Susanna Hofmann)
Homicide House [1950] (Frome, David)
Honey in the Flesh [1959] (Fickling, G. G.)
Honey on Her Tail [1971] (Fickling, G. G.)
Honeymoon with Murder [1988] (Hart, Carolyn G.) ★
Honolulu Murder Story [1946] (Ford, Leslie)
Honolulu Story [1946] (Ford, Leslie)
Hoofprints [1996] (Crum, Laura)
∎ Hope Against Hope [1990] (Kelly, Susan B.)
Hope Will Answer [1993] (Kelly, Susan B.)
∎ Hopeless Case [1992] (Beck, K. K.)
Horror House [1931] (Wells, Carolyn)
Horror on the Ruby X [1956] (Crane, Frances)
∎ Horse of a Different Killer [1995] (Jaffe, Jody)
Horse You Came in On [1993] (Grimes, Martha)
Hot Money [1993] (Woods, Sherryl)
∎ Hot Property [1991] (Woods, Sherryl)
Hot Schemes [1994] (Woods, Sherryl)
Hot Secret [1992] (Woods, Sherryl)
Hot Ticket [1995] (Woods, Sherryl)
∎ Hot Water [1990] (Gunning, Sally)
Hotel Morgue [1991] (Laurence, Janet)
Hounded to Death [1993] (Cleary, Melissa)
Hour of Our Death [1995] (Fallon, Ann C.)
∎ Hour of the Knife [1991] (Zukowski, Sharon)
House in Hook Street [1978] (Erskine, Margaret)
House of Blues [1995] (Smith, Julie)
House of Cards [1991] (Hooper, Kay) ☆
House of Green Turf [1969] (Peters, Ellis)
House of the Enchantress [1959] (Erskine, Margaret)

H . . . continued

House of the Whispering Pines [1910] (Green, Anna K.)
House Without the Door [1942] (Daly, Elizabeth)
Houston in the Rear View Mirror [1990] (Cooper, Susan R.)
Houston Town [1992] (Powell, Deborah)
How I Spent My Summer Vacation [1994] (Roberts, G.)
How to Kill a Man [1972] (Wells, Tobias)
How to Murder the Man of Your Dreams [1995] (Cannell, D.)
How to Murder Your Mother-in-law [1994] (Cannell, D.)
Huckleberry Fiend [1987] (Smith, Julie)
Huddle [1936] (Wells, Carolyn)
Hunter and the Hunted [1979] (Egan, Lesley)
1 Hush, Gabriel! [1940] (Johns, Veronica Parker)
1 Hush, Money [1989] (Femling, Jean)
1 Hush-Hush Murders [1937] (Yates, Margaret Evelyn T.)
Hyde Park Headsman [1994] (Perry, Anne)

I

I Am the Only Running Footman [1986] (Grimes, Martha)
1 I Give You Five Days [1983] (Curzon, Clare)
"I" is for Innocent [1992] (Grafton, Sue) ★
I Knew MacBean [1948] (Erskine, Margaret)
1 I Left My Heart [1991] (Maiman, Jaye)
I Met Murder [1985] (Ferrars, E. X.)
I. O. U. [1991] (Pickard, Nancy) ★ ★ ☆
I Want to Go Home [1948] (Lockridge, Frances & Richard)
I'd Rather Be in Philadelphia [1991] (Roberts, Gillian)
I'll Be Leaving You Always [1993] (Scoppettone, Sandra)
Ice Water [1993] (Gunning, Sally)
Iced [1995] (Clark, Carol Higgins)
Iced [1994] (Robitaille, Julie)
Idol Bones [1993] (Greenwood, Diane M.)
1 If Ever I Return, Pretty Peggy-O [1990] (McCrumb, S.) ★ ☆
If I'd Killed Him When I Met Him [1995] (McCrumb, S.)
1 If Looks Could Kill [1995] (Furie, Ruthe)
Ill Wind [1995] (Barr, Nevada)
Ill-Met by Moonlight [1937] (Ford, Leslie)
Illusion [1984] (Warner, Mignon)
Immortal in Death [1996] (Robb, J. D.)
Imperfect Spy [1995] (Cross, Amanda)
Importance of Being Murdered [1939] (Wells, Carolyn)
Improbable Cause [1988] (Jance, J. A.)
Improbable Fiction [1970] (Woods, Sara)
In at the Deep End [1994] (Donald, Anabel)
In at the Kill [1978] (Ferrars, E. X.)
1 In Blacker Moments [1994] (Schenkel, S. E.)
1 In Murder We Trust [1995] (Hyde, Eleanor)
In Remembrance of Rose [1986] (Meek, M. R. D.)
In Serena's Web [1987] (Hooper, Kay)
In Stony Places [1991] (Mitchell, Kay)
In the Balance [1941] (Wentworth, Patricia)
In the Bleak Midwinter [1996] (Hall, Patricia)
1 In the Dark [1994] (Brennan, Carol)
In the Dead of Summer [1995] (Roberts, Gillian)
In the Death of a Man [1970] (Egan, Lesley)
1 In the Game [1991] (Baker, Nikki)
1 In the Last Analysis [1964] (Cross, Amanda) ☆
In the Midnight Hour [1995] (Tyre, Peg)
In the Onyx Lobby [1920] (Wells, Carolyn)
In the Presence of the Enemy [1996] (George, Elizabeth)
1 In the Shadow of King's [1984] (Kelly, Nora)
In the Teeth of Adversity [1990] (Babson, Marian)
In the Teeth of the Evidence [1939] (Sayers, Dorothy L.)
In the Tiger's Cage [1936] (Wells, Carolyn)

Incident at Parga [1987] (Livingston, Nancy)
1 Indemnity Only [1982] (Paretsky, Sara)
Indigo Necklace [1945] (Crane, Frances)
Inherited Murder [1994] (Martin, Lee)
Initials Only [1911] (Green, Anna Katherine)
Injustice for All [1986] (Jance, J. A.)
Innocent Bottle [1945] (Gilbert, Anthony)
Innocent Flower [1945] (Armstrong, Charlotte)
1 Inspector and Mrs. Jeffries [1993] (Brightwell, Emily)
Inspector's Holiday [1971] (Lockridge, Frances & Richard)
Intersection of Law and Desire [1995] (Redmann, J. M.)
Interview with Mattie [1995] (Singer, Shelley)
1 Introducing Amanda Valentine [1992] (Beecham, Rose)
1 Introducing C. B. Greenfield [1979] (Kallen, Lucille)
1 Invisible Worm [1941] (Millar, Margaret)
Irene at Large [1992] (Douglas, Carole Nelson)
Irene's Last Waltz [1994] (Douglas, Carole Nelson)
Irish Chain [1995] (Fowler, Earlene)
Iron Clew [1947] (Tilton, Alice)
Iron Hand [1947] (Tilton, Alice)
Iron Gates [1945] (Millar, Margaret)
Iron Hand of Mars [1992] (Davis, Lindsey)
Is She Dead Too? [1955] (Gilbert, Anthony)
1 Is There a Traitor in the House [1964] (McGerr, Patricia)
Island Girl [1991] (Berry, Carole)
It Takes a Thief [1989] (Hooper, Kay)
It's Her Funeral [1992] (Christmas, Joyce)
It's Murder Mr. Potter [1961] (Foley, Rae)
It's Murder with Dover [1973] (Porter, Joyce)
Ivory Dagger [1951] (Wentworth, Patricia)

J

1 J. Alfred Prufrock Murders [1988] (Sawyer, Corinne H.) ☆
"J" is for Judgment [1993] (Grafton, Sue)
1 Jacoby's First Case [1980] (Smith, J. C. S.)
James Joyce Murder [1967] (Cross, Amanda)
Javelin for Jonah [1974] (Mitchell, Gladys)
Jazz Funeral [1993] (:)
Jemima Shore at the Sunny Grave [1993] (Fraser, A.)
Jemima Shore's First Case & Other Stories [1986]
    (Fraser, Antonia)
Jersey Monkey [1992] (Gallison, Kate)
Jerusalem Inn [1984] (Grimes, Martha)
Jethro Hammer [1944] (Venning, Michael)
1 Jinx [1992] (Robitaille, Julie)
Jinx High [1991] (Lackey, Mercedes)
Johnny Underground [1965] (Moyes, Patricia)
Judge Is Reversed [1960] (Lockridge, Frances & Richard)
Julius Hose [1995] (Harris, Charlaine)
1 June Mail [1986] (Warmbold, Jean)
1 Just Another Day in Paradise [1985] (Maxwell, A. E.)
1 Just Desserts [1991] (Daheim, Mary) ☆
1 Just Desserts [1995] (McKevett, G. A.)
Just Enough Light to Kill [1988] (Maxwell, A. E.)
Justice [1995] (Kellerman, Faye)
1 Justice for Some [1993] (Wilhelm, Kate)

K

"K" is for Killer [1994] (Grafton, Sue) ★ ☆
Kahuna Killer [1951] (Sheridan, Juanita)
Kansas Troubles [1996] (Fowler, Earlene)
1 Karma [1981] (Dunlap, Susan)
Kat's Cradle [1991] (Kijewski, Karen)
Katapult [1990] (Kijewski, Karen)

K . . . *continued*

- Katwalk [1988] (Kijewski, Karen) ★ ★ ★
- Keeper at the Shrine [1995] (Highsmith, Domini)
  Keeper of the Mill [1995] (Kelly, Mary Ann)
- Keeping Secrets [1994] (Mickelbury, Penny)
  Key [1944] (Wentworth, Patricia)
  Key to Death [1954] (Lockridge, Frances & Richard)
  Kick Back[1993] (McDermid, Val)
  Kid's Stuff [1994] (Kelly, Susan B.)
  Kill Flash [1987] (MacGregor, T. J.)
  Kill or Cure [1995] (Kittredge, Mary)
  Kill with Kindness [1968] (Shannon, Dell)
  Killer [1938] (Wells, Carolyn)
  Killer in the Crowd [1954] (Tey, Josephine)
- KILLER.app [1996] (D'Amato, Barbara)
  Killer Dolphin [1966] (Marsh, Ngaio) ☆
  Killer in the Street [1967] (Nielsen, Helen)
  Killer Pancake [1995] (Davidson, Diane Mott)
- Killing Circle [1981] (Wiltz, Chris)
  Killing Cousins [1990] (Knight, Alanna)
  Killing Critics [1996] (O'Connell, Carol)
  Killing Cure [1993] (Hart, Ellen)
  Killing in Real Estate [1996] (McClellan, Tierney)
- Killing of Ellis Martin [1993] (Grindle, Lucretia)
  Killing of Monday Brown [1994] (Prowell, Sandra West) ☆
  Killing Orders [1985] (Paretsky, Sara)
  Killing the Goose [1944] (Lockridge, Frances & Richard)
  Killing with Kindness [1975] (Morice, Anne)
- Killings at Badger's Drift [1987] (Graham, Caroline) ★ ☆
  Killjoy [1995] (Cleeves, Ann)
  Kin Dread [1990] (MacGregor, T. J.)
  Kind of Healthy Grave [1986] (Mann, Jessica)
- Kindred Crimes [1990] (Dawson, Janet) ★ ☆ ☆ ☆
  King Is Dead [1992] (Shankman, Sarah)
  King of Hearts [1995] (Moody, Susan)
  King of Nothing [1992] (Maxwell, A. E.)
  King of the Mountain [1995] (Wren, M. K.)
  Kingdom of Death [1933] (Allingham, Margery)
  Kingsbridge Plot [1993] (Meyers, Maan)
  Kiss for a Killer [1960] (Fickling, G. G.)
  Kiss Yourself Goodbye [1989] (Fennelly, Tony)
  Kissing the Gunner's Daughter [1993] (Rendell, Ruth)
  Knave of Hearts [1962] (Shannon, Dell) ☆
  Knavish Crows [1971] (Woods, Sara)
  Knife at the Opera [1988] (Stacey, Susannah)
  Knife to Remember [1994] (Churchill, Jill)
- Knight Fall [1987] (Pulver, Mary Monica)
- Knight Must Fall [1985] (Wender, Theodora)
  Knives Have Edges [1968] (Woods, Sara)
  Knock, Knock, Who's There? [1964] (Gilbert, Anthony)
  Knocked for a Loop [1957] (Rice, Craig)
  Knocker on Death's Door [1970] (Peters, Ellis)

L

"L" is for Lawless [1995] (Grafton, Sue)
- Lace Curtain Murders [1986] (Belfort, Sophie)
  Ladies' Bane [1952] (Wentworth, Patricia)
- Ladies' Night [1988] (Bowers, Elisabeth)
  Lady Chapel [1994] (Robb, Candace M.)
  Lady Killer [1951] (Gilbert, Anthony)
- Lady on the Line [1983] (Tone, Teona)
- Lady with a Cool Eye [1973] (Moffat, Gwen)
  Ladybug, Ladybug [1994] (McShea, Susanna Hofmann)
  Ladykiller [1984] (O'Donnell, Lillian)

Lamb to the Slaughter [1996] (Quinn, Elizabeth)
Lament for a Dead Cowboy [1994] (Dain, Catherine) ☆
Lament for a Lady Laird [1982] (Arnold, Margot)
Lament for Christabel [1991] (Peterson, Audrey)
Lament for Leto [1971] (Mitchell, Gladys)
Lament for the Bride [1951] (Reilly, Helen)
Lament for Two Ladies [1991] (Hart, Jeanne)
- Larkspur [1990] (Simonson, Sheila)
  Last Act in Palmyra [1994] (Davis, Lindsey)
  Last Annual Slugfest [1986] (Dunlap, Susan)
- Last Billable Hour [1989] (Wolfe, Susan) ★
  Last Camel Died at Noon [1991] (Peters, Elizabeth) ☆
  Last Chance Country [1983] (Moffat, Gwen)
  Last Chants [1996] (Matera, Lia)
  Last Dinosaur [1994] (Dengler, Sandy)
  Last Ditch [1977] (Marsh, Ngaio)
  Last Gamble [1956] (Foley, Rae)
- Last Judgment [1985] (Clarke, Anna)
  Last of Her Lies [1996] (Taylor, Jean)
  Last Plane from Nice [1988] (Watson, Clarissa)
  Last Resort [1991] (Girdner, Jaqueline)
  Last Resort [1995] (Manthorne, Jackie)
  Last Respects [1982] (Aird, Catherine)
  Last Seen Alive [1985] (Simpson, Dorothy) ★
  Last Seen in London [1987] (Clarke, Anna)
  Last Straw [1954] (Disney, Doris Miles)
  Last Suppers [1994] (Davidson, Diane Mott)
  Last Tango of Delores Delgado [1992] (Day, Marele) ★
  Last Walk Home [1982] (Page, Emma)
- Last Will and Testament [1978] (Ferrars, E. X.)
  Late and Cold [1967] (Torrie, Malcolm)
  Late Lady [1992] (Stacey, Susannah)
  Late, Late in the Evening [1976] (Mitchell, Gladys)
  Late of This Parish [1992] (Eccles, Marjorie)
  Late Phoenix [1970] (Aird, Catherine)
  Latter End [1947] (Wentworth, Patricia)
  Laughing Corpse [1994] (Hamilton, Laurell K.)
  Laughing Policeman [1970] (Sjöwall, Maj & Per W.) ★
  Laurels are Poson [1942] (Mitchell, Gladys)
  Lavender House Murder [1992] (Baker, Nikki)
  Law's Delay [1977] (Woods, Sara)
- Lay It on the Line [1992] (Dain, Catherine) ☆
- Lay on, Mac Duff! [1942] (Armstrong, Charlotte)
  Leap of Faith [1994] (Zukowski, Sharon)
  Leave a Message for Willie [1984] (Muller, Marcia)
  Leave the Grave Green [1995] (Crombie, Deborah)
- Leavenworth Case [1878] (Green, Anna Katherine)
  Ledger [1970] (Uhnak, Dorothy) ★
  Left Leg [1940] (Tilton, Alice)
  Legacy in Blood [1936] (Allingham, Margery)
  Legacy of Danger [1970] (McGerr, Patricia)
  Legend of the Slain Soldiers [1985] (Muller, Marcia)
  Leisure Dying [1976] (O'Donnell, Lillian)
  Leper of St. Giles [1981] (Peters, Ellis)
- Lesson in Dying [1990] (Cleeves, Ann)
- Lessons [1994] (McAllester, Melanie)
- Lessons in Murder [1988] (McNab, Claire)
  Let Dead Enough Alone [1956] (Lockridge, Frances & R.)
  Let or Hindrane [1973] (Lemarchand, Elizabeth)
  Let's Choose Executors [1966] (Woods, Sara)
  Let's Rob Roy [1989] (Kraft, Gabrielle)
  Lethal Fixation [1993] (Shepherd, Stella)
  Lethal Genes [1996] (Grant, Linda)
  Lethal Legacy [1995] (Hendricksen, Louise)
- Letter of the Law [1987] (Berry, Carole)
  Library: No Murder Aloud [1993] (Steiner, Susan)

L . . . *continued*

🔳 Lickety Split [1996] (Trocheck, Kathy Hogan)
Lie Direct [1983] (Woods, Sara)
Lies That Bind [1993] (Van Gieson, Judith) ☆
🔳 Life and Crimes of Harry Lavender [1988] (Day, Marele)
🔳 Life of Adventure [1992] (Grant-Adamson, Lesley)
Lifeblood [1990] (Elrod, P. N.)
Lift up the Lid [1945] (Gilbert, Anthony)
Light Thickens [1982] (Marsh, Ngaio)
Light through the Glass [1984] (Lemarchand, Elizabeth)
🔳 Lighthearted Quest [1956] (Bridge, Ann)
Lights, Camera, Death [1988] (Fulton, Eileen)
Lily-White Boys [1991] (Fraser, Anthea)
🔳 Limping Man [1938] (Erskine, Margaret)
Line-up [1934] (Reilly, Helen)
Lion in the Valley [1986] (Peters, Elizabeth)
Lion in Wait [1963] (Gardiner, Dorothy)
Lion? or Murderer? [1963] (Gardiner, Dorothy)
Listening Eye [1955] (Wentworth, Patricia)
Literary Murder [1993] (Gur, Batya)
Little Boy Lost [1983] (Egan, Lesley)
Little Class on Murder [1989] (Hart, Carolyn G.) ★ ☆ ☆
Little Gentle Sleuthing [1990] (Rowlands, Betty)
Little Madness [1986] (Kallen, Lucille)
🔳 Little Neighborhood Murder [1989] (Orde, A. J.)
🔳 Lively Form of Death [1990] (Mitchell, Kay)
Lobster Pick Murder [1940] (Heberden, M. V.)
Locked Room [1973] (Sjöwall, Maj & Per Wahlöö)
Lockout [1994] (O'Donnell, Lillian)
London Particular [1953] (Brand, Christianna)
Lonesome Road [1939] (Wentworth, Patricia)
Long Body [1955] (McCloy, Helen)
Long Goodbyes [1993] (Baker, Nikki)
Long Revenge [1974] (Thomson, June)
Long Search [1990] (Holland, Isabelle)
Long Shadow [1932] (Gilbert, Anthony)
Long Skeleton [1958] (Lockridge, Frances & Richard)
Long Slow Whistle of the Moon [1996] (Ayres, Noreen)
Long Time Dead [1995] (Orde, A. J.)
Longer Bodies [1930] (Mitchell, Gladys)
Longer the Thread [1971] (Lathen, Emma)
Look Behind You Lady [1952] (Erskine, Margaret)
Look to the Lady [1931] (Allingham, Margery)
Looking for the Aardvark [1993] (Orde, A. J.)
Looking Glass Murder [1966] (Gilbert, Anthony)
Loose Connection [1989] (Meek, M. R. D.)
Lord Edgeware Dies [1933] (Christie, Agatha)
Lord Peter Views the Body [1929] (Sayers, Dorothy L.)
🔳 Lost Madonna [1983] (Holland, Isabelle)
Lost Man's Lane [1898] (Green, Anna Katherine)
Lost to Sight [1996] (Knight, Phyllis)
Lotus Affair [1971] (Wells, Tobias)
Love and Murder [1991] (Bowen, Gail)
Love Bytes [1994] (Chapman, Sally)
Love Lies Bleeding [1989] (Blackmur, L. L.)
🔳 Love Lies Slain [1989] (Blackmur, L. L.)
Love Me in Death [1951] (Olsen, D. B.)
Love nor Money [1991] (Grant, Linda) ☆
🔳 Love to Die For [1994] (Jorgensen, Christine T.)
Lovely in Her Bones [1985] (McCrumb, Sharyn)
Lover Scorned [1986] (Holland, Isabelle)
Lovers, Make Moan [1981] (Mitchell, Gladys)
Luck Runs Out [1979] (MacLeod, Charlotte)
Lucky Stiff [1945] (Rice, Craig)
Lullaby of Murder [1984] (Davis, Dorothy Salisbury)

Luminous Face [1921] (Wells, Carolyn)
Lunatic Cafe [1996] (Hamilton, Laurell K.)
Lying in Wait [1994] (Jance, J. A.)
Lying Jade [1953] (Ford, Leslie)

M

MacLurg Goes West [1968] (Petrie, Rhona)
MacPherson's Lament [1992] (McCrumb, Sharyn)
🔳 Madison Avenue Murder [1989] (Bennett, Liza)
Madness in Maggody [1991] (Hess, Joan)
Maggody in Manhattan [1992] (Hess, Joan)
🔳 Magic Mirror [1988] (Friedman, Mickey)
🔳 Mail-Order Murder [1993] (Meier, Leslie)
Main Course [1996] (Davidson, Diane Mott)
🔳 Main Line Is Murder [1995] (Murray, Donna Huston)
Major Vices [1995] (Daheim, Mary)
Make Me a Murderer [1961] (Butler, Gwendoline)
Makeover Murders [1993] (Rowe, Jennifer)
Making Good Blood [1989] (Melville, Jennie)
Malady in Madeira [1969] (Bridge, Ann)
🔳 Malice Domestic [1986] (Hardwick, Mollie)
Malice Domestic [1962] (Woods, Sara)
🔳 Malice in Maggody [1987] (Hess, Joan)
Malice Poetic [1995] (Rowlands, Betty)
Malicious Mischief [1971] (Egan, Lesley)
🔳 Malignant Heart [1958] (Sibley, Celestine)
🔳 Mallory's Oracle [1994] (O'Connell, Carol) ☆ ☆
Maltese Puppy [1995] (Cleary, Melissa)
Mamo Murders [1952] (Sheridan, Juanita)
Man from Scotland Yard [1932] (Frome, David)
Man in Gray [1958] (Crane, Frances)
🔳 Man in the Green Chevy [1988] (Cooper, Susan Rogers)
Man in the Moonlight [1940] (McCloy, Helen)
🔳 Man in the Queue [1929] (Tey, Josephine)
🔳 Man Lay Dead [1934] (Marsh, Ngaio)
Man Missing [1954] (Eberhart, Mignon G.)
Man on the Balcony [1968] (Sjöwall, Maj & Per Wahlöö)
Man Who Cast Two Shadows [1995] (O'Connell, Carol)
Man Who Fell Through the Earth [1919] (Wells, Carolyn)
Man Who Grew Tomatoes [1959] (Mitchell, Gladys)
🔳 Man Who Slept All Day [1942] (Venning, Michael)
🔳 Man Who Understood Cats [1993] (Dymmoch, M. A.) ★
Man Who Was Too Clever [1935] (Gilbert, Anthony)
Man Who Wasn't There [1937] (Gilbert, Anthony)
Man Who Went Up in Smoke [1969] (Sjöwall, Maj & P. W.)
🔳 Man with a Load of Mischief [1981] (Grimes, Martha)
Many Deadly Returns [1970] (Moyes, Patricia) ☆
Mark of Cain [1917] (Wells, Carolyn)
Mark of Murder [1964] (Shannon, Dell)
🔳 Mark Twain Murders [1989] (Skom, Edith) ☆ ☆ ☆
Marriage Is Murder [1987] (Pickard, Nancy) ★ ☆
Marshal and the Forgery [1995] (Nabb, Magdalen)
Marshal and the Madwoman [1988] (Nabb, Magdalen)
Marshal and the Murderer [1987] (Nabb, Magdalen)
Marshal at the Villa Torrini [1994] (Nabb, Magdalen)
Marshal Makes His Report [1991] (Nabb, Magdalen)
Marshal's Own Case [1990] (Nabb, Magdalen)
Martians in Maggody [1994] (Hess, Joan)
Martini Effect [1992] (Morison, B. J.)
Marvell College Murders [1991] (Belfort, Sophie)
🔳 Masculine Ending [1987] (Smith, Joan)
Masks and Faces [1984] (Curzon, Clare)
Masquerade in Blue [1991] (Brod, D. C.)
Master Murderer [1933] (Wells, Carolyn)
Match for a Murderer [1971] (Dunnett, Dorothy)

M . . . continued

Matricide at St. Martha's [1994] (Edwards, Ruth Dudley)
1 Matter of Love and Death [1966] (Wells, Tobias)
Matter of Millions [1890] (Green, Anna Katherine)
Maxwell Mystery [1913] (Wells, Carolyn)
May's Newfangled Mirth [1989] (Adamson, M. J.)
Mayhem in Parva [1990] (Livingston, Nancy)
McCone Files [1995] (Muller, Marcia)
McKee of Centre Street [1934] (Reilly, Helen)
Meadowlark [1996] (Simonson, Sheila)
Meddler and Her Murder [1972] (Porter, Joyce)
1 Medium for Murder [1976] (Warner, Mignon)
Memorial Hall Murder [1978] (Langton, Jane)
Memory Can Be Murder [1995] (Squire, Elizabeth Daniels)
Men in Her Death [1981] (Morice, Anne)
Menehune Murders [1989] (Arnold, Margot)
Mensa Murders [1990] (Martin, Lee)
1 Merely Murder [1935] (Heyer, Georgette)
Merlin's Furlong [1953] (Mitchell, Gladys)
Mermaid [1982] (Millar, Margaret)
Method in Madness [1957] (Disney, Doris Miles)
Miami, It's Murder [1994] (Buchanan, Edna) ☆
Midas Murders [1995] (Arnold, Margot)
Midnight Baby [1993] (Hornsby, Wendy)
Midway to Murder [1941] (Yates, Margaret Evelyn Tayler)
Milk and Honey [1990] (Kellerman, Faye)
Mill on the Shore [1994] (Cleeves, Ann)
Mind Readers [1965] (Allingham, Margery)
Mind to Murder [1963] (James, P. D.)
1 Minerva Cries Murder [1993] (Ballard, Mignon)
Mingled with Venom [1974] (Mitchell, Gladys)
Ministering Angel [1986] (Cohen, Anthea)
Minor in Possession [1990] (Jance, J. A.)
Mint Julep Murder [1995] (Hart, Carolyn G.)
1 Minuteman Murder [1976] (Langton, Jane)
Miracles in Maggody [1995] (Hess, Joan)
Mirror Crack'd [1962] (Christie, Agatha)
Mirror Crack'd from Side to Side [1962] (Christie, Agatha)
Miscast for Murder [1954] (Fenisong, Ruth)
Mischief in Maggody [1988] (Hess, Joan) ☆
Miser [1981] (Egan, Lesley)
Misfortune of Others [1993] (Dank, Gloria)
1 Miss Melville Regrets [1986] (Smith, Evelyn E.)
Miss Melville Returns [1987] (Smith, Evelyn E.)
Miss Melville Rides a Tiger [1991] (Smith, Evelyn E.)
Miss Melville Runs for Cover [1995] (Smith, Evelyn E.)
Miss Melville's Revenge [1989] (Smith, Evelyn E.)
Miss Pink at the Edge of the World [1975] (Moffat, Gwen)
Miss Pink's Mistake [1982] (Moffat, Gwen)
1 Miss Pinkerton [1932] (Rinehart, Mary Roberts)
Miss Pinnegar Disappears [1952] (Gilbert, Anthony)
Miss Seeton at the Helm [1990] (Crane, Hamilton)
Miss Seeton, Bewitched [1971] (Crane, Hamilton)
Miss Seeton, by Appointment [1990] (Crane, Hamilton)
Miss Seeton by Moonlight [1992] (Crane, Hamilton)
Miss Seeton Cracks the Case [1991] (Crane, Hamilton)
Miss Seeton Draws the Line [1969] (Crane, Hamilton)
Miss Seeton Goes to Bat [1993] (Crane, Hamilton)
Miss Seeton Paints the Town [1991] (Crane, Hamilton)
Miss Seeton Plants Suspicion [1993] (Crane, Hamilton)
Miss Seeton Rocks the Cradle [1992] (Crane, Hamilton)
Miss Seeton Rules [1994] (Crane, Hamilton)
Miss Seeton Sings [1973] (Crane, Hamilton)
Miss Seeton Undercover [1994] (Crane, Hamilton)
Miss Silver Comes to Stay [1949] (Wentworth, Patricia)

Miss Silver Deals in Death [1943] (Wentworth, Patricia)
Miss Silver Intervenes [1943] (Wentworth, Patricia)
Miss Zukas and the Island Murders [1995] (Dereske, Jo)
1 Miss Zukas and the Library Murders [1994] (Dereske, Jo)
Miss Zukas and the Raven's Dance [1996] (Dereske , Jo)
Miss Zukas and the Stroke of Death [1996] (Dereske, Jo)
Missing Duchess [1994] (Knight, Alanna)
Missing Eden [1996] (Lee, Wendi)
Missing from Her Home [1969] (Gilbert, Anthony)
Missing Joseph [1993] (George, Elizabeth)
Missing Link [1938] (Wells, Carolyn)
Missing Madonna [1988] (O'Marie, Sister Carol Anne)
1 Missing Members [1990] (Vlasopolos, Anca)
Missing Susan [1991] (McCrumb, Sharyn)
Missing Widow [1947] (Gilbert, Anthony)
1 Missing Woman [1980] (Page, Emma)
Mistress of the Bones [1995] (MacGregor, T. J.)
Model Murder [1993] (Dengler, Sandy)
Model Murder [1991] (Quest, Erica)
Money Burns [1991] (Maxwell, A. E.)
Money Musk [1936] (Wells, Carolyn)
Money to Burn [1993] (White, Gloria)
Monk's Hood [1980] (Peters, Ellis) ★
1 Monkey Puzzle [1985] (Gosling, Paula) ★
Monkey Wrench [1994] (Cody, Liza)
Monstrous Regiment of Women [1995] (King, Laurie R.)
Morbid Kitchen [1995] (Melville, Jennie)
1 Morbid Symptoms [1984] (Slovo, Gillian)
1 Morbid Taste for Bones [1977] (Peters, Ellis)
More Deaths Than One [1990] (Eccles, Marjorie)
More Perfect Union [1988] (Jance, J. A.)
More Work for the Undertaker [1949] (Allingham, Margery)
Morning Raga [1969] (Peters, Ellis)
Moroccan Traffic [1992] (Dunnett, Dorothy)
Mortal Remains [1974] (Yorke, Margaret)
Mortal Remains in Maggody [1991] (Hess, Joan)
Mortal Sins [1987] (Porter, Anna)
Mortal Spoils [1996] (Greenwood, Diane M.)
Mortal Words [1990] (Knight, Kathryn Lasky)
Most Deadly Hate [1986] (Woods, Sara)
Most Grievous Murder [1982] (Woods, Sara)
Most Likely to Die [1996] (Girdner, Jaqueline)
Mother Love [1995] (Wright, L. R.)
1 Mother Shadow [1989] (Howe, Melodie Johnson) ☆ ☆ ☆
Motive in Shadow [1980] (Egan, Lesley)
Motive on Record [1982] (Shannon, Dell)
Mourned on Sunday [1941] (Reilly, Helen)
Mouse Trapped [1993] (Dengler, Sandy)
Mouse Who Wouldn't Play Ball [1943] (Gilbert, Anthony)
Mouthful of Sand [1988] (Meek, M. R. D.)
Moving Finger [1942] (Christie, Agatha)
Mr. Brading's Collection [1950] (Wentworth, Patricia)
Mr. Campion's Falcon [1970] (Allingham, Margery)
Mr. Campion's Farthing [1969] (Allingham, Margery)
Mr. Campion's Quarry [1970] (Allingham, Margery)
Mr. Cromwell is Dead [1939] (Ford, Leslie)
Mr. Crook Lifts the Mask [1970] (Gilbert, Anthony)
1 Mr. Donaghue Investigates [1995] (Shone, Anna)
Mr. Pinkerton and the Old Angel [1939] (Frome, David)
Mr. Pinkerton at the Old Angel [1939] (Frome, David)
Mr. Pinkerton Finds a Body [1934] (Frome, David)
Mr. Pinkerton Goes to Scotland Yard [1934] (Frome, D.)
Mr. Pinkerton Grows a Beard [1935] (Frome, David)
Mr. Pinkerton Has the Clue [1936] (Frome, David)
Mr. Simpson Finds a Body [1932] (Frome, David)
Mr. Smith's Hat [1936] (Reilly, Helen)

M . . . continued

Mr. Splitfoot [1968] (McCloy, Helen)
Mr. Watson Intervenes [1934] (Gardiner, Dorothy)
Mrs. Jeffries Dusts for Clues [1993] (Brightwell, Emily)
Mrs. Jeffries on the Ball [1994] (Brightwell, Emily)
Mrs. Jeffries on the Trail [1995] (Brightwell, Emily)
Mrs. Jeffries Plays the Cook [1995] (Brightwell, Emily)
Mrs. Jeffries Takes Stock [1994] (Brightwell, Emily)
Mrs. Malory and the Festival Murders [1993] (Holt, Hazel)
Mrs. Malory: Detective in Residence [1994] (Holt, Hazel)
❶ Mrs. Malory Investigates [1989] (Holt, Hazel)
Mrs. Malory Wonders Why [1995] (Holt, Hazel)
Mrs. McGinty's Dead [1952] (Christie, Agatha)
Mrs. Pollifax and the Golden Triangle [1988] (Gilman, D.)
Mrs. Pollifax and the Hong Kong Buddha [1985] (Gilman, D.)
Mrs. Pollifax and the Lion Killer [1996] (Gilman, Dorothy)
Mrs. Pollifax and the Second Thief [1993] (Gilman, D.)
Mrs. Pollifax and the Whirling Dervish [1990] (Gilman, D.)
Mrs. Pollifax on Safari [1976] (Gilman, Dorothy)
Mrs. Pollifax on the China Station [1983] (Gilman, D.)
Mrs. Pollifax Pursued [1995] (Gilman, Dorothy)
❶ Mrs. Porter's Letter [1982] (McConnell, Vickie P.)
Much Ado in Maggody [1989] (Hess, Joan)
Mudflats of the Dead [1979] (Mitchell, Gladys)
Mudlark [1993] (Simonson, Sheila)
❶ Mulch [1994] (Ripley, Ann)
Multitude of Sins [1975] (Wren, M. K.)
Mum's the Word [1990] (Cannell, Dorothy)
Mumbo Jumbo [1991] (Knight, Kathryn Lasky)
Mummy Case [1985] (Peters, Elizabeth)
Murder a la Mode [1963] (Moyes, Patricia)
Murder After Hours [1946] (Christie, Agatha)
Murder Against the Grain [1967] (Lathen, Emma) ★
Murder Among Friends [1995] (Jacobs, Jonnie)
❶ Murder Among Neighbors [1994] (Jacobs, Jonnie)
Murder Among the Angels [1996] (Matteson, Stefanie)
Murder Among Us [1993] (Granger, Ann)
Murder and a Muse [1994] (Farrell, Gillian B.)
Murder Anonymous [1968] (Gilbert, Anthony)
Murder at Arroways [1950] (Reilly, Helen)
❶ Murder at Government House [1937] (Huxley, Elspeth)
❶ Murder at Markham [1988] (Sprinkle, Patricia H.)
Murder at Monticello [1994] (Brown, Rita Mae)
❶ Murder at Moot Point [1992] (Millhiser, Marlys)
Murder at Plum's [1989] (Myers, Amy)
❶ Murder at Red Rook Ranch [1990] (Tell, Dorothy)
❶ Murder at St. Adelaide's [1995] (Hollingsworth, Gerelyn)
Murder at Teatime [1991] (Matteson, Stefanie)
Murder at the Blue Owl [1988] (Martin, Lee)
Murder at the Casino [1941] (Wells, Carolyn)
Murder at the Cat Show [1972] (Babson, Marian)
❶ Murder at the Class Reunion [1993] (Stein, Triss)
Murder at the Falls [1993] (Matteson, Stefanie)
Murder at the Feast of Rejoicing [1996] (Robinson, L. S.)
Murder at the Gardner [1988] (Langton, Jane)
Murder at the God's Gate [1995] (Robinson, Lynda S.)
❶ Murder at the Kennedy Center [1989] (Truman, Margaret)
Murder at the Masque [1991] (Myers, Amy)
Murder at the Mendel [1991] (Bowen, Gail)
Murder at the Murder at the Mimosa Inn [1986] (Hess, J.)
Murder at the Music Hall [1995] (Myers, Amy)
Murder at the National Cathedral [1990] (Truman, M.)
Murder at the National Gallery [1995] (Truman, Margaret)
Murder at the Nightwood Bar [1986] (Forrest, K. V.)
Murder at the Old Vicarage [1989] (McGown, Jill)

❶ Murder at the Pentagon [1992] (Truman, Margaret)
❶ Murder at the PTA Luncheon [1987] (Wolzien, Valerie)
Murder at the Savoy [1971] (Sjöwall, Maj & Per Wahlöö)
❶ Murder at the Spa [1990] (Matteson, Stefanie)
❶ Murder at the Vicarage [1930] (Christie, Agatha)
❶ Murder at the War [1987] (Pulver, Mary Monica)
Murder at Vassar [1987] (Taylor, Elizabeth Atwood)
❶ Murder Beach [1993] (McKenna, Bridget)
❶ Murder Before Breakfast [1938] (Offord, Lenore Glen)
Murder Being Once Done [1972] (Rendell, Ruth)
Murder by an Aristocrat [1932] (Eberhart, Mignon G.)
Murder by Deception [1989] (Meredith, D. R.) ☆
❶ Murder by Experts [1936] (Gilbert, Anthony)
❶ Murder by Impulse [1988] (Meredith, D. R.) ☆
Murder by Masquerade [1990] (Meredith, D. R.)
Murder by Owl Light [1992] (Sawyer, Corinne Holt)
Murder by Precedent [1964] (Petrie, Rhona)
Murder by Proxy [1978] (Morice, Anne)
❶ Murder by Proxy [1951] (Nielsen, Helen)
Murder by Reference [1991] (Meredith, D. R.)
Murder by Sacrilege [1993] (Meredith, D. R.)
Murder by Tale [1987] (Shannon, Dell)
Murder by the Book [1963] (Lockridge, Frances & R.)
❶ Murder by theBook [1989] (Rowe, Jennifer)
Murder by the Book [1979] (Schier, Norma)
❶ Murder by the Book [1990] (Welch, Pat)
❶ Murder by the Day [1953] (Johns, Veronica Parker)
Murder by the Yard [1942] (Yates, Margaret Evelyn Tayler)
Murder by Tradition [1991] (Forrest, Katherine V.) ★
❶ Murder Can Kill Your Social Life [1994] (Eichler, Selma)
Murder Can Ruin Your Looks [1995] (Eichler, Selma)
Murder Can Stunt Your Growth [1996] (Eichler, Selma)
Murder Can Wreck Your Reunion [1996] (Eichler, Selma)
Murder Can't Wait [1964] (Lockridge, Frances & Richard)
❶ Murder Cancels All Debts [1946] (Heberden, M. V.)
Murder Cheats the Bride [1945] (Gilbert, Anthony)
Murder Comes Caller [1995] (Page, Emma)
Murder Comes First [1951] (Lockridge, Frances & R.)
Murder Comes Hme [1950] (Gilbert, Anthony)
❶ Murder Draws a Line [1940] (Barber, Willetta Ann)
Murder Enters the Picture [1942] (Barber, Willetta Ann)
Murder Fantastical [1967] (Moyes, Patricia)
Murder Follows Desmond Shannon [1942] (Heberden, M. V.)
Murder for Christmas [1938] (Christie, Agatha)
Murder Gets a Degree [1986] (Wender, Theodora)
Murder Goes Astray [1943] (Heberden, M. V.)
Murder Goes Mumming [1981] (Craig, Alisa)
Murder Greets Jean Holton [1936] (Knight, Kathleen M.)
Murder Has a Pretty Face [1981] (Melville, Jennie)
Murder Has Its Points [1961] (Lockridge, Frances & R.)
Murder Has No alories [1994] (Sawyer, Corinne Holt)
Murder Has No Tongue [1937] (Gilbert, Anthony)
Murder Hurts [1993] (Maxwell, A. E.)
Murder in a Good Cause [1990] (Sale, Medora)
Murder in a Hot Flash [1995] (Millhiser, Marlys)
Murder in a Hurry [1950] (Lockridge, Frances & Richard)
Murder ina Mummy Case [1985] (Beck, K. K.)
❶ Murder in a Nice Neighborhood [1994] (Roberts, Lora)
❶ Murder in Bandora [1993] (Karr, Leona)
Murder in Blue Hour [1951] (Crane, Frances)
Murder in Blue Street [1951] (Crane, Frances)
❶ Murder in Brief [1995] (Lachnit, Carroll)
Murder in Bright Red [1953] (Crane, Frances)
Murder in Burgundy [1989] (Peterson, Audrey)
❶ Murder in C Major [1993] (Frommer, Sara Hoskinson)
Murder in Focus [1972] (Dunnett, Dorothy)

M . . . continued

Murder in Focus [1989] (Sale, Medora)
Murder in Gray & White [1989] (Sawyer, Corinne Holt)
Murder in High Place [1970] (Dominic, R. B.)
▪ Murder in Hospital [1937] (Bell, Josephine)
Murder in Married Life [1971] (Morice, Anne)
▪ Murder in Mellingham [1993] (Oleksiw, Susan)
▪ Murder in Mendocino [1987] (Kittredge, Mary)
Murder in Mesopotamia [1936] (Christie, Agatha)
Murder in Mimicry [1977] (Morice, Anne)
Murder in My Backyard [1991] (Cleeves, Ann)
Murder in Ordinary Time [1991] (O'Marie, Sister Carol A.)
Murder in Outline [1979] (Morice, Anne)
Murder in Paradise [1989] (Cleeves, Ann)
▪ Murder in Pug's Parlour [1987] (Myers, Amy)
Murder in Retrospect [1941] (Christie, Agatha)
▪ Murder in Scorpio [1995] (Lawrence, Martha)
Murder in Shinbone Alley [1940] (Reilly, Helen)
▪ Murder in Store [1989] (Brod, D. C.)
Murder in the Bookshop [1936] (Wells, Carolyn)
Murder in the Calais Coach [1934] (Christie, Agatha)
Murder in the Charleston Manner [1990] (Sprinkle, P. H.)
▪ Murder in the Collective [1984] (Wilson, Barbara)
▪ Murder in the Cotswolds [1989] (Rowlands, Betty)
Murder in the Dog Days [1990] (Carlson, P. M.) ☆
Murder in the Garden [1989] (Melville, Jennie)
Murder in the Limelight [1987] (Myers, Amy)
Murder in the Marketplace [1995] (Roberts, Lora)
▪ Murder in the Maze [1993] (Mason, Sarah Jill)
Murder in the Mews [1937] (Christie, Agatha)
Murder in the Mews [1931] (Reilly, Helen)
Murder in the Mist [1940] (Popkin, Zelda)
Murder in the O.P.M. [1942] (Ford, Leslie)
▪ Murder in the Place of Anubis [1994] (Robinson, Lynda S.)
Murder in the Round [1970] (Dunnett, Dorothy)
Murder in the Smokehouse [1994] (Myers, Amy)
Murder in Three Acts [1934] (Christie, Agatha)
Murder in Volume 2 [1941] (Daly, Elizabeth)
Murder in Writing [1988] (Clarke, Anna)
Murder Is Academic [1985] (Carlson, P. M.) ☆
▪ Murder Is Academic [1976] (Mackay, Amanda)
Murder Is Announced [1950] (Christie, Agatha)
Murder Is Cheap [1944] (Gilbert, Anthony)
Murder Is Germane [1992] (Saum, Karen)
Murder Is Material [1994] (Saum, Karen)
▪ Murder Is Only Skin Deep [1987] (Sims, L. V.)
Murder is Pathological [1986] (Carlson, P. M.)
▪ Murder Is Relative [1990] (Saum, Karen)
Murder Is Served [1948] (Lockridge, Frances & Richard)
Murder IsSuggested [1959] (Lockridge, Frances & R.)
Murder Listens In [1949] (Daly, Elizabeth)
Murder Machree [1992] (Boylan, Eleanor)
Murder Makes a Pilgrimmage [1993] (O'Marie, Sister C. A.)
Murder Makes a Racket [1942] (Heberden, M. V.)
Murder Makes an Entree [1992] (Myers, Amy)
Murder Makes Me Nervous [1948] (Scherf, Margaret)
Murder Makes the Wheels Go 'Round [1966] (Lathen, E.)
Murder Makes Tracks [1985] (Linscott, Gillian)
Murder Mile-High [1996] (Roberts, Lora)
Murder Misread [1990] (Carlson, P. M.)
Murder Most Beastly [1996] (Cleary, Melissa)
Murder Most Fouled Up [1968] (Wells, Tobias)
Murder Most Fowl [1991] (Morgan, Kate)
▪ Murder Most Grizzly [1993] (Quinn, Elizabeth)
Murder Most Mellow [1992] (Girdner, Jaqueline)

Murder Most Strange [1981] (Shannon, Dell)
Murder Must Advertise [1933] (Sayers, Dorothy L.)
Murder My Suite [1995] (Daheim, Mary)
▪ Murder Needs a Face [1942] (Fenisong, Ruth)
Murder Needs a Name [1942] (Fenisong, Ruth)
Murder Now and Then [1993] (McGown, Jill)
Murder Observed [1990] (Boylan, Eleanor)
Murder of a Fifth Columnist [1941] (Ford, Leslie)
Murder of a Stuffed Shirt [1944] (Heberden, M. V.)
Murder of a Suicide [1941] (Ferrars, E. X.)
Murder of Busy Lizzie [1973] (Mitchell, Gladys)
▪ Murder of Crows [1987] (Duffy, Margaret)
Murder of Miranda [1979] (Millar, Margaret)
Murder of Mrs. Davenport [1928] (Gilbert, Anthony)
Murder of Roger Ackroyd [1926] (Christie, Agatha)
▪ Murder Offscreen [1994] (Osborne, Denise)
Murder on a Tangent [1945] (Disney, Doris Miles)
Murder on Angler's Island [1945] (Reilly, Helen)
Murder on Campus [1994] (Holt, Hazel)
▪ Murder on Cue [1983] (Dentinger, Jane)
Murder on French Leave [1973] (Morice, Anne)
▪ Murder on Her Mind [1991] (Steiner, Susan)
Murder on High [1994] (Matteson, Stefanie)
Murder on Parade [1940] (Wells, Carolyn)
Murder on Peachtree Street [1991] (Sprinkle, Patricia H.)
▪ Murder on Russian Hill [1938] (Offord, Lenore Glen)
Murder on Safari [1938] (Huxley, Elspeth)
Murder on Show [1972] (Babson, Marian)
Murder on the Ballarat Train [1991] (Greenwood, Kerry)
Murder on the Cliff [1991] (Matteson, Stefanie)
Murder on the Flying Scotsman [1997] (Dunn, Carola)
▪ Murder on the Iditarod Trail [1991] (Henry, Sue) ★ ★
Murder on the Kibbutz: A Communal Case [1994] (Gur, B.) ☆
Murder on the Links [1923] (Christie, Agatha)
Murder on the Merry-Go-Round [1956] (Bell, Josephine)
Murder on the Mount [1994] (Dengler, Sandy)
Murder on the Orient Express [1934] (Christie, Agatha)
Murder on the Potomac [1994] (Truman, Margaret)
Murder on the Purple Water [1947] (Crane, Frances)
▪ Murder on the Run [1986] (Sale, Medora) ★
▪ Murder on the Run [1991] (White, Gloria) ☆
Murder on the Silk Road [1992] (Matteson, Stefanie)
Murder on the Square [1950] (Frome, David)
Murder on Wheels [1992] (Frankel, Valerie)
▪ Murder Once Removed [1993] (Kunz, Kathleen)
Murder Out of Commission [1976] (Dominic, R. B.)
Murder Out of Turn [1941] (Lockridge, Frances & Richard)
Murder Plus [1940] (Wells, Carolyn)
Murder Post-Dated [1983] (Morice, Anne)
Murder Rides the Express [1955] (Reilly, Helen)
Murder Roundabout [1966] (Lockridge, Frances & R.)
Murder Runs a ever [1943] (Fenisong, Ruth)
▪ Murder Sunny Side Up [1968] (Dominic, R. B.)
Murder Superior [1993] (Haddam, Jane)
Murder: The Musical [1993] (Meyers, Annette)
Murder Through the Looking Glass [1943] (Venning, M.)
Murder To Go [1969] (Lathen, Emma)
Murder Too Many [1988] (Ferrars, E. X.)
Murder Under the Kissing Bough [1992] (Myers, Amy)
Murder Under the Mistletoe [1988] (Jordan, Jennifer)
Murder Unlimited [1953] (Heberden, M. V.)
Murder Unrenovated [1987] (Carlson, P. M.) ☆ ☆
Murder Waiting to Happen [1989] (Taylor, L. A.)
Murder Well-Bred [1995] (Banks, Carolyn)
Murder Well-Done [1996] (Bishop, Claudia)
Murder Will In [1942] (Wells, Carolyn)

M . . . continued

1 Murder Will Out [1994] (Yeager, Dorian)
Murder with Love [1972] (Shannon, Dell)
Murder with Mirrors [1952] (Christie, Agatha)
Murder Within Murder [1946] (Lockridge, Frances & R.)
Murder Without Icing [1972] (Lathen, Emma)
Murder's a Waiting Game [1972] (Gilbert, Anthony)
Murder's Out of Tune [1984] (Woods, Sara)
Murderer's Houses [1964] (Melville, Jennie)
Murderer's Tale [1996] (Frazer, Margaret)
Murdering Kind [1958] (Butler, Gwendoline)
Murderous Remedy [1990] (Shepherd, Stella)
Murders of Mrs. Austin & Mrs. Beale [1991] (McGown, Jill)
Murders of Richard III [1974] (Peters, Elizabeth)
Music When Sweet Voices Die [1979] (Yarbro, Chelsea Q.)
My Bones Will Keep [1962] (Mitchell, Gladys)
My Father Sleeps [1974] (Mitchell, Gladys)
My Kingdom for a Hearse [1957] (Rice, Craig)
My Life Is Done [1976] (Woods, Sara)
My Name Is Death [1964] (Egan, Lesley)
My Sister's Keeper [1992] (Kelly, Nora)
My Sweet Untraceable You [1994] (Scoppettone, Sandra)
1 Mysterious Affair at Styles [1920] (Christie, Agatha)
Mystery Bred in Buckhead [1994] (Sprinkle, Patricia H.)
Mystery Girl [1922] (Wells, Carolyn)
Mystery in the Woodshed [1942] (Gilbert, Anthony)
Mystery Lady [1986] (Clarke, Anna)
Mystery Loves Company [1992] (Morgan, Kate)
Mystery Mile [1930] (Allingham, Margery)
Mystery of a Butcher's Shop [1929] (Mitchell, Gladys)
Mystery of Hunting's End [1930] (Eberhart, Mignon G.)
Mystery of the Blue Train [1928] (Christie, Agatha)
Mystery of the Cape Cod Players [1933] (Taylor, P. A.)
Mystery of the Cape Cod Tavern [1934] (Taylor, P. A.)
Mystery of the Hasty Arrw [1911] (Green, Anna K.)
Mystery of the Open Window [1929] (Gilbert, Anthony)
Mystery of the Sycamore [1921] (Wells, Carolyn)
Mystery of the Tarn [1937] (Wells, Carolyn)
Mystery of the Woman in Red [1941] (Gilbert, Anthony)

N

N or M? [1941] (Christie, Agatha)
1 Naked in Death [1995] (Robb, J. D.)
Naked Once More [1989] (Peters, Elizabeth) ★ ★
Naked Villainy [1987] (Woods, Sara)
Name Is Malone [1958] (Rice, Craig)
Name Withheld [1995] (Jance, J. A.)
Name Your Poison [1942] (Reilly, Helen)
Nameless Coffin [1966] (Butler, Gwendoline)
Nameless Ones [1967] (Egan, Lesley)
Nantucket Diet Murders [1985] (Rich, Virginia)
1 Napoleon Must Die [1993] (Fawcett, Quinn)
Natural Death [1996] (Furie, Ruthe)
Natural Enemy [1982] (Langton, Jane)
1 Necessary End [1986] (Fraser, Anthea)
Neck in a Noose [1942] (Ferrars, E. X.)
Necrochip [1993] (Harrod-Eagles, Cynthia)
Neither a Candle nor a Pitchfork [1969] (Porter, Joyce)
Nell Alone [1966] (Melville, Jennie)
Nemesis [1971] (Christie, Agatha)
Nest of Vipers [1979] (Mitchell, Gladys)
Never Let a Stranger in Your House [1995] (Logan, M.)
New Kind of Killer [1970] (Melville, Jennie)
New Lease on Death [1967] (Rendell, Ruth)

1 New Leash on Death [1989] (Conant, Susan)
New Orleans Beat [1994] (Smith, Julie)
1 New Orleans Mourning [1990] (Smith, Julie) ★
Nice Cup of Tea [1950] (Gilbert, Anthony)
Nice Derangement of Epitaphs [1965] (Peters, Ellis)
Nice Girls Finish Last [1996] (Hayter, Sparkle)
Nice Little Killing [1974] (Gilbert, Anthony)
Nice People [1995] (Curzon, Clare)
1 Nice Way to Die [1976] (Warner, Mignon)
Night at the Vulcan [1951] (Marsh, Ngaio)
1 Night Butterfly [1992] (McFall, Patricia)
Night Encounter [1968] (Gilbert, Anthony)
Night Ferry to Death [1985] (Moyes, Patricia)
Night Game [1993] (Gordon, Alison)
Night of the Fog [1930] (Gilbert, Anthony)
1 Night She Died [1981] (Simpson, Dorothy)
Night Shift [1993] (Fromer, Margot J.)
Night Songs [1995] (Mickelbury, Penny)
Night Train to Memphis [1994] (Peters, Elizabeth) ☆
Night Walk [1947] (Daly, Elizabeth)
Night Walker [1990] (Hager, Jean)
Nightcap [1984] (Smith, J. C. S.)
Nightmare Honeymoon [1963] (Foley, Rae)
Nine Bright Shiners [1988] (Fraser, Anthea)
Nine Tailors [1934] (Sayers, Dorothy L.)
Ninth Life [1989] (Douglas, Lauren Wright)
No. 9 Belmont Square [1963] (Erskine, Margaret)
No Birds Sing [1996] (Bannister, Jo)
No Body [1986] (Pickard, Nancy) ☆
No Business Being a Cop [1979] (O'Donnell, Lillian)
No Crime for a Lady [1942] (Popkin, Zelda)
No Dust in the Attic [1962] (Gilbert, Anthony)
No Evil Angel [1964] (Linington, Elizabeth)
No Flowers by Request [1987] (Thomson, June)
No Forwarding Address [1991] (Bowers, Elisabeth)
1 No Harm [1987] (Hornsby, Wendy)
No Holiday for Crime [1973] (Shannon, Dell)
No Honeymoon for Death [1995] (Kruger, Mary)
No Lady in the House [1982] (Kallen, Lucille)
No Laughing Matter [1993] (Simpson, Dorothy)
No Love Lost [1954] (Allingham, Margery)
No Man's Island [1983] (Mann, Jessica)
No More Dying Then [1971] (Rendell, Ruth)
1 No One Dies in Branson [1994] (Buckstaff, Kathryn)
1 No Place for Secrets [1995] (Lewis, Sherry)
No Place Like Home [1996] (Lewis, Sherry)
No Use Dying Over Spilled Milk [1996] (Myers, Tamar)
No Vacation from Murder [1973] (Lemarchand, Elizabeth)
No Villian Need Be [1979] (Linington, Elizabeth)
1 No Wind of Blame [1939] (Heyer, Georgette)
No Winding-Sheet [1984] (Mitchell, Gladys)
No Word from Winifred [1986] (Cross, Amanda)
Nobody's Child [1995] (Dawson, Janet)
1 Nocturne Murder [1988] (Peterson, Audrey)
Nodding Canaries [1961] (Mitchell, Gladys)
Noonday and Night [1977] (Mitchell, Gladys)
Noose Is Drawn [1945] (Barber, Willetta Ann)
Nor Live so Long [1986] (Woods, Sara)
1 North of Montana [1994] (Smith, April)
1 North of the Border [1988] (Van Gieson, Judith)
North Star Conspiracy [1993] (Monfredo, Miriam Grace)
1 Norths Meet Murder [1940] (Lockridge, Frances & R.)
Northwest Murders [1992] (Taylor, Elizabeth Atwood)
1 Not a Creature Was Stirring [1990] (Haddam, Jane) ☆ ☆
Not Exactly a Brahmin [1985] (Dunlap, Susan)
Not I, Said the Sparrow [1973] (Lockridge, Frances & R.)

N . . . continued

Not Me, Inspector [1959] (Reilly, Helen)
🔟 Not One of Us [1971] (Thomson, June)
Not That Kind of Place [1990] (Fyfield, Frances)
🔟 Not Till a Hot January [1987] (Adamson, M. J.)
Nothing Can Rescue Me [1943] (Daly, Elizabeth)
Nothing To Do with the Case [1981] (Lemarchand, E.)
Nothing's Certain but Death [1978] (Wren, M. K.)
🔟 Novena for Murder [1984] (O'Marie, Sister Carol Anne)
🔟 Novice's Tale [1992] (Frazer, Margaret)
Now Let's Talk of Graves [1990] (Shankman, Sarah)
🔟 Now You Don't [1988] (Greth, Roma)
Numbered Account [1960] (Bridge, Ann)
Nun's Tale [1995] (Robb, Candace M.)
Nurse Dawes Is Dead [1994] (Shepherd, Stella)
Nursery Tea and Poison [1975] (Morice, Anne)
Nursing-Home Murder [1935] (Marsh, Ngaio)

O

O Little Town of Maggody [1993] (Hess, Joan) ☆ ☆
Obscure Grave [1985] (Woods, Sara)
Obstacle Course [1990] (Montgomery, Yvonne E.)
Octagon House [1937] (Taylor, Phoebe Atwood)
Odd Job [1995] (MacLeod, Charlotte)
Odds on Miss Seeton [1975] (Crane, Hamilton)
Of Graves, Worms and Epitaphs [1988] (Wells, Tobias)
Off Key [1992] (McNab, Claire)
Off with His Head [1956] (Marsh, Ngaio)
🔟 Ogilvie, Tallant and Moon [1976] (Yarbro, Chelsea Quinn)
Oh Bury Me Not [1977] (Wren, M. K.)
Old Contemptibles [1990] (Grimes, Martha)
Old Enemies [1993] (La Pierre, Janet) ☆
Old Faithful Murder [1992] (Wolzien, Valerie)
Old Fox Deceived [1982] (Grimes, Martha)
Old Lady Dies [1934] (Gilbert, Anthony)
Old Lover's Ghost [1940] (Ford, Leslie)
Old Mrs. Ommanney Is Dead [1955] (Erskine, Margaret)
Old Silent [1989] (Grimes, Martha)
Old Sinners Never Die [1959] (Davis, Dorothy Salisbury)
Oldest Sin [1997] (Hart, Ellen)
On Ice [1989] (MacGregor, T. J.)
Once and Always Murder [1990] (Papazoglou, Orania)
🔟 One Coffee With [1981] (Maron, Margaret)
One Corpse Too Many [1979] (Peters, Ellis)
One Fell Sloop [1990] (Kenney, Susan)
🔟 One for the Money [1993] (Borton, D. B.)
🔟 One for the Money [1994] (Evanovich, Janet) ☆ ☆ ☆ ☆
One in One and All Alone [1996] (Fraser, Anthea)
1(900)D-E-A-D [1996] (Fennelly, Tony)
One of My Sons [1901] (Green, Anna Katherine)
One That Got Away [1945] (McCloy, Helen)
One, Two, Buckle My Shoe [1940] (Christie, Agatha)
🔟 One, Two, What Did Daddy Do? [1992] (Cooper, S. R.)
🔟 Only Half a Hoax [1984] (Taylor, L. A.)
🔟 Only Security [1972] (Mann, Jessica)
Only with a Bargepole [1971] (Porter, Joyce)
Open and Shut [1991] (McDermid, Val)
Open House [1995] (Welch, Pat)
Opening Door [1944] (Reilly, Helen)
Opening Night [1951] (Marsh, Ngaio)
🔟 Orchestrated Death [1991] (Harrod-Eagles, Cynthia)
Original Sin [1994] (James, P. D.)
Original Sin [1991] (Pulver, Mary Monica)
🔟 Osprey Reef [1990] (McKernan, Victoria)

🔟 Other David [1984] (Coker, Carolyn)
Other Devil's Name [1986] (Ferrars, E. X.)
Other People's Houses [1990] (Cooper, Susan Rogers)
Other People's Skeletons [1993] (Smith, Julie)
Other Side of Death [1991] (Van Gieson, Judith)
Other Side of the Door [1987] (O'Donnell, Lillian)
Other Woman [1992] (McGown, Jill)
Otherworld [1993] (Dreher, Sarah)
Out for the Kill [1960] (Gilbert, Anthony)
Out of Order [1936] (Taylor, Phoebe Atwood)
Out of the Darkness [1992] (Kelly, Susan)
Out of the Past [1953] (Wentworth, Patricia)
Outlaw Derek [1988] (Hooper, Kay)
Outlaw's Fortune [1993] (Lee W. W.)
Outlaw's Tale [1994] (Frazer, Margaret)
Ovation by Death [1995] (Yeager, Dorian)
Over the Edge [1993] (Rowlands, Betty)
Over the Sea to Death [1976] (Moffat, Gwen)
Overture to Death [1939] (Marsh, Ngaio)
🔟 Owl in the Cellar [1945] (Scherf, Margaret)
Owl Too Many [1991] (MacLeod, Charlotte) ☆
Oxford Blood [1985] (Fraser, Antonia)
Oxford Exit [1995] (Stallwood, Veronica)
Oxford Mourning [1996] (Stallwood, Veronica)

P

Package Included Murder [1975] (Porter, Joyce)
Pageant of Murder [1965] (Mitchell, Gladys)
🔟 Painted Mask [1938] (Erskine, Margaret)
Painted Truth [1995] (McClendon, Lise)
Palace Guard [1981] (MacLeod, Charlotte)
Palm for Mrs. Pollifax [1973] (Gilman, Dorothy)
Paper Chase [1972] (Egan, Lesley)
Paragon Walk [1981] (Perry, Anne)
🔟 Parklane South, Queens [1990] (Kelly, Mary Ann)
Parrot Blues [1995] (Van Gieson, Judith)
Parsley, Sage, Rosemary and Crime [1995] (Myers, T.)
Parson's Pleasure [1987] (Hardwick, Mollie)
Parting Breath [1977] (Aird, Catherine)
🔟 Partners in Crime [1991] (Gray, Gallagher)
Partners in Crime [1929] (Christie, Agatha)
Passenger to Nowhere [1965] (Gilbert, Anthony)
Passing Strange [1980] (Aird, Catherine)
Passover Murder [1996] (Harris, Lee)
Past Imperfect [1991] (Maron, Margaret)
Past Praying For [1968] (Woods, Sara)
Past Pretense [1994] (Short, Sharon Gwyn)
Past Reckoning [1990] (Thomson, June)
🔟 Patient in Room 18 [1929] (Eberhart, Mignon G.)
Patriotic Murders [1940] (Christie, Agatha)
Patterns in the Dust [1985] (Grant-Adamson, Lesley)
Paws Before Dying [1992] (Conant, Susan)
Pay Dirt [1995] (Brown, Rita Mae)
Pay the Piper [1996] (Kingsbury, Kate)
Paying the Piper [1988] (McCrumb, Sharyn) ☆ ☆
Payment in Blood [1989] (George, Elizabeth)
Payment in Kind [1991] (Jance, J. A.)
Payoff for the Banker [1945] (Lockridge, Frances & R.)
🔟 Peacock Is a Bird of Prey [1955] (Foley, Rae)
Peanut Butter Murders [1993] (Sawyer, Corinne Holt)
Pearls Before Swine [1945] (Allingham, Margery)
🔟 Pedigree to Die For [1995] (Berenson, Laurien)
Pencil Points to Murder [1941] (Barber, Willetta Ann)
Pennies on a Dead Woman's Eyes [1992] (Muller, Marcia)
🔟 Penny Black [1984] (Moody, Susan)
Penny Dreadful [1984] (Moody, Susan)

P . . . continued

Penny Pinching [1989] (Moody, Susan)
Penny Post [1985] (Moody, Susan)
Penny Royal [1986] (Moody, Susan)
Penny Saving [1993] (Moody, Susan)
Penny Wise [1988] (Moody, Susan)
Pentecost Alley [1996] (Perry, Anne)
People vs. Withers and Malone [1963] (Rice, Craig)
Perchance of Death [1977] (Linington, Elizabeth)
Perennial Border [1941] (Taylor, Phoebe Atwood)
Perfect Day for Dying [1994] (Christmas, Joyce)
Perfect Fools [1982] (Green, Edith Pinero)
■ Perfect Match [1983] (McGown, Jill)
Perfectly Pure and Good [1994] (Fyfield, Frances)
Peril at End House [1932] (Christie, Agatha)
Peril Under the Palms [1989] (Beck, K. K.)
Perish in July [1989] (Hardwick, Mollie)
Personal Effects [1991] (Piesman, Marissa)
■ Personal Possession [1987] (Hart, Jeanne) ☆
Persons Unknown [1978] (Moffat, Gwen)
■ Pet Peeves [1990] (McCafferty, Taylor)
Philadelphia Murder Story [1945] (Ford, Leslie)
Philly Stakes [1989] (Roberts, Gillian) ☆
■ Phoebe's Knee [1986] (Comfort, Barbara)
■ Phone Calls [1972] (O'Donnell, Lillian)
Photo-Finish [1980] (Marsh, Ngaio)
■ Photogenic Soprano [1968] (Dunnett, Dorothy)
Piano Bird [1984] (Kallen, Lucille)
Pick up Sticks [1970] (Lathen, Emma)
■ Picture Miss Seeton [1968] (Crane, Hamilton) ☆
Picture of David [1993] (Singer, Shelley)
Piece of Justice [1995] (Walsh, Jill Paton)
Pilgrim of Hate [1984] (Peters, Ellis)
Pilgrim's Rest [1946] (Wentworth, Patricia)
Pinch of Poison [1995] (Bishop, Claudia)
Pinch of Poison [1941] (Lockridge, Frances & Richard)
Pink Umbrella [1943] (Crane, Frances)
■ Pint of Murder [1980] (Craig, Alisa)
■ Pious Deception [1989] (Dunlap, Susan)
Piper on the Mountain [1966] (Peters, Ellis)
■ Pizza House Crash [1989] (Danks, Denise)
Place for Murder [1963] (Lathen, Emma)
Plague of Kinfolks [1995] (Sibley, Celestine)
Plain Murder [1989] (Greth, Roma)
Plain Old Man [1985] (MacLeod, Charlotte)
Play with Fire [1995] (Stabenow, Dana)
Players Come Again [1990] (Cross, Amanda)
Playing for the Ashes [1994] (George, Elizabeth)
Please Omit Funeral [1975] (Dolson, Hildegarde)
Plymouth Cloak [1992] (Sedley, Kate)
Pocket Full of Rye [1953] (Christie, Agatha)
■ Pocketful of Karma [1993] (Cannon, Taffy)
Poetic Justice [1970] (Cross, Amanda)
Point Deception [1992] (McKernan, Victoria)
Poirot Investigates [1924] (Christie, Agatha)
Poirot Loses a Client [1937] (Christie, Agatha)
Poison Flowers [1991] (Cooper, Natasha)
Poison for the Prince [1994] (Eyre, Elizabeth)
Poison Fruit [1991] (Yarbro, Chelsea Quinn)
Poison in the Blood [1994] (Zachary, Fay)
Poison in the Pen [1957] (Wentworth, Patricia)
Poison Pen [1990] (Kittredge, Mary)
■ Poison Pool [1993] (Hall, Patricia)
Poisoned Pins [1993] (Hess, Joan)
Police at the Funeral [1931] (Allingham, Margery)

Policeman's Lot [1968] (Linington, Elizabeth)
Political Death [1994] (Fraser, Antonia)
Polkadot Murder [1951] (Crane, Frances)
Poor Man's Shilling [1936] (Knight, Kathleen Moore)
■ Poor, Poor Ophelia [1972] (Weston, Carolyn)
Port and a Star Border [1984] (Morison, B. J.)
■ Port of London [1938] (Bell, Josephine)
Portion for Foxes [1995] (Mitchell, Kay)
Portrait of Lilith [1982] (Thomson, June)
Portuguese Escape [1958] (Bridge, Ann)
Poseidon's Gold [1993] (Davis, Lindsey)
Postern of Fate [1973] (Christie, Agatha)
■ Postmortem [1990] (Cornwell, Patricia) ★ ★ ★ ★
Postscript to Murder [1996] (Meek, M. R. D.)
Potter's Field [1993] (Fallon, Ann C.)
Potter's Field [1989] (Peters, Ellis) ☆
Practice to Deceive [1971] (Linington, Elizabeth)
Practice to Deceive [1957] (Lockridge, Frances & Richard)
Practice to Deceive [1992] (Smith, Janet L.)
■ Pray God to Die [1993] (Roberts, Carey)
Precious Blood [1991] (Haddam, Jane)
Prelude to Death [1996] (Zukowski, Sharon)
Prelude to Murder [1959] (Gilbert, Anthony)
Prescription for Death [1993] (McGiffin, Janet)
Pretty Maids All in a Row [1986] (Fraser, Anthea)
Prey to Murder [1989] (Cleeves, Ann)
■ Price You Pay [1987] (Wakefield, Hannah)
Prilligirl [1924] (Wells, Carolyn)
Prima Donna at Large [1985] (Paul, Barbara)
Primary Target [1988] (Wallace, Marilyn) ☆
■ Prime Suspect [1993] (La Plante, Lynda)
Prime Suspect 2 [1993] (La Plante, Lynda)
Prime Suspect 3 [1994] (La Plante, Lynda)
■ Prime Time Corpse [1972] (Babbin, Jacqueline)
Prime Time for Murder [1994] (Frankel, Valerie)
■ Principal Defense [1992] (Hartzmark, Gini) ☆
Printer's Error [1939] (Mitchell, Gladys)
Prior Convictions [1991] (Matera, Lia) ☆
Priority Murder [1942] (Ford, Leslie)
Private Crime [1991] (O'Donnell, Lillian)
■ Private Lies [1993] (Cail, Carol)
Prized Possessions [1993] (Wright, L. R.)
■ Probe [1985] (Douglas, Carole Nelson)
Proceed to Judgement [1979] (Woods, Sara)
Proof of the Pudding [1945] (Taylor, Phoebe Atwood)
Proper Burial [1993] (Welch, Pat)
Prospect of Death [1995] (Duffy, Margaret)
Publish and Be Killed [1986] (Morice, Anne)
Pumpkin Shell Wife [1992] (McShea, Susannah Hofman)
Punch with Care [1946] (Taylor, Phoebe Atwood)
■ Punjat's Ruby [1990] (Jackson, Marian J. A.)
Puppet for a Corpse [1983] (Simpson, Dorothy)
Pursued by Shadows [1992] (Sale, Medora)
Pursuit in Peru [1946] (Leonard, Charles L.)
Pursuit of a Parcel [1942] (Wentworth, Patricia)
Pushing Murder [1993] (Boylan, Eleanor)
Pushover [1992] (O'Donnell, Lillian)
Pussyfoot [1993] (Douglas, Carole Nelson)
Put on by Cunning [1981] (Rendell, Ruth)
Put out the Light [1985] (Woods, Sara)

Q

■ Quaker Silence [1992] (Allen, Irene)
Quaker Witness [1993] (Allen, Irene)
Queen Is Dead [1994] (Dentinger, Jane)

Q . . . continued

Quest for K [1986] (Curzon, Clare)
1 Question of Guilt [1988] (Fyfield, Frances) ☆ ☆ ☆
Question of Identity [1977] (Thomson, June)
Question of Inheritance [1980] (Bell, Josephine)
Question of Max [1976] (Cross, Amanda)
Question of Murder [1955] (Gilbert, Anthony)
Question of Preference [1994] (Lamb, J. Dayne)
1 Questionable Behavior [1993] (Lamb, J. Dayne)
Quiche Before Dying [1993] (Churchill, Jill)
Quick and the Dead [1995] (Dengler, Sandy)
1 Quiet as a Nun [1977] (Fraser, Antonia)
Quiet Death [1991] (Knight, Alanna)
Quiet Murder [1992] (Livingston, Nancy)
Quiet Road to Death [1983] (Radley, Sheila)
Quiet Violence [1957] (Disney, Doris Miles)
Quoth the Raven [1991] (Haddam, Jane)

R

Radical Departure [1987] (Matera, Lia) ☆
Radio Studio Murder [1937] (Wells, Carolyn)
Rafferty's Wife [1987] (Hooper, Kay)
Rage [1990] (Moffat, Gwen)
Rage of Innocence [1996] (Mitchell, Kay)
Rage of Maidens [1994] (Douglas, Lauren Wright)
Raggedy Man [1995] (O'Donnell, Lillian)
Rain with Violence [1967] (Shannon, Dell)
Rainbow's End [1995] (Grimes, Martha)
Rainbow's End [1978] (Peters, Ellis)
Rancher's Blood [1991] (Lee W. W.)
1 Random Access Murder [1988] (Grant, Linda) ☆
Random Death [1982] (Egan, Lesley)
Raptor [1990] (Van Gieson, Judith)
Raspberry Jam [1920] (Wells, Carolyn)
1 Rather a Common Sort of Crime [1970] (Porter, Joyce)
Raven in the Foregate [1986] (Peters, Ellis)
Raven on the Wing [1987] (Hooper, Kay)
1 Ravenmocker [1992] (Hager, Jean)
1 Raw Data [1991] (Chapman, Sally)
1 Real Murders [1990] (Harris, Charlaine) ☆
1 Real Shot in the Arm [1989] (Roome, Annette) ★
Really Cute Corpse [1988] (Hess, Joan)
Recipe for Death [1992] (Laurence, Janet)
1 Reckless [1989] (Woods, Sherryl)
Recording Angel [1991] (Cohen, Anthea)
Recycled Citizen [1987] (MacLeod, Charlotte)
Red Roses for a Dead Trucker [1996] (Collins, Anna Ashwood)
1 Red Scream [1994] (Walker, Mary Willis) ★ ☆
1 Red Sea, Dead Sea [1991] (Stevens, Serita)
Red-Haired Girl [1926] (Wells, Carolyn)
Redbird's Cry [1994] (Hager, Jean)
Redemption [1988] (McGown, Jill)
Redneck Riviera [1995] (Dunbar, Sophie)
1 Reel Murder [1986] (Babson, Marian)
Rehearsal for Murder [1988] (Carlson, P. M.)
Rehearsals for Murder [1940] (Ferrars, E. X.)
Relative Innocence [1996] (Shelton, Connie)
1 Relative Stranger [1991] (Lucke, Margaret) ☆
1 Religious Body [1966] (Aird, Catherine)
Remember March [1988] (Adamson, M. J.)
Remember Me, Irene [1996] (Burke, Jan)
Remember the Alibi [1994] (Squire, Elizabeth Daniels)
Remodeled to Death [1995] (Wolzien, Valerie)

Remove the Bodies [1940] (Ferrars, E. X.)
1 Rendezvous with the Past [1940] (Knight, Kathleen M.)
1 Renewable Virgin [1984] (Paul, Barbara)
Reno Rendezvous [1939] (Ford, Leslie)
Repent at Leisure [1962] (Foley, Rae)
1 Report for Murder [1987] (McDermid, Val)
Requiem for a Dove [1990] (Eccles, Marjorie)
Requiem for a Mezzo [1996] (Dunn, Carola)
Rest in Pieces [1992] (Brown, Rita Mae)
1 Rest You Merry [1978] (MacLeod, Charlotte)
Resurrection Man [1992] (MacLeod, Charlotte)
Resurrection Row [1981] (Perry, Anne)
Return of Dr. Sam: Johnson, Detector [1984] (de la Torre, L.)
Rich, Radiant Slaughter [1988] (Papazoglou, Orania)
Riddle of a Lady [1956] (Gilbert, Anthony)
Right Jack [1987] (Maron, Margaret)
Right Murder [1941] (Rice, Craig)
Right on the Money [1993] (Lathen, Emma)
Rigor Mortis [1991] (Kittredge, Mary)
Ring for a Noose [1963] (Gilbert, Anthony)
Ringer [1971] (Shannon, Dell)
Ripley Under Water [1992] (Highsmith, Patricia)
Ripley Underground [1970] (Highsmith, Patricia)
Ripley's Game [1974] (Highsmith, Patricia)
Rising of the Moon [1945] (Mitchell, Gladys)
Risky Way to Kill [1969] (Lockridge, Frances & Richard)
1 Ritual Bath [1986] (Kellerman, Faye) ★
Ritual Murder [1982] (Haymon, S. T.) ★
Robber's Trail [1992] (Lee W. W.)
Robber's Wine [1996] (Hart, Ellen)
Rockefeller Gift [1982] (Winslow, Pauline Glen)
Rogue Wave [1991] (Dunlap, Susan)
1 Rogue's Gold [1989] (Lee W. W.)
Roll Over and Play Dead [1991] (Hess, Joan)
Roll-Top Desk Mystery [1932] (Wells, Carolyn)
Rook-Shoot [1991] (Duffy, Margaret)
Room for a Body [1963] (Bell, Josephine)
1 Room with a Clue [1993] (Kingsbury, Kate)
1 Room with the Tassels [1918] (Wells, Carolyn)
Root of All Evil [1984] (Ferrars, E. X.)
Root of All Evil [1964] (Shannon, Dell)
Roots of Evil [1994] (Mitchell, Kay)
Ropedancer's Fall [1990] (Lorens, M. K.)
Rose Rent [1986] (Peters, Ellis)
1 Roseanna [1967] (Sjöwall, Maj & Per Wahlöö)
Rosemary for Remembrance [1988] (Thomson, June)
Rosemary Remembered [1995] (Albert, Susan Wittig)
Rosewood Casket [1996] (McCrumb, Sharyn)
Rotten Apples [1995] (Cooper, Natasha)
1 Rotten Apples [1977] (Green, Edith Pinero)
Rotten Lies [1995] (Elkins, Charlotte & Aaron)
Rough Water [1994] (Gunning, Sally)
Rouse the Demon [1976] (Weston, Carolyn)
Ruddy Gore [1995] (Greenwood, Kerry)
Ruffled Feathers [1992] (McCafferty, Taylor)
Ruffly Speaking [1993] (Conant, Susan)
Run for Your Life [1956] (Foley, Rae)
Run from Nightmare [1981] (O'Callaghan, Maxine)
Run to Evil [1963] (Egan, Lesley)
Runaway [1985] (Watson, Clarissa)
Running Deep [1965] (Petrie, Rhona)
Running for Shelter [1995] (Spring, Michelle)
1 Running from the Law [1995] (Scottoline, Lisa)
Rustler's Venom [1990] (Lee W. W.)
Rutland Place [1983] (Perry, Anne)

S

Sabotage Murder Mystery [1941] (Allingham, Margery)
Sacred and Profane [1987] (Kellerman, Faye)
Sad Cypress [1939] (Christie, Agatha)
Safe at Home [1991] (Gordon, Alison)
Safe Place to Die [1993] (Law, Janice)
∎ Safe Place to Sleep [1992] (Jordan, Jennifer)
Salmon in the Soup [1990] (O'Brien, Meg)
Saltmarsh Murders [1932] (Mitchell, Gladys)
∎ Samson's Deal [1983] (Singer, Shelley)
Sanctuary [1994] (Kellerman, Faye)
Sanctuary Sparrow [1983] (Peters, Ellis)
Sandbar Sinister [1934] (Taylor, Phoebe Atwood)
Sarsen Place [1974] (Butler, Gwendoline)
∎ Satan's Lambs [1993] (Hightower, Lynn S.) ★
Satan's Silence [1997] (Matthews, Alex)
∎ Saturday Morning Murder [1988] (Gur, Batya)
Say It with Flowers [1960] (Mitchell, Gladys)
∎ Say It with Poison [1991] (Granger, Ann)
Say No to Murder [1985] (Pickard, Nancy) ★
Scales of Justice [1955] (Marsh, Ngaio) ★
∎ Scalpel's Edge [1991] (Fromer, Margot J.)
Scandal in Fair Haven [1994] (Hart, Carolyn G.) ☆
Scared to Death [1977] (Morice, Anne)
Scarlet Button [1944] (Gilbert, Anthony)
Scarlet Night [1980] (Davis, Dorothy Salisbury)
∎ Scavengers [1987] (Montgomery, Yvonne E.)
Scenes of Crime [1976] (Egan, Lesley)
Scent of Death [1985] (Page, Emma)
School of English Murder [1990] (Edwards, Ruth Dudley)
Schooled to Kill [1969] (Shannon, Dell)
∎ Screaming Bones [1990] (Burden, Pat) ☆
Screwdriver [1988] (Kraft, Gabrielle)
Sea Fever [1991] (Cleeves, Ann)
∎ Sea of Troubles [1990] (Smith, Janet L.) ☆
Search for a Scientist [1948] (Leonard, Charles L.)
Searching for Sara [1994] (Singer, Shelley)
Season for Murder [1992] (Granger, Ann)
Season of Knives [1996] (Chisholm, P. F.)
Season of Snows and Sins [1971] (Moyes, Patricia) ★
Seasons of Death [1981] (Wren, M. K.)
Second Guess [1994] (Beecham, Rose)
Second Shot in the Dark [1990] (Roome, Annette)
∎ Secret Adversary [1922] (Christie, Agatha)
Secret of the Spa [1944] (Leonard, Charles L.)
∎ Secret's Shadow [1996] (Matthews, Alex)
Secrets for Sale [1950] (Leonard, Charles L.)
Seeing Eye [1958] (Bell, Josephine)
Seminar for Murder [1985] (Gill, B. M.)
Send a Fax to the Kasbah [1992] (Dunnett, Dorothy)
∎ Seneca Falls Inheritance [1992] (Monfredo, M. G.) ☆ ☆
Serious Investigation [1968] (Egan, Lesley)
Serpent's Tooth [1971] (Woods, Sara)
Servant's Problem [1958] (Johns, Veronica Parker)
Servant's Tale [1993] (Frazer, Margaret) ☆
Service for Two [1994] (Kingsbury, Kate)
Set-Up [1991] (O'Callaghan, Maxine)
Setting for Murder [1988] (Fulton, Eileen)
Seven Black Stones [1995] (Hager, Jean)
Seven Kinds of Death [1992] (Wilhelm, Kate)
Seven Stars [1995] (Fraser, Anthea)
Seven Were Suspect [1937] (Knight, Kathleen Moore)
Seven Were Veiled [1937] (Knight, Kathleen Moore)
Seventh Avenue Murder [1990] (Bennett, Liza)

Seventh Mourner [1958] (Gardiner, Dorothy)
∎ Seventh Sinner [1972] (Peters, Elizabeth)
77th Street Requiem [1995] (Hornsby, Wendy)
Severed Key [1973] (Nielsen, Helen)
Shades of Darkness [1970] (Torrie, Malcolm)
Shades of Gray [1988] (Hooper, Kay)
∎ Shadow of a Child [1996] (O'Callaghan, Maxine)
Shadow of a Doubt [1981] (Thomson, June)
Shadow of Death [1995] (Gilpatrick, Noreen)
∎ Shadow of Doubt [1996] (Jacobs, Jonnie)
Shadow of the Palms [1980] (Law, Janice)
Shadow Play [1993] (Fyfield, Frances)
Shadow Walkers [1993] (Romberg, Nina)
∎ Shadowdance [1989] (Bushell, Agnes)
Shadows in Bronze [1990] (Davis, Lindsey)
Shadows in Their Blood [1993] (Babson, Marian)
∎ Shadows on the Mirror [1989] (Fyfield, Frances)
Shady Doings [1941] (Johns, Veronica Parker)
Shake Hands Forever [1975] (Rendell, Ruth)
Shape of a Stain [1942] (Ferrars, E. X.)
Shape of Dread [1989] (Muller, Marcia) ★ ☆
∎ Share in Death [1993] (Crombie, Deborah) ☆ ☆
Sharkbait [1993] (Geason, Susan)
∎ Shattered Moon [1986] (Green, Kate) ☆
Shattered Rhythms [1994] (Knight, Phyllis)
Shattered Silk [1986] (Michaels, Barbara)
∎ Shaved Fish [1993] (Geason, Susan)
She Came Back [1945] (Wentworth, Patricia)
She Came by the Book [1995] (Wings, Mary)
She Came in a Flash [1990] (Wings, Mary)
∎ She Came Too Late [1987] (Wings, Mary)
She Shall Die [1961] (Gilbert, Anthony)
She Vanished in the Dawn [1941] (Gilbert, Anthony)
She Walks in Beauty [1991] (Shankman, Sarah)
She Walks These Hills [1994] (McCrumb, Sharyn) ★ ★ ★
Shed Light on Death [1985] (Taylor, L. A.)
Sheriff & the Branding Iron Murders [1985] (Meredith, D. R.)
Sheriff & the Folsom Man Murders [1987] (Meredith, D. R.)
∎ Sheriff & the Panhandle Murders [1984] (Meredith, D. R.)
Sheriff & the Pheasant Hunt Murders [1993] (Meredith, D. R.)
Shilling for Candles [1936] (Tey, Josephine)
Shocking Pink Hat [1946] (Crane, Frances)
Shoot, Don't Shoot [1995] (Jance, J. A.)
Shooting at Loons [1994] (Maron, Margaret)
∎ Shore to Die [1996] (Wolzien, Valerie)
Short Cut to Santa Fe [1994] (Sale, Medora)
Short Time to Live [1976] (Moffat, Gwen)
Shortest Day [1995] (Langton, Jane)
Shortest Journey [1992] (Holt, Hazel)
Shortest Way to Hades [1985] (Caudwell, Sarah)
Shot on Location [1990] (Jones, Hazel Wynn)
Show of Violence [1975] (Woods, Sara)
Show Red for Danger [1960] (Lockridge, Frances & R.)
Show Stopper [1992] (Pulver, Mary Monica)
∎ Showcase [1992] (Glen, Alison)
Shred of Evidence [1995] (McGown, Jill)
Shroud for a Lady [1956] (Daly, Elizabeth)
Shroud for a Nightingale [1971] (James, P. D.) ★ ☆
Shroud for a Scholar [1995] (Peterson, Audrey)
∎ Shroud for the Bride [1945] (Olsen, D. B.)
Shroud for Delilah [1986] (Fraser, Anthea)
Shy Tulip Murders [1995] (Rothenberg, Rebecca)
∎ Sick of Shadows [1984] (McCrumb, Sharyn)
Signs of Murder [1993] (Bedford, Jean)
Silence in Hanover Close [1988] (Perry, Anne)
Silence of the Hams [1996] (Churchill, Jill)

S . . . continued

1 Silent Buddy [1995] (Flora, Kate Clark)
Silent Pool [1954] (Wentworth, Patricia)
Silent Witness [1972] (Yorke, Margaret)
Silhouette in Scarlet [1983] (Peters, Elizabeth)
Silver Ghost [1987] (MacLeod, Charlotte)
Silver Ladies [1950] (Erskine, Margaret)
Silver Leopard [1946] (Reilly, Helen)
1 Silver Moon [1990] (McNab, Claire)
1 Silver Pigs [1989] (Davis, Lindsey)
Silver Scalpel [1993] (Jacobs, Nancy Baker)
1 Silverlake Heat [1993] (Schmidt, Carol)
Simisola [1994] (Rendell, Ruth)
Simple Way of Poison [1937] (Ford, Leslie)
Simply to Die For [1989] (Christmas, Joyce)
Sing a Song of Death [1993] (Dain, Catherine)
Singing in the Shrouds [1958] (Marsh, Ngaio)
Singing Sands [1952] (Tey, Josephine)
Single Stone [1991] (Wallace, Marilyn) ☆
Sinister Assignment [1960] (Fenisong, Ruth)
Sinister Shelter [1949] (Leonard, Charles L.)
Sins of the Fathers [1970] (Rendell, Ruth)
Sins of the Heart [1994] (Bannister, Jo)
Sins of the Wolf [1994] (Perry, Anne)
Siren in the Night [1943] (Ford, Leslie)
Sirens Sang of Murder [1989] (Caudwell, Sarah) ★ ☆
1 Sister Beneath the Sheet [1991] (Linscott, Gillian)
Sister Death [1980] (Winslow, Pauline Glen)
Sister's Keeper [1994] (Lorden, Randye)
Sisters of the Road [1986] (Wilson, Barbara)
Six Feet Under [1982] (Simpson, Dorothy)
Six Iron Spiders [1942] (Taylor, Phoebe Atwood)
Six Proud Walkers [1989] (Fraser, Anthea)
Six-Letter Word for Death [1983] (Moyes, Patricia)
Skeleton at the Feast [1931] (Wells, Carolyn)
Skeleton Island [1967] (Mitchell, Gladys)
1 Skeleton Key [1943] (Offord, Lenore Glen)
Skeletons in the Closet [1982] (Linington, Elizabeth)
1 Skins [1993] (O'Connell, Catherine)
Skull and Dog Bones [1994] (Cleary, Melissa)
Skull Beneath the Skin [1982] (James, P. D.)
Skylark [1992] (Simonson, Sheila)
Slash of Scarlet [1992] (Jacobs, Nancy Baker)
1 Slay at the Races [1990] (Morgan, Kate)
Sleep No More [1958] (Erskine, Margaret)
Sleep of Death [1982] (Morice, Anne)
Sleep of the Innocent [1991] (Sale, Medora)
Sleep of the Unjust [1990] (Ferrars, E. X.)
Sleep While I Sing [1986] (Wright, L. R.)
Sleep with Slander [1960] (Hitchens, Dolores)
1 Sleep with Strangers [1957] (Hitchens, Dolores)
1 Sleeping Dogs [1929] (Wells, Carolyn)
Sleeping Lady [1996] (Henry, Sue)
Sleeping Life [1978] (Rendell, Ruth) ☆
Sleeping Murder [1976] (Christie, Agatha)
Sleeping Witness [1951] (Heberden, M. V.)
Slight Mourning [1975] (Aird, Catherine)
Slow Burn [1993] (Bland, Eleanor Taylor)
Slow Squeeze [1994] (Pugh, Dianne G.)
1 Small Favors [1988] (Wallace, Patricia)
Small Sacrifice [1994] (Hart, Ellen) ★
Smart House [1989] (Wilhelm, Kate)
1 Smart Money [1988] (Matera, Lia)
1 Smile, Honey [1991] (Donald, Anabel)
Smiling at Death [1996] (Rowlands, Betty)

Smiling Tiger [1949] (Offord, Lenore Glen)
Smoke Without Fire [1990] (Ferrars, E. X.)
Snagged [1993] (Clark, Carol Higgins)
Snake Dance [1992] (Mariz, Linda French)
Snake in the Grass [1954] (Gilbert, Anthony)
Snake Tattoo [1989] (Barnes, Linda)
Snake, the Crocodile and the Dog [1992] (Peters, E.) ☆
Snapshot [1993] (Barnes, Linda)
Snare [1987] (Moffat, Gwen)
Snares of Death [1993] (Charles, Kate)
Sneaks [1979] (Green, Edith Pinero)
Snow-White Murder [1939] (Ford, Leslie)
1 Snowstorms in a Hot Climate [1988] (Dunant, Sarah)
So Little to Die For [1994] (Grindle, Lucretia)
Sold to Miss Seeton [1995] (Crane, Hamilton)
Solitary Twist [1993] (Pincus, Elizabeth)
Some Avenger, Rise [1966] (Egan, Lesley)
Some Die Eloquent [1979] (Aird, Catherine)
Some Die Young [1990] (Hart, Jeanne)
Some Lie and Some Die [1973] (Rendell, Ruth)
Somebody Killed the Messenger [1988] (Watson, C.)
Somebody's Dead in Snellville [1992] (Sprinkle, P. H.)
Someone Is Killing the Great Chefs of America ['93] (Lyons)
1 Someone Is Killing the Great Chefs of Europe ['76] (Lyons)
Someone to Watch [1995] (Maiman, Jaye)
Something About Midnight [1950] (Olsen, D. B.)
Something in the Air [1988] (Lathen, Emma)
Something in the Cellar [1995] (Shepherd, Stella)
Something in the Water [1994] (MacLeod, Charlotte)
Something Nasty in the Woodshed [1942] (Gilbert, A.)
Something Shady [1986] (Dreher, Sarah)
Something the Cat Dragged In [1983] (MacLeod, C.)
1 Something To Kill For [1994] (Holtzer, Susan) ★
1 Something Wicked [1983] (Ferrars, E. X.)
Something Wicked [1988] (Hart, Carolyn G.) ★ ★
Something Wrong [1967] (Linington, Elizabeth)
1 Something's Cooking [1993] (Pence, Joanne)
Somewhere in the House [1946] (Daly, Elizabeth)
Sorrowheart [1993] (Lorens, M. K.)
Sound Evidence [1984] (Thomson, June)
1 Sour Cream with Everything [1966] (Porter, Joyce)
Sourdough Wars [1984] (Smith, Julie)
Southern Discomfort [1993] (Maron, Margaret) ☆ ☆
Southern Ghost [1992] (Hart, Carolyn G.) ☆ ☆
1 Speak Daggers to Her [1994] (Edghill, Rosemary)
Speak No Evil [1985] (Warner, Mignon)
Speaker of Mandarin [1983] (Rendell, Ruth)
1 Speedy Death [1929] (Mitchell, Gladys)
Spin Your Web, Lady! [1949] (Lockridge, Frances & R.)
Spinster's Secret [1946] (Gilbert, Anthony)
Spinsters in Jeopardy [1953] (Marsh, Ngaio)
1 Spirit Stalker [1989] (Romberg, Nina)
Spit in the Ocean [1987] (Singer, Shelley)
Splash of Red [1981] (Fraser, Antonia)
Split Code [1976] (Dunnett, Dorothy)
Split Second [1985] (Meek, M. R. D.)
Spoils of Time [1989] (Thomson, June)
1 Spoilt Kill [1961] (Kelly, Mary) ★
Spooky Hollow [1923] (Wells, Carolyn)
1 Sports Freak [1980] (OCork, Shannon)
Spotlight [1947] (Wentworth, Patricia)
Spotted Hemlock [1958] (Mitchell, Gladys)
Spree [1992] (MacGregor, T. J.)
Spring Harrowing [1939] (Taylor, Phoebe Atwood)
Spring of Violence [1973] (Shannon, Dell)
St. Patrick's Day Murder [1994] (Harris, Lee)

S . . . continued

St. Peter's Fair [1981] (Peters, Ellis)
St. Peter's Finger [1938] (Mitchell, Gladys)
St. Valentine's Day Murders [1985] (Edwards, Ruth D.)
Stage Fright [1992] (Hart, Ellen)
Stage Fright [1993] (Linscott, Gillian)
Staircase 4 [1949] (Reilly, Helen)
Stalker [1984] (Cody, Liza)
Stand up and Die [1952] (Lockridge, Frances & Richard)
1 Stand-in for Murder [1994] (Bradley, Lynn)
Star-Spangled Murder [1993] (Wolzien, Valerie)
Starring Miss Seeton [1994] (Crane, Hamilton)
Stately Home Murder [1969] (Aird, Catherine)
Stately Homicide [1984] (Haymon, S. T.)
Steel Guitar [1991] (Barnes, Linda)
Step in the Dark [1976] (Lemarchand, Elizabeth)
Stiff as a Broad [1972] (Fickling, G. G.)
Stiff Critique [1995] (Girdner, Jaqueline)
1 Still Explosion [1993] (Logue, Mary)
Still Water [1996] (Gunning, Sally)
1 Still Waters [1991] (Tucker, Kerry)
Still Waters [1992] (Welch, Pat)
Stillness in Bethlehem [1992] (Haddam, Jane)
Stitch in Time [1968] (Lathen, Emma)
Stitches in Time [1995] (Michaels, Barbara)
Stolen Moments [1990] (Woods, Sherryl)
1 Stolen Squadron [1942] (Leonard, Charles L.)
Stone Hawk [1989] (Moffat, Gwen)
1 Stoner McTavish [1985] (Dreher, Sarah)
Storm Front [1995] (Silva, Linda Kay)
Storm Shelter [1993] (Silva, Linda Kay)
Storm Surge [1993] (MacGregor, T. J.)
Straight as an Arrow [1992] (Sibley, Celestine)
Strange Desire [1994] (Mitchell, Kay)
Strange Disappearance [1880] (Green, Anna Katherine)
Strange Felony [1986] (Linington, Elizabeth)
1 Strange Files of Fremont Jones [1995] (Day, Dianne)
1 Stranger and Afraid [1971] (Ferrars, E. X.)
1 Strangers in the Night [1994] (Tyre, Peg)
1 Strangled Prose [1986] (Hess, Joan) ☆
1 Strangled Witness [1934] (Ford, Leslie)
Stranglehold [1994] (Rowe, Jennifer)
Straw Man [1951] (Disney, Doris Miles)
Strawgirl [1994] (Padgett, Abigail)
Street of the Five Moons [1978] (Peters, Elizabeth)
Streets of Death [1976] (Shannon, Dell)
Striking Out [1995] (Gordon, Alison)
1 Striving with Gods [1984] (Bannister, Jo)
Strong Poison [1930] (Sayers, Dorothy L.)
Student Body [1986] (Borthwick, J. S.)
1 Study in Lilac [1987] (Oliver, Maria Antonia)
Stunning Way to Die [1991] (Christmas, Joyce)
Subscription to Murder [1940] (Heberden, M. V.)
1 Sudden Death at the Norfolk Cafe [1993] (Sullivan, W.) ★
Sudden Exposure [1996] (Dunlap, Susan)
Sudden, Fearful Death [1993] (Perry, Anne)
Suddenly at His Residence [1946] (Brand, Christianna)
1 Suddenly in Her Sorbet [1988] (Christmas, Joyce)
Suddenly While Gardening [1978] (Lemarchand, E.)
Suicide King [1988] (Singer, Shelley)
Suitable for Framing [1995] (Buchanan, Edna)
Suitable Vengeance [1991] (George, Elizabeth)
Summer of the Danes [1991] (Peters, Ellis)
Summer School Mystery [1950] (Bell, Josephine)
Summer Will End [1995] (Yeager, Dorian)

Summerhouse [1956] (Wentworth, Patricia)
Summertime Soldiers [1986] (Kelly, Susan)
1 Sunday Pigeon Murders [1942] (Rice, Craig)
Sunken Treasure [1994] (Jackson, Marian J. A.)
1 Sunrise [1994] (West, Chassie) ☆
Sunset Over Soho [1943] (Mitchell, Gladys)
Superfluous Death [1995] (Holt, Hazel)
Superior Death [1994] (Barr, Nevada)
Surfeit of Guns [1997] (Chisholm, P. F.)
Surfeit of Lampreys [1940] (Marsh, Ngaio)
Susannah Screaming [1975] (Weston, Carolyn)
1 Suspect [1985] (Wright, L. R.) ★
1 Suspect [1980] (Gill, B. M.)
Suspicious Characters [1931] (Sayers, Dorothy L.)
Suspicion of Guilt [1995] (Parker, Barbara)
1 Suspicion of Innocence [1994] (Parker, Barbara) ☆
Suspicious Death [1988] (Simpson, Dorothy)
Sweet and Low [1974] (Lathen, Emma)
Sweet Cherry Wine [1994] (Schmidt, Carol)
Sweet Danger [1933] (Allingham, Margery)
Sweet Death, Kind Death [1984] (Cross, Amanda)
Sweet Dreams, Irene [1994] (Burke, Jan)
1 Sweet Narcissus [1990] (Lorens, M. K.)
1 Sweet, Savage Death [1984] (Papazoglou, Orania) ☆
Sweet, Sweet Poison [1990] (Wilhelm, Kate)
Swing, Brother, Swing [1949] (Marsh, Ngaio)
1 Switching the Odds [1992] (Knight, Phyllis) ☆
Symbols at Your Door [1990] (Fraser, Anthea)

T

1 Tail of Two Murders [1992] (Cleary, Melissa)
Tainted Token [1938] (Knight, Kathleen Moore)
Take a Dark Journey [1965] (Erskine, Margaret)
Take a Number [1993] (Dawson, Janet)
1 Take One for Murder [1988] (Fulton, Eileen)
Taken at the Flood [1948] (Christie, Agatha)
1 Taken by Storm [1991] (Silva, Linda Kay)
1 Takeout Double [1993] (Moody, Susan)
Taking the Fifth [1987] (Jance, J. A.)
Talent for Destruction [1982] (Radley, Sheila)
1 Talented Mr. Ripley [1955] (Highsmith, Patricia) ☆
Talked to Death [1995] (Shaffer, Louise)
Tangled Roots [1995] (Cannon, Taffy)
Tanglewood Murder [1980] (Kallen, Lucille)
1 Tango Key [1988] (Drake, Alison)
Tannahill Tangle [1928] (Wells, Carolyn)
Tapestry Room Murder [1929] (Wells, Carolyn)
Tarot Murders [1978] (Warner, Mignon)
Tarry and Be Hanged [1969] (Woods, Sara)
Taste for Burning [1995] (Bannister, Jo)
Taste for Death [1986] (James, P. D.) ★ ★
1 Taste for Murder [1994] (Bishop, Claudia)
Taste of Fears [1963] (Woods, Sara)
Tasty Way to Die [1990] (Laurence, Janet)
Tea-Totally Dead [1994] (Girdner, Jaqueline)
Tell Her It's Murder [1954] (Reilly, Helen)
1 Tell Me What You Like [1993] (Allen, Kate)
1 Telling Lies [1992] (Hornsby, Wendy)
Temporary Ghost [1989] (Friedman, Mickey)
Ten Were Missing [1958] (Allingham, Margery) ★
Tenant for the Tomb [1971] (Gilbert, Anthony)
Tender Death [1990] (Meyers, Annette)
1 Tensleep [1994] (Andrews, Sarah)
Tenth Life [1977] (Lockridge, Frances & Richard)
Termination Dust [1995] (Henry, Sue)

T . . . continued

Terrible Drag for Dover [1971] (Porter, Joyce)
Terror by Twilight [1942] (Knight, Kathleen Moore)
Terrorists [1976] (Sjöwall, Maj & Per Wahlöö)
Tether's End [1958] (Allingham, Margery) ★
Thanksgiving Day Murder [1995] (Harris, Lee)
That Affair Next Door [1897] (Green, Anna Katherine)
That's the Spirit [1950] (Heberden, M. V.)
Theban Mysteries [1972] (Cross, Amanda)
Then Hang All the Liars [1989] (Shankman, Sarah)
There Hangs the Knife [1988] (Muller, Marcia)
There is a Tide [1948] (Christie, Agatha)
There is No Justice [1971] (Dominic, R. B.)
There Lies Your Love [1965] (Melville, Jennie)
There's Nothing To Be Afraid Of [1985] (Muller, Marcia)
There's Something in a Sunday [1989] (Muller, Marcia)
These Bones Were Made for Dancin' [1995] (Meyers, A.)
They Can't All Be Guilty [1947] (Heberden, M. V.)
They Do It with Mirrors [1952] (Christie, Agatha)
They Found Him Dead [1937] (Heyer, Georgette)
They Love Not Poison [1972] (Woods, Sara)
They Stay for Death [1980] (Woods, Sara)
Thief or Two [1977] (Woods, Sara)
Thin Skins [1994] (McCafferty, Taylor)
∎ Thin Woman [1984] (Cannell, Dorothy)
∎ Think of Death [1947] (Lockridge, Frances & Richard)
Thinner Than Blood [1992] (Shepherd, Stella)
Thinner Than Water [1981] (Ferrars, E. X.)
Third Crime Lucky [1959] (Gilbert, Anthony)
Third Encounter [1963] (Woods, Sara)
Third Girl [1966] (Christie, Agatha)
∎ Third Victim [1987] (Waltch, Lilla M.)
Third Way [1989] (Warmbold, Jean)
Thirteen at Dinner [1933] (Christie, Agatha)
Thirteen White Tulips [1953] (Crane, Frances)
30 Days to Live [1943] (Gilbert, Anthony)
This Blessed Plot [1990] (Meek, M. R. D.)
∎ This Business Is Murder [1993] (Christmas, Joyce)
This Fatal Writ [1979] (Woods, Sara)
∎ This Girl for Hire [1957] (Fickling, G. G.)
This Little Measure [1964] (Woods, Sara)
∎ This Little Piggy Went to Murder [1994] (Hart, Ellen)
This Way Out [1989] (Radley, Sheila)
∎ Those Who Hunt the Night [1988] (Hambly, Barbara)
Though I Know She Lies [1965] (Woods, Sara)
Threatening Eye [1988] (Grant-Adamson, Lesley)
Three Bedrooms, One Corpse [1994] (Harris, Charlaine)
Three Bright Pebbles [1938] (Ford, Leslie)
Three Is a Crowd [1994] (Borton, D. B.)
Three of Diamonds [1953] (Knight, Kathleen Moore)
Three Plots for Asey Mayo [1942] (Taylor, Phoebe A.)
Three Quick and Five Dead [1968] (Mitchell, Gladys)
Three, Three the Rivals [1992] (Fraser, Anthea)
Three Women in Black [1941] (Reilly, Helen)
Three-Act Tragedy [1934] (Christie, Agatha)
Three-Core Lead [1988] (Curzon, Clare)
Threnody for Two [1991] (Hart, Jeanne)
Through a Glass Darkly [1950] (McCloy, Helen)
Through a Gold Eagle [1996] (Monfredo, Miriam Grace)
Through the Wall [1950] (Wentworth, Patricia)
∎ Throw Darts at a Cheesecake [1993] (Dietz, Denise)
Thursday Turkey Murders [1943] (Rice, Craig)
∎ Thus Was Adonis Murdered [1981] (Caudwell, Sarah)
∎ Thyme of Death [1992] (Albert, Susan Wittig) ☆ ☆
∎ Ticking Heart [1940] (Olsen, D. B.)

Tickled to Death [1994] (Hess, Joan)
Tied up in Tinsel [1972] (Marsh, Ngaio) ☆
Ties That Bind [1991] (Woods, Sherryl)
Tiger in the Smoke [1952] (Allingham, Margery)
Tiger's Heart [1992] (Douglas, Lauren Wright)
Tightrope [1986] (White, Teri)
Till the Butchers Cut Him Down [1994] (Muller, Marcia)
Till the Old Men Die [1993] (Dawson, Janet)
Time Expired [1993] (Dunlap, Susan)
Time Lapse [1992] (Law, Janice)
Time of Hope [1990] (Kelly, Susan B.)
Time Off for Murder [1940] (Popkin, Zelda)
Time to Depart [1995] (Davis, Lindsey)
Time to Die [1944] (Lawrence, Hilda)
Tinkling Symbol [1935] (Taylor, Phoebe Atwood)
Tippy-Toe Murder [1994] (Meier, Leslie)
Tis the Season To Be Murdered [1994] (Wolzien, Valerie)
To Cache a Millionaire [1972] (Scherf, Margaret)
To Kill a Queen [1992] (Knight, Alanna)
To Live and Die in Dixie [1993] (Trocheck, Kathy H.) ☆ ☆
To Love and Be Wise [1950] (Tey, Josephine)
∎ To Make a Killing [1990] (Bedford, Jean)
To Make a Killing [1982] (Thomson, June)
To Play the Fool [1995] (King, Laurie R.)
To Sleep, Perchance to Kill [1988] (Sims, L. V.)
∎ To Spite Her Face [1971] (Dolson, Hildegarde) ☆
Toby's Folly [1990] (Arnold, Margot)
Tom Brown's Body [1949] (Mitchell, Gladys)
Tombstone Courage [1994] (Jance, J. A.)
Too Close to the Edge [1987] (Dunlap, Susan)
Too Lovely to Live [1954] (Fenisong, Ruth)
Too Many Cooks [1994] (Pence, Joanne)
∎ Too Many Crooks Spoil the Broth [1994] (Myers, Tamar)
∎ Too Many Questions [1991] (Grant-Adamson, Lesley)
∎ Too Sane a Murder [1984] (Martin, Lee)
∎ Touch a Cold Door [1989] (Roberts, Carey)
Touch & Go [1993] (Meek, M. R. D.)
Touch of Mortality [1996] (Granger, Ann)
Touch of Panic [1994] (Wright, L. R.) ☆
Tour de Force [1955] (Brand, Christianna)
Tourist Trap [1986] (Smith, Julie)
Tourists are for Trapping [1989] (Babson, Marian)
Toxic Shock [1988] (Paretsky, Sara) ★ ☆ ☆
∎ Trace Elements [1986] (Knight, Kathryn Lasky)
∎ Track of the Cat [1993] (Barr, Nevada) ★ ★
Trade-Off [1994] (O'Callaghan, Maxine)
∎ Tragedy at Freyne [1927] (Gilbert, Anthony)
Tragic Target [1952] (Heberden, M. V.)
∎ Trail of Murder [1992] (Andreae, Christine) ☆
Trail of the Dragon [1988] (Kelly, Susan)
Traitor's Gate [1995] (Perry, Anne)
Traitor's Purse [1941] (Allingham, Margery)
∎ Transatlantic Ghost [1933] (Gardiner, Dorothy)
∎ Transcendental Murder [1964] (Langton, Jane)
Trap for Fools [1989] (Cross, Amanda)
Traveling with the Dead [1995] (Hambly, Barbara)
Traveller Returns [1945] (Wentworth, Patricia)
Treachery in Trieste [1951] (Leonard, Charles L.)
Treason in My Breast [1938] (Gilbert, Anthony)
Treble Exposure [1987] (Morice, Anne)
∎ Tree of Death [1983] (Muller, Marcia)
Trial by Fire [1990] (Fyfield, Frances)
Trial by Fury [1986] (Jance, J. A.)
Trial by Fury [1941] (Rice, Craig)
Trick or Treat [1955] (Disney, Doris Miles)
Triple Murder [1929] (Wells, Carolyn)

T . . . continued

Trojan Gold [1987] (Peters, Elizabeth)
Trojan Hearse [1985] (Curzon, Clare)
Trophies and Dead Things [1990] (Muller, Marcia)
Tropical Issue [1983] (Dunnett, Dorothy)
■ Trouble at Aquitaine [1985] (Livingston, Nancy)
Trouble at Turkey Hill [1946] (Knight, Kathleen Moore)
Trouble in the Brasses [1989] (Craig, Alisa)
Trouble in Transylvania [1993] (Wilson, Barbara)
Trouble Looking for a Place to Happen [1995] (Kelner, T.)
■ Trouble of Fools [1987] (Barnes, Linda) ★ ☆ ☆
Trouble with a Bad Fit [1996] (Crespi, Camilla)
■ Trouble with a Small Raise [1991] (Crespi, Camilla)
Trouble with Going Home [1995] (Crespi, Camilla)
Trouble with Moonlighting [1991] (Crespi, Camilla)
Trouble with Thin Ice [1993] (Crespi, Camilla)
Trouble with Too Much Sun [1992] (Crespi, Camilla)
■ Troublecross [1972] (Mann, Jessica)
Troubled Water [1993] (Gunning, Sally)
Troubled Waters [1982] (Lemarchand, Elizabeth)
■ True-Life Adventure [1985] (Smith, Julie)
Trunk Show [1995] (Glen, Alison)
Trusted Like the Fox [1964] (Woods, Sara)
Tunnel Vision [1994] (Paretsky, Sara)
Turkey Tracks [1994] (Brown, Lizbie)
■ Turquoise Shop [1941] (Crane, Frances)
■ Turquoise Tattoo [1991] (Jacobs, Nancy Baker)
Turtle Baby [1995] (Padgett, Abigail)
Twelve Horses and the Hangman's Noose [1956] (Mitchell, Gladys)
27-Ingredient Chili Con Carne Murders [1993] (Rich, V.)
Twenty-Third Man [1957] (Mitchell, Gladys)
Twice in a Blue Moon [1993] (Moyes, Patricia)
Twilight [1995] (Pickard, Nancy)
Twister [1994] (Block, Barbara)
Two Against Scotland Yard [1931] (Frome, David)
Two for the Dough [1996] (Evanovich, Janet)
Two Points for Murder [1993] (Borton, D. B.)
■ Two-Bit Tango [1992] (Pincus, Elizabeth)
Two-thirds of a Ghost [1956] (McCloy, Helen)

U

Ultraviolet Widow [1956] (Crane, Frances)
Umbrella Murder [1931] (Wells, Carolyn)
■ Unbalanced Accounts [1986] (Gallison, Kate)
Uncertain Death [1961] (Gilbert, Anthony)
Uncertain Death [1993] (Holt, Hazel)
Uncoffin'd Clay [1980] (Mitchell, Gladys)
Uncommon Murder [1993] (Donald, Anabel)
Under Contract [1986] (Cody, Liza)
Under My Skin [1995] (Dunant, Sarah)
Under My Skin [1993] (Maiman, Jaye)
Under Orion [1978] (Law, Janice)
Under the Beetle's Cellar [1995] (Walker, Mary Willis)
■ Under the Influence [1989] (Travis, Elizabeth)
Under Water [1992] (Gunning, Sally)
Underdog [1996] (Berenson, Laurien)
Uneaseful Death [1988] (Hardwick, Mollie)
Unexpected Corpse [1990] (Oliphant, B. J.)
Unexpected Death [1970] (Shannon, Dell)
Unexpected Developments [1984] (Dominic, R. B.)
■ Unexpected Mrs. Pollifax [1966] (Gilman, Dorothy)
■ Unexpected Night [1940] (Daly, Elizabeth)
Unforgiving Minutes [1988] (Pulver, Mary M.)

Unhappy Returns [1977] (Lemarchand, Elizabeth)
Unholy Ghosts [1992] (Greenwood, Diane M.)
Union Jack [1993] (McDermid, Val)
Unkindness of Ravens [1985] (Rendell, Ruth) ☆
Unmasking Kelsey [1988] (Hooper, Kay)
Unnatural Causes [1967] (James, P. D.)
Unnatural Death [1927] (Sayers, Dorothy L.)
■ Unorthodox Methods [1989] (Valentine, Deborah)
■ Unorthodox Practices [1989] (Piesman, Marissa)
Unpleasantness at the Bellona Club [1928] (Sayers, D. L.)
Unquestioned Loyalty [1995] (Lamb, J. Dayne)
■ Unquiet Grave [1987] (La Pierre, Janet) ☆
Unsafe Keeping [1995] (Cail, Carol)
■ Unsuitable Job for a Woman [1972] (James, P. D.) ☆
Untidy Murder [1947] (Lockridge, Frances & Richard)
■ Until Death [1994] (Whitney, Polly) ☆
Until It Hurts [1996] (Whitney, Polly)
Until Justice is Done [1994] (McGuire, Christine)
■ Until Proven Guilty [1985] (Jance, J. A.)
■ Until Proven Guilty [1993] (McGuire, Christine)
Until Proven Innocent [1990] (Kelly, Susan)
Until the End of Time [1995] (Whitney, Polly)
Unwilling to Vegas [1991] (Livingston, Nancy)
Up Jumps the Devil [1996] (Maron, Margaret)
■ Upfold Witch [1964] (Bell, Josephine)
Urn Burial [1996] (Greenwood, Kerry)
Used to Kill [1993] (O'Donnell, Lillian)
■ User Deadly [1989] (Danks, Denise)

V

Vacations Can Be Murder [1995] (Shelton, Connie)
Valse Macabre [1952] (Knight, Kathleen Moore)
Vane Pursuit [1989] (MacLeod, Charlotte)
Vanishing Corpse [1941] (Gilbert, Anthony)
Vanishing of Betty Varian [1922] (Wells, Carolyn)
Vanishing Point [1953] (Wentworth, Patricia)
Veiled One [1988] (Rendell, Ruth)
Velvet Hand [1953] (Reilly, Helen)
Venetian Reckoning [1995] (Leon, Donna)
Venus in Copper [1991] (Davis, Lindsey)
Veronica's Sisters [1992] (Moffat, Gwen)
Very Good Hater [1981] (Challis, Mary)
Very Particular Murder [1989] (Haymon, S. T.)
Vial Murders [1995] (Landreth, Marsha)
Vicious Pattern [1945] (Heberden, M. V.)
Vicky Van [1918] (Wells, Carolyn)
■ Victims [1980] (Gill, B. M.)
Villains by Necessity [1982] (Woods, Sara)
Vintage Murder [1937] (Marsh, Ngaio)
Vintage Murder [1994] (Smith, Janet L.)
Violent End [1988] (Page, Emma)
Virgin in the Ice [1982] (Peters, Ellis)
Visiting Villain [1934] (Wells, Carolyn)
Visitor [1967] (Gilbert, Anthony)
Vital Lies [1991] (Hart, Ellen)
Voice [1964] (Gilbert, Anthony)
Voice of Murder [1965] (Erskine, Margaret)
Voice of the House [1947] (Erskine, Margaret)
Voice of the Past [1981] (Leek, Margaret)
Vow of Chastity [1992] (Black, Veronica)
Vow of Devotion [1994] (Black, Veronica)
Vow of Felicity [1996] (Black, Veronica)
Vow of Obedience [1993] (Black, Veronica)
Vow of Penance [1994] (Black, Veronica)
Vow of Poverty [1995] (Black, Veronica)

V . . . *continued*

Vow of Sanctity [1993] (Black, Veronica)
∎ Vow of Silence [1990] (Black, Veronica)
Voyage into Violence [1956] (Lockridge, Frances & R.)
Voyage of the Chianti [1987] (Morison, B. J.)

W

Wages of Sin [1994] (Woods, Sherryl)
Waikiki Widow [1953] (Sheridan, Juanita)
Wait for the Dark [1993] (Crowleigh, Ann)
Wake Her Dead [1992] (Simpson, Dorothy)
Wake Up, Darlin' Corey [1984] (Wren, M. K.)
Walk a Crooked Mile [1994] (Dain, Catherine)
Walking Dead Man [1992] (Kittredge, Mary)
Walking Shadow [1959] (Offord, Lenore Glen)
∎ Wall of Eyes [1943] (Millar, Margaret)
Wandering Arm [1995] (Newman, Sharan)
Wandering Knife [1952] (Rinehart, Mary Roberts)
Wandering Soul Murders [1993] (Bowen, Gail)
Wanted Dude or Alive [1994] (Morgan, Kate)
Washington Whispers Murder [1953] (Ford, Leslie)
Watersplash [1951] (Wentworth, Patricia)
Watson's Choice [1955] (Mitchell, Gladys)
∎ We Know Where You Live [1995] (Taylor, Jean)
∎ We Must Have a Trial [1980] (Leek, Margaret)
We Wish You a Merry Murder [1991] (Wolzien, Valerie)
Weak-Eyed Bat [1942] (Millar, Margaret)
Weathering the Storm [1994] (Silva, Linda Kay)
Weaver's Tale [1993] (Sedley, Kate)
Weep for Her [1980] (Woods, Sara)
Well-Known Face [1960] (Bell, Josephine)
Well-Schooled in Murder [1990] (George, Elizabeth)
Wench Is Dead [1953] (Fenisong, Ruth)
∎ What Crime Is It? [1956] (Gardiner, Dorothy)
What Men Say [1993] (Smith, Joan)
What Mrs. McGillicuddy Saw! [1957] (Christie, Agatha)
What Should You Know of Dying? [1967] (Wells, Tobias)
What To Do Until the Undertaker Comes [1971] (Wells, T.)
∎ What's a Girl Gotta Do? [1994] (Hayter, Sparkle) ★
Wheel That Turned [1936] (Knight, Kathleen Moore)
Wheel Turns [1983] (Lemarchand, Elizabeth)
Wheels Within Wheels [1923] (Wells, Carolyn)
∎ When Death Comes Stealing [1994] (Wesley, Valerie W.) ☆
When Dover Gets Knotted [1977] (Porter, Joyce)
When in Greece [1969] (Lathen, Emma) ☆
When in Rome [1970] (Marsh, Ngaio)
When Last I Died [1941] (Mitchell, Gladys)
Where Death Lies [1991] (Fallon, Ann C.)
Where Echoes Live [1991] (Muller, Marcia) ☆
Where Is Mary Bostwick? [1958] (Foley, Rae)
∎ Where Lawyers Fear to Tread [1986] (Matera, Lia) ☆
Where Nobody Dies [1986] (Wheat, Carolyn)
∎ Where Old Bones Lie [1993] (Granger, Ann)
Where Should He Die? [1983] (Woods, Sara)
Where There's a Will [1980] (Burton, Anne)
Where's Emily? [1927] (Wells, Carolyn)
Whiff of Sulphur [1987] (Linscott, Gillian)
While the Coffin Waited [1952] (Sheridan, Juanita)
While the Patient Slept [1930] (Eberhart, Mignon G.)
Whim to Kill [1971] (Shannon, Dell)
Whispering House [1947] (Erskine, Margaret)
Whispering Knights [1980] (Mitchell, Gladys)
White Alley [1915] (Wells, Carolyn)
White Hand [1988] (Warmbold, Jean)

White Lightning [1995] (Woods, Sherryl)
∎ White Male Running [1985] (Webb, Martha G.)
Whitelands Affair [1989] (Clarke, Anna)
Who Dropped Peter Pan? [1995] (Dentinger, Jane)
Who Goes Home? [1986] (Lemarchand, Elizabeth)
Who Is Simon Warwick? [1979] (Moyes, Patricia)
Who Killed Caldwell? [1942] (Wells, Carolyn)
Who Killed Chloe? [1937] (Allingham, Margery)
Who Killed Cock Robin? [1990] (Duffy, Margaret)
∎ Who Killed What's-Her-Name? [1994] (Squire, Elizabeth D.)
Who Lies Here? [1965] (Peters, Ellis)
Who Saw Her Die? [1970] (Moyes, Patricia) ☆
Who Saw Him Die? [1987] (Radley, Sheila)
Who the Heck Is Sylvia? [1977] (Porter, Joyce)
Who's Calling? [1942] (McCloy, Helen)
Whom the Gods Love [1995] (Ross, Kate)
∎ Whose Body? [1923] (Sayers, Dorothy L.)
Why Aren't They Screaming? [1988] (Smith, Joan)
Wicked Designs [1980] (O'Donnell, Lillian)
Wicked, Loving Murder [1985] (Papazoglou, Orania)
∎ Wicked Slice [1989] (Elkins, Charlotte & Aaron)
Wicked Uncle [1947] (Wentworth, Patricia)
Widow's Club [1988] (Cannell, Dorothy) ☆ ☆
Widow's Peak [1994] (Linscott, Gillian)
∎ Widows [1983] (La Plante, Lynda)
Widows II [1985] (La Plante, Lynda)
Widows' Watch [1995] (Herndon, Nancy)
Wild and Lonely Place [1995] (Muller, Marcia)
Wild Island [1978] (Fraser, Antonia)
Wild Justice [1987] (Grant-Adamson, Lesley)
Wild Kat [1994] (Kijewski, Karen)
Wilderness Trek [1990] (Tell, Dorothy)
Windsor Knot [1990] (McCrumb, Sharyn)
Windsor Red [1988] (Melville, Jennie)
Windy City Blues [1995] (Paretsky, Sara)
Windy Side of the Law [1965] (Woods, Sara)
Wine of Life [1985] (Egan, Lesley)
Wine of Violence [1969] (Egan, Lesley)
Wink a Hopeful Eye [1994] (Danks, Denise)
Winking at the Brim [1974] (Mitchell, Gladys)
Winter Garden Mystery [1995] (Dunn, Carola)
∎ Winter Widow [1992] (Weir, Charlene) ★ ☆
∎ Wish You Were Here [1990] (Brown, Rita Mae)
Witch Hill Murder [1977] (Winslow, Pauline Glen)
Witch Miss Seeton [1971] (Crane, Hamilton)
Witches' Bane [1993] (Albert, Susan Wittig)
Witching Murder [1990] (Melville, Jennie)
With a Vengeance [1966] (Shannon, Dell)
With Child [1996] (King, Laurie R.)
∎ With Deadly Intent [1993] (Hendricksen, Louise)
∎ With Flowers That Fell [1983] (Meek, M. R. D.)
With Friends Like These [1993] (Roberts, Gillian)
With Intent to Kill [1972] (Shannon, Dell)
With One Stone [1961] (Lockridge, Frances & Richard)
With Option to Die [1967] (Lockridge, Frances & Richard)
Withdrawing Room [1980] (MacLeod, Charlotte)
Without Due Process [1992] (Jance, J. A.) ★
Witness [1969] (Uhnak, Dorothy)
Wolf in Death's Clothing [1995] (Quinn, Elizabeth)
Wolf in Man's Clothing [1942] (Eberhart, Mignon G.)
Wolf in the Shadows [1993] (Muller, Marcia) ★ ☆ ☆
Wolf Path [1992] (Van Gieson, Judith)
Wolf to Slaughter [1967] (Rendell, Ruth)
Wolf Whispered Death [1986] (Moore, Barbara)
∎ Wolf! Wolf! [1979] (Bell, Josephine)
Woman at Belguardo [1961] (Erskine, Margaret)

W . . . continued

Woman in Black [1947] (Ford, Leslie)
Woman in Red [1941] (Gilbert, Anthony)
Woman in the Alcove [1906] (Green, Anna Katherine)
Woman Slaughter [1989] (Ferrars, E. X.)
Woman Who Was Not There [1996] (Melville, Jennie)
Woman's Own Mystery [1990] (Wakefield, Hannah)
Woman's Place [1994] (Grant, Linda)
Wooden Indian [1935] (Wells, Carolyn)
1 Working Murder [1989] (Boylan, Eleanor) ☆
1 World the Color of Salt [1992] (Ayres, Noreen)
Worm of Doubt [1987] (Meek, M. R. D.)
Worse Than a Crime [1981] (Burton, Anne)
Worse Than Death [1992] (Bedford, Jean)
Worsted Viper [1943] (Mitchell, Gladys)
Wrack and Rune [1982] (MacLeod, Charlotte)
Wraiths and Changelings [1978] (Mitchell, Gladys)
Wreath for Rivera [1949] (Marsh, Ngaio)
1 Wreath for the Bride [1990] (O'Donnell, Lillian)
Wreath of Honesty [1990] (Burden, Pat)
1 Writers of the Purple Sage [1994] (Smith, Barbara B.) ☆
Written in Blood [1995] (Graham, Caroline)
Wrong Body [1950] (Gilbert, Anthony)
Wrong Murder [1940] (Rice, Craig)
Wrong Rite [1992] (Craig, Alisa)
Wrong Way Down [1946] (Daly, Elizabeth)
1 Wychford Murders [1986] (Gosling, Paula)
1 Wyndham Case [1993] (Walsh, Jill Paton)

Y

Yakuza, Go Home! [1993] (Wingate, Anne)
Year of the Monkey [1988] (Berry, Carole)
Yellow Violet [1943] (Crane, Frances)
Yet She Must Die [1973] (Woods, Sara)
Yom Kippur Murder [1992] (Harris, Lee)
You Bet Your Life [1995] (Jorgensen, Christine T.)
You Have the Right to Remain Silent [1992] (Paul, B.)
You'll Fry Tomorrow [1950] (Heberden, M. V.)
Young Can Die Protesting [1969] (Wells, Tobias)
Your Neck in a Noose [1942] (Ferrars, E. X.)
Your Royal Hostage [1987] (Fraser, Antonia)
Your Secret Friend [1968] (Torrie, Malcolm)

Z

1 Zach's Law [1987] (Hooper, Kay)
Zadock's Treasure [1979] (Arnold, Margot)
1 Zero at the Bone [1991] (Walker, Mary Willis) ★ ★ ☆
Zombies of the Gene Pool [1992] (McCrumb, Sharyn)

Seven

Pseudonyms

Pseudonym P	Author Identity	Series Character(s)
ABBEY, Kiernan	Helen Reilly	nonseries mystery
ADAMSON, Yvonne	M. J. Adamson & Yvonne E. Montgomery	historical romance
AIRD, Catherine	Kinn Hamilton McIntosh	Insp. C. D. "Seedy" Sloan
ALLAN, Dennis	Elinore Denniston	nonseries
ALLEN, Irene	Elsa Kirsten Peters	Elizabeth Elliot
ALLEN, Kate	unknown Denver author	Alison Kaine
AMOS, Alan	Kathleen Moore Knight	nonseries
ARNOLD, Margot	Petronelle Cook	Penny Spring & Toby Glendower, Sir
BAKER, Nikki	undisclosed	Virginia Kelly
BANE, Diana	Dianne Day	romantic suspense
BEATON, M. C.	Marion Chesney	Agatha Raisin; Hamish Macbeth
BECK, K. K.	Katherine Marris	Iris Cooper; Jane da Silva
BELFORT, Sophie	Kate Auspitz	Molly Rafferty
BELL, Josephine	Doris Bell Collier Ball	Tupper; Warrington-Reeve; Wintringham; Frost; Mitchell
BENNETT, Elizabeth	Cynthia Harrod-Eagles	nonmystery
BIRKLEY, Dolan	Dolores B. Olsen Hitchens	nonseries
BISHOP, Claudia	Mary Stanton	Sarah & Meg Quilliam
BLACK, Malacai	Barbara D'Amato	nonseries
BLACK, Veronica	Maureen Peters	Sister Joan
BLACKMUR, L. L.	Lydia Long	Galen Shaw & Julian Baugh
BLAISDELL, Anne	Elizabeth Linington	nonseries
BLAKE, Margaret	Barbara Margaret Trimble	romantic suspense
BORDILL, Judith	Marjorie Eccles	romantic suspense
BORTHWICK, J. S.	Joan Scott Creighton	Sarah Deane & Dr. Alex McKenzie
BORTON, D. B.	Lynette Carpenter	Cat Caliban
BRAND, Christianna	Mary Christianna Lewis	Insp. Cockrill
BRIDGE, Ann	Lady Mary Dolling Saunders O'Malley	Julia Probyn Jamieson
BRIGHTWELL, Emily	Cheryl Arguiles	Insp. Witherspoon & Mrs. Jeffries
BRILL, Toni	husband and wife	Midge Cohen
BROWN, Lizbie	Mary Marriott	Elizabeth Blair

Pseudonym P	Author Identity	Series Character(s)
BUCHANAN, Marie	Eileen-Marie Duell Buchanan	nonseries
BUCKINGHAM, Nancy	Nancy Buckingham Sawyer & John Sawyer	historical; romantic suspense
BURKE, Noel	Dolores B. Olsen Hitchens	nonseries
BURTON, Anne	Sara (Hutton) Bowen-Judd	Richard Trenton
BUTTERS, Dorothy G.	Dorothy Gilman	children's books
CAUDWELL, Sarah	Sarah Cockburn	Hilary Tamar
CHALLIS, Mary	Sara (Hutton) Bowen-Judd	Jeremy Locke
CHAPLIN, Elizabeth	Jill McGown	nonseries mystery
CHARLES, Kate	Carol Chase	Lucy Kingsley & David Middleton-Brown
CHISHOLM, P. F.	Pauline Finney	Sir Robert Carey
CHURCHILL, Jill	Janice Young Brooks	Jane Jeffry
CODY, Liza	Liza Nassim	Anna Lee
COHEN, Anthea	Doris Simpson	Agnes Carmichael
CONRAD, Brenda	Zenith Jones Brown	medical thrillers
COOPER, Natasha	Daphne Wright	Willow King & Cressida Woodruffe
CORTLAND, Tyler	Marsha Landreth	medical thrillers
CRAIG, Alisa	Charlotte MacLeod	Dittany Henbit & Osbert Monk; Madoc & Janet Rhys
CRAIG, Anne	Mary Stanton	hardboiled suspense
CRAMPTON, Helen	Marion Chesney	historical romance
CRANE, Hamilton	Heron Carvic	Emily D. Seeton
CRANE, Hamilton	Hampton Charles	Emily D. Seeton
CRANE, Hamilton	Sarah J. Mason	Emily D. Seeton
CROSS, Amanda	Carolyn G. Heilbrun	Kate Fansler
CROWLEIGH, Ann	Barbara Cummings & Jo-Ann Power	Mirinda & Clare Clively
CURZON, Clare	Eileen-Marie Duell Buchanan	Mike Yeadings
DAIN, Catherine	Judith Garwood	Freddie O'Neal
DARBY, Catherine	Maureen Peters	romantic suspense
DOMINIC, R. B.	Mary Latsis & Martha Henissart	Ben Safford
DRAKE, Alison	Trish Janeshutz MacGregor	Aline Scott
DUNNETT, Dorothy	Dorothy Halliday	Johnson Johnson
DYMMOCH, Michael A.	EM Grant	John Thinnes & Dr. Jack Caleb
EARLY, Jack	Sandra Scoppettone	Lauren Laurano
EDGHILL, Rosemary	Eluki bes-Shahar	Karen Hightower
EGAN, Lesley	Elizabeth Linington	Jesse Falkenstein; Vic Varallo
ERSKINE, Margaret	Margaret Wetherby Williams	Septimus Finch
EYRE, Elizabeth	Jill Staynes & Margaret Storey	Sigismondo
FAIRFAX, Ann	Marion Chesney	historical romance
FAWCETT, Quinn	Chelsea Quinn Yarbro & Bill Fawcett	Victoire Vernet
FERRARS, E. X.	Morna Doris MacTaggart Brown	Basnett; Ditteridge; Dyke; Freer
FICKLING, G. G.	Gloria & Forrest E. Fickling	Erik March; Honey West
FOLEY, Rae	Elinore Denniston	Hiram Potter
FORBES, Stanton	DeLoris Florine Stanton Forbes	nonseries mystery
FORD, Leslie	Zenith Jones Brown	Col. John Primrose & Grace Latham
FRAZER, Margaret	Mary Pulver Kuhfeld & Gail Bacon	Sister Frevisse
FRIEDMAN, Mickey	Michaele Thompson Friedman	Georgia Lee Maxwell
FROME, David	Zenith Jones Brown	Evan Pinkerton
FYFIELD, Frances	Frances Hegarty	Helen West; Sarah Fortune

Pseudonym Ⓟ	Author Identity	Series Character(s)
GALLANT, Jennie	Joan G. Smith	historical romance
GILBERT, Anthony	Lucy Beatrice Malleson	Arthur G. Crook; Scott Egerton
GILL, B. M.	Barbara Margaret Trimble	Tom Maybridge
GILMOUR, Barbara	Barbara Margaret Trimble	romantic suspense
GIROUX, E. X.	Doris Shannon	Robert Forsythe & Abigail Sanderson
GLEN, Alison	Cheryl Meredith Lowry & Louise Vetter	Charlotte Sams
GRANT, Linda	Linda V. Williams	Catherine Sayler
GRAY, Dulcie	Dulcie Winifred Catherine Dennison	Insp. Supt. Cardiff
GRAY, Gallagher	Katy Munger	Theodore S. Hubbert & Auntie Lil
HADDAM, Jane	Orania Papazoglou	Gregor Demarkian
HADLEY, Joan	Joan Hess	Theo Bloomer
HANOVER, Terri	Tanya Huff	science fiction
HARRIS, Lee	Syrell Rogovin Leahy	Christine Bennett
HART, Ellen	Patricia Boenhardt	Jane Lawless; Sophie Greenway
HOCKABY, Stephen	Gladys Mitchell	nonmystery
HORANSKY, Ruby	Rebecca Holland	Nikki Trakos
HUFF, T. S.	Tanya Huff	science fiction
HYDE, Jennifer	Marjorie Eccles	romantic suspense
JAMES, Susannah	Susan Moody	nonmystery
JANESHUTZ, Trish	T. J. MacGregor	nonseries thrillers
KEITH, J. Kilmeny	Lucy Beatrice Malleson	nonseries
KENT, Roberta	Doreen Roberts	romantic suspense
KINGSBURY, Kate	Doreen Roberts	Cecily Sinclair
LASKY, Kathryn	Kathryn Lasky Knight	children's books
LATHEN, Emma	Mary Latsis & Martha Henissart	John Putnam Thatcher
LEE, W. W.	Wendi Lee	western P. I.
LEEK, Margaret	Sara (Hutton) Bowen-Judd	Stephen Marryat
LEONARD, Charles L.	M(ary) V(iolet) Heberden	Paul Kilgerrin
LOWELL, Elizabeth	Ann Maxwell	romantic suspense
MALONE, Ruth	Georgiana Ann Randolph Craig	nonseries mystery
MARTIN, Lee	Anne Wingate	Deb Ralston
MARTIN, Stella	Georgette Heyer	historical romance
MAXWELL, A. E.	Ann & Evan Maxwell	Fiddler & Fiora Flynn
MAXWELL, Helen	Elinore Denniston	nonseries
MCALLISTER, Amanda	Jean Hager	romantic suspense
MCCLELLAN, Tierney	Barbara Taylor McCafferty	Schuyler Ridgway
MELVILLE, Jennie	Gwendoline Butler	Charmian Daniels
MEREDITH, Anne	Lucy Beatrice Malleson	nonseries
MEYERS, Maan	Martin & Annette Meyers	The Tonnemans
MICHAELS, Barbara	Barbara Mertz	Georgetown house
MORGAN, Claire	Patricia Highsmith	lesbian romance
MORGAN, Kate	Ann Hamilton Whitman	Dewey James
MORICE, Anne	Felicity Shaw	Tessa Crichton
NEEL, Janet	Janet Cohen	John McLeish & Francesca Wilson
NORTH, Sara	Jean Hager	romantic suspense
OLIPHANT, B. J.	Sheri S. Tepper	Shirley McClintock
OLSEN, D. B.	Dolores B. Olsen Hitchens	Prof. Pennyfather; R. & J. Murdock; Lt. Mayhew

Pseudonym P	Author Identity	Series Character(s)
O'NEILL, Egan	Elizabeth Linington	nonseries mystery
ORDE, A. J.	Sheri S. Tepper	Jason Lynx
OWENS, Marissa	Maxine O'Callaghan	nonmystery
PAGE, Emma	Honoria Tirbutt	Insp. Kelsey
PAIGE, Robin	Susan Wittig Albert & Bill Albert	Kathryn Ardleigh
PARIS, Ann	Orania Papazoglou	nonseries
PETERS, Elizabeth	Barbara Mertz	Amelia Peabody; Jacqueline Kirby; Vicky Bliss
PETERS, Ellis	Edith Mary Pargeter	Brother Cadfael
PETRIE, Rhona	Eileen-Marie Duell Buchanan	Marcus MacLurg
QUEST, Erica	Nancy Buckingham Sawyer & John Sawyer	Kate Maddox
RADLEY, Sheila	Sheila Robinson	Douglas Quantrill & Hilary Lloyd
RICE, Craig	Georgiana Ann Randolph Craig	Bingo Riggs & Handsome Kusak; John J. Malone
ROBB, J. D.	Nora Roberts	Eve Dallas
ROBBINS, Kay	Kay Hooper	romantic suspense
ROBERTS, Gillian	Judith Greber	Amanda Pepper
ROTHMAN, Judith	Maureen Peters	romantic suspense
ROWAN, Hester	Sheila Robinson	romantic thrillers
RYDELL, Forbes	DeLoris Forbes & Helen B. Rydell	nonseries mystery
SANDERS, Daphne	Georgiana Ann Randolph Craig	nonseries
SANDERS, Madelyn	Dianne Day	romantic suspense
SEDLEY, Kate	Brenda Margaret Lilian Honeyman Clarke	Roger the Chapman
SHANNON, Dell	Elizabeth Linington	Luis Mendoza
SMITH, J. C. S.	Jane S. Smith	Quentin Jacoby
SMITH, Lora Roberts	Lora Roberts	Palo Alto mystery
STACEY, Susannah	Jill Staynes & Margaret Storey	Robert Bone
STOREY, Alice	Sarah Shankman	Samantha Adams
STOUT, Ruth	Ruthe Furie	nonseries
TEY, Josephine	Elizabeth Mackintosh	Alan Grant
TILTON, Alice	Phoebe Atwood Taylor	Leonidas Witherall
TORRIE, Malcolm	Gladys Mitchell	Timothy Herring
TREMAINE, Jennie	Marion Chesney	historical romance
VENNING, Michael	Georgiana Ann Randolph Craig	Melville Fairr
VINE, Barbara	Ruth Rendell	nonseries
WAKEFIELD, Hannah	Sarah Burton & Judith Holland	Dee Street
WARD, Charlotte	Marion Chesney	historical romance
WEBB, Martha G.	Anne Wingate	Tommy Inman
WELLS, Tobias	DeLoris Florine Stanton Forbes	Knute Severson
WENTWORTH, Patricia	Dora Amy Elles Dillon Turnbull	Insp. Ernest Lamb; Maud Silver
WESTMACOTT, Mary	Agatha Christie	romantic suspense
WHITBY, Sharon	Maureen Peters	romantic suspense
WOODHOUSE, Emma	Cynthia Harrod-Eagles	nonmystery
WOODS, Sara	Sara (Hutton) Bowen-Judd	Antony Maitland
WREN, M. K.	Martha Kay Renfroe	Conan Flagg
WRIGHT, Rowland	Carolyn Wells	nonseries mystery
YORKE, Margaret	Margaret Beda Larminie Nicholson	Dr. Patrick Grant

Eight

Short stories

The short story was once the predominant form of crime fiction. In fact, the origin of the genre is often traced to the stories of Edgar Allen Poe. And everyone knows the stories of Sherlock Holmes. But short stories were more than art or entertainment—they were an economic necessity for writers of the time. Actually, until well into the 20th century, book publishing continued to be a luxury most writers could not afford. As a result, some of the best-known sleuths of the Golden Age of Detection, perhaps now better-known for their appearances in full-length novels, were also featured in numerous short stories. Among them are Albert Campion, created by Margery Allingham, Hercule Poirot from the pen of Agatha Christie, and Lord Peter Wimsey, the fantasy detective of Dorothy L. Sayers.

Short stories, particularly those featured in anthologies, are regaining popularity in detective fiction. The bonus for readers is finding detectives who also appear in longer works of fiction. Reading short stories can lead you to authors whose work you might like to know more about. To that end, we've selected 25 anthologies with over 350 short stories written by women.

Using the story-grid laid out on the following eight pages, you can locate stories by authors you are already familiar with, as well as those who might be new to you. Many of the 188 writers featured in our short story grid have series detectives identified in the Master List of Chapter 1. And some of them are well-known for their series novels. If you thought you had run out of Kinsey, Sharon and V. I. tales, you'll be happy to find 22 stories that can help you avoid some of the withdrawal symptoms experienced while waiting for the next installment of the big three.

So, find your favorite author in the story-grid and wherever you see a black square, you'll know there's an entry by that author in the anthology identified at the top of the column. Short stories that have been nominated for or awarded mystery prizes are identified by the familiar stars (solid stars denote winners; open stars nominees). At the end of this chapter you'll find a complete list of awards won by the author of these stories.

If you're a fan of the mystery short story, you'll want to check out three magazines that feature short fiction—*Alfred Hitchcock Mystery Magazine* (*AHMM*), *Ellery Queen Mystery Magazine* (*EQMM*), and *Murderous Intent*. *AHMM* and *EQMM* are published monthly by Dell Magazines, Inc., in a format the size of *Reader's Digest*. *Murderous Intent* is a quarterly publication, new in 1995, from a Vancouver press with its own Web site. These magazines can be found in many bookstores. Subscription information is shown in Chapter 10, Other Resources, under the heading, "Magazines & Periodicals."

Author	CH	Culp1	Culp2	DA1	DA2	Mal1	Mal2	Mal3	Mal4	MsM	MMD	PC
Adams, Deborah								Mal3★☆				
Adamson, M. J.												
Aird, Catherine		Culp1	Culp2									
Albert, Susan & Bill								Mal3				
Aldrich, Pearl G.												
Anders, K. T.												
Andrews, Sarah				DA1								
Armstrong, Charlotte										MsM☆		
Ballard, Mignon									Mal4			
Barnes, Linda												
Baxter, Alida		Culp1										
Beatty, Terry											MMD	
Beck, K. K.							Mal2☆☆		Mal4		MMD	
Bentley, Phylis										MsM		
Biederman, Marcia												
Braun, Lilian Jackson												
Burnham, Brenda Melton												
Burt, Elizabeth												
Cannell, Dorothy	CH							Mal3★				
Carlson, P. M.	CH				DA2	Mal1☆			Mal4			
Carpenter, Helen & Lorri												
Cash-Domingo, Lea												
Caudwell, Sarah			Culp2									
Chehak, Susan Taylor												
Christie, Agatha										MsM		
Clark, Mary Higgins							Mal2					
Cody, Liza		Culp1	Culp2									
Collins, Anna Ashwood												
Collins, Barbara											MMD	
Collins, Dorothy A.												
Costa, Carol												
Craig, May Shura												
Crespi, Camilla T.								Mal3				
Cross, Amanda										MsM̂		
Dalton, Elizabeth A.												
D'Amato, Barbara	CH				DA2							PC☆
Dain, Catherine											MMD	
Dale, Celia		Culp1										
Davidson, Diane Mott						Mal1						
Davis, Dorothy Salisbury												
Dawson, Janet												
de la Torre, Lillian												
Dearmore, Ellen												
Douglas, Carole Nelson							Mal2		Mal4			
Duke, Madelaine			Culp2									
Dunlap, Susan	CH			DA1	DA2		Mal2★★					PC
Eberhart, Mignon G.										MsM		
Elkins, Charlotte & Aaron						Mal1★						
Fiedler, Jean												
Forbes, DeLoris Stanton											MMD	

CH = Crimes of the Heart Culp = 1st & 2nd Culprit DA = Deadly Allies Mal = Malice Domestic
MsM = Ms. Murder MMD = Murder Most Delicious PC = Partners in Crime

Author	SC1	SC2	SC3	SC4	SC5	Web	Eye	WSA1	WSA2	WSA3	WM1	WM2	Wiles
Adams, Deborah													
Adamson, M. J.			SC3										
Aird, Catherine													
Albert, Susan & Bill													
Aldrich, Pearl G.												WM2	
Anders, K. T.					SC5					WSA3			
Andrews, Sarah													
Armstrong, Charlotte						Web							
Ballard, Mignon													
Barnes, Linda	SC1★☆												
Baxter, Alida													
Beatty, Terry													
Beck, K. K.					SC5								
Bentley, Phylis													
Biederman, Marcia			SC3										
Braun, Lilian Jackson			SC3										
Burnham, Brenda Melton										WSA3			
Burt, Elizabeth								WSA1					
Cannell, Dorothy	SC1		SC3☆										
Carlson, P. M.		SC2			SC5								
Carpenter, Helen & Lorri								WSA1	WSA2	WSA3			
Cash-Domingo, Lea										WSA3			
Caudwell, Sarah													
Chehak, Susan Taylor					SC5								
Christie, Agatha						Web							
Clark, Mary Higgins		SC2									WM1		
Cody, Liza							EyeH						
Collins, Anna Ashwood								WSA1					
Collins, Barbara													
Collins, Dorothy A.													Wiles
Costa, Carol								WSA1	WSA2	WSA3			
Craig, May Shura	SC1												
Crespi, Camilla T.													
Cross, Amanda							Eye				WM1	WM2	
Dalton, Elizabeth A.											WM1		
D'Amato, Barbara				SC4									
Dain, Catherine													
Dale, Celia													
Davidson, Diane Mott					SC5★								
Davis, Dorothy Salisbury	SC1		SC3				Eye				WM1☆		Wiles
Dawson, Janet				SC4									
de la Torre, Lillian						Web							
Dearmore, Ellen								WSA1		WSA3			
Douglas, Carole Nelson													
Duke, Madelaine													
Dunlap, Susan	SC1	SC2★			SC5	Web	Eye						Wiles
Eberhart, Mignon G.						Web							
Elkins, Charlotte & Aaron													
Fiedler, Jean		SC2		SC4									
Forbes, DeLoris Stanton													

SC = Sisters in Crime **Web** = The Web She Weaves **Eye** = A Woman's Eye
WSA = The Womansleuth Anthologies **WM** = Women of Mystery **Wiles** = Women's Wiles

Author	CH	Culp1	Culp2	DA1	DA2	Mal1	Mal2	Mal3	Mal4	MsM	MMD	PC
Frankel, Valerie						Mal1						
Fraser, Anthea			Culp2									
Fraser, Antonia		Culp1	Culp2							MsM		
Fremlin, Celia												
Friedman, Mickey												
Fyfield, Frances							Mal2					
George, Elizabeth												
Giles, Gail												
Girdner, Jaqueline												
Grafton, Sue			Culp2★	DA1★								
Grant, Linda									Mal4			
Grant-Adamson, Lesley		Culp1										
Grape, Jan				DA1	DA2		Mal2					PC
Greenwood, L. B.						Mal1		Mal3				
Grindle, Lucretia							Mal2					
Gunning, Sally							Mal2					
Haddam, Jane												
Hager, Jean									Mal4			
Hall, Mary Bowen												
Hanson, Deborah												
Harrington, Joyce												
Hart, Carolyn G.	CH			DA1	DA2	Mal1★			Mal4			PC
Hart, Jeanne												
Haugh, Wendy Hobday												
Healey, Rose Million												
Hearndon, Nancy R.												
Hershey, Kathleen												
Hess, Joan	CH				DA2	Mal1☆		Mal3				
Highsmith, Patricia												
Hornsby, Wendy								Mal3				
Howe, Melodie Johnson												
Hughes, Dorothy B.												
Jackson, Shirley												
James, P. D.												
Jance, J. A.												PC
Jesse, F. Tennyson										MsM		
Kellerman, Faye					DA2							
Kelly, Susan		Culp1	Culp2									
Kelman, Judith												
Kijewski, Karen												
Komo, Dolores												
Knight, Tracy											MMD	
Kraft, Gabrielle												
Krich, Rochelle Majer									Mal4			
Laiken, Deidre												
La Pierre, Janet						Mal1						
Lee, Wendi											MMD	
Lind, Judi												
Livingston, Nancy			Culp2									
Lowndes, Marie Belloc												

CH = Crimes of the Heart Culp = 1st & 2nd Culprit DA = Deadly Allies Mal = Malice Domestic
MsM = Ms. Murder MMD = Murder Most Delicious PC = Partners in Crime

Author	SC1	SC2	SC3	SC4	SC5	Web	Eye	WSA1	WSA2	WSA3	WM1	WM2	Wiles
Frankel, Valerie													
Fraser, Anthea												WM2	
Fraser, Antonia							Eye				WM1		
Fremlin, Celia						Web					WM1		
Friedman, Mickey	SC1	SC2											
Fyfield, Frances													
George, Elizabeth		SC2											
Giles, Gail										WSA3			
Girdner, Jaqueline					SC5					WSA3			
Grafton, Sue	SC1	SC2☆☆		SC4			Eye						
Grant, Linda			SC3	SC4									
Grant-Adamson, Lesley													
Grape, Jan													
Greenwood, L. B.													
Grindle, Lucretia													
Gunning, Sally													
Haddam, Jane				SC4									
Hager, Jean					SC5								
Hall, Mary Bowen				SC4									
Hanson, Deborah								WSA1					
Harrington, Joyce		SC2			SC5	Web						WM2	Wiles
Hart, Carolyn G.		SC2					Eye						
Hart, Jeanne		SC2											
Haugh, Wendy Hobday										WSA3			
Healey, Rose Million								WSA1	WSA2				
Hearndon, Nancy R.										WSA3			
Hershey, Kathleen													Wiles
Hess, Joan		SC2★★		SC4							WM1	WM2	
Highsmith, Patricia						Web							
Hornsby, Wendy				SC4★									
Howe, Melodie Johnson				SC4									
Hughes, Dorothy B.							Eye						
Jackson, Shirley						Web							
James, P. D.						Web							
Jance, J. A.													
Jesse, F. Tennyson													
Kellerman, Faye	SC1		SC3				Eye				WM1		
Kelly, Susan	SC1		SC3										
Kelman, Judith				SC4									
Kijewski, Karen			SC3		SC5								
Komo, Dolores									WSA2				
Knight, Tracy													
Kraft, Gabrielle			SC3		SC5l								
Krich, Rochelle Majer					SC5								
Laiken, Deidre		SC2											
La Pierre, Janet			SC3		SC5								
Lee, Wendi													
Lind, Judi									WSA2				
Livingston, Nancy													
Lowndes, Marie Belloc						Web							

SC = Sisters in Crime Web = The Web She Weaves Eye = A Woman's Eye
WSA = The Womansleuth Anthologies WM = Women of Mystery Wiles = Women's Wiles

Author	CH	Culp1	Culp2	DA1	DA2	Mal1	Mal2	Mal3	Mal4	MsM	MMD	PC
MacGregor, T. J.												
MacLeod, Charlotte						Mal1						
Mansfield, Katherine												
Maron, Margaret	CH			DA1			Mal2☆					PC
Matthews, Christine					DA2							
Matera, Lia	CH			DA1								
McCafferty, Taylor							Mal2	Mal3☆				
McCloy, Helen												
McConnell, Jean			Culp2									
McCrumb, Sharyn	CH					Mal1☆		Mal3				PC
McGerr, Patricia										MsM		
McGlamry, Beverly												
McQuillan, Karin												
Meredith, D. R.	CH					Mal1		Mal3				
Meyers, Annette									Mal4			
Michaels, Barbara												
Millar, Margaret												
Millay, Edna St. Vincent												
Millhiser, Marlys								Mal3				
Mitchell, Gladys										MsM		
Moody, Susan		Culp1	Culp2									
Morgan, Jill											MMD	
Morris, Bonnie												
Mosiman, Billie Sue											MMD	
Muller, Marcia					DA2							
Neville, Katherine												
Oates, Joyce Carol												
O'Brien, Meg												
O'Callaghan, Maxine					DA2							
O'Marie, Sr. Carol Anne												
Oliver, Maria Antonia												
Olsen, D. B.										MsM		
Orczy, Baroness												
Paretsky, Sara		Culp1		DA1						MsM		
Paul, Barbara						Mal1					MMD	
Penfold, Nita												
Perry, Anne												
Peters, Elizabeth												
Peters, Ellis			Culp2									
Peterson, Audrey	CH					Mal1						
Pickard, Nancy	CH			DA1				Mal3				
Pickens, Cathy					DA2							
Pincus, Elizabeth												
Post, Judith												
Prucha, Lynette												
Ramer, Edie												
Rawcliffe, Carole			Culp2									
Rendell, Ruth		Culp1								MsM		
Rice, Craig												
Richardson, D. L.												

CH = Crimes of the Heart Culp = 1st & 2nd Culprit DA = Deadly Allies Mal = Malice Domestic
MsM = Ms. Murder MMD = Murder Most Delicious PC = Partners in Crime

Author	SC1	SC2	SC3	SC4	SC5	Web	Eye	WSA1	WSA2	WSA3	WM1	WM2	Wiles
MacGregor, T. J.		SC2			SC5								
MacLeod, Charlotte													
Mansfield, Katherine						Web							
Maron, Margaret		SC2		SC4			Eye★★					WM2	
Matthews, Christine													
Matera, Lia	SC1	SC2											
McCafferty, Taylor													
McCloy, Helen						Web							
McConnell, Jean													
McCrumb, Sharyn		SC2☆		SC4								WM2	
McGerr, Patricia											WM1	WM2	
McGlamry, Beverly								WSA1					
McQuillan, Karin				SC4									
Meredith, D. R.													
Meyers, Annette													
Michaels, Barbara	SC1												
Millar, Margaret						Web							Wiles
Millay, Edna St. Vincent						Web							
Millhiser, Marlys													
Mitchell, Gladys													
Moody, Susan													
Morgan, Jill													
Morris, Bonnie									WSA2				
Mosiman, Billie Sue													
Muller, Marcia	SC1	SC2		SC4☆		Web	Eye					WM2☆	
Neville, Katherine				SC4									
Oates, Joyce Carol					SC5	Web							
O'Brien, Meg			SC3										
O'Callaghan, Maxine				SC4									
O'Marie, Sr. Carol Anne					SC5								
Oliver, Maria Antonia							Eye						
Olsen, D. B.													
Orczy, Baroness						Web							
Paretsky, Sara	SC1		SC3		SC5		Eye			WSA3	WM1		
Paul, Barbara			SC3	SC4									
Penfold, Nita								WSA1					
Perry, Anne											WM1		
Peters, Elizabeth	SC1												
Peters, Ellis													
Peterson, Audrey													
Pickard, Nancy	SC1★★	SC2		SC4			Eye						
Pickens, Cathy													
Pincus, Elizabeth									WSA2	WSA3			
Post, Judith								WSA1		WSA3			
Prucha, Lynette										WSA3			
Ramer, Edie									WSA2				
Rawcliffe, Carole													
Rendell, Ruth						Web					WM1	WM2	
Rice, Craig						Web							
Richardson, D. L.												WM2	

SC = Sisters in Crime　Web = The Web She Weaves　Eye = A Woman's Eye
WSA = The Womansleuth Anthologies　WM = Women of Mystery　Wiles = Women's Wiles

Author	CH	Culp1	Culp2	DA1	DA2	Mal1	Mal2	Mal3	Mal4	MsM	MMD	PC
Richter, Joan												
Rinehart, Mary Roberts										MsM		
Roberts, Gillian							Mal2					
Rozan, S. J.					DA2							
Rusch, Kristine Katheryn											MMD	
Sayers, Dorothy L.										MsM		
Scoppettone, Sandra				DA1								
Shankman, Sarah					DA2		Mal2					
Shaw, Viola Brothers										MsM		
Singer, Shelley												
Slovo, Gillian												
Smith, Julie				DA1								
Sprinkle, Patricia									Mal4			
Squire, Elizabeth Daniels									Mal4			
Stafford, Caroline												
Stevens, Bonnie K.												
Stockey, Janet												
Strichartz, Naomi												
Sucher, Dorothy												
Taylor, L. A.												
Trocheck, Kathy Hogan									Mal4			
Trott, Susan												
Valentine, Deborah												
Wagner, Linda												
Wallace, Marilyn	CH			DA1	DA2			Mal3				
Wallace, Penelope		Culp1										
Watts, Carolyn Jensen												
Wharton, Edith												
Wheat, Carolyn												
White, Ethel Lina										MsM		
White, Teri												
Wilson, Barbara												
Wilson, Karen												
Wingate, Anne												
Wings, Mary												
Wright, Betty Ren										MsM		
Yarbro, Chelsea Quinn												
Yorke, Margaret		Culp1	Culp2									

CH = Crimes of the Heart Culp = 1st & 2nd Culprit DA = Deadly Allies Mal = Malice Domestic
MsM = Ms. Murder MMD = Murder Most Delicious PC = Partners in Crime

Author	SC1	SC2	SC3	SC4	SC5	Web	Eye	WSA1	WSA2	WSA3	WM1	WM2	Wiles
Richter, Joan													Wiles
Rinehart, Mary Roberts						Web							
Roberts, Gillian	SC1		SC3		SC5							WM2	
Rozan, S. J.												WM2	
Rusch, Kristine Katheryn													
Scoppettone, Sandra	SC1												
Shankman, Sarah			SC3☆	SC4									
Shaw, Viola Brothers													
Sayers, Dorothy L.						Web							
Singer, Shelley	SC1☆		SC3				Eye						
Slovo, Gillian							Eye						
Smith, Julie	SC1	SC2					Eye						
Sprinkle, Patricia													
Squire, Elizabeth Daniels													
Stafford, Caroline										WSA3			
Stevens, Bonnie K.											WM1	WM2	
Stockey, Janet											WM1		
Strichartz, Naomi									WSA2	WSA3			
Sucher, Dorothy					SC5								
Taylor, L. A.									WSA2				
Trocheck, Kathy Hogan													
Trott, Susan			SC3										
Valentine, Deborah		SC2											
Wagner, Linda									WSA2	WSA3			
Wallace, Marilyn	SC1		SC3☆				Eye						
Wallace, Penelope													
Watts, Carolyn Jensen											WM1		
Wharton, Edith						Web							
Wheat, Carolyn	SC1	SC2		SC4			Eye						
White, Ethel Lina													
White, Teri	SC1		SC3										
Wilson, Barbara							Eye						
Wilson, Karen								WSA1					
Wingate, Anne												WM2	
Wings, Mary							Eye						
Wright, Betty Ren													
Yarbro, Chelsea Quinn			SC3										
Yorke, Margaret													

SC = Sisters in Crime   Web = The Web She Weaves   Eye = A Woman's Eye
WSA = The Womansleuth Anthologies   WM = Women of Mystery   Wiles = Women's Wiles

For a complete list of the 25 anthologies presented in this short story grid, see Chapter 10, Other Resources.

Short Story Award Winners and Nominees

2nd Culprit `Culp2`
Deadly Allies I `DA1`
Grafton, Sue. (1993) "A Little Missionary
Work." *Shamus nominee* ☆

Malice Domestic 1 `MD1`
Carlson, P. M. (1992) "The Jersey Lily; or,
Make Me Immortal with a Kiss."
Agatha nominee ☆
Elkins, Aaron & Charlotte. (1992)
"Nice Gorilla." *Agatha winner* ★
Hart, Carolyn G. (1992) "Henrie O's Holiday."
Macavity winner ★
Hess, Joan. (1992) "The Last to Know."
Agatha nominee ☆
McCrumb, Sharyn. (1992) "Happiness is a
Dead Poet." *Agatha nominee* ☆

Malice Domestic 2 `MD2`
Beck, K. K. (1992) "A Romance in the Rockies."
Agatha & Anthony nominee ☆ ☆
Dunlap, Susan. (1992) "Checkout." *Anthony &
Macavity winner* ★ ★ *Agatha nominee* ☆
Maron, Margaret. (1992) "...That Married Dear
Old Dad." *Agatha nominee* ☆

Malice Domestic 3 `MD3`
Adams, Deborah. (1994) "Cast Your Fate to the
Wind." *Macavity winner* ★
Agatha nominee ☆
Cannell, Dorothy. (1994) "The Family Jewels."
Agatha winner ★
McCafferty, Taylor. (1994) "The Dying Light."
Agatha nominee ☆

Ms. Murder `MsM`
Armstrong, Charlotte. (1966) "The Splintered
Monday." *Edgar nominee* ☆

Partners in Crime `PC`
D'Amato, Barbara. (1994) "Soon to be a Minor
Motion Picture." *Agatha nominee* ☆

Sisters in Crime 1 `SC1`
Anthony nominee for best anthology ☆
Barnes, Linda. (1986) "Lucky Penny."
Anthony winner ★ *Shamus nominee* ☆
Pickard, Nancy. (1989) "Afraid All the Time."
*Amer. Mystery Award, Anthony & Macavity
winner* ★ ★ ★ *Agatha & Edgar nominee* ☆ ☆
Singer, Shelley. (1989) "A Terrible Thing."
Anthony nominee ☆

Sisters in Crime 2 `SC2`
Dunlap, Susan. (1990) "The Celestial Buffet."
Anthony winner ★
Grafton, Sue. (1990) "A Poison that Leaves No
Trace." *Edgar & Shamus nominee* ☆ ☆
Hess, Joan. (1990) "Too Much to Bare."
Agatha & Macavity winner ★ ★
McCrumb, Sharyn. (1990) "The Luncheon."
Anthony nominee ☆

Sisters in Crime 3 `SC3`
Cannell, Dorothy. (1990) "The High Cost of
Living." *Agatha nominee* ☆
Shankman, Sarah. (1990) "Say You're Sorry."
Anthony nominee ☆
Wallace, Marilyn. (1990) "A Tale of Two
Pretties." *Anthony nominee* ☆

Sisters in Crime 4 `SC4`
Hornsby, Wendy. (1991) "Nine Sons."
Edgar winner ★
Muller, Marcia. (1989) "Deadly Fantasies."
Shamus nominee ☆
Wheat, Carolyn. (1991) "Life, for Short."
Macavity nominee ☆

Sisters in Crime 5 `SC5`
Davidson, Diane Mott. (1992) "Cold Turkey."
Anthony winner ★
Kraft, Gabrielle. (1992) "One Hit Wonder."
Edgar nominee ☆

The Web She Weaves `Web`
Jackson, Shirley. (1965) "The Possibility of
Evil." *Edgar winner* ★

A Woman's Eye `Eye`
Anthony winner for best anthology ★
Cody, Liza. (1991) "Lucky Dip."
Anthony winner ★
Grafton, Sue. (1991) "Full Circle."
Shamus nominee ☆
Maron, Margaret. (1991) "Deborah's
Judgment." *Macavity & Agatha winner* ★ ★

Women of Mystery I `WM1`
Davis, Dorothy Salisbury. (1975) "Old Friends."
Edgar nominee ☆

Women of Mystery II `WM2`
Muller, Marcia. (1989) "Deadly Fantasies."
Shamus nominee ☆

Awards and Organizations

American Crime Writers League (ACWL), founded in 1987, is a professional organization for published authors only. The group does not confer awards but has taken strong stands on a number of controversial issues such as unsigned reviews, which ACWL members find particularly distasteful.

Bouchercon (rhymes with "ouch," as in BOUCH-er-con), the popular name for the World Mystery Convention, is mystery fiction's largest fan and author convention attracting up to 1500 people when held in the U. S. 1000 writers and fans convened in Nottingham, England September 28 through October 1, 1995 for Bouchercon 26. The 1996 event will be held in St. Paul, Minnesota, October 9-13, with Mary Higgins Clark as the Author Guest of Honor and Jeremiah Healy as Toastmaster. Bouchercon 28 is scheduled for October 30 to November 2, 1997 in Monterey, California, with Sara Paretsky and Ross Thomas as Author Guests of Honor and Julie Smith as Toastmaster. **Anthony Awards**, voted each year by the membership, are presented at Bouchercon for work published during the prior year.

The Anthony Awards are named for famed mystery critic **Anthony Boucher** whose real name was William Anthony Parker White. For 17 years Boucher wrote a weekly column *Criminals at Large* for *The New York Times Review of Books*. He also wrote eight novels and doz-

ens of short stories, edited a science fiction magazine and reviewed plays, opera and science fiction.

The **Anthony Awards** include:

Best Novel
Best First Novel
Best True Crime
Best Individual Short Story
Best Short Story Collection/Anthology
Best Critical Work

The British **Crime Writers Association** (CWA), formed in 1953, was patterned after its counterpart, the Mystery Writers of America. In 1955 CWA began awarding special honors to the best crime fiction novel of the year. Originally named the Crossed Red Herrings Award, the prize later became known as the **Gold Dagger**. A **Silver Dagger** is awarded to the runner-up. Beginning in 1978 CWA also gave an award for best true crime book. Starting in 1986, Cartier and the CWA confer the **Diamond Dagger Award** based on a writer's lifetime achievement.

CWA also awards annually the **John Creasey Memorial Award** for best first novel, in honor of the famous British mystery writer (1908-1973) who produced almost 600 titles of mystery, crime, romance, western and suspense under 28 pseudonyms. He sometimes wrote two full-length books a month and often consoled aspiring writers with tales of the 743 rejection slips received before his first sale.

Arthur Ellis Awards, given by the **Crime Writers of Canada**, were established in 1984 and named after the nom de travail of Canada's official hangman. The Ellis Awards include:

> Best Novel
> Best First Novel
> Best Short Story
> Best True Crime
> Best Juvenile
> Best Play

The **Gargoyle Award**, presented for the first time in 1995, honors the best historical novel of the preceding year and is awarded at Historicon, the convention honoring historical mysteries. The first Gargoyle recipient was Kate Ross for *A Broken Vessel* (1994).

Historicon, convened for the first time in 1995, is one of the newer author and fan conventions. Historicon II, scheduled for June 7-9, 1996, is billed as the Chautauqua Historical Mystery Conference. For information write to Historicon II, PO Box 4119, Boulder CO 80306.

The **International Association of Crime Writers** (North American Branch) was established in 1987 to provide information about crime-writing worldwide and publishing opportunities around the world. Membership is open to published authors and professionals (agents, editors, booksellers) in the mystery field. This association presents the North American **Hammett Prize** annually for the best work (fiction or nonfiction) of literary excellence in crime-writing.

Left Coast Crime (LCC), typically the first regional mystery gathering of the year, has convened in February each year since 1991, drawing a crowd of 300 to 500 authors and fans primarily from the West Coast. LCC 6 is scheduled for Boulder, Colorado, March 1-3, 1996, with Kinky Friedman as Author Guest of Honor and Nevada Barr as Toastmaster. Former Hollywood Squares producer and Cleveland mystery writer Les Roberts will produce a Satur-day night cabaret at LCC 6 with mystery writers performing song and dance numbers and stand-up comedy. In 1997 LCC will be held in Seattle, Washington, February 14-17, 1997, with Faye and Jonathan Kellerman as Author Guests of Honor and Lia Matera as Toastmaster. For information about LCC 7 write to 8616 Linden Ave. N., Seattle WA 98103 or query online <Roscoe@Halycon.com>.

Magna Cum Murder, The Mid-America Mystery Convention, has been held in October each year since 1994 at Ball State University in Muncie, Indiana. For information about Magna Cum Murder III, October 25-27, 1996, call Kathryn Kennison at 317-285-8975 or send a fax request to 317-747-9566. Author Guest of Honor for 1996 will be Sara Paretsky with Margaret Maron and Edward Marston serving as Toastmasters. Peter Lovesey will be honored as Mystery Masters Award Winner and Sharan Newman as Magna Luminary.

The Mid Atlantic Mystery Book Fair and Convention is held in November each year in Philadelphia. More than 85 authors and several hundred fans attended in 1995. For information about the sixth Annual Mid Atlantic to be held November 8-10, 1996, write to Deen Kogan, Society Hill Playhouse, 507 S. 8th St., Philadelphia PA 19147 or call 215-923-0211.

Malice Domestic is an annual author and fan convention held in Bethesda, Maryland in late April or early May. Dedicated to cozy and traditional mysteries and their creators, this convention bestows the **Agatha Award** in honor of Dame Agatha Christie. The actual award is in the form of a teapot. Malice Domestic and St. Martin's Press also sponsor a Best First Novel contest for cozy mysteries. Malice VIII (April 26-28, 1996) is sold out, but you can send on-line queries about future Malice conventions to the Malice Registrar Bill Starck at <wsta@loc.gov> or write to Malice Domestic, PO Box 31137, Bethesda MD 20824-1137.

Mystery Readers of America presents the **Macavity Awards** in a variety of categories each year. The awards are voted by the readership of the *Mystery Readers Journal* of Mystery Readers International.

Mystery Writers of America (MWA) was formed in 1945 with the purpose of offering membership to all writers of good repute in the mystery field, including fiction, fact, books, magazines, film and radio. Associate membership was also available to interested editors, critics, publishers, actors, directors and accredited fans. The organization now has nine regional chapters.

Each year, usually in April or May, MWA awards the **Edgar Awards** (named for Edgar Allen Poe) in a variety of categories, including:

Best Novel
Best First Novel
Best Short Story
Best Original Paperback
Best Juvenile
Best Episode in a TV series
Best Fact Crime
Best TV Feature
Best Critical/Biographical
Best Motion Picture
Best Young Adult
Robert L. Fish Award for best short story
    from the MWA training program
Ellery Queen Award

Beginning with its selection of Agatha Christie in 1955, MWA began naming **Grand Masters** which now include 35 best-of-the-best:

1994	Lawrence Block
1993	Donald Westlake
1992	Elmore Leonard
1991	Tony Hillerman
1990	**Helen McCloy**
1989	Hillary Waugh
1988	**Phyllis A. Whitney**
1987	Michael Gilbert
1986	Ed McBain
1985	**Dorothy Salisbury Davis**
1984	John le Carre
1983	**Margaret Millar**
1982	Julian Symons
1981	Stanley Ellin
1980	W. R. Burnett
1979	Aaron Marc Stein
1976	**Daphne du Marier**
	Dorothy B. Hughes
	Ngaio Marsh
1975	Graham Greene

1976	Eric Ambler
1975	*no award given*
1974	Ross Macdonald
1973	Judson Philips
1972	John D. MacDonald
1971	**Mignon G. Eberhart**
1970	James M. Cain
1969	John Creasey
1968	*no award given*
1967	Baynard Kendrick
1966	Georges Simenon
1965	*no award given*
1964	George Harmon Coxe
1963	John Dickson Carr
1962	Erle Stanley Gardner
1961	Ellery Queen
1960	*no award given*
1959	Rex Stout
1958	Vincent Starrett
1957	*no award given*
1956	*no award given*
1955	**Agatha Christie**

The **Private Eye Writers of America** (PWA), formed in early 1982, gave its first **Shamus Awards** (for works published in 1981) at Bouchercon XIII in San Francisco. In recent years the category of P. I. has been expanded to include investigators who are paid for services rendered as part of their investigative work, such as news reporters and attorneys who do their own investigating.

Shamus Awards, honoring the private eye in mystery fiction, include:

Best Private Eye Novel
Best Private Eye Paperback Original
Best Private Eye Short Story
    (beginning in 1983)
Best First Private Eye Novel
    (beginning in 1984)
The Eye Life Achievement Award

In 1986 PWA and St. Martin's Press launched a contest for **Best First Private Eye Novel** which has become an annual event. The award-winning P. I. novel is published simultaneously in the U.S. by St. Martin's Press and in England by Macmillan.

Shamus Awards for works published in 1994, including the PWA/SMP Award, were presented at **EyeCon '95**—the first ever PWA Conference, June 15-18, 1995, in Milwaukee, Wisconsin, with Sue Grafton as Author Guest of Honor and Les Roberts as Toastmaster. The next EyeCon will be held in Indianapolis in 1997. For information contact Murder & Mayhem Mystery Bookstore, 6411 Carrollton Ave., Indianapolis, IN 46220.

Sisters in Crime was founded in 1986 "to combat discrimination against women in the mystery field, educate publishers and the general public as to inequalities in the treatment of female authors, and raise the level of awareness of their contribution to the mystery field." With chapters in more than 20 states, Sisters in Crime has over 3,000 members worldwide including 1,000 published authors, as well as editors, agents, librarians, booksellers and fans. Chicago mystery writer Sara Paretsky was the founding president. For membership information, write to M. Beth Wasson, Executive Secretary, **Sisters in Crime**, P.O. Box 442124, Lawrence KS 66044-8933.

The **World Mystery Convention**, also known as **Bouchercon**, is the site of Anthony Award presentations and mystery fiction's largest fan and author convention. One thousand writers, editors, publishers, reviewers and fans convened in Nottingham, England, September 28 through October 1, 1995 for four days of double- and triple-track author panels, readings and book signings, films, meetings, the Anthony Awards banquet and other special events.

In 1996 the World Mystery Convention moves to St. Paul, Minnesota for **Bouchercon 27** with Mary Higgins Clark as Author Guest of Honor and Jeremiah Healy as Toastmaster. For more information about the St. Paul Bouchercon (October 9-13, 1996) write to **Bouchercon 27**, P. O. Box 8296, Minneapolis MN 55408-0296. Send your fax requests to 612-671-8880. On-line information is available from <71201.657@compuserve.com>. **Bouchercon 28** will be held in Monterey, California with Sara Paretsky and Ross Thomas as Author Guests of Honor and Julie Smith as Toastmaster. For information write to **Bouchercon 28**, P. O. Box 6202, Hayward CA 94540.

Ten

Other Resources 10

Magazines & Newsletters

The magazines and newsletters listed here are excellent sources for author interviews, book reviews, news about future book releases and upcoming events in the mystery field, as well as dealers, both mail order and retail store, who specialize in out-of-print and hard-to-find titles.

Single copies are frequently available at mystery and other independent bookstores and national bookstore chains. Try one or more each month and you're sure to find several to please you. If you're feeling adventuresome, try one of the mystery publications from Canada or Great Britain. Subscription information is apt to change.

Subscriptions to the **Alfred Hitchcock Mystery Magazine** (AHMM) are $19.97 per year or 18 issues for $29.97. Outside the U.S., 12 issues for $27.97 or 18 issues for $39.97. All foreign orders must be paid in U.S. funds. Published monthly by Dell Magazines, Inc. Editor: Cathleen Jordan.

> Alfred Hitchcock
> P.O. Box 5124
> Harlan IA 51593
> 1-800-333-3311

Subscriptions to **The Armchair Detective** (TAD) are $31 per year (2 years $57) in the U.S., $35 surface mail outside the U.S. (2 years $65) or $48 per year air mail (2 years $90). Published quarterly by The Armchair Detective Magazine, Inc. Typical length is 130 pages. Absolutely the best place to find booksellers worldwide—retail and mail-order. Everybody advertises in TAD. These magazines are ones for the keeper shelf—bona fide collectibles. Individual issues are $9.00. Publisher: Judi Vause. Editor-in-Chief: Kate Stine.

> The Armchair Detective
> 129 West 56th Street
> New York NY 10019-3808
> 212-765-0902
> 212-265-5478 fax

Subscriptions to **Bookcase** are $29.95 per year in the U.S. and $65.00 elsewhere. Published monthly by Tumbleweed Productions. Typical length 36 pages. New in 1995 with an emphasis on author interviews. Columns on collecting, SF/fantasy, mystery reviews and signings. Individual issues are $4.00. Publisher: Angela Maria Ortiz Editor: Kathleen Lawrence.

> Bookcase Magazine
> P.O. Box 41-1507
> Los Angeles, CA 90041
> 213-257-9269
> 213-256-1600 fax

CADS is an irregular magazine of comment and criticism about crime and detective stories, published by Geoff Bradley of Essex, England, approximately three times a year. Serious mystery fans will be richly rewarded for the extra effort required to obtain it. With each issue you get a reservation form for the next issue, which you return with your payment. Oh so British and decidedly masculine, but fascinating reading. Typical length 80 pages. To get started, send a mail request to Geoff Bradley.

CADS
Geoff Bradley, Editor
9 Vicarage Hill
South Benfleet, Essex
England SS7 1PA

Subscriptions to **Clues: A Journal of Detection** are $12.50 per year or $23 for two years. Slightly higher for institutions and subscribers outside the U.S. Published twice yearly by Bowling Green State University Popular Press. Typical length 124 pages. Covers all aspects of detective material in print, television and movies. Editor: Pat Browne.

Clues: A Journal of Detection
Popular Press
Bowling Green State University
Bowling Green OH 43403
419-372-7865
419-372-8095 fax

Crime Time is a new magazine that made its debut at the World Mystery Conference in Nottingham, England in October 1995. From the U.S., fax your request for subscription information to 011-44-120-331-5864, or ask your favorite bookseller to inquire about *Crime Time*. To be published every two months by Crime Time Enterprises with news, interviews, reviews and listings of all the books coming out in England during the next two months. Typical length 54 pages. Editor: Paul Duncan.

Crime Time Enterprises
17 Tregullan Road
Exhall, Coventry
England CV7 9NG

Subscriptions to **The Criminal Record** are $7.00 per year in the U.S. or $12 in Canada and abroad. A sample copy is free. Published quarterly since 1987 by Ann M. Williams. Typical length 15 pages. Reviews and commentary by a longtime fan whose own mystery (*Flowers for the Dead*) was an Agatha nominee for best first novel in 1991.

The Criminal Record
3131 E. 7th Avenue
Denver CO 80206

Subscriptions to **Deadly Pleasures** are $14 per year U.S., $16 per year Canadian and $24 per year overseas. Sample issues are $3.50. Prior issues can be ordered with prepayment of $3 each. Checks should be payable to George Easter in U.S. funds. Published quarterly. Typical length 64 pages. Includes an interesting feature called "Reviewed to Death" where six or more reviewers have a go at the same book with fascinating results. Lots of other wonderful stuff. Editor and Publisher: George A. Easter.

Deadly Pleasures
Box 839
Farmington UT 84025-0839

Subscriptions to **Deadly Serious: References for Writers** are $36 per year. $41 in Canada. $46 elsewhere. Foreign subscribers should send U.S. funds in money orders or checks with U.S. routing numbers. Published monthly except July and December by Deadly Serious Press, which also publishes the Deadly Directory ($18). Ten newsletter issues per year. Subjects covered include art thefts, poisons, cults, legal procedures, etc. Editor and Publisher: Sharon Villines.

Deadly Serious Press
PO Box 1045 Cooper Station
New York NY 10003
212-473-5723

Subscriptions to **The Drood Review of Mystery** are $14 per year or $25 for two years in the U.S.; $18 per year or $34 for two years in Canada and Mexico; $24 per year and $44 for two years overseas. Published six times per year by The Drood Review. Typical length is 24 pages. Some of the most respected reviews in the field. No advertising. Editor & Publisher: Jim Huang.

> The Drood Review of Mystery
> Box 50267
> Kalamazoo MI 49005
> 616-349-3006
> 73717.663@compuserve.com

Subscriptions to the **Ellery Queen Mystery Magazine** (EQMM) are $19.97 per year or 18 issues for $29.97. Outside the U.S., 12 issues for $27.97 or 18 issues for $39.97. All foreign orders must be paid in U.S. funds. Published monthly by Dell Magazines, Inc. Editor: Janet Hutchings.

> Ellery Queen
> P.O. Box 5127
> Harlan IA 51593
> 1-800-333-3053

Subscriptions to **Gothic Journal** are $24 per year ($30 in Canada; $36 foreign). Published 6 times a year. Back issues are $4 each plus $2 per order for postage. The only publication solely about gothic and romantic suspense novels. Includes some mystery. Typical length 56 pages. Editor and Publisher: Kristi Lyn Glass.

> Gothic Journal
> 10489 169th Street North
> Hugo MN 55038-9331
> 800-7GOTHIC
> 612-433-4249
> 612-433-4655 fax
> kglass@GothicJournal.com

Subscriptions to **Mostly Murder** are $10 for one year and $18 for two years. Also available free at selected bookstores and public libraries throughout the U.S. Published quarterly by Mostly Book Reviews Inc. Typical length is 18 pages tabloid style. Reviewers include Texas bookstore owners, librarians, and mystery aficionados. Editor & Publisher: Jay W. Setliff.

> Mostly Murder
> P.O. Box 191207
> Dallas TX 75219
> 214-821-9493
> JWKS@aol.com

Subscriptions to **Murder Most Cozy** are $15 a year for 6 issues ($22 foreign). Published every other month with information on the latest cozies for the cozy mystery lover. First issue Sept-Oct 1995. Send $2 for a sample copy. Typical length 10 pages. Editor and Publisher: Jan Dean.

> Murder Most Cozy
> P.O. Box 561153
> Orlando FL 32856
> 407-481-9481 voice & fax

Subscriptions to **Murderous Intent, a Magazine of Mystery and Suspense**, new in 1995, are $15 per year in the U.S. Canada $22 and foreign $35 by surface mail. Individual issues are $5 U.S., $6.50 Canada and $8 foreign, all in U.S. funds. Published quarterly by Madison Publishing Company. Typical length is 64 pages. Includes new short fiction and guest columns, including Polly Whitney on research and Andi Schechter on the convention scene. Editor and Publisher: Margo Power.

> Murderous Intent
> PO Box 5947
> Vancouver WA 98668-5947
> madison@teleport.com

Subscriptions to **Mystery & Detective Monthly**, the "Magazine of Great Letterature," are $30 per year U.S. and Canada, $46 Europe and $48 Far East. Published about 11 times per year by Snapbrim Press. Sample issues are $3 each. MDM, as it is affectionately known among its fans, is a letterzine—a collection of letters that regular subscribers write to Cap'n Bob Napier and each other for all to read. More than 100 back issues available. This one's for insiders and those who aspire to be. If you love the gossip, here's where to find some of the good stuff. Regular letter writers include authors, booksellers, serious fans and even a mystery editor.

> Mystery & Detective Monthly
> 5601 North 40th Street
> Tacoma WA 98407

Subscriptions to **Mystery News** are $15 per year. Washington residents add 7.9% sales tax. Additional postage for Canada and overseas. Individual issues are $2.75 U.S., $4.25 Canadian. Published six times per year by Mystery News. Typical length is 36 pages tabloid style. Each issue highlights a particular mystery author as the subject of an in-depth interview and "cover story," most often written by Harriet herself. Reviewers are some of the best in the business, from all over the country. Publisher: Laurence Stay. Editor: Harriet Stay.

> Mystery News
> P.O. Box 1201
> Port Townsend WA 98368-0901

Subscriptions to **Mystery Readers Journal** are $24 per year ($36 overseas air mail) including membership in Mystery Readers International, which allows each member to vote for the annual Macavity awards. Published quarterly as a thematic journal. Typical length is 64 pages. Individual issues are $6. 1995 issues focused on Suburban Mysteries (spring), San Francisco (summer), Regional British Mysteries I (fall) and Regional British Mysteries II (winter). Issues in 1996 will include Technological Mysteries, New Orleans, Sports Mysteries II and Academic Mysteries II. Editor: Janet A. Rudolph.

> Mystery Readers Journal
> P.O. Box 8116
> Berkeley CA 94707-8116
> 510-339-8309 fax
> JRudolph2@aol.com

Subscriptions to **The Mystery Review, A Quarterly Publication for Mystery Readers** are $21.50 per year in Canada, $20 U.S. in the United States and $28 U.S. elsewhere. Individual issues are $5.95 on the newsstand.

Published quarterly by C. von Hessert & Associates Ltd. Typical length is 76 pages. Includes reviews and features, including Book Store Beat, which profiles a mystery bookshop. Publisher: Christian von Hessert. Editor: Barbara Davey.

> C. von Hessert & Associates Ltd.
> P.O. Box 233
> Colborne, Ontario K0K 1S0 Canada
> 613-475-4440
> 613-475-3400 fax
> 71554.551@compuserve.com

Subscriptions to **Mystery Scene** magazine are $35 per year in the U.S. and $63.50 elsewhere. Foreign subscriptions are sent surface mail. Published six times per year by Mystery Enterprises. Typical length is 88 pages. Regional news, features, columns and reviews written by names you'll recognize. Lots and lots of tidbits about the mystery scene. Publisher: Martin H. Greenburg. Editor: Joe Gorman.

> Mystery Scene
> P.O. Box 669
> Cedar Rapids IA 52406-0669
> 414-728-0793

Subscriptions to **New Mystery Magazine** are $27.77 per year or $47.77 for two years in the U.S. Foreign rates are $37.77 and $57.77 surface mail or $47.77 and $77.77 air mail. Individual issues are $3.95 on the newsstand. Published quarterly by Friends of New Mystery. Typical length is 62 pages. Short fiction from established and new authors, features and mystery products. Editor: Charles Raisch, 3rd.

> New Mystery Magazine
> 175 Fifth Ave., Suite 2001
> New York NY 10010
> 212-353-1582
> 212-353-3495 fax

Subscriptions to **Over My Dead Body!**, the Mystery Magazine, are $12 per year. Published quarterly. Typical length is 72 pages. While the magazine has a similar name to the computer bulletin board (BBS) offered by the same group, they try not to duplicate each other. The BBS offers mostly book reviews and e-mail mystery chatter, while the magazine strives for 50% new fiction and 50% nonfiction. Publisher: Cherie Jung.

Over My Dead Body!
PO Box 1778
Auburn WA 98071-1778
OMDB@aol.com

Short Story Anthologies

1st Culprit, *Annual Anthology of the Crime Writers' Association*, edited by Liza Cody and Michael Z Lewin. New York: St. Martin's Press, 1992. 314 pages, $5.99, softcover.

2nd Culprit, *Annual Anthology of the Crime Writers' Association*, edited by Liza Cody and Michael Z Lewin. New York: St. Martin's Press, 1995. 309 pages, $5.99, softcover.

Crimes of the Heart, edited by Carolyn G. Hart. New York: Berkley Prime Crime, 1995. 288 pages, $9.00, softcover.

Deadly Allies, *Private Eye Writers of America and Sisters in Crime Collaborative Anthology*, edited by Robert J. Randisi and Marilyn Wallace. New York: Doubleday, 1992, 369 pages, hardcover.

Deadly Allies II, *Private Eye Writers of American and Sisters in Crime Collaborative Anthology*, edited by Robert J. Randisi and Susan Dunlap. New York: Bantam, 1995. $557 pages, $4.99, softcover.

Malice Domestic 1, presented by Elizabeth Peters, an anthology of original traditional mystery stories, edited by Martin Greenburg. New York: Pocket Books, 1992. 275 pages, $4.99, softcover.

Malice Domestic 2, presented by Mary Higgins Clark, an anthology of original traditional mystery stories, edited by Martin Greenburg. New York: Pocket Books, 1993. 255 pages, $4.99, softcover.

Malice Domestic 3, presented by Nancy Pickard, an anthology of original traditional mystery stories, edited by Martin Greenburg. New York: Pocket Books, 1994. 240 pages, $4.99, softcover.

Malice Domestic 4, presented by Carolyn G. Hart. an anthology of original traditional mystery stories, edited by Martin Greenburg, New York: Pocket Books, 1995, 273 pages, $5.50, softcover.

Ms. Murder, edited by Marie Smith. New York: Carol Publishing Group, Citadel Press, 1989. 274 pages, $14.95, hardcover.

Murder Most Delicious, edited by Martin H. Greenburg. New York: Signet, 1995. 272 pages, $4.99, softcover.

Partners in Crime, *Mysteries that Take Two to Untangle*, edited by Elaine Raco Chase. New York: Signet, 1994. 269 pages, $4.99, softcover.

Sisters in Crime, edited by Marilyn Wallace. New York: The Berkley Publishing Group, 1989. 306 pages, $4.95, softcover.

Sisters in Crime 2, edited by Marilyn Wallace. New York: The Berkley Publishing Group, 1990. 292 pages, $4.99, softcover. *Anthony nominee* ☆

Sisters in Crime 3, edited by Marilyn Wallace. New York: The Berkley Publishing Group, 1990. 324 pages, $4.50, softcover.

Sisters in Crime 4, edited by Marilyn Wallace. New York: The Berkley Publishing Group, 1991. 352 pages, $4.99, softcover.

Sisters in Crime 5, edited by Marilyn Wallace. New York: The Berkley Publishing Group, 1992. 278 pages, $4.99, softcover.

The Web She Weaves, *An Anthology of Mystery & Suspense Stories by Women*, edited by Marcia Muller & Bill Pronzini. New York: William Morrow & Co, 1983. 514 pages, $17.50, hardcover.

Women of Mystery, 15 stories previously published in Ellery Queen's Mystery Magazine, edited by Cynthia Manson. New York: Berkley Books, 1992. 317 pages, $5.50, softcover.

Women of Mystery II, 15 stories previously published in Ellery Queen's Mystery Magazine, edited by Cynthia Manson. New York: Berkley Books, 1994. 337 pages, $5.99, softcover.

A Woman's Eye, edited by Sara Paretsky. New York: Dell Publishing, 1991. 448 pages, $4.99, softcover. *Anthony winner for best anthology* ★

Women's Wiles, *An Anthology of Mystery Stories by the Mystery Writers of America*, edited by Michele Slung. New York: Harcourt Brace Jovanovich, 1979. 288 pages, $9.95, hardcover.

The WomanSleuth Anthology, *Contemporary Mystery Stories by Women*, edited by Irene Zahava. California: The Crossing Press, 1988. 177 pages, $6.95, softcover.

The WomanSleuth Anthology, *Second Edition, Contemporary Mystery Stories by Women*. edited by Irene Zahava, California: The Crossing Press, 1989. softcover.

The WomanSleuth Anthology, *Third Edition, Contemporary Mystery Stories by Women*, edited by Irene Zahava. California: The Crossing Press, 1990. 204 pages, $8.95, softcover.

References

And Then There Were Nine...More Women of Mystery. Jane Bakerman, editor. Bowling Green: Bowling Green State University Popular Press, 1985. 219 pages, $10.95, softcover.

> *Essays on the lives and work of Margery Allingham, Daphne du Marier, E. X. Ferrars, Patricia Highsmith, Shirley Jackson, Anne Morice, Lillian O'Donnell, Craig Rice and Dorothy Uhnak.*

The Armchair Detective Book of Lists, A Complete Guide to the Best Mystery, Crime, and Suspense Fiction. Kate Stine, editor. New York: Otto Penzler Books, 1995. 267 pages, $12.95, softcover.

> *Includes both nominees and winners for major mystery awards; favorite authors and books of famous mystery authors, critics, and booksellers. Plus information about mystery organizations, conventions and publications.*

By a Woman's Hand, A Guide to Mystery Fiction by Women. Jean Swanson and Dean James. New York: Berkley Books, 1994. 254 pages, $10.00, softcover. *Agatha & Macavity winner* ★ ★ *Anthony & Edgar nominee* ☆ ☆

> *Profiles of more than 200 contemporary women mystery writers with recommendations of what to read if you enjoy the writing of a featured author.*

Crime Fiction II: A Comprehensive Bibliography, 1749-1990, Volumes 1 and 2. Allen J. Hubin. New York & London: Garland Publishing, Inc., 1994. 1568 pages, $195.00, hardcover. *Special Edgar award* ★

> *Crime Fiction II is the mother of all bibliographic resources in crime fiction. These volumes weigh in at a combined 9.5 pounds.*

The Crown Crime Companion. Compiled by Mickey Friedman. New York: Crown Publishers, 1995. 190 pages, $12.00, softcover.

The top 100 mystery novels of all time selected by the Mystery Writers of America, annotated by Otto Penzler and compiled by Mickey Friedman in her role as MWA publications chair.

Deadlier Than the Male: Why Are Respectable English Women So Good at Murder? Jessica Mann. New York: Macmillan Publishing Co., Inc.

An examination of the lives and work of Dorothy L. Sayers, Margery Allingham, Agatha Christie and Ngaio Marsh by a woman crime writer.

The Deadly Directory. Compiled by Sharon Villines. New York: Deadly Serious Press, 1994. $18.00, softcover.

Includes listings for bookstores specializing in mystery; booksellers of rare, out-of-print and first-edition mysteries; general bookstores with strong mystery collections; organizations for mystery writers; mystery publications; mystery conventions; and online services and bulletin boards for mysteries.

Doubleday Crime Club Compendium, 1928-1991. Ellen Nehr. Martinez, California: Offspring Press, 1992. 682 pages, $75.00, hardcover.

Contains dust jacket description and cover blurbs from all the novels of the Crime Club's 62 years. Also includes name of the leading or series character, setting and subject where known.

Encyclopedia Mysteriosa, A Comprehensive Guide to the Art of Detection in Print, Film, Radio, and Television. William L. DeAndrea. New York: Prentice Hall General Reference, 1994. 405 pages, $29.95, hardcover. *Anthony, Edgar & Macavity winner ★ ★ ★ Agatha nominee for best critical work* ☆

More than 1400 entries arranged alphabetically with lots of cross references and essays by experts. Edited by a two-time Edgar winner for fiction.

Fine Art of Murder, The Mystery Reader's Indispensable Companion. Ed Gorman, Martin H. Greenburg, Larry Segriff, editors with Jon L. Breen. New York: Carroll & Graf, 1993. 390 pages, $17.95, softcover. Anthony winner for best critical work ★

Dozens of well-known mystery authors writing on everything from religious mysteries to true crime, including favorite settings for American crime fiction, TV mysteries, lists of favorites, nostalgia and much more.

The Girl Sleuth. Bobbie Ann Mason. The University of Georgia Press, 1995. 145 pages, $10.95, softcover, with a new preface. Originally published by Feminist Press, Old Westbury NY, 1975.

On the trail of Nancy Drew, Judy Bolton and Cherry Ames. This little gem was first written in 1973 during recess periods of the televised Watergate hearings. The author is the winner of the 1994 Southern Book Critics Circle Award for Fiction for Feather Crowns.

Girl Sleuth on the Couch: The Mystery of Nancy Drew. Betsy Caprio. Source Books, 1992. 195 pages, $14.95, softcover.

Nancy Drew as seen through the prism of Jungian psychology by a Los Angeles art therapist and life-long fan of the fictional virgin detective goddess.

Murder by the Book, Feminism and the Crime Novel. Sally Rowena Munt. Routledge, 1994. 264 pages, $16.95, softcover.

A look at the blossoming genre of the feminist crime novel in Britain and the United States by a professor from Nottingham Trent University. Academics are calling this a pioneering work in the field.

Murderess Ink, The Better Half of the Mystery. Dilys Winn. New York: Workman Publishing Co., 1979. 304 pages, softcover.

More than 50 contributors including Josephine Bell with a "Face-to-Face Encounter with Sayers," Ngaio Marsh with a "Portrait of Troy," Dell Shannon on "My Problems with the Police" and much more.

Mystery & Crime: The New York Public Library Book of Answers. Jay Pearsall. New York: Simon & Schuster, 1995. 175 pages, $11.00, softcover.

Entertaining questions and answers about the who's who and what's what of whodunits; some incorrect answers according to critics.

Mystery Writers Market Place and Sourcebook. Donna Collingwood, editor. Cincinnati: Writer's Digest Books, 1993. 312 pages, $17.95, hardcover.

Mystery editors talk about their work and what they look for in new fiction; a writing and marketing companion for aspiring crime writers.

The Nancy Drew Scrapbook. Karen Plunkett-Powell. New York: St. Martin's Press, 1995. $10.95, softcover.

An affectionate tribute to Nancy Drew including reproductions of book covers, history of the series from 1932 to the present and tips on collecting.

The New Bedside, Bathtub & Armchair Companion to Agatha Christie. Dick Riley and Pam McAllister, editors. New York: Ungar Publishing Company, 1993. 362 pages, $12.95, softcover.

Everything you ever wanted to know about the life and work of Agatha Christie.

100 Great Detectives. Maxim Jakubowski, editor. New York: Carroll & Graf Publishers, Inc., 1991. 255 pages, $9.95, softcover. Anthony winner for best critical work ★

100 famous writers examine their favorite fictional investigators, including Sue Dunlap on Chief Inspector Wilfred Dover, Patricia Moyes on Amelia Peabody Emerson, Susan Moody on Gervase Fen, Gwendoline Butler on Henry Gamadge, Jill McGown on Alan Grant, Deborah Valentine on Cordelia Grey, Margaret Maron on Johnson Johnson, Bill Pronzini on Sharon McCone, Sharyn McCrumb on Sir Henry Merrivale, Simon Brett on Kinsey Millhone, Barbara Wilson on Mrs. Pollifax, Lesley Grant-Adamson on Rebecca Schwartz, Elizabeth Peters on Peter Shandy, Catherine Aird on John Putnam Thatcher, Sarah Caudwell on Henry and Emmy Tibbett, Linda Semple on V. I. Warshawski, Melodie Johnson Howe and Catherine Kenney on Lord Peter Wimsey, Carolyn G. Hart on Leonidas Witherall, Paula Gosling on Nero Wolfe, Frances Fyfield on Aurelio Zen.

1001 Midnights, The Aficionado's Guide to Mystery and Detective Fiction. Bill Pronzini and Marcia Muller. New York: Arbor House, 1986. 879 pages, $39.95, hardcover. *Edgar nominee for best critical work ☆*

1001 plot summaries, author biographies and critical evaluations of classic crime and espionage novels written by Muller and Pronzini and 26 contibutors including Sue Dunlap and Julie Smith. Out of print but well worth the hunt.

A Reader's Guide to The American Novel of Detection. Marvin Lachman. New York: G. K. Hall & Co., 1993. 435 pages, $45.00, hardcover. *Anthony nominee for best critical work ☆*

Fully annotated entries on 1314 titles featuring mostly amateur detectives by 166 authors through 1991.

A Reader's Guide to the Classic British Mystery. Susan Oleksiw. New York: Mysterious Press, 1989. 585 pages, $19.95, softcover. Originally published by G. K. Hall & Co., Boston, 1988.

Fully annotated entries on 1440 titles by 121 authors, including all their work through 1985. Oleksiw read most of them.

A Reader's Guide to the Police Procedural. Jo Ann Vicarel. New York: G. K. Hall & Co., 1995. $45.00, hardcover.

A Reader's Guide to The Private Eye Novel. Neibuhr, Gary Warren. New York: G. K. Hall & Co., 1993. 323 pages, $45.00, hardcover. *Anthony nominee for best critical work* ☆

Fully annotated entries on over 1000 titles by 90 authors through 1991.

Recipes for Crime. Kerry Greenwood and Jenny Pausacker. McPhee Gribble Penguin Books, Australia Ltd., 1995. 220 pages, Aust. $16.95, softcover.

A smorgasbord for crime lovers—a potted history of the detective story, recipes to die for and nine new stories in the style of the greats. Including breakfast with Sherlock Holmes, Dinner with Lord Peter Wimsey, Afternoon Tea with Miss Marple, Snacks on the Run with Philip Marlowe and Supper with Phryne Fisher and four others.

Silk Stalkings: When Women Write of Murder. Victoria Nichols and Susan Thompson. Berkeley: Black Lizard Books, 1988.

Survey of series characters created by women authors prior to 1988. Out of print but worth the hunt.

Sisters in Crime: Feminism and the Crime Novel. Maureen T. Reddy. New York: The Continuum Publishing Company, 1988.

Focuses on women mystery writers with women protagonists.

A Suitable Job for a Woman: Inside the World of Women Private Eyes. Val McDermid. London: HarperCollins Publishers, 1995. 278 pages, UK £5.99, softcover.

Former investigative reporter and crime writer Val McDermid collected 800 pages of interview notes after talking with working women private eyes on both sides of the Atlantic during 1994. This is the fascinating result. Available in Britain.

The Woman Detective, Gender & Genre. Kathleen Gregory Klein. Urbana and Chicago: University of Illinois Press, 1988. 261 pages, $27.95, hardcover.

Traces the appearance of paid female professional private investigators in British, Canadian and American novels from 1864 to 1987.

Writing Mysteries: A Handbook by the Mystery Writers of America. Sue Grafton, editor. Cincinnati: Writer's Digest Books, 1992. 208 pages, hardcover.

Includes Faye and Jonathan Kellerman on "Expertise and Research," Sara Paretsky on "Writing a Series Character," Nancy Pickard on "The Amateur Sleuth," Sandra Scoppettone on "Vivid Villains," Julie Smith on "Background, Location and Setting," Marilyn Wallace on "Sparks, Triggers and Flashes" and 20 other chapters.

Eleven

Glossary

Agatha Awards, in honor of Agatha Christie, are presented annually in late April in various categories by the Malice Domestic Mystery Convention which is devoted to the traditional or cozy mystery. The actual award is in the form of a teapot.

Amateur detectives typically do not have special training or education in investigative techniques. Unlike private investigators or police, they are not paid for the work of investigating and are likely to be volunteers. They are also likely to be working professionals in other fields, such as journalism, academia, law or medicine. In some cases, the amateur detective is independently wealthy or retired and can thus afford to spend time investigating.

The **American Crime Writers League** (ACWL), founded in 1987, is a professional organization for published authors only. Applicants must have published a novel, three short stories or a work of non-fiction.

The **American Mystery Awards**, given annually in various categories, are voted by the readership of *Mystery Scene* magazine.

The **Anthony Awards**, named in honor of Anthony Boucher, are voted annually in various categories by members of the World Mystery Convention. They are presented at Bouchercon in early October.

The **Baker Street Irregulars,** named for the street gang that used to help Sherlock Holmes with some of his cases, was founded by Christopher Morley in 1934. It is a loosely organized literary society devoted to the study of Sherlock Holmes. Although there are no formal requirements, members must have a thorough knowledge of Sherlock Holmes and be invited to join. Membership is maintained at 52. As older members die, their names (taken from Holmes' short story titles) are passed on to new members. In addition to the parent society, there are Scion Societies all over the country.

A **book plate** is a label or sticker that can be pasted inside the front cover of a book to show the name of its owner. Typically book plates have a special design or coat of arms and may include the words "ex libris" which means literally "from the library of."

Bouchercon is the name given to the World Mystery Convention held in early October each year since 1970 to honor the work of **Anthony Boucher** (1911-1968), a prolific mystery writer. From 1951 until his death he wrote the weekly column *Criminals at Large* for the *New York Times Review of Books*. He also wrote eight novels and dozens of short stories, edited a science fiction magazine and reviewed plays, opera and science fiction. His real name was William Anthony Parker White.

Caper mysteries are usually told from the point of view of the perpetrator, often with a lighthearted or comical tone. The crime is usually theft rather than murder, with art or jewelry being a favorite target.

C.I.D. is the Criminal Investigation Department of Scotland Yard, the Metropolitan Police Force responsible for Greater London.

Constable or Detective Constable is the lowest officer rank in the County or Metropolitan Police Force in Great Britain.

Cozy or traditional mysteries are classically English and most often feature an inspired amateur detective who restores order to the town or village by solving an elaborate puzzle. Violence is most likely off stage and the murderer, often devilishly clever, uses ingenious methods for murder and mayhem. Agatha Christie is the quintessential creator of the cozy mystery.

The John **Creasey Memorial Award** is conferred annually by the British Crime Writers Association (CWA) for best first novel, in honor of the British mystery writer who was a significant force in the founding of CWA. John Creasey (1908-1973) was a prolific writer of romance, crime, suspense, mystery and western novels—close to 600 titles under 28 pseudonyms. He sometimes wrote two full-length books a month and often consoled aspiring writers with tales of receiving 743 rejections before his first sale.

Crime fiction includes both mystery and suspense. Police procedurals, private eye fiction and cozy or traditional mysteries are all part of crime fiction.

The British **Crime Writers Association** (CWA), formed in 1953, was patterned after its counterpart, the Mystery Writers of America. Since 1955 the Crime Writers Association has conferred awards (Gold and Silver Daggers) for best novel and best true crime book. Beginning in 1986, Cartier and CWA have sponsored the Diamond Dagger Award, given in honor of lifetime achievement in crime writing.

Cross-genre novels include strong elements of two or more genres and are thought to appeal to a wider audience. More often they are the result of the talent and writing preferences of their creators, who are experienced writers in multiple genres. Examples include Wendi Lee's Western private eye, Jefferson Birch (written as W. W. Lee), and Barbara Hambly's Victorian detective and London vampire hunter, Professor James Asher. Lynn Hightower's Alien series features an alien cop partner for David Silver, while J. D. Robb's 21st century NYPD stories have a strong romantic thread.

The **Detection Club**, sometimes called the London Detection Club, was founded in 1928 by Anthony Berkeley who put the organization, under a thinly disguised title, in a book called the *The Poisoned Chocolates Case*. The Club's first president was G. K. Chesterton who served until his death in 1936. Membership in the oldest association of mystery writers is kept by charter relatively small, but has included the most distinguished names in British detective fiction, including Agatha Christie, Dorothy L. Sayers, Lucy Beatrice Malleson and Josephine Bell. Headquartered in London, the group issues anthologies from time to time to finance the organization.

The **Diamond Dagger Award** is given in honor of lifetime achievement in crime writing. Since its origin in 1986, it has been conferred by the British Crime Writers Association and Cartier.

Dime novels were a distinctly American phenomenon dating from 1860 to 1901, when a change in postal laws eliminated their second-class mailing privileges. Immensely popular during the Civil War era, these ten-cent paperbacks were reportedly shipped by the traincar load to soldiers in the field.

Edgar Allen Poe (1809-1849) is widely recognized as the inventor of the detective story with "The Murders in the Rue Morgue," first published in the Philadelphia periodical *Graham's Magazine* in 1841. Some think he would also be credited with the first novel of detection if not for his early, untimely death.

The **Edgar Awards**, in honor of Edgar Allen Poe, are awarded in April each year by the Mystery Writers of America in various categories. The award is a Poe statuette.

The **Ellis Awards** are given annually by the Crime Writers of Canada in various categories. The award takes its name from Arthur Ellis, the nom de travail of Canada's official hangman.

Ex-lib. or ex libris literally means from the library of. The phrase is often inscribed inside the cover of a book, in front or above the name of the owner. Book plate designs often include the words "ex libris."

A **fanzine** is a magazine or newsletter produced inexpensively by and for fans, typically of science fiction, fantasy of mystery fiction.

Genre is a term created by publishers to describe a book, making it easier to classify and therefore easier to target the book's audience. Included in genre fiction would be horror, fantasy, science fiction, western, romance, suspense, thriller, espionage, private eye fiction, cozy or traditional mysteries. True crime is also a genre.

The **Gold Dagger**, which was originally called the Crossed Red Herrings, is the top award given annually in various categories by the British Crime Writers Association. Runners up are awarded the Silver Dagger.

Golden Age of Mystery, sometimes called the Golden Age of Detection, was ushered in by Agatha Christie's 1920 debut novel, *The Mysterious Affair at Styles*, followed shortly by Lord Peter Wimsey's arrival in Dorothy Sayers' 1923 novel *Whose Body?* It is thought that detectives became more believable during this period between the First and Second World Wars, when greater emphasis was placed on period and character rather than simply constructing clever puzzles.

Gothic mysteries have a dark and scary tone, often with supernatural elements woven into the story. Likely to be set on an old estate, a gothic mystery will also contain elements of romantic suspense.

The **Grand Master Award** is given by the Mystery Writers of America (elected by its board of directors) in recognition of a lifetime of excellence in crime fiction. The first to be named to this mystery hall of fame was Agatha Christie in 1955. See *Chapter 9, Awards and Organizations*, for a list of Grand Masters.

The **Hammett Prize**, established in 1988 by the International Association of Crime Writers, is given for excellence in crime writing, either fiction or non-fiction. Nominations are made by members of the publishing and reading committees and a trophy is presented at the Edgar ceremonies in New York City in April.

Hard-boiled mysteries, typically narrated by a cynical private investigator walking the mean streets of anytown, are generally thought to be an American invention.

The **heist** is a mystery involving a theft, but typically more serious than a caper. The focus is likely to be on planning and executing the theft, in addition to solving the crime.

A **house name** is a pseudonym belonging to the publisher, frequently used by a number of writers to produce a long-running or many-titled series. A good example would be the house name Carolyn Keene, author of more than 60 years' worth of Nancy Drew books.

A **house series** is a series belonging to the publisher and written by one or more pseudonymous authors. The author-for-hire may be responsible for the storylines, but the publisher owns the copyright. *The Inspector and Mrs. Jeffries* series is an example of a current house series—this one owned by Berkeley.

Howdunits are mysteries which focus on how a particular crime was committed. Locked room mysteries are good examples of howdunits, as opposed to whodunits, which concentrate on determining the identity of the murderer.

Inverted mysteries are those where the identity of the murderer is known at the outset and the question is not whodunit but howtoget'em. That rumpled-raincoat police detective of TV fame, Sgt. Columbo, is typically working an inverted mystery while the viewing audience matches wits in the race to find a fatal flaw in the perfect crime.

Lambda Literary Awards, nominated by readers of the Lambda Book Report, include awards for best gay and lesbian mystery novel. They are awarded annually at a banquet held the night before opening of the American Booksellers Association (ABA) national convention in June.

Locked room mysteries are a classic mystery format where the murder takes place inside a locked room with no visible means of entry or exit for the murderer. The room is typically locked from the inside.

Macavity Award winners in various categories are selected by the readers of the *Mystery Readers Journal* of Mystery Readers International. See *Chapter 10, Other Resources*, for subscription information.

A **McGuffin**, according to Alfred Hitchcock, is the thing in the story that the characters are looking for—the prize to win, or the disaster to be averted, that sets the plot in motion. In the movie *Psycho*, the McGuffin is the money the woman steals.

Mass market paperbacks are softcover books intended for a general audience and wide circulation. Often called pocket books, they typically measure 4 by 7 inches and are sold in drugstores, grocery stores, discount stores and airports, as well as in bookstores.

The **Nero Wolfe Award** is given in recognition of the best detective novel first published in the United States during the current year (September to September). The trophy, a bust of Nero Wolfe, is awarded annually at the Wolfe Pack's Black Orchid Banquet the first Saturday in December. The prize was established in 1979 in honor of Rex Stout's Nero Wolfe mystery series.

One-off is the British term for a non-series novel. When an author says she's going back to one-offs, you can expect she'll be taking a break from her series characters and writing stand alone novels.

A **pastiche** can be literary, musical or artistic and consists of motifs or techniques borrowed from someone else. A Sherlock Holmes pastiche would be a story or novel strongly resembling the work of Sir Arthur Conan Doyle, Holmes' creator.

Pen name, from the French *nom de plume*, is another term for pseudonym or alias used by an author to conceal identity.

Penny dreadful, chiefly a British term circa 1870-1875, is a sensational novel of adventure, crime or violence, typically produced with very little expense. The writers of these novels were often paid only a penny per line and later a penny per word.

Police procedurals are mystery novels, film or television dramas that deal realistically with police work.

Police rank order in Great Britain's **County Police Force** is (from the top down):

Watch Committee
Chief Constable
Deputy Chief Constable
(Detective) Chief Superintendent
(Detective) Superintendent
(Detective) Chief Inspector
(Detective) Inspector
(Detective) Sergeant
(Detective) Constable

Members of the police are assigned to either the uniformed or the detective branch. The ranks are the same in both branches, with the term "detective" added to distinguish that branch.

Police rank order in Great Britain's Metropolitan Police Force, popularly known as **Scotland Yard**, is (from the top down):

Home Secretary
Commissioner
Deputy Commissioner
Assistant Commissioner
Deputy Assistant Commissioner
Commander
Deputy Commander
(Detective) Chief Superintendent
(Detective) Superintendent
(Detective) Chief Inspector
(Detective) Inspector
(Detective) Sergeant
(Detective) Constable

Police rank order in U. S. police departments is (from the top down):

Chief
Assistant Chief
Major(s)
Captain(s)
Lieutenant(s)
Sergeants(s)
Officer(s)

The **Private Eye Writers of America** (PWA), founded in 1982 to promote and recognize private-eye writers, confers the annual Shamus Awards in a variety of categories. Prior to 1995 they were typically awarded at Bouchercon in October, but last year PWA held its own convention, EyeCon, in June and Shamus Awards were presented then. The next EyeCon is scheduled for 1997.

The **protagonist** is the leading character or hero of a literary work, from the Greek term for the first actor and main character in a drama.

Pseudonymns are literally false names used by authors and their publishers to hide the identity of the writer. In some cases, a pseudonym is used when an author's most recent work is a radical departure from earlier work and the publisher fears confusing the reader. Writers who work in multiple genres frequently use pseudonyms at the insistence of their publishers. Where once women mystery writers used initials or androgynous names to hide their sex, men are now using female pseudonyms or initials to lead readers to believe a certain series is written by a woman. A good example would be the series featuring cat-loving actress, Alice Nestleton, published under Lydia Adamson, but written by a man.

Pulp fiction got its name originally from the rough and low-quality paper (manufactured from wood pulp) on which it was printed. The term is often synonymous with fiction involving lurid and sensational subjects.

A **red herring** was once an actual smoked herring (more brown than red) that was dragged across a hunting trail for the purpose of confusing the tracking dogs. The term in crime fiction is used to describe any false clue planted for the purpose of confusing the reader.

Regency novels are historical novels set during that period of British history (1811-1820) when George, Prince of Wales, later George IV, was regent. A prodigious number of novels and their dedicated readers and fans are focused on this 10-year slice of English history.

The Rita Awards, open only to members of the Romance Writers of America (RWA), include an award for best romantic suspense novel.

Romantic suspense includes strong elements of romance, usually between the detective and the victim or the detective and a suspect. The emphasis is on the tension which builds in anticipation of the outcome.

Scotland Yard is the popular name for the Metropolitan Police Force responsible for Greater London. The term comes from a short street in central London which was once the site of the police headquarters, later moved (1890) to a Thames embankment and renamed the New Scotland Yard. On the original site was once a 13th century palace used by Scottish kings and queens on state visits to London and hence the name, Scotland Yard.

Shamus is a slang expression for private eye or police detective, originating around 1925. The term is thought to come from either the Yiddish expression for custodian of a synagogue (*shames*) or the Irish male given name *Seamus*.

Shamus Awards are given annually by the Private Eye Writers of America (PWA) in various categories pertaining to the P. I. story and novel. Nominations, which are made by publishers and voted by PWA members, are open to novels or short stories featuring any investigator not employed by or paid by a unit of government.

Sherlockiana is the term for all things related to Sherlock Holmes. Sherlockians are those in the U.S. who enjoy promoting Sherlock Holmes, while their British counterparts are known as Holmesians. Their shared goal is "to keep green the memory of the Master." Sherlockian interests range from serious scholarship to reenacting Holmes' adventures, collecting Victorian artifacts and rare manuscripts to developing authentic costumes. It is estimated that more than 350 organizations worldwide are devoted to Sherlockian interests.

The **Silver Dagger** is awarded annually by the British Crime Writers Association in various categories as a runner-up to the Gold Dagger winner.

Sisters in Crime International was founded in 1986 to combat discrimination against women in the mystery field and to raise the level of awareness regarding the contribution of women to the genre. The organization now has more than 3000 members worldwide including writers, editors, literary agents, librarians, booksellers and fans. Chicago mystery writer Sara Paretsky was the founding president. Elaine Raco Chase is the '95–'96 president.

In a **suspense story** or **novel of suspense** is one in which the main action (crime or murder) has not yet taken place. Instead the emphasis is on the tension which builds in anticipation of the outcome. Although mystery and suspense are often used interchangeably, a mystery starts with a murder and emphasizes solving the crime or figuring out whodunit.

Trade paperbacks are softcover books typically measuring 5 by 8 inches, available mostly in bookstores and intended for a general audience, as opposed to textbooks, reference books or other specialty publications. Originally they were printed with the same plates used to produce the hardcover edition, but on smaller pages with narrower margins. Trade paperbacks are usually priced somewhere between the cost of a mass market paperback and a hard cover book.

True crime stories or novels are works of nonfiction about actual murders or serial killings. Truman Capote's *In Cold Blood* is perhaps the best known example of a true crime novel, described once as a book about people doing things which, if put in a novel, no one would believe.

Tuckerize is an expression that takes its name from popular '50s and '60s science fiction writer, Bob Wilson Tucker, who had the habit of naming characters (who were often later killed) after friends and acquaintances. The opportunity to be "tuckerized" has became a favorite at charity auctions where fans bid money to have themselves named in an upcoming novel by their favorite mystery writer. Not all authors are enthusiastic about the practice.

A **Watson** is a friend or helper of the detective, whose job it often is to narrate the story and describe the detective's brilliance at solving crimes. By definition, the Watson should be not as smart or clever as the actual detective. And ideally the Watson should also be less intelligent than the average mystery reader who will enjoy feeling superior to the Watson. The term comes from that able assistant to Sherlock Holmes, Dr. Watson.

Whodunits are mysteries which concentrate on determining the identity of the murderer, as opposed to howdunits which focus on exactly how a particular crime was committed.

The **World Mystery Convention**, also known as Bouchercon (rhymes with "ouch," as in BOUCH-er-con), is held each year in early October in a different city around the world to honor the work of Anthony Boucher (1911-1968), a prolific mystery writer. Bouchercon 26 was held in Nottingham, England, September 28 to October 1, 1995. Bouchercon 27 will convene in St. Paul, Minnesota, October 9-13, 1996, with Bouchercon 28 moving to Monterey, California, October 30 to November 2, 1997.

Whydunits are mysteries which empahsize why the murder took place, as opposed to who committed the murder or how they accomplished it. Greatly influenced by the growth of psychology, whydunit are sometimes called psychological novels.

Twelve

Bibliography

The Armchair Detective, Vols. 27-28. Stine, Kate, editor-in-chief. 1994-95. New York: The Armchair Detective, Inc.

And Then There Were Nine...More Women of Mystery. Bakerman, Jane, editor. Bowling Green, Ohio: Bowling Green State University Popular Press, 1985.

Bouchercon 25 and 26 Program Books.

BuffCon '95 Program Book, 1995.

By a Woman's Hand, A Guide to Mystery Fiction by Women. Swanson, Jean and Dean James. New York: Berkley Books, 1994.

CADS, Crime and Detective Stories, Nos. 20-26, 1993-1995. Bradley, Geoff, editor. Essex, England.

Crime Fiction II, A Comprehensive Bibliography 1749-1990. Vols. 1-2. Hubin, Allen J. New York & London: Garland Publishing, Inc. 1994.

The Crown Crime Companion. Compiled by Mickey Friedman. New York: Crown Publishers, 1995.

Deadly Pleasures, Nos. 1-11, 1993-1995. Easter, George A., editor. 1994-95.

Deadly Serious, References for Writers of Detective, Mystery and Crime Fiction. Villines, Sharon, editor. 1995.

Doubleday Crime Club Compendium, 1928-1991. Nehr, Ellen. Martinez, California: Offspring Press. 1992.

The Drood Review of Mystery, Nos. 133-139, 1994-1995. Huang, Jim, editor and publisher. Kalamazoo, Michigan: The Drood Review.

Encyclopedia Mysteriosa, A Comprehensive Guide to the Art of Detection in Print, Film, Radio, and Television. DeAndrea, William L. New York: Prentice Hall General Reference, 1994.

EyeCon '95 Program Book, 1995.

Fine Art of Murder, The Mystery Reader's Indispensable Companion. Gorman, Ed, Martin H. Greenburg, Larry Segriff, editors with Jon L. Breen. New York: Carroll & Graf, 1993.

Genreflecting, A Guide to Reading Interests in Genre Fiction. Rosenberg, Betty and Diana Tixier Herald, editors. Third Edition, 1991. Englewood, Colorado: Libraries Unlimited, Inc.

Magna Cum Murder Program Book, 1995.

Malice Domestic I-VII Program Books, 1989-1995.

Mid Atlantic Mystery Book Fair and Convention Program Book, 1995.

Mostly Murder, Your Guide to Reading Mysteries. Setliff, Jay W. K., editor and publisher. 1994-1995. Dallas, Texas: Mostly Book Reviews, Inc.

Murderess Ink, The Better Half of Mystery. Winn, Dilys, editor. New York: Workman Publishing. 1979.

Murderous Intent, A Magazine of Mystery & Suspense, Volume 1. 1995. Power, Margo, editor. Vancouver, Washington: Madison Publishing Co.

Mystery News, 1994-95. Stay, Harriet, editor. Port Townsend, Washington.

Mystery & Detective Monthly, 1995. Napier, Robert S., editor. Tacoma, Washington: Snapbrim Press.

Mystery Readers Journal, The Journal of Mystery Readers International. Vols. 10-11. Rudolph, Janet A., editor. Berkeley, California.

The Mystery Review, A Quarterly Publication for Mystery Readers. 1994-1995. Davey, Barbara, editor. Colborne, Ontario, Canada.

Mystery Scene Magazine, Nos. 41-48, 1994-1995. Gorman, Joe W., editor. Cedar Rapids, Iowa: Mystery Enterprises.

Mystery Writers Market Place and Sourcebook. Collingwood, Donna, editor. Cincinnati: Writer's Digest Books, 1993.

The New Bedside, Bathtub & Armchair Companion to Agatha Christie, Second Edition, 1993. Riley, Dick and Pam McAllister, editors. New York: Ungar.

100 Great Detectives. Jakubowski, Maxim, editor. New York: Carroll & Graf Publishers, Inc., 1991.

1001 Midnights, The Aficionado's Guide to Mystery and Detective Fiction. Pronzini, Bill and Marcia Muller. New York: Arbor House, 1986.

Publishers Weekly, The International News Magazine of Book Publishing and Bookselling. 1995. A Cahners/R. R. Bowker Publication.

A Reader's Guide to The American Novel of Detection. Lachman, Marvin. New York: G. K. Hall & Co., 1993.

A Reader's Guide to the Classic British Mystery. Oleksiw, Susan. New York: Mysterious Press, 1989. Originally published by G. K. Hall & Co., Boston, 1988.

A Reader's Guide to The Private Eye Novel. Neibuhr, Gary Warren. New York: G. K. Hall & Co., 1993.

Sisters in Crime, Vols. 1-5. Wallace, Marilyn, editor. New York: The Berkley Publishing Group, 1989-1992.

Sisters in Crime Books-in-Print, 1994-1995. Compiled by Sue Henry. Available from Rowan Mountain Literary Associates, Blacksburg, Virginia.

Sisters in Crime Newsletters, 1994-1995.

Twentieth-Century Crime and Mystery Writers. Reilly, John M., editor. London: St. James Press. Second Edition, 1985.

What Do I Read Next? A Reader's Guide to Current Genre Fiction, 1990-1993. Detroit and London: Gale Research Inc.

The Woman Detective, Gender & Genre. Klein, Kathleen Gregory. Urbana and Chicago: University of Illinois Press, 1988.

Thirteen

 Index

100 Great Detectives 352, 362
1001 Midnights, The Aficionado's Guide to Mystery 352, 362
1st Culprit anthology 349
2nd Culprit anthology 340, 349

A

A. Pennyfather 150, 209, 223, 244, 329
Abbey, Kiernan 162, 327
Abby Abagnarro 196, 218, 223, 251
Abigail Doyle 44, 212, 223, 250
Abigail Patience Danforth 100, 207, 216, 223, 254
Abigail Sanderson 218, 223, 257, 329
Adam Dalgleish 101, 204, 223, 258
➡ Adams, Deborah 19, 222, 232, 253, 285, 286, 291, 295, 332, 333, 340
Adams, Samantha 330
➡ Adamson, M. J. 19, 203, 224, 239, 255, 278, 279, 280, 296, 306, 312, 316, 318, 327, 332, 333
Adamson, Yvonne 19, 140, 327
Addie Devore 104, 217, 223, 245
Agatha Awards 342, 355
Agatha Raisin 26, 212, 221, 223, 256, 327
Agatha Welch 102, 220, 223, 246
Agnes Carmichael 43, 219, 223, 255, 328
➡ Aird, Catherine 20, 203, 226, 258, 272, 273, 274, 275, 276, 278, 286, 293, 295, 300, 301, 307, 308, 309, 311, 317, 318, 320, 321, 327, 332, 333, 352
Al Krug 195, 206, 223, 245
Alan Grant 183, 206, 223, 258, 330, 352
Alan Markby 81, 204, 223, 256
Alan Stewart 106, 210, 223, 248
Albenia "Benni" Harper 70, 210, 223, 244
Albert Campion 21, 220, 223, 257
Albert, Susan & Bill 152, 330, 332, 333
➡ Albert, Susan Wittig 20, 212, 226, 253, 285, 286, 289, 291, 308, 319, 322, 325
Alden Chase 193, 209, 223, 248
Aldrich, Pearl G. 332, 333
Alex Jensen 93, 210, 214, 223, 243
Alex McKenzie 31, 209, 223, 248, 327
Alex Sinclair 88, 204, 223, 255
Alex Tanner 56, 206, 218, 223, 257
Alex Winter 181, 208, 223, 243
Alfred Hitchcock Mystery Magazine 331, 345

Aline Scott 57, 203, 223, 246, 328
Alison Hope 105, 213, 223, 257
Alison Kaine 21, 203, 214, 223, 245, 327
Alix Thorssen 129, 210, 224, 254
Allan, Dennis 68, 69, 327
➡ Allen, Irene 20, 221, 228, 252, 285, 286, 318, 327
➡ Allen, Kate 20, 203, 214, 223, 245, 286, 291, 307, 322, 327
➡ Allingham, Margery 21, 220, 223, 257, 264, 265, 266, 268, 269, 270, 271, 272, 296, 297, 298, 299, 300, 303, 305, 306, 307, 308, 309, 310, 311, 312, 313, 315, 316, 317, 319, 322, 323, 325, 351
Alonzo Hawkin 107, 207, 224, 245
Amanda Hazard 65, 212, 220, 224, 252
Amanda Knight 73, 219, 224, 246
Amanda Mackay 122
Amanda Pepper 166, 209, 224, 253, 330
Amanda Roberts 200, 216, 224, 247
Amanda Valentine 27, 203, 214, 224, 260
amateur detectives 355, see also Chapter 2
Amelia Butterworth 82, 83
Amelia Peabody 155, 216, 222, 224, 257, 330, 352
American Booksellers Association 358
American Crime Writers League 341, 355
American Mystery Awards 355
➡ Amey, Linda 21, 212, 225, 253, 285, 291, 296, 298
Amos, Alan 108, 327
Amy Prescott 93, 219, 224, 254
Amy Tupper 28, 224, 257, 327
Ana Grey 177, 206, 224, 244
And Then There Were Nine…More Women of Mystery 350, 361
Anders, K. T. 332, 333
Andrea Perkins 44, 210, 224, 248
➡ Andreae, Christine 22, 220, 234, 249, 285, 289, 308, 323
Andrew Basnett 67, 209, 224, 255
➡ Andrews, Sarah 22, 214, 228, 254, 289, 291, 306, 322, 332, 333
Angela Benbow 169, 221, 224, 245
Angela Matelli 116, 207, 224, 248
Angelina Amalfi 154, 215, 224, 245
Angie DaVito 172, 218, 220, 224, 251
Anita Blake 88, 213, 224, 249
Anna Lee 43, 206, 224, 257, 328

Anna Peters 115, 207, 224, 246
Anna Pigeon 26, 203, 214, 224, 255
Anna Southwood 27, 206, 224, 259
Annabel Reed 186, 218, 224, 246
Anne "Davvie" Davenport McLean 201, 217, 222, 224, 260
Anne Fitzhugh 165, 205, 224, 246
Anne Menlo 147, 219, 224, 243
Anneke Haagen 97, 213, 224, 249
Annie Laurance 90, 211, 224, 253
Annie MacPherson 178, 218, 224, 254
Annie McGrogan 65, 207, 224, 250
anthologies see Chapters 8 & 10
Anthony Awards 341, 355
Antony Maitland 199, 219, 224, 256, 330
April Woo 78, 204, 224, 250
Arguiles, Cheryl 33, 327
Arly Hanks 94, 204, 222, 224, 243
Armchair Detective magazine 345, 361
Armchair Detective Book of Lists 350
➡ Armstrong, Charlotte 22, 209, 235, 250, 267, 268, 298, 310, 311, 332, 333, 340
➡ Arnold, Margot 22, 209, 237, 240, 260, 275, 276, 280, 282, 283, 285, 289, 291, 298, 299, 303, 304, 306, 311, 312, 323, 326, 327
Arthur Ellis Awards 342
Arthur G. Crook 76, 218, 224, 255, 329
Arthur "Snooky" Randolph 51, 211, 224, 246
Asey Mayo 183, 220, 224, 249
Ashley Johnson 129, 205, 224, 254
associations see Chapter 9
➡ Atherton, Nancy 23, 220, 224, 255, 285, 289, 293, 296
Auguste Didier 144, 215, 216, 224, 256
Aunt Dimity 23, 220, 224, 255
Auntie Lil 82, 212, 221, 224, 250, 329
Aurora Teagarden 89, 211, 212, 224, 247
Auspitz, Kate 28, 327
awards see Chapter 9
➡ Ayres, Noreen 23, 203, 238, 244, 285, 289, 293, 298, 311, 325

B

➡ Babbin, Jacqueline 23, 218, 226, 250, 273, 280, 297, 318
➡ Babson, Marian 23, 212, 222, 227, 228, 240, 257, 273, 278, 280, 282, 286, 291, 297, 300, 305, 309, 313, 315, 318, 320, 323

➡ denotes authors in Master List

Bacon, Gail 328
➦ Baker, Nikki 24, 212, 214, 241, 247, 283, 285, 286, 309, 311, 327
Baker Street Irregulars 355
Ball, Doris Bell Collier 327
➦ Ballard, Mignon 24, 220, 228, 254, 286, 312, 332, 333
Balthazar Marten 19, 203, 224, 255
Bane, Diana 53, 327
➦ Banks, Carolyn 24, 210, 238, 253, 286, 289, 291, 302, 308, 315
➦ Bannister, Jo 24, 203, 210, 219, 225, 226, 229, 230, 234, 255, 256, 276, 280, 282, 286, 289, 291, 293, 297, 298, 299, 307, 316, 320, 321, 322
Barbara Havers 75, 204, 224, 257
Barbara Holloway 196, 219, 224, 252
Barbara Joan "Bo" Bradley 152, 208, 224, 244
➦ Barber, Willetta Ann 25, 203, 226, 250, 266, 267, 268, 303, 304, 314, 316, 317
➦ Barnes, Linda 25, 206, 225, 236, 248, 276, 278, 280, 282, 283, 286, 291, 297, 299, 300, 301, 308, 321, 323, 332, 333, 340
➦ Barr, Nevada 26, 203, 214, 224, 255, 286, 289, 291, 293, 306, 309, 322, 323, 342
Barrett Lake 176, 209, 224, 244
Barry Vaughan 103, 211, 225, 258
Basil Willing 130, 219, 225, 251
Basnett, Andrew 328
Baxter, Alida 332, 333
➦ Beaton, M. C. 26, 203, 212, 221, 223, 230, 256, 259, 277, 278, 279, 280, 282, 283, 285, 286, 289, 291, 295, 302, 303, 327
Beatrice Lestrange Bradley 138, 221, 225, 258
Beatty, Terry 332, 333
➦ Beck, K. K. 27, 216, 222, 231, 244, 254, 276, 277, 280, 285, 286, 289, 291, 295, 299, 302, 305, 309, 314, 317, 327, 332, 333, 340
Becky Belski 86, 213, 225, 247
➦ Bedford, Jean 27, 206, 224, 259, 282, 285, 286, 320, 323, 325
➦ Beecham, Rose 27, 203, 214, 224, 260, 285, 289, 291, 306, 310, 319
➦ Belfort, Sophie 28, 209, 236, 248, 278, 283, 285, 306, 310, 312, 327
➦ Bell, Josephine 28, 203, 218, 219, 220, 224, 226, 227, 230, 239, 257, 265, 266, 267, 268, 269, 270, 271, 272, 275, 295, 297, 299, 300, 302, 303, 305, 306, 307, 314, 315, 318, 319, 321, 324, 325, 327
Ben Haskell 37, 220, 225, 256
Ben Porter 185, 212, 225, 246
Ben Safford 56, 215, 218, 225, 246, 328
Benjamin Jurnet 92, 204, 225, 258
Bennett, Elizabeth 90, 327
➦ Bennett, Liza 29, 212, 237, 250, 280, 282, 312, 319
Bentley, Phylis 332, 333
➦ Berenson, Laurien 29, 210, 222, 230, 235, 246, 250, 289, 291, 293, 303, 304, 317, 323
Bernadette Hebert 63, 214, 219, 225, 248
Bernard Woodrull 51, 211, 225, 246
➦ Berry, Carole 29, 212, 225, 250, 278, 279, 282, 283, 289, 293, 302, 308, 310, 311, 326
bes-Shahar, Eluki 328
Bessie Petty 115, 221, 225, 255
Betty Trenka 41, 212, 221, 225, 246
Beulah Pond 115, 221, 225, 255
Biederman, Marcia 332, 333
Bill Hastings 149, 220, 225, 245
Bill Slider 90, 204, 225, 256
Bill Smith 168, 208, 225, 251
Bingo Riggs 164, 220, 225, 254, 330
Birdie Linnet 119, 222, 225, 256
Birkley, Dolan 327
➦ Bishop, Claudia 29, 211, 235, 238, 250, 289, 291, 293, 301, 315, 317, 322, 327
Black, Malacai 49, 327

➦ Black, Veronica 30, 213, 232, 256, 282, 285, 286, 289, 291, 293, 324, 327
➦ Blackmur, L. L. 30, 210, 229, 232, 255, 280, 311, 327
Blackwater Bay 79, 225, 255
Blaine Stewart 202, 208, 225, 252
Blair Emerson 21, 212, 225, 253
Blaisdell, Anne 118, 172, 327
Blake, Margaret 77, 327
Blanche White 146, 211, 213, 225, 252
➦ Bland, Eleanor Taylor 30, 203, 211, 235, 247, 285, 286, 289, 291, 301, 304, 307, 320
Blevins, Haskell 129
➦ Block, Barbara 30, 210, 238, 252, 289, 299, 323
Bloomer, Theo 329
Blue Maguire 196, 206, 225, 244
Boenhardt, Patricia 90, 329
Bonnie Indermill 29, 212, 225, 250
Bordill, Judith 61, 327
➦ Borthwick, J. S. 31, 209, 223, 239, 248, 276, 277, 278, 282, 285, 289, 291, 297, 298, 304, 321, 327
➦ Borton, D. B. 31, 206, 221, 226, 252, 286, 289, 291, 293, 306, 307, 316, 322, 323, 327
Boucher, Anthony 355, 360
Bouchercon 341, 343, 344, 355, 359, 360
➦ Bowen, Gail 31, 209, 232, 259, 282, 283, 286, 289, 300, 301, 311, 313, 324
Bowen-Judd, Sara Hutton 35, 38, 116, 198, 328, 329, 330
➦ Bowers, Elisabeth 31, 206, 235, 259, 279, 283, 310, 316
➦ Boylan, Eleanor 32, 221, 226, 250, 280, 282, 285, 286, 314, 315, 318, 325
➦ Bradley, Lynn 32, 206, 227, 253, 289, 321
➦ Brand, Christianna 32, 203, 227, 257, 266, 267, 268, 269, 270, 300, 303, 307, 308, 311, 321, 323, 327
➦ Braun, Lilian Jackson 32, 209, 217, 232, 233, 241, 255, 272, 278, 279, 280, 282, 283, 285, 286, 289, 291, 293, 298, 299, 332, 333
➦ Brennan, Carol 33, 212, 222, 228, 234, 250, 283, 285, 289, 291, 299, 307, 308, 309
Brett Nightingale 104, 214, 225, 259
➦ Bridge, Ann 33, 217, 221, 232, 255, 270, 271, 272, 300, 305, 311, 312, 316, 318, 327
➦ Brightwell, Emily 33, 216, 221, 231, 257, 286, 287, 289, 291, 307, 310, 313, 327
Brigid Donovan 169, 211, 215, 225, 248
➦ Brill, Toni 34, 210, 236, 250, 283, 287, 301, 327
British Crime Writers Association 341, 356, 357
Britt Montero 35, 217, 225, 246
➦ Brod, D. C. 34, 206, 238, 247, 280, 282, 283, 287, 298, 305, 307, 312, 314
Brooke Cassidy 110, 216, 225, 253
Brooks, Janice Young 41, 328
Brother Cadfael 156, 214, 225, 258, 330
➦ Brown, Lizbie 34, 210, 228, 256, 285, 289, 298, 323, 327
Brown, Morna Doris MacTaggart 66, 328
➦ Brown, Rita Mae 34, 209, 235, 254, 282, 285, 289, 291, 313, 317, 319, 325
Brown, Zenith Jones 69, 328
➦ Buchanan, Edna 35, 217, 225, 246, 285, 289, 291, 293, 295, 300, 312, 321
Buchanan, Eileen-Marie Duell 49, 157, 328, 330
Buckingham, Nancy 161, 328
➦ Buckstaff, Kathryn 35, 216, 236, 246, 289, 316
Bunty Felse 156, 205, 225, 258
➦ Burden, Pat 35, 203, 230, 257, 282, 285, 287, 298, 306, 319, 325
➦ Burke, Jan 35, 217, 230, 245, 287, 289, 291, 293, 301, 308, 318, 322
Burke, Noel 328
Burnham, Brenda Melton 332, 333
Burt, Elizabeth 332, 333

➦ Burton, Anne 35, 116, 199, 212, 238, 255, 275, 301, 324, 325, 328
Burton, Sarah 188, 330
➦ Bushell, Agnes 36, 206, 241, 248, 280, 287, 302, 320
➦ Butler, Gwendoline 36, 134, 203, 232, 257, 270, 271, 272, 274, 278, 279, 280, 283, 285, 287, 289, 291, 299, 300, 301, 302, 304, 312, 315, 319, 329, 352
Butters, Dorothy G. 77, 328
By a Woman's Hand 350, 361

C

C. B. Greenfield 103, 217, 225, 246
C. Donovan 256
C.I.D. 356
CADS, Crime and Detective Stories 346, 361
➦ Cail, Carol 36, 217, 235, 245, 287, 291, 318, 324
Caitlin Reece 57, 206, 214, 225, 259
Cal Donovan 25, 203, 225
Caleb Sweetwater 82, 204, 225, 250
Caledonia Wingate 169, 221, 225, 245
Caley Burke 133, 207, 225, 244
Calista Jacobs 109, 212, 225, 248
Callahan Garrity 186, 213, 225, 247
➦ Cannell, Dorothy 37, 220, 225, 228, 256, 276, 277, 279, 282, 285, 289, 291, 304, 306, 309, 313, 322, 325, 332, 333, 340
Cannon, Eileen E. 37
➦ Cannon, Taffy 37, 218, 236, 244, 287, 291, 293, 299, 317, 322
Caper mysteries 356
Cardiff, Insp. Supt. 82, 204, 225, 255, 329
Carl Pedersen 91, 204, 225, 243
Carlos Cruz 188, 206, 225, 244
Carlotta Carlyle 25, 206, 225, 248
➦ Carlson, P. M. 37, 203, 209, 235, 247, 250, 277, 278, 279, 282, 283, 285, 291, 296, 297, 308, 314, 315, 318, 332, 333, 340
Carmen Ramirez 87, 214, 217, 225, 252
Carol Ashton 133, 205, 214, 225, 259
Carpenter, Helen & Lorri 332, 333
Carpenter, Lynette 31, 327
Carrie Porter 185, 212, 225, 246
Carter, Philip Youngman 21
Carvic, Heron 47, 328
Casey Kellog 195, 206, 226, 245
Cash-Domingo, Lea 332, 333
Cass Jameson 195, 219, 226, 251
Cassandra Reilly 197, 213, 226, 258
Cassandra Swann 141, 220, 226, 256
Cassidy McCabe 128, 209, 219, 226, 247
Cassie Newton 178, 209, 226, 259
Cat Caliban 31, 206, 221, 226, 252, 327
Cat Marsala 49, 216, 226, 247
Catherine LeVendeur 146, 213, 215, 226, 259
Catherine Sayler 81, 207, 226, 245, 329
Catherine Wilde 168, 210, 221, 226, 254
➦ Caudwell, Sarah 38, 209, 230, 258, 275, 277, 280, 320, 322, 328, 332, 333, 352
Cecile Buddenbrooks 181, 208, 226, 248
Cecily Sinclair 107, 211, 216, 226, 256, 329
➦ Challis, Mary 38, 116, 199, 218, 231, 255, 275, 298, 300, 307, 324, 328
Chaplin, Elizabeth 132, 328
➦ Chapman, Sally 38, 206, 213, 232, 245, 283, 289, 293, 300, 311, 318
character names see Chapter 3
Charles, Hampton 47, 328
➦ Charles, Kate 38, 213, 227, 234, 257, 283, 287, 289, 291, 296, 301, 304, 306, 321, 328
Charles Matthews 135, 205, 226, 253
Charles Spotted Moon 201, 219, 226, 245
Charlie Greene 137, 222, 226, 244
Charlie Meiklejohn 196, 208, 226, 252
Charlie Parker 174, 213, 226, 250

➦ denotes authors in Master List

Charlotte Graham 128, 221, 222, 226, 251
Charlotte Kent 107, 211, 226, 246
Charlotte Pitt 154, 205, 216, 226, 258
Charlotte Sams 79, 211, 226, 252, 329
Charmian Daniels 135, 205, 226, 257, 329
Chase, Carol 38, 328
➥ Chase, Elaine Raco 39, 217, 236, 238, 246, 278, 279, 300, 349
Chautauqua Historical Mystery Conference 342
Chehak, Susan Taylor 332, 333
Chesney, Marion 26, 327, 328, 330
Chicago Nordejoong 133, 222, 226, 246
China Bayles 20, 212, 226, 253
➥ Chisholm, P. F. 39, 216, 238, 255, 291, 293, 294, 306, 319, 322, 328
➥ Christie, Agatha 39, 206, 221, 230, 231, 240, 257, 258, 264, 265, 266, 267, 268, 269, 270, 271, 272, 273, 274, 295, 296, 297, 298, 299, 300, 301, 302, 303, 304, 305, 306, 307, 308, 309, 311, 312, 313, 314, 315, 316, 317, 318, 319, 320, 322, 324, 330, 332, 333, 343, 351, 352, 355, 362
Christine Bennett 89, 213, 226, 250, 329
Christine Martin 166, 217, 226, 256
Christine Opara 187, 206, 226, 251
➥ Christmas, Joyce 41, 212, 220, 221, 225, 235, 246, 250, 279, 280, 282, 283, 285, 287, 289, 291, 302, 306, 307, 310, 317, 320, 321, 322
Christopher Dennis "Seedy" Sloan 20, 203, 226, 258, 327
Christopher "Kit" Storm 25, 203, 226, 250
Christopher McKee 162, 205, 226, 251
➥ Churchill, Jill 41, 222, 231, 247, 280, 283, 287, 289, 291, 293, 299, 306, 307, 308, 310, 318, 320, 328
Claire Aldington 97, 213, 226, 251
Claire Breslinsky 105, 217, 226, 251
Claire Camden 157, 209, 226, 258
Claire Claiborne 59, 220, 226, 248
Claire Conrad 99, 207, 226, 245
Claire Malloy 94, 211, 226, 243
Claire Sharples 167, 212, 226, 244
Clara Gamadge 221, 226, 250
Clare Clively 48, 216, 226, 257, 328
➥ Clark, Carol Higgins 41, 206, 238, 244, 285, 287, 291, 303, 309, 321
➥ Clark, Carolyn Chambers 42, 206, 219, 235, 240, 246, 287, 289, 300, 301
Clark, Mary Higgins 332, 333, 341, 349
➥ Clarke, Anna 42, 209, 237, 257, 277, 278, 279, 280, 283, 289, 298, 311, 314, 315, 325
Clarke, Brenda Margaret Lilian Honeyman 330
Claude Warrington-Reeve 28, 218, 226, 257, 327
Claudia Valentine 53, 206, 226, 259
➥ Cleary, Melissa 42, 209, 210, 231, 249, 285, 287, 289, 291, 293, 301, 304, 306, 309, 312, 314, 320, 322
➥ Cleeves, Ann 42, 203, 214, 221, 229, 236, 239, 255, 258, 278, 280, 282, 283, 285, 287, 289, 291, 293, 296, 297, 300, 301, 308, 309, 310, 311, 312, 314, 318, 319
Clio Browne 109, 207, 211, 226, 249
Clio Rees 25, 210, 219, 226, 255
Clovis Kelly 23, 218, 226, 250
Clues: A Journal of Detection 346
Cockburn, Sarah 38, 328
Cockrill, Insp. 32, 203, 227, 257, 327
Coco Hastings 149, 220, 227, 245
➥ Cody, Liza 43, 206, 222, 228, 257, 275, 276, 277, 278, 283, 287, 289, 296, 298, 304, 308, 313, 321, 323, 328, 332, 333, 340, 349
➥ Coel, Margaret 43, 214, 232, 241, 254, 291, 293, 305, 307
➥ Cohen, Anthea 43, 219, 223, 255, 276, 277, 278, 279, 280, 283, 285, 287, 291, 296, 303, 306, 308, 312, 318, 328
Cohen, Janet 145, 329

➥ Coker, Carolyn 44, 210, 224, 248, 276, 278, 282, 287, 296, 308, 316
Coleman January 32, 206, 227, 253
➥ Collins, Anna Ashwood 44, 212, 223, 250, 289, 293, 301, 318, 332, 333
Collins, Barbara 332, 333
Collins, Dorothy A. 332, 333
➥ Comfort, Barbara 44, 210, 221, 240, 253, 278, 280, 287, 291, 298, 305, 308, 317
Conan Flagg 200, 212, 227, 252, 330
➥ Conant, Susan 44, 210, 230, 248, 280, 282, 283, 285, 287, 291, 297, 301, 307, 315, 317, 319
Connor O'Neill 83, 204, 227, 257
Conrad, Brenda 69, 328
Constance Ethel Morrison Burke 159, 221, 227, 256
Constance Leidl 196, 208, 227, 252
Cook, Petronelle 22, 327
➥ Cooper, Natasha 45, 210, 215, 227, 241, 257, 282, 283, 285, 287, 291, 297, 300, 306, 317, 319, 328
➥ Cooper, Susan Rogers 45, 203, 210, 222, 228, 233, 236, 252, 253, 279, 282, 283, 285, 287, 289, 291, 293, 299, 301, 304, 307, 308, 309, 312, 316, 317
Cordelia Gray 101, 207, 227, 258, 352
➥ Cornwell, Patricia 46, 219, 233, 254, 282, 283, 285, 287, 289, 291, 295, 297, 300, 307, 318
Cortland, Tyler 112, 328
Costa, Carol 332, 333
cozy mysteries 356
➥ Craig, Alisa 46, 123, 203, 212, 227, 231, 235, 237, 259, 275, 277, 278, 279, 280, 282, 285, 287, 304, 308, 314, 317, 323, 325, 328
Craig, Anne 29, 328
Craig, Georgiana Ann Randolph 163, 187, 329, 330
Craig, May Shura 332, 333
Crampton, Helen 26, 328
➥ Crane, Frances 46, 222, 231, 237, 260, 266, 267, 268, 269, 270, 271, 295, 296, 297, 298, 299, 300, 302, 303, 307, 308, 309, 310, 312, 314, 315, 317, 318, 320, 322, 323, 326
➥ Crane, Hamilton 47, 209, 221, 228, 257, 272, 273, 274, 282, 283, 285, 287, 289, 291, 295, 308, 312, 316, 317, 321, 325, 328
Creasey, John 341, 356
Creighton, Joan Scott 31, 327
➥ Crespi, Camilla 47, 215, 239, 250, 283, 285, 287, 291, 294, 323, 332, 333
Cressida Woodruffe 210, 215, 227, 257, 328
crime fiction 356
Crime Fiction II 350, 361
Crime Time 346
Crime Writers of Canada 342, 357
Criminal Investigation Department 356
Criminal Record 346
➥ Crombie, Deborah 48, 203, 227, 229, 257, 287, 289, 291, 295, 311, 320
➥ Cross, Amanda 48, 209, 233, 250, 271, 272, 273, 274, 275, 276, 278, 280, 282, 291, 302, 309, 310, 316, 317, 318, 322, 323, 328, 332, 333
cross-genre novels 356
Crossed Red Herrings 357
➥ Crowleigh, Ann 48, 216, 226, 236, 257, 287, 301, 324, 328
Crown Crime Companion 351, 361
➥ Crum, Laura 48, 210, 229, 245, 289, 294, 300, 308, 309
Cummings, Barbara 48, 328
➥ Curzon, Clare 49, 157, 203, 236, 258, 276, 277, 278, 279, 282, 285, 287, 289, 291, 297, 299, 303, 306, 309, 312, 316, 318, 322, 323, 328

D

D. S. Trewley 127, 205, 227, 256
➥ Daheim, Mary 50, 211, 217, 228, 232, 254, 283, 285, 287, 289, 291, 294, 295, 296, 304, 306, 307, 309, 310, 312, 315
➥ Dain, Catherine 50, 206, 229, 249, 285, 287, 289, 291, 296, 311, 320, 324, 328, 332, 333
Daisy Dalrymple 60, 216, 227, 257
Dale, Celia 332, 333
Dalton, Elizabeth A. 332, 333
➥ Daly, Elizabeth 32, 51, 211, 230, 250, 266, 267, 268, 269, 296, 297, 301, 305, 309, 314, 316, 320, 321, 323, 325
➥ D'Amato, Barbara 49, 203, 213, 216, 219, 226, 229, 237, 239, 247, 275, 282, 283, 285, 287, 289, 291, 294, 306, 308, 310, 327, 332, 333, 340
Dan Claiborne 59, 220, 227, 248
➥ Dank, Gloria 51, 211, 224, 225, 246, 280, 282, 285, 287, 296, 307, 312
➥ Danks, Denise 51, 213, 217, 229, 257, 280, 285, 289, 307, 317, 324, 325
Darby, Catherine 30, 328
Darina Lisle 114, 215, 227, 256
David Middleton-Brown 38, 213, 227, 257, 328
David Silver 95, 204, 213, 227, 254
David Webb 70, 204, 227, 255
David Wintringham 28, 219, 227, 257, 327
➥ Davidson, Diane Mott 52, 215, 229, 245, 282, 285, 287, 289, 291, 294, 299, 304, 310, 311, 312, 332, 333, 340
➥ Davis, Dorothy Salisbury 52, 203, 222, 231, 232, 237, 250, 270, 274, 275, 276, 278, 302, 303, 307, 308, 311, 316, 319, 332, 333, 340, 343
➥ Davis, Lindsey 52, 206, 215, 235, 260, 280, 282, 283, 285, 287, 289, 291, 294, 304, 305, 310, 311, 318, 320, 323, 324
➥ Dawson, Janet 53, 206, 231, 244, 282, 287, 289, 291, 304, 310, 316, 322, 323, 332, 333
➥ Day, Dianne 53, 212, 216, 229, 245, 291, 294, 297, 306, 321, 327, 330
➥ Day, Marele 53, 206, 226, 259, 279, 282, 285, 289, 298, 304, 311
➥ de la Torre, Lillian 54, 211, 216, 231, 238, 257, 268, 270, 276, 278, 303, 304, 306, 319, 332, 333
Deadlier Than the Male 351
Deadly Allies anthologies 340, 349
Deadly Directory 351
Deadly Pleasures 346, 361
Deadly Serious 346, 361
DeAndrea, William 86, 153
Dearborn V. Pinch 83, 221, 227, 250
Dearmore, Ellen 332, 333
Deb Ralston 126, 205, 227, 253, 329
Deborah Knott 125, 219, 227, 252
Dee Street 188, 218, 227, 258, 330
Dee Vaughan 103, 211, 225, 227, 258
Delia Ross-Merlani 68, 220, 227, 250
Delilah West 147, 208, 227, 244
Delta Stevens 175, 205, 215, 227, 243
➥ Dengler, Sandy 54, 203, 214, 231, 232, 243, 255, 287, 289, 291, 298, 303, 307, 311, 313, 315, 318
Dennison, Dulcie Winifred Catherine 329
Denniston, Elinore 68, 327, 328, 329
➥ Dentinger, Jane 54, 222, 232, 250, 276, 279, 285, 289, 291, 301, 302, 306, 315, 318, 325
➥ Dereske, Jo 55, 211, 230, 254, 289, 291, 294, 313
Desiree Shapiro 63, 206, 227, 250
Desmond Shannon 92, 207, 227, 251
Detection Club 356
Devon MacDonald 101, 207, 227, 249
Dewey James 141, 212, 221, 227, 250, 329

➥ denotes authors in Master List

Diamond Dagger Award 341, 356
Diana Tregarde 111, 207, 213, 227, 246
↦ Dietz, Denise 55, 215, 228, 254, 287, 289, 296, 322
dime novels 356
Dino Rossi 73, 220, 222, 227, 250
↦ Disney, Doris Miles 55, 203, 206, 231, 232, 246, 248, 267, 268, 269, 270, 271, 273, 296, 298, 299, 300, 301, 304, 306, 308, 311, 312, 315, 318, 321, 323
Dittany Henbit Monk 46, 212, 227, 259, 328
Ditteridge, Supt. 67, 204, 227, 255, 328
Dixie T. Struthers 176, 206, 227, 245
Dolly Rawlins 113, 227, 256
↦ Dolson, Hildegarde 56, 119, 221, 231, 234, 246, 273, 274, 296, 304, 317, 323
Dominic Felse 156, 205, 227, 258
↦ Dominic, R. B. 56, 113, 215, 218, 225, 246, 272, 273, 274, 275, 276, 296, 305, 314, 315, 322, 323, 328
↦ Donald, Anabel 56, 206, 218, 223, 257, 283, 287, 289, 291, 307, 309, 320, 323
Doran Fairweather 89, 210, 227, 257
Doubleday Crime Club Compendium 361
↦ Douglas, Carole Nelson 56, 209, 213, 216, 219, 230, 233, 236, 240, 249, 259, 277, 282, 285, 287, 289, 292, 294, 298, 299, 300, 308, 310, 318, 332, 333
↦ Douglas, Lauren Wright 57, 206, 214, 225, 259, 278, 280, 283, 285, 287, 289, 295, 301, 307, 316, 318, 323
Douglas Perkins 24, 212, 227, 257
Douglas Quantrill 161, 205, 227, 258, 330
↦ Drake, Alison 57, 122, 203, 223, 246, 279, 280, 285, 297, 306, 309, 322, 328
↦ Dreher, Sarah 57, 214, 222, 239, 248, 277, 278, 282, 287, 292, 296, 298, 308, 317, 321
Drew, Nancy 351
Drood Review of Mystery 347, 361
du Maurier, Daphne 343
↦ Duffy, Margaret 58, 206, 211, 230, 232, 237, 255, 256, 278, 279, 280, 282, 283, 287, 289, 292, 297, 303, 304, 307, 315, 318, 319, 325
Duke, Madelaine 332, 333
↦ Dunant, Sarah 58, 206, 209, 230, 235, 254, 257, 279, 285, 287, 292, 297, 306, 321, 323
↦ Dunbar, Sophie 59, 220, 226, 227, 248, 287, 292, 294, 296, 318
Duncan Kincaid 48, 203, 227, 257
↦ Dunlap, Susan 59, 203, 206, 214, 232, 233, 240, 243, 244, 275, 276, 277, 278, 280, 282, 283, 285, 287, 289, 294, 296, 297, 302, 304, 305, 309, 310, 311, 316, 317, 319, 321, 323, 332, 333, 340, 349, 352
↦ Dunn, Carola 59, 216, 227, 257, 289, 292, 294, 302, 315, 319, 325
↦ Dunnett, Dorothy 60, 210, 222, 232, 260, 272, 273, 274, 276, 285, 304, 312, 313, 314, 317, 319, 321, 323, 328
↦ Dymmoch, Michael A. 60, 203, 219, 231, 232, 247, 287, 292, 303, 312, 328

E

E. J. Pugh 45, 210, 228, 253
Early, Jack 171, 328
Ebenezer Gryce 83, 204, 228, 250
↦ Eberhart, Mignon G. 60, 203, 234, 239, 250, 264, 265, 267, 269, 307, 312, 314, 315, 317, 324, 325, 332, 333, 343
↦ Eccles, Marjorie 61, 203, 229, 255, 279, 280, 282, 285, 287, 289, 292, 295, 298, 300, 303, 311, 313, 319, 327, 329
Eddie Brown 159, 221, 228, 256
Edgar Awards 343, 356
↦ Edghill, Rosemary 61, 220, 233, 250, 289, 292, 297, 321, 328

↦ Edwards, Ruth Dudley 61, 204, 215, 231, 238, 255, 275, 277, 282, 285, 289, 299, 300, 305, 312, 319, 321
Edwina Charles 190, 220, 221, 228, 257
Edwina Crusoe 107, 219, 228, 246
↦ Egan, Lesley 62, 118, 172, 204, 218, 232, 241, 244, 271, 272, 273, 274, 275, 276, 277, 295, 296, 297, 298, 299, 300, 303, 304, 309, 311, 312, 313, 315, 317, 318, 319, 321, 325, 328
↦ Eichler, Selma 62, 206, 227, 250, 289, 292, 294, 314
Elena Jarvis 94, 204, 228, 253
Elena Oliverez 144, 210, 228, 245
Elisha Macomber 108, 212, 221, 228, 248
Eliza Figg 24, 220, 228, 254
Elizabeth Austin 177, 209, 228, 255
Elizabeth Blair 34, 210, 228, 256, 327
Elizabeth Chase 115, 207, 220, 228, 244
Elizabeth Elliot 20, 221, 228, 252, 327
Elizabeth Lamb Worthington 42, 220, 228, 248
Elizabeth MacPherson 131, 209, 228, 255
Elizabeth Mendoza 129, 205, 228, 254
Elizabeth Will 202, 210, 213, 228, 249
↦ Elkins, Charlotte & Aaron 63, 222, 229, 234, 254, 280, 292, 319, 325, 332, 333, 340
Ella Clah 184, 206, 214, 228, 250
Ellery Queen Mystery Magazine 331, 347
Elles, Dora Amy 193
Ellie Bernstein 55, 215, 228, 254
Ellie Haskell 37, 220, 228, 256
Ellis Awards 342, 357
↦ Elrod, P. N. 63, 213, 217, 231, 247, 282, 283, 285, 296, 297, 306, 311
Elvira 95, 213, 215, 228, 257
Em Hansen 22, 214, 228, 254
Emily Bryce 170, 210, 228, 251
Emily D. Seeton 47, 209, 221, 228, 257, 328
Emily Pollifax 77, 221, 222, 228, 249, 260, 352
Emily Silver 33, 222, 228, 250
Emma Chizzit 87, 221, 228, 244
Emma Lord 50, 217, 228, 254
Emma Shaw 103, 217, 228, 260
Emma Victor 197, 208, 215, 228, 245
Emmy Tibbett 143, 205, 228, 258, 352
Encyclopedia Mysteriosa 351, 361
↦ Ennis, Catherine 63, 214, 219, 225, 248, 283, 287, 299
Enrico Caruso 154, 222, 228, 251
Erik March 68, 207, 228, 243, 328
Ernest Lamb 193, 206, 228, 258, 330
↦ Erskine, Margaret 63, 204, 239, 255, 266, 268, 269, 270, 271, 272, 273, 274, 296, 298, 301, 303, 304, 306, 307, 308, 309, 311, 316, 317, 320, 322, 324, 325, 328
Eugenia Potter 164, 215, 221, 228, 248
Eva Wylie 43, 222, 228, 257
Evan Pinkerton 72, 220, 228, 255, 328
↦ Evanovich, Janet 64, 206, 239, 249, 289, 294, 316, 323
Eve Dallas 165, 205, 220, 228, 251, 330
Eve Elliott 115, 210, 212, 228, 248
Eve Sinclair 24, 222, 228, 257
EyeCon 359
↦ Eyre, Elizabeth 64, 180, 215, 239, 260, 285, 287, 289, 294, 296, 297, 300, 303, 317, 328

F

Fairfax, Ann 26, 328
Faith Sibley Fairchild 152, 215, 228, 248
↦ Fallon, Ann C. 65, 218, 231, 258, 282, 283, 285, 287, 292, 297, 301, 309, 318, 324
Fanny Zindel 181, 221, 228, 255
Fansler, Kate 328
fanzine 357
↦ Farrell, Gillian B. 65, 207, 224, 250, 285, 289, 295, 313
Fawcett, Bill 65, 328

↦ Fawcett, Quinn 65, 216, 241, 259, 287, 303, 315, 328
↦ Feddersen, Connie 65, 212, 220, 224, 252, 287, 289, 292, 294, 301
Felix Freer 67, 219, 228, 255, 328
↦ Femling, Jean 65, 207, 235, 245, 280, 283, 307, 309
↦ Fenisong, Ruth 66, 204, 229, 250, 267, 269, 270, 271, 297, 298, 301, 303, 308, 312, 315, 320, 323, 324
↦ Fennelly, Tony 66, 207, 214, 217, 235, 248, 277, 278, 280, 289, 294, 295, 299, 307, 309, 310, 316
↦ Ferrars, E. X. 66, 204, 209, 219, 220, 224, 227, 228, 240, 241, 255, 266, 267, 273, 274, 275, 276, 277, 278, 279, 280, 282, 285, 289, 292, 296, 299, 300, 302, 303, 304, 307, 309, 311, 315, 316, 318, 319, 320, 321, 322, 325, 326, 328
↦ Fickling, G. G. 67, 207, 228, 230, 243, 270, 271, 273, 297, 298, 300, 304, 307, 308, 309, 310, 321, 322, 328
Fickling, Gloria & Forrest E. 328
Fiddler Flynn 128, 212, 228, 245, 329
Fiedler, Jean 332, 333
Finch, Insp. 184, 206, 228, 257
Fine Art of Murder 351, 361
Finney, Pauline 39, 328
Finny Aletter 140, 212, 229, 246
Fiora Flynn 128, 212, 229, 245, 329
1st Culprit anthology 349
Fleming Stone 191, 208, 229, 251
↦ Flora, Kate Clark 68, 209, 212, 238, 240, 248, 289, 292, 299, 302, 320
↦ Florian, S. L. 68, 220, 227, 250, 285, 297
↦ Foley, Rae 68, 220, 230, 250, 270, 271, 273, 296, 298, 300, 301, 302, 305, 306, 310, 311, 316, 317, 319, 324, 328
Forbes, DeLoris Florine Stanton 192, 328, 330, 332, 333
Forbes, Stanton 192, 328
↦ Ford, Leslie 69, 219, 229, 232, 246, 265, 266, 267, 268, 269, 295, 298, 300, 304, 306, 309, 312, 313, 314, 315, 316, 317, 318, 319, 320, 321, 322, 324, 325, 328
↦ Forrest, Katherine V. 69, 204, 214, 233, 244, 277, 280, 283, 295, 296, 313, 314
↦ Fowler, Earlene 70, 210, 223, 244, 289, 292, 294, 307, 310
Fran Kirk 73, 207, 229, 250
Fran Wilson (Green, Christine) 83, 204, 229, 257
Frances Finn 97, 207, 229, 247
Francesca Wilson (Neal, Janet) 145, 205, 215, 229, 256, 329
Frank Carver 189, 214, 229, 252
Frank Shapiro 25, 203, 229, 256
↦ Frankel, Valerie 70, 207, 241, 250, 283, 285, 289, 292, 297, 301, 315, 318, 334, 335
↦ Fraser, Anthea 70, 204, 227, 255, 277, 278, 279, 280, 282, 283, 285, 289, 292, 294, 296, 303, 308, 311, 315, 316, 318, 319, 320, 322, 334, 335
↦ Fraser, Antonia 71, 218, 231, 257, 274, 275, 276, 277, 278, 283, 287, 289, 299, 300, 310, 317, 318, 321, 325, 326, 334, 335
↦ Frazer, Margaret 71, 213, 229, 258, 285, 287, 289, 292, 294, 297, 315, 316, 317, 319, 328
Fred Vickery 118, 221, 229, 245
Freda Pedersen 91, 204, 229, 243
Freddie O'Neal 50, 206, 229, 249, 328
Frederika Bascomb 184, 219, 229, 254
Fremlin, Celia 334, 335
Fremont Jones 53, 212, 216, 229, 245
Frevisse, Sister 71, 213, 229, 258, 328
↦ Friedman, Mickey 71, 211, 229, 259, 279, 280, 301, 312, 322, 328, 334, 335, 351, 361
↦ Froetschel, Susan 72, 212, 231, 243, 289, 295

↦ denotes authors in Master List

➡ Frome, David 69, 72, 220, 228, 255, 265, 266, 269, 296, 297, 298, 305, 308, 309, 312, 313, 315, 323, 328
➡ Fromer, Margot J. 73, 219, 224, 246, 283, 287, 316, 319
➡ Frommer, Sara Hoskinson 73, 210, 222, 232, 247, 287, 289, 298, 314
➡ Fulton, Eileen 73, 220, 222, 227, 237, 250, 279, 280, 303, 305, 306, 311, 319, 322
➡ Furie, Ruthe 73, 207, 229, 250, 292, 294, 301, 309, 315, 330
➡ Fyfield, Frances 74, 218, 230, 239, 255, 257, 279, 280, 282, 283, 287, 289, 299, 303, 316, 317, 318, 320, 323, 328, 334, 335, 352

G

G. D. H. Pringle 119, 221, 229, 256
Gail Connor 153, 218, 229, 246
Gail McCarthy 49, 210, 229, 245
Gale Grayson 96, 211, 229, 257
Galen Shaw 30, 210, 229, 255, 327
Gallant, Jennie 178, 329
➡ Gallison, Kate 74, 207, 213, 234, 236, 249, 278, 285, 292, 294, 298, 303, 304, 310, 323
➡ Gardiner, Dorothy 74, 204, 220, 236, 241, 243, 246, 265, 270, 271, 298, 304, 311, 313, 319, 323, 324
Gargoyle Award 342
Garwood, Judith 328
➡ Geason, Susan 75, 207, 239, 259, 287, 304, 320
Gemma James 48, 203, 229, 257
genre 357
Genreflecting, A Guide to Reading 361
➡ George, Elizabeth 75, 204, 224, 240, 257, 279, 280, 282, 283, 285, 287, 289, 294, 307, 308, 309, 313, 317, 321, 324, 334, 335
George Felse 156, 205, 229, 258
George Palmer-Jones 42, 214, 221, 229, 258
Georgia Lee Maxwell 72, 211, 229, 259, 328
Georgina Powers 51, 213, 217, 229, 257
Georgine Wyeth 149, 211, 229, 243
Gerritt DeGraaf 49, 219, 229, 247
Gianna Maglione 136, 205, 214, 217, 229, 246
Gil Mayo 61, 203, 229, 255
➡ Gilbert, Anthony 75, 215, 218, 224, 239, 255, 264, 265, 266, 267, 268, 269, 270, 271, 272, 273, 274, 295, 296, 297, 298, 299, 300, 301, 302, 303, 304, 306, 307, 308, 310, 311, 312, 313, 314, 315, 316, 317, 318, 319, 320, 321, 322, 323, 324, 325, 329
Giles, Gail 334, 335
➡ Gill, B. M. 77, 204, 240, 255, 275, 277, 282, 306, 319, 322, 324, 329
Gillian Adams 105, 209, 229, 259
➡ Gilman, Dorothy 77, 221, 222, 228, 249, 260, 272, 273, 274, 276, 277, 279, 282, 287, 292, 294, 295, 305, 313, 317, 323, 328
Gilmour, Barbara 77, 329
➡ Gilpatrick, Noreen 77, 204, 233, 254, 287, 292, 306, 320
Ginger Struve Barnes 144, 220, 229, 253
Ginny Trask 189, 214, 229, 252
➡ Girdner, Jaqueline 78, 212, 233, 244, 283, 285, 287, 289, 292, 294, 295, 306, 311, 313, 314, 321, 322, 334, 335
Girl Sleuth on the Couch 351
➡ Giroux, E. X. 78, 218, 223, 238, 257, 277, 278, 279, 280, 282, 283, 287, 302, 329
Glad Gold 193, 209, 229, 248
➡ Glass, Leslie 78, 204, 224, 250, 287, 292, 298, 308
➡ Glen, Alison 79, 211, 226, 252, 285, 292, 320, 323, 329
Glory Day 171, 222, 229, 260
glossary see Chapter 11
Glynis Tryon 140, 216, 229, 252

Gold Dagger award 341, 356, 357, 360
Golden Age of Detection 357
Golden Age of Mystery 357
Goldy Bear 52, 215, 229, 245
➡ Gordon, Alison 79, 217, 233, 259, 280, 283, 287, 292, 301, 316, 319, 321
Gordon Christy 141, 210, 229, 250
➡ Gosling, Paula 79, 204, 225, 231, 233, 234, 252, 255, 277, 278, 280, 283, 285, 289, 292, 296, 297, 301, 303, 306, 313, 325, 352
gothic mysteries 357
Grace Latham 69, 219, 229, 246, 328
Grace Rossi 171, 218, 229, 253
Grace Severance 170, 219, 229, 243
➡ Grafton, Sue 80, 207, 233, 245, 276, 277, 278, 279, 280, 282, 283, 285, 287, 289, 292, 295, 296, 298, 300, 305, 306, 307, 308, 309, 310, 334, 335, 340, 353
➡ Graham, Caroline 80, 204, 240, 255, 278, 280, 287, 292, 302, 303, 310, 325
Graham Sheldon 63, 222, 229, 254
Grand Master Award 357
Grand Masters, list of 343
➡ Granger, Ann 80, 204, 223, 236, 256, 283, 285, 287, 289, 292, 294, 298, 299, 306, 307, 313, 319, 323, 324
Grant, EM 328
➡ Grant, Linda 81, 207, 226, 245, 279, 282, 283, 289, 294, 297, 311, 318, 325, 329, 334, 335
➡ Grant-Adamson, Lesley 81, 207, 217, 220, 232, 234, 238, 255, 257, 277, 278, 282, 284, 285, 287, 289, 300, 303, 306, 307, 308, 311, 317, 322, 323, 325, 334, 335, 352
Grape, Jan 334, 335
➡ Gray, Dulcie 82, 204, 225, 255, 270, 272, 304, 305, 329
➡ Gray, Gallagher 82, 212, 221, 224, 240, 250, 284, 285, 292, 298, 303, 317, 329
Greber, Judith 165, 330
➡ Green, Anna Katherine 82, 204, 225, 228, 250, 264, 295, 296, 299, 304, 308, 309, 310, 311, 312, 315, 316, 321, 322, 325
➡ Green, Christine 83, 204, 219, 227, 229, 233, 255, 257, 284, 285, 289, 292, 294, 301, 302, 304, 306
➡ Green, Edith Pinero 83, 221, 227, 250, 274, 275, 276, 317, 319, 321
➡ Green, Kate 83, 204, 220, 237, 240, 244, 278, 287, 297, 320
➡ Greenwood, Diane M. 84, 213, 240, 255, 284, 285, 287, 289, 292, 294, 299, 305, 309, 313, 323
➡ Greenwood, Kerry 84, 216, 237, 259, 280, 282, 284, 285, 287, 289, 292, 294, 297, 299, 302, 307, 308, 315, 319, 324
Greenwood, L. B. 334, 335
Gregor Demarkian 86, 207, 221, 229, 252, 329
Gregory Toye 116, 205, 229, 256
➡ Greth, Roma 84, 220, 230, 252, 279, 280, 316, 317
Gridley Nelson 66, 204, 229, 250
➡ Grimes, Martha 85, 204, 238, 257, 275, 276, 277, 278, 280, 282, 287, 292, 296, 303, 304, 306, 308, 309, 310, 312, 316, 318, 325
➡ Grindle, Lucretia 85, 204, 230, 255, 287, 289, 310, 321, 334, 335
Guido Brunetti 117, 205, 230, 260
➡ Gunning, Sally 85, 212, 237, 248, 282, 285, 287, 290, 294, 309, 319, 321, 323, 334, 335
➡ Gur, Batya 86, 204, 236, 260, 279, 287, 290, 311, 315, 319
Gwen Harding 29, 222, 230, 250
Gwenn Ramadge 148, 208, 230, 251

H

H. W. Ross 85, 204, 230, 255
➡ Haddad, Carolyn A. 86, 213, 225, 247, 285, 299
➡ Haddam, Jane 86, 207, 221, 229, 252, 282, 284, 285, 287, 290, 292, 295, 297, 301, 306, 307, 308, 315, 316, 318, 321, 329, 334, 335
➡ Haddock, Lisa 87, 214, 217, 225, 252, 290, 292, 305, 306
Hadley, Joan 94, 329
Hagen 98, 221, 230, 254
➡ Hager, Jean 87, 204, 211, 214, 236, 240, 249, 252, 280, 282, 285, 290, 292, 294, 297, 301, 303, 306, 307, 308, 316, 318, 319, 329, 334, 335
➡ Hall, Mary Bowen 87, 221, 228, 244, 280, 282, 285, 287, 305, 334, 335
➡ Hall, Patricia 88, 204, 217, 223, 233, 234, 236, 255, 258, 287, 290, 292, 294, 302, 304, 309, 317
Halliday, Dorothy 328
➡ Hambly, Barbara 88, 213, 216, 231, 257, 279, 292, 322, 323
➡ Hamilton, Laurell K. 88, 213, 224, 249, 287, 290, 292, 294, 299, 308, 311
Hamish Macbeth 27, 203, 230, 259
Hammett Prize 342, 357
Hana Shaner 85, 220, 230, 252
Handsome Kusak 164, 220, 230, 254, 330
Hannah Barlow 111, 218, 230, 244
Hannah Land 123, 209, 230, 252
Hannah Wolfe 58, 206, 230, 257
Hannasyde, Supt. 94, 204, 230, 256
Hanover, Terri 99, 329
Hanson, Deborah 334, 335
hard-boiled mysteries 357
➡ Hardwick, Mollie 88, 210, 227, 257, 278, 279, 280, 282, 296, 304, 312, 317, 323
Harriet Jeffries 168, 205, 217, 230, 259
Harriett Hubley 124, 214, 230, 259
Harrington, Joyce 334, 335
➡ Harris, Charlaine 89, 211, 212, 224, 247, 282, 285, 290, 292, 294, 297, 301, 310, 318, 322
➡ Harris, Lee 89, 213, 226, 250, 285, 287, 290, 292, 294, 299, 308, 317, 321, 322, 326, 329
➡ Harrison, Jamie 89, 204, 232, 249, 292, 305
➡ Harrod-Eagles, Cynthia 90, 204, 225, 256, 284, 285, 287, 290, 294, 297, 301, 303, 308, 315, 316, 327, 330
Harry Marsh 25, 210, 219, 230, 255
➡ Hart, Carolyn G. 90, 211, 217, 221, 224, 230, 235, 253, 278, 279, 280, 282, 284, 285, 287, 290, 292, 294, 299, 301, 302, 303, 309, 311, 312, 319, 321, 334, 335, 340, 349, 352
➡ Hart, Ellen 90, 214, 215, 216, 231, 239, 249, 280, 284, 285, 287, 290, 292, 294, 306, 307, 308, 310, 316, 319, 320, 321, 322, 324, 329
➡ Hart, Jeanne 91, 204, 225, 229, 243, 278, 282, 284, 306, 311, 317, 321, 322, 334, 335
➡ Hartzmark, Gini 91, 218, 233, 247, 285, 290, 292, 297, 306, 318
Haskell Blevins 207, 230, 247
Haugh, Wendy Hobday 334, 335
➡ Haymon, S. T. 91, 204, 225, 258, 275, 276, 277, 278, 280, 284, 290, 296, 302, 303, 319, 321, 324
➡ Hayter, Sparkle 92, 218, 238, 251, 290, 294, 316, 324
Healey, Rose Million 334, 335
Hearndon, Nancy R. 334, 335
➡ Heberden, M. V. 92, 117, 207, 227, 238, 251, 266, 267, 268, 269, 295, 298, 303, 304, 305, 306, 307, 311, 314, 315, 320, 321, 322, 323, 324, 326, 329
Hedley Nicholson 104, 207, 230, 256
Hegarty, Frances 74, 328
Heilbrun, Carolyn G. 48, 328
heist 357
Helen Black 191, 208, 215, 230, 245

➡ denotes authors in Master List

Helen Marsh Shandy 123, 209, 230, 248
Helen West 74, 218, 230, 257, 328
Helma Zukas 55, 211, 230, 254
Hemingway, Insp. 95, 204, 230, 256
➡ Hendricksen, Louise 93, 219, 224, 254, 287, 290, 292, 308, 311, 325
Henissart, Martha 56, 113, 328, 329
Henrietta O'Dwyer Collins 217, 221, 230, 253
Henry Bassett 35, 203, 230, 257
Henry Bryce 170, 210, 230, 251
Henry Frost 28, 219, 230, 257, 327
Henry Gamadge 51, 211, 230, 250, 352
Henry Merrivale 352
➡ Henry, Sue 93, 210, 214, 223, 232, 243, 284, 292, 294, 315, 320, 322, 362
Henry Tibbett 143, 205, 230, 258, 352
Hercule Poirot 39, 206, 230, 257
➡ Herndon, Nancy 93, 204, 228, 253, 292, 295, 325
Hershey, Kathleen 334, 335
➡ Hess, Joan 94, 204, 211, 222, 224, 226, 243, 278, 279, 280, 284, 285, 287, 290, 292, 298, 301, 302, 304, 312, 313, 316, 317, 318, 319, 321, 322, 329, 334, 335, 340
➡ Heyer, Georgette 94, 204, 230, 256, 265, 266, 267, 269, 296, 297, 302, 303, 304, 305, 312, 316, 322, 329
➡ Highsmith, Domini 95, 213, 215, 228, 239, 257, 292, 310
➡ Highsmith, Patricia 95, 213, 240, 256, 270, 273, 274, 275, 285, 297, 319, 322, 329, 334, 335
➡ Hightower, Lynn S. 95, 204, 207, 213, 227, 234, 239, 247, 252, 254, 285, 287, 290, 292, 295, 307, 319
Hilary Lloyd 161, 205, 230, 258, 330
Hilary Tamar 38, 209, 230, 258, 328
Hilda Adams 164, 219, 230, 256
Hiram Potter 69, 220, 230, 250, 328
Historicon 342
➡ Hitchens, Dolores 96, 150, 207, 232, 244, 270, 271, 320, 327, 328, 329
Hockaby, Stephen 137, 185, 329
➡ Holbrook, Teri 96, 211, 229, 257, 292, 294, 306, 308
➡ Holland, Isabelle 96, 213, 226, 251, 276, 277, 278, 280, 282, 302, 306, 307, 311
Holland, Judith 188, 330
Holland, Rebecca 98, 329
➡ Hollingsworth, Gerelyn 97, 207, 229, 247, 292, 313
Hollis Carpenter 160, 215, 217, 230, 253
Holly Winter 45, 210, 230, 248
➡ Holt, Hazel 97, 216, 239, 257, 280, 284, 285, 287, 290, 292, 294, 300, 302, 307, 313, 315, 320, 322, 323
➡ Holtzer, Susan 97, 213, 224, 249, 290, 292, 300, 321
Homer Kelly 112, 204, 230, 248
Honey West 68, 207, 230, 243, 328
➡ Hooper, Kay 98, 207, 221, 234, 240, 247, 254, 279, 280, 284, 295, 298, 300, 306, 309, 310, 317, 318, 320, 324, 326, 330
➡ Horansky, Ruby 98, 204, 236, 251, 282, 290, 301, 329
➡ Hornsby, Wendy 98, 204, 217, 233, 235, 238, 243, 245, 279, 282, 285, 287, 290, 292, 295, 296, 308, 312, 316, 320, 322, 334, 335, 340
house name 357
house series 357
howdunits 357
➡ Howe, Melodie Johnson 99, 207, 226, 235, 245, 280, 290, 296, 313, 334, 335, 352
➡ Huff, Tanya 99, 207, 213, 241, 259, 285, 287, 297, 329
Hughes, Dorothy B. 334, 335, 343
➡ Huxley, Elspeth 99, 204, 214, 240, 260, 266, 295, 303, 313, 315

➡ Hyde, Eleanor 100, 216, 234, 251, 292, 294, 296, 309
Hyde, Jennifer 61, 329

I

Ike Tygart 196, 218, 230, 251
Imogen Quy 189, 209, 219, 230, 256
Ingrid Langley 58, 211, 230, 255
International Association of Crime Writers 342, 357
inverted mysteries 357
Irene Adler 57, 216, 230, 259
Irene Kelly 35, 217, 230, 245
Iris Cooper 27, 216, 231, 244, 327
Iris Thorne 213, 231, 244
Ivor Maddox 118, 205, 212, 231, 244

J

J. J. Jamison 182, 213, 231, 249
J. P. Beaumont 102, 204, 231, 254
Jack Caleb 60, 203, 219, 231, 247, 328
Jack Fleming 63, 213, 217, 231, 247
Jack Prester 54, 203, 214, 231, 255
Jack Stryker 79, 204, 231, 252
Jackie Walsh 42, 209, 210, 231, 249
➡ Jackson, Marian J. A. 100, 207, 216, 223, 254, 282, 284, 285, 290, 296, 299, 304, 318, 322
➡ Jackson, Muriel Resnick 100, 220, 236, 252, 285, 307
Jackson, Shirley 334, 335, 340
➡ Jacobs, Jonnie 100, 218, 222, 233, 244, 245, 290, 292, 294, 313, 320
➡ Jacobs, Nancy Baker 100, 207, 227, 249, 284, 285, 287, 320, 323
Jacqueline Kirby 155, 211, 231, 251, 330
➡ Jaffe, Jody 101, 210, 217, 236, 252, 292, 294, 299, 309
Jake 42, 209, 210, 231, 249
Jake Samson 176, 208, 231, 244
James Asher 88, 213, 216, 231, 257
James Boswell 54, 211, 216, 231, 257
James Fleming 65, 218, 231, 258
James McDougal 56, 221, 231, 246
James Milton 62, 204, 215, 231, 255
James Owens Mega 131, 209, 231, 254
➡ James, P. D. 101, 204, 207, 223, 227, 258, 271, 272, 273, 274, 276, 278, 280, 290, 297, 300, 303, 312, 316, 320, 322, 324, 334, 335
James, Susannah 140, 329
➡ Jance, J. A. 102, 204, 231, 232, 243, 254, 277, 278, 279, 280, 282, 284, 285, 287, 290, 292, 303, 304, 306, 309, 310, 312, 313, 315, 317, 320, 322, 323, 324, 325, 334, 335
Jane da Silva 27, 222, 231, 254, 327
Jane Jeffry 41, 222, 231, 247, 328
Jane Lawless 91, 214, 215, 231, 249, 329
Jane Marple 40, 221, 231, 258, 353
Jane McBride 72, 212, 231, 243
Jane Tennison 113, 205, 231, 258
Jane Winfield 157, 217, 231, 258
Janeshutz, Trish 122, 329
Janet Rhys 46, 203, 231, 259, 328
Janice Cameron 174, 208, 231, 247
Jason Lynx 151, 210, 231, 246, 330
Jasper Tully 52, 203, 231, 250
Jay Goldstein 188, 206, 231, 244
Jazz Jasper 134, 214, 231, 260
Jean Abbot 46, 222, 231, 260
Jeff Di Marco 55, 206, 231, 248
Jefferson Birch 116, 207, 216, 231, 255
Jeffries, Mrs. 34, 216, 221, 231, 257, 327
Jemima Shore 71, 218, 231, 257
Jennifer Murdock 150, 209, 221, 231, 244, 329
Jenny Cain 157, 213, 231, 249
Jeremy Faro 108, 204, 216, 231, 259
Jeremy Locke 38, 218, 231, 255, 328

Jeri Howard 53, 206, 231, 244
Jerry North 120, 212, 231, 251
Jerry Zalman 109, 212, 231, 244
Jesse, F. Tennyson 334, 335
Jesse Falkenstein 62, 218, 232, 244, 328
Jessica James 147, 217, 232, 252
Jessica Randolph 122, 207, 232, 245
Jessie Arnold 93, 210, 214, 232, 243
Jessie Drake 110, 204, 232, 244
Jesus Creek, TN 19, 222, 253
Jill Smith 59, 203, 232, 243
Jim O'Neill 55, 203, 232, 246
Jim Qwilleran 32, 209, 217, 232, 255
Jim Rush 81, 220, 232, 255
Jim Sader 96, 207, 232, 244
Jo Hughes 127, 220, 232, 254
Joan, Sister 30, 213, 232, 256, 327
Joan Spencer 73, 210, 222, 232, 247
Joanna Brady 102, 204, 232, 243
Joanna MacKenzie 206, 232, 256
Joanna McKenzie 58
Joanna Stark 144, 207, 232, 244
Joanne Kilbourn 31, 209, 232, 259
Jocelyn O'Roarke 54, 222, 232, 250
Joe Rodriguez 54, 203, 232, 243
Joe Silva 149, 205, 232, 249
John Aloysius O'Malley 43, 214, 232, 254
John Coffin 36, 203, 232, 257
John Creasey Memorial Award 341, 356
John Farrel 96
John J. Malone 164, 218, 232, 247, 330
John Lloyd Branson 135, 218, 232, 253
John McLeish 145, 205, 215, 232, 256, 329
John Morrissey 139, 205, 232
John Primrose 69, 219, 232, 246, 328
John Putnam Thatcher 114, 212, 232, 251, 329, 352
John Sanders 168, 205, 217, 232, 259
John Thinnes 60, 203, 219, 232, 247, 328
➡ Johns, Veronica Parker 102, 211, 220, 221, 222, 223, 241, 246, 251, 266, 267, 269, 270, 309, 314, 319, 320
Johnson Johnson 60, 210, 222, 232, 260, 328, 352
Jolie Wyatt 177, 211, 232, 253
➡ Jones, Hazel Wynn 102, 217, 228, 260, 279, 282, 302, 320
Jones, Zenith Brown 328
➡ Jordan, Jennifer 103, 211, 220, 225, 227, 233, 258, 279, 282, 285, 287, 297, 306, 308, 315, 319
➡ Jorgensen, Christine T. 103, 217, 220, 239, 246, 290, 292, 294, 300, 311, 326
Josie Pigeon 198, 213, 222, 232, 255
Judith Hayes 159, 217, 232, 259
Judith McMonigle 50, 211, 232, 254
Judy Hill 132, 205, 232, 257
Jules Clement 89, 204, 232, 249
Julia Probyn Jamieson 33, 217, 221, 232, 255, 327
Julian Baugh 30, 210, 232, 255, 327
Julian Kestrel 167, 216, 232, 258
Julie Hayes 52, 222, 232, 250
Juliet Blake 38, 206, 213, 232, 245

K

Kali O'Brien 100, 218, 233, 244
➡ Kallen, Lucille 103, 217, 225, 235, 246, 275, 276, 277, 278, 310, 311, 316, 317, 322
Karen Hightower 61, 220, 233, 250, 328
Karen Levinson 148, 205, 233, 251
➡ Karr, Leona 104, 217, 223, 245, 287, 314
Kat Colorado 106, 207, 233, 244
Kate Austen 100, 222, 233, 245
Kate Baeier 177, 208, 233, 258
Kate Brannigan 131, 207, 233
Kate Delafield 70, 204, 214, 233, 244

Kate Driscoll 188, 210, 233, 253
Kate Fansler 48, 209, 233, 250
Kate Frederick 170, 205, 233, 249
Kate Henry 79, 217, 233, 259
Kate Ivory 180, 211, 233, 258
Kate Jasper 78, 212, 233, 244
Kate Kincaid Mulcay 175, 217, 233, 247
Kate Kinsella 83, 219, 233, 255
Kate Maddox 161, 205, 233, 256, 330
Kate Martinelli 107, 207, 233, 245
Kate McLean 78, 204, 233, 254
Kate Murray 186, 217, 233, 250
Kate Shugak 180, 208, 214, 233, 243
Kate Teague 98, 204, 233, 245
Kate Trevorne 79, 204, 233, 252
Kate Weston 88, 204, 233, 255
Katharine Craig 187, 210, 233, 244
Katherine Prescott Milholland 91, 218, 233, 247
Kathleen Mallory 147, 205, 233, 251
Kathryn Ardleigh 152, 211, 216, 233, 257, 330
Kathryn Mackay 132, 218, 233, 244
Kay Barth 171, 218, 233, 245
Kay Engles 181, 217, 233, 254
Kay Scarpetta 46, 219, 233, 254
Keith, J. Kilmeny 75, 329
➾ Kellerman, Faye 104, 204, 237, 238, 244, 278, 279, 282, 285, 287, 290, 292, 301, 306, 308, 310, 312, 319, 334, 335, 342, 353
➾ Kelly, Mary 104, 204, 207, 225, 230, 256, 259, 270, 271, 299, 301, 304, 321
➾ Kelly, Mary Ann 104, 217, 226, 251, 282, 285, 292, 307, 310, 317
➾ Kelly, Nora 105, 209, 229, 259, 277, 285, 287, 296, 309, 315
➾ Kelly, Susan 105, 216, 234, 248, 277, 278, 279, 282, 284, 285, 296, 307, 317, 321, 323, 324, 334, 335
➾ Kelly, Susan B. 105, 213, 223, 236, 257, 282, 287, 290, 294, 302, 309, 310, 323
Kelman, Judith 334, 335
➾ Kelner, Toni L. P. 106, 207, 234, 252, 287, 290, 292, 301, 304, 323
Kelsey, Insp. 152, 205, 233, 256, 330
Kendra MacFarlane 158, 220, 233, 254
Kenneth Carlisle 192, 208, 233, 251
➾ Kenney, Susan 106, 210, 223, 238, 248, 276, 277, 282, 307, 308, 316
Kent, Roberta 107, 329
Kevin Blake 57, 213, 219, 233, 249
Kevin Bryce 187, 210, 233, 244
Kiernan O'Shaughnessy 59, 206, 233, 244
➾ Kijewski, Karen 106, 207, 233, 244, 279, 282, 284, 285, 290, 292, 295, 300, 310, 325, 334, 335
Kimmey Kruse 45, 222, 233, 253
➾ King, Laurie R. 106, 207, 216, 224, 233, 235, 245, 258, 287, 290, 292, 294, 296, 308, 313, 323, 325
➾ Kingsbury, Kate 107, 211, 216, 226, 256, 288, 290, 292, 294, 299, 304, 305, 308, 317, 319, 329
Kinsey Millhone 80, 207, 233, 245, 352
Kit Powell 166, 218, 222, 233, 245
➾ Kittredge, Mary 107, 211, 219, 226, 228, 246, 279, 280, 282, 284, 285, 288, 292, 298, 301, 303, 306, 310, 314, 317, 319, 324
➾ Knight, Alanna 108, 204, 216, 231, 259, 279, 280, 282, 284, 285, 288, 290, 292, 297, 298, 301, 305, 306, 310, 313, 318, 323
➾ Knight, Kathleen Moore 108, 212, 221, 228, 235, 248, 251, 265, 266, 267, 268, 269, 270, 295, 296, 298, 299, 302, 303, 306, 307, 314, 318, 319, 322, 323, 324, 327
➾ Knight, Kathryn Lasky 109, 212, 225, 248, 278, 282, 284, 290, 301, 313, 323, 329
➾ Knight, Phyllis 109, 207, 214, 222, 234, 248, 285, 290, 294, 311, 320, 322
Knight, Tracy 334, 335
Knute Severson 192, 206, 233, 248, 330
Koko 32, 209, 217, 233, 255
➾ Komo, Dolores 109, 207, 211, 226, 249, 279, 299, 334, 335
Kori Price Brichter 160, 205, 233, 247
➾ Kraft, Gabrielle 109, 212, 231, 244, 279, 281, 282, 297, 298, 311, 319, 334, 335, 340
➾ Kreuter, Katherine E. 110, 207, 211, 237, 254, 290, 307
➾ Krich, Rochelle Majer 110, 204, 232, 244, 288, 290, 296, 306, 334, 335
Kristin Ashe 103, 220, 233, 258
➾ Kruger, Mary 110, 216, 225, 235, 253, 290, 292, 303, 316
Kuhfeld, Mary Pulver 160, 328
➾ Kunz, Kathleen 110, 212, 240, 249, 288, 294, 302, 315
Kyra Keaton 185, 208, 216, 233, 246

L

➾ La Pierre, Janet 113, 204, 235, 241, 244, 279, 281, 282, 284, 288, 299, 300, 308, 316, 324, 334, 335
➾ La Plante, Lynda 113, 205, 227, 231, 256, 258, 276, 277, 288, 290, 318, 325
➾ Lacey, Sarah 110, 139, 212, 234, 258, 286, 288, 290, 292, 306
➾ Lachnit, Carroll 111, 218, 230, 244, 292, 294, 297, 314
➾ Lackey, Mercedes 111, 207, 213, 227, 246, 281, 282, 284, 298, 299, 310
Laiken, Deidre 334, 335
➾ Lamb, J. Dayne 111, 212, 240, 248, 288, 290, 292, 318, 324
Lambda Literary Awards 358
➾ Lambert, Mercedes 112, 218, 241, 244, 284, 304
Lance O'Leary 61, 203, 234, 250
➾ Landreth, Marsha 112, 219, 238, 254, 286, 288, 292, 299, 309, 324, 328
Lane Montana 98, 207, 234, 247
Laney Samms 171, 215, 234, 244
➾ Langton, Jane 112, 204, 230, 248, 271, 274, 276, 277, 278, 279, 284, 286, 288, 292, 300, 301, 304, 305, 307, 312, 313, 315, 320, 323
Lark Dailey 175, 212, 234, 244
Lasky, Kathryn 109, 329
➾ Lathen, Emma 56, 113, 212, 232, 251, 271, 272, 273, 274, 275, 276, 279, 284, 288, 295, 296, 298, 300, 303, 304, 305, 307, 308, 311, 313, 314, 315, 317, 319, 321, 322, 324, 329
Latsis, Mary 56, 113, 328, 329
Laura Ackroyd 88, 204, 217, 234, 258
Laura Di Palma 127, 218, 234, 245
Laura Fleming 106, 207, 234, 252
Laura Flynn 81, 207, 234, 257
Laura Ireland 125, 209, 234, 254
Laura Malloy 121, 217, 234, 249
Laura Principal 179, 208, 234, 256
Lauren Laurano 171, 208, 215, 234, 251, 328
Lauren Maxwell 161, 214, 234, 243
➾ Laurence, Janet 114, 215, 227, 256, 281, 282, 284, 286, 288, 290, 292, 294, 301, 302, 303, 304, 309, 318, 322
Lavinia Grey 74, 213, 234, 249
➾ Law, Janice 114, 207, 224, 246, 274, 275, 286, 288, 290, 296, 303, 307, 319, 320, 323
➾ Lawrence, Hilda 115, 207, 221, 225, 235, 255, 267, 268, 297, 302, 323
➾ Lawrence, Martha 115, 207, 220, 228, 244, 292, 314
Leah Hunter 111, 212, 234, 258
Leahy, Syrell Rogovin 89, 329
➾ Lee, Barbara 115, 210, 212, 228, 248, 292, 302
➾ Lee, Marie 115, 209, 235, 249, 292, 300
Lee Ofsted 63, 222, 234, 254
Lee Squires 22, 220, 234, 249
➾ Lee, W. W. 116, 207, 216, 224, 231, 248, 255, 281, 282, 284, 286, 288, 290, 292, 294, 298, 307, 313, 317, 318, 319, 329
Lee, Wendi 116, 329, 334, 335
➾ Leek, Margaret 116, 199, 218, 239, 256, 275, 308, 324, 329
Left Coast Crime 342
Leigh Ann Warren 194, 206, 211, 222, 234, 252
➾ Lemarchand, Elizabeth 116, 205, 229, 240, 256, 272, 273, 274, 275, 276, 277, 278, 279, 295, 298, 299, 300, 303, 307, 311, 316, 321, 323, 324, 325
Lena Padget 96, 207, 234, 247
Lennox Kemp 134, 218, 234, 258
➾ Leon, Donna 117, 205, 230, 260, 286, 288, 290, 292, 294, 295, 296, 301, 302, 304, 324
➾ Leonard, Charles L. 92, 117, 207, 237, 246, 267, 268, 269, 296, 301, 306, 307, 318, 319, 320, 321, 323, 329
Leonidas Witherall 185, 212, 234, 248, 330, 352
Leslie Wetzon 136, 212, 222, 234, 251
Lewis, Mary Christianna 327
➾ Lewis, Sherry 118, 221, 229, 245, 292, 294, 316
Libby Kincaid 186, 217, 234, 251
Lil Ritchie 109, 207, 214, 222, 234, 248
Lily Wu 174, 208, 234, 247
Lind, Judi 334, 335
Lindsay Gordon 131, 214, 217, 234, 259
➾ Linington, Elizabeth 62, 118, 172, 205, 212, 231, 244, 271, 272, 273, 274, 275, 276, 277, 278, 300, 301, 306, 308, 316, 317, 318, 320, 321, 327, 328, 330
➾ Linscott, Gillian 118, 216, 222, 225, 236, 256, 277, 279, 284, 286, 288, 290, 292, 300, 305, 308, 314, 320, 321, 324, 325
Lisa Davis 189, 217, 234, 248
➾ Livingston, Nancy 119, 221, 229, 256, 277, 278, 279, 281, 282, 284, 286, 302, 306, 309, 312, 318, 323, 324, 334, 335
Liz Broward 202, 213, 219, 234, 243
Liz Connors 105, 216, 234, 248
Liz Graham 25, 203, 234, 256
Liz Sullivan 166, 211, 234, 244
Liz Wareham 33, 212, 234, 250
Lloyd, Chief Insp. 132, 205, 234, 257
locations *see Chapter 4*
locked room mysteries 358
➾ Lockridge, Frances & Richard 56, 119, 205, 212, 231, 236, 237, 250, 251, 266, 267, 268, 269, 270, 271, 272, 273, 274, 295, 298, 299, 300, 301, 302, 303, 304, 306, 307, 308, 309, 310, 311, 314, 315, 316, 317, 318, 319, 320, 321, 322, 324, 325
➾ Logan, Margaret 121, 210, 237, 248, 290, 292, 305, 315
➾ Logue, Mary 121, 217, 234, 249, 288, 321
London Detection Club 356
Long, Lydia 327
Lonia Guiu 150, 208, 234, 260
➾ Lorden, Randye 121, 207, 239, 251, 288, 290, 298, 320
➾ Lorens, M. K. 121, 209, 241, 251, 282, 284, 286, 288, 303, 304, 319, 321, 322
Loretta Lawson 178, 209, 234, 258
Louise Eldridge 165, 212, 234, 246
➾ Lovett, Sarah 121, 219, 239, 250, 292, 294, 295, 300
Lowell, Elizabeth 128, 329
Lowndes, Marie Belloc 334, 335
Lowry, Cheryl Meredith 79, 329
Lucia Ramos 141, 205, 214, 234, 253
➾ Lucke, Margaret 122, 207, 232, 245, 284, 294, 297, 318
Lucy Kingsley 38, 213, 234, 257, 328
Lucy Ramsdale 56, 221, 234, 246
Lucy Stone 134, 222, 234, 248

➾ denotes authors in Master List

Luis Mendoza 173, 205, 234, 244, 330
Luke Abbott 79, 204, 234, 255
Luke Thanet 175, 206, 234, 256
Lydia Chin 168, 208, 234, 251
Lydia Fairchild 135, 218, 234, 253
Lydia Miller 100, 216, 234, 251
➡ Lyons, Nan & Ivan 122, 215, 236, 254, 274, 288, 321

M

Macavity Award 342, 358
MacDougal Duff 22, 209, 235, 250
➡ MacGregor, T. J. 57, 122, 207, 236, 238, 246, 278, 279, 281, 282, 284, 286, 288, 290, 292, 297, 300, 302, 303, 310, 313, 316, 321, 328, 329, 336, 337
➡ Mackay, Amanda 209, 230, 252, 274, 275, 303, 314
Mackenzie Smith 186, 218, 235, 246
Mackintosh, Elizabeth 183, 330
➡ MacLeod, Charlotte 46, 123, 207, 209, 230, 235, 237, 239, 248, 274, 275, 276, 277, 278, 279, 281, 284, 286, 290, 292, 296, 300, 306, 307, 311, 316, 317, 318, 319, 320, 321, 324, 325, 328, 336, 337
Madoc Rhys 46, 203, 235, 259, 328
magazines see Chapter 10
Magdalena Yoder 145, 211, 235, 252
Maggie Elliott 182, 208, 235, 245
Maggie Garrett 182, 208, 215, 235, 245
Maggie Hill 99, 207, 235, 245
Maggie MacGowen 99, 217, 235, 243
Maggie Rome 103, 217, 235, 246
Maggie Ryan 37, 209, 235, 250
Magna Cum Murder 342
➡ Maiman, Jaye 123, 207, 211, 214, 238, 251, 284, 286, 288, 292, 300, 309, 321, 323
Malice Domestic anthologies 340, 349
Malice Domestic Mystery Convention 342, 355
Malleson, Lucy Beatrice 75, 329
➡ Malmont, Valerie S. 124, 211, 240, 252, 290, 303
Malone, Ruth 163, 187, 329
➡ Maney, Mabel 124, 214, 236, 247, 288, 290, 292, 298, 307
➡ Mann, Jessica 124, 209, 240, 256, 273, 274, 276, 277, 278, 279, 284, 298, 302, 306, 307, 308, 310, 316, 323
Mansfield, Katherine 336, 337
Manson, Cynthia 350
➡ Manthorne, Jackie 124, 214, 230, 259, 290, 292, 301, 307, 311
Marcus Didius Falco 52, 206, 215, 235, 260
Marcus MacLurg 157, 205, 235, 256, 330
Margaret Priam 41, 220, 235, 250
Margo Fortier 66, 217, 235, 248
Margo Simon 181, 218, 235, 245
Margot Blair 212, 235, 251
Marguerite Smith 115, 209, 235, 249
Marian Larch 154, 205, 235, 251
Marian Winchester 166, 214, 235, 253
➡ Mariz, Linda 125, 209, 234, 254, 286, 297, 321
Mark East 115, 207, 221, 235, 255
Mark Shigata 197, 206, 235, 253
Marla Masterson 58, 209, 235, 254
➡ Maron, Margaret 125, 205, 219, 227, 239, 251, 252, 275, 277, 279, 281, 284, 286, 288, 290, 292, 294, 296, 297, 300, 302, 307, 316, 317, 319, 320, 321, 324, 336, 337, 340, 342, 352
Marriott, Mary 327
Marris, Katherine 327
➡ Marsh, Ngaio 125, 205, 238, 258, 265, 266, 267, 268, 269, 270, 271, 272, 273, 274, 275, 276, 296, 297, 299, 300, 301, 302, 303, 304, 305, 306, 308, 310, 311, 312, 316, 317, 319, 320, 321, 322, 324, 325, 343, 351
Martha "Moz" Brant 66, 207, 235, 245
Marti MacAlister 30, 203, 211, 235, 247

Martin Beck 176, 206, 235, 260
Martin Buell 170, 214, 235, 249
Martin Karl Alberg 201, 206, 235, 259
➡ Martin, Lee 126, 190, 197, 205, 227, 253, 277, 278, 279, 280, 281, 282, 286, 288, 290, 292, 297, 300, 301, 303, 308, 310, 312, 313, 323, 329
Martin, Stella 94, 329
Martine LaForte Hopkins 37, 203, 235, 247
Mary Carner 158, 208, 235, 251
Mary DiNunzio 171, 218, 235, 253
Mary Helen 149, 213, 235, 245
Mary Minor Haristeen 34, 209, 235, 254
Mary Russell 107, 207, 216, 235, 258
➡ Mason, Sarah Jill 47, 127, 205, 227, 239, 256, 288, 290, 300, 304, 307, 314, 328
mass market paperbacks 358
➡ Matera, Lia 91, 127, 218, 234, 241, 245, 278, 279, 280, 281, 282, 284, 286, 290, 292, 294, 303, 306, 307, 308, 309, 311, 318, 320, 324, 336, 337, 342
➡ Mather, Linda 127, 220, 232, 254, 290, 292, 296, 297, 307
➡ Mathews, Francine 127, 205, 236, 249, 290, 292, 302
Matt Devlin 110, 216, 235, 253
➡ Matteson, Stefanie 128, 221, 222, 226, 251, 282, 284, 286, 288, 290, 294, 313, 314, 315
Matthew Arthur Sinclair 66, 207, 214, 235, 248
➡ Matthews, Alex 128, 209, 219, 226, 247, 294, 319
Matthews, Christine 336, 337
Maud Silver 193, 208, 221, 235, 258, 330
Max Bittersohn 123, 207, 235, 248
Max Darling 90, 211, 235, 253
Maxene St. Clair 132, 219, 235, 254
Maxey Burnell 36, 217, 235, 245
➡ Maxwell, A. E. 128, 212, 228, 229, 245, 277, 278, 279, 280, 281, 284, 286, 288, 296, 307, 310, 313, 314, 329
Maxwell, Helen K. 68, 69, 329
➡ McAllester, Melanie 129, 205, 224, 228, 254, 290, 311
McAllister, Amanda 87, 329
➡ McCafferty, Taylor 129, 207, 230, 247, 282, 286, 290, 292, 296, 308, 317, 319, 322, 3329, 336, 337, 340
➡ McClellan, Tierney 129, 212, 239, 247, 292, 294, 299, 308, 310, 329
➡ McClendon, Lise 129, 210, 224, 254, 290, 292, 297, 317
➡ McCloy, Helen 130, 219, 225, 251, 266, 267, 268, 269, 270, 272, 275, 295, 298, 300, 301, 303, 307, 310, 311, 312, 313, 316, 322, 323, 325, 336, 337, 343
McConnell, Jean 336, 337
➡ McConnell, Vickie P. 130, 214, 217, 237, 246, 276, 277, 280, 298, 304, 313
➡ McCrumb, Sharyn 130, 205, 209, 228, 231, 239, 253, 254, 255, 277, 278, 280, 282, 284, 286, 290, 292, 294, 297, 308, 309, 311, 312, 313, 317, 319, 320, 325, 326, 336, 337, 340, 352
McCue, Lillian de la Torre Bueno 54
➡ McDermid, Val 131, 207, 214, 217, 233, 234, 258, 259, 279, 281, 284, 286, 288, 290, 292, 294, 297, 299, 300, 301, 306, 310, 316, 319, 324, 353
➡ McFall, Patricia 131, 209, 237, 260, 286, 316
➡ McGerr, Patricia 132, 221, 239, 256, 271, 273, 310, 311, 336, 337
➡ McGiffin, Janet 132, 219, 235, 254, 286, 288, 292, 305, 318
McGlamry, Beverly 336, 337
➡ McGown, Jill 132, 205, 232, 234, 257, 276, 280, 281, 282, 284, 286, 288, 292, 307, 313, 315, 317, 320, 328, 352
McGuffin 358

➡ McGuire, Christine 132, 218, 233, 244, 288, 290, 324
McIntosh, Kinn Hamilton 20, 327
➡ McKenna, Bridget 133, 207, 225, 244, 288, 290, 292, 299, 301, 314
➡ McKernan, Victoria 133, 222, 226, 246, 282, 286, 290, 300, 316, 317
➡ McKevett, G. A. 133, 207, 239, 245, 292, 294, 297, 310
➡ McNab, Claire 133, 205, 214, 225, 259, 280, 281, 282, 284, 286, 290, 292, 297, 300, 301, 302, 304, 306, 311, 316, 320
➡ McQuillan, Karin 133, 214, 231, 260, 282, 288, 290, 299, 301, 305, 336, 337
➡ McShea, Susannah Hofman 134, 221, 236, 246, 282, 286, 290, 309, 310, 318
➡ Meek, M. R. D. 134, 218, 234, 258, 276, 277, 278, 279, 280, 281, 282, 288, 294, 308, 309, 311, 313, 318, 321, 322, 323, 325
Meg Halloran 113, 204, 235, 244
Meg Lacey 31, 206, 235, 259
Meg Quilliam 30, 211, 235, 250, 327
Megan Baldwin 42, 219, 235, 246
➡ Meier, Leslie 134, 222, 234, 248, 288, 290, 312, 323
Melanie Travis 29, 210, 222, 235, 246
Melinda Pink 139, 211, 236, 253
Melissa Craig 167, 211, 236, 257
Melville Fairr 187, 218, 236, 251, 330
➡ Melville, Jennie 36, 134, 205, 226, 257, 271, 272, 273, 275, 280, 281, 283, 288, 290, 292, 294, 296, 298, 300, 301, 302, 304, 307, 312, 313, 314, 315, 320, 322, 325, 329
Meredith, Anne 75, 329
➡ Meredith, D. R. 135, 205, 218, 226, 232, 234, 253, 277, 279, 280, 281, 283, 284, 288, 292, 309, 314, 320, 336, 337
Meredith "Merry" Folger 128, 205, 236, 249
Meredith Mitchell 81, 204, 236, 256
Meren, Lord 166, 208, 215, 236, 259
Merlin Capricorn 198, 206, 236, 256
Merrie Lee Spencer 100, 220, 236, 252
Merton Heimrich 120, 205, 236, 250
Mertz, Barbara 136, 155, 329, 330
Metropolitan Police Force 359
➡ Meyers, Annette 135, 212, 222, 234, 241, 251, 281, 283, 284, 286, 288, 292, 294, 296, 297, 301, 308, 315, 322, 336, 337
➡ Meyers, Maan 135, 136, 216, 240, 251, 286, 288, 290, 292, 304, 309, 310, 329
Michael Ohayon 86, 204, 236, 260
Michael Spraggue III 206, 236, 248
Michael Thackeray 88, 204, 217, 236, 258
➡ Michaels, Barbara 136, 155, 220, 229, 246, 272, 278, 293, 296, 320, 321, 329, 336, 337
Michelle "Micky" Knight 162, 208, 215, 236, 248
Mici Anhalt 148, 205, 236, 251
➡ Mickelbury, Penny 136, 205, 214, 217, 229, 236, 246, 290, 293, 310, 316
Mid Atlantic Mystery Book Fair and Convention 342
Midge Cohen 34, 210, 236, 250, 327
Midnight Louie 57, 209, 236, 249
Mike McCleary 122, 207, 236, 246
Mike Yeadings 49, 203, 236, 258, 328
Mildred Bennett 134, 221, 236, 246
➡ Millar, Margaret 137, 205, 218, 219, 237, 238, 240, 243, 259, 267, 268, 274, 275, 276, 296, 303, 310, 312, 315, 324, 336, 337, 343
Millay, Edna St. Vincent 336, 337
➡ Millhiser, Marlys 137, 222, 226, 244, 286, 288, 293, 303, 313, 314, 336, 337
Millie Ogden 122, 215, 236, 254
Milton Kovak 45, 203, 236, 252
Mimi Patterson 136, 205, 214, 217, 236, 246
Mirinda Clively 48, 216, 236, 257, 328
Mitch Bushyhead 87, 204, 236, 252

➡ denotes authors in Master List

➡ Mitchell, Gladys 137, 185, 221, 225, 258, 264, 265, 266, 267, 268, 269, 270, 271, 272, 273, 274, 275, 276, 277, 295, 297, 299, 300, 301, 302, 303, 304, 305, 306, 308, 309, 310, 311, 312, 313, 315, 316, 317, 318, 319, 320, 321, 322, 323, 324, 325, 329, 330, 336, 337
➡ Mitchell, Kay 139, 205, 232, 258, 283, 284, 290, 293, 294, 309, 311, 318, 319, 321
➡ Moffat, Gwen 139, 211, 236, 253, 273, 274, 276, 277, 279, 281, 283, 286, 298, 304, 308, 310, 311, 312, 317, 318, 320, 321, 324
Mollie Cates 188, 217, 236, 253
Molly Bearpaw 87, 214, 236, 252
Molly DeWitt 200, 222, 236, 246
Molly Palmer-Jones 42, 214, 221, 236, 258
Molly Rafferty 28, 209, 236, 248, 327
➡ Monfredo, Miriam Grace 140, 216, 229, 252, 286, 288, 293, 294, 297, 316, 319, 322
➡ Montgomery, Yvonne E. 140, 212, 229, 246, 279, 283, 316, 319, 327
➡ Moody, Susan 140, 211, 217, 220, 226, 237, 256, 277, 278, 280, 281, 288, 290, 293, 294, 303, 304, 308, 310, 317, 322, 329, 336, 337, 352
➡ Moore, Barbara 141, 210, 229, 250, 276, 278, 304, 325
➡ Morell, Mary 141, 205, 214, 234, 253, 284, 288, 306
Morgan, Claire 95, 329
Morgan, Jill 336, 337
➡ Morgan, Kate 141, 212, 221, 227, 250, 283, 284, 286, 290, 301, 309, 314, 315, 320, 324, 329
Morgana Dalton 35, 216, 236, 246
➡ Morice, Anne 142, 222, 240, 256, 273, 274, 275, 276, 277, 278, 279, 280, 301, 302, 303, 306, 307, 309, 310, 312, 314, 315, 316, 318, 319, 320, 323, 329
➡ Morison, B. J. 142, 220, 228, 248, 276, 277, 279, 286, 296, 299, 312, 318, 324
Morris, Bonnie 336, 337
Mosiman, Billie Sue 336, 337
Moss Magill 74, 204, 236, 246
Mostly Murder 347, 362
➡ Moyes, Patricia 143, 205, 228, 230, 258, 270, 271, 272, 273, 274, 275, 276, 277, 281, 288, 296, 297, 299, 300, 301, 302, 303, 304, 306, 310, 312, 313, 314, 316, 319, 320, 323, 325, 352
Ms. Murder anthology 340, 349
➡ Muller, Marcia 143, 207, 210, 228, 232, 239, 244, 245, 274, 276, 277, 278, 279, 280, 281, 283, 284, 286, 288, 290, 293, 294, 296, 298, 299, 301, 304, 305, 306, 307, 311, 312, 317, 320, 322, 323, 324, 325, 336, 337, 340, 350, 352, 362
Munger, Katy 82, 329
Murder by the Book 351
Murder Most Cozy 347
Murder Most Delicious anthology 349
Murderess Ink, The Better Half of Mystery 352, 362
Murderous Intent magazine 331, 347, 362
➡ Murray, Donna Huston 144, 220, 229, 253, 293, 294, 306, 312
MWA Grand Masters 343
➡ Myers, Amy 144, 215, 216, 224, 256, 276, 279, 281, 284, 286, 290, 293, 313, 314, 315
➡ Myers, Tamar 145, 211, 235, 252, 290, 293, 294, 316, 317, 323
Mystery & Crime: The New York Public Library Book 352
Mystery & Detective Monthly 347, 362
Mystery News 348, 362
Mystery Readers Journal 348, 362
Mystery Readers of America 342
Mystery Review magazine 348, 362
Mystery Scene magazine 348, 362

Mystery Writers Market Place and Sourcebook 352, 362
Mystery Writers of America 343, 356, 357

N

➡ Nabb, Magdalen 145, 205, 238, 260, 275, 276, 277, 279, 280, 283, 284, 290, 293, 302, 303, 312
Nan Robinson 37, 218, 236, 244
Nancy Clue 124, 214, 236, 247
Nancy Drew Scrapbook 352
Nassim, Liza 43, 328
Nassim Pride 156
Natalie Gold 101, 210, 217, 236, 252
Natasha O'Brien 122, 215, 236, 254
Neal Rafferty 197, 208, 236, 248
➡ Neel, Janet 145, 205, 215, 229, 232, 256, 280, 281, 284, 288, 301, 303, 329
➡ Neely, Barbara 146, 211, 213, 225, 252, 286, 290, 297
Neil Hamel 187, 218, 236
Nell Bray 119, 216, 236, 256
Nell Fury 158, 208, 214, 236, 245
Neville, Katherine 336, 337
New Mystery Magazine 348
➡ Newman, Sharan 146, 213, 215, 226, 259, 288, 290, 293, 302, 303, 324
Nicholson, Margaret Beda Larminie 202, 330
Nick Magaracz 74, 207, 236, 249
Nick Trevellyan 105, 213, 236, 257
Nicky Titus 169, 205, 236, 252
➡ Nielsen, Helen 146, 218, 239, 245, 269, 272, 273, 274, 295, 298, 301, 307, 310, 314, 320
Nikki Holden 39, 217, 236, 246
Nikki Trakos 98, 204, 236, 251, 329
Nina Fischman 158, 218, 236, 251
Nina McFall 73, 220, 222, 237, 250
Nora James 132, 209, 237, 260
Norah Mulcahaney 148, 205, 237, 251
Norm Bennis 49, 203, 213, 237, 247
Norris, Mrs. 52, 203, 237, 250
North, Sara 87, 329
➡ North, Suzanne 146, 217, 237, 259, 290, 308
Nyla Wade 130, 214, 217, 237, 246

O

Oates, Joyce Carol 336, 337
➡ O'Brien, Meg 146, 217, 232, 252, 283, 284, 286, 300, 305, 308, 319, 336, 337
➡ O'Callaghan, Maxine 147, 208, 219, 224, 227, 243, 244, 275, 281, 284, 290, 294, 296, 302, 309, 319, 320, 323, 330, 336, 337
➡ O'Connell, Carol 147, 205, 233, 251, 290, 293, 294, 310, 312
➡ O'Connell, Catherine 148, 205, 233, 251, 288, 320
➡ OCork, Shannon 149, 217, 240, 251, 275, 276, 305, 308, 321
➡ O'Donnell, Lillian 148, 205, 208, 230, 236, 237, 251, 273, 274, 275, 276, 277, 279, 281, 283, 284, 286, 288, 290, 293, 295, 296, 298, 299, 300, 304, 306, 308, 310, 311, 316, 317, 318, 324, 325
➡ Offord, Lenore Glen 149, 211, 220, 225, 227, 229, 240, 243, 245, 266, 267, 268, 270, 299, 307, 314, 315, 320, 324
➡ Oleksiw, Susan 149, 205, 232, 249, 288, 290, 293, 304, 306, 314, 353, 362
➡ Oliphant, B. J. 150, 151, 214, 239, 245, 283, 286, 290, 294, 299, 301, 302, 303, 323, 329
Oliver Jardino 84, 204, 220, 237, 244
➡ Oliver, Maria Antonia 150, 208, 234, 260, 279, 281, 296, 321, 336, 337
Olivia Chapman 121, 210, 237, 248

➡ Olsen, D. B. 96, 150, 205, 209, 221, 231, 238, 244, 266, 267, 268, 269, 270, 295, 297, 298, 299, 301, 303, 304, 305, 307, 311, 320, 321, 322, 329, 336, 337
O'Malley, Lady Mary Dolling Saunders 33, 327
➡ O'Marie, Carol Anne, Sister 148, 213, 235, 245, 277, 278, 280, 284, 288, 293, 295, 302, 313, 314, 316, 336, 337
O'Neill, Egan 118, 172, 330
one-off 358
100 Great Detectives 352, 362
1001 Midnights, The Aficionado's Guide to Mystery 352, 362
Orczy, Baroness 336, 337
➡ Orde, A. J. 150, 151, 210, 231, 246, 281, 283, 286, 288, 293, 301, 302, 311, 330
organizations *see Chapter 9*
Osbert Monk 46, 212, 237, 259, 328
➡ Osborne, Denise 151, 211, 238, 244, 290, 293, 300, 315
Over My Dead Body! 348
Owen Archer 165, 214, 237, 256
Owens, Marissa 147, 330

P

➡ Padgett, Abigail 151, 208, 224, 244, 288, 290, 293, 299, 321, 323
➡ Page, Emma 152, 205, 233, 256, 275, 276, 277, 279, 280, 293, 299, 305, 306, 311, 313, 314, 319, 324, 330
➡ Page, Katherine Hall 152, 215, 228, 248, 283, 284, 286, 288, 290, 294, 297
➡ Paige, Robin 152, 211, 216, 233, 257, 290, 293, 302, 330
Paige Taylor 110, 207, 211, 237, 254
Pam Nilsen 197, 215, 237, 254
Pam North 120, 212, 237, 251
➡ Papazoglou, Orania 86, 152, 211, 237, 251, 277, 278, 280, 283, 303, 316, 319, 322, 325, 329, 330
➡ Paretsky, Sara 153, 208, 240, 247, 276, 277, 279, 280, 283, 284, 290, 293, 297, 298, 301, 308, 310, 323, 325, 336, 337, 341, 342, 350, 353
Pargeter, Edith Mary 156, 330
Paris, Ann 86, 153, 330
Paris Chandler 172, 208, 237, 244
➡ Parker, Barbara 154, 218, 229, 246, 290, 293, 322
Partners in Crime anthology 340, 349
pastiche 358
Pat Abbot 46, 222, 237, 260
Patience Campbell McKenna 153, 211, 237, 251
Patricia Delaney 174, 208, 237, 252
Patrick Gillard 58, 211, 237, 255
Patrick Grant 202, 209, 237, 258, 330
➡ Paul, Barbara 154, 205, 222, 228, 235, 251, 277, 279, 281, 286, 288, 293, 296, 298, 299, 306, 307, 308, 318, 319, 326, 336, 337
Paul Kilgerrin 117, 207, 237, 246, 329
Paul MacDonald 179, 211, 237, 245
Paul Prye 137, 219, 237, 259
Paula Glenning 42, 209, 237, 257
Peaches Dann 180, 221, 237, 252
Peg Goodenough 29, 212, 237, 250
➡ Pence, Joanne 154, 215, 224, 245, 288, 290, 293, 294, 300, 321, 323
Penfold, Nita 336, 337
Pennington Wise 192, 208, 237, 251
penny dreadful 358
Penny Spring 22, 209, 237, 260, 327
Penny Wanawake 141, 211, 217, 237, 256
periodicals *see Chapter 10*
➡ Perry, Anne 154, 205, 216, 226, 240, 241, 256, 258, 275, 276, 277, 279, 280, 283, 284, 286, 288, 290, 293, 294, 296, 297, 298, 299, 300, 302, 303, 306, 309, 317, 319, 320, 321, 323, 336, 337

➡ denotes authors in Master List

Persis Willum 190, 210, 237, 250
Peter Bartholomew 85, 212, 237, 248
Peter Brichter 160, 205, 237, 247
Peter Decker 104, 204, 237, 244
Peter Shandy 123, 209, 237, 248, 352
Peter Wimsey 169, 220, 237, 258, 352, 353
➠ Peters, Elizabeth 136, 155, 210, 211, 216, 222,
   224, 231, 241, 251, 257, 260, 272, 273, 274,
   275, 276, 277, 278, 279, 280, 281, 284, 286,
   290, 297, 300, 303, 304, 311, 313, 315, 316,
   320, 321, 323, 330, 336, 337, 349, 352
➠ Peters, Ellis 156, 205, 214, 225, 227, 229, 258,
   269, 271, 272, 273, 274, 275, 276, 277, 278,
   279, 280, 281, 284, 286, 290, 297, 298, 299,
   300, 301, 302, 303, 304, 306, 307, 308, 309,
   310, 311, 313, 316, 317, 318, 319, 321, 324,
   325, 330, 336, 337
Peters, Elsa Kirsten 20, 327
Peters, Maureen 30, 327, 328, 330
➠ Peterson, Audrey 157, 209, 217, 226, 231, 258,
   280, 281, 283, 284, 286, 290, 293, 301, 302,
   303, 305, 311, 314, 316, 320, 336, 337
➠ Petrie, Rhona 49, 157, 205, 235, 256, 271,
   272, 301, 302, 312, 314, 319, 330
Philip Marlowe 353
Phoebe Fairfax 146, 217, 237, 259
Phoebe Siegel 160, 208, 237, 249
Phryne Fisher 84, 216, 237, 259, 353
➠ Pickard, Nancy 157, 164, 213, 231, 249, 277,
   278, 279, 280, 281, 284, 288, 290, 293, 298,
   300, 301, 307, 309, 312, 316, 319, 323, 336,
   337, 340, 349, 353
Pickens, Cathy 336, 337
➠ Piesman, Marissa 158, 218, 236, 251, 281,
   284, 288, 290, 293, 295, 299, 308, 317, 324
➠ Pincus, Elizabeth 158, 208, 214, 236, 245, 286,
   288, 293, 308, 321, 323, 336, 337
Pinkerton, Miss 219, 230, 256
Plangman, Mary Patricia 95
Poe, Edgar Allen 356
police procedurals 358, see also Chapter 2
police rank (Brit) 358
police rank (U.S.) 359
➠ Popkin, Zelda 158, 208, 235, 251, 266, 267,
   301, 303, 314, 316, 323
Poppy Dillworth 183, 215, 221, 237, 253
➠ Porath, Sharon 158, 220, 233, 254, 293, 301
➠ Porter, Anna 159, 217, 232, 259, 277, 279,
   309, 313
➠ Porter, Joyce 159, 205, 221, 227, 228, 241,
   256, 271, 272, 273, 274, 275, 298, 299, 301,
   304, 310, 312, 315, 316, 317, 318, 321, 322,
   324, 325
Post, Judith 336, 337
➠ Powell, Deborah 160, 215, 217, 230, 253, 284,
   286, 296, 309
Power, Jo-Ann 48, 328
Private Eye Writers of America 343, 359
private eyes see Chapter 2
Pronzini, Bill 117, 143, 151, 163, 192, 350, 352
protagonist 359
➠ Prowell, Sandra West 160, 208, 237, 249, 288,
   290, 293, 298, 303, 310
Prucha, Lynette 336, 337
pseudonymns 359, see also Chapter 7
Publishers Weekly 362
➠ Pugh, Dianne G. 160, 213, 231, 244, 288, 290,
   299, 320
pulp fiction 359
➠ Pulver, Mary Monica 160, 205, 233, 237, 247,
   279, 280, 284, 286, 296, 310, 314, 316, 320,
   323

Queenie Davilow 151, 211, 238, 244
Quentin Jacoby 178, 208, 238, 251, 330

➠ Quest, Erica 161, 205, 233, 256, 280, 283,
   284, 299, 303, 313, 330
Quin St. James 122, 207, 238, 246
➠ Quinn, Elizabeth 161, 214, 234, 243, 288, 293,
   294, 310, 314, 325
Quint McCauley 34, 206, 238, 247

Rachel Murdock 150, 209, 221, 238, 244
➠ Radley, Sheila 161, 205, 227, 230, 258, 275,
   276, 277, 279, 281, 286, 290, 297, 299, 300,
   302, 306, 318, 322, 325, 330
Rain Morgan 81, 217, 238, 257
Ramer, Edie 336, 337
Rawcliffe, Carole 336, 337
Ray Frederick 170, 205, 238, 249
Reader's Guide to the
   American Novel of Detection 352, 362
   Classic British Mystery 353, 362
   Police Procedural 353
   Private Eye Novel 353, 362
Rebecca Schwartz 179, 218, 238, 245, 352
Recipes for Crime 353
red herring 359
➠ Redmann, J. M. 162, 208, 215, 236, 248, 283,
   288, 293, 302, 303, 310
Regan Reilly 41, 206, 238, 244
regency novels 359
Reginald Wexford 163, 205, 238, 258
➠ Reilly, Helen 162, 205, 226, 251, 265, 266,
   267, 268, 269, 270, 271, 295, 298, 299, 300,
   301, 302, 304, 306, 307, 311, 312, 313, 314,
   315, 316, 320, 321, 322, 324, 327
➠ Rendell, Ruth 163, 205, 238, 258, 271, 272,
   273, 274, 275, 276, 277, 280, 288, 290, 296,
   302, 307, 308, 310, 314, 315, 316, 318, 320,
   321, 324, 325, 330, 336, 337
Renfroe, Martha Kay 330
➠ Rice, Craig 163, 187, 218, 220, 225, 230, 232,
   247, 254, 266, 267, 268, 270, 271, 272, 295,
   296, 298, 300, 304, 305, 307, 308, 310, 311,
   315, 317, 319, 322, 323, 325, 330, 336, 337
➠ Rich, Virginia 164, 215, 221, 228, 248, 276,
   277, 288, 295, 296, 300, 315, 323
Richard Jury 85, 204, 238, 257
Richard Montgomery 174, 205, 238
Richard Trenton 36, 212, 238, 255, 328
Richardson, D. L. 336, 337
Richter, Joan 338, 339
Rick Vanner 93, 207, 238, 251
Rina Lazarus 104, 204, 238, 244
➠ Rinehart, Mary Roberts 164, 219, 230, 256,
   265, 267, 269, 308, 312, 324, 338, 339
➠ Ripley, Ann 165, 212, 234, 246, 290, 293, 303,
   313
Rita Awards 359
Rita Morrone Hamilton 171, 218, 238, 253
➠ Robb, Candace M. 165, 214, 237, 256, 288,
   290, 293, 296, 310, 316
➠ Robb, J. D. 165, 205, 220, 228, 251, 293, 294,
   307, 309, 315, 330
Robbins, Kay 98, 330
Robert Amiss 62, 204, 215, 238, 255
Robert Bone 180, 206, 238, 256, 330
Robert Carey 39, 216, 238, 255, 328
Robert Forsythe 218, 238, 257, 329
➠ Roberts, Carey 165, 205, 224, 246, 281, 288,
   318, 323
Roberts, Doreen 107, 329
➠ Roberts, Gillian 165, 209, 224, 253, 279, 281,
   284, 288, 290, 293, 299, 309, 317, 325, 330,
   338, 339
➠ Roberts, Lora 166, 211, 234, 244, 291, 293,
   294, 314, 330
Roberts, Nora 165, 330
Robin Hudson 92, 218, 238, 251
Robin Light 30, 210, 238, 252

Robin Miller 123, 207, 211, 214, 238, 251
Robin Vaughn 24, 210, 238, 253
➠ Robinson, Lynda S. 166, 208, 215, 236, 259,
   291, 293, 294, 313, 314
Robinson, Sheila 161, 330
➠ Robitaille, Julie 166, 218, 222, 233, 245, 286,
   291, 309, 310
Roderick Alleyn 126, 205, 238, 258
Roger Tejeda 98, 204, 238, 245
Roger the Chapman 172, 215, 238, 256, 330
Roman Cantrell 39, 217, 238, 246
romantic suspense 359
➠ Romberg, Nina 166, 214, 235, 253, 281, 288,
   320, 321
➠ Roome, Annette 166, 217, 226, 256, 281, 283,
   318, 319
Rosie Vicente 176, 208, 238, 244
➠ Ross, Kate 167, 216, 232, 258, 288, 291, 293,
   298, 300, 325
Ross McIntyre 68, 209, 238, 248
➠ Rothenberg, Rebecca 167, 212, 226, 244, 284,
   291, 293, 298, 300, 320
Rothman, Judith 30, 330
Rowan, Hester 161, 330
➠ Rowe, Jennifer 167, 218, 240, 259, 281, 284,
   286, 288, 291, 302, 308, 312, 314, 321
➠ Rowlands, Betty 167, 211, 236, 257, 281, 283,
   288, 291, 293, 294, 306, 311, 312, 314, 317,
   320
Roz Howard 106, 210, 238, 248
➠ Rozan, S. J. 168, 208, 225, 234, 251, 291, 293,
   299, 300, 338, 339
Rudd, Insp. 184
➠ Ruryk, Jean 168, 210, 221, 226, 254, 291, 299
Rusch, Kristine Katheryn 338, 339
Ryan, Lt. 170, 205, 238, 251
Rydell, Forbes 192, 330
Rydell, Helen B. 330

Sabina Swift 181, 208, 238, 246
➠ Sale, Medora 168, 205, 217, 230, 232, 259,
   278, 281, 283, 284, 286, 291, 314, 315, 318,
   320
Salvatore Guarnaccia 145, 205, 238, 260
Sam Titus 169, 205, 238, 252
Samantha Adams 172, 217, 238, 247
Samantha Holt 197, 210, 238, 246
Samantha "Smokey" Brandon 23, 203, 238, 244
Samantha Turner 112, 219, 238, 254
Samuel Johnson 54, 211, 216, 238, 257
Sanders, Daphne 163, 187, 330
Sanders, Madelyn 53, 330
Sands, Insp. 137, 205, 238, 259
➠ Sandstrom, Eve K. 168, 205, 236, 238, 252,
   283, 284, 288, 302, 303, 304
Sarah Calloway 217, 239, 245
Sarah Deane 31, 209, 239, 248, 327
Sarah Drexler 196, 219, 239, 252
Sarah Fortune 218, 239, 255, 328
Sarah Keate 61, 203, 239, 250
Sarah Kelling 123, 207, 239, 248
Sarah Nelson 198, 206, 239, 245
Sarah Quilliam 30, 211, 238, 250, 327
➠ Saum, Karen 169, 211, 215, 225, 248, 283,
   286, 291, 314
Savannah Reid 133, 207, 239, 245
➠ Sawyer, Corinne Holt 169, 221, 224, 225, 245,
   280, 281, 286, 288, 291, 293, 309, 310, 314,
   317
Sawyer, John 161, 328, 330
Sawyer, Nancy Buckingham 161, 328, 330
➠ Sayers, Dorothy L. 169, 220, 237, 258, 264,
   265, 266, 298, 299, 301, 307, 308, 309, 311,
   315, 316, 321, 322, 324, 325, 338, 339, 351
➠ Schenkel, S. E. 170, 205, 233, 238, 249, 291,
   293, 302, 309

➠ denotes authors in Master List

➥ Scherf, Margaret 170, 205, 210, 214, 219, 228, 229, 230, 235, 238, 243, 249, 251, 268, 269, 270, 271, 272, 273, 275, 295, 296, 299, 300, 302, 304, 305, 307, 308, 314, 317, 323
➥ Schier, Norma 171, 218, 233, 245, 275, 302, 303, 314
➥ Schmidt, Carol 171, 215, 234, 244, 288, 291, 298, 320, 322
Schuyler Ridgway 129, 212, 239, 247, 329
➥ Scoppettone, Sandra 171, 208, 215, 234, 251, 284, 288, 291, 305, 309, 315, 328, 338, 339, 353
Scotland Yard 356, 359
Scott Egerton 77, 215, 239, 255, 329
➥ Scott, Rosie 171, 222, 229, 260, 281, 307
➥ Scottoline, Lisa 171, 218, 229, 235, 238, 253, 288, 291, 293, 305, 306, 319
2nd Culprit anthology 340, 349
➥ Sedley, Kate 172, 215, 238, 256, 284, 286, 288, 291, 294, 302, 305, 308, 309, 317, 324, 330
Selena Mead 132, 221, 239, 256
Septimus Finch 63, 204, 239, 255, 328
settings see Chapter 4
➥ Shaffer, Louise 172, 218, 220, 224, 251, 291, 293, 295, 322
➥ Shah, Diane K. 172, 208, 237, 244, 283, 286, 296, 304
Shamus Awards 343, 344, 359
➥ Shankman, Sarah 172, 217, 238, 247, 280, 281, 283, 284, 286, 288, 306, 308, 310, 316, 320, 322, 330, 338, 339, 340
➥ Shannon, Dell 62, 118, 172, 205, 234, 244, 271, 272, 273, 274, 275, 276, 277, 278, 279, 295, 296, 297, 298, 299, 300, 302, 303, 304, 306, 310, 312, 313, 314, 315, 316, 318, 319, 321, 323, 324, 325, 330
Shannon, Doris 329
Sharon Dair 188, 206, 239, 249
Sharon McCone 144, 207, 239, 245, 352
Shaw, Felicity 142, 329
Shaw, Viola Brothers 338, 339
Sheila Malory 97, 216, 239, 257
Sheila Travis 179, 213, 239, 247
➥ Shelton, Connie 173, 213, 226, 250, 293, 294, 301, 318, 324
➥ Shepherd, Stella 174, 205, 238, 258, 281, 283, 286, 288, 291, 293, 297, 311, 315, 316, 321, 322
➥ Sheridan, Juanita 174, 208, 231, 234, 247, 268, 269, 299, 310, 312, 324
Sherlockiana 359
Shirley McClintock 150, 214, 239, 245, 329
➥ Shone, Anna 174, 208, 240, 259, 293, 313
➥ Short, Sharon Gwyn 174, 208, 237, 252, 291, 293, 296, 303, 317
short story anthologies 349–350, see also Chapters 8 & 10
➥ Sibley, Celestine 175, 217, 233, 247, 270, 284, 286, 288, 293, 295, 304, 312, 317, 321
Sigismondo 64, 215, 239, 260, 328
Sigrid Harald 125, 205, 239, 251
Silk Stalkings 353
➥ Silva, Linda Kay 175, 205, 215, 227, 243, 284, 288, 291, 293, 321, 322, 324
Silver Dagger award 341, 356, 357, 360
Simeon, Father 95, 213, 215, 239, 257
Simon Drake 146, 218, 239, 245
Simona Griffo 48, 215, 239, 250
➥ Simonson, Sheila 175, 212, 234, 244, 283, 286, 288, 294, 311, 312, 313, 320
Simpson, Doris 43, 328
➥ Simpson, Dorothy 175, 206, 234, 256, 276, 277, 278, 279, 280, 281, 284, 286, 288, 293, 299, 301, 304, 305, 311, 316, 318, 320, 322, 324
➥ Sims, L. V. 176, 206, 227, 245, 279, 280, 302, 314, 323

➥ Singer, Shelley 176, 208, 209, 224, 231, 238, 244, 276, 277, 278, 279, 280, 288, 291, 293, 294, 296, 307, 310, 317, 319, 321, 338, 339, 340
Sisters in Crime 344, 360
   anthologies 340, 349, 362
   Books-in-Print 362
   Newsletters 362
Sisters in Crime: Feminism and the Crime Novel 353
Sixto Cardenas 19, 203, 239, 255
➥ Sjöwall, Maj 176, 206, 235, 260, 272, 273, 274, 295, 300, 304, 306, 311, 312, 314, 319, 322
Skip Langdon 179, 206, 239, 248
➥ Skom, Edith 177, 209, 228, 255, 281, 293, 307, 312
➥ Slovo, Gillian 177, 208, 233, 258, 277, 279, 280, 291, 293, 299, 302, 313, 338, 339
➥ Smith, April 177, 206, 244, 291, 316
➥ Smith, Barbara Burnett 177, 211, 232, 253, 291, 293, 294, 299, 325
➥ Smith, Evelyn E. 177, 210, 239, 251, 278, 279, 281, 284, 293, 312
➥ Smith, J. C. S. 178, 208, 238, 251, 275, 277, 310, 316, 330
Smith, Jane S. 330
➥ Smith, Janet L. 178, 218, 224, 254, 283, 286, 291, 318, 319, 324
➥ Smith, Joan 178, 209, 234, 258, 279, 280, 283, 288, 293, 304, 307, 312, 324, 325
➥ Smith, Joan G. 178, 209, 226, 259, 281, 283, 298, 329
➥ Smith, Julie 178, 206, 211, 218, 237, 238, 239, 245, 248, 276, 277, 278, 279, 283, 284, 288, 291, 293, 296, 301, 303, 309, 316, 317, 321, 323, 338, 339, 341, 353
Smith, Lora Roberts 166, 330
Snooky Randolph 51, 211, 224, 246
Sonora Blair 96, 204, 239, 252
Sophie Greenway 91, 215, 216, 239, 249, 329
Spaceman Kowalski 196, 206, 239, 244
Spencer Arrowood 131, 205, 239, 253
➥ Spring, Michelle 179, 208, 234, 256, 291, 293, 305, 319
➥ Sprinkle, Patricia H. 179, 213, 239, 247, 280, 283, 284, 286, 288, 291, 293, 301, 303, 313, 314, 315, 321, 338, 339
➥ Squire, Elizabeth Daniels 179, 221, 237, 252, 291, 293, 312, 318, 325, 338, 339
➥ Stabenow, Dana 180, 208, 214, 233, 243, 286, 288, 291, 293, 294, 297, 299, 300, 301, 306, 317
➥ Stacey, Susannah 64, 180, 206, 238, 256, 279, 280, 283, 286, 288, 293, 297, 301, 308, 310, 311, 330
Stafford, Caroline 338, 339
➥ Stallwood, Veronica 180, 211, 233, 258, 288, 293, 294, 302, 317
Stanton, Mary 29, 327, 328
Staynes, Jill 64, 180, 328, 330
➥ Stein, Triss 180, 217, 233, 254, 288, 313
➥ Steinberg, Janice 181, 218, 235, 245, 293, 302, 303
➥ Steiner, Susan 181, 208, 223, 243, 284, 288, 311, 315
Stella the Stargazer 103, 217, 220, 239, 246
Stephanie Plum 64, 206, 239, 249
Stephen Marryat 116, 218, 239, 256, 329
Stephen Mayhew 151, 205, 209, 239, 244, 329
Stephen Ramsey 43, 203, 239, 255
Steven Mitchell 28, 203, 239, 257, 327
Stevens, Bonnie K. 338, 339
➥ Stevens, Serita 181, 221, 228, 255, 284, 288, 296, 318
Stockey, Janet 338, 339
Stone, Sgt. 127, 205, 239, 256
Stoner McTavish 58, 214, 222, 239, 248

Storey, Alice 172, 330
Storey, Margaret 64, 180, 328, 330
Stout, Ruth 73, 330
Strichartz, Naomi 338, 339
String 95, 204, 213, 239, 254
➥ Sucher, Dorothy 181, 208, 238, 246, 280, 281, 301, 338, 339
Suitable Job for a Woman 353
➥ Sullivan, Winona 181, 208, 226, 248, 288, 294, 301, 321
➥ Sumner, Penny 182, 208, 212, 241, 256, 286, 293, 300, 305
Susan Henshaw 198, 222, 239, 246
Susan Melville 177, 210, 239, 251
Susan Wren 190, 206, 239, 247
suspense story 360
Suze Figueroa 49, 203, 213, 239, 247
Syd Fish 75, 207, 239, 259
Sydney Bryant 189, 208, 239, 245
Sydney Sloane 121, 207, 239, 251
Sylvia Strange 122, 219, 239, 250

T

Tamara Hayle 194, 208, 211, 240, 249
Tamara Hoyland 124, 209, 240, 256
➥ Taylor, Elizabeth Atwood 182, 208, 235, 245, 276, 279, 286, 298, 314, 316
➥ Taylor, Jean 182, 208, 215, 235, 245, 293, 294, 311, 324
➥ Taylor, L. A. 182, 213, 231, 249, 277, 278, 281, 301, 315, 316, 320, 338, 339
➥ Taylor, Phoebe Atwood 182, 185, 220, 224, 249, 265, 266, 267, 268, 269, 296, 298, 300, 301, 302, 303, 304, 306, 307, 315, 316, 317, 318, 319, 320, 321, 322, 323, 330
Teal Stewart 111, 212, 240, 248
➥ Tell, Dorothy 183, 215, 221, 237, 253, 283, 284, 308, 313, 325
Temple Barr 57, 209, 240, 249
Tepper, Sheri S. 150, 151, 329, 330
Terry Girard 110, 212, 240, 249
Tess Darcy 87, 211, 240, 249
Tessa Crichton 142, 222, 240, 256, 329
➥ Tey, Josephine 183, 206, 223, 258, 264, 265, 268, 269, 301, 307, 312, 320, 323, 330
Thea Crawford 124, 209, 240, 256
Thea Kozak 68, 212, 240, 248
Theo Bloomer 94
Theodora Braithwaite 84, 213, 240, 255
Theodore S. Hubbert 82, 212, 221, 240, 250, 329
Theresa Fortunato 84, 204, 220, 240, 244
Theresa Franco 42, 206, 240, 246
Theresa Tracy Baldwin 149, 217, 240, 251
Thomas Lynley 75, 204, 240, 257
Thomas Pitt 154, 205, 216, 240, 258
➥ Thompson, Joyce 184, 219, 229, 254, 284, 297
➥ Thomson, June 184, 206, 228, 257, 273, 274, 275, 276, 277, 278, 279, 280, 281, 283, 284, 294, 295, 298, 301, 302, 304, 307, 308, 311, 316, 317, 318, 319, 320, 321, 323
Thorne, Iris 160
➥ Thurlo, Aimée & David 184, 206, 214, 228, 250, 293, 294, 297, 303
➥ Tilton, Alice 182, 185, 212, 234, 248, 266, 267, 268, 296, 299, 300, 301, 306, 309, 310, 311, 330
Timothy Herring 185, 210, 240, 256, 330
Tirbutt, Honoria 152, 330
Tish McWhinney 44, 210, 221, 240, 253
Toby Dyke 67, 220, 240, 255, 328
Toby Glendower 22, 209, 240, 260, 327
Todd McKinnon 149, 211, 240, 243
Tom Aragon 137, 218, 240, 243
Tom Barnaby 80, 204, 240, 255
Tom Maybridge 77, 204, 240, 255, 329
Tom Pollard 116, 205, 240, 256
Tom Ripley 95, 213, 240, 256

➥ denotes authors in Master List

Tommy Beresford 40, 221, 240, 257
Tommy Inman 190, 206, 240, 253, 330
➡ Tone, Teona 185, 208, 216, 233, 246, 276, 278, 307, 310
Tonnemans 136, 216, 240, 251, 329
Tori Miracle 124, 211, 240, 252
➡ Torrie, Malcolm 137, 185, 210, 240, 256, 272, 273, 297, 299, 308, 311, 320, 326, 330
trade paperbacks 360
traditional mysteries 356
➡ Travis, Elizabeth 185, 212, 225, 246, 281, 283, 306, 323
Tremaine, Jennie 26, 330
Trey Fortier 98, 207, 240, 247
Trimble, Barbara Margaret 77, 327, 329
Trixie Dolan 24, 222, 240, 257
➡ Trocheck, Kathy Hogan 186, 213, 217, 221, 225, 240, 246, 247, 286, 288, 291, 293, 294, 305, 308, 309, 311, 323, 338, 339
Trott, Susan 338, 339
true crime stories 360
Truman Kicklighter 186, 217, 221, 240, 246
➡ Truman, Margaret 186, 218, 224, 235, 246, 281, 283, 286, 291, 293, 313, 315
➡ Tucker, Kerry 186, 217, 234, 251, 284, 286, 288, 291, 299, 302, 304, 321
Tuckerize 360
Tuppence Beresford 40, 221, 240, 257
Turnbull, Dora Amy Elles Dillon 330
Twentieth-Century Crime and Mystery Writers 362
types of mysteries see Chapter 2
➡ Tyre, Peg 186, 217, 233, 250, 291, 293, 309, 321

U

➡ Uhnak, Dorothy 187, 206, 226, 251, 272, 273, 296, 311, 325
Ulysses Finnegan Donaghue 174, 208, 240, 259

V

V. I. Warshawski 153, 208, 240, 247, 352
Vachell, Supt. 99, 204, 214, 240, 260
➡ Valentine, Deborah 187, 210, 233, 244, 281, 284, 300, 306, 324, 338, 339, 352
➡ Van Gieson, Judith 187, 218, 236, 250, 280, 283, 284, 286, 288, 293, 311, 316, 317, 318, 325
Vejay Haskell 59, 214, 240, 244
➡ Venning, Michael 163, 187, 218, 236, 251, 267, 310, 312, 315, 330
Verity "Birdie" Birdwood 167, 218, 240, 259
Veronica "Ronnie" Ventana 195, 208, 240, 245
Vetter, Louise 79, 329
Vic Varallo 62, 204, 241, 244, 328
Vicki Nelson 99, 207, 213, 241, 259
Vicky Bliss 155, 210, 241, 260, 330
Vicky Holden 43, 214, 241, 254
Victoire Vernet 65, 216, 241, 259, 328
Victoria Bowering 202, 222, 241, 252
Victoria Cross 182, 208, 212, 241, 256
Vince Gutierrez 113, 204, 241, 244
Vine, Barbara 330
Virginia Freer 67, 219, 241, 255, 328
Virginia Kelly 24, 212, 214, 241, 247, 327
➡ Vlasopolos, Anca 188, 206, 239, 249, 283, 313

W

Wagner, Linda 338, 339
➡ Wahlöö, Per 176, 206, 235, 260, 272, 273, 274, 295, 300, 304, 306, 311, 312, 314, 319, 322
➡ Wakefield, Hannah 188, 218, 227, 258, 279, 283, 306, 318, 325, 330
➡ Walker, Mary Willis 188, 210, 217, 233, 236, 253, 284, 291, 293, 318, 323, 326
➡ Wallace, Marilyn 188, 206, 225, 231, 244, 278, 280, 284, 298, 318, 320, 338, 339, 340, 349, 350, 353, 362
➡ Wallace, Patricia 188, 208, 239, 245, 280, 281, 284, 291, 297, 301, 320
Wallace, Penelope 338, 339
➡ Wallingford, Lee 189, 214, 229, 252, 284, 288, 299, 300
➡ Walsh, Jill Paton 189, 209, 219, 230, 256, 288, 293, 317, 325
➡ Waltch, Lilla M. 189, 217, 234, 248, 279, 280, 306, 322
Wanda Mallory 70, 207, 241, 250
Ward, Charlotte 26, 330
➡ Warmbold, Jean 189, 217, 239, 245, 278, 280, 281, 310, 322, 324
➡ Warner, Mignon 190, 220, 221, 228, 257, 274, 275, 276, 277, 278, 302, 304, 307, 309, 312, 316, 321, 322
➡ Watson, Clarissa 190, 210, 237, 250, 274, 275, 278, 280, 297, 307, 311, 319, 321, 360
Watson, Mr. 74, 220, 241, 243
Watts, Carolyn Jensen 338, 339
Web She Weaves anthology 340, 350
➡ Webb, Martha G. 126, 190, 197, 206, 240, 253, 278, 305, 324, 330
Webster Flagg 102, 211, 221, 222, 241, 251
➡ Weir, Charlene 190, 206, 239, 247, 286, 288, 293, 300, 306, 325
➡ Welch, Pat 190, 208, 215, 230, 245, 283, 286, 288, 293, 314, 316, 318, 321
➡ Wells, Carolyn 191, 208, 229, 233, 237, 251, 264, 265, 266, 267, 295, 296, 297, 298, 299, 300, 301, 304, 306, 307, 309, 310, 312, 313, 314, 315, 318, 319, 320, 321, 322, 323, 324, 325, 330
➡ Wells, Tobias 192, 206, 233, 248, 272, 273, 274, 280, 297, 300, 301, 304, 307, 308, 309, 311, 312, 314, 316, 324, 326, 330
➡ Wender, Theodora 193, 209, 223, 229, 248, 278, 310, 314
➡ Wentworth, Patricia 193, 206, 208, 221, 228, 235, 258, 264, 266, 267, 268, 269, 270, 271, 295, 296, 297, 298, 299, 300, 301, 302, 305, 306, 307, 308, 309, 310, 311, 312, 313, 317, 318, 320, 321, 322, 323, 324, 325, 330
➡ Wesley, Valerie Wilson 194, 208, 211, 240, 249, 291, 293, 304, 324
➡ West, Chassie 194, 206, 211, 222, 234, 252, 291, 322
Westmacott, Mary 39, 330
➡ Weston, Carolyn 194, 206, 223, 226, 245, 273, 274, 318, 319, 322
Wharton, Edith 338, 339
What Do I Read Next? 362
➡ Wheat, Carolyn 195, 219, 226, 251, 276, 278, 293, 301, 307, 324, 338, 339, 340
Whitby, Sharon 30, 330
White, Ethel Lina 338, 339
➡ White, Gloria 195, 208, 240, 245, 284, 288, 293, 299, 313, 315
➡ White, Teri 195, 206, 225, 239, 244, 277, 278, 297, 323, 338, 339
Whitman, Ann Hamilton 329
Whitney Logan 112, 218, 241, 244
Whitney, Phyllis 343
➡ Whitney, Polly 196, 218, 223, 230, 251, 291, 293, 294, 324
whodunits 360
whydunits 360
Wilder & Wilson 36, 206, 241, 248
Wilford Dover 352
Wilfred Dover 159, 205, 241, 256
➡ Wilhelm, Kate 196, 208, 219, 224, 226, 227, 239, 252, 279, 280, 281, 283, 284, 286, 288, 291, 293, 296, 300, 303, 307, 308, 310, 319, 320, 322
Willa Jansson 127, 218, 241, 245
William Marlowe Sherman 209, 241, 251
William Monk 155, 205, 216, 241, 256
Williams, Linda V. 81, 329
Williams, Margaret Wetherby 63, 328
Willow King 210, 215, 241, 257, 328
Wilson & Wilder 36, 206, 241, 248
➡ Wilson, Barbara 196, 213, 215, 226, 237, 254, 258, 277, 278, 281, 283, 288, 304, 307, 314, 320, 323, 338, 339, 352
Wilson, Karen 338, 339
➡ Wilson, Karen Ann 197, 210, 238, 246, 291, 293, 300, 305
➡ Wiltz, Chris 197, 208, 236, 248, 276, 279, 284, 304, 305, 310
➡ Wingate, Anne 126, 190, 197, 206, 235, 253, 280, 281, 284, 286, 288, 298, 302, 306, 326, 329, 330, 338, 339
➡ Wings, Mary 197, 208, 215, 228, 245, 279, 283, 294, 320, 338, 339
➡ Winslow, Pauline Glen 198, 206, 236, 256, 274, 275, 276, 297, 300, 303, 319, 320, 325
Winston Marlowe Sherman 121
Witherspoon, Insp. 34, 216, 221, 241, 257, 327
➡ Wolfe, Susan 198, 206, 239, 245, 281, 311
➡ Wolzien, Valerie 198, 213, 222, 232, 239, 246, 255, 279, 281, 284, 286, 289, 291, 293, 294, 295, 305, 307, 308, 314, 316, 318, 320, 321, 323, 324
Woman Detective, Gender & Genre 353, 362
Woman's Eye anthology 340, 350
WomanSleuth Anthologies 350
Women of Mystery anthologies 340, 350
Women's Wiles anthology 350
Woodhouse, Emma 90, 330
➡ Woods, Sara 198, 219, 224, 256, 271, 272, 273, 274, 275, 276, 277, 278, 279, 296, 297, 298, 300, 301, 303, 304, 305, 306, 309, 310, 311, 312, 313, 315, 316, 317, 318, 319, 320, 322, 323, 324, 325, 326, 330
➡ Woods, Sherryl 200, 216, 222, 224, 236, 246, 247, 281, 283, 284, 286, 289, 291, 293, 296, 297, 301, 309, 318, 321, 323, 324
World Mystery Convention 344, 355, 360
➡ Wren, M. K. 200, 212, 227, 252, 273, 274, 275, 276, 277, 289, 293, 300, 301, 310, 313, 316, 319, 324, 330
Wright, Betty Ren 338, 339
Wright, Daphne 45, 328
➡ Wright, L. R. 200, 206, 235, 259, 278, 283, 284, 289, 291, 293, 299, 306, 313, 318, 320, 322, 323
Wright, Rowland 191, 330
Writing Mysteries 353

X

Xenia Smith 136, 212, 222, 241, 251

Y

➡ Yarbro, Chelsea Quinn 65, 201, 219, 226, 245, 274, 275, 283, 284, 286, 296, 299, 306, 315, 316, 317, 328, 338, 339
➡ Yates, Margaret Evelyn T. 201, 217, 222, 224, 260, 266, 267, 303, 309, 312, 314
➡ Yeager, Dorian 201, 210, 213, 222, 228, 241, 249, 252, 286, 289, 291, 293, 298, 305, 315, 317, 321
➡ Yorke, Margaret 202, 209, 237, 258, 273, 274, 298, 301, 308, 313, 320, 330, 338, 339
Yum Yum 32, 209, 217, 241, 255

Z

➡ Zachary, Fay 202, 213, 219, 234, 241, 243, 291, 297, 317
Zack James 202, 213, 219, 241, 243
Zahava, Irene 350
➡ Zukowski, Sharon 202, 208, 225, 252, 284, 286, 291, 294, 300, 309, 311, 318

➡ denotes authors in Master List

Fourteen

About the author

Willetta L. Heising is the author and publisher of **Detecting Women** and **Detecting Women 2**, reader's guides for mystery series written by women. Before launching Purple Moon Press in 1994, she spent 20 years in the corporate world, chiefly with NBD Bank, where she held positions in facilities planning, market research, product management and private banking.

A former Certified Financial Planner, Willetta has worked as a site location analyst, city planner and instructor in geography at Wayne State University. She developed her newswriting style as a reporter and campus news editor for the Valparaiso University *Torch* while earning a BA in geography and sociology in the late '60s.

Born in Coronado, California, she has lived in the Detroit area since 1969. Growing up in a large Navy family, she attended schools in six states, Norway and France. In 1995 she attended the 30-year (and first ever) reunion of Dreux American High School and is now the editor of the Dreux Alumni newsletter (readership 700).

She is a member of Mid America Publishers Association (MAPA), Publishers Marketing Association (PMA), Women's National Book Association (WNBA), Sisters in Crime (SinC) and the American Association of University Women (AAUW). A collector of cast iron building banks, she is an amateur genealogist and counts herself lucky to still find time for one or two mysteries a week.

In October 1995 **Detecting Women** received the MAPA Book Award for Best First Book by a New Publisher.

You can reach Willetta at:

Purple Moon Press
3319 Greenfield Road, Suite 317
Dearborn, Michigan 48120-1212
phone   313-593-1033
fax   313-593-4087
e-mail   nrgx40a@prodigy.com

Genealogy anyone?

If you are an amateur genealogist with any of these family connections, Willetta would like to hear from you.

Birdwell (AL, KY, IL, WA)
Boozer (KY, IL, WA)
Brand (KY, MO, WA)
DeGood (PA, IA, WA)
Garrett (SC, IL)
Grossherr (Ger., MO)
Hawkins (MO, WA)
Heising(er) (Ger., MO)
Hysing(er) (Ger., MO)
Koch (Ger., MO)
Moak (IL, OR)
Nickell (IA, WA)
Philips (TN, AL, WA)
Rott (Ger., MO)
Scheibe (Ger., MO)
Schmidt (Ger., PA, MO)
Westerman (Ger., MO)
Zulow (Ger., MO)

Calling all Willettas

It's fairly unlikely I'll ever come across a sleuth named Willetta, but when Catherine Parsons (from Albany's Haven't Got a Clue mystery bookstore) told me she had an aunt named Willetta, it occurred to me I'd never met one—a Willetta, that is—with the exception of my mother. And when mystery bibliographer extraordinaire, Al Hubin, told me there were 400 Willettas in the Social Security Death Benefits Register, I was floored. Sadly, those 400 Willettas are no longer with us. But assuming some of them passed along the name, I'd like to find any living Willettas. I'd especially like to find Willetta Ann Barber to tell her what a thrill it was for me to discover a bona fide mystery writer named Willetta. So, if you're a Willetta, or you know one personally, ask her to please get in touch with me at:

Purple Moon Press
3319 Greenfield Road, Suite 317
Dearborn, Michigan 48120-1212
phone   313-593-1033
fax   313-593-4087
e-mail   nrgx40a@prodigy.com

Appendix A

✒ Preview of future editions

In the original **Detecting Women** we unwittingly announced our intention to produce a new and updated edition of this book every year. Silly us. We now know that's just about an impossible task for a small press publisher. Especially if we continue offering a pocket guide to accompany the full-size edition of **Detecting Women**. And now that we've been "convinced" to undertake **Detecting Men** we're really going to be busy. The current plan is to publish Detecting Men and Women in alternate years, with the first **Detecting Men** to be released in late 1996, followed by **Detecting Women 3** (DW3) in late 1997. The discerning reader will recognize that we intend to keep **Detecting Women** one step ahead of **Detecting Men**.

To accomplish this we're going to need your help in keeping up with new authors, titles and series. To encourage your participation in this effort, we've included a feedback form which you can fax or mail back to us with your comments, suggestions, corrections and revisions. We are also happy to receive e-mail.

More than 85 women authors with over 250 series titles are currently in our follow-up files for **Detecting Women 3.** Author names you can expect to see in the next edition are shown in the following list.

New Authors for Detecting Women 3

Ashton, Winifred
Bailey, Michele
Behrens, Margaret
Benke, Patricia D.
Berne, Karin

Blackstock, Terri
Bolitho, Janie
Boniface, Marjorie
Bookluck, Adelaide
Bowers, Dorothy

Branch, Pamela J.
Brown, Molly
Burnes, Caroline
Castle, Jayne
Chan, Melissa

Chittenden, Meg
Clayton, Mary
Coles, Manning
Coles, Cyril Henry
Corrigan, John W.

Corrigan, Joyce H.
Dams, Jeanne M.
Dane , Clemence
Dawber, Carol
Dawkins, Cecil

Dewhurst, Eileen
Dreyer, Eileen
Durham, Mary
Edmonds, Janet
Epstein, Charlotte

Evans, Geraldine
Evermay, March
Fairstein, Linda
Fell, Doris E.
Fitt, Mary

Fleming, Joan
Flower, Patricia
Foster, Marion
Francis, Robin
Freeman, Lucy
Garcia-Aguilera, Carolina

George, Ann
Godfrey, Ellen
Gordon, Mildred
Gordon, Gordon
Gresham, Elizabeth

Grimes, Terris M.
Haffner, Margaret
Hall, Linda
Hamilton, Nan
Hebden, Juliet

Hite, Mollie
Hocker, Karla
Infante, Anne
Jernigan, Brenda
Jesse, F. Tennyson

Johnston, Jane
Kemp, Sarah
Kershaw, Valerie
Lawrence, Cynthia
Lynds, Gayle H.

MacInnes, Helen
Manning , Adelaide
Marlett, Melba
Masters, Priscilla
Matthews, Patricia

Matthews, Clayton
Mavity, Nancy Barr
Maxwell, Jan
Meade, Lillie T.
Mills, Deanie F.

O'Kane, Leslie
Owens, Virginia S.
Quinton, Ann
Rayner, Claire
Richards, Emilie

Rippon, Marion E.
Rooth, Anne Reed
Rosemoor, Patricia
Russell, E. S.
Simpson, Helen

Smith, Sarah
Stephenson, Anne
Struthers, Betsy
Symons, Beryl
Todd, Marilyn

Van Folly, Soeur
Williams, Amanda
Woodward, Caroline
Zaremba, Eve

How you can help

Every effort has been made to identify all the women who are currently writing and have written mystery series, to identify their detectives and correctly list series titles in the proper order, all the while spelling everyone's name correctly. No small task indeed. Among the readers of this book are experts on just about everything. So let us hear from you—about our sins of omission or unintentional blunders, large and small.

If you are an author or an expert on something we've overlooked, or worse, something we've botched, please let us know. You won't hurt our feelings if you tell us we got it wrong. After all, this is reference book so it's important to get it right. We'll consider it a favor if you help.

If you have suggestions, comments, or ideas for improvement, we want to hear from you. If you would like to make a contribution to **Detecting Men**, please send material before June 30, 1996 to be included in the forthcoming book. If you think we might need to follow up with you, please provide an address, fax number or phone number where you can be reached. We look forward to hearing from you.

And thanks for your help.

Feedback Form ✍

Detecting Women at Purple Moon Press

Fax: 313-593-4087

Mail: 3319 Greenfield Rd., Suite 317
            Dearborn, MI 48120-1212

E-mail: nrgx40a@prodigy.com

☐ Additions & Suggestions
for New Information

☐ Corrections, Revisions, Errors
(please note page numbers)

Name (optional): _____

Contact me at: _____

Best time: _____

Feedback Form

Detecting Women at Purple Moon Press

Fax: 313-593-4087

Mail: 3319 Greenfield Rd., Suite 317
            Dearborn, MI 48120-1212

E-mail: nrgx40a@prodigy.com

☐ Additions & Suggestions
  for New Information

☐ Corrections, Revisions, Errors
  (please note page numbers)

Name (optional): _____

Contact me at: _____

Best time: _____

Appendix B

✎ Pocket guide changes

The Pocket Guide edition of **Detecting Women 2** includes 558 authors with their 681 series characters and 3,495 series titles. The full-size edition includes the same 558 authors and 681 series characters but 3,595 series titles—a net increase of 100 titles over the Pocket Guide.

This net increase of 100 titles is comprised of 116 series titles which were added and 16 which were deleted. Deleted titles include 11 short story collections (which are still shown in the Master List but are now unnumbered)

and five discards for other reasons (duplicate titles and nonseries novels).

Please use this list of additions and deletions to make corrections to your Pocket Guide. Wherever you find a discrepancy between the Pocket Guide and the full-size edition of **Detecting Women 2**, use the big book as your guide. Because the full-size edition went to press three months after the Pocket Guide, it includes corrections that became available later.

Pocket Guide Additions (+)

Author	Character(s)	Series #	Title (Date)
Aird, Catherine	Christopher Dennis "Seedy" Sloan	13	After Effects (1996)
Babson, Marian	Eve Sinclair & Trixie Dolan	4	Even Yuppies Die (1993)
Babson, Marian	Eve Sinclair & Trixie Dolan	5	Break a Leg Darlings (1995)
Bannister, Jo	Frank Shapiro, et al	4	No Birds Sing (1996)
Beecham, Rose	Amanda Valentine	3	Fair Play (1995)
Berenson, Laurien	Melanie Travis	3	Dog Eat Dog (1996)
Berry, Carole	Bonnie Indermill	6	The Death of a Dancing Fool (1996)
Black, Veronica	Joan, Sister	7	Vow of Poverty (1995)
Black, Veronica	Joan, Sister	8	Vow of Felicity (1996)
Brightwell, Emily	Insp. Witherspoon & Mrs. Jeffries	7	Mrs. Jeffries Plays the Cook (1995)
Butler, Gwendoline	John Coffin	24	A Dark Coffin (1995)
Cannon, Taffy	Nan Robinson	3	Class Reunions are Murder (1996)
Charles, Kate	Lucy Kingsley & David Middleton-Brown	5	Evil Angels Among Them (1995)
Chisholm, P. F.	Robert Carey, Sir	3	A Surfeit of Guns (1997)
Clarke, Anna	Paula Glenning	4	Last Seen in London (1987)
Cleary, Melissa	Jackie Walsh & Jake	6	Dead and Buried (1994)
Cleary, Melissa	Jackie Walsh & Jake	8	Murder Most Beastly (1996)
Cleeves, Ann	George & Molly Palmer-Jones	8	High Island Blues (1996)
Cohen, Anthea	Agnes Carmichael	10	Recording Angel (1991)
Cohen, Anthea	Agnes Carmichael	11	Angel in Action (1992)

Author	Character(s)	Series #	Title (Date)
Cohen, Anthea	Agnes Carmichael	12	Angel in Love (1993)
Cohen, Anthea	Agnes Carmichael	13	Angel in Autumn (1995)
Collins, Anna A.	Abigail Doyle	2	Red Roses for a Dead Trucker (1996)
Cooper, Susan Rogers	E. J. Pugh	2	Hickory, Dickory Stock (1996)
Crespi, Camilla	Simona Griffo	6	The Trouble with a Bad Fit (1996)
Crum, Laura	Gail McCarthy	2	Hoofprints (1996)
Dank, Gloria	Bernard Woodrull & A. 'Snooky' Randolph	3	As the Sparks Fly Upward (1992)
Dank, Gloria	Bernard Woodrull & A. 'Snooky' Randolph	4	The Misfortune of Others (1993)
Davidson, Diane Mott	Goldy Bear	6	The Main Course (1996)
Davis, Lindsey	Marcus Didius Falco	8	A Dying Light in Corduba (1996)
Dereske , Jo	Helma Zukas	4	Miss Zukas and the Raven's Dance (1996)
Douglas, Carole Nelson	Temple Barr & Midnight Louie	5	Cat in a Diamond Dazzle (1996)
Duffy, Margaret	Ingrid Langley & Patrick Gillard	6	Gallows Bird (1993)
Duffy, Margaret	Joanna McKenzie	2	Prospect of Death (1995)
Dunn, Carola	Daisy Dalrymple	3	Requiem for a Mezzo (1996)
Dunn, Carola	Daisy Dalrymple	4	Murder on the Flying Scotsman (1997)
Eccles, Marjorie	Gil Mayo	6	The Company She Kept (1993)
Eccles, Marjorie	Gil Mayo	7	An Accidental Shroud (1994)
Eccles, Marjorie	Gil Mayo	8	A Death of Distinction (1995)
Eichler, Selma	Desiree Shapiro	3	Murder Can Stunt Your Growth (1996)
Eichler, Selma	Desiree Shapiro	4	Murder Can Wreck Your Reunion (1996)
Eyre, Elizabeth	Sigismondo	5	Axe for an Abbot (1996)
Feddersen, Connie	Amanda Hazard	4	Dead in the Dirt (1996)
Ferrars, E. X.	Andrew Basnett	8	A Choice of Evils (1995)
Fickling, G. G.	Erik March	1	Naughty But Dead (1962)
Fraser, Anthea	David Webb	3	Pretty Maids All in a Row (1986)
Fraser, Anthea	David Webb	4	Death Speaks Softly (1987)
Fraser, Anthea	David Webb	7	The April Rainers (1989)
Fraser, Anthea	David Webb	8	Symbols at Your Door (1990)
Fraser, Anthea	David Webb	12	Seven Stars (1995)
Fraser, Anthea	David Webb	13	One is One and All Alone (1996)
Furie, Ruthe	Fran Kirk	3	A Deadly Paté (1997)
Gallison, Kate	Lavinia Grey, Mother	2	The Devil's Workshop (1996)
Gallison, Kate	Nick Magaracz	3	The Jersey Monkey (1992)
George, Elizabeth	Thomas Lynley & Barbara Havers	8	In the Presence of the Enemy (1996)
Gilpatrick , Noreen	Kate McLean	2	Shadow of Death (1995)
Gosling, Paula	Blackwater Bay Mystery	2	The Dead of Winter (1995)
Granger, Ann	Alan Markby, Insp. & Meredith Mitchell	8	Candle for a Corpse (1995)
Granger, Ann	Alan Markby, Insp. & Meredith Mitchell	9	A Touch of Mortality (1996)
Greenwood, Diane M.	Theodora Braithwaite, Rev.	6	Mortal Spoils (1996)
Hall, Patricia	Alex Sinclair & Kate Weston	4	In the Bleak Midwinter (1996)
Hamilton, Laurell K.	Anita Blake	4	The Lunatic Cafe (1996)
Harrod-Eagles, Cynthia	Bill Slider	5	Blood Lines (1996)
Hart, Ellen	Jane Lawless	7	Robber's Wine (1996)
Hart, Ellen	Sophie Greenway	3	The Oldest Sin (1997)

Author	Character(s)	Series #	Title (Date)
Holt, Hazel	Sheila Malory	7	Death of a Dean (1996)
Hyde, Eleanor	Lydia Miller	2	Animal Instincts (1996)
Jorgensen, Christine T.	Stella the Stargazer	3	Curl Up and Die (1996)
Kelly, Mary Ann	Claire Breslinsky	3	Keeper of the Mill (1995)
Kelly, Susan B.	Alison Hope & Nick Trevellyan	5	Death is Sweet (1996)
Kingsbury, Kate	Cecily Sinclair	7	Pay the Piper (1996)
Knight, Alanna	Jeremy Faro	9	The Bull Slayers (1995)
Kruger, Mary	Matt Devlin & Brooke Cassidy	2	No Honeymoon for Death (1995)
Laurence, Janet	Darina Lisle	8	Diet for Death (1996)
Lee, Wendi	Angela Matelli	2	Missing Eden (1996)
Leon, Donna	Guido Brunetti	5	Acqua Alta (1996)
Lewis, Sherry	Fred Vickery	2	No Place Like Home (1996)
Linscott, Gillian	Nell Bray	5	Crown Witness (1995)
Livingston, Nancy	G. D. H. Pringle	7	Unwilling to Vegas (1991)
Livingston, Nancy	G. D. H. Pringle	8	Quiet Murder (1992)
Manthorne, Jackie	Harriett Hubley	3	Last Resort (1995)
Maron, Margaret	Deborah Knott	4	Up Jumps the Devil (1996)
Mather, Linda	Jo Hughes	3	Gemini Doublecross (1995)
Matteson, Stefanie	Charlotte Graham	7	Murder Among the Angels (1996)
McCrumb, Sharyn	Spencer Arrowood	4	The Rosewood Casket (1996)
McDermid, Val	Kate Brannigan	5	Blue Genes (1996)
McGuire, Christine	Kathryn Mackay	2	Until Justice is Done (1994)
McKevett, G. A.	Savannah Reid	2	Bitter Sweets (1996)
McNab, Claire	Carol Ashton	7	Double Bluff (1995)
Meek, M. R. D.	Lennox Kemp	10	Postscript to Murder (1996)
Melville, Jennie	Charmain Daniels	16	The Morbid Kitchen (1995)
Melville, Jennie	Charmain Daniels	17	The Woman Who Was Not There (1996)
Mitchell, Kay	John Morrissey	4	A Rage of Innocence (1996)
Moody, Susan	Cassandra Swann	4	Doubled in Spades (1996)
Muller, Marcia	Sharon McCone	18	The Broken Promise Land (1996)
Myers, Amy	Auguste Didier	8	Murder at the Music Hall (1995)
Myers , Tamar	Magdalena Yoder	3	No Use Dying Over Spilled Milk (1996)
Nabb, Magdalen	Salvatore Guarnaccia	11	The Marshal and the Forgery (1995)
O'Connell, Carol	Kathleen Mallory	3	Killing Critics (1996)
Oliphant, B. J.	Shirley McClintock	6	A Ceremonial Death (1996)
Page, Emma	Inspector Kelsey	8	Murder Comes Caller (1995)
Paul, Barbara	Marian Larch	2	He Huffed and He Puffed (1989)
Paul, Barbara	Marian Larch	3	Good King Sauerkraut (1989)
Pence, Joanne	Angelina Amalfi	4	Cooking Most Deadly (1996)
Perry, Anne	Thomas and Charlotte Pitt	16	Pentecost Alley (1996)
Quest, Erica	Kate Maddox	3	Model Murder (1991)
Quinn, Elizabeth	Lauren Maxwell	3	Lamb to the Slaughter (1996)
Ripley, Ann	Louise Eldridge	2	Death of a Garden Pest (1995)
Robb, J. D.	Eve Dallas	3	Immortal in Death (1996)
Roberts, Lora	Liz Sullivan	3	Murder Mile-High (1996)

Pocket Guide Additions (+)

Author	Character(s)	Series #	Title (Date)
Rowlands, Betty	Melissa Craig	7	Smiling at Death (1996)
Sedley, Kate	Roger the Chapman	6	Eve of St. Hyacinth (1996)
Simonson, Sheila	Lark Dailey	4	Meadowlark (1996)
Stabenow, Dana	Kate Shugak	6	Blood Will Tell (1996)
Sullivan, Winona	Cecile Buddenbrooks, Sister	2	Dead South (1996)
Thomson, June	Inspector Rudd	18	Burden of Innocence (1996)

Pocket Guide Deletions (–)

Author	Character(s)	Series #	Title (Date)
Daly, Elizabeth	Henry Gamadge [APA title]	17	Shroud for a Lady (1956)
Grant-Adamson, Lesley	nonseries	5	Threatening Eye (1988)
Krich, Rochelle Majer	nonseries	3	Speak No Evil (1996)
O'Brien, Meg	nonseries	5	Thin Ice (1993)
Wallace, Patricia	nonseries	5	Dark Intent (1994)